THE ESSENTIAL HUSSERL

Studies in Continental Thought

John Sallis, general editor

THE ESSENTIAL HUSSERL

Basic Writings in Transcendental Phenomenology

EDITED BY DONN WELTON

INDIANA UNIVERSITY PRESS
Bloomington and Indianapolis

This book is a publication of

Indiana University Press
601 North Morton Street
Bloomington, Indiana 47404-3797 USA

http://iupress.indiana.edu

Telephone orders 800-842-6796
Fax orders 812-855-7931
Orders by e-mail iuporder@indiana.edu

The paper used in this publication meets the minimum
requirements of American National Standard for Information
Sciences—Permanence of Paper for Printed Library Materials,
ANSI Z39.48-1984.

Manufactured in the United States of America

Library of Congress Cataloging-in-Publication Data

Husserl, Edmund. 1859–1938.
[Selections. English. 1999]
The essential Husserl : basic writings in transcendental
phenomenology / edited by Donn Welton.
    p.   cm. — (Studies in Continental thought)
Includes bibliographical references and index.
ISBN 978-0-253-21273-3 (pbk. : alk. paper)
1. Phenomenology. I. Welton, Donn.   II. Title.   III. Series.
B3279.H92E52   1999
193—dc21   98-34973

6   7   8   9   12   11   10

CONTENTS

PART TWO: TRANSCENDENTAL PHENOMENOLOGY AND THE PROBLEM OF THE LIFE-WORLD

ACKNOWLEDGMENTS

Grateful acknowledgment is made to the following publishers for permission to reprint works by Edmund Husserl in this anthology:

Kluwer Academic Publishers for selections from *Cartesian Meditations,* translated by Dorion Cairns. ©1960 by Kluwer Academic Publishers; *Formal and Transcendental Logic,* translated by Dorion Cairns. ©1969 by Kluwer Academic Publishers; *Ideas Pertaining to a Pure Phenomenology and to a Phenomenological Philosophy,* First Book, translated by Fred Kersten. ©1982 by Kluwer Academic Publishers; *Ideas Pertaining to a Pure Phenomenology and to a Phenomenological Philosophy,* Second Book, translated by R. Rojcewicz and A. Schuwer. ©1989 by Kluwer Academic Publishers; *On the Phenomenology of the Consciousness of Internal Time (1893–1917),* translated and edited by John Barnett Brough. ©1991 by Kluwer Academic Publishers.

Northwestern University Press for selections from *Crisis of European Sciences and Transcendental Phenomenology,* translated by David Carr. ©1970 by Northwestern University Press; and *Experience and Judgment,* translated by James S. Churchill and Karl Ameriks. ©1973 by Northwestern University Press.

Routledge & Kegan Paul for selections from *Logical Investigations,* translated by J. N. Findlay. © 1968 by Routledge & Kegan Paul.

University of Notre Dame Press for "Philosophy as Rigorous Science," in *Husserl: Shorter Works,* edited by Peter McCormick and Frederick Elliston. ©1981 by University of Notre Dame, Ind.

I am greatly indebted to Anthony Steinbock for his help in selecting the materials to be included in this collection, to Gina Zavota and Lanei Rodemeyer for their help with the task of editing and preparing them for publication, and especially to Lanei Rodemeyer for her skill and exceptional dedication to the task of proofing and indexing this volume. The reader should understand that they were more than assistants and were collaborators in this project, for without their special contributions this collection would not be what it is.

INTRODUCTION

The Development of Husserl's Phenomenology

From what rests on the surface one is led into the depths.
—Husserl (1936)[1]

As we look back upon the course of Continental philosophy in the twentieth century, there is one work, a work which introduced a novel conception of the relationships between language and experience, meaning and reference, and subject and object, that stands at its threshold. This work established an opening that would eventually take philosophy beyond the older, tired alternatives of psychologism and formalism, realism and idealism, objectivism and subjectivism. Its efforts to integrate a theory of meaning with one of truth, a theory of the subject with one of the object, turned philosophical thought in a direction that it had not envisioned. In this sense we might say that this work made twentieth-century Continental philosophy possible. The new work was Edmund Husserl's *Logical Investigations,* published in two volumes in the years 1900 and 1901,[2] and the opening it created was called phenomenology.

If the *Logical Investigations* established a new opening for Continental philosophy, the course of Husserl's own thought, culminating in his last work, *The Crisis of European Sciences and Transcendental Phenomenology,* imaged its movement. He progressed from foundational studies in mathematics and logic, through a phenomenology of intentional acts, to a reframing of his phenomenology as transcendental, and, finally, into a diachronic, dynamic phenomenology of phenomena, well beyond the scope of his synchronic, structural account. Disciplined yet restless in his thinking, he would often move beyond what he discovered before it was solidified and brought to publication. Behind the published works there is a rich profusion of lectures and work-ing manuscripts (some forty thousand pages) in which we find him building, and then rebuilding, the very foundations upon which his phenomenology stands. In many ways, he remained a fellow traveler of seminal thinkers along the winding course of philosophy throughout the century. Perhaps this is why, as we read him today, we sense that he is our contemporary.

While there have been translations of individual volumes for some time, this collection is the first anthology in English of Husserl's major writings. It is designed to be a first reader, providing access to the scope of his philosophical studies. Though it concentrates on materials that he published, it also contains excerpts from some of the works that remained in manuscript form. This introduction will not attempt to provide a systematic analysis of either the specific ideas or the method of Husserl's phenomenology as a whole. That task, made unusually complicated by the existence of his manuscript materials, has been done in a volume that one might consider a companion to this collection.[3] Here I will restrict myself to a brief historical sketch of Husserl's career in order to explain why I have included the texts that I have and why I have placed them in the order found here.

I

Husserl was born on April 8, 1859, in Proß-nitz in Mähren. He began his university studies with three semesters in Leipzig but then spent six semesters in Berlin, where he studied mathematics and philosophy, attending lectures by the mathematicians Karl Weier-

straß and Leopold Kronecker and by the philosopher Friedrich Paulsen.[4] He then moved
to Vienna, where he completed his doctoral
dissertation, *Beiträge zur Theorien der Varia-
tionsrechnung,* in 1882. After another year in
Berlin (with Weierstraß) and military service,
he attended lectures by Franz Brentano in
Vienna. As a result, he decided to devote himself to the study of philosophy. At the recom-
mendation of Brentano, he moved in 1886 to
Halle an der Saale to do his Habilitation with
Carl Stumpf.[5] He concentrated on the intersection of philosophy and mathematics, writing
his Habilitation dissertation, *Über den Begriff
der Zahl,* on the concept of number. Four years
later he published his first book, *Philosophie der Arithmetik,*[6] in which he attempted to
ground certain basic concepts, such as manifold, unity, and number, in a descriptive, psychological analysis of acts.[7] Husserl remained
in Halle as a Privatdozent until the publication of his *Logical Investigations,* in which he
turned from questions of mathematics to issues
in logic and developed his groundbreaking
theory of intentionality. Altogether, he spent
fifteen years in Halle.

Husserl's critiques of psychologism (Selection 1), developed in the *Investigations,* and
historicism (Selection 2), published nine years
later but very much a part of his thinking in
this first period, open this collection (Section
I). "Philosophy as Rigorous Science" (Selection 2) also sketches Husserl's concept of philosophy as a strict discipline; its developed
form promised to dispel the fog of ungrounded
philosophical speculation and place thinking
on sure foundations. This promise opens the
question of what should be our point of access
to philosophical analysis. Husserl's own path
in his First Investigation (Section II, Selection
3) was through an analysis of signs, in particular of expressions, and of the way in which their
meaning can be connected to intentional acts,
an idea he developed further in the Fifth and
Sixth Investigations (see Selection 4).[8]

II

After the publication of his *Investigations*
and his move from Halle to Göttingen in 1901,

Husserl began to rethink both the content and
the methodological framework of his theory
of intentionality. The changes took place gradually in his lectures during this period, finding
their first published formulations in his *Ideas
Pertaining to a Pure Phenomenology and to a
Phenomenological Philosophy,* Book 1: *General Introduction to a Pure Phenomenology*
(1913).[9] This was to be followed by two other
volumes, but they remained in manuscript form
and were not printed during his lifetime. We
now know them as Book 2: *Studies in the Phenomenology of Constitution* (first published in
1950),[10] and Book 3: *Phenomenology and the
Foundations of the Sciences* (first published in
1952).[11]

In *Ideas I* Husserl introduced needed modifications into his theory of intentional acts.
He argued that their structure consists of an a
priori correlation between what he called noesis and noema (Section IV). In addition, he
stressed the importance of securing different
kinds of claims through various types of evidence (Section V, Selection 7) and continued
to employ his crucial distinction between sensuous and categorial intuition developed in
the *Investigations* (Selection 8), a contrast that
Heidegger valued above all others in Husserl.[12]
During his years at Göttingen, he further expanded the scope of his interests, devoting extensive lectures and manuscript studies to
new problems, in particular to a phenomenology of time and space. These studies, for reasons I will indicate in a moment, belong to Part
2 of this collection. At the same time, he also
became convinced that phenomenology could
become philosophy proper only if it became
transcendental, as Kant had taught. Rejecting
the hypothetical, deductive approach of Kant
and the Neo-Kantians, however, he developed
his famous theory of the transcendental reduction, using Descartes to give insight into how
the region of pure consciousness could be se-
cured as the absolute and irreducible foundation for philosophical analysis (Section III).

Husserl's first formulation of the reduction
was Cartesian, as he came to put it, and thus
faced the threat of solipsism. Husserl attempted to handle this problem within the scope of
the Cartesian program by developing a theory

of intersubjectivity consistent with its starting point. The result is what we find in the now famous Fifth Meditation of his *Cartesian Meditations*[13] (Section VI). The introduction of the idea of transcendental intersubjectivity gave Husserl a notion commensurate with the concept of the world, which he already understood in *Ideas I* in terms of the notion of horizons (Selection 6, Horizons). Though it is a later text published in 1931, the Fifth Meditation is best understood, I would suggest, as employing what Husserl calls "static analysis," an idea I will introduce momentarily.

III

In 1916 Husserl assumed a post as full professor *(Ordinarius)* in Freiburg, where he taught until his retirement in 1928. After the personal and political difficulties of the first World War, Husserl envisioned writing a major work on the system of phenomenology. At the level of method he began to distinguish between what he called static and genetic phenomenology (Selection 18), and to differentiate various paths or ways into the transcendental reduction. In 1922 he wrote to Adolf Grimme that "this year was a time of great interpretative reflections *[Besinnungen]*. I thought through yet a final time *[sic]* the principle, basic ideas and lines of direction of phenomenology."[14] Four years earlier he had even written to Paul Natorp that "for more than a decade I have already overcome the stage of static Platonism and have framed the idea of transcendental genesis as the main theme of phenomenology."[15] In another letter to Natorp in 1922 Husserl spoke of both the upheaval in his thinking and the frustration of bringing his new ideas to publication:

I am in a much worse situation than you because the greatest part of my work is stuck in my manuscripts. I almost curse my inability to bring my works *[mich]* to an end, and that first quite late, partly only now, the universal, systematic thoughts have come to me, which, though demanded by my previous, particular investigations, now also compel me to rework them all. Everything is in the stage of recrystallization! Perhaps I am working, with all the humanly possible expenditure of energy, only for my posthumous works.[16]

This anthology is organized from the perspective of Husserl's belief that phenomenology is systematic in nature. From this perspective we can say that the foundations discovered in *Ideas I* turn out to be provisional, being themselves in need of deeper grounds. Part 2 of this collection is designed both to reflect Husserl's effort to complement his earlier synchronic, structural phenomenology with a genetic analysis, his first Cartesian way with other "paths" into transcendental analysis, and to follow Husserl as he expanded his initial notion of the world with his important concept of the life-world. His "systematic" reflections not only required a transcendental grounding to logic, the program of both *Ideas I* and *Formal and Transcendental Logic*,[17] but also attempted to situate within that ground an expanded transcendental aesthetics (Section VII) before the transcendental analytics, which itself grounds logical reason (Section VIII).[18] In other words, he developed not just a certain protologic to his logic, but also, within that protologic, a difference between a transcendental analysis of different types of what he called "passive" syntheses (Section VII) and that of different types of "active" syntheses (Section VIII). Some of the selections in Part 2 deepen the content of Part 1—as in the analyses gathered under Section VIII—and some extend it into new areas—as in his treatment of the body, time, and perception in Section VII. As a whole, however, they reconstruct the ground upon which the studies in Part 1 stand.

The "recrystallization" of Husserl's thought in the early 1920s, first of all, cast his earlier studies in a new light. His important theories of spatial orientation and the body (Selection 10), which were first developed between 1907 and 1912, contribute to our understanding of the inescapable background of all speech and understanding. They also account for the interconnection between motility, action, and conscious life, a nexus richly explored by Merleau-Ponty in his *Phenomenology of Perception*.[19] Husserl's earlier studies on the consciousness of time (Selection 11), which he expressly eliminated from consideration in *Ideas I*, become part of an analysis of how our experience of perceptual objects involves a process and is built up over time. The distinction he makes between retention and recollection, on the one hand, and protention and expectation, on the other, contributes much to our understanding of how the present spans what is past and what is future, and how presence includes absence. Husserl extensively reworked his theory of the consciousness of time in 1917 and 1918, as he was speaking to Natorp of "transcendental genesis"; but these texts are still being prepared for publication.[20] It will be interesting to see how they compare with his first theory.

The second result of Husserl's recrystallization was to introduce a new and richer theory of perception, which integrated the account of horizons into an account of phenomena, and which partially replaced his earlier form-content scheme with a theory of interlocking aesthetic syntheses.[21] Anthony Steinbock has provided a translation of a sample from Husserl's important lectures from 1920–1926 on the analysis of passive synthesis (Selection 12).[22]

The outlines of what Husserl thought about the relationship between formal and transcendental logic in general (Selection 13), and about the constitution of individuals, sets, and universals in particular (Selections 14 and 15), are captured in Section VIII. His theory of eidetic variation (Selection 15) has been of value in a wide range of disciplines. This is another case where a notion used in his earlier writings, that of eidetic intuition, is reconstructed in an effort to do justice to the diachronic process of constitution involved.

Husserl's attempt to connect time to the self-constitution of the ego gives us unusual insight into what he meant both by the ego and by genetic phenomenology (Selection 17). This selection is complemented by a sketchy, working manuscript, also translated by Anthony Steinbock, devoted expressly to the distinction between static and genetic method (Selection 18). While not easy to interpret, this text is especially valuable in outlining the range of issues and areas that are to be covered by genetic analysis.

Husserl was asked to write an article on phenomenology for the *Encyclopaedia Britannica*, which appeared in 1927. His efforts to co-author it with Heidegger led to exchanges of manuscripts but ultimately came to naught. The occasion, however, did produce a short, dense summary of Husserl's own approach about 1925, and a clear case of an "indirect" way (in contrast to the "direct" way of his first Cartesian approach) in which Husserl employed an existing science as his "guiding thread" into the realm of transcendental phenomenology. In this article (Selection 19) he chose psychology and used its differences from transcendental phenomenology as a way of clarifying *both* disciplines.

The way through psychology, however, brought with it a new threat of psychologism at a deeper level, namely transcendental psychologism. Husserl thought he could overcome the danger, but he eventually found that this way was not as productive as ones that use other regional ontologies or the notion of the life-world as their leading clue. The final readings are from his last work, *The Crisis of European Sciences;* they employ a genetic analysis, expanded by the concept of history, in an effort to understand the development of the concept of nature in the physical sciences at the beginning of the modern age (Selection 20), and to frame an alternative approach to the world, employing the concept of the life-world, one of the most important and fruitful ideas in all of Husserl's writings (Selection 21).

IV

Husserl labored with exceptional energy between 1918 and 1936. As we look at the content of Husserl's ongoing studies, we can see that the expansion of his phenomenology through the genetic method facilitated the development of rich theories of perception, genetic logic, cultural renewal, the life-world, and history. Ongoing efforts to bring his new ideas to publication, however, met with failure time and time again. One very brief and programmatic essay, the *Encyclopaedia Britannica* article, did reach the public in 1927 (see Selection 19), but there was a gap of some sixteen years between *Ideas I* and *Formal and Transcendental Logic* (1929). Even at that, the latter was yet another "introduction" that did not apprise the reader of the full scope of the changes in Husserl's thought, though it did contain new ideas on the grounds of logical reason (Selections 13 and 16), and clear indications that Husserl had progressed beyond the method of *Ideas I* in his understanding of the genesis of logical formations. Two other works published around this time also failed to alert the public to the most recent developments in his understanding of phenomenology. The bulk of his *Phenomenology of the Consciousness of Internal Time* (1928),[23] while moving into an area of study excluded from consideration in *Ideas I* but essential to genetic analysis, consisted of older materials written between 1905 and 1909. The *Cartesian Meditations,* published only in a French translation in 1931,[24] introduced an important expansion to his constitutive phenomenology, as we see in Section VI. But it was deemed unsuitable for a "German" public and, after several attempts to rework the materials, it was finally abandoned. Husserl had also worked with Ludwig Landgrebe on the text of *Experience and Judgment* (1938)[25] during this period; using manuscripts from as far back as about 1915, he concentrated, as he had in *Formal and Transcendental Logic,* entirely on a genealogy of logic (Selections 14 and 15). Husserl finally left the *Cartesian Meditations* in the hands of Eugen Fink[26] and *Experience and Judgment* in the hands of Landgrebe as he turned to the text that we know as *The Crisis,* a project that occupied him until his death in 1938 but was not published until some fourteen years later.

As a result, a number of Husserl's new ideas were developed not in print but in his lecture courses given between 1920 and 1926 and in countless working manuscripts composed between 1918 and 1937. Of course, an anthology of this kind, designed to introduce the reader to the broad range of Husserl's writings, cannot do justice to his published works, let alone these manuscripts. But this collection does include translations of a lecture manuscript (Selection 12) and a working manuscript (Selection 18), both previously unpublished in English translation, from the early 1920s. In addition, Selections 10, 20, and 21 contain manuscript materials. Fortunately, there is already a translation of *Phenomenological Psychology,*[27] a lecture course given in 1925, and forthcoming translations of two additional courses: *Analyses Concerning Passive Synthesis,* given three times between 1920 and 1926, and *First Philosophy,* given in 1923 and 1924. One would hope that this anthology will give the reader the sources necessary not only to understand the main contours of Husserl's transcendental phenomenology and to glimpse how that phenomenology deepened as it dealt with the problem of the life-world, but also to situate the forthcoming translations of these lecture courses from the 1920s.

Except for correction of obvious errors and regularization of minor discrepancies in punctuation and spelling, the selections published in this anthology have not been changed from their original translations. Creating a uniform terminology for some key terms throughout would have made for greater consistency, but requirements of the copyright holders precluded this. Cross-references by Husserl and/ or his editors to his own texts are preserved only if they refer to a text in this collection. All square brackets "[]" in the text indicate translator's insertions; all angle brackets "<>" indicate editors' interpolations. Critical apparatus and many of the translators' comments from the sources reprinted here have not been included, except in the case of *Crisis.*

Notes

1. Edmund Husserl, *Die Krisis der europäischen Wissenschaften und die transzendentale Phänomenologie: Eine Einleitung in die phänomenologische Philosophie,* ed. Walter Biemel, *Husserliana,* vol. 6 (The Hague: Martinus Nijhoff, 1954), p. 366; *The Crisis of European Sciences and Transcendental Phenomenology: An Introduction to Phenomenological Philosophy,* trans. David Carr (Evanston, Ill.: Northwestern University Press, 1970), p. 355.

2. Edmund Husserl, *Logische Untersuchungen,* 2 vols. (Halle a.d. Saale: Max Niemeyer, 1900 and 1901). The second edition appeared in 1913 and 1921. *Logische Untersuchungen,* 2nd rev. ed., 2 vols. (Halle a.d. Saale: Max Niemeyer, 1913 and 1921); *Logical Investigations,* trans. J. N. Findlay, 2 vols. (London: Routledge & Kegan Paul, 1970).

3. Donn Welton, *The Other Husserl: The Horizons of Transcendental Phenomenology* (forthcoming). For a recent study that moves even further into Husserl's later thought, see Anthony J. Steinbock, *Home and Beyond* (Evanston, Ill.: Northwestern University Press, 1996).

4. For an overview of Husserl's career, see *Edmund Husserl und die Phänomenologische Bewegung: Zeugnisse in Text und Bild,* ed. Hans Rainer Sepp (Freiburg: Karl Alber, 1988). On his student years, see pp. 131–132. For a detailed chronology of Husserl's life, see Karl Schuhmann, *Husserl-Chronik: Denk- und Lebensweg Husserls, Husserliana Dokumente,* vol. 1 (The Hague: Martinus Nijhoff, 1977).

5. *Edmund Husserl und die Phänomenologische Bewegung,* p. 159. In the German university system the Habilitation is a degree over and above the doctorate. It requires an additional dissertation.

6. Edmund Husserl, *Philosophie der Arithmetik: Psychologische und logische Untersuchungen,* vol. 1 (Halle a.d. Saale: C.E.M. Pfeffer, 1891).

7. *Edmund Husserl und die Phänomenologische Bewegung,* p. 160.

8. Since we get a fuller, revised theory of intentionality in Husserl's *Ideas I* (see Section IV), I do not include further selections from the *Investigations.*

9. Edmund Husserl, *Ideen zu einer reinen Phänomenologie und phänomenologischen Philosophie,* vol. 1: *Allgemeine Einführung in die reine Phänomenologie,* in *Jahrbuch für Philosophie und phänomenologische Forschung,* vol. 1 (Halle a.d. Saale: Max Niemeyer, 1913), pp. 1–323; *Ideas Pertaining to a Pure Phenomenology and to a Phenomenological Philosophy,* First Book: *General Introduction to a Pure Phenomenology,* trans. F. Kersten, *Collected Works,* vol. 2 (The Hague: Martinus Nijhoff, 1983).

10. Edmund Husserl, *Ideen zu einer reinen Phänomenologie und phänomenologischen Philosophie,* vol. 2: *Phänomenologische Untersuchungen zur Konstitution,* ed. Marly Biemel, *Husserliana,* vol. 4 (The Hague: Martinus Nijhoff, 1952); *Ideas Pertaining to a Pure Phenomenology and to a Phenomenological Philosophy,* Second Book: *Studies in the Phenomenology of Constitution,* trans. Richard Rojcewicz and André Schuwer, *Collected Works,* vol. 3 (Dordrecht: Kluwer Academic Publishers, 1989).

11. Edmund Husserl, *Ideen zu einer reinen Phänomenologie und phänomenologischen Philosophie,* vol. 3: *Die Phänomenologie und die Fundamente der Wissenschaften,* ed. Marly Biemel, *Husserliana,* vol. 5 (The Hague: Martinus Nijhoff, 1952); *Ideas Pertaining to a Pure Phenomenology and to a Phenomenological Philosophy,* Third Book: *Phenomenology and the Foundations of the Sciences,* trans. Ted Klein and William Pohl, *Collected Works,* vol. 1 (The Hague: Martinus Nijhoff, 1980).

12. See Jacques Taminiaux, "Remarques sur Heidegger et les *Recherches Logiques* de Husserl," *Le regard et l'excédent, Phaenomenologica,* vol. 75 (The Hague: Martinus Nijhoff, 1977), pp. 156–182; "Heidegger and Husserl's *Logical Investigations,*" *Dialectic and Difference,* ed. and trans. Robert Crease and James Decker (Atlantic Highlands, N.J.: Humanities Press, 1985), pp. 91–114.

13. Edmund Husserl, *Cartesianische Meditationen und Pariser Vorträge,* ed. S. Strasser, *Husserliana,* vol. 1 (The Hague: Martinus Nijhoff, 1963); *Cartesian Meditations: An Introduction to Phenomenology,* trans. Dorion Cairns (The Hague: Martinus Nijhoff, 1960).

14. Letter to Adolf Grimme, September 1, 1922, *Briefwechsel,* ed. Karl Schuhmann with Elisabeth Schuhmann, *Husserliana Dokumente,* 3/3 (Dordrecht: Kluwer Academic Publishers, 1994), p. 85.

15. Letter to Paul Natorp, June 29, 1918, *Briefwechsel,* vol. 3/5, p. 137.

16. Letter to Paul Natorp, February 1, 1922, *Briefwechsel,* vol. 3/5, pp. 151–152.

17. Edmund Husserl, *Formale und transzendentale Logik: Versuch einer Kritik der logischen Vernunft,* in *Jahrbuch für Philosophie und phänomenologische Forschung,* vol. 10 (Halle a.d. Saale: Max Niemeyer, 1929), pp. v–xiii, 1–298; *Formal and Transcendental Logic,* trans. Dorion Cairns (The Hague: Martinus Nijhoff, 1969).

18. See Edmund Husserl, *Analysen zur passiven Synthese: Aus Vorlesungs- und Forschungsmanuskripten 1918–1926,* ed. Margot Fleischer, *Husserliana,* vol. 11 (The Hague: Martinus Nijhoff, 1966), pp. 295, 361–362, and esp. 498.

19. Maurice Merleau-Ponty, *Phénoménologie de la perception* (Paris: Gallimard, 1945); *Phenomenology of Perception,* trans. Colin Smith (London: Routledge & Kegan Paul, 1962).

20. They are being prepared by Rudolf Bernet in Louvain.

21. For an account of this see Donn Welton, *The Origins of Meaning: A Critical Study of the Thresholds of Husserlian Phenomenology, Phaenomenologica,* vol. 88 (The Hague: Martinus Nijhoff, 1983), Part 2.

22. His complete translation of *Analysen zur passiven Synthesis* is forthcoming from Kluwer Academic Publishers.

23. Edmund Husserl, *Vorlesungen zur Phänomenologie des inneren Zeitbewusstseins,* ed. Martin Heidegger, *Jahrbuch für Philosophie und phänomenologische Forschung,* vol. 9 (Halle a.d. Saale: Max Niemeyer, 1928), pp. viii–ix, 367–498; *On the Phenomenology of the Consciousness of Internal Time (1893–1917),* trans. John Brough, *Collected Works,* vol. 4 (Dordrecht: Kluwer Academic Publishers, 1991).

24. Edmund Husserl, *Méditations Cartésiennes,* trans. E. Levinas and G. Pilfer (Paris: A. Colin, 1931).

25. Edmund Husserl, *Erfahrung und Urteil: Untersuchungen zur Genealogie der Logik,* ed. L. Landgrebe (Prague: Academia-Verlag, 1938; Hamburg: Claasen, 1954); *Experience and Judgment: Investigations in a Genealogy of Logic,* trans. James S. Churchill and Karl Ameriks (Evanston, Ill.: Northwestern University Press, 1973).

26. See Eugen Fink, *VI. Cartesianische Meditation,* Part 1: *Die Idee einer transzendentalen Methodenlehre,* Part 2: *Ergänzungsband, Husserliana Dokumente,* vol. 2/1 and 2/2 (Dordrecht: Kluwer Academic Publishers, 1988); *Sixth Cartesian Meditation: The Idea of a Transcendental Theory of Method,* trans. Ronald Bruzina (Bloomington: Indiana University Press, 1994).

27. Edmund Husserl, *Phänomenologische Psychologie: Vorlesungen Sommersemester 1925,* ed. Walter Biemel, *Husserliana,* vol. 9 (The Hague: Martinus Nijhoff, 1968); *Phenomenological Psychology: Lectures, Summer Semester, 1925,* trans. John Scanlon (The Hague: Martinus Nijhoff, 1977).

ABBREVIATIONS FOR WORKS BY HUSSERL

APS   *Analyses Concerning Passive and Active Synthesis: Lectures on Transcendental Logic.* Trans. Anthony J. Steinbock (Boston: Kluwer Academic Publishers, forthcoming).

CES   *The Crisis of European Sciences and Transcendental Phenomenology: An Introduction to Phenomenological Philosophy,* trans. David Carr (Evanston, Ill.: Northwestern University Press, 1970).

CM   *Cartesian Meditations: An Introduction to Phenomenology,* trans. Dorion Cairns (The Hague: Martinus Nijhoff, 1960).

EJ   *Experience and Judgment: Investigations in a Genealogy of Logic,* trans. James S. Churchill and Karl Ameriks (Evanston, Ill.: Northwestern University Press, 1973).

FTL   *Formal and Transcendental Logic,* trans. Dorion Cairns (The Hague: Martinus Nijhoff, 1969).

Ideas I   Ideas Pertaining to a Pure Phenomenology and to a Phenomenological Philosophy, First Book: *General Introduction to a Pure Phenomenology,* trans. F. Kersten, *Collected Works,* vol. 2 (The Hague: Martinus Nijhoff, 1982).

Ideas II   Ideas Pertaining to a Pure Phenomenology and to a Phenomenological Philosophy, Second Book: *Studies in the Phenomenology of Constitution,* trans. Richard Rojcewicz and André Schuwer, *Collected Works,* vol. 3 (Dordrecht: Kluwer Academic Publishers, 1989).

LI   *Logical Investigations,* trans. J. N. Findlay, 2 vols. (London: Routledge & Kegan Paul, 1970).

PCIT   *On the Phenomenology of the Consciousness of Internal Time (1893–1917),* trans. John Brough, *Collected Works,* vol. 4 (Dordrecht: Kluwer Academic Publishers, 1991).

PRS   "Philosophy as Rigorous Science," in *Phenomenology and the Crisis of Philosophy,* trans. Quentin Lauer (New York: Harper and Row, 1965), pp. 71–147. Reprinted in *Husserl: Shorter Works,* ed. Peter McCormick and Frederick Elliston, 1981.

SW   *Husserl: Shorter Works,* ed. Peter McCormick and Frederick Elliston (Notre Dame, Ind.: University of Notre Dame Press, 1981).

PART ONE

Contours of a Transcendental Phenomenology

Edmund Husserl, 1894. Courtesy of Anna-Maria Husserl.

I.

Antitheses

1. The Critique of Psychologism

Normative and Theoretical Disciplines*

§11. Logic or theory of science as normative discipline and as technology

From our discussions up to this point logic—in the sense of the theory of science here in question—emerges as a *normative discipline*. Sciences are mental creations which are directed to a certain end, and which are for that reason to be judged in accordance with that end. The same holds of theories, validations and in short of everything that we call a "method." Whether a science is truly a science, or a method a method, depends on whether it accords with the aims that it strives for. Logic seeks to search into what pertains to genuine, valid science as such, what constitutes the Idea of Science, so as to be able to use the latter to measure the empirically given sciences as to their agreement with their Idea, the degree to which they approach it, and where they offend against it. In this logic shows itself to be a normative science, and separates itself off from the comparative mode of treatment which tries to conceive of the sciences, according to their *typical* communities and peculiarities, as concrete cultural products of their era, and to explain them through the relationships which obtain in their time. For it is of the essence of a normative science that it establishes general prop-

ositions in which, with an eye to a normative standard, an Idea or highest goal, certain features are mentioned whose possession guarantees conformity to that standard, or sets forth an indispensable condition of the latter. A normative science also establishes cognate propositions in which the case of non-conformity is considered or the absence of such states of affairs is pronounced. Not as if one had to state general marks in order to say what an object should be to conform to its basic norm: a normative discipline never sets forth universal criteria, any more than a therapy states universal symptoms. Special criteria are what the theory of science particularly gives us, and what it alone can give us. If it maintains that, having regard to the supreme aim of the sciences and the human mind's actual constitution, and whatever else may be invoked, such and such methods M_1, M_2 . . . arise, it states general propositions of the form: "Every group of mental activities of the sorts AB . . . which realize the combinatory form M_1 (or M_2 . . .) yield a case of correct method," or, what amounts to the same "Every (soi-disant) methodical procedure of the form M_1 (or M_2 . . .) is a correct one." If one could really formulate all intrinsically possible valid propositions of this and like sort, our normative science would certainly possess a measuring rod for every pretended method, but then also only in the form of special criteria.

Where the basic norm is an end or can be-

*LI, I, 70–72, 87–88 (Sections 11 and 16).

come an end, the normative discipline by a ready extension of its task gives rise to a technology. This occurs in this case too. If the theory of science sets itself the further task of investigating such conditions as are subject to our power, on which the realization of valid methods depends, and if it draws up rules for our procedure in the methodical tracking down of truth, in the valid demarcation and construction of the sciences, in the discovery and use, in particular, of the many methods that advance such sciences, and in the avoidance of errors in all of these concerns, then it has become a *technology of science*. This last plainly includes the whole normative theory of science, and it is therefore wholly appropriate, in view of the unquestionable value of such a technology, that the concept of logic should be correspondingly widened, and should be defined in its sense.

§16. Theoretical disciplines as the foundation of normative disciplines

It is now easy to see that each normative, and, *a fortiori,* each practical discipline, presupposes one or more theoretical disciplines as its foundations, in the sense, namely, that it must have a theoretical content free from all normativity, which as such has its natural location in certain theoretical sciences, whether these are already marked off or yet to be constituted.

The basic norm (or basic value, or ultimate end) determines, we saw, the unity of the discipline: it also is what imports the thought of normativity into all its normative propositions. But alongside of this general thought of measurement in terms of a basic norm, these propositions have their own theoretical content, which differs from one case to another. Each expresses the thought of a measuring relation between norm and what it is a norm for, but this relation is itself objectively characterized—if we abstract from valuational interest—as a relation between condition and conditioned, which relation is set down as existent or non-existent in the relevant normative propositions. Every normative proposition of, e.g., the form "An *A* should be *B*" implies the theoretical proposition "Only an *A* which is *B* has the properties *C,*" in which "*C*" serves to indicate the constitutive content of the standard-setting predicate "good" (e.g., pleasure, knowledge, whatever, in short, is marked down as good by the valuation fundamental to our given sphere). The new proposition is purely theoretical: it contains no trace of the thought of normativity. If, conversely, a proposition of the latter form is true, and thereupon a novel valuation of a *C* as such emerges, and makes a normative relation to the proposition seem requisite, the theoretical proposition assumes the normative form "Only an *A* which is *B* is a good *A,*" i.e., "An *A* should be *B*." Normative propositions can therefore make an appearance even in theoretical contexts: our theoretical interest in such contexts attaches value to the being of a state of affairs of a sort—to the equilateral form, e.g., of a triangle about to be determined—and then assesses other states of affairs, e.g., one of equiangularity, in relation to this: If the triangle is *to be* equilateral, it must be equiangular. Such a modification is, however, merely passing and secondary in theoretical sciences, since our last intention is here directed to the theoretical coherence of the things themselves. Enduring results are not therefore stated in normative form, but in the forms of this objective coherence, in the form, that is, of a general proposition.

It is now clear that the theoretical relations which our discussion has shown to lie hidden in the propositions of normative sciences, must have their logical place in certain theoretical sciences. If the normative science is to deserve its name, if it is to do scientific work on the relations of the facts to be normatively considered to their basic norms, it must study the content of the theoretical nucleus of these relations, and this means entering the spheres of the relevant theoretical sciences. In other words: Every normative discipline demands that we know certain non-normative truths: these it takes from certain theoretical sciences, or gets by applying propositions so taken to the constellation of cases determined by its normative interest. This naturally holds, likewise, in the more special case of a technology, and plainly to a greater extent. The theoretical knowledge is there added which will provide a basis for a fruitful realization of ends and means.

The Arguments of Psychologism*

§17. The disputed question as to whether the essential theoretical foundations of normative logic lie in psychology

If we now apply the general results arrived at in the last chapter to logic as a normative discipline, a first, very weighty question arises: Which theoretical sciences provide the essential foundations of the theory of science? And to this we forthwith add the further question: Is it correct that the theoretical truths we find dealt with in the framework of traditional and modern logic, and above all those belonging to its essential foundations, have their theoretical place in the sciences that have been already marked off and independently developed?

Here we encounter the disputed question as to the relation between psychology and logic, since one dominant tendency of our time has a ready answer to the questions raised: The essential theoretical foundations of logic lie in psychology, in whose field those propositions belong—as far as their theoretical content is concerned—which give logic its characteristic pattern. Logic is related to psychology just as any branch of chemical technology is related to chemistry, as land-surveying is to geometry, etc. This tendency sees no need to mark off a new theoretical discipline, and, in particular, not one that would deserve the name of logic in a narrower and more pointed sense. Often people talk as if psychology provided the sole, sufficient, theoretical foundation for logical technology. So we read in Mill's polemic against Hamilton: "Logic is not a science separate from and coordinate with psychology. To the extent that it is a science at all,

it is a part or branch of psychology, distinguished from it on the one hand as the part is from the whole, and on the other hand as the art is from the science. It owes all its theoretical foundations to psychology, and includes as much of that science as is necessary to establish the rules of the art" (*An Examination of Sir William Hamilton's Philosophy*, p. 461). According to Lipps it even seems that logic is to be ranked as a mere constituent of psychology for he says: "The fact that logic is a specific discipline of psychology distinguishes them satisfactorily from one another" (Lipps, *Grundzüge der Logik* [1893], §3).

§18. The line of proof of the psychologistic thinkers

If we ask for the justification of such views, a most plausible line of argument is offered, which seems to cut off all further dispute *ab initio*. However one may define logic as a technology—as a technology of thinking, judging, inferring, knowing, proving, of the courses followed by the understanding in the pursuit of truth, in the evaluation of grounds of proof, etc.—we find invariably that mental activities or products are the objects of practical regulation. And just as, in general, the artificial working over of a material presupposes the knowledge of its properties, so this will be the case here too, where we are specially concerned with psychological material. The scientific investigation of the rules according to which this stuff should be worked over naturally leads back to the scientific investigation of these properties. Psychology therefore provides the theoretical basis for constructing a logical technology, and, more particularly, the psychology of cognition.†

Any glance at the contents of logical literature will confirm this. What is being talked of throughout? Concepts, judgments, syllogisms, deductions, inductions, definitions, classifications, etc.—all psychology, except that they are

---

*LI, I, 90–97 (Sections 17–20).

†"Logic is a psychological discipline just as surely as knowing only arises in the mind, and as thinking which terminates in knowledge is a mental happening." Lipps, op. cit.

selected and arranged from normative and practical points of view. Draw the bounds of pure logic as tightly as one likes, it will not be possible to keep out what is psychological. This is implicit in the concepts constitutive for logical laws: truth and falsehood, affirmation and negation, universality and particularity, ground and consequent, etc.

§19. The usual arguments of the opposition and the psychologistic rejoinder

Remarkably enough, the opposition believes that it can base a sharp separation of the two disciplines on precisely the normative character of logic. Psychology, it is said, deals with thinking as it is, logic with thinking as it should be. The former has to do with the natural laws, the latter with the normative laws of thinking. It reads in this sense in Jäsche's version of Kant's Lectures on Logic: "Some logicians presuppose psychological principles for logic, but to introduce such principles into logic is as absurd as to derive morality from Life. If we take principles from psychology, i.e., from observations of our understanding, we shall only see how thought proceeds, and what happens under manifold subjective hindrances and conditions. Those would only lead to a knowledge of merely *contingent* laws. Logic does not however ask after *contingent,* but after *necessary* laws—not how we think but how we ought to think. The rules of logic must therefore be taken, not from the *contingent,* but from the *necessary* use of reason, which one finds in oneself apart from all psychology. In logic we do not wish to know what the understanding is like and how it thinks, nor how it has hitherto proceeded in its thinking, but how it ought to proceed in its thinking. It should teach us the correct use of the understanding, the use in which it is consistent with itself" (Introduction, I. Concept of Logic. Kant's *Werke,* ed. Hartenstein [1867], VIII, p. 15). Herbart takes up a similar position when he objects to the logic of his time and "the would be psychological stories about understanding and reason with which it starts," by saying that this is as

badly in error as a moral theory which tried to begin with the natural history of human tendencies, urges and weaknesses, and by pointing to the normative character of logic as of ethics (Herbart, *Psychologie als Wissenschaft,* II, §119, original ed. II, p. 173).

Such arguments do not dismay the psychologistic logicians. They answer: A necessary use of the understanding is none the less a use of the understanding, and belongs, with the understanding itself, to psychology. Thinking as it should be, is merely a special case of thinking as it is. Psychology must certainly investigate the natural laws of thinking, the laws which hold for all judgments whatever, whether correct or false. It would, however, be absurd to interpret this proposition as if such laws only were psychological as applied with the most embracing generality to *all* judgments whatever, whereas special laws of judgment, like the laws of correct judgment, were shut out from its purview. (Cf., e.g., Mill, *An Examination,* pp. 459f.) Or does one hold a different opinion? Can one deny that the normative laws of thinking have the character of such special laws? This also will not do. Normative laws of thought, it is said, only try to say how one must proceed *provided* one wants to think *correctly.* "We think correctly, in the material sense, when we think of things as they are. But for us to say, certainly and indubitably, that things are like this or like that, means that the nature of our mind prevents us from thinking of them otherwise. For one need not repeat what has been so often uttered, that one can obviously not think of a thing as it is, without regard to the way in which one must think of it, nor can one make of it so isolated an object of knowledge. The man, therefore, who compares his thought of things with the things themselves can in fact only measure his contingent thinking, influenced by custom, tradition, inclination and aversion, against a thinking that is free from such influences, and that heeds no voice but that of its own inherent lawfulness."

"The rules, therefore, on which one must proceed in order to think rightly are merely rules on which one must proceed in order to think as the nature of thought, its specific lawfulness, demands. They are, in short, identical with the natural laws of thinking itself. Logic is a physics of thinking or it is nothing at all." (Lipps, "Die Aufgabe der Erkenntnistheorie," *Philos. Monatshefte* XVI [1880], pp. 530f.)

It may perhaps be said from the antipsychologistic side:* Of course the various kinds of presentations, judgments, syllogisms, etc., also have a place in psychology as mental phenomena and dispositions, but psychology has a different task in regard to them than logic. Both investigate the laws of these activities, but "law" means something quite different in the two cases. The task of psychology is to investigate the laws governing the real connections of mental events with one another, as well as with related mental dispositions and corresponding events in the bodily organism. "Law" here means a comprehensive formula covering coexistent and successive connections that are without exception and necessary. Such connections are causal. The task of logic is quite different. It does not inquire into the causal origins or consequences of intellectual activities, but into their truth-content: it inquires what such activities *should* be like, or how they *should* proceed, in order that the resultant judgments should be true. Correct judgments and false ones, evident ones and blind ones, come and go according to natural laws, they have causal antecedents and consequences like all mental phenomena. Such natural connections do not, however, interest the logician; he looks rather for ideal connections that he does not always find realized, in fact only exceptionally finds realized in the actual course of thoughts. He aims not at a physics, but an ethics of thinking. Sigwart therefore rightly stresses the point that, in the psychological treatment of thought, "the opposition of true and false has as little part to play as the opposition of good or bad in human conduct is a psychological matter."†

We cannot be content—such will be the psychologistic rejoinder—with such half-truths. The task of logic is of course quite different from that of psychology: who would deny it? It is a technology of knowledge, but how could such a technology ignore questions of causal connection, how could it look for ideal connections without studying natural ones? "As if every 'ought' did not rest on an 'is,' every ethics did not also have to show itself a physics." (Lipps, "Die Aufgabe der Erkenntnistheorie," op. cit., p. 529.) "A question as to what should be done always reduces to a question as to what must be done if a definite goal is to be reached, and this question in its turn is equivalent to a question as to how this goal is *in fact reached"* (Lipps, *Grundzüge der Logik,* §1). That psychology, as distinct from logic, does not deal with the opposition of true and false "does not mean that psychology treats these different mental conditions on a like footing, but that it renders both intelligible in a like manner" (Lipps, op. cit., §2, p. 2). Theoretically regarded, Logic therefore is related to psychology as a part to a whole. Its main aim is, in particular, to set up propositions of the form: Our intellectual activities must, either generally, or in specifically characterized circumstances, have such and such a form, such and such an arrangement, such and such combinations and no others, if the resultant judgments are to have the character of evidence, are to achieve knowledge in the pointed sense of the word. Here we have an obvious causal relation. The psychological character of evidence is a causal consequence of certain antecedents. What sort of antecedents? This is just what we have to explore.‡

The following often repeated argument is no more successful in shaking the psychologistic ranks: Logic, it is said, can as little rest on psychology as on any other science; since each science is only a science in virtue of its

---

*Cf., e.g., W. Hamilton's Lectures III, p. 78, Drobisch, *Neue Darstellung der Logik,* ed. IV, §2; cf. also B. Erdmann, *Logik* I, p. 18.

†*Logik,* vol. I, p. 10. Sigwart's own way of treating logic (as we shall see in Ch. VIII) is altogether on psychologistic lines.

‡This point of view is expressed with increasing clearness in the works of Mill, Sigwart, Wundt, and Höfler-Meinong. Cf. on this the quotations and criticisms in Ch. VIII, §49f.

harmony with logical rules, it presupposes the validity of these rules. It would therefore be circular to try to give logic a first foundation in psychology.*

The opposition will reply: That this argument cannot be right, is shown by the fact that it would prove the impossibility of all logic. Since logic itself must proceed logically, it would itself commit the same circle, would itself have to establish the validity of rules that it presupposes.

Let us, however, consider more closely what such a circle could consist in. Could it mean that psychology presupposes the validity of logical laws? Here one must notice the equivocation in the notion of "presupposing." That a science presupposes the validity of certain rules may mean that they serve as premises in its proofs: it may also mean that they are rules in accordance with which the science must proceed in order to be a science at all. Both are confounded in our argument for which reasoning *according* to logical rules, and reasoning *from* logical rules, count as identical. There would only be a circle if the reasoning were *from* such rules. But, as many an artist creates beautiful works without the slightest knowledge of aesthetics, so an investigation may construct proofs without ever having recourse to logic. Logical laws cannot therefore have been premises in such proofs. And what is true of single proofs is likewise true of whole sciences.

§20. A gap in the psychologistic line of proof

In these and similar arguments the anti-psychologistic party seems undoubtedly to have got the worst of it. Many think the battle quite at an end, they regard the rejoinders of the psychologistic party as completely victorious. One thing only might arouse our philosophical wonder, that there was and is such a battle at all, that the same arguments have repeatedly been adduced while their refutations have not been acknowledged as cogent. If everything really were so plain and clear as the psychologistic trend assures us, the matter would not be readily understandable, since there are unprejudiced, serious and penetrating thinkers on the opposite side as well. Is this not again a case where the truth lies in the middle? Has each of the parties not recognized a valid portion of the truth, and only shown incapacity for its sharp conceptual circumscription, and not even seen that they only had part of the whole? Is there not perhaps an unresolved residuum in the arguments of the anti-psychologists—despite much unclearness and error in detail which has made refutation easy; are they not informed by a true power, which always re-emerges in unbiased discussion? I for my part would answer "Yes." It seems to me that the greater weight of truth lies on the anti-psychologistic side, but that its key thoughts have not been properly worked out, and are blemished by many mistakes.

Let us go back to the question we raised above regarding the essential foundations of normative logic. Have the arguments of psychologistic thinkers really settled this? Here a weak point at once appears. The argument only proves one thing, that psychology *helps* in the foundation of logic, not that it has the only or the main part in this, not that it provides logic's *essential foundation* in the sense above defined (§16). The possibility remains open that another science contributes to its foundation, perhaps in a much more important fashion. Here may be the place for the "pure logic" which on the other party's view, has an existence independent of all psychology, and is a naturally bounded, internally closed-off science. We readily grant that what Kantians and Herbartians have produced under this rubric does not quite accord with the character that our suggested supposition would give it. For

---

*Cf. Lotze's *Logik,* ed. II, 332, pp. 543–544; Natorp, "Über objektive und subjektive Begründungen der Erkenntnis," *Philos. Monatshefte* XXIII, p. 264; Erdmann's *Logik,* vol. I, p. 18. As against this cf. Stumpf, "Psychologie und Erkenntnistheorie," p. 5 *(Proceedings of Kais. Bay. Akad. d. Wiss.,* I Kl., vol. XIX, Section II, p. 469). That Stumpf is discussing epistemology, not logic, obviously makes no essential difference.

they always talk of normative laws of thinking and particularly of concept-formation, judgment-framing, etc. Proof enough, one might say, that their subject-matter is neither theoretical nor wholly unpsychological. But this objection would lose weight if closer investigation confirmed the surmise suggested to us above in §13, that these schools were unlucky in defining and building up the intended discipline, yet none the less approached it closely, in so far as they discerned an abundance of interconnected theoretical truths in traditional logic, which did not fit into psychology, nor into any other separate science, and so permitted one to divine the existence of a peculiar realm of truth. And if these were the truths to which all logical regulation in the last resort related, truths mainly to be thought of when "logical truths" were in question, one could readily come to see in them what was essential to the whole of logic, and to give the name of "pure logic" to their theoretical unity. That this hits off the true state of things I hope actually to prove.

The Prejudices of Psychologism*

§41. First prejudice

A first prejudice runs: Prescriptions which regulate what is mental must obviously have a mental basis. It is accordingly self-evident that the normative principles of knowledge must be grounded in the psychology of knowledge.

One's delusion vanishes as soon as one abandons general argumentation and turns to the "things themselves."

We must first put an end to a distorted notion which both parties share, by pointing out that logical laws, taken in and for themselves, are not normative propositions at all in the sense of prescriptions, i.e., propositions which tell us, as part of their *content,* how one *should* judge. One must always distinguish between laws that *serve as norms* for our knowledge-activities, and laws which include normativity in their thought-content, and *assert* its universal obligatoriness.

Let us take as an example the well-known syllogistic principle we expressed in the words: A mark of a mark is also a mark of the thing itself. This statement would be commendably brief if its expression were not also an obvious falsehood.† To express it concretely, we shall have to adjust ourselves to a few more words. "It is true of every pair of characters *A, B,* that if every object which has the character *A* also has the character *B,* and if any definite object *S* has the character *A,* then it also has the character *B.*" That this proposition contains the faintest thought of normativity must be strongly denied. We can employ our proposition for normative purposes, but it is not therefore a norm. Anyone who judges that every *A* is also *B,* and that a certain *S* is *A,* ought also to judge that this *S* is *B.* Everyone sees, however, that this proposition is not the original proposition of logic, but one that has been derived from it by bringing in the thought of normativity.

The same obviously holds of all syllogistic laws, as of all laws of pure logic as such.‡

---

*LI, I, 168–174, 177–182, 185–196 (Sections 41, 42, 44–46, and 48–51).

†A mark of a mark is, generally speaking, plainly *not* a mark of the thing. If the principle meant what it literally says, we could infer: This blotting-paper is red, Red is a color, therefore this blotting-paper is a color.

‡In this view, that the normative notion of "ought" does not form part of the content of logical laws, I am glad to find myself in agreement with Natorp, who has recently made the brief and clear remark in his *Sozialpädagogik* (Stuttgart, 1899), §4, that "logical principles, we maintain, are as little about what people actually think in such and such circumstances, as they are about what they ought to think." He says of the equational reasoning "If *A = B* and *B = C, A = C"* that "I perceive its truth when only the terms to be compared, and the relations given together with them, are before me, without having to think in the least of the actual or proper conduct of some corresponding act of thought" (pp. 20–21). There are certain other equally important *rapprochements* between these Prolegomena and the distinguished thinker's present work, which unhappily came too late to assist in forming and expounding these thoughts. Two previous writings of Natorp, the above quoted article from *Phil. Monatshefte* XXIII and the *Einleitung in die Psychologie,* stimulated me, however—though other points in them provoked me to controversy.

But not of such laws alone. A capacity for normative use is shared by the truths of other theoretical disciplines, and above all by those of pure mathematics, which are usually kept separate from logic.* The well-known principle

$$(a+b)(a-b) = a^2-b^2$$

tells us, e.g., that the product of the sum and the difference of any two numbers equals the difference of their squares. Here there is no reference to our judging and the manner in which it *should* be conducted; what we have before us is a theoretical law, not a practical rule. If, however, we consider the corresponding practical proposition: "To arrive at the product of the sum and difference of two numbers, one should find the difference of their squares," we have conversely uttered a practical rule and not a theoretical law. Here, too, the transformation of law into rule involves a bringing in of the notion of normativity; the rule is the obvious, apodeictic consequence of the law, but it none the less differs from it in thought-content.

We can even go further. It is clear that *any* theoretical truth belonging to *any* field of theory can be used in a like manner as the foundation for a universal norm of correct judgment. The laws of logic are not at all peculiar in this respect. In their proper nature, they are not normative but theoretical truths, and as such we can employ them, as we can the truths of all other disciplines, as norms for our judgment.

We cannot, however, treat the general persuasion that the laws of logic are norms of thinking as quite baseless, nor the obviousness with which it impresses us as a mere delusion. These laws must have some intrinsic *prerogative* in the regulation of our thought. But does this mean that the idea of regulation, or of an "ought," must therefore form part of the content of such laws? Can it not *follow* from that content with self-evident necessity? In other words: May not the laws of logic and pure mathematics have a distinctive meaning-content which gives them a *natural right* to regulate our thought?

This simple treatment shows us how both sides have made their mistakes.

The anti-psychologists went wrong by making the regulation of knowledge the "essence," as it were, of the laws of logic. The purely theoretical character of formal logic, and its identity of character with formal mathematics, were thereby insufficiently recognized. It was correctly seen that the set of laws treated in traditional syllogistic theory were remote from psychology. Their natural right to regulate knowledge was recognized, for which reason they must be made the kernel of all practical logic. The difference between the proper content of these laws, and their function, their practical application, was, however, ignored. Men failed to see that so-called basic laws of logic were not in themselves norms, though they could be used normatively. Concern with this normative use had led men to speak of such laws as laws of thought, and so it appeared that these laws, too, had a psychological content, and that their only difference from what are ordinarily called psychological laws lay in this normative function, not possessed by other psychological laws.

The psychologistic thinkers, on the other hand, went wrong in putting forward a presumed axiom whose invalidity we may expose in a few words: It is entirely obvious that each general truth, whether psychological or not, serves to found a rule for correct judgment, but this not only assures us of the meaningful possibility, but even of the actual existence of rules of judgment which do not have their basis in psychology.

Not all rules which set standards for correct judgment are on that account *logical* rules. It is, however, evident that, of the genuinely logical rules which form the nucleus of a technology of scientific thinking, only one set per-

*"Pure" or "formal" mathematics, as I use the term, includes all pure arithmetic and theory of manifolds, but not geometry. Geometry corresponds in pure mathematics to the theory of a three-dimensional Euclidean manifold. This manifold is the generic Idea of space, but not space itself.

mits and demands a psychological establishment: the technical precepts concerning the acquisition and criticism of scientific knowledge. The remaining, much more important group consists of normative transformations of laws, which belong solely to the objective or ideal content of the science. Psychological logicians, even such as are of the stature of a Mill or a Sigwart, treat science from its subjective side (as a methodology of the specifically human acquisition of knowledge), rather than from its objective side (as the Idea of the theoretical unity of truth), and therefore lay one-sided stress on the methodological tasks of logic. In doing so they ignore the *fundamental difference between the norms of pure logic and the technical rules of a specifically human art of thought.* These are totally different in character in their content, origin and function. The laws of logic, seen in their original intent, concern only what is ideal, while these methodological propositions concern only what is real. If the former spring from immediately evident axioms, the latter spring from empirical facts, belonging mainly to psychology. If the formulation of the former promotes our purely theoretical interests, and gives only subsidiary practical help, the latter, on the other hand, have an immediate practical aim, and they only give indirect help to our theoretical interests, in so far as they aim at the methodical progress of scientific knowledge.

§42. Elucidations

Every theoretical statement, we saw above, permits of a normative transformation. But the rules for correct judgment which thus arise are not, in general, such as logic, considered as a technology, requires: few of them are, as it were, predestined to normativity. If such a logical technology is to be of real help in our scientific endeavors, it must not presuppose that full knowledge of the complete sciences which we hope to achieve by its means. We shall not be helped by the mechanical restatement of all given theoretical knowledge as norms: what we need are general norms, extending beyond all particular sciences to the critical evaluation of theoretical knowledge and its methods in general, as well as practical rules for its promotion.

This is exactly what logic as a technology aims at, and if it aims at this as a scientific discipline, it must itself presuppose certain items of theoretical knowledge. It is clear from the start that it must attach exceptional worth to all knowledge resting only on the notions of Truth, Proposition, Subject, Predicate, Object, Property, Ground and Consequent, Relation and Relatum, etc. For all science in its objective, theoretical aspects, i.e., in respect of *what* it tells us, consists of truths, truth pertains to propositions, all propositions have subjects and predicates, and refer by way of these to things or properties, propositions are connected as grounds and consequents, etc. Those truths, it is now clear, which have their roots in such *essential constituents of all science considered as an objective theoretical unity,* truths which, accordingly, cannot be thought away without thinking away all that gives science as such its objective purchase and sense, such truths obviously provide the fundamental standards by which we can decide whether anything claiming to be a science, or to belong to one, whether as premiss, conclusion, syllogism, induction, proof or theory, really lives up to its intentions, or does not rather stand in an a priori conflict with the ideal conditions of the possibility of theory and science as such. Men should admit that truths which have their roots in the concepts which constitute the objectively conceived Idea of Science, cannot also belong to the field of any particular science. They should see that such truths, being ideal, cannot have their home-ground in the sciences of matter of fact, and therefore not in psychology. If these facts were realized, our case would be won, and it would be impossible to dispute the existence of a peculiar science of pure logic, absolutely independent of all other scientific disciplines, which delimits the concepts constitutive of the Idea of System or of theoretical unity, and which goes on to investigate the theoretical connections whose roots lie solely in these concepts. This science would have the unique peculiarity of itself, *qua* form, underlying the content of its laws; the elements and theoretical connections of which it, as a systematic unity of truths, consists, are governed by the very laws which form part of its theoretical content.

That the science which deals with all sciences in respect of their form should *eo ipso* deal with itself, may sound paradoxical, but involves no inner conflict. The simplest example will make this clear. The law of contradiction governs all truth, and since it is itself a truth, governs itself. To realize what such self-government means one need only apply the law of contradiction to itself: the resultant proposition is an obvious truism, having none of the marks of the remarkable or the questionable. This is invariably the case where pure logic is used to regulate itself.

This pure logic is therefore the first and most essential foundation of methodological logic. The latter, however, has other quite different foundations contributed by psychology. Every science, as we stated above, permits of a double treatment: it is, on the one hand, an aggregate of human devices for acquiring, systematically delimiting and expounding this or that territory of truth. These devices are called methods, e.g., calculation by abacus or slide-rule, by written signs on a slate, by this or that computer, by logarithmic, sine- or tangent-tables, astronomical methods involving cross-wires or telescopes, physiological methods involving microscopy, staining, etc. All these methods, and also all forms of exposition, are adapted to the human constitution as it at present normally is, and are in fact in part expressive of contingent, national features. Even physiological organization has a not unimportant part to play. Would our most refined optical instruments be of much use to a being whose sense of sight was attached to an end-organ differing considerably from our own?

But all science permits of quite another treatment; it can be considered in regard to *what* it teaches, in regard to its theoretical content. What each statement states is—in the ideal case—a truth. No truth is, however, iso-

lated in science: it occurs in combination with other truths in theoretical connections bound by relations of ground and consequent. This objective content of science, to the extent that it really lives up to its intent, is quite independent of the scientist's subjectivity, of the peculiarities of human nature in general. It is objective truth.

Pure logic aims at this ideal side of science, in respect of its form. It does not aim at the peculiar material of the various special sciences, or the peculiarity of their truths and forms of combination: it aims at what relates to truths and theoretical combinations of truths as such. For this reason *every* science must, on its objective, theoretical side, conform to the laws of logic, which are of an entirely ideal character.

In this way these ideal laws acquire a methodological significance, which they also have since mediate justification is provided by proofs whose norms are merely normative transformations of the ideal laws whose sole grounds lie in logical categories. The characteristic peculiarities of proofs mentioned in the first chapter of this work (§7) all have their origin and complete explanation in the fact that inner evidence in demonstration—whether in the syllogism, in connected, apodeictic proof, or in the unity of the most comprehensive, rational theory, or also in the unity of an argument in probabilities—is simply our consciousness of an ideal law. Purely logical reflection, whose first historic awakening occurred in the genius of Aristotle, abstracts the underlying law itself, and then brings the multiplicity of laws discoverable in this manner, and at first seen in isolation, under primitive basic laws, and so creates a scientific system which, in a purely deductive order, permits the derivation of all possible laws of pure logic, all possible forms of syllogisms, proofs, etc. The forms of logic transform themselves into norms or rules telling us how we should conduct proofs, and—in relation to possible illegal formations—into rules telling us how we should not conduct them.

Norms accordingly fall into two classes. One class of norms regulates all proof and all apodeictic connection a priori; it is purely ideal, and only relates to our human knowledge by way of a self-evident application. The other class is empirical, and relates essentially to the specifically human side of the science. It consists of what might be called mere auxiliary devices or substitutes for proofs (above §9). It has its roots in our general human constitution, in the main, in our mental constitution, since this is more important for logical technology, but also in part in our physical constitution.*

§44. Second prejudice

To confirm its first prejudice that rules for cognition must rest on the psychology of cognition, the psychologistic party appeals to the actual content of logic (cf. the arguments of §18 above, pp. 3–4, par. 2). What is logic about? Everywhere it concerns itself with presentations and judgments, with syllogisms and proofs, with truth and probability, with necessity and possibility, with ground and consequent, and with other closely related or connected concepts. But what can be thought of under such headings but mental phenomena and formations? This is obvious in the case of presentations and judgments. Syllogisms, however, are proofs of judgments by means of judgments, and proof is plainly a mental activity. Talk of truth, probability, necessity, possibility, etc., likewise concerns judgments: what they refer to can only be manifested or experienced in judgments. Is it not, therefore, strange that one should wish to exclude from psychology propositions and theories which relate to psychological phenomena? In this regard the distinction between purely logical and methodological propositions is pointless, the objection affects both equally. Every attempt, therefore, to extrude even a part of logic from psychology, on ground of its pretended "purity," must count as radically mistaken.

§45. Refutation. Pure mathematics would likewise be made a branch of psychology

Obvious as all this may seem, it *must* be mistaken. This is shown by the absurd consequences which, as we know, psychologism cannot escape. There is, however, another reason for misgiving: the natural affinity between purely logical and mathematical doctrine, which has often led to an assertion of their theoretical unity.

We have already mentioned by the way that even Lotze taught that mathematics must be regarded as "an independently developed branch of general logic." "Only a practically motivated division of teaching" can, he thinks, blind us to the fact that mathematics "has its whole home-ground in the general field of logic" *(Logik,* ed. II, §18, p. 34 and §112, p. 138). To which Riehl adds that "one could well say that logic coincides with the general part of purely formal mathematics (taken in the sense of H. Hankel)" (A. Riehl, *Der philosophische Kritizismus und seine Bedeutung für die positive Wissenschaft,* vol. II, Part 1, p. 226). However this may be, an argument that is correct for logic must be approved in the case of arithmetic as well. Arithmetic sets up laws for numbers, for their relations and combinations: numbers, however, are the products of colligation and counting, which are mental activities. Relations arise from relating activities, combinations from acts of combination. Adding and multiplying, subtracting and dividing—these are merely mental processes. That they require sensuous supports makes no difference, since this is true of any and every act of thinking. Sums, products, differences and quotients, and whatever may be determined in arithmetical propositions, are merely mental processes, and must as such obey mental laws. It may be highly desirable that modern psychology with its earnest pursuit of exactness

---

*Elementary arithmetic provides good examples of this last. A being that could intuit three-dimensional arrangements (with difference of sign) as clearly and with as much practical mastery as men are able to intuit two-dimensional arrangements would possibly have quite different methods of calculation. My *Philosophie der Arithmetik* deals with such questions, and, in particular, with the influence of physical circumstances on methodical set-up, pp. 275f., 312ff.

should be widened to include mathematical theories, but it would hardly be much elevated by the inclusion of mathematics itself as one of its parts. For the heterogeneity of the two sciences cannot be denied. The mathematician, on the other hand, would merely smile if psychological studies were pressed upon him as supposedly providing a better and deeper grounding for his theoretical pronouncements. He would rightly say that mathematics and psychology belong to such different worlds that the very thought of interchange among them was absurd: here, if anywhere, talk of a μετάβασις εἰς ἄλλο γένος is applicable.*

§46. *The territory to be investigated by pure logic is, like that of mathematics, an ideal territory*

These objections may have taken our argument far afield, but, when we attend to their content, they help us to state the basic errors of our opponents' position. *The comparison of pure logic with pure mathematics,* its mature sister discipline, which no longer needs fight for its right to independent existence, provides us with a reliable *Leitmotiv.* We shall first glance at mathematics.

No one regards the theories of pure mathematics, e.g., the pure theory of numbers, as "parts or branches of psychology," though we should have no numbers without counting, no sums without addition, no products without multiplication, etc. The patterns of all arithmetical operations refer back to certain mental acts of arithmetical operation, and only in reflection upon these can we "show" what a total, sum, product, etc., is. In spite of the "psychological origin" of arithmetical concepts, everyone sees it to be a fallacious μετάβασις to demand that mathematical laws should be

psychological. How is this to be explained? Only *one* answer is possible. Counting and arithmetical operation as *facts,* as mental acts proceeding in time, are of course the concern of psychology, since it is the empirical science of mental facts in general. Arithmetic is in a totally different position. Its domain of research is known, it is completely and exhaustively determined by the familiar series of ideal species 1, 2, 3 . . . In this sphere there can be no talk of individual facts, of what is temporally definite. Numbers, Sums and Products and so forth are not such casual acts of counting, adding and multiplying, etc., as proceed here and there. They also differ obviously from *presentations* in which they are given. The number Five is not my own or anyone else's counting of five, it is also not my presentation or anyone else's presentation of five. It is in the latter regard a possible *object* of acts of presentation, whereas, in the former, it is the ideal *species* of a form whose concrete *instances* are found in what becomes objective in certain acts of counting, in the collective whole that these constitute. In no case can it be regarded without absurdity as a *part* or *side* of a mental experience, and so not as something real. If we make clear to ourselves what the number Five truly is, if we conceive of it adequately, we shall first achieve an articulate, collective presentation of this or that set of five objects. In this act a collection is intuitively given in a certain formal articulation, and so as an instance of the number-species in question. Looking at this intuited individual, we perform an "abstraction," i.e., we not only isolate the non-independent moment of collective form in what is before us, but we apprehend the Idea in it: the number Five as the species of the form swims into our conscious sphere of reference. What we are now meaning is not

---

*See in addition the fine statement of Natorp "Über objektive und subjektive Begründung der Erkenntnis," *Philos. Monatshefte* XXIII, pp. 265f. Cf. also G. Frege's stimulating work *Die Grundlagen der Arithmetik* (1884), pp. vif. I need hardly say that I no longer approve of my own fundamental criticisms of Frege's antipsychologistic position set forth in my *Philosophie der Arithmetik,* I, pp. 124–132. I may here take the opportunity, in relation to all of the discussions of these Prolegomena, to refer to the Preface of Frege's later work *Die Grundgesetze der Arithmetik,* vol. I (Jena, 1893).

this individual instance, not the intuited object as a whole, not the form immanent in it but still inseparable from it: what we mean is rather the *ideal form-species,* which is absolutely one in the sense of arithmetic, in whatever mental act it may be individuated for us in an intuitively constituted collective, a species which is accordingly untouched by the contingency, temporality and transience of our mental acts. Acts of counting arise and pass away and cannot be meaningfully mentioned in the same breath as numbers.

Arithmetical propositions are concerned with such ideal unities ("lowest species" in a heightened sense quite different from that of empirical classes), and this holds both of numerical propositions (arithmetical singulars) and of algebraic propositions (arithmetical generalizations). They tell us nothing about what is real, neither about the real things counted, nor about the real acts in which they are counted, in which such and such indirect numerical characteristics are constituted for us. Concrete numbers and numerical propositions belong in the scientific fields to which the relevant concrete units belong: propositions about arithmetical thought-processes belong in psychology. In strict propriety, arithmetical propositions say nothing about "what is contained in our mere number-presentations": as little as they speak of other presentations, do they speak of ours. They are rather concerned with absolute numbers and number-combinations in their abstract purity and ideality. The propositions of universal arithmetic—the nomology of arithmetic we may call it—are laws rooted *in the ideal essence of the genus Number.* The *ultimate* singulars which come within the range of these laws are *ideal singulars:* they are the determinate numbers, i.e., the lowest specific differences of the genus number. It is to these singulars that arithmetically singular propositions relate, propositions which belong to the arithmetic of definite numbers. These arise through the application of universal arithmetical laws to numerically specific numbers, they express what is purely part of the ideal essence of these numbers. None of these propositions

reduces to one that has empirical generality, not even to the widest case of such generality, one that applies without exception to the entire real world.

What we have here said in regard to pure arithmetic carries over at all points to *pure logic.* In the latter case, too, we accept as obvious the fact that logical concepts have a psychological origin, but we deny the psychologistic conclusion to which this seems to lead. In consideration of the domain that must be granted to logic in the sense of a *technology* of scientific knowledge, we naturally do not doubt that logic is to a large extent concerned with our mental states. Naturally the methodology of scientific research and proof must take full cognizance of the nature of the mental states in which research and proof take their course. Logical terms such as "presentation," "concept," "judgment," "syllogism," "proof," "theory," "necessity," "truth," etc., may therefore, and must therefore, come up as general names for psychical experiences and dispositions. We deny, however, that this ever occurs in the purely logical parts of logical technology. We deny that the theoretical discipline of pure logic, in the independent separateness proper to it, has any concern with mental facts, or with laws that might be styled "psychological." We saw that the laws of pure logic, e.g., the primitive "laws of thought," or the syllogistic formulae, totally lose their basic sense if one tries to interpret them as psychological. It is therefore clear from the start *that the concepts which constitute these and similar laws have no empirical range.* They cannot, in other words, have the character of those mere universal notions whose range is that of individual singulars, but they must be notions truly *generic, whose range is exclusively one of ideal singulars, genuine species.* It is clear, for the rest, that the terms in question, and all such as function in purely logical contexts, must be *equivocal;* they must, on the one hand, stand for class-concepts of mental states such as belong in psychology, but, on the other hand, for generic concepts covering ideal singulars, which belong in a sphere of pure law.

§48. The fundamental differences

We shall conclude by stressing the fundamental differences on whose recognition or non-recognition one's total response to the psychologistic line of argument depends. These are as follows:

1. There is an essential, quite unbridgeable difference between sciences of the ideal and sciences of the real. The former are a priori, the latter empirical. The former set forth ideal general laws, grounded with intuitive certainty in certain general concepts: the latter establish real general laws, relating to a sphere of fact, with probabilities into which we have insight. The extension of general concepts is, in the former case, one of lowest specific differences, in the latter case one of individual, temporally determinate singulars. Ultimate objects are, in the former case, ideal species, in the latter case, empirical facts. The essential differences between natural laws and ideal laws, between universal propositions of fact (perhaps disguised as general propositions: "All ravens are black," "The raven is black") and genuine generalizations (such as the universal propositions of pure mathematics), between the notion of an empirical class and that of an ideal genus, etc. A correct assessment of these differences presupposes the complete abandonment of the empiricistic theory of abstraction, whose present dominance renders all logical matters unintelligible. We shall have to speak in detail of this matter later on (cf. Investigation II).

2. In all knowledge, and particularly in all scientific knowledge, there are three fundamentally distinct patterns of connection:

(a) A pattern of connection of *cognitive experiences,* in which science is subjectively realized, a *psychological pattern of connection* among the presentations, judgments, insights, surmises, questions, etc., in which research is carried out, in which a theory already discovered receives its insightful thinking out.

(b) A pattern of connection among the *matters* investigated and theoretically known in the science, which constitute its sphere a territory. The pattern of connection of investigation and

knowing is plainly quite different from that of what is investigated and known.

(c) The logical pattern of connection, i.e., the specific pattern of connection of the theoretical Ideas in which the unity of the truths of a scientific discipline, and those, in particular, of a scientific theory or proof or inference, are constituted (the unity of concepts in a true proposition, of simple truths in truth-combinations, etc.).

In the case, e.g., of physics we distinguish between the pattern of connection of the mental states of the physical thinker from that of the physical nature that he knows, and both from the ideal pattern of connection of the truths in physical theory, e.g., in the unity of analytical mechanics, of theoretical optics, etc. Even the form of an argument in probability, which governs the connection between facts and hypotheses, is part of this logical line. The logical pattern of connection is the ideal form for the sake of which we speak *in specie* of the same truth, the same syllogism or proof, the same theory and rational discipline, by whomsoever these "same things" may be thought. This unity of form is one of legal validity, of the validity of laws under which all these "same things" stand, the validity, i.e., of the laws of pure logic, which accordingly overshadow all science, and do so, not in respect of the psychological or objective content of science, but in respect of its ideal meaning-load. The peculiar patterns of combination of the concepts, propositions and truths which form the ideal unity of a particular science can of course only be called "logical," in so far as they are *instances* falling under logic. They do not belong among the actual parts of logic.

The three patterns of combination just distinguished naturally concern logic and arithmetic like all other sciences. Only in their case, the matters investigated are not, as in physics, real matters of fact, but ideal species. The specific nature of logic involves the previously noted peculiarity that the ideal patterns of combination which make up its theoretical unity are themselves subordinate instances of the laws that it sets up. Logical laws are at once parts and rules of such patterns of combination: they belong to the *theoretical structure,* but at the same time to the *field,* of logical science.

§49. *Third prejudice. Logic as the theory of inner evidence*

We shall state a third prejudice—one particularly to the fore in the arguments of chapter 11, §19—in the following words: All truth pertains to judgment. Judgment, however, is only recognized as true when it is *inwardly evident.* The term "inner evidence" stands, it is said, for a peculiar mental character, well-known to everyone through his inner experience, a peculiar feeling which guarantees the truth of the judgment to which it attaches. If logic is the technology which will assist us to know the truth, logical laws are obviously psychological propositions. They are, in fact, propositions which cast light on the psychological conditions on which the presence or absence of this "feeling of inner evidence" depends. Practical prescriptions are naturally connected with such propositions, and help us to achieve judgments having this distinctive character. Such psychologically based rules of thought must surely be meant where we speak of logical laws or norms.

Mill hits on this conception when he attempts to draw a line between logic and psychology, and says: "The properties of thought which concern logic are some of its contingent properties, those namely on the presence of which depends good thinking as distinguished from bad" *(An Examination of Sir William Hamilton's Philosophy,* p. 462). In his further statements, he repeatedly calls logic the (psychologically conceived) "theory" or "philosophy of evidence" (op. cit., pp. 473, 475–76, 478); he was of course not immediately concerned with the propositions of pure logic. In Germany this point of view occasionally crops

up in Sigwart. "Logic," he says, "can only proceed by becoming conscious of the way this subjective feeling of necessity [the 'inner feeling' of the evident of our previous paragraph] makes its appearance, and then expressing these conditions in a general manner" *(Logik,* I, ed. 2, p. 16). Many statements of Wundt's tend in a similar direction. We read, e.g., in his *Logik* that "the properties of self-evidence and universal validity involved in certain thought-connections, permit us to derive the logical from the psychological laws of thought." The normative character of the former "has its sole foundation in the fact that certain psychological thought-connections actually *do* have self-evidence and universal validity, without which it would not be possible for us to approach thought with the demand that it *should* satisfy the conditions of the self-evident and universally valid." "The conditions that must themselves be fulfilled if we are to have self-evidence and universal validity are called the logical laws of thought." But Wundt emphasizes that "psychological thinking is always the more comprehensive form of thinking."*

In the logical literature at the end of last century the interpretation of logic as a practically applied psychology of the inwardly evident certainly became more penetrating and more widely entertained. The *Logik* of Höfler and Meinong here deserves special mention, since it may be regarded as the first properly carried out attempt to make a thorough, consistent use of the notion of the psychology of inward evidence over the whole field of logic. Höfler says that the main task of logic is the investigation of "those laws, primarily psychological, which express the dependence of emergent inward evidence on the particular properties of our presentations and judgments" *(Logik* [Vienna, 1890], p. 16). "Among all actually given thought-phenomena, or even such as we can conceive possible, logic must pick

---

*Wundt, *Logik,* I, ed. 2, p. 91. Wundt regularly couples inner evidence with universal validity in this passage. As regards the latter, he distinguishes between a subjective form of universal validity, a mere consequence of inner evidence, and an objective form, which also covers the postulate of the intelligibility of experience. But as the justification and adequate fulfillment of this postulate itself rests on inner evidence, it does not seem feasible to drag in "universal validity" into discussions of basic principles.

out the types or forms of thinking to which inner evidence attaches directly, or which are necessary conditions for the emergence of inner evidence" (op. cit., p. 17). The seriousness of such psychologism is shown by the rest of the treatment. Thus the method of logic, in its concern with the theoretical groundwork of correct thinking, is said to be the same method that psychology applies to *all* mental phenomena: it must *describe* such phenomena, in this case those of correct thinking, and reduce them as far as may be to simple laws, i.e., explain more complex laws by way of simple ones (op. cit., p. 18). Further on, one reads that the logical doctrine of the syllogism is given the task of "formulating the laws, which tell us what features in our premisses determine whether a certain judgment can be deduced from them with inward evidence." Etc., etc.

§50. Transformation of logical propositions into equivalent propositions about the ideal conditions for inner evidence. The resultant propositions are not psychological

We turn to criticism. We are far from regarding as unobjectionable the nowadays commonplace but far from clear assumption with which the argument starts, that all truth lies in our judgments. We do not of course doubt that to know truth and to utter it justifiably presupposes the prior seeing of it. Nor do we doubt that logic as a technology must look into the psychological conditions in which inner evidence illuminates our judgments. We may even go a further step in the direction of the conception we are refuting. While we seek to preserve the distinction between purely logical and methodological propositions, we expressly concede that the former have a relation to the psychological datum of inner evidence, that they in a sense state its psychological conditions.

Such a relation must, however, be regarded as purely ideal and indirect. The pure laws of logic say absolutely nothing about inner evidence or its conditions. We can show, we hold, that they only achieve this relation through a process of application or transformation, the same sort of process, in fact, through which every purely conceptual law permits application to a generally conceived realm of empirical cases. The propositions about inner evidence which arise in this manner keep their a priori character, and the conditions of inner evidence that they assert bear no trace of the psychological or the real. They are purely conceptual propositions, transformable, as in every like case, into statements about *ideal* incompatibilities or possibilities.

A little reflection will make matters clear. Every law of pure logic permits of an (inwardly evident) transformation, possible a priori, which allows one to read off certain propositions about inward evidence, certain conditions of inward evidence, from it. The combined principles of contradiction and excluded middle are certainly equivalents to the proposition: One and only *one* of two mutually contradictory judgments *can* manifest inner evidence.* The mood *Barbara* is likewise certainly equivalent to the proposition: The inner evidence of the necessary truth of a proposition of the form *All A's are C's* (more precisely, its truth as a necessary consequence), may appear in a syllogizing act whose premisses are of the forms *All A's are B's* and *All B's are C's*. The like holds of every proposition of pure logic.

---

*If we really had to interpret the theory of inner evidence in the manner of Höfler on p. 133, op. cit., it would have been corrected by our previous critique of empiricistic misunderstandings of logical principles (see §23). Höfler's statement "that an affirmative and a negative judgment about the same object are incompatible" is, as an exact statement, false, and can even less count as a statement of the logical principle. A similar mistake slips into the definition of the correlatives "ground" and "consequence": if it were correct, it would falsify all syllogistic rules. It runs: "A judgment *C* is the consequence of a ground *G*, if the *belief* in the falsity of *C* is incompatible with the (imagined) *belief* in the truth of *G*" (op. cit., p. 136). Note that Höfler explains incompatibility in terms of evident non-coexistence (op. cit., p. 129). He plainly confuses the ideal non-coexistence (i.e., lack of joint truth) of the propositions in question, with the real non-coexistence of the corresponding acts of affirmation, presentation, etc.

Understandably so, since there evidently is a general equivalence between the proposition *A is true* and *It is possible for anyone to judge A to be true in an inwardly evident manner.* The propositions, therefore, whose sense lies in stating what necessarily is involved in the notion of truth, that the truth of propositions of certain forms determines the truth of propositions of corresponding other forms, can certainly be transformed into equivalent propositions which connect the possible emergence of inner evidence with the forms of our judgments.

Our insight into such connections will, however, provide us with the means to refute the attempt to swallow up pure logic in a psychology of inner evidence. In itself, plainly, the proposition *A is true* does not state the same thing as the equivalent proposition *It is possible for anyone and everyone to judge that A is the case.* The former says nothing about anyone's judgment, not even about judgments of anyone in general. The position here resembles that of propositions of pure mathematics. The statement that $a + b = b + a$ states that the numerical value of the sum of two numbers is independent of their position in such a sum, but it says nothing about anyone's acts of counting or addition. The latter first enters the picture in an inwardly evident, equivalent transformation. It is an a priori truth that no number can be given *in concreto* unless we count, and no sum unless we add.

But even when we abandon the original forms of the propositions of pure logic, and turn them into corresponding equivalents regarding inward evidence, nothing results which psychology could claim as its own. Psychology is an empirical science, the science of mental facts, and psychological possibility is accordingly a case of real possibility. Such possibilities of inner evidence are, however, real ones, and what is psychologically impossible may very well be ideally possible. The solution of the generalized "3-body problem," or "*n*-body problem" may transcend all human cognitive capacity, but the problem *has* a solution, and the inner evidence which relates to it is therefore possible. There are decimal numbers with trillions of places, and there are truths relating to them. No one, however, can actually imagine such numbers, nor do the additions, multiplications, etc., relating to them. Inward evidence is here a psychological impossible, yet, *ideally* speaking, it undoubtedly represents a possible state of mind.

The turning of the notion of truth into the notion of the possibility of evident judgment has its analogue in the relation of the concepts *Individual Being* and *Possibility of Perception.* The equivalence of these concepts, if by "perception" we mean adequate perception, is undeniable. A perception is accordingly *possible* in which the whole world, with the endless abundance of its bodies, is perceived at *one* glance. But this ideal possibility is of course no real possibility, we could not attribute it to any empirical subject, particularly since such a vision would be an endless continuum of vision: unitarily conceived, it would be a Kantian Idea.

Though we stress the ideality of the possibilities of evident judgment which can be derived from logical principles, and which we see to reveal their a priori validity in cases of apodeictic self-evidence, we do not deny their *psychological utility.* If we take the law that, out of two contradictory propositions, one is true and one is false, and deduce from it the truth that, one only out of every pair of possible contradictory judgments can have the character of inward evidence, we may note this to be a self-evidently correct deduction, if self-evidence be defined as the experience in which the correctness of his judgment is brought home to a judging subject, the new proposition utters a truth about the compatibilities or incompatibilities of certain *mental experiences.* In this manner, however, every proposition of pure mathematics tells us something about possible and impossible happenings in the mental realm. No empirical enumeration or calculation, no mental act of algebraical transformation or geometrical construction, is possible which conflicts with the ideal laws of mathematics. These laws accordingly have a psychological use. We can read off from each of them a priori possibilities and impossibilities relating to certain sorts of mental acts, acts of counting, of additive and multiplicative combination, etc. These laws are not thereby made into psychological laws. Psychology, the natural science concerned with what we mentally live through, has to look into the *natural conditions* of our experience. In its field are specifically to be found the empirically real relationships of our mathematical and logical activities, whose *ideal* relations and laws make up an independent realm. This latter realm is set up in purely universal propositions, made up out of "concepts" which are not class-concepts of mental acts but ideal concepts of essence, each with its concrete foundation in such mental acts or in their objective correlates. The number Three, the Truth named after Pythagoras, etc., are, as our discussion showed, neither empirical singulars nor classes of singulars: they are ideal objects ideationally apprehended in the correlates of our acts of counting, of inwardly evident judging, etc.

In relation to inner evidence, psychology has therefore merely the task of tracking down the *natural* conditions of the experiences which fall under this rubric, of investigating the real contexts in which, as experience shows, inward evidence arises and perishes. Such natural conditions are concentration of interest, a certain mental freshness, practice, etc. Their investigation does not lead to knowledge which is exact in its content, to inwardly evident, truly lawlike generalizations, but only to vague, empirical generalizations. The inward evidence of our judgments does not merely depend on such psychological conditions, conditions that one might also call external and empirical, since they are rooted not purely in the specific form and matter of our judgment, but in its empirical context in mental life: it depends also on *ideal* conditions. Each truth stands as an ideal unit over against an endless, unbounded possibility of correct statements which have its form and its matter in common. Each actual judgment, which belongs to this ideal manifold, will fulfill, either in its mere form or in its matter, the ideal conditions for its own possible inward evidence. The laws of pure logic are truths rooted in the concept of truth, and in

concepts essentially related to this concept. They state, in relation to possible acts of judgment, and on the basis of their mere form, the ideal conditions of the possibility or impossibility of their inner evidence. Of these two sorts of conditions of the inwardly evident, the former relates to the special constitution of the sorts of psychical being which the psychology of the period recognizes, psychological induction being limited by experience. The other conditions, however, have the character of ideal laws, and hold generally for every possible consciousness.

§51. *The decisive points in this dispute*

A final clearing-up of our present dispute depends likewise on a correct discernment of the most fundamental of epistemological distinctions, the distinction between the real and the ideal, or the correct discernment of all the distinctions into which this distinction can be analyzed. We are here concerned with the repeatedly stressed distinctions between real and ideal truths, laws, sciences, between real and ideal (individual and specific) generalities and also singularities, etc. Everyone, no doubt, has some acquaintance with these distinctions: even so extreme an empiricist as Hume draws a fundamental distinction between "relations of ideas" and "matters of fact," a distinction which the great idealist Leibniz drew before him, using the rubrics *vérités de raison* and *vérités de fait*. To draw an epistemologically important distinction does not, however, mean that one has as yet grasped its epistemological essence. One must clearly grasp what the ideal is, both intrinsically and in its relation to the real, how this ideal stands to the real, how it can be immanent in it and so come to knowledge. The basic question is whether ideal objects of thought are—to use the prevailing jargon—mere pointers to "thought-economies," verbal abbreviations whose true content merely reduces to individual, singular experiences, mere presentations and judgments concerning individual facts, or whether the idealist is right in holding that such an empiricistic doctrine, nebulous in its generality, can indeed be uttered, but in no wise thought out, that all attempts to reduce ideal unities to real singulars are involved in hopeless absurdities, that its splintering of concepts into a range of singulars, without a concept to unify such a range in our thought, cannot be thought, etc.

The understanding of our distinction between the real and the ideal "theory of inner evidence" presupposes, on the other hand, correct concepts of *inner evidence* and *truth.* In the psychologistic literature of the last decades we have seen inner evidence spoken of as a casual feeling which attends on certain judgments, and is absent from others, which at best has a universally human linkage with certain judgments and not with others, a linkage in every normal human being in normal circumstances of judgment. There are certain normal circumstances in which every normal person feels self-evidence in connection with the proposition $2 + 1 = 1 + 2$, just as he feels pain when he gets burnt. One might then well ask what gives such a special feeling authority, how it manages to guarantee the truth of our judgment, "impress the stamp of truth" on it, "proclaim its truth," or whatever the other metaphor one cares to use. One might also ask what such vague talk of normal endowment and normal circumstances precisely covers, and might point to the fact that even this recourse to normality will not make inwardly evident judgments coincide with true ones. It is in the last resort undeniable that even the normal man in normal circumstances must pass, in an unnumbered majority of cases, possible correct judgments which lack inner evidence. One would surely not wish to conceive the "normality" in question in such a way that no actual human being, and no possible human being living in our finite natural conditions, could be called "normal."

Empiricism altogether misunderstands the relation between the ideal and the real: it likewise misunderstands the relation between truth and inner evidence. Inner evidence is no accessory feeling, either casually attached, or attached by natural necessity, to certain judgments. It is not the sort of mental character that simply lets itself be attached to any and every

judgment of a certain class, i.e., the so-called "true" judgments, so that the phenomenological content of such a judgment, considered in and for itself, would be the same whether or not it had this character. The situation is not at all like the way in which we like to conceive of the connection between sensations and the feelings which relate to them: two persons, we think, have the same sensations but are differently affected in their feelings. Inner evidence is rather nothing but the "experience" of truth. Truth is of course only experienced in the sense in which something ideal can be an experience in a real act. Otherwise put: *Truth is an Idea, whose particular case is an actual experience in the inwardly evident judgment.* The inwardly evident judgment is, however, an experience of primal givenness: the non-self-evident judgment stands to it much as the arbitrary positing of an object in imagination stands to its adequate perception. A thing adequately perceived is not a thing merely meant in some manner or other: it is a thing primarily given in our act, and as what we mean it, i.e., as itself given and grasped without residue. In like fashion what is self-evidently judged is not merely judged (meant in a judging, assertive, affirmative manner) but is given in the judgment-experience as itself present—present in the sense in which a state of affairs, meant in this or that manner, according to its kind, whether singular or general, empirical or ideal, etc., can be "present." The analogy which connects all experiences of primal givenness then leads to analogous ways of speaking, and inner evidence is called a seeing, a grasping of the self-given (true) state of affairs, or, as we say with tempting equivocation, of the truth. And, as in the realm of perception, the unseen does not at all coincide with the nonexistent, so lack of inward evidence does not amount to untruth. *The experience of the agreement* between meaning and what is itself present, meant, between the actual *sense of an assertion* and the self-given *state of affairs,* is inward evidence: the *Idea* of this agreement is truth, whose ideality is also its objectivity. It is not a chance fact that a propositional thought, occurring here and now, agrees with a given state of affairs: the agreement rather holds between a self-identical propositional meaning, and a self-identical state of affairs. "Validity" or "objectivity," and their opposites, do not pertain to an assertion as a particular temporal experience, but to the assertion *in specie,* to the pure, self-identical assertion $2 \times 2 = 4$, etc.

This conception alone accords with the fact that it makes no difference whether we perform a judgment (a judgment with the content, the meaning J) insightfully, or whether we have insight into the truth, the being of J. We accordingly also have insight into the fact that no one's insight can be at variance with our own (to the extent that either of us really has insight). This has its source in the essential relation between the experience of truth and truth.

Our conception alone escapes the doubt which the conception of inner evidence as a causally connected feeling never can escape, and which plainly amounts to a complete skepticism: the doubt whether, when we have insight that J is the case, another might not have the insight that J', incompatible with J, is the case, that insights in general might not clash with insights, without a hope of settlement. We understand, accordingly, why the "feeling" of inner evidence has no other essential precondition but the truth of the judged content in question. It is obvious that where there is nothing, nothing can be seen, but it is no less obvious that where there is no truth, there can be no seeing something to be true, i.e., no inward evidence (cf. Investigation VI, chapter 5).

2. The Critique of Historicism

"Philosophy as Rigorous Science"*

Historicism and Weltanschauung philosophy

Historicism takes its position in the factual sphere of the empirical life of the spirit. To the extent that it posits this latter absolutely, without exactly naturalizing it (the specific sense of nature in particular lies far from historical thinking and in any event does not influence it by determining it in general), there arises a relativism that has a close affinity to naturalistic psychologism and runs into similar skeptical difficulties. Here we are interested only in what is characteristic of historical skepticism, and we want to familiarize ourselves more thoroughly with it.

Every spiritual formation—taking the term in its widest possible sense, which can include

every kind of social unity, ultimately the unity of the individual itself and also every kind of cultural formation—has its intimate structure, its typology, its marvelous wealth of external and internal forms which in the stream of spirit-life itself grow and transform themselves, and in the very manner of the transformation again cause to come forward differences in structure and type. In the visible outer world the structure and typology of organic development afford us exact analogies. Therein there are no enduring species and no construction of the same out of enduring organic elements. Whatever seems to be enduring is but a stream of development. If by interior intuition we enter vitally into the unity of spirit-life, we can get a feeling for the motivations at play therein and consequently "understand" the essence and development of the spiritual structure in question, in its dependence on a spiritually motivated unity and development. In this man-

*PRS, pp. 122–129. Also reprinted in *Husserl: Shorter Works,* edited by Peter McCormick and Frederick Elliston (Notre Dame, Ind.: University of Notre Dame Press, 1981), pp. 185–188.

ner everything historical becomes for us "understandable," "explicable," in the being peculiar to it, which is precisely "spiritual being," a unity of interiorly self-questioning moments of a sense and at the same time a unity of intelligible structuration and development according to inner motivation. Thus in this manner also art, religion, morals, etc., can be intuitively investigated, and likewise the *Weltanschauung* that stands so close to them and at the same time is expressed in them. It is this *Weltanschauung* that, when it takes on the forms of science and after the manner of science lays claim to objective validity, is customarily called metaphysics, or even philosophy. With a view to such a philosophy there arises the enormous task of thoroughly investigating its morphological structure and typology as well as its developmental connections and of making historically understandable the spiritual motivations that determine its essence, by reliving them from within. That there are significant and in fact wonderful things to be accomplished from this point of view is shown by W. Dilthey's writings, especially the most recently published study on the types of *Weltanschauung*.*

Up to this point we have obviously been speaking of historical science, not of historicism. We shall grasp most easily the motives that impel toward the latter if in a few sentences we follow Dilthey's presentation. We read as follows: "Among the reasons that constantly give new nourishment to skepticism, one of the most effective is the anarchy of philosophical systems" (p. 3). "Much deeper, however, than the skeptical conclusions based on the contradictoriness of human opinions go the doubts that have attached themselves to the progressive development of historical consciousness" (p. 4). "The theory of development (as a theory of evolution based on natural science, bound up with a knowledge of cultural structures based on developmental history) is necessarily linked to the knowledge of the relativity proper to the historical life form. In face of

the view that embraces the earth and all past events, the absolute validity of any particular form of life-interpretation, of religion, and of philosophy disappears. Thus the formation of a historical consciousness destroys more thoroughly than does surveying the disagreement of systems a belief in the universal validity of any of the philosophies that have undertaken to express in a compelling manner the coherence of the world by an ensemble of concepts" (p. 6).

The factual truth of what is said here is obviously indubitable. The question is, however, whether it can be justified when taken as universal in principle. Of course, *Weltanschauung* and *Weltanschauung* philosophy are cultural formations that come and go in the stream of human development, with the consequences that their spiritual content is definitely motivated in the given historical relationships. But the same is true of the strict sciences. Do they for that reason lack objective validity? A thoroughly extreme historicist will perhaps answer in the affirmative. In doing so he will point to changes in scientific views—how what is today accepted as a proved theory is recognized tomorrow as worthless, how some call certain things laws that others call mere hypotheses and still others vague guesses, etc. Does that mean that in view of this constant change in scientific views we would actually have no right to speak of sciences as objectively valid unities instead of merely as cultural formations? It is easy to see that historicism, if consistently carried through, carries over into extreme skeptical subjectivism. The ideas of truth, theory, and science would then, like all ideas, lose their absolute validity. That an idea has validity would mean that it is a factual construction of spirit which is held as valid and which in its contingent validity determines thought. There would be no unqualified validity, or validity-in-itself, which is what it is even if no one has achieved it and though no historical humanity will ever achieve it. Thus too there would then be no validity to the principle of contradiction

---

*Wilhelm Dilthey et al., *Weltanschauung, Philosophie und Religion in Darstellungen* (Berlin: Reichel & Co., 1911).

nor to any logic, which latter is nevertheless still in full vigor in our time. The result, perhaps, will be that the logical principles of non-contradiction will be transformed into their opposites. And to go even further, all the propositions we have just enunciated and even the possibilities that we have weighed and claimed as constantly valid would in themselves have no validity, etc. It is not necessary to go further here and to repeat discussions already given in another place. We shall certainly have said enough to obtain recognition that no matter what great difficulties the relation between a sort of fluid worth and objective validity, between science as a cultural phenomenon and science as a valid systematic theory, may offer an understanding concerned with clarifying them, the distinction and opposition must be recognized. If, however, we have admitted science as a valid idea, what reason would we still have not to consider similar differences between the historically worthwhile and the historically valid as at least an open possibility—whether or not we can understand this idea in the light of a critique of reason? The science of history, or simply empirical humanistic science in general, can of itself decide nothing, either in a positive or in a negative sense, as to whether a distinction is to be made between art as a cultural formation and valid art, between historical and valid law, and finally between historical and valid philosophy. It cannot decide whether or not there exists, to speak Platonically, between one and the other the relation between the idea and the dim form in which it appears. And even if spiritual formations can in truth be considered and judged from the standpoint of such contraries of validity, still the scientific decision regarding validity itself and regarding its ideal normative principles is in no way the affair of empirical science. Certainly the mathematician too will not turn to historical science to be taught about the truth of mathematical theories. It will not occur to him to relate the historical development of mathematical representations with the question of truth. How, then, is it to be the historian's task to decide as to the truth of given philosophical systems and, above all, as to the very

possibility of a philosophical science that is valid in itself? And what would he have to add that could make the philosopher uncertain with regard to his idea, i.e., that of a true philosophy? Whoever denies a determined system, and even more, whoever denies the ideal possibility of a philosophical system as such, must advance reasons. Historical facts of development, even the most general facts concerning the manner of development proper to systems as such, may be reasons, good reasons. Still, historical reasons can produce only historical consequences. The desire either to prove or to refute ideas on the basis of facts is nonsense—according to the quotation Kant used: *ex pumice aquam.*

Consequently, just as historical science can advance nothing relevant against the possibility of absolute validities in general, so it can advance nothing in particular against the possibility of an absolute (i.e., scientific) metaphysics or any other philosophy. It can as historical science in no way prove even the affirmation that up to the present there has been no scientific philosophy; it can do so only from other sources of knowledge, and they are clearly philosophical sources. For it is clear that philosophical criticism, too, in so far as it is really to lay claim to validity, is philosophy and that its sense implies the ideal possibility of a systematic philosophy as a strict science. The unconditional affirmation that any scientific philosophy is a chimaera, based on the argument that the alleged efforts of millennia make probable the intrinsic impossibility of such a philosophy, is erroneous not merely because to draw a conclusion regarding an unlimited future from a few millennia of higher culture would not be a good induction, but erroneous as an absolute absurdity, like $2 \times 2 = 5$. And this is for the indicated reason: if there is something there whose objective validity philosophical criticism can refute, then there is also an area within which something can be grounded as objectively valid. If problems have demonstrably been posed "awry," then it must be possible to rectify this and pose straight problems. If criticism proves that philosophy in its historical growth has operated with confused concepts, has been guilty of mixed concepts and specious conclusions, then if one does not wish to fall into nonsense, that very fact makes it undeniable that, ideally speaking, the concepts are capable of being pointed, clarified, distinguished, that in the given area correct conclusions can be drawn. Any correct, profoundly penetrating criticism itself provides means for advancing and ideally points to correct goals, thereby indicating an objectively valid science. To this would obviously be added that the historical untenableness of a spiritual formation as a fact has nothing to do with its untenableness from the standpoint of validity. And this applies both to all that has been discussed so far and to all spheres whatever where validity is claimed.

What may still lead the historicist astray is the circumstance that by entering vitally into a historically reconstructed spiritual formation, into the intention or signification that is dominant in it as well as into the ensembles of motivations that belong to it, we not only can understand its intrinsic sense but also can judge its relative worth. If by a sort of assumption we make use of the premises a past philosopher had at his disposition, then we can eventually recognize and even marvel at the relative "consistency" of his philosophy. From another point of view, we can excuse the inconsistencies along with shifts and transformations of problems that were inevitable at that stage of the problematic and of the analysis of signification. We can esteem as a great accomplishment the successful solution of a scientific problem that would today belong to a class of problems easily mastered by a high-school student. And the same holds true in all fields. In this regard we obviously still maintain that the principles of even such relative evaluations lie in the ideal sphere, which the evaluating historian who will understand more than mere developments can only presuppose and not—as historian—justify. The norm for the mathematical lies in mathematics, for the logical in logic, for the ethical in ethics, etc. He would have to seek reasons and methods of verification in these disciplines if he also wanted to be really scientific in his evaluation. If from this standpoint there are no strictly developed sciences, then he evaluates on his own responsibility— let us say, as an ethical or as a religious man, but in any case not as a scientific historian.

If, then, I look upon historicism as an epistemological mistake that because of its consequences must be just as unceremoniously rejected as was naturalism, I should still like to emphasize expressly that I fully recognize the extraordinary value of history in the broadest sense for the philosopher. For him the discovery of the common spirit is just as significant as the discovery of nature. In fact, a deeper penetration into the general life of the spirit offers the philosopher a more original and hence more fundamental research material than does penetration into nature. For the realm of phenomenology, as a theory of essence, extends immediately from the individual spirit over the whole area of the general spirit; and if Dilthey has established in such an impressive way that psychophysical psychology is not the one that can serve as the "foundation for the humanistic sciences," I would say that it is the phenomenological theory of essence alone that is capable of providing a foundation for a philosophy of the spirit.

II.

Phenomenological Clues

3. Expression and Meaning

Essential Distinctions*

§1. An ambiguity in the term "sign"

The terms "expression" and "sign" are often treated as synonyms, but it will not be amiss to point out that they do not always coincide in application in common usage. Every sign is a sign for something, but not every sign has "meaning," a "sense" that the sign "expresses." In many cases it is not even true that a sign "stands for" that of which we may say it is a sign. And even where this can be said, one has to observe that "standing for" will not count as the "meaning" which characterizes the expression. For signs in the sense of indications (notes, marks, etc.) *do not express* anything, unless they happen to fulfill a significant as well as an indicative function. If, as one unwillingly does, one limits oneself to expressions employed in living discourse, the notion of an indication seems to apply more widely than that of an expression, but this does not mean that its content is the genus of which an expression is the species. To mean is *not a particular way of being a sign in the sense of indicating something.* It has a narrower application only because meaning—in communicative speech—is always bound up with such an indicative relation, and this in its turn leads to a wider concept, since meaning is also capable of occurring without such a connection.

Expressions function meaningfully even in *isolated mental life, where they no longer serve to indicate anything.* The two notions of sign do not therefore really stand in the relation of more extensive genus to narrower species.

The whole matter requires more thorough discussion.

§2. The essence of indication

Of the two concepts connected with the word "sign," we shall first deal with that of an *indication.* The relation that here obtains we shall call the *indicative relation.* In this sense a brand is the sign of a slave, a flag the sign of a nation. Here all marks belong, as characteristic qualities suited to help us in recognizing the objects to which they attach.

But the concept of an indication extends more widely than that of a mark. We say the Martian canals are signs of the existence of intelligent beings on Mars, that fossil vertebrae are signs of the existence of prediluvian animals, etc. Signs to aid memory, such as the much-used knot in a handkerchief, memorials, etc., also have their place here. If suitable things, events or their properties are deliberately produced to serve as such indications, one calls them "signs" whether they exercise this function or not. Only in the case of indications deliberately and artificially brought about does one speak of standing for, and that both in re-

*LI, I, 269–271, 273–295 (First Investigation, Sections 1, 2, and 4–15).

spect of the action which produces the marking (the branding or chalking, etc.), and in the sense of the indication itself, i.e., taken in its relation to the object it stands for or that it is to signify.

These distinctions and others like them do not deprive the concept of indication of its essential unity. A thing is only properly an indication if and where it in fact serves to indicate something to some thinking being. If we wish to seize the pervasively common element here present we must refer back to such cases of "live" functioning. In these we discover as a common circumstance the fact that certain objects or states of affairs *of whose reality someone has actual knowledge* indicate to him *the reality of certain other objects or states of affairs,* in the sense that *his belief in the reality of the one is experienced* (though not at all evidently) *as motivating a belief or surmise in the reality of the other.* This relation of "motivation" represents a *descriptive unity* among our acts of judgment in which indicating and indicated states of affairs become constituted for the thinker. This descriptive unity is not to be conceived as a mere form-quality founded upon our acts of judgment, for it is in their unity that the essence of indication lies. More lucidly put: the "motivational" unity of our acts of judgment has itself the character of a unity of judgment; before it as a whole an objective correlate, a unitary state of affairs, parades itself, is meant in such a judgment, appears to be in and for that judgment. Plainly such a state of affairs amounts to just this: that certain things *may* or *must* exist, *since* other things have been given. This "since," taken as expressing an objective connection, is the objective correlate of "motivation" taken as a descriptively peculiar way of combining acts of judgment into a single act of judgment.

§4. Digression on the associative origin of indication

The mental facts in which the notion of indication has its "origin," i.e., in which it can be abstractively apprehended, belong to the wider group of facts which fall under the historical rubric of the "association of ideas." Under this rubric we do not merely have those facts which concern the "accompaniment" and "reactivation" of ideas stated in the laws of association, but the further facts in which association operates creatively, and produces peculiar descriptive characters and forms of unity.* Association does not merely restore contents to consciousness and then leave it to them to combine with the contents there present, as the essence or generic nature of either may necessarily prescribe. It cannot indeed disturb such unified patterns as depend solely on our mental contents, e.g., the unity of visual contents in the visual field. But it can create additional phenomenological characters and unities which do not have their necessary, law-determined ground in the experienced contents themselves, nor in the generic forms of their abstract aspects.† If *A* summons *B* into consciousness, we are not merely simultaneously or successively conscious of both *A* and *B,* but we usually *feel* their connection forcing itself upon us, a connection in which the one points to the other and seems to belong to it. To turn mere coexistence into mutual pertinence, or, more precisely, to build cases of the former into intentional unities of things which seem mutually pertinent, is the constant result of associative functioning. All unity of experience, all empirical unity, whether of a thing, an event or of the order and relation of things, becomes a phenomenal unity through the felt mutual belongingness of the sides and

---

*To use personification and to talk of association as "creating" something, and to employ other similar figurative expressions in common use, is too convenient to be abandoned. Important as a scientifically exact but circumlocutory description of the relevant facts may be, ready understanding absolutely requires that we talk figuratively wherever ultimate exactness is not needed.

†I talk above of "experienced contents," not of meant, apparent objects or events. Everything that really helps to constitute the individual, "experiencing" consciousness is an experienced content. What it perceives, remembers, inwardly presents, etc., is a meant or intentional object. This point will be further discussed in Investigation V.

parts that can be made to stand out as units in the apparent object before us. That one thing points to another, in definite arrangement and connection, is itself apparent to us. The single item itself, in these various forward and backward references, is no mere experienced content, but an apparent object (or part, property, etc., of the same) that appears only in so far as experience *(Erfahrung)* endows contents with a new phenomenological *character,* so that they no longer count separately, but help to present an object different from themselves. In this field of facts the fact of indication also has its place, in virtue whereof an object or state of affairs not merely recalls another, and so points to it, but also provides evidence for the latter, fosters the presumption that it likewise exists, and makes us immediately feel this in the manner described above.

§5. Expressions as meaningful signs. Setting aside of a sense of "expression" not relevant for our purpose

From indicative signs we distinguish *meaningful* signs, i.e., *expressions.* We thereby employ the term "expression" restrictively: we exclude much that ordinary speech would call an "expression" from its range of application. There are other cases in which we have thus to do violence to usage, where concepts for which only ambiguous terms exist call for a fixed terminology. We shall lay down, for provisional intelligibility, that each instance or part of *speech,* as also each sign that is essentially of the same sort, shall count as an expression, whether or not such speech is actually uttered, or addressed with communicative intent to any persons or not. Such a definition excludes facial expression and the various gestures which involuntarily accompany speech without communicative intent, or those in which a man's mental states achieve understandable "expression" for his environment, without the added help of speech. Such "utterances" are not expressions in the sense in which a case of speech is an expression, they are not phenomenally one with the experiences made manifest in them in the consciousness of the man who manifests

them, as is the case with speech. In such manifestations one man communicates nothing to another: their utterance involves no intent to put certain "thoughts" on record expressively, whether for the man himself, in his solitary state, or for others. Such "expressions," in short, have properly speaking, *no meaning.* It is not to the point that another person may interpret our involuntary manifestations, e.g., our "expressive movements," and that he may thereby become deeply acquainted with our inner thoughts and emotions. They "mean" something to him in so far as he interprets them, but even for him they are without meaning in the special sense in which verbal signs have meaning: they only mean in the sense of indicating.

In the treatment which follows these distinctions must be raised to complete conceptual clarity.

§6. Questions as to the phenomenological and intentional distinctions which pertain to expressions as such

It is usual to distinguish two things in regard to every expression:

1. The expression physically regarded (the sensible sign, the articulate sound-complex, the written sign on paper, etc.);

2. A certain sequence of mental states, associatively linked with the expression, which make it be the expression of something. These mental states are generally called the "sense" or the "meaning" of the expression, this being taken to be in accord with what these words ordinarily mean. But we shall see this notion to be mistaken, and that a mere distinction between physical signs and sense-giving experiences is by no means enough, and not at all enough for logical purposes.

The points here made have long been observed in the special case of names. We distinguish, in the case of each name, between what it "shows forth" (i.e., mental states) and what it means. And again between what it means (the sense or "content" of its naming presentation) and what it names (the object of that presentation). We shall need similar distinctions in the case of all expression and shall have to explore their nature precisely. Such distinctions have led to our distinction between the notions of "expression" and "indication," which is not in conflict with the fact that an expression in living speech also functions as an indication, a point soon to come up for discussion. To these distinctions other important ones will be added which will concern the relations between meaning and the intuition which illustrates meaning and on occasion renders it evident. Only by paying heed to these relations can the concept of meaning be clearly delimited and can the fundamental opposition between the symbolic and the epistemological function of meanings be worked out.

§7. Expressions as they function in communication

Expressions were originally framed to fulfill a communicative function: let us, accordingly, first study expressions in this function, so that we may be able to work out their essential logical distinctions. The articulate sound-complex, the written sign, etc., first becomes a spoken word or communicative bit of speech, when a speaker produces it with the intention of "expressing himself about something" through its means; he must endow it with a sense in certain acts of mind, a sense he desires to share with his auditors. Such sharing becomes a possibility if the auditor also understands the speaker's intention. He does this inasmuch as he takes the speaker to be a person who is not merely uttering sounds but *speaking to him,* who is accompanying those sounds with certain sense-giving acts which the sounds reveal to the hearer, or whose sense they seek to communicate to him. What first makes mental commerce possible, and turns connected speech into discourse, lies in the correlation among the corresponding physical and mental experiences of communicating persons which is effected by the physical side of speech. Speaking and hearing, intimation of mental states through speaking and reception thereof in hearing, are mutually correlated.

If one surveys these interconnections, one sees at once that all expressions in *communi-cative* speech function as *indications.* They serve the hearer as signs of the "thoughts" of the speaker, i.e., of his sense-giving inner experiences, as well as of the other inner experiences which are part of his communicative intention. This function of verbal expressions we shall call their *intimating function.* The content of such intimation consists in the inner experiences intimated. The sense of the predicate "intimated" can be understood more narrowly or more widely. The *narrower* sense we may restrict to *acts which impart sense,* while the *wider* sense will cover *all* acts that a hearer may introject into a speaker on the basis of what he says (possibly because he tells us of such acts). If, e.g., we state a wish, our judgment concerning that wish is what we intimate in the narrower sense of the word, whereas the wish itself is intimated in the wider sense. The same holds of an ordinary statement of perception, which the hearer forthwith takes to belong to some actual perception. The act of perception is there intimated in the wider sense, the judgment built upon it in the narrower sense. We at once see that ordinary speech permits us to call an experience which is intimated an experience which is *expressed.*

To understand an intimation is not to have conceptual knowledge of it, not to judge in the sense of asserting anything about it: it consists simply in the fact that the hearer *intuitively* takes the speaker to be a person who is expressing this or that, or as we certainly can say, *perceives* him as such. When I listen to someone, I perceive him as a speaker, I hear him recounting, demonstrating, doubting, wishing, etc. The hearer perceives the intimation in the same sense in which he perceives the intimating person—even though the mental phenomena which make him a person cannot fall, for what they are, in the intuitive grasp of another. Common speech credits us with percepts even of other people's inner experiences; we "see" their anger, their pain, etc. Such talk is quite correct, as long as, e.g., we allow outward bodily things likewise to count as perceived, and as long as, in general, the notion of perception is not restricted to the adequate, the strictly intuitive percept. If the essential mark of perception lies in the intuitive persuasion that a thing or event is itself before us for our grasping—such a persuasion is possible, and in the main mass of cases actual, without verbalized, conceptual apprehension—then the receipt of such an intimation is the mere perceiving of it. The essential distinction just touched on is of course present here. The hearer perceives the speaker as manifesting certain inner experiences, and to that extent he also perceives these experiences themselves: he does not, however, himself experience them, he has not an "inner" but an "outer" percept of them. Here we have the big difference between the real grasp of what is in adequate intuition, and the putative grasp of what is on a basis of inadequate, though intuitive, presentation. In the former case we have to do with an experienced, in the latter case with a presumed being, to which no truth corresponds at all. Mutual understanding demands a certain correlation among the mental acts mutually unfolded in intimation and in the receipt of such intimation, but not at all their exact resemblance.

§8. Expressions in solitary life

So far we have considered expressions as used in communication, which last depends essentially on the fact that they operate indicatively. But expressions also play a great part in uncommunicated, interior mental life. This change in function plainly has nothing to do with whatever makes an expression an expression. Expressions continue to have meanings as they had before, and the same meanings as in dialogue. A word only ceases to be a word when our interest stops at its sensory contour, when it becomes a mere sound-pattern. But when we live in the understanding of a word, it expresses something and the same thing, whether we address it to anyone or not.

It seems clear, therefore, that an expression's meaning, and whatever else pertains to it essentially, cannot coincide with its feats of intimation. Or shall we say that, even in solitary mental life, one still uses expressions to intimate something, though not to a second person? Shall one say that in soliloquy one speaks

to oneself, and employs words as signs, i.e., as indications, of one's own inner experiences? I cannot think such a view acceptable. Words function as signs here as they do everywhere else: everywhere they can be said to point to something. But if we reflect on the relation of expression to meaning, and to this end break up our complex, intimately unified experience of the sense-filled expression, into the two factors of word and sense, the word comes before us as intrinsically indifferent, whereas the sense seems the thing aimed at by the verbal sign and meant by its means: the expression seems to direct interest away from itself towards its sense, and to point to the latter. But this pointing is not an indication in the sense previously discussed. The existence of the sign neither "motivates" the existence of the meaning, nor, properly expressed, our belief in the meaning's existence. What we are to use as an indication must be perceived by us as existent. This holds also of expressions used in communication, but not for expressions used in soliloquy, where we are in general content with imagined rather than with actual words. In imagination a spoken or printed word floats before us, though in reality it has no existence. We should not, however, confuse imaginative presentations, and the image-contents they rest on, with their imagined objects. The imagined verbal sound, or the imagined printed word, does not exist, only its imaginative presentation does so. The difference is the difference between imagined centaurs and the imagination of such beings. The word's nonexistence neither disturbs nor interests us, since it leaves the word's expressive function unaffected. Where it *does* make a difference is where intimation is linked with meaning. Here thought must not be merely expressed as meaning, but must be communicated and intimated. We can only do the latter where we actually speak and hear.

One of course speaks, in a certain sense, even in soliloquy, and it is certainly possible to think of oneself as speaking, and even as speaking to oneself, as, e.g., when someone says to himself: "You have gone wrong, you can't go on like that." But in the genuine sense of communication, there is no speech in such cases, nor does one tell oneself anything: one merely conceives of oneself as speaking and communicating. In a monologue words can perform no function of indicating the existence of mental acts, since such indication would there be quite purposeless. For the acts in question are themselves experienced by us at that very moment.

§9. Phenomenological distinctions between the phenomena of physical expression and the sense-giving and sense-fulfilling act

If we now turn from experiences specially concerned with intimation and consider expressions in respect of distinctions that pertain to them equally whether they occur in dialogue or soliloquy, two things seem to be left over: the expressions themselves, and what they express as their meaning or sense. Several relations are, however, intertwined at this point, and talk about "meaning," or about "what is expressed," is correspondingly ambiguous. If we seek a foothold in pure description, the concrete phenomenon of the sense-informed expression breaks up, on the one hand, into the *physical phenomenon* forming the physical side of the expression, and, on the other hand, into the *acts* which give it *meaning* and possibly also *intuitive fullness,* in which its relation to an expressed object is constituted. In virtue of such acts, the expression is more than a merely sounded word. It *means* something, and in so far as it means something, it relates to what is objective. This objective somewhat can either be actually present through accompanying intuitions, or may at least appear in representation, e.g., in a mental image, and where this happens the relation to an object is realized. Alternatively this need not occur: the expression functions significantly, it remains more than mere sound of words, but it lacks any basic intuition that will give it its object. The relation of expression to object is now un-

realized as being confined to a mere meaning-intention. A *name,* e.g., names its object whatever the circumstances, in so far as it *means* that object. But if the object is not intuitively before one, and so not before one as a named or meant object, mere meaning is all there is to it. If the originally *empty* meaning-intention is now fulfilled, the relation to an object is realized, the naming becomes an actual, conscious relation between name and object named.

Let us take our stand on this fundamental distinction between meaning-intentions void of intuition and those which are intuitively fulfilled: if we leave aside the sensuous acts in which the expression, *qua* mere sound of words, makes its appearance, we shall have to distinguish between two acts or sets of acts. We shall, on the one hand, have acts essential to the expression if it is to be an expression at all, i.e., a verbal sound infused with sense. These acts we shall call the *meaning-conferring acts* or the *meaning-intentions.* But we shall, on the other hand, have acts, not essential to the expression as such, which stand to it in the logically basic relation of *fulfilling* (confirming, illustrating) it more or less adequately, and so actualizing its relation to its object. These acts, which become fused with the meaning-conferring acts in the unity of knowledge or fulfillment, we call the *meaning-fulfilling* acts. The briefer expression "meaning-fulfillment" can only be used in cases where there is no risk of the ready confusion with the *whole* experience in which a meaning-intention finds fulfillment in its correlated intuition. In the realized relation of the expression to its objective correlate,* the sense-informed expression becomes one with the act of meaning-fulfillment. The sounded word is first made one with the meaning-intention, and this in its turn is made one (as intentions in general are made one with their fulfillments) with its corresponding meaning-fulfillment. The word "expression" is normally understood—wherever, that is, we do not speak of a "mere" expression—as the *sense-*

---

*I often make use of the vaguer expression "objective correlate" *(Gegenständlichkeit)* since we are here never limited to objects in the narrower sense, but have also to do with states of affairs, properties, and non-independent forms, etc., whether real or categorial.

informed expression. One should not, therefore, properly say (as one often does) that an expression *expresses its meaning* (its intention). One might more properly adopt the alternative way of speaking according to which the *fulfilling act* appears as *the act expressed by the complete expression:* we may, e.g., say that a statement "gives expression" to an act of perceiving or imagining. We need not here point out that both meaning-conferring and meaning-fulfilling acts have a part to play in intimation in the case of communicative discourse. The former in fact constitute the inmost core of intimation. To make them known to the hearer is the prime aim of our communicative intention, for only in so far as the hearer attributes them to the speaker will he understand the latter.

§10. The phenomenological unity of these acts

The above distinguished acts involving the expression's appearance, on the one hand, and the meaning-intention and possible meaning-fulfillment, on the other, do not constitute a mere aggregate of simultaneously given items in consciousness. They rather form an intimately fused unity of peculiar character. Everyone's personal experience bears witness to the differing weight of the two constituents, which reflects the asymmetry of the relation between an expression and the object which (through its meaning) it expresses or names. Both are "lived through," the presentation of the word and the sense-giving act: but, while we experience the former, we do not live *in* such a presentation at all, but solely in enacting its sense, its meaning. And in so far as we do this, and yield ourselves to enacting the meaning-intention and its further fulfillment, our whole interest centers upon the object intended in our intention, and named by its means. (These two ways of speaking have in fact the same meaning.) The function of a word (or rather of an intuitive word-presentation) is to awaken a sense-conferring act in ourselves, to point to what is intended, or perhaps given intuitive fulfillment in this act, and to guide our interest exclusively in this direction.

Such pointing is not to be described as the mere objective fact of a regular diversion of interest from one thing to another. The fact that two presented objects *A* and *B* are so linked by some secret psychological coordination that the presentation of *A* regularly arouses the presentation of *B*, and that interest is thereby shifted from *A* to *B*—such a fact does not make *A* the expression of the presentation of *B*. To be an expression is rather a descriptive aspect of the *experienced unity* of sign and thing signified.

What is involved in the descriptive difference between the physical sign-phenomenon and the meaning-intention which makes it into an expression becomes most clear when we turn our attention to the sign *qua* sign, e.g., to the printed word as such. If we do this, we have an external percept (or external intuitive idea) just like any other, whose object loses its verbal character. If this object again functions as a word, its presentation is wholly altered in character. The word (*qua* external singular) remains intuitively present, maintains its appearance, but we no longer intend it, it no longer properly is the object of our "mental activity." Our interest, our intention, our thought—mere synonyms if taken in sufficiently wide senses—point exclusively to the thing meant in the sense-giving act. This means, phenomenologically speaking, that the intuitive presentation, in which the physical world-phenomenon is constituted, undergoes an essential phenomenal modification when its object begins to count as an *expression.* While what constitutes the object's appearing remains unchanged, the intentional character of the experience alters. There is constituted (without need of a fulfilling or illustrative intuition) an act of meaning which finds support in the verbal presentation's intuitive content, but which differs in essence from the intuitive intention directed upon the word itself. With this act, the new acts or act-complexes that we call "fulfilling" acts or act-complexes are often peculiarly blended, acts whose object coincides with the object meant in the meaning, or named through this meaning.

In our next chapter we shall have to conduct additional researches into the question as to whether the "meaning-intention," which on our view characteristically marks off an expression from empty "sound of words," consists in the mere association of mental imagery of the intended object with the sounded words, or at least necessarily involves such an act of fancy, or whether, on the other hand, mental imagery lies outside of the essence of an expression, and rather performs a fulfilling role, even if only of a partial, indirect or provisional character. In order not to blur the main outlines of our thought, we shall not here enter more deeply into phenomenological questions. In this whole investigation, we need only do as much phenomenology as is required to establish essential, primary distinctions.

The provisional description so far given will have shown how complex is the correct description of a phenomenological situation. Such complexity appears inevitable once we clearly see that all objects and relations among objects only are what they are for us, through acts of thought essentially different from them, in which they become present to us, in which they stand before us as unitary items that we *mean.* Where not the phenomenological but the naively objective interest dominates, where we live in intentional acts without reflecting upon them, all talk of course becomes plain sailing and clear and devoid of circumlocution. One then, in our case, simply speaks of "expression" and of "what is expressed," of name and thing named, of the steering of attention from one to the other, etc. But where the phenomenological interest dominates, we endure the hardship of having to describe phenomenological relationships which we may have experienced on countless occasions, but of which we were not normally conscious as objects, and we have also to do our describing with expressions framed to deal with objects whose appearance lies in the sphere of our normal interests.

§11. The ideal distinctions between (I) expression and meaning as ideal unities

We have so far considered "the well-understood expression" as a concrete experience. Instead of considering its two types of factor, the phenomenal expression and the sense-conferring or sense-fulfilling experience, we wish to consider what is, in a certain fashion, given "in" these: the expression itself, its sense and its objective correlate. We turn therefore from the real relation of acts to the ideal relation of their objects or contents. A subjective treatment yields to one that is objective. The ideality of the relationship between expression and meaning is at once plain in regard to both its sides, inasmuch as, when we ask for the meaning of an expression, e.g., "quadratic remainder," we are naturally not referring to the sound-pattern uttered here and now, the vanishing noise that can never recur identically: we mean the expression *in specie.* "Quadratic remainder" is the same expression by whomsoever uttered. The same holds of talk about the expression's meaning, which naturally does not refer to some meaning-conferring experience.

Every example shows that an essential distinction must here be drawn.

If I sincerely say—we shall always presume sincerity—"The three perpendiculars of a triangle intersect in a point," this is of course based on the fact that I judge so. If someone hears me and understands my assertion, he likewise knows this fact; he "apperceives" me as someone who judges thus. But is the judging here *intimated* the meaning of my assertion, is it what my assertion asserts, and in that sense expresses? Plainly not. It would hardly occur to anyone, if asked as to the sense or meaning of my assertion, to revert to my judgment as an inner experience. Everyone would rather reply by saying: What this assertion asserts is *the same* whoever may assert it, and on whatever occasion or in whatever circumstances he may assert it, and what it asserts is precisely this, *that the three perpendiculars of a triangle intersect in a point,* no more and no less. One therefore repeats what is in essence "the same" assertion, and one repeats it because it is the one, uniquely adequate way of expressing the same thing, i.e., its meaning. In this selfsame meaning, of whose identity we are conscious whenever we repeat the statement, nothing at all about judging or about one who judges is discoverable. We thought we were sure that a state of affairs held or obtained objectively, and what we were sure of we expressed by way of a declarative sentence. The state of affairs is what it is whether we assert that it obtains or not. It is intrinsically an item, a unity, which is capable of so obtaining or holding. But such an obtaining is what appeared before us, and we set it forth as it appeared before us: we said "So the matter is." Naturally we could not have done this, we could not have made the assertion, if the matter had not so appeared before us, if, in other words, we had not so judged. This forms part of an assertion as a psychological fact, it is involved in its intimation. But only in such intimation; for while what is intimated consists in inner experiences, what we assert in the judgment involves nothing subjective. My act of judging is a transient experience: it arises and passes away. But what my assertion asserts, the content *that the three perpendiculars of a triangle intersect in a point,* neither arises nor passes away. It is an identity in the strict sense, one and the same geometrical truth.

It is the same in the case of all assertions, even if what they assert is false and absurd. Even in such cases we distinguish their ideal content from the transient acts of affirming and asserting it: it is the meaning of the assertion, a unity in plurality. We continue to recognize its identity of intention in evident acts of reflection: we do not arbitrarily attribute it to our assertions but discover it in them.

If "possibility" or "truth" is lacking, an assertion's intention can only be carried out symbolically: it cannot derive any "fullness" from intuition or from the categorial functions performed on the latter, in which "fullness" its value for knowledge consists. It then lacks, as one says, a "true," a "genuine" meaning. Later we shall look more closely into this distinction between intending and fulfilling meaning. To characterize the various acts in which the relevant ideal unities are constituted, and to throw light on the essence of their actual "coincidence" in knowledge, will call for difficult, comprehensive studies. It is plain, however, that each assertion, whether representing an exercise of knowledge or not—whether or not, i.e., it fulfills or can fulfill its intention in corre-

sponding intuitions, and the formative acts involved in these—involves a thought, in which thought, as its unified specific character, its meaning is constituted.

It is this ideal unity men have in mind when they say that "the" judgment is the meaning of "the" declarative sentence. Only the fundamental ambiguity of the word "judgment" at once tends to confuse the evidently grasped ideal unity with the real act of judging, to confuse what the assertion intimates with what it asserts.

What we have here said of complete assertions readily applies also to actual or possible parts of assertions. If I judge *If the sum of the angles in a triangle does not equal two right angles, the axiom of parallels does not hold,* the hypothetical antecedent is no assertion, for I do not say that such an inequation holds. None the less it says something, and what it says is once more quite different from what it intimates. What it says is not my mental act of hypothetical presumption, though I must of course have performed this in order to speak sincerely as I do. But it is rather the case that, when this subjective act is intimated, something objective and ideal is brought to expression: the hypothesis whose conceptual content can appear as the same intentional unity in many possible thought-experiences, and which evidently stands before us in its unity and identity in the objectively-ideal treatment characteristic of all thinking.

The same holds of the other parts of our statements, even of such as do not have the form of propositions.

§12. Continuation: The objective correlate of an expression

Talk of *what an expression expresses* has, in the discussion so far, several essentially different meanings. It relates, *on the one hand,* to intimation in general, and especially in that connection to sense-giving acts, at times also to sense-fulfilling acts (if these are present at all). In an assertion, e.g., we express our judgment (we intimate it), but we also express percepts and other sense-fulfilling acts which illustrate our assertion's meaning. *On the other hand,* such talk relates to the "contents" of such acts, and primarily to the meanings, which are often enough said to be "expressed."

It is doubtful whether the examples analyzed, in our last section, would suffice even to lend provisional intelligibility to the notion of meaning, if one could not forthwith introduce a new sense of "expression" for purposes of comparison. The terms "meaning," "content," "state of affairs" and all similar terms harbor such powerful equivocations that our intention, even if expressed most carefully, still can promote misunderstanding. The third sense of "being expressed," which we must now discuss, concerns the *objective correlate* meant by a meaning and expressed by its means.

Each expression not merely says something, but says it *of* something: it not only has a meaning, but refers to certain *objects.* This relation sometimes holds in the plural for one and the same expression. But the object never coincides with the meaning. Both, of course, only pertain to an expression in virtue of the mental acts which give it sense. And, if we distinguish between "content" and object in respect of such "presentations," one's distinction means the same as the distinction between what is meant or said, on the one hand, and what is spoken of, by means of the expression, on the other.

The necessity of distinguishing between meaning (content) and object becomes clear when a comparison of examples shows us that several expressions may have the same meaning but different objects, and again that they may have different meanings but the same object. There is of course also the possibility of their differing in both respects and agreeing in both. The last occurs in the cases of synonymous expressions, e.g., the corresponding expressions in different languages which mean and name the same thing ("London," "Londres"; "zwei," "deux," "duo," etc.).

Names offer the plainest examples of the separation of meaning from the relation to objects, this relation being in their case usually spoken of as "naming." Two names can differ in meaning but can name the same object, e.g., "the victor at Jena"—"the vanquished at Waterloo"; "the equilateral triangle"—"the equiangular triangle." The meaning expressed in our pairs of names is plainly different, though the same object is meant in each case. The same applies to names whose indefiniteness gives them an "extension." The expressions "an equilateral triangle" and "an equiangular triangle" have the same objective reference, the same range of possible application.

It can happen, conversely, that two expressions have the same meaning but a different objective reference. The expression "a horse" has the same meaning in whatever context it occurs. But if on one occasion we say "Bucephalus is a horse," and on another "That carthorse is a horse," there has been a plain change in our sense-giving presentation in passing from the one statement to the other. The expression "a horse" employs the same meaning to present Bucephalus on one occasion and the carthorse on the other. It is thus with all general names, i.e., names with an "extension." "One" is a name whose meaning never differs, but one should not, for that reason, identify the various "ones" which occur in a sum: they all mean the same, but they differ in objective reference.

The case of proper names is different, whether they name individual or general objects. A word like "Socrates" can only name different things by meaning different things, i.e., by becoming *equivocal.* Wherever the word has *one* meaning, it also names *one* object. The same holds of expressions like "the number two," "redness," etc. We therefore distinguish equivocal names that have *many meanings* from general or class-names that have *many values.*

The same holds of other types of expression, though in their case talk of objective reference involves certain difficulties in virtue of its manifoldness. If we consider, e.g., statements of the form *"S is P"* we generally regard the subject of the statement as the object about which the statement is made. Another view is, however, possible, which treats the *whole* state of affairs which corresponds to the statement as an analogue of the object a name names, and distinguishes this from the object's meaning. If this is done one can quote as examples pairs of sentences such as *"a is bigger* than *b*"—"*b* is smaller than *a,*" which plainly say different things. They are not merely grammatically but also "cogitatively" different, i.e., different in meaning-content. But they express the same state of affairs: the same "matter" is predicatively apprehended and asserted in two different ways. Whether we define talk of the "object" of a statement in one sense or the other—each has its own claims—statements are in either case possible which differ in meaning while referring to the same object.

§13. Connection between meaning and objective reference

Our examples entitle us to regard the distinction between an expression's meaning and its power to direct itself as a name to this or that objective correlate—and of course the distinction between meaning and object itself—as well-established. It is clear for the rest that the sides to be distinguished in each expression are closely connected: an expression only refers to an objective correlate *because* it means something, it can be rightly said to signify or name the object *through* its meaning. An act of meaning is the determinate manner in which we refer to our object of the moment, though this mode of significant reference and the meaning itself can change while the objective reference remains fixed.

A more profound phenomenological clarification of this relation can be reached only by research into the way expressions and their meaning-intentions function in knowledge. This would show that talk about *two distinguishable sides* to each expression, should not be taken seriously, that the essence of an expression lies solely in its meaning. But the same intuition (as we shall show later) can offer fulfillment of different expressions: it can be categorially apprehended in varying ways and synthetically linked with other intuitions. Expressions and their meaning-intentions do not take their measure, in contexts of thought and knowledge, from mere intuition—I mean phenomena of external or internal sensibility—but

from the varying intellectual forms through which intuited objects first become intelligibly determined, mutually related objects. And so expressions, even when they function outside of knowledge, must, as symbolic intentions, point to categorially *formed* unities. Different meanings may therefore pertain to the same intuitions regarded in differing categorial fashion, and may therefore also pertain to the same object. But where a whole range of objects corresponds to a single meaning, this meaning's own essence must be *indeterminate:* it must permit a sphere of possible fulfillment.

These indications may suffice for the moment. They must guard in advance against the error of seriously thinking that sense-giving acts have two distinct sides, one which gives them their meaning, while the other gives them their determinate direction to objects.*

§14. Content as object, content as fulfilling sense, and content as sense or meaning simpliciter

Relational talk of "intimation," "meaning" and "object" belongs *essentially* to every expression. Every expression intimates something, means something and names or otherwise designates something. In each case, talk of "expression" is equivocal. As said above, relation to an actually given objective correlate, which fulfills the meaning-intention, is *not* essential to an expression. If this last important case is also taken into consideration, we note that there are two things that can be said to be expressed in the realized relation to the object. We have, on the one hand, the *object itself* and the object as meant in this or that manner. On the other hand, and more properly, we have the object's ideal correlate in the acts of meaning-fulfillment which constitute it, *the fulfilling sense.* Wherever the meaning-intention is fulfilled in a corresponding intuition, i.e., wherever the expression actually serves to name a given object, there the object is constituted as one "given" in certain acts, and, to the extent that our expression really measures up to

---

*Cf. with this Twardowski's assumption of a "presentative activity moving in two directions" in his work *Zur Lehre vom Inhalt und Gegenstand der Vorstellungen* (Vienna, 1894), p. 14.

the intuitive data, as given *in the same manner* in which the expression *means* it. In this unity of coincidence between meaning and meaning-fulfillment, the essence of the meaning-fulfillment corresponds with, and is correlative to, the essence of meaning: the essence of the meaning-fulfillment is the *fulfilling* sense of the expression, or, as one may also call it, the sense expressed by the expression. One says, e.g., that a statement of perception expresses a perception, but also that it expresses the *content* of a perception. We distinguish, in a perceptual statement, as in every statement, between *content* and *object;* by the "content" we understand the self-identical meaning that the hearer can grasp even if he is not a percipient. We must draw the same distinction in the case of fulfilling acts, in the case, therefore, of perceptions and their categorial formations. Through these acts the objective correlate of our act of meaning stands before us intuitively as the very object we mean. We must, I say, distinguish again, in such fulfilling acts, between their *content,* the meaning-element, as it were, in the categorially formed percept, and the *object* perceived. In the unity of fulfillment, the fulfilling content coincides with the intending content, so that, in our experience of this unity of coincidence, the object, at once intended and "given," stands before us, not as two objects, but as *one* alone. The ideal conception of the act which *confers meaning* yields us the Idea of the *intending meaning,* just as the ideal conception of the correlative essence of the act which *fulfills* meaning, yields the *fulfilling meaning,* likewise *qua* Idea. This is the *identical content* which, in perception, pertains to the totality of possible acts of perception which intended the same object perceptually, and intend it actually as the same object. This content is therefore the ideal correlate of this *single* object, which may, for the rest, be completely imaginary.

The manifold ambiguities in talk about what an expression expresses, or about an *expressed content,* may therefore be so ordered that one distinguishes between a content in a *subjective,*

and a content in an *objective* sense. In the latter respect we must distinguish between:

The content as intending sense, or as sense, *meaning simpliciter,*
the content as fulfilling sense, and
the content as object.

§15. The equivocations in talk of meaning and meaninglessness connected with these distinctions

The application of the terms "meaning" and "sense," not merely to the content of the meaning-intention inseparable from the expression, but also to the content of the meaning-fulfillment, engenders a most unwelcome ambiguity. It is clear from previous indications, where we dealt with the fact of fulfillment, that the acts on either side, in which intending and fulfilling sense are constituted, need not be the same. What tempts us to transfer the same terms from intention to fulfillment, is the peculiar way in which the unity of fulfillment is a unity of identification or coincidence: the equivocation which one hoped a modifying adjective might render innocuous can scarcely be avoided. We shall continue, of course, to understand by "meaning" *simpliciter* the meaning which, as the identical element in our intention, is essential to the expressions as such.

"Meaning" is further used by us as synonymous with "sense." It is agreeable to have parallel, interchangeable terms in the case of this concept, particularly since the sense of the term "meaning" is itself to be investigated. A further consideration is our ingrained tendency to use the two words as synonymous, a circumstance which makes it seem rather a dubious step if their meanings are differentiated, and if (as G. Frege has proposed)* we use one for meaning in our sense, and the other for the objects expressed. To this we may add that both terms are exposed to the same equivocations, which we distinguished above in connection with the term "expression," and to many more besides, and that this is so both in scientific and

*G. Frege, *Über Sinn und Bedeutung, Zeitschr. f. philos. Kritik,* vol. 100, p. 25; "On Sense and Reference," *Translations from the Philosophical Writings of Gottlob Frege,* ed. Peter Geach and Max Black (Oxford, 1966), pp. 56–78.

in ordinary speech. Logical clarity is much impaired by the manner in which the sense or meaning of an expression is, often in the same thought-sequence, now looked upon as the acts intimated by it, now as its ideal sense, now as the objective correlate that it expresses. Since fixed terminological landmarks are lacking, the concepts themselves run confusedly into one another.

Fundamental confusions arise from these facts. General and equivocal names are, e.g., repeatedly lumped together, since both can be predicatively referred to a plurality of objects. Lacking fixed concepts, men did not know how to distinguish the *multiple senses* of the equivocal names from the *multiple values* of the general ones. Here we also meet with the frequent unclearness as to the true essence of the difference between collective and general names. For, where collective meanings are fulfilled, we intuit a plurality of items: fulfillment is articulated into a plurality of individual intuitions, and so, if intention and fulfillment are not kept apart, it may well seem that the collective expression in question has many meanings.

It is more important for us to set forth precisely the most detrimental equivocations in talk which concerns *meaning* and *sense,* on the one hand, or *meaningless* or *senseless* expressions, on the other. If we separate the blurred concepts, the following list emerges:

1. It is part of the notion of an expression to have a meaning: this precisely differentiates an expression from the other signs mentioned above. A meaningless expression is, therefore, properly speaking, no expression at all: it is at best something that claims or seems to be an expression, though, more closely considered, it is not one at all. Here belong articulate, word-like sound-patterns such as "Abracadabra," and also combinations of genuine expressions to which no unified meaning corresponds, though their outer form seems to pretend to such a meaning, e.g., "Green is or."

2. In meaning, a relation to an object is constituted. To use an expression significantly, and to refer expressively to an object (to form a presentation of it), are one and the same. It makes no difference whether the object exists or is fictitious or even impossible. But if one gives a very rigorous interpretation to the proposition that an expression, in so far as it has meaning, relates to an object, i.e., in a sense which involves the existence of the object, then an expression has *meaning* when an object corresponding to it exists, and it is *meaningless* when no such object exists. Meanings are often spoken of as signifying the *objects* meant, a usage that can scarcely be maintained consistently, as it springs from a confusion with the genuine concept of meaning.

3. If the meaning is identified with the objective correlate of an expression, a name like "golden mountain" is meaningless. Here men generally distinguish objectlessness from meaninglessness. As opposed to this, men tend to use the word "senseless" of expressions infected with contradiction and obvious incompatibilities, e.g., "round square," or to deny them meaning by some equivalent phrase. Sigwart,* e.g., says that a self-contradictory formula such as "square circle" expresses no concept we can think, but that it uses words to set up an insoluble task. The existential proposition "There is no square circle," on his view denies the possibility of connecting a concept with these words, and by a concept he expressly wants us to understand (if we get him right) the "general meaning of a word," which is just what we mean by it. Erdmann† has similar opinions in regard to the instance "A square circle is frivolous." We should, in consistency, have to apply the word "senseless" not merely to expressions immediately absurd, but to those whose absurdity is mediate, i.e., the countless expressions shown by mathematicians, in lengthy indirect demonstrations, to be objectless a priori. We should likewise have to deny that concepts like *regular decahedron,* etc., are concepts at all.

Marty raises the following objection to the thinkers just mentioned. "If the words are sense-

*Die Impersonalien, p. 62.
†Logik, I, p. 233.

less, how could we understand the question as to whether such things exist, so as to answer it negatively? Even to reject such an existence, we must, it is plain, somehow form a presentation of such contradictory material"* . . . "If such absurdities are called senseless, this can only mean that they have no rational sense."† These objections are clinching, in so far as these thinkers' statements suggest that they are confusing the true meaninglessness mentioned above under 1, with another quite different meaninglessness, i.e., *the* a priori *impossibility of a fulfilling sense.* An expression has meaning in this sense if a possible fulfillment, i.e., the possibility of a unified intuitive illustration, corresponds to its intention. This possibility is plainly meant ideally. It concerns no contingent acts of expression or fulfillment, but their ideal contents: meaning as an ideal unity, here to be called "intending meaning," on the one hand, and fulfilling meaning, standing to it in a certain relation of precise adequacy, on the other. We apprehend this ideal relation by ideative abstraction based on an act of unified fulfillment. In the contrary case we apprehend the real impossibility of meaning-fulfillment through an experience of the incompatibility of the partial meanings in the intended unity of fulfillment.

The phenomenological clarification of these relationships calls for long, difficult analyses, as will appear in a later investigation.

4. If we ask what an expression means, we naturally recur to cases where it actually contributes to knowledge, or, what is the same, where its meaning-intention is intuitively fulfilled. In this manner the "notional presentation," i.e., the meaning-intention, gains clarity, it shows itself up as "correct," as "really" capable of execution. The draft it makes on intuition is as it were cashed. Since in the unity of fulfillment the act of intention coincides with the fulfilling act, and fuses with it in the most intimate fashion—if indeed there is any dif-

ference left over here at all—it readily seems as if the expression first got its meaning here, as if it drew meaning from the act of fulfillment. The tendency therefore arises to treat the *fulfilling intuitions*—categorially formative acts are here in general passed over—as meanings. But fulfillment is often imperfect—we shall have to devote closer study to all such possibilities—and expressions often go with remotely relevant, only partially illustrative intuitions, if with any at all. Since the phenomenological differences of these cases have not been closely considered, men have come to locate the significance of expressions, even of such as could make no claim to adequate fulfillment, in accompaniments of intuitive imagery. This naturally led to a total denial of meaning to absurd expressions.

The new concept of meaning therefore originates in a confusion of meaning with fulfilling intuition. On this conception, an expression has meaning if and only if its intention—we should say its "meaning-intention"—is in fact fulfilled, even if only in a partial, distant and improper manner. The understanding of the expression must be given life through certain "ideas of meaning" (it is commonly said), i.e., by certain *illustrative* images.

The final refutation of highly attractive, opposed notions is an important task which requires lengthy discussions. These we shall postpone to the next chapter, and here go on enumerating different concepts of meaning.

Fluctuation in Meaning and the Ideality of Unities of Meaning‡

§24. Introduction

In our last chapter we dealt with the act of meaning. But among the conclusions of our first chapter was a distinction between the act of meaning, on the one hand, and meaning itself,

---

*A. Marty, "Über subjektlose Sätze und das Verhältnis der Grammatik zur Logik und Psychologie," Art. VI, *Vierteljahrsschrift f. wiss. Phil.* XIX, 80f.
†Ibid., p. 81 note. Cf. Art. V, Vol. XVIII, p. 464.
‡LI, I, 312–326 (First Investigation, Sections 24–29).

on the other, the ideal unity as against the multiplicity of possible acts. This distinction, like the others which go along with it—the distinction between expressed content taken in a subjective, and the same taken in an objective sense, and, in the latter respect, the distinction between content as significatum and content as nominatum—are in countless cases undoubtedly clear. This holds of all expressions which occur in the context of an adequately expounded scientific theory. There are, however, cases where the situation is different, which require particular consideration if they are not to plunge all our hard-won distinctions back into confusion. Expressions whose meaning shifts, especially such as are occasional or vague, here raise serious problems. To solve these problems by distinguishing between shifting acts of meaning, on the one hand, and ideal units of meaning, on the other, is the theme of the present chapter.

§25. Relations of coincidence among the contents of intimation and naming

Expressions may relate to the contemporary mental state of the person using them as much as they relate to other objects. They accordingly divide into those that also *intimate what they name* (or what they generally stand for) and those in whose case *named and intimated contents fall asunder.* Instances of the former class are interrogative, optative and imperative sentences, of the latter, statements relating to external things, to one's own past experiences, to mathematical relationships, etc. If someone utters the wish "I should like a glass of water," this serves to indicate to the hearer the speaker's wish, which is also the object of the statement. What is intimated and what is named here coincide in part. I say "in part," since the intimation obviously goes further. It extends to the judgment expressed in the words "I should like, etc." The like naturally holds of statements about the ideas, judgments, and surmises of the speaker which are of the forms "I imagine that . . . ," "I am of the opinion that . . . ," "I judge that . . . ," "I conjecture that . . . ." A case even of total coincidence seems at first sight

possible, in, e.g., the words "the state of mind intimated by the words I am now uttering," though the interpretation of our example breaks down on closer examination. But intimation and the state of affairs asserted fall quite apart in statements such as "$2 \times 2 = 4$." This statement does not say what is said by "I judge that $2 \times 2 = 4$." They are not even equivalent statements, since the one can be true when the other is false.

One must of course stress that if the notion of "intimation" is given the *narrower* sense defined above, the objects named in the above examples are *not* among the experiences they intimate. A man saying something about his contemporary mental state communicates its presence through a judgment. Only as intimating such a judgment (whose content is that he wishes, hopes, etc., this or that) is the man apperceived by the hearer as one who wishes, hopes, etc. The meaning of such a statement lies in this judgment, whereas the inner experiences in question are among the objects judged *about.* If we limit intimation in the narrower sense to experiences which carry an expression's meaning, the contents of intimation and naming remain as distinct here as they are generally.

§26. Essentially occasional and objective expressions

The expressions which name the momentary content of intimation belong to a wider class of expressions whose meaning varies from case to case. This happens, however, in so peculiar a manner that one hesitates to speak of "equivocation" in this case. The same words "I wish you luck" which express my wish, can serve countless other persons to express wishes having "the same" content. Not only do the wishes themselves differ from case to case, but the meanings of the wish-utterances do so too. At one time a person A confronts a person B, at another time a person M confronts a person N. If A wishes B "the same" that M wishes N, the sense of the wish-utterances, which includes the idea of the confronting persons, is plainly different. This ambiguity is, however, quite different from that of the word "dog," which at one time means a type of animal, and at another a foot or a grate.* The class of ambiguous expressions illustrated by this last example are what one usually has in mind when one speaks of "equivocation." Ambiguity in such cases does not tend to shake our faith in the ideality and objectivity of meanings. We are free, in fact, to limit our expression to a *single* meaning. The ideal unity of each of the differing meanings will not be affected by their attachment to a common designation. But how do things stand in the case of the other expressions? Can we there still stick to self-identical meaning-unities, elsewhere made clear in their opposition to varying persons and their experiences, when here our meanings must vary *with* such persons and their experiences? Obviously we are here dealing with a case of unavoidable rather than chance ambiguity, one that cannot be removed from our language by an artificial device or convention.

To promote clearness we shall define the following distinction between *essentially subjective and occasional* expressions, on the one hand, and *objective* expressions, on the other. For simplicity's sake we shall deal only with expressions in their normal use.

We shall call an expression *objective* if it pins down (or can pin down) its meaning merely by its manifest, auditory pattern, and can be understood without necessarily directing one's attention to the person uttering it, or to the circumstances of the utterance. An objective expression may be in varying ways equivocal: it may stand in the stated relation to several meanings, so that it depends on the psychological context (on the chance drift of the hearer's thoughts, on the tenor of the talk already in progress and the tendencies it arouses, etc.) which of these meanings it arouses and means. It may be that a glance at the speaker and his situation may help all this. But whether or not the word *can* be understood in one or other of such meanings does not depend on this glance as a *sine qua non*.

On the other hand, we call an expression essentially subjective and occasional, or, more briefly, *essentially occasional,* if it belongs to a conceptually unified group of possible meanings, in whose case it is essential to orient actual meaning to the occasion, the speaker and the situation. Only by looking to the actual circumstances of utterance can one definite meaning out of all this mutually connected class be constituted for the hearer. Since we regularly understand such expressions in normal circumstances, the very idea of these circumstances, and of their regular relation to the expression, involves the presence of generally graspable, sufficiently reliable clues to guide the hearer to the meaning intended in the case in question.

Among objective expressions we have, e.g., all expressions in theory, expressions out of which the principles and theorems, the proofs and theories of the "abstract" sciences are made up. What, e.g., a mathematical expression means, is not in the least affected by the circumstances of our actual use of it. We read and understand it without thinking of a speaker at all. The case is different with expressions which serve the practical needs of ordinary life and with expressions which, in the sciences, prepare the way for theoretical results. I mean by the latter expressions with which the investigator accompanies his own thought, or acquaints others with his considerations and endeavors, with his methodical preparations and his provisional beliefs.

Every expression, in fact, that includes a *personal pronoun* lacks an objective sense. The word "I" names a different person from case to case, and does so by way of an ever altering meaning. What its meaning is at the moment, can be gleaned only from the living utterance and from the intuitive circumstances which surround it. If we read the word without knowing who wrote it, it is perhaps not meaningless but is at least estranged from its normal sense. Certainly it strikes us differently from a wanton arabesque: we know it to be a word, and a

---

*Husserl's example is of the German word *Hund,* meaning both a dog and a truck used in mines. —Translator's note.

word with which whoever is speaker designates himself. But the conceptual meaning thus evoked is not what the word "I" means, otherwise we could simply substitute for it the phrase "whatever speaker is designating himself." Such a substitution would lead to expressions, not only unusual, but also divergent in sense, if, e.g., instead of saying "I am pleased" I said "Whatever speaker is now designating himself is pleased." It is the universal *semantic function* of the word "I" to designate whoever is speaking, but the notion through which we express this function is not the notion immediately constitutive of its meaning.

In solitary speech the meaning of "I" is essentially realized in the immediate idea of one's own personality, which is also the meaning of the word in communicated speech. Each man has his own I-presentation (and with it his individual notion of I) and this is why the word's meaning differs from person to person. But since each person, in speaking of himself, says "I," the word has the character of a universally operative indication of this fact. Through such *indication* the hearer achieves understanding of the meaning, he takes the person who confronts him intuitively, not merely as the speaker, but also as the immediate object of this speaker's speech. The word "I" has not itself directly the power to arouse the specific I-presentation; this becomes fixed in the actual piece of talk. It does not work like the word "lion," which can arouse the idea of a lion in and by itself. In its case, rather, an indicative function mediates, crying as it were, to the hearer "Your *vis-à-vis* intends himself."

We must, however, add something to what has been said. Properly speaking, we should not suppose that the immediate presentation of the speaker sums up the entire meaning of the word "I." The word is certainly not to be regarded as an equivocal expression, with meanings to be identified with all possible proper names of persons. Undoubtedly the idea of self-reference, as well as an implied pointing to the individual idea of the speaker, also belong, *after a certain fashion,* to the word's meaning. We shall have to admit that two meanings are here built upon one another in peculiar fash-

ion. The one, relating to the word's general function, is so connected with the word that its indicative function can be exercised once something is actually presented: this indicative function is, in its turn, exercised *for* the other, singular presentation, and, by subsumption, makes the latter's object known as what is here and now meant. The former meaning can be called the *indicating* meaning, the latter the meaning *indicated.*

What is true of personal pronouns is of course also true of demonstratives. If someone says "this," he does not directly arouse in the hearer the idea of what he means, but in the first place the idea or belief that he means something lying within his intuitive or thought-horizon, something he wishes to point out to the hearer. In the concrete circumstances of speech, this thought is an adequate guide to what is really meant. "This" read in isolation likewise lacks its proper meaning, and is understood only to the extent that it arouses the notion of its demonstrative function (which we call its indicating meaning). In each case of normal use, its full, actual meaning can only grow out of the prominent presentation of the thing that it makes its object.

We must grant, of course, that a demonstrative often works in a manner that can claim equivalence with an objective use. A "this" in a mathematical context points to something determined in a conceptually fixed manner, that is, understood as meant in this manner, without our needing to regard the actual utterance. A mathematical exposition, after expressly stating a proposition, may go on to say "This follows from the fact that. . . ." Here the proposition in question could itself have been substituted for the word "this" without greatly altering the sense; this follows from the exposition's objective sense. One must of course attend to the continuous exposition since, not the intended meaning, but only the thought of an indication, belongs to the demonstrative considered by itself. Mediation by indicating meanings merely promotes brevity and increases mastery over the main drift of one's thought-intentions. The same plainly does not apply in the common case where the demonstrative "this" and similar forms stand for the house confronting the speaker, for the bird flying up before him, etc. Here individual intuition, varied from case to case, must do duty: it is not enough to look back to previously uttered objective thoughts.

In the sphere of essentially occasional expressions one has also the subject-bound determinations "here," "there," "above," "below," "now," "yesterday," "tomorrow," "later," etc. "Here" (to think out a last example) designates the speaker's vaguely bounded spatial environment. To use the word is to refer to one's place on the basis of an intuitive, believing presentation of one's own person and location. This changes from case to case, and changes likewise from person to person, though each can say "here." It is again the general function of the word to name the spatial environment of the speaker, so that the genuine meaning of the word is first constituted in the variable presentation of this place. The meaning of "here" is in part universal and conceptual, inasmuch as it always names a place as such, but to this universal element the direct place-presentation attaches, varying from case to case. In the given circumstances of speech, it acquires heightened intelligibility by subsumption under the conceptual indicating presentation of "here."

An essentially indicating character naturally spreads to all expressions which include these and similar presentations as parts: this includes all the manifold speech-forms where the speaker gives normal expression to something concerning himself, or which is thought of in relation to himself. All expressions for percepts, beliefs, doubts, wishes, fears, commands belong here, as well as all combinations involving the *definite article,* in which the latter relates to something individual and merely pinned down by class- or property-concepts. When we Germans speak of *the* Kaiser we of course mean the present German Kaiser. When we ask for *the* lamp in the evening, each man means his own.

Note. Expressions with essentially occasional meaning, as dealt with in this section, do not fit into Paul's useful division of expressions into those of usual and those of occasional meaning. His division is based on the fact "that the meaning which a word has in each application need not coincide with what usage accords in it in and for itself" (H. Paul, *Prinzipien der Sprachgeschichte,* p. 68). Paul has, however, included our essentially occasional expressions in his treatment, for he says: "There are some words in occasional use which are essentially framed to designate the concrete, but which none the less lack their own relation to a definite concretum till individual application gives them one. Here belong personal pronouns, possessive and demonstrative adjectives, demonstrative adverbs, also words like "now," "today," "yesterday.""* It seems to me that occasional expressions in this sense fall outside of Paul's definitory antithesis. For it pertains to the *usual* sense of this class of expressions, that they owe their determinate meaning to the occasion, and are therefore occasional in a somewhat *different* sense. Expressions of usual meaning (in Paul's sense) can be divided into those usually univocal and those usually equivocal, and the latter into expressions usually varying among definite meanings assignable in advance (such as the casual equivoca "cock," "bear," etc.) and those in which this is not so, since their meaning is oriented in each case to the individual instance, though the manner of this orientation is a matter of usage.

§27. Other sorts of fluctuating expressions

The variation of essentially occasional expressions is heightened by the incompleteness with which they often express the speaker's meaning. The distinction between essentially occasional and objective expressions cuts across many other distinctions standing for new forms of ambiguity, the distinctions, e.g., between complete and incomplete (enthymematic) expressions, between expressions functioning normally and expressions functioning

---

*The restriction to concreta is not essential. Demonstratives, e.g., can also refer to abstracta.

abnormally, between exact and vague expressions. The impersonalia of ordinary speech are good examples as to how apparently firm, objective expressions really vary subjectively in virtue of enthymematic abbreviation. No one would understand the sentence "There are cakes" as he understands the mathematical sentence "There are regular solids." In the first case we do not mean that cakes exist absolutely and in general, but that there are cakes *here* and *now*—for coffee. "It is raining," likewise, does not have the general meaning that rain is falling, but that it is doing so *now, outside*. What the expression lacks is not merely unspoken, it is not even expressly thought: it certainly belongs, however, to what our speech means. If additions are made, we plainly get expressions that must be called "essentially occasional" in the sense defined above.

There is an even greater difference between the properly expressed content of speech, i.e., the content picked out and pinned down by the uniform meaning-functions of the words involved, and its meaning on occasions when expressions are so shortened as not to express complete thoughts without the aids given to understanding by the fortuitous occasion, e.g., "Onward!," "You!," "Man alive!," "But my dear, my dear," etc. Through the common intuitive situation in which both speaker and hearer find themselves, these last can supplement or differentiate mutilated and subjectively indeterminate meanings: the defective expressions thus become understandable.

Among the distinctions relating to ambiguity of expressions, we mentioned those between *exact* and *vague* expressions. Most expressions used in ordinary life, such as "tree," "shrub," "animal," "plant," etc., are vague, whereas all expressions integral to pure theories and laws are exact. Vague expressions have no single meaning-content, the same in all cases of their application: their meaning is oriented towards types, only partially conceived with clearness and definiteness, types which tend to vary from case to case, perhaps even in a single train of

thought. The types, stemming from what are, or from what seem to be, genuinely unified fields, yield a number of concepts, more or less cognate or related, which emerge in turn according to the circumstances of our talk and its varied thought-promptings. These do not permit, for the most part, of definite identifications and distinctions such as might guard against unnoticed confusions among closely connected concepts.

Similar to the haziness of such vague expressions, is the haziness of expressions standing for relatively simple genera and species of phenomenal properties, which shade continuously into one another, whether spatially, temporally, qualitatively or intensively. The typical characters which press in upon us in perception and experience, characters, e.g., of space- and time-pattern, of color- and tone-pattern, etc., lead to significant expressions which, in virtue of the fluid transitions among such types (i.e., among their higher genera) must themselves be fluid. Within certain ranges and limits their application is unhesitant, i.e., in fields where the type appears clearly, where it can be evidently identified and evidently distinguished from remotely unlike characters, e.g., "signal-red" and "coal-black," *andante* and *presto*. But these fields have vague borders, and flow over into correlative spheres comprehended in the same genus, and so give rise to transitional regions where application varies and is wholly uncertain.*

§28. Variations in meanings as variations in the act of meaning

We have become acquainted with various classes of expressions changeable in meaning, which count as subjective and occasional, since chance circumstances of speaking influence their change. To these expressions other expressions stand opposed, which are, in a correspondingly wide sense, objective and fixed, their meaning being normally free from all variation. If we take this freedom from all varia-

*Cf. B. Erdmann, "Theorie der Typeneinteilungen," *Philos. Monatshefte* XXX.

tion quite strictly, only exact expressions are ranged on this side, whereas vague expressions and expressions which, for differing reasons, vary with the occasion, stand ranged on the other side.

We have now to consider whether these important facts of fluctuation of meaning are enough to shake our conception of meanings as ideal (i.e., rigorous) unities, or to restrict its generality significantly. Those ambiguous expressions we called *essentially* subjective, in particular, as also our distinction between vague and exact expressions, might make us doubtful on this point. Do meanings *themselves* divide into objective and subjective, into meanings fixed and meanings changeable on occasion? Must we, in other words, so interpret this difference, with seeming obviousness, that it becomes one between meanings that are ideal unities, on the one hand, fixed species untouched by the flux of our subjective picturing and thinking, and such, on the other hand, as live submerged in the flux of subjective mental experiences, and are transitory events, at one time there, and at the next moment not?

We shall have to look on such a notion as invalid. The content meant by the subjective expression, with sense oriented to the occasion, is an ideal unit of meaning in precisely the same sense as the content of a fixed expression. This is shown by the fact that, ideally speaking, each subjective expression is replaceable by an objective expression which will preserve the identity of each momentary meaning-intention.

We shall have to concede that such replacement is not only impracticable, for reasons of complexity, but that it cannot in the vast majority of cases, be carried out at all, will, in fact, never be so capable.

Clearly, in fact, to say that each subjective expression could be replaced by an objective expression is no more than to assert the *unbounded range of objective reason*. Everything that is, can be known "in itself." Its being is a being definite in content, and documented in such and such "truths in themselves." What is, has its intrinsically definite properties and relations, and if it has natural, thinglike reality, then it has also its quite definite extension

and position in space and time, its quite definite ways of persisting and changing. But what is objectively quite definite must permit objective determination, and what permits objective determination must, ideally speaking, permit expression through wholly determinate word-meanings. To being-in-itself correspond truths-in-themselves, and, to these last, fixed, unambiguous assertions. Of course, to be able to say all this actually, would require, not merely the necessary number of well-distinguished *verbal signs,* but a corresponding number of *expressions* having precise meanings—in the strict sense of expressions. We must be able to build up all expressions covering all meanings entering into our theory, and to identify or distinguish such meanings with self-evidence.

We are infinitely removed from this ideal. One need only think of the defective way in which we pin down time- and space-positions, our necessary recourse to relations to previously given individual existents, these last themselves inaccessible to an exact pinning down without making use of expressions having an essentially subjective sense. Strike out the essentially occasional expressions from one's language, try to describe any subjective experience in unambiguous, objectively fixed fashion: such an attempt is always plainly vain.

Plainly therefore, considered as such, meanings do not differ essentially among themselves. Actual word-meanings are variable, often changing in a single spell of thought, by their nature mainly adjusted to the occasion. Rightly seen, however, such change in meanings is really *change in the act of meaning.* In other words, the subjective acts which confer meaning on expressions are variable, and that not merely as individuals, but, more particularly, in respect of the specific characters in which their meaning consists. But the meanings themselves do not alter: this is in fact an absurd manner of speech if we adhere to our view of meanings as ideal unities, whether in the case of equivocal, subjectively defective expressions, or in the case of univocal, objectively fixed ones. This is not merely a view demanded by our ordinary orientation to fixed expressions, and by our talk of meanings which stay the same, whenever anyone uses the same expression; it fits in with the whole guiding aim of our analyses.

§29. Pure logic and ideal meanings

Pure logic, wherever it deals with concepts, judgments, and syllogisms, is exclusively concerned with the *ideal* unities that we here call "meanings." If we take the trouble to detach the ideal essence of meanings from their psychological and grammatical connections, if we try, further, to clear up their a priori relations of adequacy, founded in this essence, to the objective correlates that they mean, we are already within the domain of pure logic.

This is clear from the start if we *first* think of the position logic takes up to the many sciences, the position of nomological science, concerned with the ideal essence of science as such, or, what is the same, the position of nomological science, of scientific thought in general, taken purely in its theoretic content and connection. It is clear, *secondly,* when we note that the theoretic content of a science is no more than the meaning-content of its theoretical statements, disembarrassed of all contingent thinkers and occasions of judgment, and that such statements are given *unity* by the theory's pattern, which in its turn acquires objective validity through the ideally guaranteed adequacy of its unified meaning to the objective correlate meant by it (which is "given" to us in self-evident knowledge). Undeniably what we call "meaning" in this sense covers only ideal unities, expressed through manifold expressions, and thought of in manifold act-experiences, but none the less clearly separable from such chance expressions and from such chance experiences of thinking subjects.

If all given theoretic unity is in essence a unity of meaning, and if logic is the science of theoretic unity in general, then logic evidently is the science of meanings as such, of their essential sorts and differences, as also of the ideal laws which rest purely on the latter. Among such essential differences we have those be-

tween meanings which have, and meanings which have no objects, between true and false meanings, and, among such laws, we have the pure "laws of thought," which express the a priori connection between the categorial form of meanings and their objectivity or truth.

This notion of logic as a science of meanings is of course at odds with the mode of speech and treatment of the traditional logic, which operates with psychological or psychologically slanted terms such as "idea," "judgment," "affirmation," "denial," "presupposition," "inference," etc., and which thinks it is really only establishing differences of psychology and tracking down psychological laws relating to these. After the critical investigations of our *Prolegomena* we can no more be taken in by all this. It only shows how far logic still is from a proper understanding of the objects which make up its own true field of research, and how much it has still to learn from the objective sciences, whose essence it none the less claims to make theoretically intelligible.

Where the sciences unfold systematic theories, when they no longer merely communicate the progress of personal research and proof, but set forth the objectively unified, ripe fruit of known truth, there is absolutely no talk of judgments, ideas and other mental acts. The objective researcher of course *defines* his expressions. He says: By *"vis viva,"* by "mass," by an "integral," by a "sine," etc., this or that is meant. But he only points thereby to the *objective meaning* of his expressions, he indicates what "contents" he has in mind, which play their part as constitutive moments in the truths of his field. He is not interested in understanding, but in the concepts, which are for him ideal unities of meaning, and also in the truths, which themselves are made up out of such concepts.

The investigator then propounds propositions, and naturally, in so doing, he asserts or judges. But he has no wish to speak of his own or of anyone else's judgments, but of the correlated *states of affairs,* and when his critical discussions concern propositions, he means by the latter the ideal meanings of statements. He does not say that judgments are true or false, but that propositions are so: his premises are propositions, and so are his conclusions. Propositions are not constructed out of mental acts of presentation or belief: when not constructed out of other propositions, they ultimately point back to concepts.

Propositions are themselves the elements of *inferences*. Here too there is a distinction between acts of inferring and their unified contents, syllogisms, i.e., the self-identical *meanings* of certain complex statements. The relation of necessary consequence in which the form of an inference consists is not an empirical-psychological connection among judgments as experiences, but an ideal relation among possible statement-meanings, among propositions. It "exists" or "subsists," i.e., it is valid, and such validity is something without essential relation to an empirical thinker. If a natural scientist deduces a machine's working from the laws of the lever, gravitation, etc., he no doubt experiences all sorts of subjective acts. What, however, he thinks of, and what he knits together in unity, are concepts and propositions together with their objective relations. An objective unity of meaning, i.e., one adequate to the objectivity which is self-evidently "given," thereby corresponds to his subjective thought-connections: this is whatever it is, whether anyone realizes this in thought or not.

This holds in general. Though the scientific investigator may have no reason to draw express distinctions between words and symbols, on the one hand, and meaningful thought-objects, on the other, he well knows that expressions are contingent, and that the thought, the ideally selfsame meaning, is what is essential. He knows, too, that he does not *make* the objective validity of thoughts and thought-connections, of concepts and truths, as if he were concerned with contingencies of his own or of the general human mind, but that he *sees* them, *discovers* them. He knows that their ideal being does not amount to a psychological "being in the mind": the authentic objectivity of the true, and of the ideal in general, suspends *all* reality, including such as is subjective. If some scientists at times think differently on this point, they do so, not in their professional scientific settings, but on subsequent reflection. If, with Hume, we may hold that men's true beliefs are better documented by their deeds than by their words, then we may twit such thinkers with not understanding themselves. They pay no unprejudiced heed to what they think in their unreflective inquiries and demonstrations, but are led astray by the supposed authority of logic, with its psychologistic fallacies and subjectively distorted terminology.

All theoretical science consists, in its objective content, of *one* homogeneous stuff: it is an ideal fabric of *meanings*. We can go even further and say that the whole, indefinitely complex web of meanings that we call the theoretical unity of science, falls under the very category that covers all its elements: it is itself a unity of meaning.

If meaning, rather than the act of meaning, concept and proposition, rather than idea and judgment, are what is essential and germane in science, they are necessarily the general object of investigation in the science whose theme is the essence of science. Everything that is logical falls under the two correlated categories of *meaning* and *object*. If we speak in the plural of *logical categories*, we have only to do with the pure species distinguishable a priori within the genus of meaning, or with the correlated forms of *categorially considered objectivity*. In such categories the laws formulable in logic have their foundation. We have, on the one hand, such laws as abstract from the ideal relations between meaning-intention and meaning-fulfillment, and so from any possible knowledge-use of meanings, and consider only how meanings can be compounded to form novel meanings (whether "real" or "imaginary").* We have, on the other hand, *logical laws,* in the more emphatic sense, which consider meanings in respect of their having or not having objects,

*More on this point in Investigation IV.

in respect of their truth or their falsity, their consistency or their absurdity, to the extent that such things are merely determined by the categorial form of such meanings. Corresponding with these latter laws, we have equivalent, correlated *laws for objects in general, objects determined in thought by mere categories.* All valid assertions regarding existence and truth, that are capable of being framed in abstraction from all material of knowledge on a mere foundation of meaning-forms, find their place among such laws.

The Phenomenological and Ideal Content of the Experiences of Meaning*

§30. The content of the expressive experience taken in its psychological sense and in the sense of a unified meaning

The essence of meaning is seen by us, not in the meaning-conferring experience, but in its "content," the single, self-identical intentional† unity set over against the dispersed multiplicity of actual and possible experiences of speakers and thinkers. The "content" of a meaning-experience, in this ideal sense, is not at all what psychology means by a "content," i.e., any real part or side of an experience. If we understand a name—whether standing for what is individual or general, physical or psychic, existent or non-existent, possible or impossible—or if we understand a statement— true in content or false, consistent or absurd, believed or figmentary—then what either expression "says"—the meaning which forms its *logical* content and which, in contexts of pure logic, is called either an idea or concept, or a judgment or proposition—is nothing which could, in a real sense, count as part of our act of understanding. This experience naturally has its psychological components, is a content, con-

sists of contents, in the ordinary sense of psychology. Here belong primarily all the sensuous elements of our experience, the appearances of words, in their purely visual, auditory or motor content, and, in the next place, the acts of objective reference which locate such words in space and time. The psychic stuff here involved is well-known to be vastly manifold, varying greatly from one individual to the next, and for the same individual from one moment to another, even in respect of "one and the same" word. The verbal presentations which accompany and support my silent thinking sometimes involve picturings of words spoken by my own voice, sometimes of letters written by *me* in shorthand or longhand—all these are individual peculiarities, and belong merely to the psychological content of *my* presentational experience. Among contents in this psychological sense are also many differences in respect of act-character, not always easily seized descriptively, such as the subjective difference which constitutes reference or understanding. If I hear the name "Bismarck" it makes not the slightest difference to my understanding of the word's unified meaning, whether I imagine the great man in a felt hat or coat, or in a cuirassier's uniform, or whatever pictorial representation I may adopt. It is not even of importance whether *any* imagery serves to illustrate my consciousness of meaning, or to enliven it less directly.

Battling against a seductive notion, we laid it down that the essence of expression lies in a meaning-intention, and not in the more or less perfect, more or less close or remote, illustration that accompanies or fulfills that intention. If, however, such illustrations are present, they will be intimately fused with the meaning-intention. It is therefore understandable that our unified experience of the meaningfully functioning expression should, from case to case, reveal considerable psychological differences even on the meaning side, whereas its meaning remains strictly the same.

---

*LI, I, 327–333 (First Investigation, Sections 30–35).

†The word "intentional" is so framed as to permit application both to the meaning and the object of the *intentio.* Intentional unity does not therefore necessarily mean the intended, the objective unity.

We have also shown that there is *something* in the correlated acts which really corresponds to such selfsameness of meaning, that what we call a meaning-intention is not an undifferentiated character to which a connection with fulfilling intuitions first imparts an *external* differentiation. Meaning-intentions of intrinsically different character belong rather with differing meanings, or with expressions used with differing meanings, whereas all expressions understood with like sense are clothed with the same meaning-intention as an invariant mental character. Through this character, expressive experiences strongly differing in psychological make-up first become experiences endowed with the same meaning. Fluctuation of meaning here certainly involves restrictions which make no essential difference.

§31. The act-character of meaning and the ideally unified meaning

We have opposed what is psychologically common to what is psychologically variable, but we have not thereby hit off the distinction we wanted to clarify: that between the psychological and logical content of our expressions and expressive acts. For the psychological content as much includes what is constant from case to case as what varies with the occasion. It is not, therefore, our doctrine that an act-character which stays the same in all cases is itself our meaning. What, e.g., the statement "π is a transcendental number" says, what *we* understand when we read it, and mean when we say it, is no individual feature in our thought-experience, which is merely repeated on many occasions. Such a feature is always individually different from case to case, whereas the sense of the sentence should remain *identical*. If we or others repeat the same sentence with like intention, each of us has his own phenomena, his own words and his own nuances of understanding. Over against this unbounded multiplicity of individual experiences is the selfsame element expressed in them all, "selfsame" in the very strictest sense. Multiplication of persons and acts does not multiply propositional meanings; the judgment in the ideal, logical sense remains single.

That we here insist on the strict identity of what is meant, and oppose it to the constant mental character of meaning it, does not spring from our personal fondness for subtle distinctions, but from the firm theoretical belief that so alone can we do justice to a fact fundamental for the understanding of logic. We are not here dealing with a mere hypothesis, justifiable only by explanatory fruitfulness; we are appealing to an immediately graspable truth, following in this the self-evidence which is the final authority in all questions of knowledge. I see that in repeated acts of presentation and judgment I mean, or can mean, the same concept or proposition: I see that, wherever there is talk of the *proposition* or *truth* that π *is a transcendental number,* there is nothing I have less in mind than an individual experience, or a feature of an individual experience of any person. I see that such reflective talk really has as its object what serves as a meaning in straightforward talk. I see lastly that what I mean by the sentence in question or (when I hear it) grasp as its meaning, is the same thing, whether I think and exist or not, and whether or not there are *any* thinking persons and acts. The same holds of all types of meanings, subject-meanings, predicate-meanings, relational and combinatory meanings, etc. It holds, above all, in the case of the ideal properties which pertain primarily to meanings. Here belong, to mention a few only of the most important, the predicates *true* and *false, possible* and *impossible, general* and *singular, determinate* and *indeterminate,* etc.

The genuine identity that we here assert is none other than the *identity of the species.* As a species, and only as a species, can it embrace in unity (ξυμβάλλειν εἰς ἕν), as an ideal unity, the dispersed multiplicity of individual singulars. The manifold singulars for the ideal unity Meaning are naturally the corresponding act-moments of meaning, the *meaning-intentions.* Meaning is related to varied acts of meaning—Logical Presentation to presentative acts, Logical Judgment to acts of judging, Logical Syllogism to acts of syllogism—just as

Redness *in specie* is to the slips of paper which lie here, and which all "have" the same redness. Each slip has, in addition to other constitutive aspects (extension, form, etc.), its own individual redness, i.e., its instance of this color-species, though this neither exists in the slip nor anywhere else in the whole world, and particularly not "in our thought," in so far as this latter is part of the domain of real being, the sphere of temporality.

Meanings constitute, we may say further, a class of concepts in the sense of "universal objects." They are not for that reason objects which, though existing nowhere in the world, have being in a τόπος οὐράνιος or in a divine mind, for such metaphysical hypostatization would be absurd. If one has accustomed oneself to understand by "being" only real being, and by "objects" only real objects, then talk of universal objects and of their being may well seem basically wrong; no offense will, however, be given to one who has first used such talk merely to assert the validity of certain judgments, such in fact as concern numbers, propositions, geometrical forms, etc., and who now asks whether he is not evidently obliged, here as elsewhere, to affix the label "genuinely existent object" to the correlate of his judgment's validity, to what it judges about. In sober truth, the seven regular solids, are, logically speaking, seven objects precisely as the seven sages are: the principle of the parallelogram of forces is as much a single object as the city of Paris.*

§32. The ideality of meanings is no ideality in the normative sense

The ideality of meanings is a particular case of the ideality of what is specific in general. It has not the sense of *normative ideality,* as if we were here dealing with an ideal of perfection, an ideal limiting value, over against particular cases which realized it more or less approximately. No doubt the "logical concept," i.e., the term in the sense of *normative* logic, is an ideal in respect of its meaning. For the demand of the craft of knowledge runs: "Use words with an absolutely selfsame meaning: exclude all meaning-variations. Distinguish meanings and keep them distinct in declarative thought, and employ sharply distinct sensible signs."

This prescription relates, however, as it only can relate, to the formation of meaningful terms, to care in the subjective sifting out and expression of one's thoughts. Meanings "in themselves" are, as we have argued, specific unities, however much the act of meaning may vary: they themselves are not ideals. Ideality in the ordinary, normative sense does not exclude reality. An ideal is a concrete original that may exist, and that may confront one in reality, as when a young artist takes the work of a great master as the ideal that he relives and that he strives after in his own creations. Even where an ideal is not realizable, it is at least an individual in our presentative intention. The ideality of what is specific is, contrariwise, the complete opposite of reality or individuality; it represents no end of possible endeavor, its ideality lies in a "unity in multiplicity." Not the species itself, but the individual falling under it, can be a practical ideal.

§33. The concepts Meaning and Concept (in the sense of Species) do not coincide

Meanings, we said, constitute a *class* of "universal objects" or species. Each species, if we wish to speak of it, presupposes a meaning, in which it is presented, and this meaning is itself a species. But the meaning in which an object is thought, and its object, the species itself, are not one and the same. Just as in the sphere of individuals we distinguish, e.g., between Bismarck himself and presentations of Bismarck, e.g., *Bismarck—the greatest of German statesmen,* etc., so also, in the field of species, we distinguish between, e.g., the number 4 itself and the presentations, i.e., meanings, which have 4 as their object, as, e.g., *the number 4—the second even number in the number-*

---

*Regarding the question of the essence of universal objects see Investigation II.

series, etc. The universality *that* we think of does not therefore resolve itself into the universality of the meanings *in which* we think of it. Meanings, although as such they are universal objects, fall, *in respect of the objects to which they refer, into individual and specific meanings,* or (to conform to a readily understandable linguistic preference) *into individual and general meanings.* Individual presentations, e.g., are therefore *generalia, qua* unities of meaning, though their objects are *individualia.*

§34. In the act of meaning we are not conscious of meaning as an object

In the actual experience of meaning an individual feature, a singular case of the species (we said) corresponds to the unitary meaning, just as to the specific difference Redness the aspect of red in the object corresponds. If we perform the act and live in it, as it were, we naturally refer to its object and not to its meaning. If, e.g., we make a statement, we judge about the thing it concerns, and not about the statement's meaning, about the judgment in the logical sense. This latter first becomes objective to us in a reflex act of thought, in which we not only look back on the statement just made, but carry out the abstraction (the Ideation) demanded. This logical reflection is not an act that takes place only under exceptional, artificial conditions: it is a normal component of *logical* thinking. What is characteristic of such thought is the context of theory, and the theoretical consideration of the latter, which is carried out in step-by-step reflections on the *contents* of the thought-acts just performed. A very common form of thoughtful pondering may serve as an instance: "Is *S P*? That could very well be. But from this proposition it would follow that *M* is the case. This cannot be, and so what I first thought possible, *that S is P,* must be false, etc." The italicized words should be noted, as well as the idealizations they express. *This* proposition, that *S is P,* which is the pervasive theme of discussion, is plainly not the fleeting moment of meaning in the thought-act in which the notion first occurred to us. Logical reflection rather sets in at later stages, and

an identical propositional meaning is continuously meant in it, idealized and identified in our unified thought-context, and thought of as one and the same. The same is the case wherever a unified theoretical demonstration is being wound up. We could utter no "therefore" unless there was also a glance at the meaning-content of the premisses. In judging the premisses, we not merely live in our judgments, but reflect on their contents: only by glancing back at these does the conclusion appear "motivated." Thus and only thus can the logical form of the premisses—which of course is not stressed in that universal, conceptual way that finds expression in syllogistic formulae—determine with insight the drawing of the conclusion.

§35. Meanings "in themselves" and meanings expressed

We have so far preferred to speak of meanings which, as the normal, relational sense of the word suggests, are meanings of expressions. There is, however, no intrinsic connection between the ideal unities which in fact operate as meanings, and the signs to which they are tied, i.e., through which they become real in human mental life. We cannot therefore say that all ideal unities of this sort are expressed meanings. Wherever a new concept is formed, we see how a meaning becomes realized that was previously unrealized. As numbers—in the ideal sense that arithmetic presupposes—neither spring forth nor vanish with the act of enumeration, and as the endless number-series thus represents an objectively fixed set of general objects, sharply delimited by an ideal law, which no one can either add to or take away from, so it is with the ideal unities of pure logic, with its concepts, propositions, truths, or in other words, with its meanings. They are an ideally closed set of general objects, to which being thought or being expressed are alike contingent. There are therefore countless meanings which, in the common, relational sense, are merely possible ones, since they are never expressed, and since they can, owing to the limits of man's cognitive powers, never be expressed.

4. Meaning-Intention and Meaning-Fulfillment*

§6. *The static union of expressive thought and expressed intuition. Recognition (das Erkennen)*

We shall now absorb ourselves in a closer investigation of the relations holding among intuitive acts, on the one hand, and expressive acts, on the other. We shall confine ourselves, in the present section entirely, to the range of the simplest possible cases, and so naturally to expressions and significant intentions which belong to the sphere of *naming*. We shall make, for the rest, no claim to treat this field exhaustively. We are concerned with nominal expressions, which refer themselves in the most perspicuous of possible fashions to "corresponding" percepts and other forms of intuition.

Let us first glance in this field at a *relationship of static union, where a sense-giving thought has based itself on intuition, and is thereby related to its object.* I speak, e.g., of my *inkpot,* and my inkpot also stands before me: I see it. The name names the object of my percept, and is enabled to name it by the significant act which expresses its character and its form in the form of the name. The relation between name and thing named has, in this state of union, a certain *descriptive character* that we previously noticed: the name "my inkpot" seems to *overlay* the perceived object, to belong *sensibly* to it. This belonging is of a peculiar kind. The words do not belong to the objective context of physical thing-hood that they express: in this context they have no place, they are not referred to as something in or attaching to the things that they name. If we turn to the experiences involved, we have, on the one hand, as said before,† the acts in which the words appear, on the other hand, the similar acts in which the things appear. As regards the latter, the inkpot confronts us in perception.

Following our repeated demonstration of the descriptive essence of perception, this means no more phenomenologically than that we undergo a certain sequence of experiences of the class of sensations, sensuously unified in a peculiar serial pattern, and informed by a certain act-character of "interpretation" *(Auffassung),* which endows it with an objective sense. This act-character is responsible for the fact that an *object,* i.e., this inkpot, is perceptually apparent to us. In similar fashion, the phenomenal word is constituted for us in an act of perception or imaginative presentation.

Not word *and* inkpot, therefore, but the act-experiences just described, in which they make their appearance, are here brought into relation: in these word and inkpot appear, while yet being nothing whatever *in* the acts in question. But how does this happen? What brings these acts into unity? The answer seems clear. The relation, as one of naming, is mediated, not merely by acts of meaning, but by acts of recognition *(Erkennen),* which are here also acts of *classification.* The perceived object is *recognized* for an inkpot, known as one, and in so far as the act of meaning is most intimately one with an act of classification, and this latter, as recognition of the perceived object, is again intimately one with the act of perception, the expression seems to be *applied* to the thing and to clothe it like a garment.

Ordinarily we speak of recognizing and classifying the object of perception, as if our act busied itself with this *object.* But we have seen that there is no object in the experience, only a perception, a thus and thus determinate mindedness *(Zumutesein): the recognitive act in the experience must accordingly base itself on the act of perception.* One must not of course misunderstand the matter and raise the objection that we are putting the matter as if perception

---

*LI, II, 687–697, 699–702 (Sixth Investigation, Sections 6–8, 10, and 11).
†*Log. Inv.* 1, 2, 10.

was classified rather than its object. We are not doing this at all. Such a performance would involve acts of a quite different, much more complex constitution, expressible through expressions of corresponding complexity, e.g., "the perception of the inkpot." It follows that the recognitive experience of this thing as "my inkpot," is nothing but a recognition which, in a definite and direct fashion, fuses an expressive experience, on the one hand, with the relevant percept, on the other.

The same holds of cases in which *picture-presentations* serve in place of percepts. The imaginatively apparent object, e.g., the identical inkpot in memory or in fancy, is felt to bear the expression which names it. This means, phenomenologically speaking, that a recognitive act in union with an expressive experience is so related to an imaginative act as to be, in objective parlance, spoken of as the recognition of an imaginatively presented object as, e.g., our inkpot. The imagined object, too, is absolutely nothing in our presentation of it, our experience is rather a certain blend of images, fancied sensations, informed by a certain interpretative act-character. To live through this act, and to have an imaginative presentation of the object, are one and the same. If we therefore express the situation in the words "I have before me an image, the image of an inkpot," we have plainly coupled *new* acts with our expressions, and, in particular, a *recognitive* act which is intimately one with our act of imagining.

§7. Recognition as a character of acts, and the "generality of words"

The following more exact argument would seem to show conclusively that, in all cases where a name is applied to a thing intuitively given, we may presume the presence of a recognitive act-character mediating between the appearance of the word-sounds, on the one hand (or the complete sense-informed word), and the intuition of the thing on the other. One often hears of the *generality of words,* and usually understands by this highly ambiguous phrase that a word is not bound to an individual intu-

ition, but belongs rather to an endless array of possible intuitions.

In what, however, does this belonging consist?

Let us deal with an extremely simple example, that of the name "red." In so far as it names a phenomenal object as red, it belongs to this object in virtue of the aspect of red that appears in this object. And each object that bears an aspect of like sort in itself justifies the same appellation: the same name belongs to each, and does so by way of an identical sense.

But in what does this appellation by way of an identical sense consist?

We observe first that the word does not attach externally, and merely through hidden mental mechanisms, to the individual, specifically similar traits of our intuitions. It is not enough, manifestly, to acknowledge the bare fact that, wherever such and such an individual trait appears in our intuition, the word also *accompanies* it as a mere pattern of sound. A mere concomitance, a mere external going with or following on one another would not forge any internal bond among them, and certainly not an intentional bond. Yet plainly we have here such an intentional bond, and one of quite peculiar phenomenological character. The word *calls* the red thing red. The red appearing before us is what is *referred* to by the name, and is referred to as *"red."* In this mode of naming reference, the name appears as *belonging* to the named and as *one* with it.

On the other hand, however, the word has its sense quite apart from an attachment to this intuition, and without attachment to *any* "corresponding" intuition. Since this sense is everywhere the same, it is plain that it is not the mere phoneme, rather the true, complete word, endowed on all occasions with the constant character of its sense, that must be held to underlie the naming relation. Even then it will not be enough to describe the union of meaningful word and corresponding intuition in terms of mere concomitance. Take the word, present in consciousness and *understood as a mere symbol* without being actually used to name anything, and set the corresponding intuition beside it: these two phenomena may at once, for genetic reasons, be brought together in the phenomenological unity of naming. Their mere togetherness is, however, not as yet this unity, which *grows out of it* with plain novelty. It is conceivable, a priori, that no such unity should emerge, that the coexistent phenomena should be phenomenologically disjoined, that the object before us should not be the thing meant or named by the meaningful word, and that the word should not *belong* to the object as its name, and so name it.

Phenomenologically we find before us no mere aggregate, but an intimate, in fact intentional, unity: we can rightly say that the two acts, the one setting up the complete word, and the other the thing, are intentionally combined in a single *unity of act.* What here lies before us can be naturally described, with equal correctness, by saying that *the name "red" calls the object red,* or that *the red object is recognized (known) as red, and called "red" as a result of this recognition.* To "call something red"— in the fully actual sense of "calling" which presupposes an underlying intuition of the thing so called—and to "recognize something as red," are in reality *synonymous* expressions: they only differ in so far as the latter brings out more clearly that we have here no mere duality, but a unity engineered by a single act-character. In the intimacy of this fusion, we must nonetheless admit, the various factors implicit in our unity—the physical word-phenomenon with its ensouling meaning, the aspect of recognition and the intuiting of what one names—do not separate themselves off clearly, but our discussion compels us to presume them all to be there. We shall have more to say on this point later on.

It is plain that the recognitive character of certain acts, which gives them their significant relation to objects of intuition, does not pertain to words as noises, but to words in their meaningful, their *semantic (bedeutungsmässigen)* essence. Very different verbal sounds, e.g., the "same" word in different languages, may involve an identical recognitive relation: the object is essentially known for the same, though with the aid of quite different noises. Naturally the complete recognition of something red, being equivalent to the actually used name,

must include the noise "red" as a part. The members of different speech-communities feel different verbal sounds to be fitting, and include these in the unity of "knowing something." But the meaning attaching to such words, and the recognitive act actually attaching this meaning to its object, remains everywhere the same, so that these verbal differences are rightly regarded as irrelevant.

The "generality of the word" means, therefore, that the unified sense of one and the same word covers (or, in the case of a nonsense-word, purports to cover) an ideally delimited manifold of possible intuitions, each of which could serve as the basis for an act of recognitive naming endowed with the same sense. To the word "red," e.g., corresponds the possibility of both knowing as, and calling "red," all red objects that might be given in possible intuitions. This possibility leads on, with an a priori guarantee, to the further possibility of becoming aware, through an *identifying synthesis* of all such naming recognitions, of a sameness of meaning of one with the other: this A is red, and that A is *the same,* i.e., *also* red: the two intuited singulars belong under the same "concept."

A dubious point emerges here. We said above that a word could be understood even if not actually used to name anything. Must we not, however, grant that a word must at least have the *possibility* of functioning as the actual name of something and so of achieving an actual recognitive relation to corresponding intuition? Must we not say that without such a possibility it could not be a word at all? The answer, of course, is that this possibility depends on the possibility of the recognitions, the "knowings," in question. Not all intended knowing is possible, not all nominal meaning can be *realized.* "Imaginary" names may be names, but they cannot *actually* be used to name anything, they have, properly speaking, no extension, they are *without generality in the sense of the possible and the true.* Their generality is *empty pretension.* But how these last forms of speech are themselves to be made clear, what phenomenological facts lie behind them, will be a matter for further investigation.

What we have said applies to *all* expressions, and not merely to such as have generality of meaning in the manner of a *class-concept.* It applies also to expressions having *individual reference,* such as proper names. The fact spoken of as the "generality of verbal meaning" does not point to the generality accorded to generic, as opposed to individual concepts, but, on the contrary, embraces either indifferently. The "recognition," the "knowing," of which we speak when a significantly functioning expression encounters corresponding intuition, must not, therefore, be conceived as an actual *classification,* the ranging of an intuitively or cogitatively presented object in a *class,* a ranging necessarily based on general concepts and verbally mediated by general names. Proper names, too, have their generality, though, when actually used to name anything, they can *eo ipso* not be said to classify it. Proper names, like other names, cannot name anything, without thereby also "knowing" it. That their relation to corresponding intuition is, in fact, as indirect as that of any other expression, can be shown by a treatment exactly analogous to the one conducted above. Each and every name obviously belongs to no definite percept, nor to a definite imagination nor to any other pictorial illustration. The same person can make his appearance in countless possible intuitions, and all these appearances have no merely intuitive but also a recognitive unity. Each appearance from such an intuitive manifold will justify a precisely synonymous use of the proper name. Whichever appearance is given, the man using the name means one and the same person or thing. And he means this not merely in being intuitively oriented to it, as when he deals with an object personally strange to him; he knows it as this definite person or thing. He knows Hans as *Hans,* Berlin as *Berlin.* To recognize a person as this person, or a city as this city, is again an act not tied to the particular sensuous content of this or that word-appearance. It is identically the same act in the case of a variety (in possibility of an infinite variety) of verbal noises, as, e.g., when several different proper names apply to the same thing.

This generality of the proper name, and of the peculiar meaning which corresponds to it, is plainly quite different in kind from that of the *general name.*

The former consists in the fact that a synthesis of possible intuitions belongs to a *single* individual object, intuitions made one by the common intentional character imparted by every relation to the same object, despite all phenomenal differences among individual intuitions. On this unified basis, the particular unity of recognitive knowing reposes, which belongs to the "generality of verbal meaning," to its range of ideally possible realizations. In this way the naming word has a recognitive relation to a boundless multitude of intuitions, whose identical object it both knows and thereby names.

The case of the *class-name* is quite different. Its generality covers a *range of objects,* to each of which, *considered apart,* a possible synthesis of percepts, a possible individual meaning and proper name belongs. The general name "covers" this range through being able to name each item in the whole range in general fashion, i.e., not by individually recognizing it in the manner of the proper name, but by classifying it, in the manner of the common name. The thing that is either directly given, or known in its authentic self-being *(Eigenheit),* or known through its properties, is now known as *an A* and named accordingly.

§8. The dynamic unity of expression and expressed intuition. The consciousness of fulfillment and that of identity

From the tranquil, as it were *static* coincidence of meaning and intuition, we now turn to that *dynamic* coincidence where an expression first functions in merely symbolic fashion, and then is accompanied by a "more or less" corresponding intuition. Where this happens, we experience a descriptively peculiar *consciousness of fulfillment:** the act of pure meaning, like a goal-seeking intention, finds its

*Cf. my *Psych. Studies of elementary Logic,* II, "Concerning Intuitions and Representations," *Philos. Monatshefte,* 1894, p. 176. I have given up the concept of intuition supported there, as the present work makes plain.

fulfillment in the act which renders the matter intuitive. In this transitional experience, the *mutual belongingness* of the two acts, the act of meaning, on the one hand, and the intuition which more or less corresponds to it, on the other, reveals its phenomenological roots. We experience how *the same* objective item which was "merely thought of" in symbol is now presented in intuition, and that it is intuited as being precisely the determinate so-and-so that it was at first merely thought or meant to be. We are merely expressing the same fact if we say that *the intentional essence of the act of intuition* gets more or less perfectly *fitted into the semantic essence of the act of expression.*

In the previously considered static relation among acts of meaning and intuition, we spoke of a *recognition,* a *knowing.* This represents the sense-informed relation of the name to the intuitive datum that it names. But the element of meaning is not here itself the act of recognition. In the purely symbolic understanding of a word, an act of meaning is performed (the word means something to us) but nothing is thereby known, recognized. The difference lies, as the foregoing paragraphs have established, not in the mere accompanying presence of the intuition of the thing named, but in the phenomenologically peculiar form of unity. What is characteristic about this unity of knowing, of recognition, is now shown up by the dynamic relationship before us. In it there is at first the meaning-intention, quite on its own: then the corresponding intuition comes to join it. At the same time we have the phenomenological unity which is now stamped as a consciousness of fulfillment. Talk about recognizing objects, and talk about fulfilling a meaning-intention, therefore express the same fact, merely from differing standpoints. The former adopts the standpoint of the object meant, while the latter has the two acts as its foci of interest. Phenomenologically the acts are always present,

while the objects are sometimes non-existent. Talk of fulfillment therefore characterizes the phenomenological essence of the recognitive relation more satisfactorily. It is a primitive phenomenological fact that acts of signification* and acts of intuition can enter into this peculiar relation. Where they do so, where some act of meaning-intention fulfills itself in an intuition, we also say: "The object of intuition is known through its concept" or "The correct name has been applied to the object appearing before us."

We can readily do justice to the obvious phenomenological difference between the static and the dynamic fulfillment or recognition. In the dynamic relationship the members of the relation, and the act of recognition which relates them, are disjoined in time: they unfold themselves in a temporal pattern. In the static relationship, which represents the lasting outcome of this temporal transaction, they occur in temporal and material *(sachlicher)* coincidence. *There* we have a first stage of mere thought (of pure conception or mere signification), a meaning-intention wholly unsatisfied, to which a second stage of more or less adequate fulfillment is added, where thoughts repose as if satisfied in the sight of their object, which presents itself, *in virtue of* this consciousness of unity, as what is thought of in this thought, what it refers to, as the more or less perfectly attained goal of thinking. In the static relationship, on the other hand, we have this consciousness of unity alone, perhaps with no noticeably marked-off, precedent stage of unfulfilled intention. The fulfillment of the intention is not here an event of self-fulfillment, but a tranquil state of being-fulfilled, not a coming into coincidence, but a being coincident.

From an objective point of view we may here also speak of a *unity of identity.* If we compare both components of a unity of fulfillment—whether treating them in dynamic transition into one another, or holding them apart

---

*I use this expression without specially introducing it as a term, since it is the mere translation of "meaning." I shall accordingly often speak of *significative* or *signitive acts,* instead of acts of meaning-intention, of meaning, etc. "Meaning-acts" can scarcely be talked of, since *expressions* are used as the normal subjects of meaning. "Signitive" also offers us a suitable terminological opposite to "intuitive." A synonym for "signitive" is "symbolic," to the extent that the modern abuse of a word "symbol" obtains—an abuse already denounced by Kant—which equates a symbol with a "sign," quite against its original and still indispensable sense.

analytically in their static unity, only to see them at once flowing back into one another—we assert their *objective identity*. For we said, and said with self-evidence, that the object of intuition is the *same* as the object of the thought which fulfills itself in it, and, where the fit is exact, that the object is seen as being exactly the same as it is thought of or (what always says the same in this context) meant. Identity, it is plain, is not first dragged in through comparative, cogitatively mediated reflection: it is there from the start as experience, as unexpressed, unconceptualized experience. In other words, the thing which, from the point of view of our acts is phenomenologically described as fulfillment, will also, from the point of view of the two objects involved in it, the intuited object, on the one hand, and the thought object, on the other, be expressively styled "experience of identity," "consciousness of identity," or "act of identification." A more or less complete *identity* is the *objective datum which corresponds to the act of fulfillment,* which "appears in it." This means that, not only signification and intuition, but also their mutual adequation, their union of fulfillment, can be called an act, since it has its own peculiar intentional correlate, an objective something to which it is "directed." Another side of the same situation is again, we saw above, expressed in talk about *recognizing* or *knowing.* The fact that our meaning-intention is united with intuition in a fulfilling manner gives to the *object* which appears in such intuition, when it primarily concerns us, the character of a thing known. If we try to say more exactly "as what" we recognize something, our objective reflection points, not to our *act* of meaning *(Bedeutens),* but to the meaning *(Bedeutung),* the self-identical "concept" itself; talk of recognition therefore expresses our view of the same unified state from the standpoint of the object of intuition (or of the fulfilling act), in its relations to the meaning-concept of the signitive act. Conversely we say, though perhaps in more special contexts, that our thought "grasps" *(begreife)* the matter, that it is the latter's concept *(Begriff)* or "grasp." After our exposition it is obvious that recognition, like

fulfillment—the former is in fact only another name for the latter—can be called an act of identification.

Addendum. I cannot here suppress a difficulty connected with the otherwise illuminating notion of the unity of identity or recognition, as an *act* of identification or recognition. This is particularly the case, since this difficulty will reveal itself as a serious one as our clarifications proceed and progress, and will inspire fruitful discussions. Closer analysis makes it plain that, in the cases detailed above, where a name is actually applied to an object of intuition, we refer to the intuited and named *object,* but not to the *identity* of this object, as something at once intuited and named. Shall we say that an emphasis of attention decides the matter? Or ought we not rather to grant that there is not here a fully constituted act of identification: the nucleus of this act, the connective union of significant intention and corresponding intuition is really present, but it "represents" no objectifying interpretation *(Auffassung).* On the experienced unity of coincidence *no act of relational identification* is founded, no intentional consciousness of identity, in which identity, as a unity referred to, first gains objective status. In our reflection on the unity of fulfillment, in analyzing and opposing its mutually connected acts, we naturally, and indeed necessarily, also framed that relational interpretation which the form of its union, with a priori necessity, permits. Our second section will deal with this question in its widest form, which concerns the categorial characters of acts (see Chapter VI, §48, and the whole of Chapter VII). Meanwhile we shall continue to treat the sort of unity in question as a full act, or we shall at least not differentiate it expressly from a full act. This will not affect the essential point in our treatment, in so far as the passage from a consciousness of unity to a relational identification always remains open, has a possibility guaranteed a priori, so that we are entitled to say that an identifying coincidence has been *experienced,* even if there is no *conscious intention* directed to identity, and no *relational* identification.

§10. The wider class of experiences of fulfillment. Intuitions as intentions which require fulfillment

We may now further characterize the consciousness of fulfillment by seeing in it an experiential form which plays a part in many other fields of mental life. We have only to think of the opposition between wishful intention and wish-fulfillment, between voluntary intention and execution, of the fulfillment of hopes and fears, the resolution of doubts, the confirmation of surmises, etc., to be clear that essentially the same opposition is to be found in very different classes of intentional experiences: the opposition between significant intention and fulfillment of meaning is merely a special case of it. We have dealt with this point previously, and delimited a class of intentional experience under the more pregnant name of "intentions": their peculiarity lies in being able to provide the basis for relations of fulfillment. In this class are ranged all the acts which are in a narrower or wider sense "logical," including the *intuitive,* whose role it is to fulfill other intuitions in knowledge.

When, e.g., a familiar melody begins, it stirs up definite intentions which find their fulfillment in the melody's gradual unfolding. The same is the case even when the melody is unfamiliar. The regularities governing melody as such, determine intentions, which may be lacking in complete objective definiteness, but which nonetheless find or can find their fulfillments. As concrete experiences, these intentions are of course fully definite: the "indefiniteness" of what they intend is plainly a descriptive peculiarity pertaining to their character. We may say, in fact, with correct paradox (as we did before in a similar case) that "indefiniteness" (i.e., the peculiarity of demanding an incompletely determined completion, which lies in a "sphere" circumscribed by a law) is a definite feature of such an intention. Such an intention has not merely a range of possible fulfillment, but imports a common fulfillment-character into each actual fulfillment from this range. The fulfillment of acts which have definite or indefinite intentions is phenomenologi-

cally different, and the same holds of fulfillments of intentions whose indefiniteness points in this or that direction of possible fulfillment.

In our previous example there is also a relation between *expectation* and *fulfillment of expectation.* It would, however, be quite wrong to think, conversely, that every relation of an intention to its fulfillment was a relationship involving expectation. *Intention is not expectancy,* it is not of its essence to be directed to future appearances. If I see an incomplete pattern, e.g., in this carpet partially covered over by furniture, the piece I see seems clothed with intentions pointing to further completions—we feel as if the lines and colored shapes go on "in the sense" of what we see—but we expect nothing. It would be possible for us to expect something, if movement promised us further views. But possible expectations, or occasions for possible expectations, are not themselves expectations.

The external perceptions of the senses offer us an indefinite number of relevant examples. The features which enter into perception always point to completing features, which themselves might appear in other possible percepts, and that definitely or more or less indefinitely, according to the degree of our "empirical acquaintance" with the object. Every percept, and every perceptual context, reveals itself, on closer analysis, as made up of components which are to be understood as ranged under two standpoints of intention and (actual or possible) fulfillment. The same applies to the parallel acts of imagining and picture-thought in general. In the normal case intentions lack the character of expectancy, they lack it in all cases of tranquil perceiving or picturing, and they acquire it only when perception is in flux, when it is spread out into a continuous series of percepts, all belonging to the perceptual manifold of one and the same object. Objectively put: the object then shows itself from a variety of sides. What was pictorially suggested from one side, becomes confirmed in full perception from another; what was merely adumbrated or given indirectly and subsidiarily as background, from one side, at least receives a portrait-sketch from another, it appears perspectively foreshortened and projected, only to appear "just as it is" from another side. All perceiving and imagining is, on our view, a web of partial intentions, fused together in the unity of a single total intention. The correlate of this last intention is the thing, while the correlate of its partial intentions are *the thing's parts and aspects.* Only in this way can we understand how consciousness reaches out beyond what it actually experiences. It can so to say mean beyond itself, and its meaning can be fulfilled.

§11. *Frustration and conflict. The synthesis of distinction*

In the wider sphere of the acts to which distinctions of intention and fulfillment apply, *frustration* may be set beside fulfillment, as its incompatible contrary. The negative expression that we normally use in this case, e.g., even the term "non-fulfillment," has no merely privative meaning: it points to a new descriptive fact, a form of synthesis as peculiar as fulfillment. This is so even in the narrower case of significant intentions as they stand to intuitive intentions. The synthesis of recognition, of "knowing," is the consciousness of a certain agreement. The possibility correlated with agreement is, however, "disagreement" or "conflict": intuition may not accord with a significant intention, but may "quarrel" with it. Conflict "separates," but the experience of conflict puts things into relation and unity: it is a form of *synthesis.* If the previously studied synthesis was one of *identification,* this new synthesis is one of *distinction* (unfortunately we possess no other positive name). This "distinction" must not be confused with the other "distinction" which stands opposed to a positive likening. The oppositions between "identification and distinction" and between "likening and distinction" are not the same, though it is clear that a close phenomenological affinity explains our use of the same word. In the "distinction" which is here in question, the *object* of the frustrating act appears *not the same as, distinct from*

the object of the intending act. These distinctions point to wider classes of cases than we have hitherto preferred to deal with. Not only significative, but even intuitive intentions are fulfilled in identifications and frustrated in conflicts. We shall have to explore the whole question of the natural circumscription of the acts to which the terms "same" and "other" (we can as well say "is" and "is not") have application.

The two syntheses are not, however, completely parallel. Each conflict presupposes something which directs its intention to the object of the conflicting act; only a synthesis of fulfillment can give it this direction. Conflict, we may say, presupposes a certain basis of agreement. If I think A to be *red,* when it shows itself to be "in fact" green, an intention to red quarrels with an intention to green in this showing forth, i.e., in this application to intuition. Undeniably, however, this can only be the case because A has been identified in the two acts of signification and intuition. Were this not so, the intention would not relate to the intuition. The total intention points to an A which is red, and intuition reveals an A which is green. It is in the coincidence of meaning and intuition in their direction to an identical A that the moments intended in union with A in the two cases come into conflict. The presumed red (i.e., red of A) fails to agree with the intuited green. It is through identity that such non-coincident aspects *correspond* with each other: instead of being "combined" by fulfillment, they are "sundered" by conflict. An intention is referred to an appropriate aspect in intuition from which it is also turned away.

What we have here said with special regard to significant intentions and the frustrations they encounter applies also to our whole previously sketched class of objectifying intentions. We may generally say: *An intention can only be frustrated in conflict in so far as it forms part of a wider intention whose completing part is fulfilled.* We can therefore not talk of conflict in the case of simple, i.e., isolated, acts.

III.

Phenomenology as Transcendental Philosophy

5. The Basic Approach of Phenomenology

The Natural Attitude and Its Exclusion*

§27. The world of the natural attitude: I and my surrounding world

We begin our considerations as human beings who are living naturally, objectivating, judging, feeling, willing *"in the natural attitude."* What that signifies we shall make clear in simple meditations which can best be carried out in the first person singular.

I am conscious of a world endlessly spread out in space, endlessly becoming and having endlessly become in time. I am conscious of it: that signifies, above all, that intuitively I find it immediately, that I experience it. By my seeing, touching, hearing, and so forth, and in the different modes of sensuous perception, corporeal physical things with some spatial distribution or other are *simply there for me, "on hand"* in the literal or the figurative sense, whether or not I am particularly heedful of them and busied with them in my considering, thinking, feeling, or willing. Animate beings too—human beings, let us say—are immediately there for me: I look up; I see them; I hear their approach; I grasp their hands; talking with them I understand immediately what they objectivate and think, what feelings stir

within them, what they wish or will. They are also present as actualities in my field of intuition even when I do not heed them. But it is not necessary that they, and likewise that other objects, be found directly in my *field of perception*. Along with the ones now perceived, other actual objects are there for me as determinate, as more or less well known, without being themselves perceived or, indeed, present in any other mode of intuition. I can let my attention wander away from the writing table which was just now seen and noticed, out through the unseen parts of the room which are behind my back, to the verandah, into the garden, to the children in the arbor, etc., to all the Objects I directly "know of" as being there and here in the surroundings of which there is also consciousness—a "knowing of them" which involves no conceptual thinking and which changes into a clear intuiting only with the advertence of attention, and even then only partially and for the most part very imperfectly.

But not even with the domain of this intuitionally clear or obscure, distinct or indistinct, *co-present*—which makes up a constant halo around the field of actual perception—is the world exhausted which is "on hand" for me in the manner peculiar to consciousness at every waking moment. On the contrary, in the fixed

Ideas I, pp. 51–62 (Sections 27–32).

order of its being, it reaches into the unlimited. What is now perceived and what is more or less clearly co-present and determinate (or at least somewhat determinate), are penetrated and surrounded by an *obscurely intended to horizon of indeterminate actuality.* I can send rays of the illuminative regard of attention into this horizon with varying results. Determining presentations, obscure at first and then becoming alive, haul something out for me; a chain of such quasi-memories is linked together; the sphere of determinateness becomes wider and wider, perhaps so wide that connection is made with the field of actual perception as my *central* surroundings. But generally the result is different: an empty mist of obscure indeterminateness is populated with intuited possibilities or likelihoods; and only the "form" of the world, precisely as "the world," is predelineated. Moreover, my indeterminate surroundings are infinite, the misty and never fully determinable horizon is necessarily there.

What is the case with the world as existing in the order of the spatial present, which I have just been tracing, is also the case with respect to its *order in the sequence of time.* This world, on hand for me now and manifestly in every waking Now, has its two-sidedly infinite temporal horizon, its known and unknown, immediately living and lifeless past and future. In the free activity of experiencing which makes what is present intuited, I can trace these interrelations of the actuality immediately surrounding me.

I can change my standpoint in space and time, turn my regard in this or that direction, forwards or backwards in time; I can always obtain new perceptions and presentations, more or less clear and more or less rich in content, or else more or less clear images in which I illustrate to myself intuitively what is possible or likely within the fixed forms of a spatial and temporal world.

In my waking consciousness I find myself in this manner at all times, and without ever being able to alter the fact, in relation to the world which remains one and the same, though changing with respect to the composition of its contents. It is continually "on hand" for me

and I myself am a member of it. Moreover, this world is there for me not only as a world of mere things, but also with the same immediacy as a *world of objects with values, a world of goods, a practical world.* I simply find the physical things in front of me furnished not only with merely material determinations but also with value-characteristics, as beautiful and ugly, pleasant and unpleasant, agreeable and disagreeable, and the like. Immediately, physical things stand there as Objects of use, the "table" with its "books," the "drinking glass," the "vase," the "piano," etc. These value-characteristics and practical characteristics also belong *constitutively to the Objects "on hand" as Objects,* regardless of whether or not I turn to such characteristics and the Objects. Naturally this applies not only in the case of the "mere physical things," but also in the case of humans and brute animals belonging to my surroundings. They are my "friends" or "enemies," my "servants" or "superiors," "strangers" or "relatives," etc.

§28. The cogito. My natural surrounding world and the ideal surrounding worlds

The complexes of my manifoldly changing *spontaneities* of consciousness then relate to this world, *the world in which I find myself and which is, at the same time, my surrounding world*—complexes of investigative inspecting, of explicating and conceptualizing in descriptions, of comparing and distinguishing, of collecting and counting, of presupposing and inferring: in short, of theorizing consciousness in its different forms and at its different levels. Likewise the multiform acts and states of emotion and of willing: liking and disliking, being glad and being sorry, desiring and shunning, hoping and fearing, deciding and acting. All of them—including the simple Ego-acts in which I, in spontaneous advertence and seizing, am conscious of the world as *immediately* present—are embraced by the one Cartesian expression, *cogito.* Living along naturally, I live continually in this *fundamental form of* "active" *[aktuellen] living* whether, while so living, I state the cogito, whether I am directed "reflectively" to the Ego and the cogitare. If I am directed to them, a new cogito is alive, one that, for its part, is not reflected on and thus is not objective for me.

I always find myself as someone who is perceiving, objectivating in memory or in phantasy, thinking, feeling, desiring, etc.; and I find myself actively related in these activities *for the most part* to the actuality continually surrounding me. For I am not always so related; not every cogito in which I live has as its cogitatum physical things, human beings, objects or affair-complexes of some kind or other that belong to my surrounding world. I busy myself, let us say, with pure numbers and their laws: Nothing like that is present in the surrounding world, this world of "real actuality." The world of numbers is likewise there for me precisely as the Object-field of arithmetical busiedness; during such busiedness single numbers of numerical formations will be at the focus of my regard, surrounded by a partly determinate, partly indeterminate arithmetical horizon; but obviously this factual being-there-for-me, like the factually existent itself, is of a different sort. *The arithmetical world is there for me only if, and as long as, I am in the arithmetical attitude.* The *natural* world, however, the world in the usual sense of the word is, and has been, *there for me continuously* as long as I go on living naturally. As long as this is the case, I am *"in the natural attitude,"* indeed both signify precisely the same thing. That need not be altered in any respect whatever if, at the same time, I appropriate to myself the arithmetical world and other similar "worlds" by effecting the suitable attitudes. In that case the natural world *remains "on hand":* afterwards, as well as before, I am in the natural attitude, *undisturbed* in it *by the new attitudes.* If my cogito is moving *only* in the worlds pertaining to these new attitudes, the natural world remains outside consideration; it is a background for my act-consciousness, but it is *not a horizon within which an arithmetical world finds a place.* The two worlds simultaneously present are *not connected,* disregarding their Ego-relation by virtue of which I can

freely direct my regard and my acts into the one or the other.

§29. The "other" Ego-subjects and the intersubjective natural surrounding world

All that which holds for me myself holds, as I know, for all other human beings whom I find present in my surrounding world. Experiencing them as human beings, I understand and accept each of them as an Ego-subject just as I myself am one, and as related to his natural surrounding world. But I do this in such a way that I take their surrounding world and mine Objectively as one and the same world of which we all are conscious, only in different modes. Each has his place from which he sees the physical things present; and, accordingly, each has different physical-thing appearances. Also, for each the fields of actual perception, actual memory, etc., are different, leaving aside the fact that intersubjectively common objects of consciousness in those fields are intended to as having different modes, different manners of apprehension, different degrees of clarity, and so forth. For all that, we come to an understanding with our fellow human beings and in common with them posit an Objective spatio-temporal actuality as *our factually existent surrounding world to which we ourselves nonetheless belong.*

§30. The general positing which characterizes the natural attitude

What we presented as a characterization of the givenness belonging to the natural attitude, and therefore as a characterization of that attitude itself, was a piece of pure description *prior to any "theory."* In these investigations, we keep theories—here the word designates preconceived opinions of every sort —strictly at a distance. Only as facts of our surrounding world, not as actual or supposed unities of validity, do theories belong in our sphere. But we do not set for ourselves now the task of continuing the pure description and raising it to the status of a systematically comprehensive characterization, exhausting the breadths and depths of what can be found as data accepted in the natural attitude (to say nothing of the attitudes which can be harmoniously combined with it). Such a task can and must be fixed—as a scientific task; and it is an extraordinarily important one, even though barely seen up to now. It is not our task here. For us, who are striving toward the entrancegate of phenomenology, everything needed along that line has already been done; we need only a few quite universal characteristics of the natural attitude which have already come to the fore with a sufficiently *full clarity* in our descriptions. Just this full clarity was of particular consequence to us.

Once more, in the following propositions we single out something most important: As what confronts me, I continually find the one spatiotemporal actuality to which I belong like all other human beings who are to be found in it and who are related to it as I am. I find the "actuality," the word already says it, as a *factually existent actuality and also accept it as it presents itself to me as factually existing.* No doubt about or rejection of data belonging to the natural world alters in any respect the *general positing which characterizes the natural attitude.* "The" world is always there as an actuality; here and there it is at most "otherwise" than I supposed; this or that is, so to speak, to be struck *out of it* and given such titles as "illusion" and "hallucination," and the like; <it is to be struck out of "the" world> which—according to the general positing—is always factually existent. To cognize "the" world more comprehensively, more reliably, more perfectly in every respect than naive experiential cognizance can, to solve all the problems of scientific cognition which offer themselves within the realm of the world, that is the aim of the *sciences belonging to the natural attitude.*

§31. Radical alteration of the natural positing. "Excluding," "parenthesizing"

Instead of remaining in this attitude, we propose to alter it radically. What we now must

do is to convince ourselves of the essential possibility of the alteration in question.

The general positing, by virtue of which there is not just any continual apprehensional consciousness of the real surrounding world, but a consciousness of it as a *factually existing* "actuality," naturally does *not consist of a particular act,* perchance an articulated judgment *about* existence. It is, after all, something that lasts continuously throughout the whole duration of the attitude, i.e., throughout natural waking life. That which at any time is perceived, is clearly or obscurely presentiated —in short, everything which is, before any thinking, an object of experiential consciousness issuing from the natural world—bears, in its total unity and with respect to all articulated saliencies in it, the characteristic "there," "on hand"; and it is essentially possible to base on this characteristic an explicit (predicative) judgment of existence agreeing with it. If we state such a judgment, we nevertheless know that in it we have only made thematic and conceived as a predicate what already was somehow inherent, as unthematic, unthought, unpredicated, in the original experiencing or, correlatively, in the experienced, as the characteristic of something "on hand."

We can now proceed with the potential and inexplicit positing precisely as we can with the explicit judgment-positing. One procedure, possible at any time, is the *attempt to doubt universally* which *Descartes* carried out for an entirely different purpose with a view toward bringing out a sphere of absolutely indubitable being. We start from here, but at the same time emphasize that the attempt to doubt universally shall serve us only as a *methodic expedient* for picking out certain points which, as included in its essence, can be brought to light and made evident by means of it.

The attempt to doubt universally belongs to the realm of our *perfect freedom:* we can attempt to doubt anything whatever, no matter how firmly convinced of it, even assured of it in an adequate evidence, we may be.

Let us reflect on what lies in the essence of such an act. Someone who attempts to doubt some "being" or other, or predicatively explicated, a "that exists," a "that is how it is," or the like. The sort of being does not matter. For example, someone who doubts whether an object, the being of which he does not doubt, is qualified thus and so, doubts precisely the *being-qualified-thus-and-so*. Obviously this is carried over from doubting to *attempting* to doubt. Furthermore, it is clear that we cannot doubt a being and, in the same consciousness (with the form of unity belonging to the simultaneous) posit the substrate of this being, thus being conscious of the substrate as having the characteristic, "on hand." Equivalently expressed: The same material of being cannot be simultaneously doubted and held to be certain. In like manner, it is clear that the *attempt* to doubt anything intended to as something *on hand* necessarily *effects a certain annulment of positing* and precisely this interests us. The annulment in question is not a transmutation of positing into counter positing, of position into negation; it is also not a transmutation into uncertain presumption, deeming possible, undecidedness, into a doubt (in any sense whatever of the word): nor indeed is anything like that within the sphere of our free choice. *Rather it is something wholly peculiar. We do not give up the positing we effected, we do not in any respect alter our conviction* which remains in itself as it is as long as we do not introduce new judgment motives: precisely this is what we do not do. Nevertheless the positing undergoes a modification: while it in itself remains what it is, *we, so to speak, "put it out of action," we "exclude it," we "parenthesize it."* It is still there, like the parenthesized in the parentheses, like the excluded outside the context of inclusion *[wie das Ausgeschaltete außerhalb des Zusammenhanges der Schaltung].* We can also say: The positing is a mental process, *but we make "no use" of it,* and this is not understood, naturally, as implying that we are deprived of it (as it would if we said of someone who was not conscious, that he made no use of a positing); rather, in the case of this expression and all parallel expressions it is a matter of indicative designations of a definite, *specifically peculiar mode of consciousness* which is added to the original positing simplic-

iter (whether this is or not an actional *[aktuelle]* and even a predicative *positing* of existence) and, likewise in a specifically peculiar manner, changes its value. *This changing of value is a matter in which we are perfectly free, and it stands over against all cogitative position-takings* coordinate with the positing and incompatible with the positing in the unity of the "simultaneous," as well as over against all position-takings in the proper sense of the term.

In the attempt to doubt which accompanies a positing which, as we presuppose, is certain and continued, the "excluding" is brought about in and with a modification of the counter positing, namely the *"supposition" of non-being* which is, therefore, part of the substratum of the attempt to doubt. In Descartes this part is so predominant that one can say that his attempt to doubt universally is properly an attempt to negate universally. Here we disregard this part; we are not interested in every analytically distinguishable component of the attempt to doubt, and consequently we are not interested in the exact and fully sufficient analysis of it. *We single out only the phenomenon of "parenthesizing" or "excluding"* which, while obviously not restricted to the phenomenon of attempting to doubt, is particularly easy to analyze out and which can, on the contrary, make its appearance *also in other combinations* and, equally well, *alone.* With regard to *any* positing we can quite freely exercise this peculiar ἐποχή, *a certain refraining from judgment which is compatible with the unshaken conviction of truth, even with the unshakable conviction of evident truth.* The positing is "put out of action," parenthesized, converted into the modification, "parenthesized positing"; the judgment simpliciter is converted into the *"parenthesized judgment."*

Naturally one must not identify this consciousness with the consciousness called "mere phantasying," let us say, that nymphs are performing a round dance. In the latter consciousness, after all, *no excluding* of a living conviction, which remains alive, takes place. The consciousness of which we are speaking is even further from being a matter of just thinking of something in the sense *of "assuming"* or *pre-*

supposing, which, in ordinary equivocal language, can also be expressed by "It seems to me (I make the assumption) that such and such is the case."

It should also be said that nothing prevents *speaking correlatively of parenthesizing* with respect to a *positable objectivity* belonging to no matter what region and category. When speaking thus, we mean that *every positing related to this objectivity is to be excluded* and converted into its parenthetical modification. Furthermore, when the metaphor of parenthesizing is closely examined it is seen to be, from the very beginning, more suitable to the object-sphere; just as the locution of "putting out of action" is better suited to the act- or consciousness-sphere.

§32. The phenomenological ἐποχή

We could now let the universal ἐποχή, in our sharply determinate and novel sense of the term, take the place of the Cartesian attempt to doubt universally. But with good reason we *limit* the universality of that. Since we are completely free to modify every positing and every judging *[Urteil]* and to parenthesize every objectivity which can be judged about if it were as comprehensive as possible, then no province would be left for unmodified judgments, to say nothing of a province for science. But our purpose is to discover a new scientific domain, one that is to be gained *by the method of parenthesizing* which, therefore, must be a definitely restricted one.

The restriction can be designated in a word. *We put out of action the general positing which belongs to the essence of the natural attitude;* we parenthesize everything which that positing encompasses with respect to being: *thus the whole natural world* which is continually "there for us," "on hand," and which will always remain there according to consciousness as an "actuality" even if we choose to parenthesize it.

If I do that, as I can with complete freedom, then I am *not negating* this "world" as though I were a sophist; I am *not doubting its factual being* as though I were a skeptic; rath-

er I am exercising the "phenomenological" ἐποχή which also *completely shuts me off from any judgment about spatiotemporal factual being.*

Thus I exclude all sciences relating to this natural world no matter how firmly they stand there for me, no matter how much I admire them, no matter how little I think of making even the least objection to them; I make *absolutely no use of the things posited in them [von ihren Geltungen].* Nor do I make my own a single one of the propositions belonging to <those sciences>, *even though it be perfectly evident; none is accepted by me; none gives me a foundation*—let this be well noted: as long as it is understood as it is presented in one of those sciences as a truth *about actualities* of this world. *I must not accept such a proposition until after I have put parenthesis around it.* That signifies that I may accept such a proposition only in the modified consciousness, the consciousness of judgment-excluding, and therefore *not as it is in science, a proposition which claims validity and the validity of which I accept and use.*

The ἐποχή in question here is not to be mistaken for the one which positivism requires, but which indeed, as we had to persuade ourselves, is itself violated by such positivism. It is not now a matter of excluding all prejudices that cloud the pure objectivity of research, not a matter of constituting a science "free of theories," "free of metaphysics," by groundings all of which go back to the immediate findings, nor a matter of means for attaining such ends, about the value of which there is, indeed, no question. What *we* demand lies in another direction. The whole prediscovered world posited in the natural attitude, actually found in experience and taken with perfect "freedom from theories" as it is actually experienced, as it clearly shows itself in the concatenations of experience, is now without validity for us; without being tested and also without being contested, it shall be parenthesized. In like manner all theories and sciences which relate to this world, no matter how well they may be grounded positivistically or otherwise, shall meet the same fate.

Consciousness as
Transcendental*

§33. Preliminary indication of "pure"
or "transcendental" consciousness as
the phenomenological residuum

We have learned to understand the sense of the phenomenological ἐποχή but not by any means its possible effect. Above all, it is not clear to what extent the previous delimitation of the total sphere of the ἐποχή actually involves a restriction of its universality. *What can remain, if the whole world, including ourselves with all our cogitare, is excluded?*

Since the reader already knows that the interest governing these meditations concerns a new eidetics, he will at first expect that, more particularly, the world as matter of fact is excluded but not the *world as Eidos,* not any other sphere of essences. Indeed, the exclusion of the world actually does not signify the exclusion of the world of, e.g., the number series or arithmetic as relating to it.

Nevertheless we shall not take this path; it does not lead toward our goal, which we can also characterize as *the acquisition of a new region of being never before delimited in its own peculiarity*—a region which, like any other genuine region, is a region of *individual* being. What that means we shall learn, more particularly, from the findings that follow.

We shall proceed, first of all, with a direct demonstrable showing and, since the being that we want to demonstrably show is nothing else than what we shall designate, for essential reasons, as "pure mental processes," "pure consciousness" with its pure "correlates of consciousness" and, on the other hand, its "pure Ego" <we shall> start with *the* Ego, *the* consciousness, and *the* mental processes which are given to us in the natural attitude.

I, the actual human being, am a real Object like others in the natural world. I effect cogitationes, acts of consciousness in both the broader and narrower sense and these acts, as belonging to this human subject, are occurrences

within the same natural actuality. And likewise all my other mental processes, out of the changing stream of which the specific Ego-acts flash in so specifically peculiar a manner, pass over into one another, become connected in syntheses, become incessantly modified. In a *broadest sense,* the expression *consciousness* comprehends (but then indeed less suitably) *all* mental processes. "In the natural attitude," as we are even in our scientific thinking, by virtue of extremely firm habits which have never been contravened, we take all these findings of psychological reflection as real worldly occurrences, just as mental processes in the lives of animate beings. So natural is it for us to see them only as such that now, when already acquainted with the possibility of an altered attitude and searching for the new Object-province, we do not even note that it is from these very spheres of mental processes that the new province arises by virtue of the new attitude. As a consequence, it follows that instead of keeping our regard turned toward those spheres, we turned it away from them and sought the new Objects in the ontological realms of arithmetic, geometry, and the like—where, after all, nothing genuinely new could be attained.

We shall therefore keep our regard fixed upon the sphere of consciousness and study what we find immanently within *it.* First of all, without as yet effecting the phenomenological judgment-exclusions, we shall subject it to a systematic, though by no means exhaustive, *eidetic* analysis. What we absolutely need is a certain universal insight into the essence of *any consciousness whatever* and also, quite particularly, of consciousness in so far as it is, in itself, by its essence consciousness of "natural" actuality. In these studies we shall go as far as is necessary to effect the insight at which we are aiming, namely the insight *that consciousness has, in itself, a being of its own which in its own absolute essence, is not touched by the phenomenological exclusion.* It therefore remains as the *"phenomenological residuum,"* as a region of being which is of essential necessity quite unique and which can

---

Ideas I, pp. 63–75, 86–104 (Sections 33–36 and 41–46).

indeed become the field of a science of a novel kind: phenomenology.

The "phenomenological" ἐποχή will deserve its name only by means of this insight; the fully conscious effecting of that ἐποχή will prove itself to be the operation necessary to *make "pure" consciousness, and subsequently the whole phenomenological region, accessible to us.* Precisely that makes it comprehensible why this region and the novel science correlated with it remained necessarily unknown: In the natural attitude nothing else but the natural world is seen. As long as the possibility of the phenomenological attitude had not been recognized, and the method for bringing about an originary seizing upon the objectivities that arise with that attitude had not been developed, the phenomenological world had to remain unknown, indeed, hardly even suspected.

Concerning our terminology we may add the following. Important motives, grounded in the epistemological problematic, justify our designating "pure" consciousness, about which we shall have so much to say, *as transcendental consciousness* and the operation by which it is reached the *transcendental ἐποχή*. As a method this operation will be divided into different steps of "excluding," "parenthesizing"; and thus our method will assume the characteristic of a step-by-step reduction. For this reason we shall, on most occasions, speak of *phenomenological reductions* (but also, with reference to their collective unity, we shall speak of *the* phenomenological reduction) and, accordingly, from an epistemological point of view, we shall refer to transcendental reductions. It should be added that these terms and *all* our others must be understood exclusively in the senses that *our* expositions prescribe for them and not in any others which history or the terminological habits of the reader may suggest.

§34. *The essence of consciousness as theme*

We begin with a series of observations which we shall make without troubling ourselves with any phenomenological ἐποχή. We are directed to the "external world" in a natural manner and, without relinquishing the natural attitude, we effect a psychological reflection on our Ego and its mental living. Quite as we should if we had heard nothing of the new sort of attitude, we engross ourselves in the *essence of the "consciousness of something,"* in which, for example, we are conscious of the factual existence of material things, animate organisms, human beings, the factual existence of technical and literary works, and so forth. We follow our universal principle that every individual event has its essence, which can be seized upon in eidetic purity and, in this purity, must belong to a field of possible eidetic research. Accordingly, the general natural fact, "I am," "I think," "I have a world over against me," and the like, has its essential content with which we shall now busy ourselves exclusively. We therefore effect, as examples, any single mental processes whatever of consciousness and take them as they themselves are given to us in the natural attitude, as real human facts; or else we presentiate such mental processes to ourselves in memory or in freely inventive phantasy. On the basis of such examples which, let us presuppose, are perfectly clear, we seize upon and fix, in an adequate ideation, the pure essences that interest us. In the process, the single facts, the facticity of the natural world taken universally, disappear from our theoretical regard—as they do wherever we carry out a purely eidetic research.

Let us limit our theme still more narrowly. Its title runs: consciousness or, more distinctly, *any mental processes whatever of consciousness* in an extraordinarily broad sense, the exact limitation of which fortunately does not matter. Such a limitation does not lie at the beginning of analyses of the sort which we are carrying on here, but is a late result of great labors. As the starting point, we take consciousness in a pregnant sense and one which offers itself first, which we can designate most simply by the Cartesian term *cogito,* by the phrase "I think." As is well known, cogito was understood so broadly by Descartes that it comprised every "I perceive, I remember, I phantasy, I judge, I feel, I desire, I will," and thus all egoical mental processes which are at all similar to them, with their countless flowing particular formations. The Ego itself, to which they are all related or which, in very different manners, lives "in" them actively, passively or spontaneously, which "comports" itself receptively and otherwise in them, shall be at first left out of consideration; more particularly, the Ego in every sense shall be left out of consideration. Later on the Ego shall be dealt with thoroughly. For now, enough is left that gives support to analysis and the apprehension of essences. In that connection, we shall find ourselves immediately referred to those comprehensive concatenations of mental processes that compel a broadening of the concept, mental process of consciousness, beyond this sphere made up of cogitationes in the specific <Cartesian> sense.

We consider mental processes of consciousness *in the entire fullness of the concreteness* within which they present themselves in their concrete context—*the stream of mental processes*—and which, by virtue of their own essence, they combine to make up. It then becomes evident that every mental process belonging to the stream which can be reached by our reflective regard has an *essence of its own* which can be seized upon intuitively, a "content" which allows of being considered *by itself in its ownness.* Our concern is to seize upon and to universally characterize this own content of the cogitation in its *pure* ownness by excluding everything which does not lie in the cogitatio with respect to what the cogitatio is in itself. It is equally our concern to characterize the *unity of consciousness* required, and therefore necessarily required, *purely by what belongs to the cogitationes as their own* such that they could not exist without that unity.

§35. The cogito as "act." Non-actionality modification

Let us begin with examples. Lying in front of me in the semi-darkness is this sheet of paper. I am seeing it, touching it. This perceptual seeing and touching of the sheet of paper, as the full concrete mental awareness *of* the sheet of paper lying here and given precisely

with respect to these qualities, appearing to me precisely with this relative obscurity, with this imperfect determinateness in this orientation, is a cogitatio, a mental process of consciousness. The sheet of paper itself, with its Objective determinations, its extension, its Objective position relative to the spatial thing called my organism, is not a cogitatio but a cogitatum; it is not a mental process of perception but something perceived. Now something perceived can very well be itself a mental process of consciousness; but it is evident that such an affair as a material physical thing, for example, this sheet of paper given in the mental process of perception, is by essential necessity not a mental process but a being of a wholly different mode of being.

Before we investigate that further, let us multiply the examples. In perceiving proper, as an attentive perceiving, I am turned toward the object, for instance, the sheet of paper; I seize upon it as this existent here and now. The seizing-upon is a singling out and seizing; anything perceived has an experiential background. Around the sheet of paper lie books, pencils, an inkstand, etc., also "perceived" in a certain manner, perceptually there, in the "field of intuition"; but, during the advertence to the sheet of paper, they were without even a secondary advertence and seizing-upon. They were appearing and yet were not seized upon and picked out, not posited singly for themselves. Every perception of a physical thing has, in this manner, a halo of *background-intuitions* (or background-seeings, in case one already includes in intuiting the advertedness to the really seen), and that is also a *"mental process of consciousness"* or, more briefly, "consciousness," and, more particularly, *"of"* all that which in fact lies in the objective "background" seen along with it. Obviously in saying this we are not speaking of that which is to be found "Objectively" in the Objective space which may belong to the seen background; we are not speaking of all the physical things and physical occurrences which valid and progressing experience may ascertain there. We speak exclusively of the halo of consciousness which belongs to the essence of a perception effected in the mode of "advertence to the Object" and, furthermore, of what is inherent in the essence proper of this halo. In it, however, there is the fact that certain modifications of the original mental process are possible which we characterize as a free turning of "regard"—not precisely nor merely of the physical, but rather of the *"mental regard" ["geistigen Blickes"]*—from the sheet of paper regarded at first, to the objects appearing, therefore intended to "implicitly" before the turning of the regard but which become explicitly intended to (either "attentively" perceived or "incidentally" heeded") *after* the regard is turned to them.

Physical things are intended to not only in perception but also in memories and in presentiations similar to memories as well as in free phantasies. All this, sometimes in "clear intuition," sometimes without noticeable intuitedness in the manner of "obscure" objectivations; in such cases they hover before us with different "characteristics" as actual physical things, possible physical things, phantasied physical things, etc. Of these essentially different mental processes obviously everything is true that we adduced about mental processes of perception. We shall not think of confusing the *objects intended to in* these modes of consciousness (for example, the phantasied water nymphs) with the mental processes themselves of consciousness which are consciousness *of* those objects. We recognize then that, to the essence of all such mental processes—these always taken in full concreteness—there belongs that noteworthy modification which converts consciousness in the *mode of actional [aktueller] advertence* into consciousness in the *mode of non-actionality [Inaktualität]* and conversely. At the one time the mental process is, so to speak, *"explicit"* consciousness of its objective something, at the other time it is implicit, merely *potential*. The objective something can be already appearing to us as it does not only in perception, but also in memory or in phantasy; however, we are *not yet "directed" to it with the mental regard,* not even secondarily—to say nothing of our being, in a peculiar sense, "busied" with it.

In the sense pertaining to the sphere of the Cartesian examples we note something similar in no matter what other cogitationes: with respect to all mental processes of thinking, feeling, or willing, except that, as the next section will show, the "directedness to," the "advertedness to," which distinguishes actionality *[Aktualität]* does not (as in the preferred—because the simplest—examples of sensuous objectivations) coincide with that heeding of Objects of consciousness which *seizes upon and picks them out.* It is likewise obviously true of all such mental processes that the actional ones are surrounded by a "halo" of non-actional mental processes; *the stream of mental processes can never consist of just actionalities.* Precisely these, when contrasted with non-actionalities, determine with the widest universality, to be extended beyond the sphere of our examples, the *pregnant* sense of the expression *"cogito,"* "I have *consciousness* of something," "I effect an *act* of consciousness." To keep this fixed concept sharply separated, we shall reserve for it exclusively the Cartesian terms, cogito and cogitationes—unless we indicate the modification explicitly by some such adjunct as "non-actional."

We can define a *"waking"* Ego as one which, within its stream of mental processes, continuously effects consciousness in the specific form of the cogito; which naturally does not mean that it continually gives, or is able to give at all, predicative expression to these mental processes. There are, after all, brute animal Ego-subjects. According to what is said above, however, it is of the essence of a waking Ego's stream of mental processes that the continuously unbroken chain of cogitationes is continually surrounded by a medium of non-actionality which is always ready to change into the mode of actionality, just as, conversely, actionality is always ready to change into non-actionality.

§36. Intentive mental processes. Mental process taken universally

However thorough the alteration which mental processes of actional consciousness undergo in consequence of their going over into non-actionality, the modified mental processes still continue to have a significant community of essence with the original ones. Universally it belongs to the essence of every actional cogito to be consciousness *of* something. In its own manner, however, according to what was set forth previously, the *modified cogitatio is also consciousness,* and consciousness of *the same thing* as that <intended to in> the corresponding unmodified consciousness. Accordingly the universal essential property pertaining to consciousness is still preserved in the modification. All mental processes having these essential properties in common are also called *"intentive mental processes"* (acts in the broadest sense of the *Logische Untersuchungen*); in so far as they are consciousness of something, they are said to be *"intentively referred"* to this something.

As a consequence, it should be well heeded that *here we are not speaking of a relation between some* psychological occurrence—called a mental process—and another real factual existence—called an object—nor of a *psychological connection* taking place *in Objective actuality* between the one and the other. Rather we are speaking of mental processes purely with respect to their essence, or of *pure essences* and of that which is "a priori" *included* in the essences *with unconditional necessity.*

That a mental process is consciousness of something—for example: that a phantasying is phantasying of the determinate centaur, but also that a perception is perception of its "real" object, that a judgment is judgment of its predicatively formed affair-complex, etc.—this concerns, rather than the fact of the mental process in the world, specifically, in the complex of psychological facts, the pure essence which is seized upon in ideation as a pure idea. In the essence of the mental process itself lies not only *that* it is consciousness but also *whereof* it is consciousness, and in which determinate or indeterminate sense it is that. It therefore also lies implicit in the essence of non-actional consciousness as to what sort of actional cogitationes non-actional consciousness can be converted into by the modification, discussed above, which we characterize as a "turning of heeding regard to the formerly unheeded."

By *mental processes in the broadest sense* we understand everything and anything to be found in the stream of mental processes; accordingly not only the intentive processes, the actional and potential cogitationes taken in their full concreteness, but also whatever is to be found in the way of really inherent moments in this stream and its concrete parts.

One easily sees, that is, that *not every really inherent moment* in the concrete unity of an intentive mental process itself has the *fundamental characteristic, intentionality,* thus the property of being "consciousness of something." That concerns, for example, all *data of sensation* which play so great a role in perceptual intuitions of physical things. Within the mental process of perceiving this sheet of white paper, more precisely, within those components of the perceiving which relate to the quality, whiteness, belonging to the sheet of paper, we find, by a suitable turning of regard, the Datum of sensation, white. This white is something which belongs inseparably to the essence of the concrete perception, and belongs to it as a *really inherent* concrete component. As the content that is "presentive" with respect to the appearing *white* of the paper, it is the bearer of an intentionality; however, it is not itself a consciousness of something. The very same thing obtains in the case of other really inherent Data, for example, the so-called *sensuous feelings.* Later on we shall discuss this in greater detail.

§41. The really inherent composition of perception and its transcendent object

Now, all of that being presupposed, *what is included in the concrete, really inherent composition of perception itself as the cogitatio?* Obviously not the physical thing as determined by physics, that utterly transcendent thing—transcendent to the whole "world of appearance." But not *even the latter,* although it is called "merely subjective," with all the particular physical things and occurrences belonging to it, is excluded from the really inherent composition of perception; it is "transcendent" to perception. Let us consider this more closely. We have already spoken, though only in passing, of the transcendence of the physical thing. We now must acquire a deeper insight into *how the transcendent stands with respect to the consciousness which is a consciousness of it,* into how this mutual relationship, which has its paradoxes, should be understood.

Let us therefore exclude the whole of physics and the whole domain of theoretical thinking. Let us remain within the limits of simple intuition and the syntheses belonging to it, among which perception is included. It is evident then that intuition and intuited, perception and perceived physical thing are, more particularly, essentially interrelated but, as a matter of essential necessity, are *not really inherently and essentially one and combined.*

Let us start with an example. Constantly seeing this table and meanwhile walking around it, changing my position in space in whatever way, I have continually the consciousness of this one identical table as factually existing "in person" and remaining quite unchanged. The table-perception, however, is a continually changing one; it is a continuity of changing perceptions. I close my eyes. My other senses have no relation to the table. Now I have no perception of it. I open my eyes; and I have the perception again. *The* perception? Let us be more precise. Returning, it is not, under any circumstances, individually the same. Only the table is the same, intended to as the same in the synthetical consciousness which connects the new perception with the memory. The perceived physical thing can exist without being perceived, without even being potentially intended to (in the already described* mode of non-actionality); and it can exist without changing. The perception itself, however, is what it is in the continuous flux of consciousness and is itself a continuous flux: continually the perceptual Now changes into the enduring consciousness of the Just-Past and simultaneously a new Now lights up, etc. Like the perceived thing as a whole, whatever parts, sides, moments accrue to it necessarily, and always for the same reasons, transcends the perception regardless of whether the particular property

be called a primary or a secondary quality. The color of the seen physical thing is, of essential necessity, not a really inherent moment of the consciousness of color; it appears, but while it is appearing the appearance can and *must,* in the case of a legitimating experience, be continually changing. *The same* color appears "in" continuous multiplicities of color *adumbrations.* Something similar is true of every sensuous quality and also of every spatial shape. One and the same shape (given "in person" *as* the same) appears continuously but always "in a different manner," always in different adumbrations of shape. That is a necessary situation, and obviously it obtains universally. Only for the sake of simplicity have we taken as our example the case of a physical thing appearing in perception as unchanging. The application to cases involving changes of any kind is obvious.

Of essential necessity there belongs to any "all-sided," continuously, unitarily, and self-confirming experiential consciousness [Erfahrungsbewußtsein] of the same physical thing a multifarious system of continuous multiplicities of appearances and adumbrations in which all objective moments falling within perception with the characteristic of being themselves given "in person" are adumbrated by determined continuities. Each determination has *its* system of adumbrations; and each of them, like the physical thing as a whole, is there as the Same for the seizing-upon consciousness which synthetically unites memory and new perception as the Same, despite any interruption of the continuous course of actional perception.

At the same time we now see what actually and indubitably is included in the really inherent composition of those concrete intentive mental processes called perceivings of physical things. Whereas the physical thing is the intentional unity, the physical thing intended to as identical and unitary in the continuously regular flow of perceptual multiplicities which interpenetrate and change into one another, the perceptual multiplicities themselves always

---

*Cf. §35, above, especially p. 69.

have their *determinate descriptional composition essentially* coordinated with that unity. For example, each phase of the perception necessarily contains a determined content of adumbrations of color, adumbrations of shape, etc. They are included among *"the Data of sensations,"* Data of an own peculiar region with determined genera and which join together with one of these genera to make up concrete unities of mental processes sui generis *("fields" of sensation)*. Furthermore, in a manner which we shall not describe here more precisely, the Data are animated by *"construings"* within the concrete unity of the perception and in the animation exercise the *"presentive function,"* or as united with the construings which animate them, they make up what we call *"appearings of"* color, shape, and so forth. These moments, combined with further characteristics, are the really inherent components making up the perception which is a consciousness of one and the same physical thing by virtue of joining together, grounded in the *essence* of those construings, to make up a *unity of construing,* and again by virtue of the possibility, grounded in the *essence* of various unities of construing, to make up *syntheses of identification.*

It must be borne clearly in mind that the Data of sensation which exercise the function of adumbrations of color, of smoothness, of shape, etc. (the function of "presentation") are, of essential necessity, entirely different from color simpliciter, smoothness simpliciter, shape simpliciter, and, in short, from all kinds of moments belonging to *physical things. The adumbration, though called by the same name, of essential necessity is not of the same genus as the one to which the adumbrated belongs.* The adumbrating is a mental process. But a mental process is possible only as a mental process, and not as something spatial. However, the adumbrated is of essential necessity possible only as something spatial (it is spatial precisely in its essence), and not possible as a mental process. In particular it is a countersense to take the adumbration of shape (e.g., the adumbration of a triangle) for something spatial and possible in space; and whoever does so confuses the adumbrating with the adumbrated, i.e., with the appearing shape. As for how the different re-

ally inherent moments of the perception as cogitatio (in contrast to the moments of the cogitatum, which is transcendent to it) are to be separated from one another and characterized with respect to their sometimes very difficult differences, is a theme for extensive investigations.

§42. Being as consciousness and being as reality. Essentially necessary difference between the modes of intuition

Our considerations have established that the physical thing is transcendent to the perception of it and consequently to any consciousness whatever related to it; it is transcendent not merely in the sense that the physical thing cannot be found in fact as a really inherent component of consciousness; rather the whole situation is an object of eidetic insight: *With an absolutely unconditional* universality and necessity it is the case that a physical thing cannot be given in any possible perception, in any possible consciousness, as something really inherently immanent. Thus there emerges a fundamentally essential difference between *being as mental process and being as a physical thing.* Of essential necessity it belongs to the regional essence, Mental Process (specifically to the regional particularization, Cogitatio) that it can be perceived in an immanental perception; fundamentally and necessarily it belongs to the essence of a spatial physical thing that it cannot be so perceived. If, as we learn from a deeper analysis, it is of the essence of any intuition presentive of a physical thing that, along with the physical-thing datum, other data analogous to physical things can be seized upon in a corresponding turn of the regard in the manner, let us say, of detachable strata and lower levels in the constitution of the appearing physical thing—e.g., *"sight thing"* with its different particularizations—still precisely the same is true of them: They are of essential necessity transcendencies.

Before tracing this contrast between something immanent and something transcendent somewhat further, let us introduce the following remark. Disregarding perception, we find intentive mental processes of many kinds that, by virtue of their essence, exclude the really inherent immanence of their intentional objects no matter what the objects may otherwise be. That holds, for example, of any presentation: of any memory, of the empathic seizing upon someone else's consciousness, etc. Naturally we must not confuse this transcendence with the transcendence with which we are concerned here. To the physical thing as physical thing, to any reality in the genuine sense, the sense of which we have yet to clarify and fix, there belongs essentially and quite "universally"* the incapacity of being immanently perceived and accordingly of being found at all in the concatenation of mental processes. Thus the physical thing is said to be, in itself, unqualifiedly transcendent. Precisely in that the essentially necessary diversity among modes of being, the most cardinal of them all, becomes manifest: the diversity between *consciousness and reality.*

Our exposition has brought out the further fact that this contrast between something immanent and something transcendent includes *an essentially fundamental difference between the corresponding kinds of givenness.* Perception of something immanent and of something transcendent do not differ merely in that the intentional object, which is there with the characteristic of something it itself, "in person," is really inherently immanent in the perceiving in one case but not in the other: rather they are differentiated by modes of givenness the essential difference between which is carried over mutatis mutandis into all the presentational modifications of perception, into the parallel memorial intuitions and phantasy intuitions. We perceive the physical thing by virtue of its being "adumbrated" in respect of all the determinations which, in a given case, "actually" and properly "fall within the scope of" perception. *A mental process is not adumbrated.* It is neither an accident of the own peculiar sense of the physical thing nor a contingency of "our human constitution," that "our" perception can arrive at physical things themselves only

through mere adumbrations of them. Rather is it evident and drawn from the essence of spatial physical things (even in the widest sense, which includes "sight things") that, necessarily a being of that kind can be given in perception only through an adumbration; and in like manner it is evident from the essence of cogitationes, from the essence of mental processes of any kind, that they exclude anything like that. For an existent belonging to their region, in other words, anything like an "appearing," a being presented, through adumbrations makes no sense whatever. Where there is no spatial being it is senseless to speak of a seeing from different standpoints with a changing orientation in accordance with different perappearances, adumbrations. On the other hand, it is an essential necessity, to be seized upon as essential in apodictic insight, that any spatial being whatever is perceivable for an Ego (for any possible Ego) only with the kind of givenness designated. A spatial being can "appear" only in a certain "orientation," which necessarily predelineates a system of possible new orientations each of which, in turn, corresponds to a certain "mode of appearance" which we can express, say, as givenness from such and such a "side," and so forth. If we understand modes of appearance in the sense of modes of *mental processes* (the phrase can also have a corresponding ontic sense, as is evident from the description just offered), then this signifies: It is essential to certain *sorts of mental processes* which have a peculiar structure, more precisely, it belongs to certain concrete perceptions which have a peculiar structure, that what is intended to in them is meant as a spatial physical thing; to their essence belongs the ideal possibility of their changing into determinately ordered continuous multiplicities of perception which can always be continued, thus which are never completed. It is then inherent in the essential structure of those multiplicities that they bring about the unity of a *harmoniously presentive* consciousness and, more particularly, of the *one* perceptual physical thing

*Here, and throughout this essay, we use the word *"prinzipiell"* in a strict sense, referring to the *highest* and therefore the most radical, eidetic universalities or necessities.

appearing ever more perfectly, from ever new sides, with an ever greater wealth of determinations. On the other hand, the spatial thing is nothing other than an intentional unity which of essential necessity can be given only as the unity of such modes of appearance.

§43. The clarification of a fundamental error

It is therefore fundamentally erroneous to believe that perception (and, after its own fashion, any other kind of intuition of a physical thing) does not reach the physical thing itself. The latter is not given to us in itself or in its being-in-itself. There belongs to any existent the essential possibility of being simply intuited as what it is and, more particularly, of being perceived as what it is in an adequate perception, one that is presentive of that existent itself, "in person," *without any mediation by "appearances."* God, the subject possessing an absolutely perfect knowledge and therefore possessing every possible adequate perception, naturally has that adequate perception of the very physical thing itself which is denied to us finite beings.

But this view is a countersense. It implies that there is no *essential difference* between something transcendent and something immanent, that, in the postulated divine intuition, a spatial physical thing is present as a really inherent constituent, that it is therefore itself a mental process also belonging to the divine stream of consciousness and divine mental processes generally. The holders of this view are misled by thinking that the transcendence belonging to the spatial physical thing is the transcendence belonging to something *depicted* or *represented by a sign.* Frequently the picture-theory is attacked with zeal and a sign theory substituted for it. Both theories, however, are not only incorrect but countersensical. The spa-

tial physical thing which we see is, with all its transcendence, still something perceived, given "in person" in the manner peculiar to consciousness. It is not the case that, in its stead, a picture or a sign is given. A picture-consciousness or a sign-consciousness must not be substituted for perception.

Between *perception,* on the one hand, and *depictive-symbolic* or *signitive-symbolic objectivation,* on the other hand, there is an unbridgeable essential difference. In the latter kinds of objectivation we intuit something in consciousness as depicting or signitively indicating something else; having the one in our field of intuition we are directed, not to it, but to the other, what is depicted or designated, through the medium of a founded apprehending. Nothing like that is involved either in perception or in simple memory or in simple phantasy.

In immediately intuitive acts we intuit an "it itself"; on their apprehendings no mediate apprehendings are built up at a higher level; thus there is no consciousness of anything *for which* the intuited might function as a "sign" or "picture." And just on that account it is said to be immediately intuited as "it itself." In perception the "it itself" is further characterized in its peculiarity as "in person" in contrast to its modified characteristic as "floating before us," as "presentiated" in memory or in free phantasy.* One would fall into a countersense if one were to confuse these modes of objectivation of essentially different structures, and if one were, accordingly, to mix up, in the usual fashion, the correlative objects given in these modes: thus confusing simple presentation with symbolizing (whether depictive or signitive) and—even worse—simple perception with both of them. The perception of a physical thing does not presentiate something non-present, as though it were a memory or a phantasy; perception makes present, seizes upon an it-itself

---

*In my Göttingen lectures (beginning with the summer semester of 1904) I substituted an improved exposition for the inadequate one which I (being still too greatly influenced by the concepts involved in the dominant psychology) had given in the *Logische Untersuchungen* concerning the relationships between these simple and founded intuitions, and offered a detailed report of my further research—which, incidentally, has meanwhile exerted both a terminological and a material influence on the literature. I hope to be able to publish these and other investigations, long since utilized in my lectures, in the next volumes of the *Jahrbuch.*

in its presence "in person." Perception does this according to its *own peculiar sense;* and to attribute something other than that to perception is precisely to contradict its sense. If we are dealing, as here, with the perception of a physical thing then it is inherent in its essence to be an adumbrative perception; and, correlatively, it is inherent in the sense of its intentional object, the physical thing *as* given in it, to be essentially perceivable only by perceptions of that kind, thus by adumbrative perceptions.

§44. Merely phenomenal being of something transcendent, absolute being of something immanent

Moreover, and this is also an essential necessity, the perception of a physical thing involves a certain *inadequacy.* Of necessity a physical thing can be given only "one-sidedly"; and that signifies, not just incompletely or imperfectly in some sense or other, but precisely what presentation by adumbrations prescribes. A physical thing is necessarily given in mere "modes of appearance" in which necessarily a *core of "what is actually presented"* is apprehended as being surrounded by a horizon of *"co-givenness," which is not givenness proper,* and of more or less vague *indeterminateness.* And the sense of this indeterminateness is, again, predelineated by the universal essence of this type of perception which we call physical-thing perception. Indeed, the indeterminateness necessarily signifies a *determinableness which has a rigorously prescribed style.* It *points ahead* to possible perceptual multiplicities which, merging continuously into one another, join together to make up the unity of one perception in which the continuously enduring physical thing is always showing some new "sides" (or else an old "side" as returning) in a new series of adumbrations. Accordingly, those moments of the physical thing which are also seized upon, but not in the proper sense of the word, gradually become actually presented, i.e., actually given; the indeterminacies become more precisely determined and are themselves eventually converted into clearly given determinations; conversely, to be sure, the clear is changed again into the unclear, the presented

into the non-presented, etc. *To be in infinitum imperfect in this manner is part of the unanullable essence of the essence of the correlation between "physical thing" and perception of a physical thing.* If the sense of the physical thing is determined by the data of physical-thing perception (and what else could determine it?), then that sense demands such an imperfection and necessarily refers us to continuously unitary concatenations of possible perceptions which, starting from any perception effected, extend in infinitely many directions in a *systematically and rigidly regular* manner and, moreover, extend in every direction without limit, being always dominated throughout by a unity of sense. Necessarily there always remains a horizon of determinable indeterminateness, no matter how far we go in our experience, no matter how extensive the continua of actual perceptions of the same thing may be through which we have passed. No god can alter that no more than the circumstance that $1 + 2 = 3$, or that any other eidetic truth obtains.

It can already be seen universally that, no matter what its genus may be, the being of something transcendent, understood as a being *for* an Ego, can become given only in a manner analogous to that in which a physical thing is given, therefore through appearances. Otherwise it would be precisely a being of something which might become immanent; but anything that is perceivable immanently is perceivable *only* immanently. Only if one is guilty of the above-indicated confusions, which now have been cleared up, can one believe it possible for one and the same affair to be given on one occasion by appearance in the form of a perception of something transcendent and, on another occasion, by a perception of something immanent.

First of all, let us still develop the other side of the specific contrast between a physical thing and a mental process. No *mental process,* we said, is presented [*stellt sich . . . nicht dar*]. That means that the perception of a mental process is a simple seeing of something which is (or can become) *perceptually given as something absolute,* and not as something identical in modes of appearance by adumbration. Everything which we have worked out about the givenness of the physical thing loses its sense here, and one must make that fully clear to oneself in detail. A mental process of feeling is not adumbrated. If I look at it, I have something absolute; it has no sides that could be presented sometimes in one mode and sometimes in another. I can think something true or something false about a feeling, but what I see when I look at it is there, with its qualities, its intensity, etc., absolutely. A violin tone, in contrast, with its objective identity, is given by adumbration, has its changing modes of appearance. These differ in accordance with whether I approach the violin or go farther away from it, in accordance with whether I am in the concert hall itself or am listening through the closed doors, etc. No one mode of appearance can claim to be the one that presents the tone absolutely although, in accordance with my practical interests, a certain appearance has a certain primacy as the normal appearance: in the concert hall and at the "right" spot I hear the tone "itself" as it "actually" sounds. In the same way we say that any physical thing in relation to vision has a normal appearance; we say of the color, the shape, the whole physical thing which we see in normal daylight and in a normal orientation relative to us, that this is how the thing actually looks; this is its actual color, and the like. But that points to what is only *a kind of secondary objectivation* within the limits of total objectivation of the physical thing, as we can easily be persuaded. For, indeed, it is clear that if we were to retain the "normal" mode of appearance while cutting off the other multiplicities of appearances and the essential relationships to them, none of the sense of the givenness of the physical thing would remain.

We therefore hold fast to the following: Whereas it is essential to givenness by appearances that no appearance presents the affair as something "absolute" instead of in a one-sided presentation, it is essential to the givenness of something immanent precisely to present something absolute which cannot ever be presented with respect to sides or be adumbrated. It is indeed evident also that the adumbrative sensation-contents themselves, which really inherently belong to the mental process of perceiving a physical thing, function, more particularly, as adumbrations of something but are not themselves given in turn by adumbrations.

The following distinction should also be noted. It is the case also of a mental process that it is never perceived completely, that it cannot be adequately seized upon in its full unity. A mental process is, with respect to its essence, in flux which we, directing the reflective regard to it, can swim along after it starting from the Now-point, while the stretches already covered are lost to our perception. Only in the form of retention do we have a consciousness of the phase which has just flowed away, or else in the form of a retrospective recollection. And my whole stream of mental processes is, finally, a unity of mental processes which, of essential necessity, cannot be seized upon completely in a perceiving which "swims along with it." But *this* incompleteness or "imperfection," pertaining to the essence of the perception of a mental process, is radically different from the incompleteness or "imperfection" pertaining to the essence of the perception of something "transcendent," perception by means of adumbrative presentation, by means of something such as appearance.

All the modes of givenness, and all the differences among modes of givenness, which we find in the sphere of perception are also present, but in a modified fashion, in the sphere of *reproductive modifications.* The presentiations of physical things make those things "present" by virtue of presentations such that the adumbrations themselves, the apprehensions and, accordingly, the whole phenomenon, are *reproductively modified throughout.* We also have reproductions of mental processes and acts of reproductively intuiting mental processes in the manner characteristic of presentation and of reflection in presentation. Naturally we do not find any reproductive adumbrations here.

We now add the following contrast. Gradual differences in relative clarity or obscurity belong to the essence of presentiations. Obviously this difference in perfection has nothing to do with the one related to givenness by virtue of adumbrative appearances. A more or less clear objectivation is not adumbrated by the degree of clarity, namely in the sense which determines our terminology, according to which a spatial shape, any quality which covers a shape, and therefore the whole "appearing physical thing as appearing" is manifoldly adumbrated—whether the objectivation of them is clear or obscure. A reproductive objectivation of a physical thing has its various possible degrees of clarity and, more particularly, for each of its modes of adumbration. One sees that it is a matter of differences that lie in different dimensions. It is also obvious that the distinctions we make within the sphere of perception itself under the headings of "clear and unclear," "distinct and indistinct" seeing do indeed exhibit a certain analogy with the differences in clarity of which we were just now speaking in so far as, in both cases, it is a matter of gradual increases and decreases in the fullness with which the objectivated affair is given; but these differences also belong to other dimensions.

§45. *Unperceived mental processes, unperceived reality*

If we penetrate more deeply into this situation we also understand the following difference in essence between mental processes and physical things with respect to their perceivableness.

The kind of being belonging to mental processes is such that a seeing regard of perception can be directed quite immediately to any actual mental process as an originary living present. This occurs in the form of *"reflection,"* which has the remarkable property that what is seized upon perceptually in reflection is characterized fundamentally not only as something which exists and endures while it is being regarded perceptually but also as something which *already existed before* this regard was turned to it. "All mental processes are intended to": This signifies, then, that in the specific case of intentive mental processes not only are they consciousness of something and present as consciousness of something when they themselves are the Objects of a reflecting consciousness, but also that they are there already as a "back-

ground" when they are not reflected on and thus of essential necessity are *"ready to be perceived"* in a sense which is, in the first place, analogous to the one in which unnoticed physical things in our external field of regard are ready to be perceived. Physical things can be ready to be perceived only in so far as already, as unnoticed things, they are intended to and this signifies: only if they are appearing. *Not all* physical things fulfill this condition: the "field of attentive regard" embracing everything which appears is not infinite. On the other hand, the mental process which is not reflected on also must fulfill certain conditions of readiness, although in quite different ways and as befits its essence. After all, it cannot be "appearing." Nevertheless it fulfills those conditions at all times by the mere mode of its existence; it fulfills them, more particularly, for the particular Ego to which it belongs, the Ego-regard which, perchance, lives "in" it. Only because reflection and the mental process have those *essential* peculiarities which have been mentioned here, is it possible for us to know something about mental processes, including reflections themselves, which are not reflected on. That reproductive (and retentional) modifications of mental processes have the same determination, correspondingly modified, is obvious.

Let us develop that contrast further. We see that *the sort of being which belongs to the mental process is such that the latter is essentially capable of being perceived in reflection.* The physical thing is also essentially *capable of being perceived,* and it is seized upon in perception as a physical thing belonging to my surrounding world. Even without being perceived it belongs to that world; and, therefore, *even when it is not perceived it is there for the Ego.* But still not in such a manner that, in general, a regard of simple heeding could be directed to it. The background field, understood as a field of simple observability, includes only a small piece of my surrounding world. That the unperceived physical thing "is there" means rather that, from my actually present perceptions, with the actually appearing background field, *possible* and, moreover, continuously-harmoniously *motivated* perception-sequences, with ever new fields of physical things (as un-heeded backgrounds), lead to those concatenations of perceptions in which the physical thing in question would make its appearance and become seized upon. Fundamentally, nothing essential is altered if, instead of a single Ego, a plurality of Egos is taken into consideration. Only by virtue of the relationship of possible mutual understanding can my experienced world become identified with that of others and, at the same time, enriched by their more extensive experience. Thus a transcendency which lacked the above-described connection by harmonious motivational concatenations with my current sphere of actually present perceptions would be a completely groundless assumption; a transcendency which lacked such a concatenation *essentially* would be *nonsensical*. Such then is the kind of presence characterizing what is not currently perceived pertaining to the world of physical things; it is something essentially different from the necessarily intended-to being of mental processes.

§46. *Indubitability of the perception of something immanent, dubitability of the perception of something transcendent*

From all of this there emerge important consequences. Every perception of something immanent necessarily guarantees the existence of its object. If reflective seizing-upon is directed to a mental process of mine, I have seized upon something absolute itself, the factual being of which is essentially incapable of being negated, i.e., the insight that it is essentially impossible for it not to exist; it would be a countersense to believe it possible that a mental process *given in that manner* does *not* in truth exist. The stream of mental processes which is mine, of the one who is thinking, no matter to what extent it is not grasped, no matter how unknown it is in the areas of the stream which have run their course and which have yet to come—: as soon as I look at the flowing life in its actual present and, while doing so, apprehend myself as the pure subject of this life (later we shall busy ourselves particularly with what that means), I say unqualifiedly and

necessarily that I am, this life is, I am living: cogito.

To each stream of mental processes and to each Ego, as Ego, there belongs the essential possibility of acquiring this evidence; each bears in itself, as an essential possibility, the guarantee of its absolute factual being. But, one might ask, is it not conceivable that an Ego have only phantasies in its stream of mental processes, that this stream consists of nothing but inventive intuitions? Such an Ego would find only phantasies *[Fiktionen]* of cogitationes; its reflections, because of the nature of these mental processes as the medium <in which it reflected> *[bei der Natur des Erlebnismediums]*, would be exclusively reflections in imagination. — But that is an obvious countersense. What hovers before one may be a mere figment; the hovering itself, the inventive consciousness, is not itself invented and there belongs to its essence, as to any other mental process, the possibility of a perceiving reflection which seizes upon absolute factual being. No countersense is implicit in the possibility that every other consciousness, which I posit in empathic experience, is non-existent. But *my* empathizing, my consciousness of whatever sort, is originarily and absolutely given not only with respect to its essence but also with respect to its existence. Only for an Ego, or a stream of mental processes, in relation to itself, does this distinctive state of affairs exist; here alone there is, and here there must be, such a thing as perception of something immanent.

In contradistinction, as we know, it is of the essence of the physical world that no perception, however perfect, presents anything absolute in that realm; and essentially connected with this is the fact that any experience, however extensive, leaves open the possibility that what is given does *not* exist in spite of the continual consciousness of its own presence "in person." According to eidetic law it is the case that *physical existence is never required as necessary* by the givenness of something physical, but is always in a certain manner contingent. This means: It can always be that the further course of experience necessitates giving up what has already been posited with a *legitimacy derived from experience*. Afterwards one says it was a mere illusion, a hallucination, merely a coherent dream, or the like. Furthermore, as a continuously open possibility in this sphere of givenness, there exists such a thing as alteration of construing, a sudden changing of one appearance into another which cannot be united harmoniously with it and thus an influx of the latter upon the earlier experiential positings owing to which the intentional objects of these earlier positings suffer afterwards, so to speak, a transformation—occurrences all of which are essentially excluded from the sphere of mental processes. In this absolute sphere there is no room for conflict, illusion, or being otherwise. It is a sphere of absolute positing.

Thus in every manner it is clear that whatever is there for me in the world of physical things is necessarily only a *presumptive actuality* and, on the other hand, that *I myself* for whom it is there (I, when the "part of me" belonging to the world of physical things is excluded) am *absolute* actuality or that the present phase of my mental processes is an absolute actuality, given by an unconditional, absolutely indefeasible positing.

Over against the positing of the world, which is a "contingent" positing, there stands then the positing of my pure Ego and Ego-life which is a "necessary," absolutely indubitable *positing. Anything physical which is given "in person" can be non-existent; no mental process which is given "in person" can be non-existent.* This is the eidetic law defining this necessity and that contingency.

Obviously that does not imply that the necessity of the being of this or that present mental process is a pure essential necessity, that is: a purely eidetic particularity subsumed under an eidetic law; it is the necessity of a fact, and is called so because an eidetic law is involved in the fact and indeed, in this case, involved in the existence of the fact as fact. The ideal possibility of a reflection having the essential characteristic of an evidently indefeasible positing of *factual existence* is grounded in the essence of *any* Ego *whatever* and of *any* mental process *whatever.*

The deliberations just carried out also make it clear that no conceivable proofs gathered from experiential consideration of the world could make the existence of the world certain for us with an absolute assurance. The world is dubitable not in the sense that rational motives are present to be taken into consideration over against the tremendous force of harmonious experiences, but rather in the sense that a doubt is *conceivable* because, of essential necessity, the possibility of the non-being of the world is never excluded. Any force of experience, no matter how great, can gradually become counterbalanced and outweighed. The absolute being of mental processes is in no respect altered thereby; in fact, they always remain presupposed by all of that.

Our considerations now have succeeded in reaching a point of culmination. We have acquired the cognitions we needed. Already included in the concatenations of essences disclosed to us are the most important premises from which we shall draw the inferences concerning the essential detachableness of the whole natural world from the domains of consciousness, of the sphere of being pertaining to mental processes; we can persuade ourselves that, in these inferences, justice is at last done to a core of Descartes's *Meditations* (which were directed to entirely different ends) which only lacked a pure, effective development. Subsequently, to be sure, we shall need some easily acquired additional supplementations in order to reach our final goal. In a preliminary way we draw our consequences within the bounds of a restricted application.

The Region of Pure Consciousness*

§47. *The natural world as a correlate of consciousness*

Taking the results of the last chapter as our point of departure, we may take the following into consideration. The *de facto* course of our

Ideas I, pp. 105–113, 128–130 (Sections 47–50 and 55).

human experiences is such that it constrains our reason to go beyond intuitionally given physical things (those of the Cartesian imaginatio) and base them on the "truth of physics." But that course might be different. It is not as though human development had never progressed, nor would ever progress, beyond the prescientific stage so that, while the world of physics indeed had its truth, we should never know anything about it. And it is not as though the world of physics were different and ordered according to laws different from the ones that in fact obtain. Rather it is conceivable that our intuited world were the ultimate one, "behind" which would be no world of physics whatever, i.e., that perceived physical things would lack mathematical or physical determination, that the data of experience would exclude any physics belonging to the same kind with ours. The concatenations of experience would then be correspondingly other and different in kind from what they in fact are in so far as the experiential motives fundamental to the fashioning of the concepts and judgments of physics would be absent. But, on the whole, within the limits of the presentive *intuitions* which we comprehend under the name "simple experience" (perception, recollection, etc.), "physical things" can still be presented as they are now as intentional unities persisting continuously in multiplicities of appearances.

But we can go further in this direction: No limits check us in the process of conceiving the destruction of the Objectivity of something physical—as the correlate of experimental consciousness. It must always be borne in mind here that *whatever physical things are*—the only physical things about which we can make statements, the only ones about the being or non-being, the being-thus or being-otherwise of which we can disagree and make rational decisions—*they are as experienceable physical things*. It is experience alone that prescribes their sense; and, since we are speaking of physical things in fact, it is actual experience alone

which does so in its definitely ordered experiential concatenations. But if the kinds of mental processes included under experience, and especially the fundamental mental process of perceiving physical things, can be submitted by us to an *eidetic* consideration, and if we can discern essential possibilities and necessities in them (as we obviously can) and can therefore eidetically trace the essentially possible variants of motivated experiential concatenations: then the result is the correlate of our factual experience, called *"the actual world,"* as *one special case among a multitude of possible worlds and surrounding worlds* which, for their part, are nothing else but the *correlates of essentially possible variants of the idea, "an experiencing consciousness,"* with more or less orderly concatenations of experience. As a consequence, one must not let oneself be deceived by speaking of the physical thing as transcending consciousness or as "existing in itself." The genuine concept of the transcendence of something physical which is the measure of the rationality of any statements about transcendence, can itself be derived only from the proper essential contents of perception or from those concatenations of definite kinds which we call demonstrative experience. The idea of such transcendence is therefore the eidetic correlate of the pure idea of this demonstrative experience.

This is true of any conceivable kind of transcendence which could be treated as either an actuality or a possibility. *An object existing in itself is never one with which consciousness or the Ego pertaining to consciousness has nothing to do.* The physical thing is a thing belonging to the *surrounding world* even if it be an unseen physical thing, even if it be a really possible, unexperienced but experienceable, or perhaps experienceable, physical thing. *Experienceableness never means a mere logical possibility*, but rather a possibility *motivated* in the concatenations of experience. This concatenation itself is, through and through, one of "motivation,"* always taking into itself new

---

*It should be noted that this fundamental phenomenological concept of motivation, which arose immediately with the isolation of the purely phenomenological sphere in the *Logische Untersuchungen* (and in contrast to the concept of causality, as relating to the transcendent sphere of reality), is a *universalization* of that concept of motivation in accor-

motivations and recasting those already formed. With respect to their apprehension-contents or determination-contents, the motivations differ, are more or less rich, are more or less definite or vague in content depending on whether it is a matter of physical things which are already "known" or "completely unknown," "still undiscovered" or in the case of the seen physical thing, whether it is a matter of what is known or unknown about it. It is exclusively a matter of the *essential structures* of such concatenations which, with respect to all their possibilities, can be made the objects of a purely eidetic exploration. It is inherent in the essence that anything whatever which exists in reality but is not yet actually experienced can become given and that this means that the thing in question belongs to the undetermined but *determinable* horizon of my experiential actuality at the particular time. This horizon, however, is the correlate of the components of undeterminateness essentially attached to experiences of physical things themselves; and those components—again, essentially—leave open possibilities of fulfillment which are by no means completely undetermined but are, on the contrary, motivated possibilities *predelineated with respect to their essential type.* Any actual experience points beyond itself to possible experiences which, in turn, point to new possible experiences and so ad infinitum. And all of that is effected involving species and regulative forms restricted to certain a priori types.

Any hypothetical formulation in practical life or in empirical science relates to this changing but always co-posited horizon whereby the positing of the world receives its essential sense.

§48. The logical possibility and the material countersense of a world outside ours

The hypothetical assumption of something real outside this world is, of course, "logically" possible; obviously it involves no formal contradiction. But when we ask about the essential conditions on which its validity would depend, about the mode of demonstration demanded by its sense, when we ask about the mode of demonstration taken universally essentially determined by the positing of something transcendent—no matter how we might legitimately universalize its essence—we recognize that something transcendent necessarily must be experienceable not merely by an Ego conceived as an empty logical possibility but by any *actual* Ego as a demonstrable unity relative to its concatenations of experience. But one can see (here, to be sure, we are not yet advanced enough to establish it in detail; only our later analyses can provide all the premises for doing so) that what is cognizable by one Ego must, of *essential necessity,* be cognizable by *any* Ego. Even though it is not *in fact* the case that each stands, or can stand, in a relationship of "empathy," of mutual understanding with every other, as, e.g., not having such relationship to mental lives living on the planets of the remotest stars, nevertheless there exist, eidetically regarded, *essential possibilities of effecting a mutual understanding* and therefore possibilities also that the worlds of experience separated in fact become joined by concatenation of actual experience to make up the one intersubjective world, the correlate of the unitary world of mental lives (the universal broadening of the community of human beings). When that is taken into account the formal-logical possibility of realities outside the world, the *one* spatiotemporal world, which is *fixed* by our *actual* experience, materially proves to be a countersense. If there are any worlds, any real physical things whatever, then the experienced motivations constituting them must be *able* to extend into my experience and into that of each Ego in the general manner characterized above. Obviously there are physical things and worlds of physical things which do not admit of being definitely demonstrated in any *human* experience; but

---

dance with which we can say, e.g., that the willing of the end motivates the willing of the means. Incidentally, the concept of motivation undergoes, for essential reasons, a variety of modifications; the corresponding equivocations become harmless, and even appear to be necessary as soon as the phenomenological situations are clarified.

that has purely factual grounds which lie within the factual limits of such experience.

§49. Absolute consciousness as the residuum after the annihilation of the world

On the other hand, all of that does not imply that there *must* be some world or some physical thing or other. The existence of a world is the correlate of certain multiplicities of experience distinguished by certain essential formations. But it *cannot* be seen that actual experiences can flow *only* in such concatenated forms; nothing like that can be seen purely on the basis of the essence of perception taken universally, and of the essences of other collaborating kinds of experiential intuition. It is instead quite conceivable that experience, because of conflict, might dissolve into illusion not only in detail, and that it might not be the case, as it is de facto, that every illusion manifests a deeper truth and that every conflict, in the place where it occurs, is precisely what is demanded by more inclusive contextures in order to preserve the total harmony; in our experiencing it is conceivable that there might be a host of irreconcilable conflicts not just for us but in themselves, that experience might suddenly show itself to be refractory to the demand that it carry on its positings of physical things harmoniously, that its context might lose its fixed regular organizations of adumbrations, apprehensions, and appearances—in short, that there might no longer be any world. Nevertheless, in that case it could be that, to some extent, crude unity-formations become constituted, transient supports for intuitions which were mere analogues of intuitions of physical things because quite incapable of constituting conservable "realities," enduring unities "which exist in themselves, whether or not they are perceived."

Now let us add the results reached at the end of the last chapter; let us recall the possibility of non-being of everything physically transcendent: it then becomes evident that *while the being of consciousness,* of any stream of mental processes whatever, *would indeed be necessarily modified by an annihilation of the world of physical things its own existence would not be touched.* Modified, to be sure. For an annihilation of the world means, correlatively, nothing else but that in each stream of mental processes (the full stream—the total stream, taken as endless in both directions, which comprises the mental processes of an Ego), certain ordered concatenations of experience and therefore certain complexes of theorizing reason oriented according to those concatenations of experience, would be excluded. But that does not mean that other mental processes and concatenations of mental processes would be excluded. *Consequently no real being,* no being which is presented and legitimated in consciousness by appearances, *is necessary to the being of consciousness itself* (in the broadest sense, the stream of mental processes).

Immanental being is therefore indubitably absolute being in the sense that by essential necessity immanental being nulla "re" indiget ad existendum.

In contradistinction, the world of transcendent "res" is entirely referred to consciousness and, more particularly, not to some logically conceived consciousness but to actual consciousness.

In so far as its most universal sense is concerned, that has already been made clear by the exposition above (in the preceding sections). A something transcendent is *given* by virtue of certain concatenations of experience. As given directly and with increasing perfection in perceptual continua which show themselves to be harmonious and in certain methodical forms of thinking based on experience, a something transcendent acquires, more or less immediately, its insightful, continually progressive determination. Let us assume that consciousness, with its *constituent mental processes* and with the *course it runs,* is actually of such a nature that the conscious subject, in his free activity of theoretical experiencing and of thinking oriented according to experience, *could* effect all such concatenations (in which connection we should also have to take into account the reinforcement received by mutual understanding with other Egos and other streams of mental processes); let us assume, furthermore, that the pertinent regularities of consciousness are actually maintained, that, in the course of consciousness taken universally, nothing whatever is lacking which is requisite for the appearance of a unitary world and for the rational theoretical cognition of such a world. All that being assumed, we now ask: is it still *conceivable* and not rather a countersense that the corresponding transcendent world *does not exist?*

Thus we see that consciousness (mental process) and real being are anything but coordinate kinds of being, which dwell peaceably side by side and occasionally become "related to" or "connected with" one another. Only things which are essentially akin, the respective proper essences of which have a like sense, can become connected in the true sense of the word, can make up a whole. An immanental or absolute being and a transcendent being are, of course, both called "existent," an "object," and have, more particularly, their objective determining contents. But it is evident that what is called "an object" and "an objective determination" in the one case, and what is called by the same name in the other case, are called so only with reference to the empty logical categories. In so far as their respective senses are concerned, a veritable abyss yawns between consciousness and reality. Here, an adumbrated being, not capable of ever becoming given absolutely, merely accidental and relative; there, a necessary and absolute being, essentially incapable of becoming given by virtue of adumbration and appearance.

Thus it becomes clear that, in spite of all our assuredly well-founded statements about the real being of the *human* Ego and its conscious mental processes, *in* the world and about everything in the way of "psychophysical" interconnections pertaining to them—that, in spite of all that, consciousness considered in its *"purity"* must be held to be a *self-contained complex of being,* a complex *of absolute being* into which nothing can penetrate and out of which nothing can slip, to which nothing is spatiotemporally external and which cannot be within any spatiotemporal complex, which cannot be affected by any physical thing and cannot exercise causation upon any physical thing—it being presupposed that causality has the normal sense of causality pertaining to Nature as a relationship of dependence between realities.

On the other hand, the whole *spatiotemporal world,* which includes human being and the human Ego as subordinate single realities is, *according to its sense, a merely intentional being,* thus one has the merely secondary sense of a being *for* a consciousness. It is a being posited by consciousness in its experiences which, of essential necessity, can be determined and intuited only as something identical belonging to motivated multiplicities of appearances: *beyond that* it is nothing.

§50. The phenomenological attitude. Pure consciousness as the field of phenomenology

Thus the sense commonly expressed in speaking of being is reversed. The being which is first for us is second in itself; i.e., it is what it is, only in "relation" to the first. <But it is> not as though there were a blind regularity such that the ordo et connexio rerum necessarily conformed to the ordo et connexio idearum. Reality, the reality of the physical thing taken singly and the reality of the whole world, lacks self-sufficiency in virtue of its essence (in our strict sense of the word). Reality is not in itself something absolute which becomes tied secondarily to something else; rather, in the absolute sense, it is nothing at all; it has no "absolute essence" whatever; it has the essentiality of something which, of necessity, is *only* intentional, *only* an object of consciousness, something presented *[Vorstelliges]* in the manner peculiar to consciousness, something apparent <as apparent>.

We now turn our thoughts back again to the first chapter, to our observations concerning the phenomenological reduction. It now becomes clear that, in contrast to the natural theoretical attitude, the correlate of which is the world, a new attitude must in fact be possible which, in spite of the "exclusion" of this psychophysical universe of Nature, leaves us something: the whole field of absolute consciousness. Instead, then, of living naively in experience and theoretically exploring what is experienced, transcendent Nature, we effect the "phenomenological reduction." In other words, instead of naively *effecting* the acts pertaining to our Nature—constituting consciousness with their positings of something transcendent, and letting ourselves be induced, by motives implicit in them, to effect ever new positings of something transcendent—instead of that, we put all those positings "out of action," we do not "participate in them"; we direct our seizing and theoretically inquiring regard to *pure consciousness in its own absolute being.* That, then, is what is left as the sought-for *"phenomenological residuum,"* though we have "excluded" the whole world with all physical things, living beings, and humans, ourselves included. Strictly speaking, we have not lost anything but rather have gained the whole of absolute being which, rightly understood, contains within itself, "constitutes" within itself, all worldly transcendencies.

§55. Conclusion. All reality existent by virtue of "sense-bestowal." Not a "subjective idealism"

In a certain way, and with some caution in the use of words, we can also say that *all real unities are "unities of sense."* Unities of sense presuppose (as I again emphasize: not because we can deduce it from some metaphysical postulates or other, but because we can show it by an intuitive, completely indubitable procedure) a *sense-bestowing* consciousness which, for its part, exists absolutely and not by virtue of another sense-bestowal. If one derives the concept of reality from *natural* realities, from unities of possible experience, then "all the world" or "all of Nature" is, of course, equivalent to the all of realities; but to identify the

latter with the all of *being,* and thus to absolutize it itself is a countersense. *An absolute reality is just as valid as a round square.* Reality and world are names here precisely for certain valid *unities of sense,* unities of "sense" related to certain concatenations of absolute, of pure consciousness which, by virtue of their *essence,* bestow sense and demonstrate sensevalidity precisely thus and not otherwise.

If anyone reading our statements objects that they mean changing all the world into a subjective illusion and committing oneself to a "Berkeleyan idealism," we can only answer that he has not seized upon the *sense* of those statements. They take nothing away from the fully valid being of the world as the all of realities, just as nothing is taken away from the fully valid geometrical being of the square by denying that the square is round (a denial admittedly based, in this case, on what is immediately obvious). The real actuality is not "reinterpreted," to say nothing of its being denied; it is rather that a countersensical interpretation of the real actuality, i.e., an interpretation which contradicts the latter's *own* sense as clarified by insight, is removed. That interpretation stems from a *philosophical* absolutizing of the world completely alien to the natural way of considering the world. This is, precisely, natural; it lives naively in the effecting of the general positing described by us; thus it can never become a countersense. The countersense only arises when one philosophizes and, while seeking ultimate intelligence about the sense of the world, never even notices that the world itself has its whole being as a certain "sense" which presupposes absolute consciousness as the field where sense is bestowed;* and when, at the same time, one fails to notice that this field, this *sphere of being of absolute origins, is accessible to insightful inquiry [schauenden Forschung]* yielding an infinite wealth of cognitions given in insight with the highest scientific dignity. The latter, to be sure, is something which we have yet to show; only

---

*Here, in passing, I am allowing myself an extraordinary and yet, in its way, admissable broadening of the concept "sense" in order to state the contrast more effectively.

as these investigations progress will it become clear.

Let us note in conclusion that the universality with which, in the deliberations carried out above, we have spoken about the constitution of the natural world in absolute consciousness, should not be found objectionable. That we have not ventured empty philosophical conceits from on high but, on the basis of systematic fundamental work in this field, have concentrated in universal statements cautiously acquired cognitions will be evident to the scientifically experienced reader from the conceptual definiteness of the exposition. The need for more detailed statements and for filling in gaps which have been left open may be felt, and rightly so. The further presentations will furnish considerable contributions to a more concrete development of the sketches previously given. It should be noted, however, that our aim here has not been to give a finished theory of that transcendental constitution and, accordingly, to project a new "theory of knowledge" pertaining to the various spheres of reality; <our aim has been instead> only to bring about insight into certain general thoughts which can help one to acquire the idea of transcendentally pure consciousness. For us what is essential is the evidence that the phenomenological reduction, as an excluding of the natural attitude, or of the latter's general positing, is possible, the evidence that, after we effect that reduction, absolute or transcendentally pure consciousness remains as a residuum to which reality cannot be ascribed without absurdity.

IV.

ل

The Structure of Intentionality

6. The Noetic and Noematic Structure of Consciousness

Noesis and Noema*

§87. Preliminary remarks

The peculiarity of the intentive mental process is easily designated in its universality; we all understand the expression "consciousness of something," especially in ad libitum exemplifications. It is so much more difficult to purely and correctly seize upon the phenomenological essence-peculiarities corresponding to it. That this heading circumscribes a large field of painfully achieved findings and, more particularly, of eidetic findings, would seem even today alien to the majority of philosophers and psychologists (if we can judge by the literature). This is because nothing is accomplished by saying and discerning that every objectivating relates to something objectivated, that every judging relates to something judged, etc. Or that, in addition, one refers to logic, theory of knowledge, ethics, with their many evidences, and now *designates* these as belonging to the essence of intentionality. This is, at the same time, a very simple way of taking the phenomenological doctrine of essences as something very old, as a new name for the old logic and those disciplines which must be ranked with it. For without having seized upon the peculiar ownness of the transcendental attitude and having actually appropriated the pure

phenomenological basis, one may of course use the word, phenomenology; but one does not have the matter itself. In addition, it does not suffice, let us say, to merely change the attitude, or to merely carry out the phenomenological reduction in order to make something like phenomenology out of pure logic. For how far logical and, in a like way, pure ontological, pure ethical, and whatever other a priori propositions one may cite, actually express something phenomenological, and to which phenomenological strata the respective <propositions> may belong, is not obvious. On the contrary, the most difficult problems of all are hidden, <problems> the sense of which is naturally concealed from all those who still have no inkling of the determinative fundamental distinctions. In fact, it is (if I may be allowed a judgment from my own experience) a long and thorny way starting from purely logical insights, from insights pertaining to the theory of signification, from ontological and noetical insights, likewise from the customary normative and psychological theory of knowledge, to arrive at seizing upon, in a genuine sense, the immanent-psychological and then phenomenological data, and finally to arrive at all at the concatenations of essence which make the transcendental relations intelligible a priori. Something similar is the case no matter from where we might set out on the way from objective insights to acquire phe-

*Ideas I, pp. 211–221, 226–233 (Sections 87–90 and 93–95).

nomenological insights which essentially belong to them.

"Consciousness of something" is therefore something obviously understandable of itself and, at the same time, highly enigmatic. The labyrinthically false paths into which the first reflections lead, easily generate a skepticism which negates the whole troublesome sphere of problems. Not a few already bar access by the fact that they cannot bring themselves to seize upon the intentive mental process, e.g., the perceptual process, with the essence proper to it as perceptual process. Rather than living in the perception, adverted to the perceived in considering and theorizing they do not manage to direct the regard instead to the perceiving, or to the own peculiarities of the *mode* of givenness of the perceived, and to take what is offered in analysis of something immanent with respect to its essence, just as it is given. If the right attitude has been won, and made secure by practice, above all, however, if one has acquired the courage to obey the clear eidetic data with a radical lack of prejudice so as to be unencumbered by all current and learned theories, then firm results are directly produced, and the same thing occurs for everyone having the same attitude; there accrue firm possibilities of communicating to others what one has himself seen, of testing descriptions, of making salient the unnoticed intrusions of empty verbal meanings, of making known and weeding out errors by measuring them again against intuition—errors which are also possible here just as in any sphere of validity. But now to the matters at hand.

§88. Really inherent and intentive components of mental processes. The noema

If, as in the present deliberations generally, we begin with the most universal distinctions which, so to speak, can be seized upon at the very threshold of phenomenology, and which are determinative for all further methodic proceedings, then with respect to intentionality we immediately confront a wholly fundamental distinction, namely the distinction between the *components proper* of intentive mental processes and their *intentional correlates* and their components. We already touched upon this distinction in the preliminary eidetical deliberations of Part II. In that connection, in making the transition from the natural to the phenomenological attitude, the distinction served us to make clear the own peculiar being of the phenomenological sphere. But that it acquired a radical signification within this sphere itself, thus in the frame of the transcendental reduction, conditioning the entire set of problems pertaining to phenomenology: of that we could not speak there. On the one side therefore, we have to discriminate the parts and moments which we find by an *analysis of the really inherent* pertaining to mental processes, whereby we deal with the mental process as an object like any other, inquiring about its pieces or non-selfsufficient moments really inherent in it which make it up. But, on the other side, the intentive mental process is consciousness of something, and it is so according to its essence, e.g., as memory, as judgment, as will, etc.; and we can therefore inquire into what is to be declared as a matter of essential necessity about the side of this "of something."

Owing to its noetic moments, every intentive mental process is precisely noetic;* it is of its essence to include in itself something such as a "sense" and possibly a manifold sense on the basis of this sense-bestowal and, in unity with that, to effect further productions *[Leistungen]* which become "senseful" precisely by <this sense-bestowal>. Such noetic moments are, e.g., directions of the regard of the pure Ego to the objects "meant" by it owing to sense-bestowal, to <the object> which is "inherent in the sense" for the Ego; furthermore, seizing upon this object, holding it fast while the regard adverts to other objects which appear in the "meaning" *["Vermeinen"]*;

*Cf. §41.

likewise, producings pertaining to explicatings, relatings, comprisings, multiple position-takings of believings, deemings likely, valuings; and so forth. All of these are to be found in the mental processes in question, no matter how differently structured and varied they are. Now, no matter to what extent this series of exemplary moments refer to really inherent components of mental processes, they nevertheless also refer to what is *not really inherent,* namely by means of the heading of sense.

Corresponding in every case to the multiplicity of Data pertaining to the really inherent noetic content, there is a multiplicity of Data, demonstrable in actual pure intuition, in a correlative *"noematic content"* or, in short, in the *"noema"*—terms which we shall continue to use from now on.

Perception, for example, has its noema, most basically its perceptual sense,* i.e., the *perceived as perceived.* Similarly, the current case of remembering has its *remembered as remembered,* just as its <remembered>, precisely as it is "meant," "intended to" in <the remembering>; again, the judging has the *judged as judged,* liking has the liked as liked, and so forth. In every case the noematic correlate, which is called "sense" here (in a very extended signification) is to be taken *precisely* as it inheres "immanently" in the mental process of perceiving, of judging, of liking; and so forth; that is, just as it is offered to us when we *inquire purely into this mental process itself.*

How we understand all of this will become clear by carrying out an exemplary analysis (which we will effect in pure intuition).

Let us suppose that in a garden we regard with pleasure a blossoming apple tree, the freshly green grass of the lawn, etc. It is obvious that the perception and the accompanying liking are not, at the same time, what is perceived and liked. In the natural attitude, the apple tree is for us something existing in the transcendent realm of spatial actuality, and the perception, as well as the liking, is for us a psychical state belonging to real people. Between the one and the other real things, between the real person or the real perception, and the real apple tree, there exist real relations. In such situations characterizing mental processes, it may be in certain cases that perception is "mere hallucination," the perceived, this apple tree before us, does not exist in "actual" reality. Now the real relation, previously meant as actually existing, is destroyed. Only the perception remains, but there is nothing actual there to which it is related.

Let us now go to the <transcendental> phenomenological attitude. The transcendent world receives its "parenthesis," we exercise the ἐποχή in relation to <positing> its actual being. We now ask what, of essential necessity, is to be discovered in the complex of noetic processes pertaining to perception and in the valuation of liking. With the whole physical and psychical world, the actual existence of the real relation between perceiving and perceived is excluded; and, nonetheless, a relation between perceiving and perceived (as well as between liking and liked) remains left over, a relation which becomes given essentially in "pure immanence," namely, purely on the ground of the phenomenologically reduced mental processes of perceiving and liking precisely as they fit into the transcendental stream of mental processes. Precisely this situation, the purely phenomenological one, will occupy us now. Concerning hallucinations, illusions and perceptual deception of whatever sort, it may be that phenomenology has something to say, and perhaps even a great deal: but it is evident that here, in the role which they played in the natural attitude, they undergo exclusion. Here, in the case of perception and also in the case of any progressive concatenation of perceptions whatever (as when we consider the blossoming tree ambulando), there is no question to be raised of the sort whether or

---

*Cf. *Logische Untersuchungen, II'* 1te Unters., §14, p. 50 <[English translation, p. 290]> on the "fulfilling sense" (in that connection, 6te Unters., §55, p. 642 <[2nd ed., p. 170; English translation, p. 807]> on "perceptual sense"); furthermore, for what follows, 5te Unters., §20, on "matter" pertaining to the act; likewise 6te Unters., §§25–29.

not something corresponds to it in "the" actuality. This posited actuality is indeed not there for us in consequence of judging. And yet, so to speak, everything remains as of old. Even the phenomenologically reduced perceptual mental process is a perceiving *of* "this blossoming apple tree, in this garden," etc., and, likewise, the reduced liking is a liking of this same thing. The tree has not lost the least nuance of all these moments, qualities, characteristics *with which it was appearing in this perception,* <with which> it <was appearing as> "lovely," "attractive," and so forth "in" *this liking.*

In our <transcendental> phenomenological attitude we can and must raise the eidetic question: *what the "perceived as perceived" is, which eidetic moments it includes in itself as this perception-noema.* We receive the answer in the pure directedness to *something given* in its essence, and we can faithfully describe the "appearing as appearing" in complete evidence. It is only another expression for this to say that we "describe perception in its noematic respect."

§89. Noematic statements and statements about actuality. The noema in the psychological sphere

It is clear that all these descriptive statements, even though they may sound like statements about actuality, have undergone a *radical* modification of sense; similarly, the described itself, even though it is given as "precisely the same," is yet something radically different by virtue of, so to speak, an inverse change of signs. "In" the reduced perception (in the phenomenologically pure mental process), we find, as indefeasibly belonging to its essence, the perceived as perceived, to be expressed as "material thing," "plant," "tree," "blossoming"; and so forth. Obviously, the *inverted commas* are significant in that they express that change in sign, the correspondingly radical significational modification of the words. The *tree simpliciter,* the physical thing belonging to Nature, is nothing less than this *perceived tree as perceived* which, as percep-

tual sense, inseparably belongs to the perception. The tree simpliciter can burn up, be resolved into its chemical elements, etc. But the sense—the sense *of this* perception, something belonging necessarily to its essence—cannot burn up; it has no chemical elements, no forces, no real properties.

Everything which is purely immanent and reduced in the way peculiar to the mental process, everything which cannot be conceived apart from it just as it is in itself, and which eo ipso passes over into the Eidos in the eidetic attitude, is separated by an abyss from all of Nature and physics and no less from all psychology—and even this image, as naturalistic, is not strong enough to indicate the difference.

Obviously the perceptual sense also belongs to the phenomenologically unreduced perception (perception in the sense of psychology). Thus one can make clear here at the same time how the phenomenological reduction can acquire for psychologists the useful methodic function of fixing the noematic sense by sharply distinguishing it from the object simpliciter, and recognizing it as something belonging inseparably to the psychological essence of the intentive mental process.

On both sides, in the psychological as well as in the phenomenological attitude, one must therefore not lose sight of the fact that the "perceived" as sense includes nothing in itself (thus nothing should be imputed to it on the ground of "indirect cognizances") other than what "actually appears" in the given case in something perceptually appearing and, more precisely, in the mode of givenness in which it is precisely something intended to in the perception. At any time a *specifically peculiar reflection* can be directed to this sense as it is immanent in the perception, and the phenomenological judgment has to conform in faithful expression to what is seized upon in it.

§90. The "noematic sense" and the distinction between "immanental" and "actual objects"

Like perception, *every* intentive mental process—just this makes up the fundamental part of intentionality—has its "intentional Object," i.e., its objective sense. Or, in other words: to have sense or "to intend to" something *[etwas "im Sinne zu haben"]*, is the fundamental characteristic of all consciousness which, therefore, is not just any mental living *[Erlebnis]* whatever, but is rather a <mental living> having sense, which is "noetic."

Certainly what has become prominent as "sense" in the analysis of our examples does not exhaust the full noema; correspondingly, the noetic side of the intentive mental process does not merely consist of the moment of "sense-bestowal" proper specifically belonging to the "sense" as correlate. It will be shown directly that the full noema consists of a complex of noematic moments, that in <that complex> the specific sense-moment only fashions one kind of necessary *core-stratum* in which further moments are essentially founded which, therefore, should likewise be designated as sense-moments, but in an extended meaning.

Nevertheless, let us remain at first with what alone has clearly emerged. Without doubt we have shown that the intentive mental process is of such a character that in a suitable focusing of regard a "sense" is to be drawn from it. The situation defining the sense for us cannot remain concealed: the circumstance, namely, that the non-existence (or the conviction of non-existence) of the objectivated or thought of Object pure and simple pertaining to the objectivation in question (and therefore to any particular intentive mental process whatever) cannot steal its something objectivated as objectivated, that therefore the distinction between both must be made. Such a striking distinction has required expression in the literature. As a matter of fact, the Scholastic distinction between the *"mental,"* *"intentional"* or *"immanental"* Object on the one hand, and the *"actual" Object* on the other hand, refers back to it. Nevertheless, it is an immense step to go from seizing upon a distinction pertaining to consciousness for the first time to its right, phenomenologically pure, fixing and correct valuation—and precisely this step, which is decisive for a harmonious, fruitful phenomenology, has not been effected. Above all, what is decisive consists of the absolute-

ly faithful description of what is actually present in phenomenological purity and in keeping at a distance all the interpretations transcending the given. Here denominations already evince interpretations, and often quite false ones. These interpretations betray themselves here in expressions such as "mental," "immanental" Object, and the expression "intentional Object" requires them the least of all.

It would even be tempting to say: In the mental process the intention is given with its intentional Object which, as intentional Object, inseparably belongs to it, therefore itself *inherently* dwells within <the intention>. Indeed, it is and remains its <Object> meant, objectivated, and the like, no matter if the corresponding "actual Object" precisely is or is not in actuality, if it has been annihilated in the meantime, etc.

But if, in *this* way, we try to separate the actual Object (in the case of perception of something external, the perceived physical thing pertaining to Nature) and the intentional Object, including the latter <as> really inherently in the mental process as "immanent" to the perception, we fall into the difficulty that now *two* realities ought to stand over against one another while only *one* <reality> is found to be present and even possible. I perceive the physical thing, the Object belonging to Nature, the tree there in the garden; that and nothing else is the actual Object of the perceptual "intention." A second immanental tree, or even an "internal image" of the actual tree standing out there before me, is in no way given, and to suppose that hypothetically leads to an absurdity. The image as a really inherent component in the psychologically real perception would be again something real—something real which would *function* as a depicturing of another something real. But that can only be by virtue of a depicturing consciousness in which something first appears—with which we would have a first intentionality—and this would function again in consciousness as a "picture Object" representing another "picture Object"— for which a second intentionality founded in the first intentionality would be necessary. It is no less evident that each particular one of these modes of consciousness already requires the distinction between the immanental and actual object, thus comprising the same problem which should have been resolved by the construction. Over and above this, in the case of perception, the construction is subject to the objection which we have discussed earlier:* to include depictive functions in the perception of something physical signifies ascribing to it a picture-consciousness which, descriptively considered, is something of an essentially different kind of constitution. Nevertheless, the main point here is that perception and, then consequently, every mental process, requires a depictive function, unavoidably (as can be seen at once from our critique) leads to an infinite regress.

In contradistinction to such errors we have to abide by what is given in the pure mental process and to take it within the frame of clarity precisely as it is given. The "actual" Object is then to be "parenthesized." Let us reflect on what that signifies: if we begin as people in the natural attitude, then the actual Object is the physical thing there, outside <us>. We see it, we stand before it, we have directed our eyes fixingly to it, and then we describe it and make our statements about it just as we find it there in space as what confronts us. Likewise we take a position toward it in valuing; what confronts us, what we see in space, pleases us, or determines us to act; we seize upon or manipulate what is given there, etc. If we now effect the phenomenological reduction, then every positing of something transcendent, thus above all what is inherent to perception itself, receives its excluding parentheses, and this is passed on to all of the founded acts, to every judgment of perception, to the positing of value, and possibly to the value judgment grounded in it. Implicit in this is that we only allow all these perceivings, judgings, etc., to be considered, to be described, as the essentialities which they are in themselves, to pin down what is evidently given with or in them. But we do not tolerate any judgment which makes use of the positing of the "actual" physical thing, nor of the whole "transcendent" Nature,

or which "joins in" <that positing>. As *phenomenologists* we abstain from all such positings. But on that account we do not reject them by not "taking them as our basis," by not "joining in" them. They are indeed there, they also essentially belong to the phenomenon. Rather we contemplate them; instead of joining in them, we make them Objects, take them as component parts of the phenomenon—the positing pertaining to perception as well as its components.

And, keeping these excludings in their clear sense, we therefore ask quite universally, then, about what is evidentially "inherent" in the whole "reduced" phenomenon. Now, inherent too precisely in perception is this: that it has its noematic sense, its "perceived as perceived," "this blossoming tree there, in space"—understood with inverted commas—precisely the *correlate* belonging to the essence of phenomenologically reduced perception. Figuratively stated: the "parenthesis" undergone by perception prevents any judgment about perceived actuality (i.e., any <judgment> having its basis in unmodified perception, thus taking up into itself its positing). But it does not prevent the judgment about the fact that perception is consciousness *of* an actuality (the positing of which, however, should not be "effected"); and it does not prevent any description of this perceptually appearing "actuality" as appearing with the particular ways in which it is here intended to, appearing only "one-sidedly," in this or that orientation; and so forth. With minute care we must now take heed against attributing to the mental process anything which is not actually included in its essence, and <we must> "attribute" <what is included> exactly and just as it precisely is "inherent" in it.

§93. Transition to the noetic-noematic structures of the higher spheres of consciousness

In the next series of considerations we wish to examine the structures which belong to the "higher" spheres of consciousness in which a *number of noeses are built up on one another in the unity of a concrete mental process* and in which, accordingly, the *noematic correlates* are likewise *founded.* Thus the eidetic law, confirmed in every case, states that there can be *no noetic moment without a noematic moment specifically belonging to it.*

Even in the case of noeses of a higher level —taken in concrete completeness—there at first emerges in the noematic composition a central core thrusting itself to the fore in a predominate way, the "meant Objectivity as Objectivity," the Objectivity in inverted commas as required by the phenomenological reduction. There this central noema must also be taken precisely in the modified Objective composition in which it is just that noema, something intended to as intended to. Because the Objective something taken in a modified way itself becomes, to be sure, under the heading of sense, as, e.g., in our scientific investigation of it, again an Objective something although of a dignity peculiar to it, one will subsequently see here that this *novel Objectivity* has its modes of givenness, its "characteristics," its manifold modes with which it is intended to in the full noema pertaining to the noetic mental process or to the species of mental process in question. Of course, here again all the distinctions in the noema must also correspond to parallel distinctions in the unmodified Objectivity.

It is then a further undertaking of more precise phenomenological study to discover what is prescribed according to eidetic law precisely by the species, and what is so prescribed by the differentiating particularities, for noemata of changing particularities of a fixed species (e.g., perception). But the restriction holds throughout: in the sphere of essences there is nothing accidental; everything is connected by eidetic relations, thus especially noesis and noema.

§94. Noesis and noema in the realm of judgment

As an example from this sphere of founded essences let us consider the *predicative judgment.* The noema of the judging, i.e., of the concrete judgmental process, is the "judged as judged"; that, however, is nothing else, or at least with respect to its main core, it is nothing else than what we usually call simply *the judgment.*

If the full noema is to be seized upon, the judgment must be taken here in the full noematic concreteness intended to in the concrete judging. What is judged must not be confused with what is judged about. If the judging is based on perceiving or on some other simply "positing" objectivating, the noema of the objectivating goes into the full concretion of the judgment (just as the objectivating noesis becomes an essential component of the concrete judgmental noesis) and takes on certain forms in the judging. That which is objectivated (as objectivated) receives the form of the apophantic subject, or that of the apophantic predicate, or some other such form. Here, for the sake of simplicity, let us disregard the higher stratum pertaining to verbal "expression." These "objects about which," especially the ones which take on <apophantic> subject <-forms> *[Subjektgegenstand]* are the objects judged *about.* The whole which is formed out of them, *the total What which is judged*—and, moreover, taken precisely in the fashion (with the *characterization,* in the *mode of givenness)* in which it is "intended to" in the mental process—makes up the *full noematic correlate,* the *"sense"* (in the *broadest* signification of the word) of the judgmental process. Stated more pregnantly, it is the "sense in the How of its mode of givenness" in so far as this mode of givenness is to be found as a characteristic belonging to it.

In this connection, we must not overlook the phenomenological reduction which requires us to "parenthesize" the making of the judgment if we wish to acquire the *pure* noema of our judgmental process. If we do so, then we have in its phenomenological purity the full concrete essence of the judgmental process or, as we now express it, the *judgment-noesis, taken concretely as an essence,* and the *judgment-noema* belonging to and necessarily united with that noesis, the *"made judgment" as an Eidos,* and it also in its phenomenological purity.

Psychologistic readers will object to all these statements; they are not inclined to distinguish between judging *[Urteilen]* as an empirical mental process and judging *[Urteil]* as an "idea," an essence. For us this distinction has already been thoroughly established. But the reader who accepts it will also be perplexed. For he is required to recognize that this one distinction is by no means sufficient and that it is necessary to fix a number of ideas which lie on two different sides within the essence of judgmental intentionality. It must above all be recognized that here, as in the case of any other intentive mental process, the two sides, noesis and noema, must by essential necessity be distinguished.

Critically it may be remarked here that the concepts of the *"intentive"* and the *"cognitional essence"* which were established in the *Logische Untersuchungen** are indeed correct but are capable of a second interpretation since they can be essentially understood as expressions not only of noetic but also of noematic essences, and that the noematic interpretation, as carried through there one-sidedly in framing the concept of the judgment in pure logic is precisely not the one to be used in framing the judgment-concept of pure logic (i.e., the concept demanded by pure logic as pure mathesis in contrast to the concept of noetic judging demanded by normative logical noetics). The difference between the *making of a judgment* and the *judgment made,* a difference already recognized in ordinary speech, can serve to point out the correct view, namely that to the judgmental mental process there belongs *correlatively* as noema *the* judgment simpliciter.

The latter, then, should be understood as the "judgment" or *proposition in the sense of the word in pure logic*—except that pure logic is interested in the noema, not with respect to its components, but only in so far as it is conceived as exclusively determined by a *narrower* essence, to the more precise definition of which the above-mentioned attempt at a distinction in the *Logische Untersuchungen* pointed the way. If we wish to obtain the full noema of a determinate judgmental process we must, as has already been said, take "the" judgment precisely as it is intended to in just that process; whereas, for formal logic, the identity of "the" judgment extends much further. An evident judgment, *S is p,* and "the same" judgment as a "blind" judgment are noematically different but identical with respect to a core of sense which alone is decisive from the standpoint of formal logic. The difference here is similar to that already mentioned between the noema of a perception and that of a parallel presentation which intends to the same object, with precisely the same set of determinations and with the same characterization (as "certainly existing," "doubtfully existing," or the like). The act-species are different, and there is wide room for phenomenological differences in other respects—but the noematic What is identical. Let us add that the idea of the judgment which has just been characterized and which functions as the fundamental concept in formal logic (that discipline within mathesis universalis pertaining to predicative significations) has as its correlate the noetic idea: "the judgment" in a second sense understood, namely, as any judging whatever, with an eidetic universality determined purely by the form. It is the fundamental concept in the formal noetic theory of correct judging.†

Everything just said is also true for other noetic mental processes; for example, it obviously holds good for all those which are es-

*Cf. op. cit, Vol. II, Part One, "Fifth Investigation," §21, pp. 391f. <[2nd ed., pp. 417f.; English translation pp. 590f.].>

†As for Bolzano's concept of the "judgment in itself" or "the proposition in itself," the exposition in the *Wissenschaftslehre* (Sulzbach, 1837) shows that Bolzano had not made clear to himself the proper sense of his pioneer conception. He never saw that we have here *two* essentially possible interpretations, each of which yields something which might be called "the judgment in itself": the specific essence of the judging process (the *noetic* idea) and the *noematic* idea correlative to the noetic idea. His descriptions and explanations are ambiguous. Given a mathematician's objective interest, he undoubtedly had the noematic concept in mind—though an occasional phrase seems to indicate the contrary (cf. op. cit., Vol. I, p. 95, the approving quotation from Mehmel's *Denklehre <scl. Versuch einer vollständigen analytische Denklehre als Vorphilosophie und im Geiste der Philosophie* (Erlangen, 1803)>). He had it in mind, pre-

sentially akin to judgings as predicative certainties: for the corresponding deemings possible, deemings likely, doubting, also rejectings. Among these the agreement can go so far that, in the noema, a sense-content occurs which is identical throughout and is merely furnished with different "characterizations." *The same* "S is p," as a *noematic core,* can be the *"content"* of a certainty, a deeming possible, a deeming likely, etc. In the noema the "S is p" does not stand alone; rather, as singled out of the noema by thinking, it is something non-selfsufficient; it is intended to with changing characterizations indispensable to the full noema: it is intended to with the characteristic of something "certain," "possible," "probable," "null," or the like—characteristics, to which the modifying inverted commas collectively belong and which, as correlates, are specifically coordinated with the noetic moments of considering-possible, considering-probable, considering-null, and the like.

With this, as we see at the same time, two fundamental concepts of *"judgment-content"* and likewise of likelihood-content, question-content, etc., are separated from one another. Not infrequently logicians use the term judgment-content in such a way that obviously (even though without the so necessary distinction) the noetic or the noematic-logical concept of judgment is meant, the two concepts which we previously characterized. The corresponding pairs of concepts pertaining to likelihoods, questions, doubts, etc., run parallel with them, naturally without ever coinciding with them or with one another. *Here,* however, a second sense of judgment-content results— as a "content" which the judgment <(or the judging)> can have identically *in common* with

a likelihood (or a deeming likely), with a question (or an asking), and with other act-noemas or noeses.

§95. The analogous distinctions in the emotional and volitional spheres.

Analogous statements hold, then, as one can easily see, for the emotional and volitional spheres, for mental processes of liking or disliking, of valuing in any sense, of wishing, deciding, acting. All these are mental processes which contain many and often heterogeneous intentive strata, the noetic and, correspondingly, also the noematic ones.

In that connection, the stratifications, generally speaking, are such that the uppermost strata of the total phenomenon can be removed without the remainder ceasing to be a concretely complete intentive mental process, and, conversely, a concrete mental process can also take on a new noetic total stratum: as when a non-selfsufficient moment of "valuing" is stratified on a concrete process of simply objectivating or, on the other hand, is removed again.

If, in this manner, a perceiving, phantasying, judging, or the like, founds a stratum of valuing which overlays it completely, we have *different noemata or senses* in the *stratified whole* which is called a concrete mental process of valuing by being designated according to the highest level within it. The perceived as perceived specifically belongs as sense to the perceiving, but it is also included in the sense of the concrete valuing, founding the *latters's* sense. We must distinguish accordingly: the objects, the physical things, the qualities, the predicatively formed affair-complexes,

cisely as the arithmetician has number in mind—being interested in operations with numbers but not in the phenomenological problem of the relationship between number and consciousness of number. Here in the sphere of logic, as well as everywhere else, phenomenology was something *quite alien* to the great logician. That cannot fail to be clear to anyone who has actually studied Bolzano's *Wissenschaftslehre* (which has unfortunately become so scarce) and who, in addition to that, is not inclined to confuse every working out of fundamental eidetic concepts—the phenomenologically naive production—with a phenomenological production. If one did this, then, in the interest of consistency one would have to say that every mathematician who creates concepts, e.g., Georg Cantor, as the genius who framed the fundamental concepts of the theory of sets, is a phenomenologist, including the unknown creator of the fundamental geometrical concepts in hoary antiquity.

which are present as valued in the valuing, or else the corresponding noemata of the objectivatings, the judgings, or the like, which found the value-consciousness; on the other hand, the value-objects themselves and the predicatively formed value-complexes themselves, or else the noematic modifications corresponding to them; and then, universally, the complete noemata belonging to the concrete value-consciousness.

By way of explanation let us say first of all that, for the sake of greater distinctness, we do well (here and in all analogous cases) to introduce distinctive relative terms in order to keep sharply separate valuable object and value-object, valuable predicatively formed affair-complex and predicatively formed value-complexes, valuable property and value-property (a term having itself two senses). We shall speak of the mere "thing" which is valuable, which has a value-characteristic, which has *value-quality;* in contradistinction, we speak of *concrete value* itself or the *value-Objectiveness [Wertobjektität]*. Likewise we shall speak of the *mere predicatively formed affair-complex* or the *mere lay of things [Sachlage]* and the *predicatively formed value-complex* or the *lay of values [Wertlage]*, namely where the valuing has a consciousness of a predicatively formed affair-complex as its founding substratum. The value-Objectiveness involves its mere materially determinate thing *[Sache]*; it introduces, as a new Objective stratum, the *value-quality*. The predicatively formed value-complex contains the mere predicatively formed affair-complex belonging to it; in like manner the value-property contains the materially determinate thing-property and, in addition the value-quality.

Here too one must distinguish between the value-Objectiveness simpliciter and the *value-Objectiveness in inverted commas* which is included in the *noema*. Just as the perceived as perceived stands over against the perceiving in a way excluding the question of whether the perceived truly exists, so the valued as valued stands over against the valuing, and likewise in a way excluding the question of the being of the value (the being of the valued thing

and the latter's being truly a value). One must exclude all actional positings in order to seize upon the noema. Moreover, careful attention must be paid to the fact that the *full* "sense" of the valuing includes its What in which it is intended to in the mental process of valuing in question, and that the value-Objectiveness in inverted commas is not, by itself, the full noema.

In like manner the distinctions made here can be made in the *volitional sphere*.

On one side we have the *deciding* which we effect together with the mental processes which it demands as a substratum, and which, when it is taken in its concreteness, it includes. To it belong many different noetic moments. Volitional positings are based on valuing positings, physical-thing positings, and the like. On the other side we find the *decision* as a peculiar kind of Objectiveness specifically belonging to the province of volition; and it is an Objectiveness obviously founded on other such noematic Objectivenesses. If, as phenomenologists, we exclude all our positings, the volitional phenomenon, as a phenomenologically pure intentive mental process, still retains its *"willed as willed,"* as a *noema belonging peculiarly to the willing: the "volition-meaning,"* precisely as it is a "meaning" in this willing (in the full essence <of the willing>) and with everything being willed and "aimed at."

We said, "the meaning." This word suggests itself in all these contexts, just as do the words "sense" and "signification." To the *meaning [Meinen]* or intending to *[Vermeinen]*, then, corresponds the meant *[Meinung]*; to *signifying*, the *signification*. But the greatest precaution is called for with respect to these words because they all have been infected with so many equivocations by transference, not least of all by equivocations which arise from slipping from one to another of the correlative strata which we are trying to separate with scientific rigor. The scope of our present observations is the broadest extension of the essential genus, "intentive mental process." "Meaning," on the other hand, is normally spoken of in referring to narrower spheres which, however, function as substrata for other phenomena in the wider sphere. As technical terms, therefore, this word and cognate expressions should be used only with reference to those narrower spheres. In referring to the universalities involved, we are undoubtedly better served by our new terms and the attached analyses of examples.

The Question of Levels*

§97. The hyletic and noetic moments as really inherent moments, the noematic moments as really non-inherent moments, of mental processes

When introducing the distinction between the noetic and the noematic in the last chapter, we used the expressions, *analysis of the really inherent* and *intentional analysis*. Let us start with that. A phenomenologically pure mental process has its really inherent components. For the sake of simplicity, let us restrict ourselves to noetic mental processes of the lowest level, namely to those which are not complicated in their intentionality by a variety of noetic strata built one upon another such as we found to be the case in acts of thinking and in emotional and volitional acts.

A sensuous perception may possibly serve as an example: the tree-perception simpliciter which we have while looking out into the garden when, in a unity of consciousness, we are looking at that tree over there which is now motionless and then appears blown by the wind, and which is also presented in greatly differing modes of appearance as we, during our continuing observation, change our spatial position relative to the tree—perhaps we go to the window or simply alter the position of our head or eyes, while perhaps at the same time relaxing and concentrating our <visual> accommodation, etc. In this way the unity of *one* perception can include a great multiplicity of modifications which we, as observers in the natural attitude, sometimes ascribe to the actual objects as *its* changes, sometimes to a real and

actual relationship to our real psychophysical subjectivity and sometimes, finally, to the latter itself. But now we must describe what is left of that as a phenomenological residuum if we reduce it to its "pure immanence" and *what therefore may* or may not *hold good for the really inherent component of the pure mental process*. And here it must be made perfectly clear that, more particularly, there belongs to the essence of the mental process of perception in itself the "perceived tree as perceived," or the full noema, which is not touched by excluding the actuality of the tree and that of the whole world; on the other hand, however, this *noema*, with its "tree" in inverted commas, *is no more contained inherently than is the tree which belongs to actuality.*

What do we find really inherent in <the perception> as pure mental process, contained in it as the parts, the pieces and the moments not divisible into pieces, of a whole? We have, on occasion, distinguished such genuine really inherent component parts by the names *stuff-*component parts and *noetic* component parts. Let us contrast them with the noematic components.

The color of the tree trunk, pure as the color of which we are perceptually conscious, is precisely the "same" as the one which, before the phenomenological reduction, we took to be the color of the actual tree (at least as "natural" human beings and prior to intervention of information provided by physics). Now, *this color,* put into parenthesis, belongs to the noema. But it does not belong to the mental process of perception as a really inherent component piece, although we can also find in it "something like color": namely, the "sensed color," that hyletic moment of the concrete mental process by which the noematic, or "objective," color is "adumbrated."

Accordingly, however, one and the same noematic color which is intended to throughout the continuous unity of changeable perceptual consciousness *as* an identical and, in itself, unchanged color, is being adumbrated

Ideas I, pp. 236–243 (Sections 97–98).

by a continuous multiplicity of sensed colors. We see a tree unchanged with respect to color —its color, the color of the tree—while the positions of the eyes <and our> relative orientations are changing and our regard is incessantly moving over the trunk and branches, and while, at the same time, we come closer and thus, in various ways, bring the mental process of perception into a flow. Let us reflect on sensations, on adumbrations: we then seize upon them as evident data and, in perfect evidence, changing the focus and direction of attention, we can also relate them and the corresponding objective moments, cognize them as corresponding and, in so doing, see at once that, e.g., the adumbrative colors pertaining to any fixed physical-thing color are related to it as a continuous "multiplicity" is related to a "unity."

Effecting the phenomenological reduction, we even acquire the generical eidetic insight that the object, tree, *can only* appear *at all* in a perception as *Objectively* determined in the mode in which it does appear in the perception if the hyletic moments (or, in the case of a continuous series of perceptions, if the continuous hyletic changes) are just those and no others. This therefore implies that any changes of the hyletic content of the perception, if it does not quite do away with perceptual consciousness, must at least result in what appears becoming objectively "other," whether in itself or in the orientation in which it is appearing, or the like.

It is also absolutely indubitable, then, that here "unity" and "multiplicity" belong to *wholly different dimensions* and, more particularly, that *everything hyletic* belongs in the concrete mental process as a *really inherent* component, whereas, in contrast, what is "presented," "adumbrated," in it as multiplicity belongs in the *noema.*

But the stuffs, we said earlier, are "animated" by noetic moments; they undergo (while the Ego is turned, not to them, but to the object) "construings," "sense-bestowals," which, in reflections, we seize upon precisely in and along with the stuffs. In view of this it immediately follows that not only the hyletic moments (the sensed colors, sounds, etc.), but also the animating construals—thus *both together:* the *appearing* of the color, the sound and thus of any quality whatever of the object—belong to the "really inherent" composition of the mental process.

Now, the following is universally true: In itself the perception is a perception of *its* object; and to every component which is singled out in the object by "objectively" directed description there corresponds a really inherent component of the perception; but, note well, only in so far as the description faithfully conforms to the object *as it "is there" in that* perception itself. Moreover, we can designate all those noetic components only by appealing to the noematic Object and its moments: thus saying, for example, consciousness, more particularly, perceptual consciousness, *of* a tree trunk, of the color of the trunk, etc.

On the other hand, our considerations have shown indeed that the really inherent unity within the mental process of hyletic and noetic component pieces is totally different from the <unity> of noematic component pieces "intended to" in the noesis; and it is also different from the unity which unites all those really inherent components in the mental process with that whereof, as a noema, we are conscious in and through them. That which is *"transcendentally constituted"* "on the ground of" the material *[stofflich]* mental processes "by" the noetic functions is, to be sure, something "given"; and in pure intuition we faithfully describe the mental process and its noematic object intended to *[sein noematisch Bewußtes],* it is something *evidently* given; but it belongs to the mental process in a sense entirely different from the sense in which the really inherent and therefore proper constituents belong to the mental process.

The characterization of the phenomenological reduction and, likewise, of the pure sphere of mental processes as "transcendental" rests precisely on the fact that we discover in this reduction an absolute sphere of stuffs and noetic forms whose determinately structured combinations possess, *according to immanental eidetic necessity,* the marvelous consciousness of something determinate and determinable, given thus and so, which is something over against consciousness itself, something fundamentally other, non-really inherent *[Irreelles]*, transcendent; <the characterization of mental processes as "transcendental" further rests on the fact> that this is the primal source in which is found the only conceivable solution of those deepest problems of cognition concerning the essence and possibility of an objectively valid knowledge of something transcendent. "Transcendental" reduction exercises the ἐποχή with respect to actuality: but what it retains of <actuality> includes the noemas with the noematic unity included within them themselves and, accordingly, the mode in which something real is intended to and, in particular, given in consciousness itself. The knowledge that everywhere it is a matter of *eidetic,* therefore unconditioned, necessary concatenations opens up a great field of research into the eidetic relations between the noetic and the noematic, between the mental process of consciousness and the correlate of consciousness. The latter term, however, includes: consciousness of objectivity as consciousness of objectivity and, at the same time, the forms of the noematic How of meantness of givenness. Within the domain from which we have taken our example, there arises, first of all, the universal evidence that perception is not an empty presentive having of the object, but that instead it belongs ("a priori") to the essence proper of perception to have "its" object, and to have it as the unity of a *certain* noematic composition which is always a different, yet always eidetically predelineated composition in the case of other perceptions of "the same" object; or that it is of the essence of the object in question, objectively determined thus and so, to be and only to be able to be a noematic object precisely in perceptions of such a descriptive sort, etc.

§98. The mode of being of the noema. Theory of forms of noeses. Theory of forms of noemata

Important supplementations are still, however, necessary. First of all, it must be careful-

ly noted that any transition from a phenomenon into the reflection which itself is an analysis of the really inherent, or into the quite differently articulated <reflection> which dissects its noema, generates new phenomena, and that we would fall into error were we to confuse the new phenomena—which, in a certain way, are recastings of the old—with the old phenomena, and were we to impute to the old what really inherently or noematically is included in the <new>. Thus it is not meant, e.g., that the material contents, let us say the adumbrative color-contents, are present in the perceptual mental process in just the same way in which they are present in the mental process of analyzing. To mention only one <difference,> in the former they were contained as really inherent moments, but they were not perceived therein, not seized upon as objects. But in the analyzing mental process they are objects, targets of noetic functions which were not present before. Although these stuffs are still laden with their presentive functions, even these have undergone essential changes (to be sure, of other dimensions). That will be discussed later. Obviously, this difference has an essential importance for the phenomenological method.

Following this remark let us turn our attention to the following points belonging to our particular theme. In the first place, every mental process is so structured that there exists the essential possibility of turning one's regard to it and its really inherent components and, likewise, in the opposite direction to the noema, perchance to the seen tree as seen. That which is given in this focusing of regard is now, more particularly, stated logically, an object, but utterly *non-selfsufficient.* Its *esse* consists exclusively of its *"percipi"*— except that this proposition does not have the Berkeleyian sense because here the esse does not include the percipi as a really inherent component piece.

This is naturally transferred to the eidetic mode of consideration: the Eidos of the noema points to the Eidos of the noetic consciousness; both belong together *eidetically.* The intentive as intentive *[Intentionale als solches]* is what it is as the intentiveness *[Intentionales]* belonging to consciousness *structured* thus and so, consciousness which is consciousness of it.

In spite of this non-selfsufficiency the noema allows for being considered by itself, compared with other noemas, explored with respect to its possible transformations, etc. One can project a *theory of the universal and pure forms of noemata* which would have as its contrasting *correlate* a *theory* of the universal and no less pure *forms of concrete noetic mental processes* with their *hyletic* and *specifically noetic* components.

Naturally these two theories would *by no means* be related as, so to speak, mutual *reflections;* nor would the one be transformed into the other by a mere change of sign, let us say, by substituting "consciousness of N" for each noema N. That already follows from what we explained before in connection with the way in which unitary qualities belong together in the physical thing—*noema* with their hyletic adumbration-multiplicities contained in possible perceptions of physical things.

It would now seem as though the same would also be true with respect to the specifically noetic moments. More particularly, one can refer to those moments which bring it about that a complex multiplicity of hyletic Data, e.g., color-Data, etc., acquire the function of a manifold adumbration of one and the same objective physical thing. Indeed, it only need be recalled that in the stuffs themselves, by virtue of their own essence, the relation to the Objective unity is not unambiguously predelineated; the same material complex, instead, can undergo a diversity of mutually discrete and shifting construings by virtue of which *different* objectivities are intended to. Is it not therefore already clear that *essential differences* lie *in the animating construings themselves* as moments of mental processes, and which are differentiated along with the attendant adumbrations and by virtue of the animation of which they constitute "sense"? One may therefore draw the following conclusion: A *parallelism* between noesis and noema is indeed the case, but it is such that one must describe the formations *on both sides* and in their essentially mutual correspondence. The noematic is the field of unities, the noetic is the field of "constituting" multiplicities. The consciousness which unites the manifold "functionally" and, at the same time, constitutes unity *never* in fact shows an identity even where an identity of the "object" is given in the noematic correlate. Where, for example, different segments of an enduring perceiving which is constituting a physical-thing unity shows something identical, the one tree unchanging according to the sense of this perceiving—given now in this, then in that orientation, now from the front, now from the back, at first indistinctly and indeterminately, then distinctly and determinately with respect to the properties of one or another place seized upon visually—: there the object found in the noema is intended to as an identical object in the literal sense, but the consciousness of it is a non-identical, only combined, continuously united consciousness in the different segments of its immanental duration.

No matter to what extent these statements contain something right, the conclusions drawn are still not wholly correct; indeed, the greatest caution is required in dealing with these difficult questions. The parallelisms obtaining here—and there are *many* which are only too easily confused with one another—involve great difficulties which are still in need of clarification. We must carefully keep in view the difference between concrete noetic mental processes, the mental processes together with their hyletic moments, and the pure noeses as mere complexes of noetic moments. Again, we must preserve the distinction between the full noema and, e.g., in the case of perception, the "appearing object as appearing." If we take this "object" and all its objective "predicates" —the noematic modifications of the predicates of the perceived physical thing, posited in normal perception simply as actual predicates—then this object and these predicates are indeed unities in contradistinction to multiplicities of constituting mental processes of consciousness (concrete noeses). But they are also unities of *noematic* multiplicities. We recognize that as soon as we take into consideration the noematic characterizations of the noematic "object" (and its "predicates"), characterizations which until now we have grossly neglected. Thus it is certain, for instance, that the appearing color is a unity in contradistinction to *noetic* multiplicities and, specifically, multiplicities of noetic construing-characteristics. But more precise investigations reveal that changes in these characteristics correspond to *noematic* parallels—if not in the "color itself," which continues to appear there, then at least in their changing "modes of givenness," e.g., in their appearing "orientation with respect to me." In this way, then noetic "characterizations" are mirrored in the noematic ones.

Expressive Acts*

§124. *The noetic-noematic stratum of "Logos." Signifying and signification*

Interwoven with all the acts considered before are the expressive act-strata, which are "logical" in the specific sense, in which the parallelism between noesis and noema is to be made evident no less than in the other acts. The universal and unavoidable ambiguity of locutions conditioned by this parallelism, and shown to be at work wherever the relevant relationships are expressed in language, is, naturally, also found in the terms expression and signification. The ambiguity is dangerous only as long as one does not recognize it as dangerous, or else has not separated the parallel structures. But if that occurs, care must be taken so that there can be no doubt as to which of the structures the terms ought to be referred.

We begin with the familiar distinction between the sensuous, so to speak, the corporeal side of the expression, and its non-sensuous

or "mental" side. We need not enter into a closer examination of the first side; likewise, we need not consider the manner of unifying both sides. Obviously they too designate headings for not unimportant phenomenological problems.

We shall restrict our regard exclusively to "signifying" and "signification." Originally, these words concerned only the linguistic sphere, that of "expressing." But one can scarcely avoid and, at the same time, take an important cognitive step, extending the signification of these words and suitably modifying them so that they can find application of a certain kind to the whole noetic-noematic sphere: thus application to all acts, be they now combined with expressive acts or not.†
Thus we have continued to speak of "sense" in the case of all intentive mental processes— a word which is used in general as equivalent to "signification." For the sake of distinctness we shall prefer the term *signification* for the old concept and, in particular, in the complex locution of *"logical"* or *"expressive" signification.* We shall continue to use the word *sense* as before in the most all-inclusive range.

For example: an object is present to perception with a determined sense, posited monothetically in determined fullness. As is our normal custom after first seizing upon something perceptually, we effect an explicating of the given and a relational positing which unifies the parts or moments singled out—perhaps according to the schema, "This is white." This process does not require the minimum of "expression," nor of expression in the sense of verbal sound, nor of anything like a verbal signifying, the latter also being capable of being present independently of the verbal sound (as when this would be "forgotten"). But if we have *"thought"* or *asserted,* "This is white," then a new stratum is co-present, unified with the purely perceptually "meant as meant." In

*Ideas I, pp. 294–297 (Section 124).
†In this respect, cf. the *Philosophie der Arithmetik,* pp. 28f. [*Husserliana,* XII, pp. 3lf.], where the distinction is already made between the "psychological description of a phenomenon" and the "declaration of its signification," and where we speak of a "logical" in contrast to the psychological "content."

this fashion anything remembered as remembered, anything phantasied as phantasied, is also explicatable and expressable. Anything "meant as meant," anything meant in the noematic sense (and, more particularly, as the noematic core) pertaining to any act, no matter which, is *expressable by means* of *"significations."* Quite universally we may say:

Logical signification is an expression.

The verbal sound can only be called an expression because the signification belonging to it expresses; expressing inheres in it originaliter. "Expression" is a distinctive form which allows for adapting to every "sense" (to the noematic "core") and raises it to the realm of "Logos," of the *conceptual* and, on that account, the *"universal."*

As a consequence, the last words are understood in a quite determinate signification to be separated from other significations of these words. Universally, what has just been indicated designates a major theme for phenomenological analysis which is fundamental for eidetically clarifying logical thinking and its correlates. In the noetic respect, a particular act-stratum should be designated under the heading of "expressing" to which, in their own peculiar way, all other acts are to conform and with which they are to fuse in a distinctive manner so that every noematic act-sense, and consequently the relationship to objectivity lying in it, is "conceptually" stamped on the noematic correlate of the expressing. An appertinent intuitional medium is present which, according to its essence, has the distinction, so to speak, of mirroring every other intentionality according to form and content, depicturing it in its own colors and hence imprinting on it its own form of "conceptuality." To be sure, these locutions of mirroring or depicturing imposed upon us are to be taken with care since their metaphorical use can easily lead to error.

Extraordinarily difficult problems are related to the phenomena subsumed under the headings of "signifying" and "signification."* Because every science is objectivated in the specifically "logical" medium, in that of expression, in accord with its theoretical content and with everything which is "doctrine" in it (theorem, proof, theory), the problems of expression and signification are the most immediate for philosophers and psychologists guided by universal logical interests; and they are, therefore, the first to require a phenomenological inquiry into essence as soon as one seriously comes to seek out their ground.† From there, on that basis, one is led to the question of how the "expressing" of the "expressed" is to be understood, how expressive mental processes are related to non-expressive ones, and what the latter undergo in supervening expressings: one finds himself referred to their "intentionality," to the "sense immanent" in them, to the "matter" and "quality" (i.e., the act-characteristic of the positing); <one is referred to> the difference between these senses, to the essential moments which lie in the pre-expressed, and to the signification of the expressive phenomenon itself and its own moments; and so forth. In many ways, one still sees in the current literature how little justice is done to the major problems indicated here with respect to their full and profound sense.

Apart from the fact that it confers expression precisely on all other intentionalities, the stratum of expression—and this makes up its own peculiarity—is not productive. Or, if one wishes: *its productivity, its noematic production, is exhausted in the expressing* and with the *form of the conceptual* which is introduced with <the expression>.

As a consequence, the expressive stratum, with respect to the posited characteristic, is perfectly identical in essence with the stratum undergoing the expression, and in the coincidence takes up its essence into itself to such

---

*As can be seen from the second volume of the *Logische Untersuchungen* where they form a major theme.

†In fact, this was the way in which the *Logische Untersuchungen* endeavored to penetrate into phenomenology. A second way, starting from the opposite side, namely from the side of experience and sensuous givenness followed by the author since the beginning of the 1890s, was not fully expressed in that work.

an extent that we call the expressive objectivating just objectivating itself, the expressive believing, <expressive> deeming likely, <expressive> doubting themselves, and as a whole, just believing, deeming likely, doubting; similarly, we call the expressive wishing or willing just wishing or willing. It is evident that even the distinction between positionality and neutrality passes over into the expressive, and we have already considered it above. The *expressive stratum can have no other qualified posited or neutral position than the stratum subject to the expression,* and in the coincidence we find not two positions which are to be separated but *only one position.*

The full clarification of the structures belonging here raises considerable difficulties. Already it is not easy to recognize that, after abstraction from the sensuous verbal sounds, a stratification of the kind we presuppose here is actually present, thus in every case—even in that of a thinking which is still quite unclear, empty, merely verbal—a stratum of expressive signifying and a substratum of the expressed; nor is it easy to understand the essential connections of these stratifications. For not too much should be expected of the metaphor stratification; expression is not something like a coat of varnish, or like a piece of clothing covering it over; it is a mental formation exercising new intentive functions on the intentive substratum and which, correlatively, is subjected to the intentive functions of the <substratum>. What this new metaphor signifies for its part must be studied in the phenomena themselves and in all their essential modifications. Of particular importance is the understanding of the different sorts of "universality" which make their appearance there: on the one side, those which belong to each expression and moment of expression, also to the non-selfsufficient "is," "not," "and," "if," and so forth; on the other side, the universality of "universal names" such as "human being" in contrast to proper names such as "Bruno"; again, those which belong to an essence which,

in itself, is syntactically formless in comparison to the different universalities of signification just touched upon.

Noema and Object*

§128. Introduction

The phenomenological excursions of the last chapter have led us into almost all spheres of intentionality. Guided by the radical point of view of the distinction between analysis of the really inherent and intentional analysis, between noetic and noematic analysis, we encountered in all cases structures which always and again became newly ramified. In the case of this distinction, we can no longer avoid the insight that it is indeed a matter of a fundamental structure pervading all intentional structures which must, therefore, determine a governing *Leitmotiv* of phenomenological methods and the course of all inquiries into problems of intentionality.

With this distinction it is clear at the same time that there becomes salient a distinction between two realms of being which are radically opposed and yet essentially related to one another. We emphasized earlier that consciousness taken universally must be accepted as a proper region of being. We recognized then, however, that eidetic description of consciousness leads back to that of what is intended to in it, that the correlate of consciousness is inseparable from consciousness and yet is not really inherent in it. The noematic became distinguished as an *objectivity* belonging to consciousness and yet *specifically peculiar.* In that connection, we notice that while objects simpliciter (understood in the unmodified sense) stand under fundamentally different highest genera, all object-senses and all noemas taken completely, no matter how different they may be otherwise, are of essential necessity of one single highest genus. It then also obtains, however, that the essences, Noema and Noesis, are

Ideas I, pp. 307–318 (Sections 128–133).

inseparable from one another: Infima species on the noematic side eidetically point back to infima species on the noetic side. That becomes extended naturally to all formations of genus and species.

Cognitions of the essential two-sidedness of intentionality, according to noesis and noema, have the consequence that a systematic phenomenology is not allowed to direct its aim one-sidedly at an analysis of what is really inherent in mental processes and specifically of intentive mental processes. The temptation to do so is, however, very great at the beginning because the historical and natural course from psychology to phenomenology brings with it that one understands the study of what is immanent in pure mental processes, the study of their own essence, as without question a study of their really inherent components.* In truth there become opened up in respect of both sides great provinces of eidetic research which are continually related to one another and which yet, as comes to light, are separated with respect to broad extents. In great measure what one has held to be act-analysis, noetic analysis, is gained entirely from the direction of regard to the "meant as meant," and thus it was noematic structures which one described in that analysis.

In our next considerations it will be our purpose to direct our attention to the universal structure of the noema from a point of view which, up to now, has often been mentioned but was still not the guiding one for noematic analysis: *The phenomenological problem of the relation of consciousness to an objectivity* has primarily its noematic side. The noema in itself has an objective relation and, more particularly, by virtue of its own "sense." If we ask, then, how the consciousness-"sense" has access to the "object" which belongs to it and can be "the same" in manifold acts of very different content, how we see this in the sense, then new structures emerge the extraordinary significance of which is evident. For, pro-

gressing in this direction and, on the other side, reflecting on the parallel noeses, we finally confront the question of what the "claim" of consciousness actually to "relate" to something objective, to be "well-founded," properly signifies, of how "valid" and "invalid" objective relations become phenomenologically clarified according to noesis and noema: and with that we confront the great *problems of reason,* the clarification of which within the realm of phenomenology, the formulation of which as *phenomenological* problems, will become our aim in this <fourth> part of <the First Book>.

§129. "Content" and "object"; the content as "sense"

In our previous analyses a universal noematic structure played its continuous role, designated by the separation of a certain *noematic "core"* from the changing *"characteristics"* belonging to it <and> with which the noematic concretion appears involved in the flow of different sorts of modifications. This core has not yet received its scientific due. It was intuitionally, unitarily, and clearly salient so that we could refer to it in general. Now the time has come to consider it more closely and place it at the center of phenomenological analysis. As soon as one does that, universally significant differences running throughout all act-species emerge which are guiding for great groups of investigations.

We begin with the usual equivocal verbal reference to the content of consciousness. As content we take the "sense," of which we say that in or through it consciousness relates to something objective as "its" something objective. So to speak, as title and aim of our discussions we take the propositions:

Each noema has a *"content,"* that is to say, its "sense," and is related through it to "its" *object.*

In recent times one often hears it praised as

---

*That is still the focus of the *Logische Untersuchungen.* However great the extent to which the nature of the matters themselves compels the carrying out of noematic analyses, the noemas are nevertheless regarded more as indices for the parallel noetic structures; the essential parallelism of the two structures has not yet attained clarity there.

a great advance, that now at last the foundation-laying differentiation among act, content, and object has been attained. The three words in this juxtaposition have become nothing short of slogans, particularly since Twardowski's fine treatise.* Yet, however great and doubtless the service of this author in having acutely discussed certain generally ordinary confusions and made their error evident, it must still be said that in the clarification of the relevant conceptual essence he did not get considerably beyond what was well-known to the philosophers of earlier generations (despite their incautious confusions). This is not, perchance, to be charged to him as a fault. A radical advance was just not at all possible before a systematic phenomenology of consciousness. With phenomenologically unclarified concepts such as "act," "content," "object" of the "objectivatings," nothing is of help to us. What is there which cannot be called *"act"* and especially which cannot be called "content of an objectivating," and an "objectivating"? And what can be called so must itself be cognized scientifically.

In this respect a first and, as it would appear to me, necessary step was attempted by means of the phenomenological distinguishing of "matter" and "quality" by means of the idea of the "intentional essence" in its distinction from the "cognitional essence." The one-sidedness of the noetic direction of regard in which these differentiations were made and meant becomes easily overcome by taking into consideration the noematic parallels. We can therefore understand the concepts as noematic; the "quality" (judgment-quality, wish-quality, and so forth) is nothing else than that which we have dealt with up to now as "posited" characteristic *["Setzungs" Charakter, "thetischen" Charakter]* in the broadest sense. The expression, originating from contemporary psychology (Brentano's), appears to me now hardly suitable; each specifically peculiar position

has its quality but it is not itself to be designated as quality. Obviously now the "matter," which is, in the particular case, the "what" which receives the posited characteristic, the "quality," corresponds to the "noematic core."

The task is now to systematically develop this beginning, to clarify it more deeply, to analyze these concepts further and to carry them through in all noetic-noematic provinces. Each actually successful advance in this direction must be of exceptional significance for phenomenology. It is indeed a question, not of side issues, but of essential moments belonging to the central structure of every intentive mental process.

In order to approach matters more closely, let us begin with the following deliberation.

The intentive mental process, so one is accustomed to say, has *"relation to something objective"*; but one also says that it is *"consciousness of something,"* for example, a blossoming apple tree, the one here in this garden. To begin with, we shall not hold it to be necessary, in the light of such examples, to discriminate the two manners of speaking. If we recall the preceding analyses, we find the full noesis related to the full noema as its intentional and full What. It is then clear, however, that this relation cannot be the one meant in speaking of the relation of consciousness to its intentional objective something; for to each noetic moment, especially to each positing noetic one, there corresponds a moment in the noema and, in the latter, there is set apart from the complex posited characteristics the noematic core characterized by them. If we recall, furthermore, the "regard-to" which, under circumstances, goes through the noesis (which goes through the actional cogito) and which converts the specifically positing moments into rays of positing actionality of the Ego, and if we heed precisely how this Ego now with them "directs" itself to something objective as seizing upon being, as deeming likely, as wishing,

---

*K. Twardowski, *Zur Lehre von Inhalt und Gegenstand der Vorstellungen [On the Theory of the Content and the Object of Objectivatings]* (Vienna, 1894).

how its regard goes through the noematic core —we then become attentive to the fact that, with the statements about the relation (and specifically the direction) of consciousness to its objective something, we are referred to an *innermost* moment of the noema. It is not the just designated core itself but rather something else which, so to speak, makes up the necessary central point of the core and functions as "bearer" for noematic peculiarities specifically belonging to the core, that is to say, the noematically modified properties of the "meant as meant."

As soon as we go into it more precisely we are immediately cognitively aware that indeed the distinction between "content" and "object" is to be made not only for the "consciousness," for the intentive mental process, but also for the *noema taken in itself.* Thus the noema too is related to an object and possesses a "content" by "means" of which it relates to the object; in which case the object is the same as that of the noesis; as then the "parallelism" again completely confirms itself.

§130. *Delimitation of the essence, "noematic sense"*

Let us bring these remarkable structures closer to us. We simplify the deliberation in such a way that we leave the attentional modifications out of consideration; we restrict ourselves further to positing acts in the positions of which we live, perhaps, according to the sequence of levels of the founding—living sometimes in the one, sometimes in the other partial position while the others are, it is true, in effect but in a secondary function. That our analyses do not suffer in the least with respect to the universality of their validity by such simplifications is to be made evident subsequently and without further ado. We are concerned precisely with an essence which is insensitive to such modifications.

If we then put ourselves into a living cogito, it has, according to its essence and in a pre-eminent sense a "direction" to something objective. In other words, there belongs to its

noema "something objective"—in inverted commas—with a certain noematic composition which becomes explicated in a description of determinate delimitation, that is to say, in such a description which, as a *description of the "meant objective something, as it is meant," avoids all "subjective" expressions.* There formal-ontological expressions are applied, such as "object," "determination," <and> "predicatively formed affair-complex"; material-ontological expressions, such as "physical thing," "bodily figure" *["Figur"],* <and> "cause"; determinations with a material content, such as "rough," "hard," <and> "colored"—all have their inverted commas, accordingly the noematic-modified sense. *Excluded,* in contrast, for the description of this meant objective something as meant are such expressions as "perceptual," "memorial," "clearly intuited," "conceptual," and "given"—they belong to another dimension of descriptions, not to the objective something *which* is an object of consciousness, but to the *mode in which it is an object of consciousness.* In contrast, in the case of an appearing physical thing-Object, it would again fall in the bounds of the description to say: a "front side" is thus and so *determined* with respect to color, shape, etc., its "rear side" has "a color" but a "not further determined" one; the appearing physical thing-Object is, in these and those respects, altogether *"undetermined"* as to whether it is thus or so.

That is true not only in the case of objects belonging to Nature but quite universally; for example, in the case of objects with value. To their description belongs that of the meant "mere thing" and, in addition, the statement of the "value," as when we say of the appearing tree, "according to the sense" of our valuing-meaning <of it>, it is covered with "delightfully" scented blossoms. Moreover, the value predicates too have their inverted commas; they are predicates, not of a valuable object *[eines Wertes]* simpliciter, but of a value noema.

With this, obviously, a quite *fixed content in each noema* is delimited. Each consciousness has its *What* and each means "its" objective something; it is evident that, in the case of each consciousness, we must, essentially speaking, be able to make such a noematic description of <"its" objective something>, "precisely as it is meant"; we acquire by explication and conceptual comprehension a closed set of formal or material, materially determined or "undetermined" ("emptily" meant) *"predicates"* and these in their *modified signification* determine that *"content"* of the object-core of the noema which is spoken of.

§131. The "Object," the "determinable X in the noematic sense"

The predicates are, however, predicates of *"something,"* and this "something" also belongs, and obviously inseparably, to the core in question: it is the central point of unity of which we spoke above. It is the central point of connection or the "bearer" of the predicates, but in no way is it a unity of them in the sense in which any complex, any combination, of the predicates would be called a unity. It is necessarily to be distinguished from them, although not to be placed alongside and separated from them; just as, conversely, they are *its* predicates: unthinkable without it, yet distinguishable from it. We say that the intentional Object is continuously intended to in the continuous or synthetical course of consciousness but again and again "presents" itself "differently"; it is *"the same";* it is only given in other predicates with a different determination-content; "it" shows itself only from different sides, whereby the predicates which remained undetermined would have become more closely determined; or "the" Object has remained unchanged in this stretch of givenness, now however "it," the identical, becomes altered, it increases in beauty through this alteration, it loses utility-value, and so forth. If this is always understood as *noematic description* of the currently meant as meant and if this description, as is possible at any time, is made in pure adequation, then the identical intentional "object" becomes evidently distinguished from the changing and alterable "predicates." It becomes separated as central noematic moment: the *"ob-*

ject" ["Gegenstand"], the *"Object" ["Objekt"],* the *"Identical,"* the "determinable subject of its possible predicates"—*the pure X in abstraction from all predicates*—and it becomes separated *from* these predicates or, more precisely, from the predicate-noemas.

With the *one* Object we coordinate multiple modes of consciousness, acts, correlatively act-noemas. Obviously this is nothing accidental; no <Object> is conceivable without there also being conceivable multiple intentive mental processes, connected in continuous or in properly synthetical (polythetical) unity—processes in which "it," the Object, is intended to as an identical object and yet in a noetically different mode: such that the characterized core is a changeable one and the "object," the pure subject of the predicating, is precisely an identical one. It is clear that we can regard each partial extent of the immanental duration of an act as an "act" and the total act as a certain harmonious unity of the continuously combined acts. We can say then: several act-noemata have here, throughout, *different cores,* yet in such a manner that, in spite of this, they are *joined together to make a unity of identity,* to make a unity in which the "something," the determinable which inheres in each core, is intended to as an identical "something."

In just the same manner, however, *separate* acts, like, for example, two perceptions or a perception and a memory, can join together to make a "harmonious" unity and by virtue of the specific character of this union, which is obviously not alien to the essence of the acts joined together, there is consciousness of the possibly at one time so and at another time otherwise determined something of the at first *separated cores* as the same something or as harmoniously the same "object."

As a consequence, therefore, there is inherent in each noema a pure object-something as a point of unity and, at the same time, we see how in a noematic respect two sorts of object-concepts are to be distinguished: this pure point of unity, this *noematic "object simpliciter,"* and the *"object in the How of its determinations"*—including undeterminednesses which for the time being "remain open" and, in this mode, are co-meant. This "How," moreover, is to be taken precisely as that which the particular act prescribes, as which it consequently belongs actually to the noema <of the act>. The *"sense,"* of which we speak repeatedly, is this noematic *"Object in the How,"* with all that which the *description characterized above* is able to find evidently in it and to express conceptually.

Let it be noted that now we cautiously said "sense," not "core." For it will turn out that, in order to gain the actual, concretely complete core of the noema, we must take into account yet another dimension of differences which finds no expression in the characterized description <but> which defines the sense for us. If at first we keep here purely to that which this <description> comprehends, the "sense" is therefore a fundamental piece of the noema. Universally it is a piece which, under circumstances, changes from noema to noema, but <which> under circumstances <is> an absolutely like <piece> and perhaps even characterized as "identical," in so far as the "object, in the How of determinations," stands there on both sides as the same and as one to be described in an absolutely like manner. In no noema, however, can it or its necessary center, the point of unity, the pure determinable X, be missing. No "sense" without the *"something"* and, again, without *"determining content."* In that connection, it is evident that the subsequent analysis and description do not first introduce such a thing but rather that, as condition for the possibility of evident description and prior to this, it inheres actually in the correlate of consciousness.

Through the sense-bearer (as empty X) belonging to the sense and through the *possibility of harmonious combination to make sense-unities of any level* whatever—a possibility grounded in the essence of the sense—not only does each sense have its "object" but also different senses relate to the *same* object, just as far as they are to be made members of sense-unities in which the *determinable X of the united senses* become *coincident with one another and with the X of the total sense of the particular unity of sense.*

Our exposition becomes extended from monothetical acts to synthetical or, more distinctly, to polythetical acts. In a positing, many-membered consciousness each member has the described noematic structure; each has its X with the latter's "determining content"; but in addition to that the noema of the synthetical total act has, with respect to the "archontic" position, the synthetical X and *its* determining content. In the effecting of the act, the ray of the pure Ego's regard, dividing itself into a plurality of rays, goes to the X which arrives at synthetical unity. With the change we call "nominalization" the synthetical total phenomenon becomes modified in such a way that a ray of actionality goes to the highest synthetic X.

§132. The core as a sense in the mode belonging to its fullness

As we have determined it, the sense is *not a concrete essence* in the total composition of the noema but a sort of abstract *form* inherent in the noema. That is to say, if we hold the sense fast, consequently the "meant," precisely with the determination-content in which it is something meant, then clearly a *second* concept of the "object in its How" is yielded—<the object> *in the How of its modes of givenness.* If, in addition, we disregard all attentional modifications, all differences of the sort to which differences in the modes of effecting belong, there come into consideration—always within the preferred sphere of positionality—the differences in fullness of clarity, which are cognitionally so very determinative. Something intended to obscurely, as obscurely intended to, and the same thing as intended to clearly are, with respect to their noematic concreteness, very different, just as the whole mental processes are. But nothing stands in the way of the determination-content with which the thing intended to obscurely is meant being absolutely the same as the determination-content of the thing intended to clearly. The descriptions would coincide, and a synthetical unity-consciousness could envelop the consciousness on one side and that on the other in such a way that it was actually a matter of the same meant something. As *full core* we shall, accordingly, count precisely the full concreteness of the noematic component in question, consequently the *sense in the mode belonging to its fullness.*

§133. The noematic positum. Posited and synthetical posita. Posita in the realm of objectivations

There would now be needed a careful carrying-through of these distinctions in all act-provinces as well as supplementary consideration of the *posited moments* which have a peculiar relation to the sense as noematic. In the *Logische Untersuchungen* they were (under the title "quality") taken into the concept of sense (of significational essence) and therefore in this unity the two components, "matter" (sense, in the present conception) and quality, were distinguished.* But it seems more suitable to define the term "sense" as merely that "matter" and then to designate the unity of sense and posited characteristic as *"positum."* We have then *one-membered posita* (as in the case of perceptions and other positional intuitions) and many-membered, *synthetical* posita, such as predicative doxic posita (judgments), uncertain likelihood-posita with predicatively membered material, etc. One-membered as well as many-membered <posita> are, furthermore, *liking-posita, wish-posita, command-posita,* etc. The concept of the positum is accordingly indeed extraordinarily and perhaps surprisingly broadened, but nevertheless within the bounds of an important essential unity. Continually it is indeed to be kept in view that the concepts sense and positum contain for us nothing pertaining to expression and conceptual signification; on the other hand, however, they comprehend under themselves all explicit posita or, correspondingly, all posita-significations.

According to our analyses these concepts designate an abstract stratum belonging to the full web of all noemata. For our cognitions it is of great significance to gain this stratum in its fully comprehensive universality, consequently to have the insight that it has its place actually in *all act-spheres.* Also in the case of *intuitions* simpliciter the concepts sense and positum have their necessary application, necessarily the particular concepts *intuition-sense* and *intuition-positum* must be coined. So, for example, in the province of perception of something external the object-sense, the *physical thing-sense of this perception,* which is a different sense (as well as with respect to "the same" physical thing) from perception to perception, is to be singled out intuitively from the "perceived object as perceived" by abstracting from the characteristic of perceivedness as something inhering in the noema prior to all explicating and conceiving thinking. If we take this sense <in its> completion, with its intuitional *fullness,* a determined and very important concept of *appearance* results. To these senses correspond posita, intuition-posita, objectivation-posita, perceptual posita, and so forth. In a phenomenology of intuition of something external which, as phenomenology has to do, not with objects simpliciter in an unmodified sense, but with noemas as correlates of noeses, concepts like those brought out here stand at the center of scientific research.

Horizons†

§19. Actuality and potentiality of intentional life

The multiplicity of the intentionality belonging to any cogito—to any that relates to

---

*Loc. cit., Fifth Investigation, §§20 and 21, pp. 336–396 [second edition, pp. 411–421; English translation, pp. 586–593]. Cf. in addition Sixth Investigation, §25, p. 559 [second edition, p. 87; English translation, pp. 737f.] Neutral having as "undecided" naturally does not now, as it does there, have for us the status of a "quality" (position) alongside other qualities, but rather the status of a modification which mirrors all qualities and therefore whole acts of whatever sort.

†CM, pp. 44–49 (Sections 19 and 20).

the world, by the very fact that such a cogito not only intends something wordly but is itself intended in the consciousness of internal time—is a theme not exhausted with the consideration of cogitationes as *actual* subjective processes. On the contrary, *every actuality involves its potentialities,* which are not empty possibilities, but rather possibilities intentionally predelineated in respect of content—namely, in the actual subjective process itself—and, in addition, having the character of possibilities *actualizable by the Ego.*

With that, *another fundamental trait of intentionality* is indicated. Every subjective process has a process "horizon," which changes with the alteration of the nexus of consciousness to which the process belongs and with the alteration of the process itself from phase to phase of its flow—an intentional *horizon of reference* to potentialities of consciousness that belong to the process itself. For example, there belongs to every external perception its reference from the "genuinely perceived" sides of the object of perception to the sides "also meant"—not yet perceived, but only anticipated and, at first, with a non-intuitional emptiness (as the sides that are "coming" now perceptually): a continuous *protention,* which, with each phase of the perception, has a new sense. Furthermore, the perception has horizons made up of other possibilities of perception, as perceptions that we *could* have, if we *actively directed* the course of perception otherwise: if, for example, we turned our eyes that way instead of this, or if we were to step forward or to one side, and so forth. In the corresponding memory this recurs in modified form, perhaps in the consciousness that, instead of the sides then visible in fact, I could have seen others—naturally, *if* I had directed my perceptual activity in a suitably different manner. Moreover, as might have been said earlier, to every perception there always belongs a horizon of the past, as a potentiality of awakenable recollections; and to every recollection there belongs, as a horizon, the continuous intervening intentionality of possible recollections (to be actualized on my initiative, ac-

tively), up to the actual Now of perception. Everywhere in this connection an "I can and do, but I can also do otherwise than I am doing" plays its part—without detriment to the fact that this "freedom," like every other, is always open to possible hindrances.

The horizons are "predelineated" potentialities. We say also: We can *ask any horizon what "lies in it,"* we can *explicate* or unfold it, and *"uncover"* the potentialities of conscious life at a particular time. Precisely thereby we uncover the *objective sense meant implicitly* in the actual cogito, though never with more than a certain degree of foreshadowing. This sense, the *cogitatum qua cogitatum,* is never present to actual consciousness [*vorstellig*] as a finished datum; it becomes "clarified" only through explication of the given horizon and the new horizons continuously awakened [*der stetig neu geweckten Horizonte*]. The predelineation itself, to be sure, is at all times imperfect; yet, with its *indeterminateness,* it has a *determinate structure.* For example: the die leaves open a great variety of things pertaining to the unseen faces; yet it is already "construed" in advance as a die, in particular as colored, rough, and the like, though each of these determinations always leaves further particulars open. This leaving open, prior to further determinings (which perhaps never take place), is a moment included in the given consciousness itself; it is precisely what makes up the "horizon." As contrasted with mere clarification by means of anticipative "imaginings," there takes place, by means of an actually continuing perception, a *fulfilling* further determination (and perhaps determination as otherwise)—but with new horizons of openness.

Thus, as consciousness of something, every consciousness has the essential property, not just of being somehow *able to change into continually new modes of consciousness of the same object* (which, throughout the unity of synthesis, is inherent in them as an identical objective sense), but of being able to do so according to—indeed, *only according to those horizon intentionalities.* The object is, so to speak, *a pole of identity,* always meant expectantly as having a sense yet to be actualized; in every moment of consciousness it is an index, pointing to a noetic intentionality that pertains to it according to its sense, an intentionality that can be asked for and explicated. All this is concretely accessible to investigation.

§20. *The peculiar nature of intentional analysis*

It becomes evident that, as intentional, the analysis of consciousness is totally different from analysis in the usual and natural sense. Conscious life, as we said once before, is not just a whole made up of "data" of consciousness and therefore "analyzable" (in an extremely broad sense, divisible) merely into its selfsufficient and non-selfsufficient *elements* —the forms of unity (the "form-qualities") being included then among the non-selfsufficient elements. To be sure, when regard is directed to certain themes, intentional "analysis" does lead *also* to such divisions, and to that extent the word can still serve in the original sense; but everywhere its peculiar attainment (as "intentional") is an uncovering of the *potentialities "implicit"* in actualities of consciousness—an uncovering that brings about, on the noematic side, an "explication" or "unfolding," a "becoming distinct" and perhaps a "clearing" of what is consciously meant (the objective sense) and, correlatively, an explication of the potential intentional processes themselves. Intentional analysis is guided by the fundamental cognition that, as a consciousness, every cogito is indeed (in the broadest sense) a meaning of its meant *[Meinung seines Gemeinten],* but that, at any moment, this something meant *[dieses Vermeinte]* is more—something meant with something more—than what is meant at that moment "explicitly." In our example, each phase of perception was a mere side of "the" object, as what was perceptually meant. This *intending-beyond-itself,* which is implicit in any consciousness, must be considered an essential moment of it. That, on the other hand, this intending is, and must be, a "meaning more"

of the Same becomes shown only by the evidence of a possible making distinct and, ultimately, of an intuitive uncovering, in the form of actual and possible continued perceiving or of possible recollecting, as something to be done on my initiative.

The phenomenologist, however, does not inquire with merely a naive devotedness to the intentional object purely as such; he does not consider the intentional object only straightforwardly and explicate its meant features, its meant parts and properties. If that were all he did, the intentionality, which makes up the intuitive or non-intuitive consciousness itself and the explicative considering, would remain "anonymous." In other words: There would remain hidden the noctic multiplicities of consciousness and their synthetic unity, by virtue of which alone, and as their essentially necessary unitary doing *[ihre wesensmässige Einheitsleistung],* we have one intentional object, and always this definite one, continuously meant —have it, so to speak, before us *as* meant thus and so; likewise the hidden constitutive performances by virtue of which (if consideration then continues as explication) we find straightforwardly, as explicata of what is meant, such things as a "feature," a "property," a "part," or mean these implicitly and can then discover them intuitively. When the phenomenologist explores everything objective, and whatever can be found in it, exclusively as a "correlate of consciousness," he does not consider and describe it only straightforwardly and only as *somehow* related back to the corresponding Ego and the *ego cogito* of which it is the *cogitatum.* Rather, with his reflective regard, he penetrates the anonymous "cogitative" life, he uncovers the *definite* synthetic courses of the manifold modes of consciousness and, further back, the modes of Ego-comportment, which make understandable the objective affair's simple meantness for the Ego, its intuitive or non-intuitive meantness. Or, stated more precisely, they make it understandable how, in itself and by virtue of its current intentional structure, consciousness makes possible and necessary the fact that such an "existing" and "thus determined" Object is intended in it, occurs in it as such a sense. Thus, in the case of perception of a spatial thing, the phenomenologist (abstracting at first from all "significance" predicates and restricting himself purely to the "res extensa") explores the manner in which the changing "sight things," and "things" of the other senses, have in themselves the character of appearances *of* this same res extensa. In the case of any spatial thing, he explores its (potential and perhaps actual) changing perspectives; furthermore, with regard to its temporal modes of givenness, the modifications of its being still intended while it sinks retentionally into the past and, with respect to the Ego, the modes of his specifically own still-having and holding, the modes of attention, and so forth. It is to be noted in this connection that phenomenological explication of the perceived as such is not restricted to that perceptual explication of it, in respect of its features, which comes about as perception continues. On the contrary, phenomenological explication makes clear what is included and only non-intuitively co-intended in the sense of the cogitatum (for example, the "other side"), by making present in phantasy the potential perceptions that would make the invisible visible. That is true of any intentional analysis. As intentional *it reaches out beyond the isolated subjective processes* that are to be analyzed. By explicating their correlative horizons, it brings the highly diverse anonymous processes into the field comprising those that function "constitutively" in relation to the objective sense of the cogitatum in question— that is to say: not only the actual but also the *potential* subjective processes, which, as such, are "implicit" and "predelineated" in the sense-producing intentionality of the actual ones and which, when discovered, have the evident character of processes that explicate the implicit sense. Thus alone can the phenomenologist make understandable to himself *how,* within the immanency of conscious life and in thus and so determined modes of consciousness belonging to this incessant flux, anything like *fixed and abiding objective unities* can become intended and, in particular, how this marvellous work of "constituting" identical objects is

done *in the case of each category of objects*— that is to say: how, in the case of each category, the constitutive conscious life looks, and must look, in respect of the correlative noetic and noematic variants pertaining to the same object. The *horizon structure* belonging to every intentionality thus prescribes for phenomenological analysis and description *methods of a totally new kind,* which come into action wherever consciousness and object, wherever intending and sense, real and ideal actuality, possibility, necessity, illusion, truth, and, on the other hand, experience, judgment, evidence, and so forth, present themselves as names for transcendental problems, to be taken in hand as genuine problems concerning "subjective origins."

Mutatis mutandis the same is manifestly true in the case of a pure "internal psychology" or a "purely intentional" psychology (within the realm of natural positivity), which we have alluded to as the parallel to constitutional transcendental phenomenology. The only radical reform of psychology consists in the pure development of an intentional psychology. Brentano demanded it; but unfortunately he failed to recognize the fundamental sense of an intentional analysis and therefore failed to recognize the method that alone makes such a psychology possible, as the latter can gain access to its genuine and truly infinite field of problems only by that method.

At first, to be sure, the possibility of a pure phenomenology of consciousness seems highly questionable, since the realm of phenomena of consciousness is so truly the realm of a Heraclitean flux. It would in fact be hopeless to attempt to proceed here with such methods of concept and judgment formation as are standard in the Objective sciences. The attempt to determine a process of consciousness as an identical object, on the basis of experience, in the same fashion as a natural Object—ultimately then with the ideal presumption of a possible explication into identical elements, which might be apprehended by means of fixed concepts—would indeed be folly. Processes of consciousness—not merely owing to our imperfect ability to know objects of that kind, but a priori—have no ultimate elements and relationships, fit for subsumption under the idea of objects determinable by fixed concepts and therefore such that, in their case, it would be rational to set ourselves the task of an approximative determination guided by fixed concepts. In spite of that, however, the idea of an intentional analysis is legitimate, since, in the flux of intentional synthesis (which creates unity in all consciousness and which, noetically and noematically, constitutes unity of objective sense), *an essentially necessary conformity to type* prevails and *can be apprehended in strict concepts.*

V.

The Question of Evidence

7. Varieties of Evidence*

If one speaks simply of objects, one normally means actual, truly existing objects belonging to the particular category of being. No matter what one says about such objects, that which is meant and stated must—if one speaks rationally—be something which can be *"grounded,"* "shown," directly *"seen"* or *mediately "seen intellectually."* In the logical sphere, in the sphere of statement, *"being truly" or "actually" and "being something which can be shown rationally" are necessarily correlated.* This holds, moreover, for all modalities of being, all doxic positional modalities. Obviously the possibility of the rational showing referred to here should be understood, not as empirical, but as "ideal," as an essential possibility.

§136. The first fundamental form of rational consciousness: Originarily presentive "seeing"

If we now ask what rational showing signifies, that is, of what *rational consciousness* consists, the intuitive presentation of examples and the beginnings of eidetic analysis performed on them offers us at once a number of differences:

First, the difference between positing mental processes in which the posited becomes *given originarily* and those in which it does *not* become given in that mode: thus, between

"perceiving" or "seeing" acts—in a broadest sense—and *non-"perceiving" acts.*

Thus a memorial consciousness—for example, of a landscape—is not originarily presentive; the landscape is not perceived as it would be in case we actually saw it. By this we do not mean to say that memorial consciousness has no competence of its own: only that it is not a "seeing" consciousness. Phenomenology brings to light an analogue of this contrast in *each of the other kinds of positing* mental processes. For example: We can assert "blindly" that two plus one is equal to one plus two; but we can also make the same judgment in the manner peculiar to intellectual seeing. When we do this, the predicatively formed affair-complex, the synthetical objectivity corresponding to the judgment-synthesis, is given originarily, seized upon in an originary manner. It is no longer given originarily *after* effecting the actual *[lebendigen]* intellectual seeing which becomes forthwith an obscured retentional modification. Even though this may have a rational superiority to just any obscure or confused consciousness with the same noematic sense—for example, an "unthinking" reproduction of something learned and, perhaps, intellectually seen on an earlier occasion—it is not an originarily presentive consciousness.

These differences do not concern the pure sense or the pure positum, since in both mem-

---

Ideas I, pp. 326–336, 344–348 (Sections 136–139 and 145).

bers of any such exemplary pair this is identical and also can always be intentively seen as identical. The difference concerns *the mode in which the bare sense or the bare positum*—which, as merely an abstract moment in the concrete noema of consciousness, requires complementary moments—*is or is not a fulfilled sense or positum.*

A fullness of the sense does not make all the difference; the How of the fulfilledness matters as well. One mode of consciousness pertaining to the sense is the *"intuitive"* mode, which is such that the "meant object as meant" is intentively intuited; and an especially preeminent case here is the one in which the mode of intuition is precisely the *originarily presentive* mode. In the perception of the landscape the sense is fulfilled perceptually; in the mode of "itself in person" there is consciousness of the perceived object with its colors, forms, and other determinations (in so far as they "are included in the perception"). Similar pre-eminent cases are found in every act-sphere. Again the situation is one which is two-sided in the sense of a parallelism; it is noetic and noematic. Focusing on the noema we find, fused with the pure sense, the characteristic "in person" (as originary fulfilledness); and *the sense, with this characteristic, now functions as the basis for the noematic posited characteristic* or, this being the same thing here: the being-characteristic. We find the parallel to this in focusing on the noesis.

But the posited characteristic has as its own a specific rational character, as a *distinguishing mark* accruing to it *essentially, if and only if* it is a position on the basis of a fulfilled, originarily presentive sense and not merely on the basis of just any sense.

Here, and in the case of any other kind of rational consciousness, the word "belong" takes on a peculiar signification. For example: Position *belongs* to any appearing "in person" on the part of a physical thing; it is not just somehow one with the appearing (perhaps even as merely a universal fact—this being out of the question here); it is one with it in a peculiar manner: it is *"motivated"* by <the appearing> and again, not just somehow, but *"ratio-*

nally motivated." That is to say, position has its *original legitimizing basis* in originary givenness. With other modes of givenness legitimizing bases need not be lacking; lacking, however, is the superiority of the *original* basis which plays its pre-eminent role in the relative estimating of other legitimizing bases.

In just the same manner, the position of the essence of predicatively formed essence-complex given "originarily" in the *seeing of essences* "belongs" to the position-"material" <of the essence or predicatively formed essence-complex>, to the "sense" in its mode of givenness. It is rational and as *certainty of believing* it is an originally motivated position; it has the specific character of an *"intellectually seeing"* position. If the position is *blind,* if the verbal significations are effected on the basis of an obscure and confusedly intentive act-substratum, then the rational character belonging to intellectual seeing is necessarily lacking; that character is *essentially incompatible* with obscure givenness of the predicatively formed affair-complex (if the word givenness is still to be used here) or with such a noematic outfitting of the sense-core. On the other hand, this does not exclude a secondary rational character, as is shown by the example of an imperfect re-presentiating of eidetic cognitions.

Intellectual seeing, evidence of any kind, is thus a wholly distinguishing occurrence; in terms of its "core" it is the *unity of a rational position with that which essentially motivates the position*—this whole situation being understandable as noetic and also as noematic. The word motivation is particularly suited to the relation between the (noetic) positing and the noematic positum in *its mode of fulfilledness.* The expression, "evident positum," is, in its noematic signification, immediately understandable.

The double sense of the word evidence, in its application, sometimes to noetic characteristics or to full acts (for example, evidence of judging) and sometimes to noematic posita (for example, evident logical judgment, evident predicative proposition), is a case of the universal and necessary double significancies of expression relating to moments of the correlation between noesis and noema. Phenomenological demonstration of their source makes these double significancies harmless and, indeed, makes it possible to recognize their indispensability.

We should note furthermore that the word fulfillment has another double sense which lies in a quite different dimension. Sometimes it signifies *"fulfillment of the intention,"* as a characteristic which the actual *positum* takes on by virtue of the particular mode of the sense; sometimes it signifies precisely the peculiarity of this mode itself or the peculiarity of the sense in question, as including a "filling" which motivates rationally.

§137. *Evidence and intellectual sight.* *"Originary" and "pure" evidence, assertoric and apodictic evidence*

The pairs of examples used above illustrate a *second* and *third* difference. What we usually call evidence and *intellectual sight (or intellectual seeing)* is a positional, doxic and *adequately* presentive consciousness which "excludes being otherwise"; the positing is motivated in a quite exceptional manner by the adequate givenness and is, in the highest sense, an act of "reason." The arithmetical example illustrates that for us. In the example of the landscape we have, it is true, a seeing, but not an evidence in the usual pregnant sense of the word, an "intellectual seeing." Observing more precisely, we note two differences. In the one example it is a matter of *essences;* in the other, a matter of something *individual;* secondly, in the eidetic example the originary givenness is *adequate,* whereas in the example from the sphere of experience it is *inadequate.* The two differences, which cross one another under some circumstances, will prove to be significant with respect to the kind of evidence.

With regard to the first difference, it is phenomenologically observable that, so to speak, the *"assertoric" seeing of something individual,* for example, the "attentive perceiving" of a physical thing or of an individual affair-complex, differs essentially in its rational character not only from an *"apodictic" seeing, from the intellectual seeing of an essence or of a predicatively formed essence-complex;* but it also differs from the modification of this intellectual seeing which may come about through mixture of the two, namely in the case where something seen intellectually is applied to something seen assertorically and in any case of *knowing the necessity of the being-thus* of a posited single particular.

Evidence and intellectual seeing, in the usual pregnant sense, are understood as signifying the same thing: apodictic intellectual seeing. We propose to separate the two in our terminology. We need a more universal term which encompasses in its signification both assertoric seeing and apodictic intellectual seeing. It should be regarded as a phenomenological cognition of the greatest importance that the two belong to *one* essential genus and that, comprehended more universally, *any rational consciousness whatever* is a highest genus of positional modalities within which the "seeing" (in the extremely broadened sense) related to originary givenness is precisely a rigidly delimited species. Now in order to name the highest genus one has the choice between extending either the signification of the term "seeing" (as has just been done, but going very much further) or that of the terms "intellectual insight" and "evidence." It seems best to choose the term *evidence* for the most universal concept; then, for every rational position characterized by a motivational relation to originariness of givenness, the expression *originary evidence* would be available. Furthermore, a distinction should be made between *assertoric* and *apodictic evidence;* and the term *intellectual seeing* should be used, as before, to designate this *apodicticity.* Going still further, one should contrast *pure* intellectual seeing and *impure* intellectual seeing (for example, cognition of the necessity pertaining to something factual, the being of which need not itself be evident) and likewise, quite universally, *pure and impure evidence.*

Yet other differences result if one inquires more deeply—differences in the motivating foundations which affect the evidence-characteristic. For example, the difference between *purely formal* ("analytic," "logical") and *material* (synthetic a priori) evidence. Here, however, we must not go beyond the first indications.

§138. *Adequate and inadequate evidence*

Let us return to the second distinction concerning evidence indicated above, with which the distinction between adequate and inadequate givenness is connected and which, at the same time, provides us with the occasion for describing a distinctive type of "impure" evidence. The positing of the *physical thing* on the ground of the appearance "itself in person" is, to be sure, a rational positing, but the appearance is always only a one-sided, "imperfect" appearance; intended to as "itself in person," what "properly" appears is not only there, but simply this physical thing itself, the whole in conformity with the total sense, though only one-sidedly intuited and, moreover, multifariously indeterminate. What "properly" appears cannot be separated from the physical thing as, let us say, a physical thing for itself; in the full sense of the physical thing, the sense-correlate <of what "properly" appears> fashions a *non-selfsufficient* part which can only have unity and selfsufficiency of sense in a whole which *necessarily* includes in itself empty components and indeterminate components.

Of essential necessity something physically real, a being with that sense, appears only *"inadequately"* in a closed appearance. Essentially tied up with this is the fact that *no* rational positing which *rests upon that sort of inadequately presentive appearance* can be *"ultimately valid,"* "insurmountable"; and that no <rational positing> is equivalent in its singularization to the <positing> simpliciter: "The physical thing is actual"; it is only equivalent to the positing: "it is actual"—assuming that the further course of experience does not bring forth "stronger rational motives" which show the original positing as a positing to be "can-

celled out" in the broader context. Accordingly, the positing is only rationally motivated by the appearance (the imperfectly fulfilled perceptual sense) in and for itself, considered in its singularization.

The phenomenology of reason must therefore study the different occurrences which are a priori predelineated in the sphere of the modes of being which are necessarily only inadequately presentive (*transcendencies* in the sense of realities). It must make clear how consciousness of inadequate givenness, how the one-sided appearing, is related to one and the same determinable X in the continuous progress to always new appearances which are continually being blended with one another; which eidetic possibilities result here; how, on the one hand, a continuation of experience is possible and always rationally motivated by continually available rational positings: precisely the course of experience in which the empty places of the previous appearance are filled out, the indeterminacies are more precisely determined and thus always in the manner of a *thoroughgoing harmonious fulfilling with a steadily increasing rational power.* On the other hand, it must make clear the contrary possibilities, the *cases of fusion or polythetical syntheses of discordancy,* the *"determination otherwise"* of the X always intended to as the same—otherwise than in the correspondingly original sense-bestowal. Moreover, it must show how positional components pertaining to the earlier perceptual flow suffer *cancellation* together with their sense; how, under circumstances, the whole perception, so to speak, *explodes* and splits up into *"conflicting physical thing-apprehensions,"* into *suppositions* concerning physical things; how the positings of these suppositions are annulled and uniquely modified in this annulment; or else how the one positing, remaining unmodified, "conditions" the cancellation of the "counter positing"; and similar processes of the same kind.

To be studied in still more detail are the relevant modifications which the original rational positings undergo such that they incur a *positive phenomenological increase* with respect to their *motivating "force"* in the further course of harmonious fulfillment, such that they continually acquire a *"weight,"* always and essentially have a weight, to be sure, but one which differs *by degrees.* There are, moreover, the other possibilities to be analyzed: how the weight of positings is affected by *"counter motives,"* how, in the case of *doubt,* they are mutually *"held in balance,"* how a positing in competition with one of "greater" weight is *"overcome," "abandoned,"* etc.

In addition, naturally, it is necessary to subject to a comprehensive eidetic analysis the processes in the sense, as the appertinent *position-materials,* which are essentially determinative for alterations in the posited characteristics (e.g., the processes of "conflict" or "rivalry" of appearances). For here, as everywhere, in the phenomenological sphere there are neither accidents nor facticities: everything is motivated by essential determination.

In the same manner *an inquiry into the essence of all kinds of immediate rational acts* is to be carried out in the context of a universal phenomenology of noetic and noematic data.

To every region and category of alleged objects there corresponds phenomenologically not only a *fundamental sort of sense,* or of *posita,* but also a *fundamental type of originarily presentive consciousness* of such senses and, belonging to it, a *fundamental type of originary evidence* which is essentially motivated by originary givenness of such a character.

Every such evidence—understanding the term in our broadened sense—is either *adequate* evidence, of essential necessity incapable of being further "strengthened" or "weakened," thus *without degrees of weight;* or the evidence is *inadequate* and thus *capable of being increased and decreased.* Whether or not this or that evidence is possible in a given sphere depends on its generic type. It is therefore a priori prefigured, and it is countersense to demand in one sphere the perfection belonging to the evidence of another sphere (e.g., that of eidetic relationships) which essentially excludes it.

It must still be noted that the original signification of the concepts of "adequate" and "inadequate" related to modes of givenness had to be extended to the essential peculiarities pertaining to the rational positings themselves which are founded by them precisely by virtue of this nexus—one of those unavoidable equivocations by extension <and> which is harmless as long as one recognizes it as such by being fully aware of the distinction between the original and the derived.

§139. The interweaving of all kinds of reason. Theoretical, axiological and practical truth

According to what has been explained so far, a positing of no matter what quality has its legitimacy as a positing of its sense when it is rational; the rational characteristic is precisely itself the characteristic of legitimation which "befits" it essentially and, therefore, not as an accidental fact among accidental circumstances pertaining to a factually positing Ego. Correlatively, *the positum* is also said to be legitimated: it is present in rational consciousness, furnished with its noematic legitimacy-characteristic which, again, essentially belongs to the positum as the noematic position qualified in this or that way, and of this or that sense-material. More precisely stated: there belongs to it a fullness of such a character which, on its side, grounds the rational distinctiveness of the position.

Here the positum has its legitimacy in itself. But it can also be that *"something speaks on behalf of the positum,"* that it can still have a share in reason without "itself" being rational. In order to remain within the doxic sphere, let us recall the relevant connection of the doxic modalities with the protodoxa to which everything refers back. If, on the other hand, we consider the rational characteristics belonging to these modalities, then at the outset the thought thrusts itself to the fore that all of them, no matter how different they may otherwise be with respect to materials and motivational foundations, refer back, so to speak, to a primal rational character belonging to the domain of primal belief, back to the case of originary and ultimately perfect evidence. It is noteworthy that profound concatenations of essences obtain between these two kinds of retroreference.

Just to indicate the following: in itself, something deemed likely can be characterized as rational. If we follow the reference, inherent in it, back to the corresponding primal believing, and if we adopt this believing in the form of a "supposing," then "something speaks for it." It is not the belief itself, simpliciter, which is characterized as rational, although it has a share in reason. We see that further rational-theoretical distinctions and inquiries related to them are needed here. Concatenations of essences are made prominent between the *different* qualities with the rational characteristics peculiar to them and, more particularly, *reciprocal* concatenations; and, *finally, all lines run back to primal believings and their primal reason;* that is to say, to primal truth, or to *"truth"* <in an absolute sense>.

Truth is manifestly the correlate of the perfect rational characteristics pertaining to protodoxa, to certainty of belief. The expression, "something posited protodoxically, for instance a predicative proposition, is true," and then the expression, "perfect rational characteristics accrue to the corresponding believing, judging"—are equivalent correlates. Naturally nothing is said about the fact of a mental process and about the one who judges, although it is eidetically unquestionable that truth can only be actually given in an actual evidential consciousness; and this holds for the truth of the unquestionableness itself, the truth of the equivalence just indicated, and so forth. If the protodoxic evidence, that of certainty of belief, is lacking to us, then for its sense-content, "S is p," we say, a doxic modality can be evident—for example, the presumed likelihood, "S ought to be p." This modal evidence is manifestly equivalent to and necessarily connected

with a protodoxic evidence of an altered sense, i.e., with the evidence or with the primal truth: "That S is p is likely (probable)"; on the other hand, <the modal evidence is also connected> with the truth: "Something speaks for S being p"; and, again: "Something speaks for Sp being true"; and so forth. With all this eidetic connections are indicated which require phenomenological inquiries into their origin.

But evidence is by no means a mere name for those sorts of rational processes in the sphere of belief (and even less in the sphere of the predicative judgment); it is rather a name for *all positional spheres* and, in particular, also for the significant rational relationships obtaining *between* them.

It therefore involves the highly difficult and far-reaching groups of problems of reason in the sphere of emotional and volitional positings* as well as their interwovenness with the "theoretical," i.e., doxic, reason. The "theoretical" or *"doxological truth,"* or *evidence,* has its parallel in the *"axiological and practical truths or evidence"* whereby the latter "truths" are given expression and cognized in doxological truths, that is to say, in specifically logical (apophantical) ones.† It need not be said that to deal with these problems there must be fundamental investigations of the sort which we tried to embark upon above: investigations involving the eidetic relationships which connect the doxic positings with all other kinds of positings, those of the emotions and the will and, again, those which lead all doxic modalities back to the protodoxa. Precisely by such investigations it is made understandable on the basis of ultimate grounds why the certainty of belief and, correspondingly, the doxological and ultimately the primal truth play such a dominant role in all of reason—a role which, at the same time, also makes it obvious that, with respect to their

---

*A first impulse in this direction was given by Brentano's brilliant work, *Vom Ursprung sittlicher Erkenntnis* (Leipzig, 1889) [*The Origin of Our Knowledge of Right and Wrong,* trans. Roderick M. Chisholm and Elizabeth H. Schneewind (New York, 1969)] a work to which I feel gratefully indebted.

†Cognition is, above all, a name for logical truth: designated from the standpoint of the subject, as the correlate of his evidential judging; but it is also a name for every sort of evidential judging itself and, finally, for every doxically rational act.

solution, the problems of reason in the doxic sphere must take precedence over those of axiological and practical reason.

§145. Critical considerations concerning the phenomenology of evidence

It is clear from considerations carried out that the *phenomenology of reason, noetics in a pregnant sense,* which will undertake an intuitive exploration not just of any consciousness, but of consciousness of reason, everywhere presupposes universal phenomenology. It is itself a phenomenological fact that— in the realm of positionality*—*positing consciousness is ruled by norms in every genus;* the norms are nothing else than eidetic laws which, with respect to their kind and form, are related to noetic-noematic concatenations to be strictly analyzed and described. In that connection, even *"non-reason"* is naturally everywhere to be regarded as the negative counterpart of reason, just as the phenomenology of evidence includes its counterpart, *absurdity.† The universal eidetic theory of evidence* with its analyses related to the most universal eidetic distinctions fashions a relatively small, though fundamental, piece of the phenomenology of reason. Accordingly, what was briefly maintained at the beginning of this Book‡ against the inverted interpretation of evidence is confirmed—and the deliberations just carried out are sufficient to see that perfectly.

Evidence is, in fact, not some sort of consciousness-index attached to a judgment (and usually one speaks of such evidence only in the case of judgment), calling to us like a mystic voice from a better world: Here is the truth; —as though such a voice would have

something to say to free spirits like us and would not have to show its title to legitimacy. We no longer need to argue with skepticism, nor take into consideration objections of the old type which cannot overcome the theory of evidence which resorts to indices and feeling: whether an evil genius (the Cartesian fiction) or a fateful change in the factual course of the world could make it happen that just any false judgment would be outfitted with this index, this feeling of intellectual necessity, of the transcendent oughtness; and the like. If one proceeds to the study of the phenomena themselves which belong here, and does so within the limits of the phenomenological reduction, then one recognizes with fullest clarity that here it is a matter of a relevant mode of positing (thus not of anything so insignificant as some sort of attached content, nor of an appendage of whatever sort) which belongs to the eidetically determined constitutions of the essence of the noema (e.g., the mode of original intellectual seenness belonging to the noematic composition of "originarily" presentive seeing of essences). One then further recognizes that once more the eidetic laws rule the relationship of those positing acts which do not have this distinctive constitution to those which do; that, e.g., there is something like consciousness of the *"fulfillment of the intention,"* of justification and confirmation specifically related to posited characteristics, just as there are the corresponding *counter characteristics* of *unjustification, disconfirmation.* One further recognizes that the logical principles require a profound phenomenological clarification, and that, e.g., the principle of contradiction leads us back to concatenations of essences of possible verification and possible disconfirmation (or rational cancel-

---

*In the sphere of phantasy and neutrality all positional processes are carried over as "mirrored" and "powerless"; thus too all processes of reason. Neutral positings are not to be confirmed, but to be "quasi" confirmed; they are not evidential, but "quasi" evidential; and so forth.

†Cf. *Logische Untersuchungen,* II. 6. Unters. §39, pp. 594ff., especially p. 598 [second edition, II, 2, §39, pp. 122ff., especially p. 126; English translation, pp. 764ff., especially pp. 768ff.]. The whole of the Sixth Investigation offers, universally, preliminary phenomenological studies for dealing with the problems of reason in the present chapter.

‡Cf. Part I, Chapter 2, especially §21.

lation).* Universally, one acquires the intellectual insight that, above all, it is a question here, not of accidental facts, but instead of eidetic processes which stand in their eidetic context, and that, therefore, what takes place in the Eidos functions as an absolutely insurmountable norm for the fact. In this phenomenological chapter one should also make clear that not every positing mental process (e.g., any mental judgment-process you please) cannot become evident in the same manner and, specifically, that not every positing mental process can become immediately evidential; furthermore, that all manners of rational positing, all types of immediate or mediate evidence, are rooted in phenomenological complexes in which the fundamentally different regions of objects are noetically-noematically distributed.

In particular, it is of concern to study systematically the continuous unions of identity and the synthetical identifications in every domain with respect to their phenomenological constitution. Once one has become acquainted—which is the first step needed—with the inner structure of intentive mental processes with respect to all universal structures, the parallelism of these structures, the stratification in the noema such as sense, subject of sense, posited characteristics, fullness: then it is necessary to make fully clear in all cases of synthetical unions how not just any act-combinations whatever take place, but rather how combination into the unity of *one* act takes place. More particularly, how identifying unions are possible, how here and there the determinable X is made to coincide, how, in that case, sense-determinations and their empty places—here that signifies their moments of indeterminateness—are related; likewise, how fullnesses, how, therefore, the forms of confirmation, of validation, of progressive cognition, at lower and higher levels of consciousness, become clear and are intellectually seen in analysis.

However, these and all parallel studies of reason are carried out in the "transcendental," in the phenomenological attitude. No judgment which occurs there is a natural judgment presupposing the positing of natural actuality as background, and not even where the phenomenology of the consciousness of actuality, of cognition of Nature, of seeing of values related to Nature and intellectual seeing of values is concerned. Everywhere we investigate the fashionings of noeses and noemata, we project a systematic and eidetic morphology, everywhere bring into relief essential necessities and essential possibilities: the latter as necessary possibilities, forms of unions of compatibility which are prescribed in the *essences* and delimited by laws of essences. Everywhere "object" is the name for eidetic concatenations of consciousness; it appears first of all as noematic X, as the subject of sense pertaining to different essential types of sense and posita. Moreover, it appears as the name, "actual object," and is then the name for certain eidetically considered rational concatenations in which the sense-conforming, unitary X inherent in them receives its rational position.

Similar names for determined, eidetically delimited groups of consciousness-formations "teleologically" belonging together, to be fixed by the inquiry into essences, are the expressions, "possible object," "probable," "dubitable" object; and so forth. The concatenations there are always again other, to be described strictly in their otherness: thus, e.g., it is easily seen intellectually that the possibili-

---

*Cf. *Logische Untersuchungen,* II, 6. Unters. §34, pp. 583ff. [second edition, II, 2, pp. 111ff.; English translation, pp. 756ff.]. It is to be regretted that W. Wundt judges otherwise here, as he does about phenomenology as a whole. The scientific inquiry, which does not in the slightest go beyond the sphere of purely intuitional data, he interprets as "Scholasticism." He designates as a "chosen formal schema" the distinction between sense-bestowing and sense-fulfilling acts *(Kleine Schriften [Shorter Writings],* I <Leipzig,> 1910/11, p. 613), and the results of our analyses, he says, are the "most primitive" "verbal repetitions": "Evidence is evidence, abstraction is abstraction." He introduces the conclusion of his critique with words which I may be permitted to quote: "Husserl's foundation of a new logic, directed more theoretically than practically, ends in each of its conceptual analyses, in so far as they possess a positive content, with the assurance that A actually = A, and that it cannot be otherwise" (ibid., pp. 613–614).

ty of an X determined thus and so is not justified simply by originary givenness of this X in its sense-composition, thus by authentication of actuality, but rather that even merely reproductively founded deeming possible can be reciprocally confirmed in the harmonious coming together; similarly, that *doubtfulness* is justified in conflicting phenomena between modalized intuitions of certain descriptive sorts; and so forth. As a result, the investigations of the theory of reason are combined which relate to the distinction of materially determinate affairs, values, practical objectivities, and which then investigate the formations

produced by consciousness constitutive for them. Phenomenology therefore actually encompasses the whole natural world and all of the ideal worlds which it excludes: phenomenology encompasses them as the "world sense" by virtue of the sets of eidetic laws connecting any object-sense and noema whatever with the closed system of noeses, and specifically by virtue of the eidetic concatenations of rational positing the correlate of which is the "actual object" which, thus, on its side, always exhibits the index for the whole determined system of teleologically unifying fashionings of consciousness.

8. Sensuous and Categorial Intuition*

§40. The problem of the fulfillment of categorial meaning-forms, with a thought leading towards its solution

In our discussions up to this point we have repeatedly and strongly felt a large gap. It had to do with the categorial objective forms, or with the synthetic functions in the sphere of objectifying acts through which these objective forms come to be constituted, through which they may come to "intuition" and thereby also to "knowledge." We shall now attempt to some extent to fill in this gap, taking our point of departure from the investigation of our first chapter; this was concerned with one limited aim of epistemological clarification: the relation of a meaning-intention as the thing to be expressed, with an expressed sensuous intuition. We shall for the time being again build on the simplest cases of perceptual and other intuitive statements, and shall use them to shed light on the theme of our next treatments, in the following manner:

In the case of a perceptual statement, not

only the inwrought nominal presentations are fulfilled: the whole sense of the statement finds fulfillment through our underlying percept. We say likewise that the whole statement gives utterance to our percept: we do not merely say "I see this paper, an inkpot, several books," and so on, but also "I see that the paper has been written on, that there is a bronze inkpot standing here, that several books are lying open," and so on. If a man thinks the fulfillment of nominal meanings clear enough, we shall ask him how we are to understand the fulfillment of total statements, especially as regards that side of them that stretches beyond their "matter," in this case beyond their nominal terms. What may and can furnish fulfillment for those aspects of meaning which make up propositional form as such, the aspects of *"categorial form"* to which, e.g., the copula belongs?

Looked at more narrowly, this question also applies to nominal meanings, in so far as these are not totally formless like the meanings for individuals. The name, like the state-

*LI, II, 773–795 (Sections 40–48).

ment, even in its grammatical appearance, possesses both "matter" and "form." If it comprises words, the form lies partly in the way these words are strung together, partly in its own form-words, partly in the mode of construction of the individual words, which allows us to draw a distinction between its moments of "matter" and its moments of "form." Such grammatical distinctions refer us back to distinctions of meaning. There is at least a rough expression of the articulations and forms which are rooted in our meaning's essence and the articulations and forms of grammar. In our meanings, therefore, parts of very different kinds are to be found, and among these we may here pay special attention to those expressed by formal words such as "the," "a," "some," "many," "few," "two," "is," "not," "which," "and," "or," etc., and further expressed by the substantival and adjectival, singular and plural inflection of our words, etc.

How does all this stand as regards fulfillment? Can the ideal of completely adequate fulfillment formulated by us in our third chapter still be maintained? *Are there parts and forms of perception corresponding to all parts and forms of meaning?* In that case we should have the *parallelism* between meaningful reference and fulfilling intuition that talk of "expression" suggests. The expression would be an image-like counterpart of the percept (i.e., in all its parts and forms to be expressed) but reconstituted in a new stuff—an *ex-pression* in the *stuff of meaning*.

The prototype for interpreting the relation between meaning and intuiting would then be the relation of the "proper" individual meaning to corresponding percepts. The man who knows Cologne itself, and therefore possesses the genuine "proper meaning" of the word "Cologne," has in his contemporary actual experience something exactly corresponding to the future confirming percept. It is not, properly speaking, a representation of the percept, as, e.g., the corresponding imagination would be. But just as the city is thought to be itself present to us in the percept, so the proper name

"Cologne," in its "proper meaning," refers, as previously argued, to the same city "directly": it means that city itself, and as it is. The straightforward percept here renders the object apparent without the help of further, superordinate acts, the object *which* the meaning-intention means, and *just as* the latter means it. The meaning-intention therefore finds in the mere percept the act which fulfills it with complete adequacy.

If instead of considering directly naming, unstructured expressions, we rather consider structured, articulated expressions, the matter seems quite the same. I *see* white paper and *say* "white paper," thereby expressing, with precise adequacy, only what I see. The same holds of complete judgments. I *see* that this paper is white, and express just this by saying: "This paper is white."

We are not to let ourselves be led astray by such ways of speaking; they are in a certain manner correct, yet are readily misunderstood. One might try to use them to show that meaning here has its seat in perception, which, as we have shown, is not so. The word "white" certainly means something attaching to the white paper itself; this "meaning" therefore coincides, in the state of fulfillment, with the partial percept which relates to the "white-aspect" of the object. But the assumption of a mere coincidence with this part-percept is not enough: we are wont to say here that the *white* thus apparent is known *as white* and is called so. In our normal talk of "knowledge," we are, however, more inclined to call the object which is our (logical) subject the thing "known." In *such* knowledge another act plainly is present, which perhaps includes the former one, but is nonetheless different from it: the *paper* is known as white, or rather as a white thing, whenever we express our percept in the words "white paper." The intention of the word "white" only partially coincides with the color-aspect of the apparent object; a surplus of meaning remains over, a form which finds nothing in the appearance itself to confirm it. White paper is paper which *is* white. Is this form not also repeated, even if it remains hidden, in the case of the noun "paper"? Only the quality-meanings contained in its "concept" terminate in perception. Here also the whole object is known as paper, and here also a supplementary form is known which includes being, though not as its sole form, in itself. The fulfillment effected by a straight percept obviously does not extend to such forms.

We have but to ask, further, what corresponds in perception to the difference between the two expressions "this white paper" and "this paper is white," which are both realized on the same perceptual basis, we have but to ask what side of perception is really brought out by this difference—the difference, that is, of the attributive and the predicative mode of statement—and what, in the case of adequate adaptation, this difference brings out with peculiar exactness, and we experience the same difficulty. Briefly we see that the case of structured meanings is not so simple as the case of a "proper" individual meaning, with its straightforward relation of coincidence with perception. Certainly one can tell one's auditors, intelligibly and unambiguously, that "I see that this paper is white," but the thought behind such talk need not be that the meaning of this spoken sentence expresses *a mere act of seeing*. It may also be the case that the epistemic essence of our seeing, in which the apparent object announces itself as self-given, serves to base certain connective or relational or otherwise formative acts, and that it is to *these* that our expression in its changing forms is adjusted, and that it is in such acts, performed on a basis of actual perception, that our expression, in respect of such changing forms, finds fulfillment. If we now combine these founded acts or rather act-forms with the acts which serve as their foundation, and give the comprehensive name "founded act" to the whole act-complexes that result from such formal "founding," we may say: Granted the possibility just sketched, our parallelism may be re-established, but it is no longer a parallelism between the meaning-intentions of expressions and the mere percepts which correspond to them: it is a parallelism between

meaning-intentions and the above mentioned *perceptually founded acts*.

§41. *Continuation. Extension of our sphere of examples*

If we suppose our range of examples widened so as to cover the whole field of predicative thinking, we shall encounter similar difficulties and similar possibilities of resolving them. Judgments in particular will come up which have no definite relation to anything individual which ought to be given through any intuition: they will give *general* expression to relations among ideal unities. The general meanings embodied in such judgments can also be realized on a basis of corresponding intuition, since they have their origin, mediately or immediately, in intuition. The intuited individual is not, however, what we mean here; it serves at best only as an individual case, an example, or only as the rough analogue of an example, for the universal which alone interests us. So, for instance, when we speak generically of "color" or specifically of "red," the appearance of a single red thing may furnish us with a documenting intuition.

It also at times happens that one calls such a general statement an expression of intuition. We say, e.g., that an arithmetical axiom expresses what we find in intuition, or we raise objection to a geometrician that he merely expresses what he sees in his figure without deducing it formally, that he borrows from his drawing and omits steps in his proof. Such talk has its good sense (as when the objection scores no mean hit against the formal validity of Euclidean geometry) but "expression" here means something different from the previous cases. Even in *their* case expression was not a mere counterpart of intuition: this is even less the case here, where our thought's intention is not aimed at intuitively given phenomena nor at their intuitive properties or relationships, and *can* in our case not be aimed at them. For a figure understood geometrically is known to be an ideal limit incapable in principle of intuitive exhibition in the concrete. Even in our case, nonetheless, and in the generic field as such, intuition has an essential relation to expression and to its meaning: these, therefore, constitute an experience of general knowledge related to intuition, no mere togetherness of them all, but a unity of felt belongingness among them. Even in our case, concept and proposition are oriented towards intuition, through which alone, after corresponding adjustment, self-evidence, the crown of knowledge, emerges. It requires little reflection, on the other hand, to see that the meaning of the expressions in question is not found in intuition at all, that such intuition only gives them a filling of clarity and in the favorable case of self-evidence. We in fact know only too well that the overwhelming majority of general statements, and in particular those of science, behave meaningfully without any elucidation from intuition, and that only a vanishing section, even of the true and the proven, are and remain open to complete intuitive illumination.

Even in the general realm, as in the realm of individuals, our natural talk has a relation to intuitively founded acts of thought. Should intuition fall wholly away, our judgment would cease to know anything. It means, in all cases, in cogitative style, just what could be known by the aid of intuition, if such judgment is indeed true at all. Knowledge always has the character of a fulfillment and an identification: this may be observed in every case where we confirm a general judgment through subsequent intuition, as in every other case of knowledge.

Our difficulty then is how identification can arise where the form of the general proposition, and in particular its form of universality, would vainly seek sympathetic elements in individual intuition. To remove this difficulty, as in the previous case, the possibility of "founded acts" suggests itself. This possibility, carried out more fully, would run more or less as follows:

Where general thoughts find fulfillment in intuition, certain new acts are built on our percepts and other appearances of like order, acts related quite differently to our appearing

object from the intuitions which constitute it. This difference in mode of relation is expressed by the perspicuous turn of phrase employed above: that the intuited object is not here itself the thing meant, but serves only as an elucidatory example of our true general meaning. But if *expressive* acts conform to these differences, their significative intention will not move towards what is to be intuitively presented, but towards what is universal, what is merely documented in intuition. Where this new intention is adequately fulfilled by an underlying intuition, it reveals its own objective possibility (or the possibility or "reality" of the universal).

§42. The distinction between sensuous stuff and categorial form throughout the whole realm of objectifying acts

After these provisional treatments have shown us our difficulty, and have provided us with a thought leading to its possible removal, we shall embark upon our actual discussion.

We started by assuming that, in the case of structured expressions, the notion of a more or less mirror-like mode of expression was quite unavailing in describing the relation which obtains between meanings to be expressed, on the one hand, and expressed intuitions, on the other. This is doubtless correct and need now only be made more precise. We need only earnestly ponder what things can be possible matter for perception, and what things possible matter for meaning, to become aware that, *in the mere form of a judgment, only certain antecedently specifiable parts of our statement can have something which corresponds to them in intuition, while to other parts of the statement nothing intuitive possibly can correspond.*

Let us consider this situation a little more closely.

Perceptual statements are, completely and normally expressed, articulate utterances of varying pattern. We have no difficulty in distinguishing such types as *"A is P"* (where *"A"* serves as index for a proper name), "An *S* is *P*," "This *S* is *P*," "All *S* are *P*," etc. Many complications arise through the modifying influence of negation, through the introduction of distinctions between absolute and relative predicates (attributes), through conjunctive, disjunctive and determinative connectives, etc. In the diversity of these types certain sharp distinctions of meaning make themselves clear. To the various letters (variables) and words in these types correspond sometimes *members,* sometimes *connective forms,* in the meanings of the actual statements which belong to these types. Now it is easy to see that *only at the places indicated by letters (variables)* in such "forms of judgment," *can* meanings be put that are themselves fulfilled in perception, whereas it is hopeless, even quite misguided, to look directly in perception for what could give fulfillment to our supplementary formal meanings. The letters (variables), on account of their merely functional meaning, can doubtless take complex thoughts as their values: statements of high complexity can be seen from the standpoint of very simple judgment-types. The same difference between "matter" and "form" therefore repeats itself in what is looked upon, in unified fashion, as a "term." But eventually, in the case of each perceptual statement, and likewise, of course, in the case of every other statement that in a certain primary sense gives expression to intuition, we shall come down to certain final elements of our terms—we may call them elements of stuff—which find direct fulfillment in intuition (perception, imagination, etc.), while the supplementary *forms,* which as forms of meaning likewise crave fulfillment, can find nothing that ever could fit them in perception or acts of like order.

This fundamental difference we call, in a natural extension of its application over the whole sphere of objectifying presentation, the *categorial* and *absolute* distinction between the *form* and *matter* of *presentation,* and at the same time separate it off from the *relative* or *functional* difference which is closely bound up with it, and which has just been subsidiarily touched on above.

We have just spoken of a natural extension of our distinction over the whole sphere of objectifying presentation. We take the constituents of the *fulfillment* which correspond to the material or formal constituents of our *meaning-intentions* as being material or formal constituents respectively, so making clear what is to count as "material" or "formal" in the general sphere of objectifying acts.

Of matter (stuff) and form we often talk in many other senses. We must expressly point out that our present talk of "matter," which has its contrast in categorial form, has nothing whatever to do with the "matter" which contrasts with the quality of acts, as when, e.g., we distinguish the "matter" in our meanings from their assertive or merely presentative quality, this "matter" being what tells us *as what,* or as *now* determined and interpreted, an object is meant in our meanings. To make the distinction easier, we shall not speak of "matter" in our categorial contrast, but of "stuff," while wherever "matter" is meant in our previous sense, we shall talk pointedly of "*intentional* matter" or of "interpretative sense."

§43. The objective correlates of categorial forms are not "real" (realen) moments

It is now time to illuminate the distinction to which we have just given a name. We shall link on, for this purpose, to our previous examples.

The form-giving flexion *Being,* whether in its attributive or predicative function, is not fulfilled, as we said, in any percept. We here remember Kant's dictum: *Being is no real predicate.* This dictum refers to being *qua* existence, or to what Herbart called the being of "absolute position," but it can be taken to be no less applicable to predicative and attributive being. In any case it precisely refers to what we are here trying to make clear. I can see color, but not *being*-colored. I can feel smoothness, but not *being*-smooth. I can hear a sound, but not that something *is* sounding. Being is nothing *in* the object, no part of it, no moment tenanting it, no quality or intensity of it, no figure of it or no internal form whatsoever, no constitutive feature of it however conceived. But being is also nothing attaching *to* an object: as it is no real *(reales)* internal feature, so also it is no real external feature, and therefore not, in the *real* sense, a "feature" at all. For it has nothing to do with the *real* forms of unity which bind objects into more comprehensive objects, tones into harmonies, things into more comprehensive things or arrangements of things (gardens, streets, the phenomenal external world). On these real forms of unity the external features of objects, the right and the left, the high and the low, the loud and the soft, etc., are founded. Among these anything like an "is" is naturally not to be found.

We have just been speaking of *objects,* their constitutive features, their factual connection with other objects, through which more comprehensive objects are created, and also, at the same time, external features in the partial objects. We said that something corresponding to *being* was not to be sought among them. For all these are perceptible, and they exhaust the range of possible percepts, so that we are at once saying and maintaining *that being is absolutely imperceptible.*

Here, however a clarifying supplement is necessary. *Perception* and *object* are concepts that cohere most intimately together, which mutually assign sense to one another, and which widen or narrow this sense conjointly. But we must emphasize that we have here made use of a certain naturally delimited, natural, but also *very narrow concept of perception (or of object).* It is well-known that one also speaks of "perceiving," and in particular of "seeing," in a greatly widened sense, which covers the grasping of whole states of affairs, and even ultimately the a priori self-evidence of laws (in the case of "insight"). In the *narrower* sense of perception (to talk roughly and popularly) we perceive everything objective that we see with our eyes, hear with our ears or can grasp with any "outer" or even "inner sense." In ordinary speech, no doubt, only *external* things and connective forms of things (together with their immediate qualities) can count as "perceived by the senses." But once talk of an "inner sense" had been introduced, one should

in consistency have widened the notion of sense-perception suitably, so as to include "inner perception," and so as to include under the name "sense-object" the correlated sphere of "inner objects," the ego and its internal experiences.

In the sphere of sense-perception thus understood, and in the sphere, likewise, of sensuous intuition in general—we adhere to our much widened talk of the "sensuous"—a meaning like that of the word "being" can find no possible *objective correlate,* and so no possible fulfillment in the acts of such perception. What holds of "being" is plainly true of the remaining categorial forms in our statements, whether these bind the constituents of terms together, or bind terms themselves together in the unity of the proposition. The "a" and the "the," the "and" and the "or," the "if" and the "then," the "all" and the "none," the "something" and the "nothing," the forms of quantity and the determinations of number, etc. —all these are meaningful propositional elements, but we should look in vain for their objective correlates (if such may be ascribed to them at all) in the sphere of *real* objects, which is in fact no other than the sphere of *objects of possible sense-perception.*

*§44. The origin of the concept of being
and of the remaining categories does
not lie in the realm of sense-perception*

This holds—we stress it expressly—both of the sphere of outer sense, and of that of "inner sense." It is a natural but quite misguided doctrine, universally put about since the time of Locke, that the meanings in question (or the corresponding substantivally hypostatized meanings)—the *logical categories* such as being and non-being, unity, plurality, totality, number, ground, consequence, etc.—arise through *reflection upon certain mental acts, and so fall in the sphere of "inner sense," of "inner perception."* In this manner, indeed, concepts like Perception, Judgment, Affirmation, Denial, Collecting, Counting, Presupposing and Inferring arise, which are all, therefore, "sensuous" concepts, belonging, that is, to the sphere of "inner sense." The previous series of concepts do not arise in this manner, since they cannot at all be regarded as concepts of mental acts, or of their real constituents. The thought of a Judgment fulfills itself in the inner intuition of an actual judgment, but the thought of an "is" does not fulfill itself in this manner. Being is not a judgment nor a constituent of a judgment. Being is as little a real constituent of some inner object as it is of some outer object, and so not of a judgment. In a judgment, a predicative statement, "is" functions as a side of our meaning, just as perhaps, although otherwise placed and functioning, "gold" and "yellow" do. The *is* itself does not enter into the judgment, it is merely meant, signitively referred to, by the little word "is." It is, however, *self-given,* or at least putatively given, in the *fulfillment* which at times invests the judgment, the *becoming aware* of the state of affairs supposed. Not only what is meant in the partial meaning *gold,* nor only what is meant in the partial meaning *yellow,* itself appears before us, but also *gold-being-yellow* thus appears. Judgment and judgmental intuition are therefore at one in the self-evident judgment, and pre-eminently so if the judgment is self-evident in the ideally limiting sense.

If one now understands by "judging" not merely meaning-intentions connected with actual assertions, but the fulfillments that in the end fit them completely, it is indeed correct that *being can only be apprehended through judging,* but this does not *at all mean* that the concept of being must be arrived at "through reflection" on certain judgments, or that it can ever be arrived at in this fashion. "Reflection" is in other respects a fairly vague word. In epistemology it has at least the relatively fixed sense that Locke gave it, that of internal perception: we can only adhere to this sense in interpreting a doctrine which imagines it can find the origin of the concept of *Being* through reflecting on judgments. The relational being expressed in predication, e.g., through "is," "are," etc., lacks independence: if we round it out to something fully concrete, we get the *state of affairs* in question, the objective correlate of the complete judgment. We can then say: *As the sensible object stands to sense-perception so the state of affairs stands to the "becoming aware" in which it is* (more or less adequately) *given*—we should like to say simply: so the state of affairs stands to the *perception* of it. As the concept *Sensuous Object (Real Object)* cannot arise through reflection upon perception, since this could only yield us the concept *Perception* (or a concept of certain real constituents of Perception), so the concept of State of Affairs cannot arise out of reflection on judgments, since this could only yield us concepts of judgments or of real constituents of judgments.

That percepts in the one case, and judgments (judgmental intuitions, percepts of states of affairs) in the other, must be *experienced,* in order that each such act of abstraction should get started, goes without saying, but to be experienced is not to be made objective. "Reflection," however, implies that what we reflect upon, the phenomenological experience, is rendered objective to us (is inwardly perceived by us), and that the properties to be generalized are really given in this objective content.

Not in reflection upon judgments, nor even upon fulfillments of judgments, but in the fulfillments of judgments themselves lies the true source of the concepts State of Affairs and Being (in the copulative sense). Not in these *acts as objects,* but in the *objects of these acts,* do we have the abstractive basis which enables us to realize the concepts in question. And naturally the appropriate modifications of these acts yield just as good a basis.

It is in fact obvious from the start that, just as any other concept (or Idea, Specific Unity) can only "arise," i.e., become *self-given* to us, if based on an act which at least sets some individual instance of it imaginatively before our eyes, so the concept of Being can arise only when *some being, actual or imaginary, is set before our eyes.* If "being" is taken to mean predicative being, some *state of affairs* must be given to us, and this by way of an *act which gives it, an analogue of common sensuous intuition.*

The like holds of all *categorial forms* (or of

all *categories*). An aggregate, e.g., is given, and can only be given, in an actual act of assembly, in an act, that is, expressed in the conjunctive form of connection *A and B and C* . . . But the concept of *Aggregate* does not arise through reflection on this act: instead of paying heed to the act which presents an aggregate, we have rather to pay heed to what it presents, to the *aggregate* it renders apparent *in concreto,* and then to lift the universal form of our aggregate to conceptually universal consciousness.

§45. Widening of the concept of Intuition, and in particular of the concepts Perception and Imagination. Sensible and categorial intuition

If we now ask: "Where do the categorial forms of our meanings find their fulfillment, if not in the 'perception' or 'intuition' which we tried provisionally to delimit in talking of 'sensibility,'" our answer is plainly prefigured in the discussions just completed.

We have taken it for granted that forms, too, can be genuinely fulfilled, or that the same applies to variously structured total meanings, and not merely to the "material" elements of such meanings, and our assumption is put beyond doubt by looking at each case of faithful perceptual assertion. This will explain also why we call the whole perceptual assertion an expression of perception, and, in a derivative sense, of whatever is intuited or itself presented in perception. But if the "categorial forms" of the expression, present together with its material aspects, have no terminus in perception, if by the latter we understand merely *sense*-perception, then talk of expressing a percept must here rest on a different meaning: there must at least be an act which renders identical services to the categorial elements of meaning that merely sensuous perception renders to the material elements. The essential homogeneity of the function of fulfillment, as of all the ideal relationships necessarily bound up with it, obliges us to give the name "perception" to each fulfilling act of confirmatory self-presentation, to each fulfilling act what-

ever the name of an "intuition," and to its intentional correlate the name of *"object."* If we are asked what it means to say that *categorially structured meanings* find fulfillment, confirm themselves in perception, we can but reply: it means only that they relate to the object itself *in its categorial structure.* The object with these categorial forms is not merely referred to, as in the case where meanings function purely symbolically, but it is set before our very eyes in just these forms. In other words: it is not merely thought of, but intuited or perceived. When we wish, accordingly, to set forth what this talk of "fulfillment" is getting at, what structured meanings and their structural elements express, what unitary or unifying factor corresponds to them objectively, we unavoidably come on "intuition" (or on "perception" and "object"). We cannot manage without these words, whose widened sense is of course evident. What shall we call the correlate of a non-sensuous subject-presentation, one involving non-sensuous structure, if the word "object" is not available to us? How shall we speak of its actual givenness, or apparent givenness, when the word "perception" is denied us? In common parlance, therefore, *aggregates, indefinite pluralities, totalities, numbers, disjunctions, predicates* (right-ness), *states of affairs,* all count as "objects," while the acts through which they seem to be given count as "percepts."

Plainly the connection between the wider and narrower, the *supersensuous* (i.e., raised above sense, or categorial) and *sensuous concept of perception,* is no external or contingent matter, but one rooted in the whole business on hand. It falls within the great class of acts whose peculiarity it is that in them something appears as "actual," as "self-given." Plainly this appearance of actuality and self-givenness (which may very well be delusive) is throughout characterized by its difference from essentially related acts through which alone it achieves full clarity—its difference from an imaginative "making present," or from a merely significative "thinking of," which both exclude "presence" (so to say appearance "in person"), though not excluding the belief in being. As regards the latter, imaginal or symbolic representation is possible in two manners: in an assertive manner, asserting something's being in imaginal or symbolic fashion, and in a non-assertive manner, as "mere" imagination or thinking without taking something to be. We need not enter more closely into the discussion of these differences after the analyses of the previous section, which permit of a sufficiently general interpretation. It is clear, in any case, that the concept of imagination must be *widened in correspondence with* the concept of perception. We could not speak of something supersensuously or categorially *perceived,* if we could not *imagine* this thing "in the same manner" (i.e., not merely sensuously). We must therefore draw a quite general distinction between *sensuous* and *categorial* intuition (or show the possibility of such a distinction).

Our extended concept of Perception permits, further, of a narrower and a wider interpretation. In the widest sense even universal states of affairs can be said to be perceived ("seen," "beheld with evidence"). In the narrower sense, perception terminates upon individual, and so upon temporal being.

§46. Phenomenological analysis of the distinction between sensuous and categorial perception

In our next treatments we shall first only discuss individual percepts, then widen our treatment to take in individual intuitions of the same order.

The division between "sensuous" and "supersensuous" percepts was only very superficially indicated and quite roughly characterized above. Antiquated talk of external and internal senses, plainly stemming from the naive metaphysic and anthropology of daily life, may be useful in pointing out the sphere to be excluded, but a true determination and circumscription of the sensory sphere is not thereby reached, so depriving the concept of categorial perception of its descriptive underpinning. To ascertain and clarify the said distinction is all the more important, since such

fundamental distinctions as that between categorial form and sensuously founded matter, and the similar distinction between categories and all other concepts, depends wholly on it. Our concern is therefore to seek more profound descriptive characterizations, which will give us some insight into the essentially different constitution of sensuous and categorial percepts (or intuitions in general).

For our immediate purposes it is, however, unnecessary to carry out an exhaustive analysis of the phenomena involved. That would be a task that would require extraordinarily comprehensive treatments. Here it is sufficient to concentrate on some weightier points, which may help to mark off both sorts of acts in their mutual relation.

It is said of every percept that it grasps its object *directly,* or grasps this object *itself.* But this direct grasping has a different sense and character according as we are concerned with a percept in the narrower or the wider sense, or according as the directly grasped object is *sensuous* or *categorial.* Or otherwise put, according as it is a *real* or an *ideal* object. Sensuous or real objects can in fact be characterized as *objects of the lowest level of possible intuition,* categorial or ideal objects as *objects of higher levels.*

In the sense of the *narrower, "sensuous" perception,* an object is directly apprehended or is itself present, if it is set up in an act of perception *in a straightforward (schlichter) manner.* What this means is this: that the object is also an *immediately given object* in the sense that, as *this object perceived with this definite objective content,* it is not *constituted* in relational, connective, or otherwise articulated acts, *acts founded on other acts which bring other objects to perception.* Sensuous objects are present in perception *at a single act-level:* they do not need to be constituted in many-rayed fashion in acts of higher level, whose objects are set up for them by way of other objects, already constituted in other acts.

Each straightforward act of perception, by itself or together with other acts, can serve as basic act for new acts which at times include it, at times merely presuppose it, acts which in their new mode of consciousness likewise bring to maturity *a new awareness of objects which essentially presupposes the old.* When the new acts of conjunction, of disjunction, of definite and indefinite individual apprehension (that—something), of generalization, of straightforward, relational and connective knowledge, arise, we do not then have *any* sort of subjective experiences, nor just acts connected with the original ones. What we have are acts which, as we said, *set up new objects,* acts in which something *appears as actual and self-given,* which was not given, and could not have been given, as what it now appears to be, in these foundational acts alone. *On the other hand, the new objects are based on the older ones, they are related to what appears in the basic acts.* Their manner of appearance is essentially determined by this relation. We are here dealing with a sphere of objects, *which can only show themselves "in person" in such founded acts.* In such founded acts we have the categorial element in intuition and knowledge, in them assertive thought, functioning expressively, finds fulfillment; the possibility of complete accord with such acts determines the truth, the rightness, of an assertion. So far we have of course only considered the sphere of perception, and only its most elementary cases. But one sees at once that the distinction of straightforward and founded acts can be extended from percepts to all intuitions. We clearly envisage the possibility of complex acts which in mixed fashion have a part-basis in straightforward percepts and a part-basis in straightforward imaginations, and the further possibility of setting up new foundations on intuitions which themselves have foundations, and so building up whole series of foundings upon foundings. We further see that signitive intentions have structures patterned on such foundings whether of lower or higher order, and that again mixtures of signitive and intuitive acts emerge out of such "founding," founded acts, in short, that are built on acts of one or the other sort. Our first task, however, is to deal with the elementary cases and elucidate them completely.

§47. Continuation. Characterization of sense-perception as "straightforward" perception

We shall now scrutinize the acts in which sensuous concreta and their sensuous constituents are presented as given; as opposed to these we shall later consider the quite different acts in which concretely determinate States of Affairs, Collections and Disjunctions are given as complex thought-objects, or as objects of higher order, *which include their foundational objects as real parts (reell) in themselves.* We shall then deal with acts of the type of generalizing or indefinitely individual apprehension, whose objects certainly are of higher level, but which do *not* include their foundational objects in themselves.

In *sense*-perception, the "external" thing appears "in one blow," as soon as our glance falls upon it. The manner in which it makes the thing appear present is *straightforward:* it requires no apparatus of founding or founded acts. To what complex mental processes it may trace back its origin, and in what manner, is of course irrelevant here.

We are not ignoring the obvious complexity that can be shown to exist in the phenomenological content of the straightforward perceptual act, and particularly in its unitary intention.

Many constitutive properties certainly pertain to the thing when it appears with a given content, some of them themselves "falling under perception," others merely intended. But we certainly do not live through all the articulated acts of perception which *would* arise were we to attend to all the details of the thing, or, more precisely, to the properties of the "side turned to us," were we to make them objects in their own right. No doubt ideas of such supplementary properties, not given in perception, are "dispositionally excited," no doubt intentions which relate to them contribute to perception, and determine its total character. But, just as the thing does not appear before us as the mere sum of its countless individual features, which a later preoccupation with detail may distinguish, and as even the latter does not dirempt the thing into such details, but takes note of them only in the ever complete, unified thing, so the act of perception also is always a homogeneous unity, which gives the object "presence" in a simple, immediate way. The unity of perception does *not* therefore arise through *our own synthetic activity*, as if only a form of synthesis, operating by way of founded acts, could give unity of objective reference to part-intentions. It requires no articulation and hence no actual linkage. The unity of perception comes into being as a *straightforward* unity, *as an immediate fusion of part-intentions, without the addition of new act-intentions.*

We may also be unsatisfied with a single glance, we may handle the thing from all sides in a *continuous perceptual series,* feeling it over as it were with our senses. But each single percept in this series is already a percept of the thing. Whether I look at this book from above or below, from inside or outside, I always see *this book.* It is always one and the same thing, and that not merely in some purely physical sense, but in the view of our percepts themselves. If individual properties dominate variably at each step, the thing itself, as a perceived unity, is not in essence set up by some overreaching act, founded upon these separate percepts.

Considering things more closely, we should not present the matter as if the one sensible object *could* be presented in a founded act (in a continuously developing act of perceiving), while it merely does not *need* to be presented in such an act. Closer analysis shows that even a continuous perceptual flux involves a *fusion* of part-acts in one act, *rather than a peculiar act founded upon such part-acts.*

To prove this we embark on the following discussion.

The individual percepts of our series have a continuous unity. Such continuity does not amount to the mere fact of temporal adjunction: the series of individual acts rather has the character of a phenomenological unity, in which the individual acts are fused. In this unity, our manifold acts are not merely fused into a phenomenological whole, but into *one act,*

more precisely, into *one concept.* In the continuous running on of individual percepts we continuously perceive the single, selfsame object. Can we now call this continuous percept, since it is built out of individual percepts, a percept *founded* upon them? It is of course founded upon them in the sense in which a whole is founded on its parts, not however in the sense here relevant, according to which a founded act manifests a new act-character, grounded in the act-characters that underlie it and unthinkable apart from these. In the case before us perception is merely, as it were, extended: it allows parts to be broken off from itself which can function as complete, independent percepts. But the unification of these percepts into a continuous percept is not the performance of some peculiar act, through which a new consciousness of something objective is set up. We find, instead, that absolutely nothing new is objectively meant in the extended act, but that the same object is continuously meant in it, the very object that the part-percepts, *taken singly,* were already meaning.

One might lay stress on this sameness, and say that our unity is plainly a *unity of identification,* that the intention of the serially arranged acts coincides continuously, and that so the unity arises. This is certainly right. But *unity of identification* is unavoidably distinct, *does not say the same as the unity of an act of identification.* An act *means* something, an act of identification means identity, presents it. In our case an identification is performed, but no identity is meant. The object meant in the differing acts of the continuous perceptual series is indeed always the same, and the acts are one through coincidence, but what is perceived in the series, what is rendered objective in it, is solely the sensible object, never its identity with self. Only when we use the perceptual series to found a novel act, only when we articulate our individual percepts, and relate their objects to each other, does the unity of continuity holding among these individual percepts—the unity of fusion through their coinciding intentions—provide a *point d'appui* for a consciousness of identity.

Identity itself is now made objective, the moment of coincidence linking our act-characters with one another, serves as *representative content for a new percept, founded upon* our articulated individual percepts. This brings to intentional awareness that what we now see and what we saw before are one and the same. Naturally we have then to do with a regular act of our second group. Our act of identification is in sober fact a new awareness of objectivity, which causes a new "object" to appear to us, an object that can only be apprehended or given in its very selfhood in a founded act of this sort.

Before we penetrate further into our new class of acts and objects, we must, however, first round off our treatment of straightforward percepts. If we may presume to have cleared up the sense of the concept of a *straightforward* percept, or, what we take for the same, of sense-perception, then we have also cleared up the concept of a *sensible* or *real object* (in the most basic sense of "real"). We define a real object as the possible object of a straightforward percept. There is a necessary parallelism between perception and *imagination,* which guarantees that a possible imagination (or more precisely a whole series of imaginations) having the same essence corresponds to each possible percept, a *straightforward* imagination is correlated with each straightforward percept, thereby giving certainty to the wider concept of *sensible intuition.* We can then define *sensible* objects as the possible objects of sensible imagination and sensible intuition in general: this of course involves no essential generalization of our previous definition. The parallelism just stressed makes both definitions equivalent.

Through the concept of a real object, the concept of a *real* part, or more particularly, the concepts of a *real piece,* and a *real* moment (real feature), and a *real form,* are determined. Each part of a real object is a real part.

In straightforward perception we say that the whole object is explicitly given, while each of its parts (in the widest sense of "parts") is implicitly given. The sum total of objects that can be *explicitly or implicitly given* in straightforward percepts constitutes *the most widely conceived sphere of sensible objects.*

Each concrete sensible object is perceptible in explicit fashion, and so also every piece of such an object. How does the matter stand in regard to abstract moments? Their nature makes them incapable of separate being: their representative content, even where there is merely representation by way of analogy, cannot be experienced alone, but only in a more comprehensive concrete setting. But this does not mean that their intuition need be a founded act. It would be one, if the apprehension of an abstract moment was necessarily preceded by the *apprehension* of the concrete whole or of its complementary moments, such an apprehension being an act of intuitive turning towards its object. This I do not find obvious. It is clear, *per contra,* that the apprehension of a moment and of a part generally *as* a part of the whole in question, and, in particular, the apprehension of a sensuous feature *as* a feature, or of a sensuous form *as* a form, point to acts which are all founded: these acts are in our case of a relational kind. This means that the sphere of "sensibility" has been left and that of "understanding" entered. We shall now subject the just mentioned group of founded acts to a closer consideration.

§48. *Characterization of categorial acts as founded acts*

A sensible object can be apprehended by us in a variety of ways. It can, first of all, of course, be apprehended in "straightforward" fashion. It is this possibility, which like all the other possibilities here in question must be throughout interpreted as "ideal," which characterizes the sensible object as a sensible object. Understood in this manner, it stands as it were simply before us: the parts which constitute it are indeed in it, but are not made our explicit objects in the straightforward act. The same object can, however, be grasped by us in explicating fashion: acts of articulation can put its parts "into relief," relational acts bring the relieved parts into relation, whether to one another or to the whole. Only through such new modes of interpretation will the connected and related members assume the character of "parts" (or of "wholes"). The articulating acts, and, taken in retrospect, the act we call "straightforward," are not merely experienced one after the other: *overreaching unities of act* are rather always present, in which, *as new objects,* the *relationships of the parts* become constituted.

Let us first look at the relationships of parts and wholes: limiting ourselves to the simplest cases, let us consider the relationships *A is or has* α and α *is in A.* To point to the founded acts in which these typical states of affairs become constituted as data, and to clear up the just employed forms of categorical statement (to lead them back to their intuitive origin and adequate fulfillment) are one and the same. We are not, however, here concerned with the qualities of acts, but only with the constitution of their interpretative forms: to that extent our analysis, if regarded as an analysis of judgment, will be defective.

An act of perception grasps *A* as a whole, at one "blow" and in straightforward fashion. A second act of perception is trained upon α, the part or dependent moment, that belongs constitutively to *A.* These two acts are not merely performed together, or after one another, in the manner of disjoined experiences; rather are they bound together in a single act in whose synthesis *A* is first given as containing α in itself. Just so, α can, with a reversal of the direction of relational perception, achieve self-givenness as pertaining to *A.*

Let us now try to penetrate a little deeper.

The total intuitive reference to our object implicitly contains an intention to α. For perception purports to grasp the object itself: its "grasping" must therefore reach to all its constituents in and with the whole object. (Naturally we are here only concerned with what constitutes the object *as* it appears in perception, and *as what* it appears in perception, and not with such constituents as may pertain to it in "objective reality," and which only later experience, knowledge and science will bring out.)

In the narrowing down of our total percept to one specific percept, the part-intention to α will not be torn out of the total appearance of *A,* so as to break up the latter's unity, but an *independent* act will have α as its own perceptual object. At the same time one's continuously operative total percept will coincide with this specific percept in respect of one implicit part-intention. The "content" which represents α, will be functioning as the same content in a twofold fashion, and, in so far as it does this, it will effect a coincidence, a peculiar unity of the two representative functions; we shall, in other words, have two coincident interpretations, both sustained by the representative content in question. But this unity of these two representative functions will now itself take on a representative role. It will not itself count in its own right as an experienced bond among acts: it will not set itself up as our object, but will help to set up another object. It will act representatively, and to such effect, that *A* will now appear to contain α in itself (or, with a reversed direction, α will appear as contained in *A*).

According, therefore, to our "interpretative standpoint," or to the "sense of our passage" from part to whole or contrariwise— which are both *novel phenomenological characters* making their contribution to the total intentional matter of the relating act—there will be two possibilities, marked off in a priori fashion, in which the "same relation" can achieve actual givenness. To these correspond two a priori possibilities of relation, objectively different, yet tied together by an ideal law, possibilities *which can only be directly constituted in founded acts of the sort in question,* which can achieve "self-givenness to perception" only in acts built up in this manner.

Our exposition obviously applies to all specific forms of the relation between a *whole* and its *parts.* All such relationships are of categorial, ideal nature. It would be a mistake to try to locate them in the straightforwardly given whole, to discover them in this whole by analysis. The part certainly lies hidden in the whole before all division into members, and is subsidiarily apprehended in our perceptual grasp of this whole. But this fact, that it thus lies hidden in the whole, is at first merely the ideal possibility of bringing the part, and the fact that it is a part, to perception in correspondingly articulated and founded acts.

The matter is plainly similar in the case of *external* relations, from which predications such as *"A* is to the right of *B,"* *"A* is larger, brighter, louder than *B,* etc.,"* take their rise. Wherever sensible objects—directly and independently perceptible—are brought together, despite their mutual exclusion, into more or less intimate unities, into what fundamentally are more comprehensive objects, then a possibility of such external relations arises. They all fall under the general type of the relation of *part to parts within a whole. Founded acts* are once more the media *in which the primary appearance of the states of affairs in question,* of such external relationships, is achieved. It is clear, in fact, that neither the straightforward percept of the complex whole, nor the specific percepts pertaining to its members, are in themselves the relational percepts which alone are possible in such a complex. Only when one member is picked out as principal member, and is dwelt on while the other members are still kept in mind, does a determination of members by members make its appearance, a determination which varies with the kind of unity that is present and plainly also with the particular members set in relief. In such cases also the choice of a principal member, or of a direction of relational apprehension, leads to phenomenologically distinct forms of relationship, correlatively characterized, which forms are not genuinely present in the unarticulated percept of the connection as a straightforward phenomenon, but which are in it only as *ideal possibilities,* the possibilities, that is, of fulfilling relevant founded acts.

A real *(reelle)* location of these relations of parts in the whole would be a confusion of distinct things: of *sensuous* or *real (realen)* forms of combination, with *categorial* or *ideal* ones. Sensible combinations are aspects of the real *(realen)* object, its actual moments, present in it, if only implicitly, and capable of being "lifted out of it" by an abstractive percept. As against this, forms of categorial combination go with the manner in which acts are synthesized: they are constituted as objects in the synthetic acts built upon our sensibility. In the formation of external relations sensuous forms may serve as foundations for the categorial forms which correspond to them, as when, in the face of the sensuously intuited contact of the contents *A* and *B* within a comprehensive whole *W,* we observe, and perhaps verbally express our observation, in the synthetic forms *"A* is in contact with *B,"* or *"B* is in contact with *A."* But, in constituting the latter forms, we bring new objects into being, objects belonging to the class of "states of affairs," which includes none but "objects of higher order." In the sensible whole, the parts *A* and *B* are made one by the sensuously combinatory form of contact. The abstraction of these parts and moments, the formation of intuitions of *A, B* and *contact,* will not yet yield the presentation *A in contact with B.* This demands a novel act which, taking charge of such presentations, shapes and combines them suitably.

VI.

From Subjectivity to Intersubjectivity

9. Empathy and the Constitution of the Other

Primordial Abstraction*

§42. Exposition of the problem of experiencing someone else, in rejoinder to the objection that phenomenology entails solipsism

As the point of departure for our new meditations, let us take what may seem to be a grave objection. The objection concerns nothing less than the claim of transcendental phenomenology to be itself transcendental *philosophy* and therefore its claim that, in the form of a constitutional problematic and theory moving within the limits of the transcendentally reduced ego, it can solve the transcendental problems pertaining to the *Objective world.* When I, the meditating I, reduce myself to my absolute transcendental ego by phenomenological epoché do I not become *solus ipse;* and do I not remain that, as long as I carry on a consistent self-explication under the name phenomenology? Should not a phenomenology that proposed to solve the problems of Objective being, and to present itself actually as philosophy, be branded therefore as transcendental solipsism?

Let us consider the matter more closely. Transcendental reduction restricts me to the stream of my pure conscious processes and the unities constituted by their actualities and potentialities. And indeed it seems obvious that such unities are inseparable from my ego and therefore belong to his concreteness itself.

But what about other egos, who surely are not a mere intending and intended *in me,* merely synthetic unities of possible verification *in me,* but, according to their sense, precisely *others?* Have we not therefore done transcendental realism an injustice? The doctrine may lack a phenomenological foundation; but essentially it is right in the end, since it looks for a path from the immanency of the ego to the transcendency of the Other. Can we, as phenomenologists, do anything but agree with this and say: "The Nature and the whole world that are constituted 'immanently' in the ego are only my 'ideas' and have behind them the world that exists in itself. The way to this world must still be sought"? Accordingly can we avoid saying likewise: "The very question of the possibility of actually transcendent knowledge—above all, that of the possibility of my going outside my ego and reaching other egos (who, after all, as others, are not actually in me but only consciously intended in me)—this question cannot be asked purely phenomenologically"? Is it not *self-understood* from the very beginning that my field of transcendental knowledge does not reach beyond my sphere of transcendental experience and what is synthetically comprised therein?

*CM, pp. 89–108 (Sections 42–49).

Is it not self-understood that all of that is included without residue in my own transcendental ego?

But perhaps there is some mistake in thoughts like these. Before one decides in favor of them and the "self-understood" propositions they exploit, and then perchance embarks on dialectical argumentations and self-styled "metaphysical" hypotheses (whose supposed possibility may turn out to be complete absurdity), it might indeed be more fitting to undertake the *task of phenomenological explication* indicated in this connection by the "alter ego" and carry it through in concrete work. We must, after all, obtain for ourselves insight into the explicit and implicit intentionality wherein the alter ego becomes evinced and verified in the realm of our transcendental ego; we must discover in what intentionalities, syntheses, motivations, the sense "other ego" becomes fashioned in me and, under the title, harmonious experience of someone else, becomes verified as existing and even as itself there in its own manner. These experiences and their works are facts belonging to my phenomenological sphere. How else than by examining them can I explicate the sense, existing others, in all its aspects?

§43. *The noematic-ontic mode of givenness of the Other, as transcendental clue for the constitutional theory of the experience of someone else*

First of all, my "transcendental clue" is the experienced Other, given to me in straightforward consciousness and as I immerse myself in examining the noematic-ontic content belonging to him (purely as correlate of my cogito, the particular structure of which is yet to be uncovered). By its remarkableness and multiplicity, that content already indicates the many-sidedness and difficulty of the phenomenological task. For example: In changeable harmonious multiplicities of experience I experience others as actually existing and, on the one hand, as world Objects—not as mere physical things belonging to Nature,

though indeed as such things in respect of one side of them. They are in fact experienced also as *governing psychically* in their respective natural organisms. Thus peculiarly involved with animate organisms, as "psychophysical" Objects, they are *"in" the world*. On the other hand, I experience them at the same time as *subjects for this world,* as experiencing it (this same world that I experience) and, in so doing, experiencing me too, even as I experience the world and others in it. Continuing along this line, I can explicate a variety of other moments noematically.

In any case then, within myself, within the limits of my transcendentally reduced pure conscious life, I *experience* the world (including others)—and, according to its experiential sense, *not* as (so to speak) my *private* synthetic formation but as other than mine alone *[mir fremde],* as an *intersubjective* world, actually there for everyone, accessible in respect of its Objects to everyone. And yet each has his experiences, his appearances and appearance-unities, his world-phenomenon; whereas the experienced world exists in itself, over against all experiencing subjects and their world-phenomena.

What is the explanation of this? Imperturbably I must hold fast to the insight that every sense that any existent whatever has or can have for me—in respect of its "what" and its "it exists and actually is"—is a sense *in* and *arising from* my intentional life, becoming clarified and uncovered for me in consequence of my life's constitutive syntheses, in systems of harmonious verification. Therefore, in order to provide the basis for answering all imaginable questions that can have any sense <here>—nay, in order that, step by step, these questions themselves may be propounded and solved—it is necessary to begin with a systematic explication of the overt and implicit intentionality in which the being of others for me becomes "made" and explicated in respect of its rightful content—that is, its fulfillment-content.

Thus the problem is stated at first as a special one, namely that of the "thereness-for-me" of others, and accordingly as the theme of a *transcendental theory of experiencing someone else,* a transcendental theory of so-called "empathy." But it soon becomes evident that the range of such a theory is much greater than at first it seems, that it contributes to the founding of a *transcendental theory of the Objective world* and, indeed, to the founding of such a theory in every respect, notably as regards Objective Nature. The existence-sense *[Seinssinn]* of the world and of Nature in particular, as Objective Nature, includes after all, as we have already mentioned, thereness-for-everyone. This is always cointended wherever we speak of Objective actuality. In addition, Objects with "spiritual" predicates belong to the experienced world. These Objects, in respect of their origin and sense, refer us to subjects, usually other subjects, and their actively constituting intentionality. Thus it is in the case of all cultural Objects (books, tools, works of any kind, and so forth), which moreover carry with them at the same time the experiential sense of thereness-for-everyone (that is, everyone belonging to the corresponding cultural community, such as the European or perhaps, more narrowly, the French cultural community, and so forth).

§44. Reduction of transcendental experience to the sphere of ownness

If the transcendental constitution of other subjects and accordingly the transcendental sense, "other subjects," are in question, and consequently a universal sense-stratum that emanates from others and is indispensible to the possibility of an Objective world for me

is also in question, then the sense, "other subjects," that is in question here cannot as yet be the sense: "Objective subjects, subjects existing in the world." As regards method, a prime requirement for proceeding correctly here is that first of all we carry out, *inside the universal transcendental sphere, a peculiar kind of epoché* with respect to our theme. For the present we exclude from the thematic field everything now in question: we *disregard all constitutional effects of intentionality relating immediately or mediately to other subjectivity* and delimit first of all the total nexus of that actual and potential intentionality in which the ego constitutes *within himself a peculiar ownness.**

This *reduction to my transcendental sphere of peculiar* ownness or to my transcendental concrete I-myself, by abstraction from everything that transcendental constitution gives me as Other, has an unusual sense. In the natural, the world-accepting attitude, I find differentiated and contrasted: myself and others. If I "abstract" (in the usual sense) from others, *I "alone"* remain. But such abstraction is not radical; such aloneness in no respect alters the natural world-sense, "experienceable by everyone," which attaches to the naturally understood Ego and would not be lost, even if a universal plague had left only me. Taken however in the transcendental attitude and at the same time with the constitutional abstraction that we have just characterized, my (the meditator's) ego in his transcendental ownness is not the usual I, this man, reduced to a mere correlate phenomenon and having his status within the total world-phenomenon. What concerns us is, on the contrary, *an essential*

---

*Originally: constitutes himself in his peculiar ownness and synthetic unities inseparable from his peculiar ownness, which are therefore to be accounted as part of it.

The following comment was appended later:

§44. "inside the universal transcendental sphere"—"peculiar epoché." But it is misleading when the text goes on to say: "in that we exclude from the theoretical <sic> field everything now in question, in that we <disregard> all constitutional effects that relate immediately or mediately to other subjectivity," etc.

The question after all concerns, not other men, but the manner in which the ego (as the transcendental onlooker experiences him transcendentally) constitutes within himself the distinction between Ego and Other Ego—a difference, however, that presents itself first of all in the phenomenon, "world": as the difference between my human Ego (my Ego in the usual sense) and the other human Ego (the other Ego <likewise in the usual sense>).

structure, which is part of the all-embracing constitution in which the transcendental ego, as constituting an Objective world, lives his life.*

What is specifically peculiar to me as ego, my concrete being as a monad, purely in myself and for myself *with an exclusive ownness,* includes <my> every intentionality and therefore, in particular, the intentionality directed to what is other; but, for reasons of method, the synthetic effect of such intentionality (the actuality for me of what is other) shall at first remain excluded from the theme. In this preeminent intentionality there becomes constituted for me the new existence-sense that goes beyond my monadic very-ownness; there becomes constituted an ego, not as "I myself," but as mirrored in my own Ego, in my monad. The second ego, however, is not simply there and strictly presented; rather is he constituted as "alter ego"—the ego indicated as one moment by this expression being I myself in my ownness. The "Other," according to his own constituted sense, points to me myself; the other is a "mirroring" of my own self and yet not a mirroring proper, an analogue of my own self and yet again not an analogue in the usual sense. Accordingly if, as a first step, the ego in his peculiar ownness has been delimited, has been surveyed and articulated in respect of his constituents—not only in the way of life-processes but also in the way of accepted unities concretely inseparable from him—the question must then be asked: *How* can my ego, within his peculiar ownness, constitute under the name, "experience of something other," precisely something *other*—something, that is, with a sense that excludes the constituted from the concrete make-up of the sense-constituting I-myself, as somehow the latter's analogue? In the first place the question concerns no matter what alter egos; then however it concerns everything that acquires sense-determinations from them—in short, an Objective world in the proper and full signification of the phrase.

These problems will become more understandable if we proceed to characterize the ego's sphere of ownness or, correlatively, to carry out explicitly the abstractive epoché that yields it. Thematic exclusion of the constitutional effects produced by experience of something other, together with the effects of all the further modes of consciousness relating to something other, does not signify merely phenomenological epoché with respect to naive acceptance of the being of the other, as in the case of everything Objective existing for us in straightforward consciousness. After all, the transcendental attitude is and remains presupposed, the attitude according to which everything previously existing for us in straightforward consciousness is taken exclusively as "phenomenon," as a sense meant and undergoing verification, purely in the manner in which, as correlate of uncoverable constitutive systems, it has gained and is gaining existential sense. We are now preparing for just this uncovering and sense-clarification by the novel epoché, more particularly in the following manner.

As Ego in the transcendental attitude I attempt first of all to delimit, within my horizon of transcendental experience, *what is peculiarly my own.* First I say that it is *non-alien [Nicht-Fremdes].* I begin by freeing that horizon abstractively from everything that is at all alien. A property of the transcendental phenomenon "world" is that of being given in harmonious straightforward experience; accordingly it is necessary to survey this world and pay attention to how something alien makes

---

*Strasser attaches here the following note, which Husserl wrote on a separate sheet:
The total appearance of the world—the world always intended in the flux.
The total appearance of Nature.
The total intending of the world, the particular intending—the particular appearance of the particular worldly object. But the intending has strata; I can abstract. Physical-thing appearance, stratum of culture or stratum of human existence as <blank-space> in the flowing present. The stream of world-"appearances," of "perceptual appearances"; what is intended ontologically. Cogito-strata, such that each stratum has a stratum of the cogitatum. The ego directed to what is intended.

its appearance as jointly determining the sense of the world and, so far as it does so, to exclude it abstractively. Thus we abstract first of all from what gives men and brutes their specific sense as, so to speak, Ego-like living beings and consequently from all determinations of the phenomenal world that refer by their sense to "others" as Ego-subjects and, accordingly, presuppose these. For example, all cultural predicates. We can say also that we abstract from everything *"other-spiritual,"* as that which makes possible, in the "alien" or "other" that is in question here, its specific sense. Furthermore the *characteristic of belonging to the surrounding world,* not merely for others who are also given at the particular time in actual experience, but also *for everyone,* the characteristic of being there for and accessible to everyone, of being capable of mattering or not mattering to each in his living and striving—a characteristic of all Objects belonging to the phenomenal world and the characteristic wherein their otherness consists—should not be overlooked, but rather excluded abstractively.

In this connection we note something important. When we thus abstract, *we retain a unitarily coherent stratum of the phenomenon world,* a stratum of the phenomenon that is the correlate of continuously harmonious, continuing world-experience. *Despite* our abstraction, we can *go on continuously in our experiencing intuition,* while remaining exclusively in the aforesaid stratum. This unitary stratum, furthermore, is distinguished by being essentially the *founding* stratum—that is to say: I obviously cannot have the "alien" or "other" as experience, and therefore cannot have the sense "Objective world" as an experiential sense, without having this stratum in actual experience; whereas the reverse is not the case.

Let us observe more closely the result of our abstraction and, accordingly, what it leaves us. From the phenomenon world, from the world appearing with an Objective sense, a substratum becomes separated, as the *"Nature" included in my ownness,* a Nature that must always be carefully distinguished from Nature, pure and simple—that is to say: from the Na-

ture that becomes the theme of the natural scientist. *This* Nature, to be sure, is likewise a result of abstraction, namely abstraction from everything psychic and from those predicates of the Objective world that have arisen from persons. But what is acquired by this abstraction on the part of the natural scientist is a stratum that belongs to the Objective world itself (viewed in the transcendental attitude, a stratum that belongs to the *objective sense:* "Objective world") and is therefore itself Objective—just as, on the other hand, what is abstracted *from* is Objective (the Objective psychic, Objective cultural predicates, and so forth). But in the case of *our* abstraction the sense "Objective," which belongs to everything worldly—as constituted intersubjectively, as experienceable by everyone, and so forth—*vanishes completely.* Thus there is included in my ownness, as purified from every sense pertaining to other subjectivity, *a sense, "mere Nature,"* that has lost precisely that "by everyone" and therefore must not by any means be taken for an abstract stratum of the world or of the world's sense. Among the bodies belonging to this "Nature" and included in my peculiar ownness, I then find my *animate organism* as *uniquely* singled out —namely as the only one of them that is not just a body but precisely an animate organism: the sole Object within my abstract world-stratum to which, in accordance with experience, I ascribe *fields of sensation* (belonging to it, however, in different manners—a field of tactual sensations, a field of warmth and coldness, and so forth), the only Object "in" which I *"rule and govern" immediately,* governing particularly in each of its "organs." Touching kinesthetically, I perceive "with" my hands; seeing kinesthetically, I perceive also "with" my eyes; and so forth; moreover I can perceive thus at any time. Meanwhile the *kinesthesias* pertaining to the organs flow in the mode "I am doing," and are subject to my "I can"; furthermore, by calling these kinesthesias into play, I can push, thrust, and so forth, and can thereby *"act" somatically*—immediately, and then mediately. As *perceptively active, I experience* (or can experience) *all of*

Nature, including my own animate organism, which therefore in the process is reflexively related to itself. That becomes possible because I "can" perceive one hand "by means of" the other, an eye by means of a hand, and so forth —a procedure in which *the functioning organ must become an Object and the Object a functioning organ.* And it is the same in the case of my generally possible original *dealing* with Nature and with my animate organism itself, by means of this organism—which therefore is reflexively related to itself *also in practice.*

Bringing to light my animate organism, reduced to what is included in my ownness, is itself part of bringing to light the *ownness-essence* of the Objective phenomenon: *"I, as this man."* If I reduce *other* men to what is included in my ownness, I get *bodies* included therein; if I reduce *myself* as a man, I get *"my animate organism"* and *"my psyche,"* or myself as a *psychophysical unity—in the latter, my personal Ego,* who operates in this animate organism and, "by means of" it, in the *"external world,"* who is affected by this world, and who thus in all respects, by virtue of the continual experience of such unique modes of Ego- and life-relatedness, is constituted as psychophysically united with the animate corporeal organism. If *ownness-purification of the external world, the animate organism, and the psychophysical whole,* has been effected, I have lost my natural sense as Ego, since every sense-relation to a possible Us or We remains excluded, and have lost likewise all my worldliness, in the natural sense. But, in my spiritual ownness, I am nevertheless the identical Ego-pole of my manifold "pure" subjective processes, those of my passive and active intentionality, and the pole of all the habitualities instituted or to be instituted by those processes.

Accordingly this peculiar abstractive sense-exclusion of what is alien leaves us a *kind of "world"* still, a Nature reduced to what is included in our ownness and, as having its place in this Nature thanks to the bodily organism, the psychophysical Ego, with "body and soul"

and personal Ego—utterly *unique* members of this reduced "world." Manifestly predicates that get significance from *this* Ego also occur in the reduced world—for example: "value" predicates and predicates of "works" as such. None of this is worldly in the natural sense (therefore all the quotation-marks); it is all exclusively what is mine in my world-experience, pervading my world-experience through and through and likewise cohering unitarily in my intuition. Accordingly the members we distinguish in this, my peculiarly own world-phenomenon, are *concretely* united, as is further shown by the fact that the *spatiotemporal form*—as reduced, however, to the form included in my ownness—also goes into this reduced world-phenomenon. Hence the reduced "Objects"—the "physical things," the "psychophysical Ego"—are likewise *outside one another.*

But here something remarkable strikes us: a sequence of evidences that yet, *in* their sequence, seem paradoxical. The psychic life of my Ego (this "psychophysical" Ego), including my whole world-experiencing life and therefore including my actual and possible experience *of* what is other, is wholly unaffected by screening off what is other. Consequently there belongs within my psychic being the whole constitution of the world existing for me and, in further consequence, the differentiation of that constitution into the systems that constitute what is included in my peculiar ownness and the systems that constitute what is other. I, the reduced "human Ego" ("psychophysical" Ego), am constituted, accordingly, as a member of the "world" with a multiplicity of "objects outside me." But I myself constitute all this in my "psyche" and bear it intentionally within me. If perchance it could be shown that everything constituted as part of my peculiar ownness, including then the reduced "world," belonged to the concrete essence of the constituting subject as an inseparable internal determination, then, in the Ego's self-explication, his peculiarly own world would be found as "inside" and, on the other hand, when running through that world straightforwardly, the Ego would find himself as a member among its "externalities" and would distinguish between himself and "the external world."

§45. The transcendental ego, and self-apperception as a psychophysical man reduced to what is included in my ownness

These last meditations, like all the others, have been carried on by us in the attitude that effects transcendental reduction—carried on, that is to say, by me (the meditator) as transcendental ego. We now ask how I, the human Ego reduced to what is purely my own and, as thus reduced, included in the similarly reduced world-phenomenon and, on the other hand, I as transcendental ego are related to one another. The transcendental ego emerged by virtue of my "parenthesizing" of the entire Objective world and all other (including all ideal) Objectivities. In consequence of this parenthesizing, I have become aware of myself as the transcendental ego, who constitutes in his constitutive life everything that is ever Objective for me—the ego of all constitutions, who exists in his actual and potential life-processes and Ego-habitualities and who constitutes in them not only everything Objective but also himself as identical ego. We can say now: In that I, as this ego, have constituted and am continually further constituting as a phenomenon (as a correlate) the world that exists for me, I have carried out a *mundanizing self-apperception*—under the title "Ego in the usual sense"—in corresponding constitutive syntheses and am maintaining a continuing acceptance and further development of it. By virtue of this mundanization everything included in the ownness belonging to me transcendentally (as this ultimate ego) enters, as something *psychic,* into "my psyche." I find the mundanizing apperception; and now, from the psyche as phenomenon and part of the phenomenon man, I can go back to the all-inclusive *absolute* ego, the *transcendental* ego. Therefore if I, as this ego, reduce my phenom-

enon, "the Objective world," to what is included in my peculiar ownness and take in addition whatever else I find as peculiarly my *own* (which can no longer contain anything "alien" or "other," after that reduction), then all this ownness of my ego is to be found again, in the reduced world-phenomenon, as the ownness of *"my psyche."* Here, however, as a component pertaining to my world-apperception, it is something *transcendentally secondary.* Restricting ourselves to the ultimate transcendental ego and the universe of what is constituted in him, we can say that a division of his whole transcendental field of experience belongs to him immediately, namely the division into the sphere of his ownness—with the coherent stratum consisting in his experience of a world reduced to what is included in his ownness (an experience in which everything "other" is "screened off")—and the sphere of what is "other." Yet every *consciousness of* what is other, every mode of appearance *of* it, belongs in the former sphere. Whatever the transcendental ego constitutes in that *first* stratum, whatever he constitutes as non-other, as his "peculiarly own"—that indeed belongs to him as *a component of his own concrete essence* (as we shall show); it is inseparable from his concrete being. Within and by means of this ownness the transcendental ego constitutes, however, the "Objective" world, as a universe of being that is other than himself—and constitutes, at the first level, the other in the mode: alter ego.

§46. Ownness as the sphere of the actualities and potentialities of the stream of subjective processes

Up to now we have characterized the fundamental concept of "my own" only indirectly: *as non-alien* or *non-other*—a characterization that is based on, and thus presupposes, the concept of another ego. In order to clarify the sense of this "my own" it is important, however, to bring out its positive characteristic, or the positive characteristic of "the ego in his ownness." This characteristic was merely indicated in the last sentences of the preceding section.

As our point of departure let us take something more general. If a concrete object stands out for us in experience as something particular, and our attentively grasping regard then becomes directed to it, it becomes appropriated in this simple grasping merely as "an undetermined object of empirical intuition." It becomes a determined object, and one undergoing further determination, in a continuation of the experience in the form of a determining experience, which at first unfolds only what is included in the object itself: a pure *explication*. In its articulated synthetic course, on the basis of the object given as self-identical in a continuous intuitive synthesis of identification, this pure explication unfolds, in a concatenation of particular intuitions the object's very own determinations, the "internal" determinations. These present themselves originaliter as determinations *in* which it, the Identical itself, is what it is and, moreover, exists in itself, "in and of itself"— determinations wherein its identical being becomes explicated as the particulars making up its ownness: what it is, in particular. This own-essential content is only generally and horizonally anticipated beforehand; it then becomes constituted originaliter—with the sense: internal, own-essential feature (specifically, part or property)—by explication.

Let us apply this. When I am effecting transcendental reduction and reflecting on myself, the transcendental ego, I am given to myself *perceptually* as this ego—in a grasping perception. Furthermore I become aware that, although not grasped before this perception, I was "already given," already there for myself continually as an object of original intuition (as perceived in the broader sense). But I am given, in any case, with an open infinite horizon of still undiscovered *internal features of my own. My* own too is discovered by explication and gets its original sense by virtue thereof. It becomes uncovered originaliter when my experiencing-explicating regard is directed to myself, to my perceptually and even apo-

dictically given "I am" and its abiding identity with itself in the continuous unitary synthesis of original self-experience. Whatever is included in this identical being's own essence is characterized as its actual or possible explicatum, as a respect in which I merely unfold my own identical being as what it, as identical, is in particular: it in itself.

Now the following is to be noted here. Though I speak rightly of *self-perception,* and indeed as regards my concrete ego, that is not to say that, like explication of a perceptually given "visual thing," self-explication always goes on in particular *perceptions,* in the proper sense, and accordingly yields just perceptual explicata and no others. After all, when explicating the horizon of being that is included in my own essence, one of the first things I run into is my immanent temporality and, with it, my existence in the form of an open infiniteness, that of a stream of subjective processes, and in the form of all those "ownnesses" of mine that are somehow included in the stream—one of which is my explicating. Since it goes on in the living present, self-explication can find, strictly *perceptively,* only what is going on in the living present. In the most original manner conceivable it uncovers my own past by means of recollections. Therefore, though I am continually given to myself originaliter and can explicate progressively what is included in my own essence, this explication is *carried out largely in acts of consciousness that are not perceptions* of the own-essential moments it discovers. Thus alone can my stream of subjective processes, the stream in which I live as the identical Ego, become accessible to me: first of all, in respect of its actualities, and then in respect of the potentialities that manifestly are likewise moments of my own essence. All possibilities of the kind subsumed under the I "can" or "could have" set this or that series of subjective processes going (including in particular: I can look ahead or look back, I can penetrate and uncover the horizon of my temporal being)— all such possibilities manifestly belong to me as moments of my own essence.

In every case, however, explication is original if, precisely on the basis of original self-experience, it unfolds the experienced itself and confers upon the experienced that self-givenness which is, for it, the *most original conceivable*. The *apodictic evidence* of transcendental self-perception (the apodictic evidence of the "I am") extends into such explication, though with a previously stated *restriction*. In unqualifiedly apodictic evidence self-explication brings out only the all-embracing structural forms in which I exist as ego—that is to say: in which I exist with an essentially necessary all-inclusiveness and without which I could not exist. They include (among others) the mode of existence in the form of a certain all-embracing life of some sort or other, that of existence in the form of the continuous self-constitution of that life's own processes, as temporal within an all-embracing time, and so forth. In this *all-embracing apodictic a priori*, with its undetermined universality and, on the other hand, its determinability, every explication of single egological data then participates—for example: as a certain, albeit imperfect, evidence contained in the recollection of my own past. The participation in apodicticity appears in the *formal law* (which is itself apodictic): So much illusion, so much being—which is only covered up and falsified thereby and which therefore can be asked about, sought, and (by following a predelineated way) found, even if only with approximation to its fully determined content. This fully determined content itself, with the sense of something firmly identifiable again and again, in respect of all its parts and moments, is an "idea," valid a priori.

§47. The intentional object also belongs to the full monadic concretion of ownness. Immanent transcendence and primordial world

Manifestly (and this is of particular importance) the own-essentially belonging to me as ego comprises more than merely the actualities and potentialities of the stream of subjective processes. Just as it comprises the constitutive systems, *it comprises the constituted unities*—but with a certain *restriction*. That is to say: Where, and *so far as, the constituted unity is inseparable from the original constitution itself*, with the inseparableness that characterizes an immediate *concrete* oneness, not only the constitutive perceiving but also the perceived existent belongs to my concrete very-ownness.

That is not only the case with sensuous data, which, taken as mere data of sensation, become constituted as peculiarly my own: as *"immanent temporalities"* within the limits of my ego. It is also the case with all my *habitualities*, which are likewise peculiarly my own: the habitualities that begin with institutive acts of my own and become constituted as abiding convictions in which *I myself* become abidingly convinced of such and such, and by virtue of which I, as polar Ego (Ego in the particular sense: mere Ego-pole), acquire determinations that are specifically Ego-determinations. But *"transcendent objects"* (for example: the objects of *"external" sensuousness*, unities belonging to multiplicities of sensuous modes of appearance) also belong here: if I, as ego, take into account just what is constituted *actually originaliter* as an appearing spatial object by my own sensuousness, my own apperceptions, *as itself concretely inseparable from them*. We see forthwith that the *entire reduced "world,"* which we previously obtained by excluding the sense-components pertaining to what is other or alien, belongs in this sphere and is rightly included in the positively defined concrete make-up of the ego: as something peculiarly his *own*. As soon as we exclude from consideration the intentional effects produced by "empathy," by our experience of others, we have a Nature (including an animate organism) that is constituted, to be sure, as a unity of spatial objects "transcending" the stream of subjective processes, yet constituted as merely a multiplicity of objects of possible experience—this experience being purely *my own* life, and what is experienced in this experience being nothing more than a synthetic unity inseparable from this life and its potentialities.

In this manner it becomes clear that *the ego, taken concretely,* has a *universe of what is peculiarly his own,* which can be uncovered by an original explication of his apodictic "ego sum"—an explication that is itself apodictic or at least predelineative of an apodictic form. *Within* this *"original sphere"* (the sphere of original self-explication) we find also a "transcendent world," which accrues on the basis of the intentional phenomenon, "Objective world," by reduction to what is peculiarly the ego's own (in the positive sense, which is now preferred). But, provided only that they are subjected to our reduction to what is included in the ego's ownness, all the corresponding illusions, phantasies, "pure" possibilities, and eidetic objectivities, which offer themselves as "transcendent," likewise belong in this domain—the domain of my peculiarly own essentiality, of what I am in myself, in my full concreteness or (as we may also say) what I am in myself as this monad.

§48. The transcendency of the Objective world as belonging to a level higher than that of primordial transcendency

That my own essence can be at all contrasted for me with something else, or that I (who am I) can become aware of someone else (who is not I but someone other than I), presupposes that *not all my own modes of consciousness are modes of my self-consciousness.* Since actual being is constituted originally by harmoniousness of experience, my own self must contain, in contrast to self-experience and the system of its harmoniousness (the system, therefore, of self-explication into components of my ownness), yet other experiences united in harmonious systems. And now the *problem* is how we are to understand the fact that the ego has, and can always go on forming, in himself such intentionalities of a different kind, intentionalities with an existence-sense whereby *he wholly transcends his own being.* How can something ac-

tually existent for me—and, as that, not just somehow meant but undergoing harmonious verification in me—be anything else than, so to speak, a point of intersection belonging to my constitutive synthesis? As concretely inseparable from my synthesis, is it peculiarly my own? But even the possibility of a vaguest, emptiest intending of something alien is problematic, if it is true that, essentially, every such mode of consciousness involves its possibilities of an uncovering of what is intended, its possibilities of becoming converted into either fulfilling or disillusioning experiences of what is meant, and moreover (as regards the genesis of the consciousness) points back to such experiences of the same intended object or a similar one.

The fact of experience of something alien (something that is not I), is present as experience of an Objective world and others in it (non-Ego in the form: other Ego); and an important result of the ownness-reduction performed on these experiences was that it brought out a substratum belonging to them, an intentional substratum in which a reduced "world" shows itself, as an "immanent transcendency." In the order pertaining to constitution of a world *alien to my Ego*—a world *"external" to my own concrete Ego* (but not at all in the natural spatial sense)—that reduced world is the intrinsically first, the *"primordial" transcendency* (or "world"); and, regardless of its *ideality* as a synthetic unity belonging to an infinite system of my potentialities, it is *still a determining part of my own concrete being,* the being that belongs to me as concrete ego.

It must now be made understandable *how,* at the founded higher level, the sense-bestowal pertaining to transcendency proper, to constitutionally secondary *Objective transcendency,* comes about—and does so as an experience. Here it is not a matter of uncovering a genesis going on in time, but a matter of *"static analysis."* The Objective world is constantly there before me as already finished, a datum of my livingly continuous Objective experience and, even in respect of what is no longer experienced, something I go on accepting habitually. It is a matter of examining this experience itself and uncovering intentionally the manner in which it bestows sense, the manner in which it can occur as experience and become verified as evidence relating to an actual existent with an explicatable essence of *its* own, which is not *my* own essence and has no place as a constituent part thereof, though it nevertheless can acquire sense and verification only in my essence.

§49. Predelineation of the course to be followed by intentional explication of experiencing what is other

Constitution of the existence-sense, "Objective world," on the basis of my primordial "world," involves a number of levels. As the *first* of these, there is to be distinguished the constitutional level pertaining to the "other ego" or to any "other egos" whatever—that is: to egos *excluded* from my own concrete being (from me as the "primordial ego"). In connection with that and, indeed, motivated by it, there occurs a *universal super-addition of sense to my primordial world,* whereby the latter becomes the *appearance "of"* a determinate "Objective" world, as the identical world for everyone, myself included. Accordingly *the intrinsically first other* (the first "non-Ego") *is the other Ego.* And the other Ego makes constitutionally possible a new infinite domain of what is "other": an *Objective Nature* and a whole Objective world, to which all other Egos and I myself belong. This constitution, arising on the basis of the *"pure"* others (the other Egos who as yet have no worldly sense), is essentially such that the "others"-for-me do not remain isolated; on the contrary, an *Ego-community,* which includes me, becomes constituted (in my sphere of ownness, naturally) as a community of Egos existing with each other and for each other—*ultimately a community of monads,* which, moreover (in its communalized intentionality) constitutes the *one identical world. In this world* all Egos again present themselves, but *in an Objectivating apperception* with the sense *"men"* or "psychophysical men as worldly Objects."

By virtue of the mentioned communal-ization <of constitutive intentionality>, the transcendental intersubjectivity has an *intersubjective* sphere of ownness, in which it constitutes the Objective world; and thus, as the transcendencental "We," it is a subjectivity for this world and also for the world of men, which is the form in which it has made itself Objectively actual. If, however, intersubjective sphere of ownness and Objective world are to be distinguished here, nevertheless, when I as ego take my stand on the basis of the intersubjectivity constituted from sources within my own essence, I can recognize that the Objective world does not, in the proper sense, *transcend* that sphere or that sphere's own intersubjective essence, but rather inheres in it as an "immanent" transcendency. Stated more precisely: The Objective world as an *idea*—the ideal correlate of an intersubjective (intersubjectively communalized) experience, which ideally can be and is carried on as constantly harmonious—is essentially related to intersubjectivity (itself constituted as having the ideality of endless openness), whose component particular subjects are equipped with mutually corresponding and harmonious constitutive systems. Consequently, *the constitution of the world essentially involves a "harmony" of the monads:* precisely this harmony among particular constitutions in the particular monads; and accordingly it involves also a harmonious generation that goes on in each particular monad. That is not meant, however, as a "metaphysical" hypothesizing of monadic harmony, any more than the monads themselves are metaphysical inventions or hypotheses. On the contrary, it is itself part of the explication of the intentional components implicit in the fact of the experiential world that exists for us. Here again it is to be noted that, as has been repeatedly emphasized, the ideas referred to are not phantasies or modes of the "as if," but arise constitutionally in integral connection with all Objective experience and have their modes of legitimation and their development by scientific activity.

What we have just presented is a preliminary view of the course to be followed, level by level, in the intentional explication that we must carry out, if we are to solve the transcendental problem in the only conceivable way and actually execute the transcendental idealism of phenomenology.

The Appresentation of the Other*

§50. The mediate intentionality of experiencing someone else, as "appresentation" (analogical apperception)

After we have dealt with the prior stage, which is very important transcendentally—namely, definition and articulation of the primordial sphere—the genuine difficulties (and in fact they are not inconsiderable) are occasioned by the *first* of the above-indicated steps toward constitution of an Objective world: *the step taking us to the "other" ego.* They lie, accordingly, in the transcendental clarification of experiencing "someone else"—in the sense in which the other has not yet attained the sense "man."

Experience is original consciousness; and in fact we generally say, in the case of experiencing a man: the other is himself there before us "in person." On the other hand, this being there in person does not keep us from admitting forthwith that, properly speaking, neither the other Ego himself, nor his subjective processes or his appearances themselves, nor anything else belonging to his own essence, becomes given in our experience originally. If it were, if what belongs to the other's own essence were directly accessible, it would be merely a moment of my own essence, and ultimately he himself and I myself would be the same. The situation would be similar as regards his animate organism, if the latter were nothing else but the "body" that is a unity constituted purely in my actual and possible experiences, a unity belonging—as a product of *my* "sensuousness" exclusively—in my primor-

dial sphere. *A certain mediacy of intentionality* must be present here, going out from the substratum, "primordial world" (which in any case is the incessantly underlying basis) and making present to consciousness a "there too," which nevertheless is not itself there and can never become an "itself-there." We have here, accordingly, a kind of *making "co-present,"* a kind of *"appresentation."*

An appresentation occurs even in external experience, since the strictly seen front of a physical thing always and necessarily appresents a rear aspect and prescribes for it a more or less determinate content. On the other hand, experiencing someone else cannot be a matter of just this kind of appresentation, which already plays a role in the constitution of primordial Nature: Appresentation of this sort involves the possibility of verification by a corresponding fulfilling presentation (the back becomes the front); whereas, in the case of that appresentation which would lead over into the other original sphere, such verification must be excluded a priori. How can appresentation of another original sphere, and thereby the sense "someone else," be motivated in my original sphere and, in fact, motivated as experience—as the word "appresentation" (making intended as co-present) already indicates? Not every non-originary making-present can do that. A non-originary making-present can do it only in combination with an originary presentation, an itself-giving proper; and only as demanded by the originary presentation can it have the character of appresentation—somewhat as, in the case of experiencing a physical thing, what is there perceptually motivates <belief in> something else being there too.

The perception proper that functions as the underlying basis is offered us by our *perception of the primordially reduced world,* with its previously described articulation—a perception going on continually within the general bounds of the ego's *incessant self-per-*

*CM, pp. 108–131, 148–151 (Sections 50–56 and 62).

ception. The problem now is: In the perception of that reduced world, what in particular must be of account here? How does the motivation run? What becomes uncovered as involved in the very complicated intentional performance of the appresentation, which does in fact come about?

Initial guidance can be furnished by the verbal sense, *an Other:* an Other Ego. "Alter" signifies alter ego. And the ego involved here is I myself, constituted within my primordial ownness, and uniquely, as the psychophysical unity (the primordial man): as "personal" Ego, governing immediately in my animate organism (the only animate organism) and producing effects mediately in the primordial surrounding world; the subject, moreover, of a concrete intentional life, <and (?)> of a psychic sphere relating to himself and the "world." All of that—with the grouping under types that arises in experiential life and the familiar forms of flow and combination—is at our disposal. As for the intentionalities by which it has become constituted (and they too are highly complicated)—admittedly we have not investigated them <in these meditations>. They belong to a distinct stratum and are the theme of vast investigations into which we did not and could not enter.

Let us assume that another man enters our perceptual sphere. Primordially reduced, that signifies: In the perceptual sphere pertaining to my primordial Nature, a body is presented, which, as primordial, is of course only a determining part of myself: an "immanent transcendency." Since, in this Nature and this world, my animate organism is the only body that is or can be constituted originally as an animate organism (a functioning organ), the body over there, which is nevertheless apprehended as an animate organism, must have derived this sense by an *apperceptive transfer from my animate organism,* and done so in a manner that excludes an actually direct, and hence primordial, showing of the predicates belonging to an animate organism specifically, a showing of them in perception proper. It is clear from the very beginning that only a

similarity connecting, within my primordial sphere, that body over there with my body can serve as the motivational basis for the *"analogizing" apprehension* of that body as another animate organism.

There would be, accordingly, a certain assimilative apperception; but it by no means follows that there would be an inference from analogy. Apperception is not inference, not a thinking act. *Every* apperception in which we apprehend at a glance, and noticingly grasp, objects given beforehand—for example, the already-given everyday world—every apperception in which we understand their sense and its horizons forthwith, points back to a *"primal instituting,"* in which an object with a similar sense became constituted for the first time. Even the physical things of this world that are unknown to us are, to speak generally, known in respect of their type. We have already seen like things before, though not precisely this thing here. Thus *each everyday experience* involves an *analogizing transfer* of an originally instituted objective sense to a new case, with its anticipative apprehension of the object as having a similar sense. To the extent that there is givenness beforehand, there is such a transfer. At the same time, that sense-component in further experience which proves to be actually new may function in turn as institutive and found a pregivenness that has a richer sense. The child who already sees physical things understands, let us say, for the first time the final sense of scissors; and from now on he sees scissors at the first glance *as* scissors—but naturally not in an explicit reproducing, comparing, and inferring. Yet the manner in which apperceptions arise —and consequently in themselves, by their sense and sense-horizon, point back to their genesis—varies greatly. There are different levels of apperception, corresponding to different layers of objective sense. Ultimately we always get back to the *radical differentiation of apperceptions* into those that, according to their genesis, belong purely to the *primordial sphere* and those that present themselves *with the sense "alter ego"* and, *upon* this sense, have built a new one—thanks to a genesis at a higher level.

§51. "Pairing" as an associatively constitutive component of my experience of someone else

If we attempt to indicate the peculiar nature of that analogizing apprehension whereby a body within my primordial sphere, being similar to my own animate body, becomes *apprehended as likewise an animate organism,* we encounter: first, the circumstance that here the *primally institutive original* is *always livingly present,* and the primal instituting itself is therefore always going on in a livingly effective manner; secondly, the peculiarity we already know to be necessary, namely that what is *appresented* by virtue of the aforesaid analogizing can never attain actual presence, never become an object of perception proper. Closely connected with the first peculiarity is the circumstance that *ego* and *alter ego* are always and necessarily given *in an original "pairing."*

Pairing, occurence in configuration as a pair and then as a group, a plurality, is a *universal* phenomenon of the transcendental sphere (and of the parallel sphere of intentional psychology); and, we may add forthwith, as far as a pairing is actually present, so far extends that remarkable kind of primal instituting of an analogizing apprehension—its continuous primal institution in living actuality—which we have already stressed as the first peculiarity of experiencing someone else. Hence it is not exclusively peculiar to this experience.

First of all, let us elucidate the essential nature of any "pairing" (or any forming of a plurality). Pairing is a *primal form of that passive synthesis* which we designate as *"association,"* in contrast to passive synthesis of "identification." In a *pairing association* the characteristic feature is that, in the most primitive case, two data are given intuitionally, and with prominence, in the unity of a consciousness and that, on this basis—essentially, already in pure passivity (regardless therefore of whether they are noticed or unnoticed)—as data appearing with mutual distinctness, they *found phenomenologically a unity of similarity* and thus are always constituted precisely as a pair. If there are more than two such data, then a phenomenally unitary group, a plurality, becomes constituted. On more precise analysis we find essentially present here an intentional overreaching, coming about genetically (and by essential necessity) as soon as the data that undergo pairing have become prominent and simultaneously intended; we find, more particularly, a living mutual awakening and an overlaying of each with the objective sense of the other. This overlaying can bring a total or a partial coincidence, which in any particular instance has its degree, the limiting case being that of complete "likeness." As the result of this overlaying, there takes place in the paired data a mutual transfer of sense—that is to say: an apperception of each according to the sense of the other, so far as moments of sense actualized in what is experienced do not annul this transfer, with the consciousness of "different."

In that case of association and apperception which particularly interests us—namely apperception of the alter ego by the ego—pairing first comes about when the Other enters my field of perception. I, as the primordial psychophysical Ego, am always prominent in my primordial field of perception, regardless of whether I pay attention to myself and turn toward myself with some activity or other. In particular, my live body is always there and sensuously prominent; but, in addition to that and likewise with primordial originariness, it is equipped with the specific sense of an animate organism. Now in case there presents itself, as outstanding in my primordial sphere, a body "similar" to mine—that is to say, a body with determinations such that it must enter into a phenomenal *pairing* with mine—it *seems* clear without more ado that, with the transfer of sense, this body must forthwith appropriate from mine the sense: animate organism. But is the apperception actually so transparent? Is it a simple apperception by transfer, like any other? What makes this organism another's, rather than a second organism of my own? Obviously what we designated as the *second fundamental characteristic* of the apperception in question plays a part here: that none of the *appropriated* sense specific to an animate organism can become actualized originarily in my primordial sphere.

§52. Appresentation as a kind of experience with its own style of verification

But now there arises for us the difficult problem of making it understandable *that such an apperception is possible* and need not be annulled forthwith. How does it happen that, as the fact tells us, the transferred sense is appropriated with existence-status, as a set of "psychic" determinations existing in combination with that body over there, even though they can never show themselves *as* themselves in the domain of originality, belonging to the primordial sphere (which alone is available)?

Let us look at the intentional situation more closely. The appresentation which gives that component of the Other which is not accessible originaliter is combined with an original presentation (of "his" body as part of the Nature given as included in my ownness). In this combination, moreover, the Other's animate body and his governing Ego are given in the manner that characterizes a *unitary transcending experience.* Every experience points to further experiences that would fulfill and verify the appresented horizons, which include, in the form of non-intuitive anticipations, potentially verifiable syntheses of harmonious further experience. Regarding experience of someone else, it is clear that its fulfillingly verifying continuation can ensue *only by means of new appresentations that proceed in a synthetically harmonious fashion,* and only by virtue of the manner in which *these appresentations owe their existence-value to their motivational connection with the* changing *presentations proper, within my ownness,* that continually appertain to them.

As a suggestive *clue* to the requisite clarification, this proposition may suffice: The ex-

perienced animate organism of another continues to prove itself as actually an animate organism, solely in its changing but incessantly *harmonious "behavior."* Such *harmonious* behavior (as having a physical side that indicates something psychic appresentatively) must present itself fulfillingly in original experience, and do so throughout the continuous change in behavior from phase to phase. The organism becomes experienced as a pseudo-organism, precisely if there is something discordant about its behavior.

The character of the existent "other" has its basis in this kind of verifiable accessibility of what is not originally accessible. Whatever can become presented, and evidently verified, *originally*—is something *I* am; or else it belongs to me as peculiarly my own. Whatever, by virtue thereof, is experienced in that founded manner which characterizes a primordially unfulfillable experience—an experience that does not give something itself originally but that consistently verifies something indicated— is "other." It is therefore conceivable only as an analogue of something included in my peculiar ownness. Because of its sense-constitution it occurs necessarily as an *"intentional modification"* of that Ego of mine which is the first to be Objectivated, or as an intentional modification of my primordial "world": the Other as phenomenologically a "modification" of myself (which, for its part, gets this character of being "my" self by virtue of the contrastive pairing that necessarily takes place). It is clear that, with the other Ego, there is appresented, in an analogizing modification, everything that belongs to his concretion: first, *his* primordial world, and then his fully concrete ego. In other words, *another monad* becomes constituted appresentatively in mine.

Similarly (to draw an instructive comparison), within my ownness and moreover within the sphere of its living present, my past is given only by memory and is characterized in memory *as* my past, a past present—that is: an intentional modification. The experiential verification of it, as a modification, then goes on necessarily in harmonious syntheses of recollection; only thus does a past as such become verified. Somewhat as my memorial past, as a modification of my living present, "transcends" my present, the appresented other being "transcends" my own being (in the pure and most fundamental sense: what is included in my primordial ownness). In both cases the modification is inherent as a sense-component in the sense itself; it is a correlate of the intentionality constituting it. Just as, in my living present, in the domain of "internal perception," my past becomes constituted by virtue of the harmonious memories occurring in this present, so in my primordial sphere, by means of appresentations occurring in it and motivated by its contents, an ego other than mine can become constituted—accordingly, in non-originary presentations [in Vergegenwärtigungen] of a new type, which have a modificatum of a new kind as their correlate. To be sure, as long as I consider non-originary presentations <of something lying> within the sphere of my ownness, the Ego in whom they center is the one identical I-myself. On the other hand, to everything alien (as long as it remains within the appresented horizon of concreteness that necessarily goes with it) centers in an appresented Ego who is not I myself but, relative to me, a modificatum: an *other* Ego.

An actually sufficient explication of the noematic complexes involved in experience of what is alien—such an explanation as is absolutely necessary to a complete clarification of what this experience does constitutively, by constitutive association—is not yet completed with what has been shown up to now. There is need of a supplement, in order to reach the point where, on the basis of cognitions already acquired, the possibility and scope of a transcendental constitution of the Objective world can become evident and transcendental-phenomenological idealism can thus become entirely manifest.

§53. Potentialities of the primordial sphere and their constitutive function in the apperception of the Other

As reflexively related to itself, my animate bodily organism (in my primordial sphere) has the central "Here" as its mode of givenness; every other body, and accordingly the "other's" body, has the mode "There." This orientation, "There," can be freely changed by virtue of my kinesthesias. Thus, in my primordial sphere, the *one spatial "Nature"* is constituted throughout the change in orientations, and constituted moreover with an intentional relatedness to my animate organism as functioning perceptually. Now the fact that my bodily organism can be (and is) apprehended as a *natural body existing and movable in space like any other* is manifestly connected with the possibility expressed in the words: By free modification of my kinesthesias, particularly those of locomotion, I can change my position in such a manner that I convert any There into a Here—that is to say, I could occupy any spatial locus with my organism. This implies that, perceiving from there, I should see the same physical things, only in correspondingly different modes of appearance, such as pertain to my being there. It implies, then, that not only the systems of appearance that pertain to my current perceiving "from here," but other quite determinate systems, corresponding to the change of position that puts me "there," belong constitutively to each physical thing. And the same in the case of every other "There."

Should not these interconnections, or rather these instances of belonging together, which are involved in the primordial constitution of "my" Nature and are themselves characterized as associative—should not they be quite essential to clarification of the associative performance, experiencing someone else? After all, I do not apperceive the other ego simply as a duplicate of myself and accordingly as having my original sphere or one completely like mine. I do not apperceive him as having, more particularly, the spatial modes of appearance that are mine from here; rather, as we find on closer examination, I apperceive him as having spatial modes of appearance like those I should have if I should go over there and be where he is. Furthermore the Other is appresentatively apperceived as the "Ego" of a primordial world, and of a monad, wherein his animate organism is originally constituted and experienced in the mode of the absolute Here, precisely as the functional center for his governing. In this appresentation, therefore, the body in the mode *There,* which presents itself in *my* monadic sphere and is apperceived as another's live body (the animate organism of the alter ego)—that body indicates "the same" body in the mode *Here,* as the body experienced by the other ego in *his* monadic sphere. Moreover it indicates the "same" body concretely, with all the constitutive intentionality pertaining to this mode of givenness in the other's experience.

§54. Explicating the sense of the appresentation wherein I experience someone else

Manifestly what has just now been brought to light points to the course of the association constituting the mode "Other." The body that is a member of my primordial world (the body subsequently of the other ego) is for me a body in the mode There. Its manner of appearance does not become paired in a direct association with the manner of appearance actually belonging at the time to my animate organism (in the mode Here); rather it awakens reproductively *another,* an immediately similar appearance included in the system constitutive of my animate organism as a body in space. It brings to mind the way my body would look "if I were there." In this case too, although the awakening does not become a memory *intuition, pairing* takes place. The first-awakened manner of appearance of my body is not the only thing that enters into a pairing; my body itself does so likewise: as the synthetic unity pertaining to this mode, and the many other familiar modes, of its appearance. *Thus the assimilative apperception becomes possible* and established, by which the external body over there receives analogically from mine the sense, animate organism, and consequently the sense, organism belonging to another "world," analogous to my primordial world.

The *general style* of this and every other apperception that arises associatively is

therefore to be described as follows: With the associative overlapping of the data founding the apperception, there takes place an association at a higher level. If the one datum is a particular mode of appearance of an intentional object, which is itself an index pointing to an associatively awakened system of manifold appearances wherein it would show itself, then the other datum is "supplemented" to become likewise an appearance *of* something, namely an analogous object. But it is not as though the unity and multiplicity "thrust upon" the latter datum merely supplemented it with modes of appearance taken from these others. On the contrary, the analogically apprehended object and its indicated system of appearances are indeed *analogically adapted* to the analogous appearance, which has awakened this whole system too. Every overlapping-at-a-distance, which occurs by virtue of associative pairing, is *at the same time a fusion* and therein, so far as incompatibilities do not interfere, an assimilation, an accommodation of the sense of the one member to that of the other.

If we return to our case, that of apperception of the alter ego, it is now self-understood that what is appresented by the "body" over there, in my primordial "surrounding world," is not something psychic of mine, nor anything else in my sphere of ownness. I am *here* somatically, the center of a primordial "world" oriented around me. Consequently my entire primordial ownness, proper to me as a monad, has the content of the Here—not the content varying with some "I can and do," which might set in, and belonging to some There or other; accordingly, not the content belonging to that definite There. Each of these contents excludes the other; they cannot both exist <in my sphere of ownness> at the same time. But, since the other body there enters into a pairing association with my body here and, being given perceptually, becomes the core of an appresentation, the core of my experience of a coexisting ego, that ego, according to the whole sense-giving course of the association, must be appresented *as an ego now coexisting in the mode There,* "such as I should be if I were there." My own ego however, the ego given in constant self-perception, is actual now with the content belonging to his Here. Therefore an ego is *appresented,* as *other* than mine. That which is primordially incompatible, in simultaneous coexistence, becomes compatible: because my primordial ego constitutes the ego who is other for him by an appresentative apperception, which, according to its intrinsic nature, never demands and never is open to fulfillment by presentation.

Likewise easy to understand is the manner in which, as the effective association goes on continuously, such an appresentation of someone else continually furnishes new appresentational contents—that is to say, brings the changing contents of the other ego to definite notice; and, on the other hand, the manner in which, by virtue of the combination with a continual presentation and the associational demands expectantly addressed to this presentation, a *consistent confirmation* becomes possible. The *first determinate content* obviously must be formed by the understanding of the other's organism and specifically organismal conduct: the understanding of the members as hands groping or functioning in pushing, as feet functioning in walking, as eyes functioning in seeing, and so forth. With this the Ego at first is determined only as governing thus somatically *[so leiblich waltendes]* and, in a familiar manner, proves himself continually, so far as the whole stylistic form of the sensible processes manifest to me primordially must correspond to the form whose type is familiar from my own organismal governing *[leibliches Walten].* It is quite comprehensible that, *as a further consequence,* an "empathizing" of definite contents belonging to the *"higher psychic sphere"* arises. Such contents too are indicated somatically and in the conduct of the organism toward the outside world—for example: as the outward conduct of someone who is angry or cheerful, which I easily understand from my own conduct under similar circumstances. Higher psychic occurrences, diverse as they are and familiar as they have become, have furthermore their style of synthetic interconnections and take

their course in forms of their own, which I can understand associatively on the basis of my empirical familiarity with the style of my own life, as exemplifying roughly differentiated typical forms. In this sphere, moreover, every successful understanding of what occurs in others has the effect of opening up new associations and new possibilities of understanding; and conversely, since every pairing association is reciprocal, every such understanding uncovers my own psychic life in its similarity and difference and, by bringing new features into prominence, makes it fruitful for new associations.

§55. Establishment of the community of monads. The first form of Objectivity: intersubjective Nature

But it is more important to clarify the *community,* developing at various levels, which is produced forthwith by virtue of experiencing someone else: the community between me, the primordial psychophysical Ego governing in and by means of my primordial organism, and the appresentatively experienced Other; then, considered more concretely and radically, between my monadic ego and his.

The first thing constituted in the form of community, and the *foundation for all other intersubjectively common things,* is the *commonness of Nature,* along with that of the *Other's organism* and *his psychophysical Ego,* as paired with *my own psychophysical Ego.*

Since other subjectivity, by appresentation within the exclusive own-essentialness of my subjectivity, arises with the sense and status of a subjectivity that is other in its own essence, it might at first seem to be a mystery how community—even the first community, in the form of a common world—becomes established. The other organism, as appearing in my primordial sphere, is first of all a body in my primordial Nature, which is a synthetic unity belonging to me and therefore, as a determining part included in my own essence, inseparable from me myself. If that body functions appresentatively, then, in union with it, the other Ego becomes an object of my consciousness—and primarily the other Ego with his organism, as given to him in the manner of appearance pertaining to his "absolute Here." How can I speak at all of *the same* body, as appearing within my primordial sphere in the mode There and within his and to him in the mode Here? These two primordial spheres, mine which is for me as ego the original sphere, and his which is for me an appresented sphere —are they not *separated* by an abyss I cannot actually cross, since crossing it would mean, after all, that I acquired an original (rather than an appresenting) experience of someone else? If we stick to our de facto experience, our experience of someone else as it comes to pass at any time, we find that actually the *sensuously seen body* is experienced forthwith as *the body of someone else* and not as merely an indication of someone else. Is not this fact an enigma?

The body belonging to my original sphere and the body constituted, after all, quite separately in the other ego become identified and are called the identical body of someone else. How does this identification come about? How *can* it come about? But the enigma appears only if the two original spheres have already been distinguished—a distinction that already presupposes that experience of someone else has done its work. Since we are not dealing here with a temporal genesis of such experience, on the basis of a temporally antecedent self-experience, manifestly only a precise explication of the intentionality actually observable in our experience of someone else and discovery of the motivations essentially implicit in that intentionality can unlock the enigma.

As we said once before, appresentation as such presupposes a core of presentation. It is a making present combined by associations with presentation, with perception proper, but a making present that is fused with the latter in the particular function of "co-perception." In other words, the two are so fused that they stand within the *functional community of one perception,* which simultaneously presents and appresents, and yet furnishes for the total object a consciousness of its being itself there.

Therefore, in the object of such a presentive-appresentive perception (an object making its appearance in the mode, itself-there), we must distinguish noematically between that part which is genuinely perceived and the rest, which is not strictly perceived and yet is indeed there too. Thus every perception of this type is transcending: it posits more as itself-there than it makes "actually" present at any time. Every external perception belongs here— for example, perception of a house (front— rear); but at bottom absolutely every perception, indeed every evidence, is thus described in respect of a most general feature, provided only that we understand "presenting" in a broader sense.

Let us apply this general cognition to the case of experiencing someone else. In this case too it should be noted that experience *can appresent only because it presents,* that here too appresentation can exist only in the aforesaid functional community with presentation. That implies, however, that, from the very beginning, *what this experience presents must belong to the unity of the very object appresented.* In other words: It is not, and cannot be, the case that the body belonging to my primordial sphere and indicating to me the other Ego (and, with him, the whole of the other primordial sphere or the other concrete ego) could appresent his factual existence and being-there-too, unless *this primordial body* acquired the sense, "a body belonging to the other ego," and, according to the whole associative-apperceptive performance, *the sense: "someone else's animate organism itself."* Therefore it is not as though the body over there, in my primordial sphere, remained separate from the animate bodily organism of the other Ego, as if that body were something like a signal for its analogue (by virtue of an obviously inconceivable motivation); it is not as though consequently, with the spreading of the association and appresentation, my primordial Nature and the other's appresented primordial Nature—therefore my concrete ego and the other concrete ego—remained separate. On the contrary, this natural body belonging to my sphere appresents the other Ego, by virtue of the pairing association with my bodily organism, and with my Ego governing in my organism, within my primordially constituted Nature. In so doing, it appresents first of all the other Ego's governing in this body, the body over there, and mediately his governing in the Nature that appears to him perceptually—identically the Nature to which the body over there belongs, identically the Nature that is my primordial Nature. It is the same Nature, but in the mode of appearance: "as if I were standing over there, where the Other's body is." The body is the same, given to me as the body there, and to him as the body here, the central body. Furthermore, "my" whole Nature is the same as the Other's. In *my* primordial sphere it is constituted as an identical unity of my manifold modes of givenness—an identical unity in changing orientations around *my* animate organism (the zero body, the body in the absolute Here), an identical unity of even richer multiplicities that, as changing modes of appearance pertaining to different "senses," or else as changeable "perspectives," belong to each particular orientation as here or there and also, in a quite particular manner, belong to my animate organism, which is inseparable from the absolute Here. All of this has for me the originality of something included in my particular ownness, something directly accessible in original explication of my own self. *In the appresented other ego* the synthetic systems are *the same,* with all their modes of appearance, accordingly with all the possible perceptions and the noematic contents of these: except that the *actual* perceptions and the modes of givenness actualized therein, and also in part the objects actually perceived, are *not the same;* rather the objects perceived are precisely those perceivable *from there,* and *as* they are perceivable from there. Something similar is true of anything else of my own and the corresponding alien thing, even where original explication does not go on in perceptions. I do not have an appresented second original sphere with a second "Nature" and, in this Nature, a second animate bodily organism (the one belonging to the other ego himself), so that I must then ask how I can apprehend my Na-

ture and this other as modes of appearance of the same Objective Nature. On the contrary, the *identity*-sense of "my" primordial Nature and the presentiated other primordial Nature is *necessarily* produced by the appresentation and the unity that it, *as* appresentation, necessarily has with the presentation co-functioning for it—this appresentation by virtue of which an Other and, consequently, his concrete ego are there for me in the first place. Quite rightly, therefore, we speak of *perceiving* someone else and then of perceiving the Objective world, perceiving that the other Ego and I are looking at the same world, and so forth—though this perceiving goes on exclusively within the sphere of my ownness. That does not at all contravene the fact that the intentionality of this sphere transcends my ownness, or the fact that accordingly my ego constitutes in himself another ego—and constitutes this ego, moreover, as existent. What I actually see is not a sign and not a mere analogue, a depiction in any natural sense of the word; on the contrary, it is someone else. And what is grasped with actual originariness in this seeing—namely that corporeality over there, or rather only one aspect of its surface—is the Other's body itself, but seen just from my position and in respect of this aspect: According to the sense-constitution involved in perceiving someone else, what is grasped originaliter is the body of a psyche essentially inaccessible to me originaliter, and the two are comprised in the unity of one psychophysical reality.

On the other hand, it is implicit in the intentional essence of this perception of the Other—the Other who exists henceforth, as I do myself, within what is henceforth the Objective world—that I as perceiver can find the aforesaid distinction between my primordial sphere and the merely presentiated primordial sphere of the Other, and consequently can trace the peculiarities of the division into two noetic strata and explicate the complexes of associative intentionality. The experiential phenomenon, Objective Nature, has, besides the primordially constituted stratum, a superimposed second, merely appresented stratum originating from my experiencing of someone else; and this fact concerns, first of all, *the Other's animate bodily organism,* which is, so to speak, *the intrinsically first Object,* just as *the other man is constitutionally the intrinsically first <Objective> man.* In the case of this primal phenomenon of Objectivity, the situation is already clear to us: If I screen off my experience of someone else, I have the lowest constitution, the one-layered presentive constitution of the other body within my primordial sphere; if I add that experience, I have appresentationally, and as coinciding synthetically with the presentational stratum, the same animate organism as it is given to the other Ego himself, and I have the further possible modes of givenness available to him.

From that, as is easily understandable, *every* natural Object experienced or experienceable by me in the lower stratum receives an appresentational stratum (though by no means one that becomes explicitly intuited), a stratum united in an identifying synthesis with the stratum given to me in the mode of primordial originality: the same natural Object in its possible modes of givenness to the other Ego. This is repeated, *mutatis mutandis,* in the case of subsequently constituted mundanities of the concrete Objective world as it always exists for us: namely as a world of men and culture.

The following should be noted in this connection. It is implicit in the sense of my successful apperception of others that their world, the world belonging to their appearance-systems, must be experienced forthwith as the same as the world belonging to my appearance-systems; and this involves an identity of our appearance-systems. Now we know very well that there are such things as *"abnormalities"* (for example: in the case of subjects who are blind or deaf); we know that therefore the appearance-systems are by no means always absolutely identical and that whole strata (though not all strata) can differ. But abnormality must first be *constituted* as such; and the constituting of abnormality is possible only on the basis of an intrinsically antecedent normality. This points to new tasks, which belong to

a higher level of phenomenological analysis of the constitutional origin of the Objective world—as the Objective world existing for us and only by virtue of our own sense-producing sources, a world that can have neither sense nor existence for us otherwise. The Objective world has existence by virtue of a harmonious confirmation of the apperceptive constitution, once this has succeeded: a confirmation thereof by the continuance of experiencing life with a consistent harmoniousness, which always becomes re-established as extending through any "corrections" that may be required to that end. Now harmoniousness is preserved also by virtue of a recasting of apperceptions through distinguishing between normality and abnormalities (as modifications thereof), or by virtue of the constitution of new unities throughout the changes involved in abnormalities. Among the problems of abnormality the problem of non-human animality and that of the levels of "higher and lower" brutes are included. Relative to the brute, man is, constitutionally speaking, the normal case—just as I myself am the primal norm constitutionally for all other men. Brutes are essentially constituted for me as abnormal "variants" of my humanness, even though *among* them in turn normality and abnormality may be differentiated. Always it is a matter of intentional modifications in the sense-structure itself, as what becomes evinced. All of that, to be sure, needs a more thorough phenomenological explication. This general account, however, is enough for our present purposes.

After these clarifications it is no longer an enigma how I can constitute in myself another Ego or, more radically, how I can constitute in my monad another monad, and can experience what is constituted in me as nevertheless other than me. At the same time, this being indeed inseparable from such constitution, it is no longer an enigma how I can identify a Nature constituted in me with a Nature constituted by someone else (or, stated with the necessary precision, how I can identify a Nature constituted in me with one constituted in me *as* a Nature constituted by someone else). This identification is no greater enigma than any other synthetic identification. It is therefore no more mysterious than any, by virtue of which, as an identification confined to my own original sphere, no matter what objective unity acquires sense and being for me through the medium of *presentations*. Let us consider the following instructive example and use it to bring out a thought that takes us further: the notion of a *connection* constituted through the medium of presentation. How does one of my own subjective processes acquire for me the sense and status of an existent process, something existing with its identical temporal form and identical temporal content? The original is gone; but, in repeated presentations, I go back to it and do so with the evidence: "I can always do so again." But these repeated presentations are evidently themselves a temporal sequence; and each is separate from the others. In spite of that, however, an identifying synthesis connects them in the evident consciousness of "the Same"—which implies the same, never repeated temporal form, filled with the same content. Here, as everywhere else, "the Same" signifies therefore an *identical intentional object of separate conscious processes,* hence an object immanent in them only as something *non-really* inherent. Another case, very important in itself, is that of the constitution of objects that are ideal in the pregnant sense —for example: all logically ideal objects. In a living, many-membered thinking action I produce a structure: a theorem or a numerical structure. Subsequently I repeat the producing, while recollecting my earlier producing. At once, and by essential necessity, an identifying synthesis takes place; furthermore a new identifying synthesis occurs with each additional repetition (a repetition performed with a consciousness that the producing can be repeated again at will): It is identically the same proposition, identically the same numerical structure, *but repeatedly produced* or, this being equivalent, repeatedly made evident. Therefore in this case, through the medium of recollective presentations, the synthesis extends—within my stream of subjective processes (which always is already consti-

tuted)—from my living present into my currently relevant separate pasts and thus makes a *connection* between my present and these pasts. With that, moreover, the supremely significant *transcendental problem of ideal objectivities* ("ideal" in the specific sense) is solved. Their supertemporality turns out to be *omnitemporality,* as a correlate of free produceability and reproduceability at all times. After constitution of the Objective world with its Objective time and its Objective men as possible thinking subjects, that obviously carries over to ideal structures, as themselves Objectivated, and to their Objective omnitemporality. Thus the contrast between them and Objective *realities,* as spatiotemporally individuated structures, becomes understandable.

If we return now to our case, the experience of someone else, we find that, with its complicated structure, it effects a similar *connection mediated by presentiation:* namely a connection between, on the one hand, the uninterruptedly living self-experience (as purely passive original self-appearance) of the concrete ego —accordingly, his primordial sphere—and, on the other hand, the *alien sphere* presentiated therein. It effects this, first, by its identifying synthesis of the *primordially given* animate body of someone else and the same animate body, but *appresented* in other modes of appearance, and secondly, spreading out from there, by its identifying synthesis of the same Nature, given and verified primordially (with pure sensuous originality) and at the same time appresentationally. In that way the *coexistence of my <polar> Ego and the other Ego,* of my whole concrete ego and his, my intentional life and his, my "realities" and his—in short, a *common time-form*—is primally instituted; and thus every primordial temporality automatically acquires the significance of being merely an original mode of appearance of Objective temporality to a particular subject. In this connection we see that the temporal community of the constitutively interrelated monads is indissoluble, because it is tied up essentially with the constitution of *a world and a world time.*

§56. *Constitution of higher levels of intermonadic community*

With these considerations we have clarified the *first and lowest level of communalization* between me, the primordial monad for myself, and the monad constituted in me, yet as other and accordingly as existing for himself but only appresentationally demonstrable to me. The only conceivable manner in which others can have for me the sense and status of existent others, thus and so determined, consists in their being constituted *in me* as others. If they get that sense and status from sources that yield a continual confirmation, then they do indeed *exist* (as I am *compelled* to say), but exclusively as having the sense with which they are constituted: as monads, existing for themselves precisely as I exist for myself, yet existing also in communion, therefore (I emphasize the expression already used earlier) in *connection with me* qua concrete ego, qua monad. To be sure, they are separate from my monad, so far as really inherent constituents are concerned, since no really inherent connection leads from their subjective processes to my subjective processes or from anything included in their peculiar ownness to anything included in mine. To that separation there corresponds, after all, the *"real,"* the mundane separation of my psychophysical existence from someone else's, a separation that shows itself as spatial, owing to the spatial character of our Objective animate organisms. On the other hand, this original communion is not just nothing. Whereas, really inherently, each monad is an absolutely separate unity, the "irreal" intentional reaching of the other into my primordiality is not irreal in the sense of being dreamt into it or being present to consciousness after the fashion of a mere phantasy. *Something that exists is in intentional communion with something else that exists.* It is an essentially *unique connectedness,* an actual community and precisely the one that makes transcendentally possible the being of a world, a world of men and things.

After the first level of communalization and (this being almost equivalent) the first consti-

tution of an Objective world, starting from the primordial world, have been sufficiently clarified, the *higher levels* offer relatively minor difficulties. Though comprehensive investigations and a progressive differentiation of problems relating to these levels are necessary for purposes of an all-round explication, here we can be satisfied with rough general indications, easily understandable on the basis already laid. Starting from me, from the one who is constitutionally the primal monad, I acquire what are for me other monads and, correlatively, others as *psychophysical* subjects. This implies that I do *not* acquire the latter *merely as over against me* somatically and —by virtue of associative pairing—as *related back to my psychophysical existence* (which indeed is universally "central," and particularly the "central member" in the communalized world of the present level because of the necessarily oriented manner in which this world is given). On the contrary (and this carries over to the sociality of brute animals), in the sense of *a community of men* and in that of *man*—who, even as solitary, has the sense: member of a community—there is implicit a *mutual being for one another,* which entails an *Objectivating equalization* of my existence with that of all others—consequently: I or anyone else, as a man among other men. If, with my understanding of someone else, I penetrate more deeply into him, into his horizon of ownness, I shall soon run into the fact that, just as his animate bodily organism lies in my field of perception, so my animate organism lies in his field of perception and that, in general, he experiences me forthwith as an Other for him, just as I experience him as *my* Other. Likewise I shall find that, in the case of a plurality of Others, they are experienced also by one another as Others, and consequently that I can experience any given Other not only as himself an Other but also as related in turn to *his* Others and perhaps—with a mediatedness that may be conceived as reiterable —related at the same time to me. It is also clear that men become apperceivable only as finding Others and still more Others, not just in the realm of actuality but likewise in the realm of possibility, at their own pleasure. Openly endless Nature itself then becomes a Nature that includes an open plurality of men (conceived more generally: animalia), distributed one knows not how in infinite space, as subjects of possible intercommunion. To this community there naturally corresponds, in transcendental concreteness, a similarly open *community of monads,* which we designate as *transcendental intersubjectivity.* We need hardly say that, as existing for me, it is constituted purely within me, the meditating ego, purely by virtue of sources belonging to my intentionality; nevertheless it is constituted thus *as* a community constituted also in every other monad (who, in turn, is constituted with the modification: "other") as the same community—only with a different subjective mode of appearance—and as necessarily bearing within itself the same Objective world. Manifestly it is essentially necessary to the world constituted transcendentally in me (and similarly necessary to the world constituted in any community of monads that is imaginable by me) that it be a *world of men* and that, *in each particular man,* it be more or less perfectly constituted *intrapsychically*—in intentional processes and potential systems of intentionality, which, as "psychic life," are themselves already constituted as existing in the world. By "the psychic constitution of the Objective world" we mean, for example, my actual and possible experience of the world, as an experience belonging to me, the Ego who experiences himself as a man. Such experience of the world is more or less perfect; it always has its open undetermined horizon. For each man, every other is implicit in this horizon—physically, psychophysically, in respect of what is internal to the other's psyche—and is thus in principle a realm of endless accessibilities, though in fact most other men remain horizonal.

§62. Survey of our intentional explication of experiencing someone else

Let us return now, at the conclusion of this chapter, to the objection by which at first we let ourselves be guided, the objection to our phenomenology, so far as, from the very beginning, it claimed to be transcendental philosophy and, as such, to have the ability to solve the problems that concern the possibility of Objective knowledge. The objection runs as follows. Starting from the transcendental ego of the phenomenological reduction and thenceforth restricted to him, phenomenology is incapable of solving those problems. Without admitting that it does so, it lapses into a transcendental solipsism; and the whole step leading to other subjectivity and to genuine Objectivity is possible only by virtue of an unacknowledged metaphysics, a concealed adoption of Leibnizian traditions.

Our actual explications have dissipated the objection as groundless. The following is to be noted above all. At no point was the transcendental attitude, the attitude of transcendental epoché, abandoned; and our "theory" of experiencing someone else, our "theory" of experiencing others, did not aim at being and was not at liberty to be anything but explication of the sense, "others," as it arises from the constitutive productivity of that experiencing: the sense, "truly existing others," as it arises from the corresponding harmonious syntheses. What I demonstrate to myself harmoniously as "someone else" and therefore have given to me, by necessity and not by choice, as an actuality to be acknowledged, is *eo ipso* the existing Other for me in the transcendental attitude: the alter ego demonstrated precisely within the experiencing intentionality of my ego. Within the bounds of positivity we say and find it obvious that, in my own experience, I experience not only myself but others—in the particular form: experiencing someone else. The indubitable transcendental explication showed us not only that this positive statement is transcendentally legitimate but also that the concretely apprehended transcendental ego (who first becomes aware of himself, with his undetermined horizon, when he effects transcendental reduction) grasps himself in his own primordial being, and likewise (in the form of his transcendental experience of what is alien) grasps others:

other transcendental egos, though they are given, not originaliter and in unqualifiedly apodictic evidence, but only in an evidence belonging to "external" experience. "In" myself I experience and know the Other; in me he becomes constituted—appresentatively mirrored, not constituted as the original. Hence it can very well be said, in a *broadened* sense, that the ego acquires—that I, as the one who meditatingly explicates, acquire by "self-explication" (explication of what I find in myself) every transcendency: as a transcendentally constituted transcendency and not as a transcendency accepted with naive positivity. Thus the *illusion* vanishes: that *everything I,* qua transcendental ego, *know as existing in consequence of myself,* and explicate as *constituted in myself,* must *belong to me as part of my own essence.* This is true only of "immanent transcendencies." As a title for the systems of synthetic actuality and potentiality that confer sense and being on me as ego in my own essentialness, constitution signifies constitution of immanent objective actuality. *At the start of phenomenology,* when my attitude is that of someone who is *only starting,* who is instituting phenomenological reduction for the first time, as a universal condition under which to pursue constitutional research, *the transcendental ego who comes into view is, to be sure, grasped apodictically*—but as having *a quite undetermined horizon,* a horizon restricted only by the general requirement that the world and all I know about it shall become a mere "phenomenon." Consequently, when I am starting in this manner, all those distinctions are lacking which are made only subsequently by intentional explication but which nevertheless (as I now see) pertain to me essentially. There is lacking, above all, self-understanding with respect to my primordial essence, my sphere of ownness in the pregnant sense, and with respect to what, within that sphere itself, becomes constituted as an Other in experiencing someone else, as something appresented but essentially non-given (and never to become given) within my primordial sphere. I must first explicate *my own as such, in order to understand that, within my own, what is not my*

own likewise receives existential sense—and does so as something appresented analogically. Therefore at the beginning I, the meditator, do not understand how I shall ever attain others and myself <as one among others>, since all other men are "parenthesized." At bottom moreover I do not yet understand, and I recognize only reluctantly, that, when I "parenthesize" myself qua man and qua human person, I myself am nevertheless to be retained qua ego. Thus I can as yet know nothing about a transcendental intersubjectivity; involuntarily I take myself, the ego, to be a *solus ipse* and still regard all constitutional components as merely contents of this one ego, even after I have acquired an initial understanding of constitutive performances. The further explications made in the present chapter were therefore necessary. Thanks to them, the *full and proper sense of phenomenological transcendental "idealism" becomes understandable* to us for the first time. The *illusion* of a solipsism is dissolved, *even though* the proposition that everything existing for me must derive its existential sense exclusively from me myself, from my sphere of consciousness retains its validity and fundamental importance. Phenomenological transcendental idealism has presented itself as a *monadology,* which, despite all our deliberate suggestions of Leibniz's metaphysics, draws its content purely from phenomenological explication of the transcendental experience laid open by transcendental reduction, accordingly from the most originary evidence, wherein all conceivable evidences must be grounded—or from the most originary legitimacy, which is the source of all legitimacies and, in particular, all legitimacies of knowledge. Actually, therefore, phenomenological explication is nothing like "metaphysical construction"; and it is neither overtly nor covertly a theorizing with adopted presuppositions or helpful thoughts drawn from the historical metaphysical tradition. It stands in sharpest contrast to all that, because it proceeds within the limits of pure "intuition," or rather of pure sense-explication based on a fulfilling givenness of the sense itself. Particularly in the case of the Objective world of realities (as well as in the case of each of the many ideal Objective worlds, which are the fields of purely a priori sciences)—and this cannot be emphasized often enough—phenomenological explication does nothing but *explicate the sense this world has for us all, prior to any philosophizing,* and obvious-ly gets solely from our experience—*a sense which philosophy can uncover but never alter,* and which, because of an essential necessity, not because of our weakness, entails (in the case of any actual experience) horizons that need fundamental clarification.

PART TWO

Transcendental Phenomenology and the

Problem of the Life-World

Edmund Husserl, 1905. Courtesy of Husserl-Archief te Leuven.

VII.

Transcendental Aesthetics

10. Perception, Spatiality, and the Body

Objective Reality, Spatial Orientation, and the Body*

§18. The subjectively conditioned factors of the constitution of the thing; the constitution of the Objective material thing†

Our entire analysis has been moving in a determinate narrow frame, the limits of which we must fix. The real unity, which was constituted for us in levels, has nevertheless, with all these levels, not reached the ultimate one, the level on which the Objective material thing is actually constituted. What it is that we have described is the thing constituted in the continuous-unitary manifold of the sense intuitions of an experiencing Ego or in the manifold of "sense-things" of various levels: multiplicities of schematic unities, of real states and real unities on various levels. It is the *thing for the solitary subject,* the subject thought of ideally as isolated, except that this subject in a certain sense remains forgotten to itself and equally forgotten by the one who is doing the analysis.

A) The intuitive qualities of the material thing in their dependencies on the experiencing subject-Body

Nevertheless, this self-forgetfulness is hardly appropriate for the restoration of the full givenness of a thing, a givenness in which the thing exhibits its actual reality. We need only consider how a thing exhibits itself as such, according to its essence, in order to recognize that such an apprehension must contain, at the very outset, components which refer back to the subject, specifically the human (or, better: animal) subject in a fixed sense.

The qualities of material things as aestheta, such as they present themselves to me intuitively, prove to be dependent on my qualities, *the make-up of the experiencing subject,* and to be related to *my Body and my "normal sensibility."*

The Body is, in the first place, the *medium of all perception;* it is the *organ of perception* and is *necessarily* involved in all perception. In seeing, the eyes are directed upon the seen and run over its edges, surfaces, etc. When it touches objects, the hand slides over them. Moving myself, I bring my ear closer in order to hear. Perceptual apprehension presupposes sensation-contents, which play their necessary role for the constitution of the schemata and, so, for the constitution of the appearances of the real things themselves. *To the possibility of experience there pertains, however, the spontaneity of the courses* of presenting acts of sensation, which are accompanied by series of kinesthetic sensations and are dependent on them as motivated: *given with the localization of the kinesthetic series in the relevant moving member of the Body is the*

---

*Ideas II, pp. 60–70, 82–95 (Sections 18a-b and 18e-h). The term "Body" (with capital B) translates German *Leib,* lived-body; the term "body" (lower case b) translates German *Körper,* physical body. —Editor's note.

†Concerning this paragraph, see also the third chapter of Section Two.

fact that in all perception and perceptual exhibition (experience) the Body is involved as freely moved sense organ, as freely moved totality of sense organs, and hence there is also given the fact that, on this original foundation, all that is thingly-real in the surrounding world of the Ego has its relation to the Body.

Furthermore, obviously connected with this is the distinction the Body acquires as the bearer of the zero point of orientation, the bearer of the here and the now, out of which the pure Ego intuits space and the whole world of the senses. Thus each thing that appears has *eo ipso* an orienting relation to the Body, and this refers not only to what actually appears but to each thing that is supposed to be able to appear. If I am imagining a centaur I cannot help but imagine it as in a certain orientation and in a particular relation to my sense organs: it is "to the right" of me; it is "approaching" me or "moving away"; it is "revolving," turning toward or away from "me" —from me, i.e., from my Body, from my eye, which is directed at it. In phantasy, I do look at the centaur; i.e., my eye, freely moved, goes back and forth, accommodating itself in this or that way, and the visual "appearances," the schemata, succeed one another in motivated "appropriate" order, whereby they produce the consciousness of an experience of an existing centaur-object viewed in various ways.

Besides its distinction as a center of orientation, the Body, in virtue of the constitutive role of the sensations, is of *significance for the construction of the spatial world.* In all constitution of spatial thinghood, two kinds of sensations, with totally different constituting functions, are involved, and necessarily so, if representations of the spatial are to be possible. The first kind are the sensations which *constitute,* by means of the apprehensions allotted to them, corresponding *features of the thing* as such by way of adumbration. For example, the sensation-colors with their sensation-expansions: it is in the apprehension of these that the corporeal colorations appear together with the corporeal extension of these colorations. Likewise, in the tactual sphere, thingly roughness appears in the apprehension of the

roughness-sensations, and corporeal warmth appears in relation to the sensation of warmth, etc.

The second kind are the "sensations" which do not undergo such apprehensions but which, on the other hand, are necessarily involved in all those apprehensions of the sensations of the first kind, insofar as, in a certain way, they *motivate* those apprehensions and thereby themselves undergo an apprehension of a completely different type, an apprehension which thus belongs correlatively to every constituting apprehension. In all constitution and on all levels, we have, by necessity, "circumstances," related one to the other, and "that which is dependent on" all the circumstances: everywhere, we find the "if-then" or the "because-therefore." Those sensations which undergo extensional apprehension (leading to the extended features of the thing) are motivated as regards the courses they take either actually or possibly and are apperceptively *related to motivating series, to systems, of kinesthetic sensations,* which freely unfold in the nexus of their familiar order in such a way that if a free unfolding of one series of this system occurs (e.g., any movement of the eyes or fingers), then from the interwoven manifold as motive, the corresponding series must unfold as motivated. In this way, from the ordered system of sensations in eye movement, in head movement freely moved, etc., there unfold such and such series in vision. That is, while this is happening, there unfold, *in motivated order,* "images" of the thing that was perceptually apprehended to begin the eye movement and, likewise, the visual sensations pertaining to the thing in each case. An apprehension of a thing as situated at such a distance, as oriented in such a way, as having such a color, etc., is unthinkable, as can be seen, without these sorts of relations of motivation. In the essence of the apprehension itself there resides the possibility of letting the perception disperse into *"possible"* series of perceptions, all of which are of the following type: *if* the eye turns in a certain way, *then* so does the "image"; if it turns differently in some definite fashion, then so does the image alter differently, in correspondence. We constantly find here this two-fold articulation: kinesthetic sensations on the one side, the motivating; and the sensations of features on the other, the motivated. The like holds, obviously, for touch and, similarly, everywhere. Perception is without exception a *unitary accomplishment* which arises essentially out of the playing together of two *correlatively related functions*. At the same time, it follows that *functions of spontaneity* belong to every perception. The processes of the kinesthetic sensations are *free processes* here, and this freedom in the consciousness of their unfolding is an essential part of the constitution of spatiality.

B) THE SIGNIFICANCE OF *NORMAL* PERCEPTUAL CONDITIONS FOR THE CONSTITUTION OF THE INTUITED THING AND THE SIGNIFICANCE OF ABNORMALITIES (CHANGE OF THE BODY, CHANGE IN THE THING)

Now the processes of perception, in virtue of which one and the same external world is present to me, do not always exhibit the same style; instead, there are distinctions which make themselves noticeable. At first, the same unchanged Objects appear, according to the changing circumstances, now this way, now in another way. The same unchanged form has a *changing appearance,* according to its position in relation to my Body; the form appears in *changing aspects,* which *present "it itself" more or less "advantageously."* If we disregard this and instead consider real properties, then we find that one and the same Object, maintaining one identical form, does have different color appearances (the form as filled), according to its position relative to an illuminating body; furthermore, the color appearances are different when it stands under different illuminating bodies, but all this happens in an ordered fashion, one which may be determined more precisely in regard to appearances. At the same time, certain conditions prove to be the *"normal"* ones: seeing in sunlight, on a clear day, without the influence of other bodies which might affect the color-appearance. The "optimum" which is thereby attained then counts as the *color itself* in opposition, for example, to the red light of the sunset which "outshines" all proper colors. All other color properties are *"aspects of,"* "appearances of," this pre-eminent color-appearance (which latter is called "appearance" only in an *other* sense: namely, with respect to a higher level, the physicalistic thing, still to be discussed). Yet it is inherent in the thing that its normal color keeps changing, precisely in dependence on whatever illuminating bodies are involved, whether the day is one of clear light or is hazy, etc., and it is only with the return of the normal circumstances that the normal color re-appears. "In itself" there belongs to a body a color as being in itself, and this color is grasped in seeing, but it ever appears differently, and the aspect it presents depends thoroughly on the Objective circumstances, and it can be distinguished there either more or less easily (with the limit case of complete invisibility). And the degree of visibility affects the form, too.

It should also be examined whether from the very start all Objective circumstances are apperceived *as causal,* as emanating from things. Certain circumstances exhibit periodic changes—e.g., the relations of night and day—and correspondingly the things which otherwise are experienced as unchanged, for instance things given as unchanged for the sense of touch, undergo periodic changes in the unfolding of their visual characters. With regard to the visual mode of givenness, which brings out the color characteristics as well as the form characteristics that become visible along with them, a privilege attaches to *clear daylight,* such that there not only does the form become visible in a particularly favorable way up to its finer details, but also in this light such global characteristics are visible through which properties of other sense spheres are co-announced at the same time, properties given in the nexus of these experiences as not affected by the change of color (e.g., the material attributes, which are disclosed when the surface structure becomes visible). Therefore in the series of possible appearances a certain givenness of the thing is privileged in that with it is given, *of the thing as a whole, what is relatively the best,* and this acquires the character of what is *especially intended:* it is the predominating focus of the "interest," what the *experience is tending toward, terminates in,* is fulfilled in; and the other modes of givenness become intentionally related to this "optimal" one.

Included *in the normal experience,* in which the world is *originally* constituted as world, *"the way it is,"* are still other *conditions of normal experience:* e.g., seeing in air—which counts as immediate seeing, seeing without any mediating things—touching by immediate contact, etc. If I interpose a foreign *medium* between my eye and the things seen, then all things undergo a change in appearance; more precisely, all phantom-unities undergo a change. It will be said: the same thing is seen, but through different media. The thing has no dependency on such changes; it remains the same. Only the "mode of appearance" of the thing (in this case, the appearance of the phantom) depends on whether this or that medium is mediating between the eye and the thing. Transparent glass is indeed a medium that can be seen through, but it changes the images of things in different ways according to its different curvatures, and, if it is colored, it transmits its color to them—all that belongs in the realm of experience. Finally, if I put on colored lenses, then everything looks changed in color. If I knew nothing of this medium, then for me all things would be colored. Insofar as I have experiential knowledge of it, this judgment does not arise. The givenness of sense-things counts, with regard to the color, as *seemingly* given, and semblance again means a mode of givenness which could possibly also occur in this way within the system of normal givenness, under the appropriate circumstances, and which would induce an *Objectively false* apprehension where there are motives prompting a mixup, something those circumstances are very likely to bring about. *The "false" lies in the contradiction with the normal system of experience.* (The change of appearance is a uniform one for all the things, recognizable as a uniform change according to type.)

The case is the same if we take, instead of an interposition of a medium between organ and thing, an *abnormal change of an organ itself.* If I am touching something with a blister on my finger, or if my hand has been abraded, then all the tactual properties of the thing are given differently. If I cross my eyes, or if I cross my fingers, then I have two "things of sight" or two "things of touch," though I maintain that only one actual thing is present. This belongs to the general question of the constitution of a thingly unity as an *apperceptive unity of a manifold of different levels* which themselves are already apperceived as unities of multiplicities. The apperception acquired in relation to usual perceptual conditions obtains a new apperceptive stratum by taking into consideration the new "experience" of the dispersion of the one thing of sight into a pair and of the fusion of the pair in the form of a continuous overlapping and convergence in the regular return to the former perceptual conditions. The doubled things of sight are indeed completely analogous with the other things of sight, but only *the latter* have the additional meaning of "things"; and the lived experience has the meaning of a *lived experience of perception only as related to a certain "position of the two eyes,"* the homologous one or one from the system of normal eye positions. If a *heterology* now occurs, then I indeed have analogous images, but they *mean* things only in *contradiction* to all normal motivations. The images now once again obtain the apprehension, "actual thing," precisely through the constitutive nexus, i.e., the *motivation which puts them in a concordant relation to the system of motivated perceptual manifolds.* If I take my eyes out of a normal position into a disparate *crossed position,* then two semblant images arise; "semblant images": i.e., images which would, each for itself, present "the thing" only if I lent them normal motivations.

A further important consideration deals with other groups of abnormalities. If I ingest santonin, then the whole world "seems" to change; e.g., it "alters" its color. The "alteration" is a "seeming." Afterwards, as is the case with every change of colored lighting, etc., I once again have a world which matches the normal: everything is then concordant and changes or does not change, moves or is at rest, as usual, and it displays the same systems of aspects as before.

But here it must be observed that rest and motion, change and permanence, get their sense by means of the constitution of thinghood as reality, in which such occurrences, especially the limit cases of rest and permanence, play an essential role.

Therefore the global coloring of all seen things can easily "change," for example when a body emits rays of light which "cast their shine" over all things. There is more to the constitution of the "change of things according to color" than just a change of the filled schemata with respect to color: *change of things is, from the very outset, constituted as causal change in relation to causal circumstances, as, for example, each advent of an illuminating body.* I can apprehend the change without seeing such an illuminating body, but in that case the causal circumstance is, in an indeterminate way, coapperceived. These causal circumstances, however, are of the order of things. *The relativity of the spatial things with reference to other ones determines the sense of the change in things. But the psychophysical conditionalities do not belong here in the least.* This must be kept in mind. It goes without saying, however, that my Body is indeed involved in the causal nexuses: if it is apprehended *as a thing in space,* it is certainly not apprehended as mere schema but instead as the point of intersection of real causalities in the real (exclusively spatio-thingly) nexus. Belonging to this sphere is, for example, the fact that a stroke of my hand (considered purely as the striking of a corporeal thing, i.e., excluding the lived experience of the "I strike") acts exactly the same as a stroke of any other material thing, and, similarly, the fall of my Corporeal body is like any other fall, etc.*

Now concerning the intake of santonin, this too is therefore, abstracting from all "concomi-tant psychic facts," a *material process,* one which could very well, if required by the constitution of the world of experience, or by the further elaboration of the constitution of the experience of this world in the course of new experiences, enter into a real relation with the optical change of the rest of the material world. In itself it is thus thinkable that I would find experiential motives for seeing a general change in the color of the entire visible world and for regarding the change, in this apprehension, as a real-causal consequence of the material process of ingesting santonin (with its Bodily-material consequences). It would be a normal perception just like any other. As long as, and whenever, I experience the change of all visible colors as an optical change of the *things,* I must assume a causal relation between whatever causing thinghoods there might be; it is *only* in the *causal* nexus that a change is precisely a change of a *thing.* As soon as experiential motives arise in opposition, then there must necessarily take place a *transformation in the apprehension,* in virtue of which the "change" that is seen loses the sense of a change and forthwith acquires the *character of "seeming."* A semblant change is a schematic transformation apprehended as a change under normal conditions, thus in relation to experiences constitutive of causality. But now it is given in a way which cancels the causal apprehension. The causal apprehension is suggested by the given schematic transformation: it is as if it would present a change, but this is, under the given circumstances, excluded. The intake of santonin is not, with respect to the general "change in color," a process which is or which could be apprehended as a cause. The shift in color of all seen things is such that there is not even an incentive to regard it at all as a real change of the illumination (e.g., in the manner of a light source emitting colored rays). It is therefore that it presents itself as a semblant change; everything looks "as though" there were a new source of light shining, or

---

*To be sure, it still remains to be discussed to what extent the solitary subject has the possibility of apprehending his Body as a material body like any other. Cf. pp. 183ff. below.

"as if," in some other way, real causes were there effecting a general optical change (even if these causes were undetermined, unknown). But such causes may not now be presupposed; they are, given the total experiential situation, excluded.

We have to ask: what can, *on the basis of a transformation in the sense-thing, totally cancel the apperception of real change* in this way, in opposition to the cases in which such an apperception, already accomplished, merely undergoes a modification (by the fact that a different causal nexus is substituted for the one that had been supposed, that is, the assumed cause abandoned but another cause accepted)? The answer is a modification in the sphere of *psychophysical "causality"* or, rather, *"conditionality,"* to say it better. (For a *causa* in the proper sense is precisely a *real* cause. The subjective, however, is, in opposition to reality, an irreality. Reality and irreality belong together essentially in the form of reality and subjectivity, which on the one hand mutually exclude one another and on the other hand, as is said, essentially require one another). Besides the relations of the real to the real, which belong to the essence of everything real as spatial, temporal, and causal relations, there also belong to this essence relations of psychophysical conditionality in possible experience. Things are "experienced," are "intuitively given" to the subject, necessarily as unities of a spatio-temporal-causal nexus, and necessarily pertaining to this nexus is a preeminent thing, "my Body," as the place where, and always by essential necessity, a system of subjective conditionality is interwoven with this system of causality and indeed in such a way that in the transition from the *natural attitude* (the regard directed in experience to nature and life) to the *subjective attitude* (the regard directed to the subject and to moments of the subjective sphere), real existence, and manifold real changes as well, are given as in conditional connection with subjective being, with a state of being in the subjective sphere. Something thingly is experienced (perceptually apperceived, to give privilege to the originary experience) in such a way that, through a

mere shift of focus, there emerge relations of dependency of the apperceived state of the thing on the sphere of sensation and on the rest of the subjective sphere. Here we have the *primordial state of psychophysical conditionality* (under this heading are included *all conditional* relations which run back and forth between thingly and subjective being). To every psychophysical conditionality there necessarily appertains *somatological causality,* which immediately always concerns the relations of the irreal, of an event in the subjective sphere, with something real, the Body: then mediately the relations with an external real thing which is in a real, hence causal, connection with the Body. . . .

E) POSSIBILITY OF THE CONSTITUTION OF AN "OBJECTIVE NATURE" ON THE SOLIPSISTIC LEVEL

We have pursued the constitution of material nature through various strata and have seen that already for the "solipsistic" subject—the subject in isolation—there exist motives for the distinction between an "appearing" thing, whose qualitative content is relative to my subjectivity, and the "Objective" thing, which remains what it is even if changes occur in my subjectivity and, dependent on it, in the "appearances" of the thing. Thereby we have to understand under the heading "true" or "Objective" thing still something double:

1) the thing as it presents itself to me under *"normal" conditions,* in opposition to all other thing-like unities which, constituted under "abnormal" conditions, are degraded to "mere semblance";

2) the identical content of qualities which, *abstraction made from all relativity,* can be worked out and fixed logico-mathematically: i.e., the physicalistic thing. Once this is known and once we have, in addition, Objective knowledge of the psychophysical character of experiencing subjects, as well as of the existing conditionalities between thing and subject, then from that it can be determined Objectively how the thing in question must be intuitive-

ly characterized for the respective subjectivity—the normal or the abnormal.*

The question now, however, is whether or not the motives for the necessary distinction between the subjectively conditioned thing and the Objective thing, motives which do present themselves in solipsistic experience, are sufficient or have to be there at all. As long as we take cases in which changes of the external world, feigned for us by an abnormal perceptual organ, are shown up as "semblances" by the testimony of the other organs, to that extent the distinction between "seeming" and what actually is is always given, even if it may remain undecided in particular cases *what* is semblant and *what* is actual. But if we assume for once that a subject would always have only normal perceptions and would never undergo a modification of any of its organs, or on the other hand would undergo a modification, but one that allowed for no possibility of correction (loss of the entire field of touch, or mental diseases which alter the entire typical character of perception), then the motives of the distinction between "semblance" and "actuality," assumed up to now, would be eliminated, and the level of "Objective nature" could not be attained by such a subject. But the danger, that under the assumed conditions the constitution of Objective nature could not be attained, is removed as soon as we lift the abstraction we have maintained up to now and take into account the conditions under which constitution takes place *de facto:* namely, that the experiencing subject is, in truth, *not a solipsistic subject* but is instead one among many.

F) TRANSITION FROM SOLIPSISTIC TO
INTERSUBJECTIVE EXPERIENCE

Let us consider a little more closely the possibility of a *solipsistic world,* something we have assumed up to now. I (everybody should substitute here his own "I") would experi-

ence a world, and it would be exactly the same as the one I actually do experience; everything would be the same, with the only exception that in my field of experience there would be no Bodies I could apprehend as Bodies of *other* psychic subjects. If this apperceptive domain is lacking, then it neither determines my apprehensions of things, and insofar as it does usually determine these apprehensions in my actual experience, then its influence would be absent from my world-image as now modified. Moreover, I now have the same manifolds of sensation; and the "same" real things, with the same properties, appear to me and, if everything is in harmony, exhibit themselves as "actually being," or otherwise, if discrepancies of a known kind occur as exceptional, the things show themselves as being "different" or as not being at all. Seemingly, nothing essential has changed; seemingly, only a fragment of my world of experience is missing, the world of animalia, as well as the group of causalities precisely involved with it in a world-nexus. Let us then imagine, however, that at a point of time within the time co-constituted along with the solipsistic world, suddenly in my domain of experience Bodies show up, things understandable as, and understood as, human Bodies. Now all of a sudden and for the first time human beings are there for me, with whom I can come to an understanding. And I come to an understanding with them about the things which are there for us in common in this new segment of time. Something very remarkable now comes out: extensive complexes of assertions about things, which *I* made in earlier periods of time on the ground of earlier experiences, experiences which were perfectly concordant throughout, are *not corroborated* by my current companions, and this not because these experiences are simply lacking to them (after all, one does not need to have seen everything others have seen, and vice versa) but because they thoroughly conflict†

---

*Thus are determined, as will later be shown in full, the tasks of physics, psychophysics, and psychology.

†Of course, this conflict should not be considered total. For a basic store of *communal* experiences is presupposed in order for mutual understanding to take place at all.

with what the others experience in experiences, we may suppose, that necessarily are harmonious and that go on being progressively confirmed. Then what about the actuality exhibited in the first period of time? And what about myself, the empirical subject of this actuality? The answer is clear. As I communicate to my companions my earlier lived experiences and they become aware of how much these conflict with their world, constituted intersubjectively and continuously exhibited by means of a harmonious exchange of experiences, then I become for them an interesting *pathological* Object, and they call my actuality, so beautifully manifest to me, the hallucination of someone who up to this point in time has been mentally ill. One may imagine perfection in the exhibition of my solipsistic world and raise that perfection to any height, still the described state of affairs as an a priori one, the ideal possibility of which is beyond question, would not change at all.

Light must now be shed on a certain problem: the relation to a multiplicity of people who have dealings with one another—how does that enter into the apprehension of a thing and come to be constitutive for the apprehension of a thing as "Objective and actual"? This "how" is at first very puzzling, because when we carry out an apprehension of a thing we do not, it *seems,* always co-posit a number of fellow men and, specifically, co-posit them as ones who are to be, as it were, invoked. One might also wonder if we are not entangled here in a circle, for surely the apprehension of one's fellow man presupposes the apprehension of the Body and consequently also presupposes thing-apprehension. There is only one way to solve this problem, the way prescribed for us by phenomenology. We must interrogate the thing-apprehension itself, there where it is an experience of an "Objectively actual" thing, and we must interrogate the experience which is not yet exhibiting, but is in want of exhibition, as to what, inherent in it, is in need of exhibition, what components

of unfulfilled intentions it harbors. (In this regard it must be observed that we have in fact described the constitution of the thing incompletely by investigating only the manifolds of sensation, the adumbrations, schemata, and, in general, visual things in all their levels. We must overcome in a decisive point the Ego's self-forgetfulness we touched upon previously.) Each thing of my experience belongs to my "environment," and that means first of all that *my Body* is part of it precisely as Body. It is not that we have here a matter of essential necessity in any sense. That is precisely what our solipsistic thought-experiment has taught us. Strictly speaking, the *solus ipse* is unaware of the *Objective Body* in the full and proper sense,* even if the *solus ipse* might possess the *phenomenon* of its Body and the corresponding system of experiential manifolds and know them in just as perfect a way as the social man. In other words, the *solus ipse* does not truly merit its name. The abstraction we carried out, for justifiable theoretical reasons, does not yield the isolated *man,* the isolated human person. This abstraction does obviously not consist in our arranging for a mass murder of the people and animals of our surrounding world, sparing one human subject alone. For in that case the remaining subject, though one and unique, would still be a human subject, i.e., still an intersubjective object, still apprehending and positing himself as such. But, on the contrary, the subject we constructed knows nothing of a human environment, knows nothing of the reality or even just the real possibility of "other" Bodies, understood in the sense of an apprehension of the human, and thus knows nothing of his own Body as understandable by others. This subject does not know that others can gaze upon the same world, one that simply appears differently to different subjects, such that the appearances are always relative to "their" Bodies, etc. It is clear that *the apprehension of the Body plays a special role for the intersubjectivity* in which all objects are apprehended "Objectively" as

---

*On this point, cf. the segments on the constitution of the Body, pp. 183ff. below.

things in the one *Objective* time and one *Objective* space of the one Objective world. (In every case the exhibition of any apprehended Objectivity whatsoever requires a relation to the apprehension of a multiplicity of subjects sharing a mutual understanding.) The thing which is constituted for the individual subject in regulated manifolds of harmonious experiences and which, as one for sense intuition, stands continuously over and against the Ego in the course of perception, obtains in that way the character of a merely subjective "appearance" of the "Objectively real" thing. Each of the subjects who are intersubjectively related in mutual understanding in regard to the same world and, within that, in regard to the same things, has his own perceptions of them, i.e., his own perceptual appearances, and in them he finds a unity in the appearances, which itself is only an appearance in a higher sense, with predicates of appearance that may not, without any further ado, count as predicates of the appearing "true thing."

Thus we come here, in considering mutual understanding, to the same distinction we already demonstrated as possible on the solipsistic level. The "true thing" is then the Object that maintains its identity within the manifolds of appearances belonging to a multiplicity of subjects, and specifically, again, it is the *intuited* Object, related to a community of normal subjects, or, abstraction made from this relativity, it is the *physicalistic* thing, determined logico-mathematically. This physicalistic thing is obviously the same, whether it is constituted solipsistically or intersubjectively. For logical Objectivity is *eo ipso* Objectivity in the intersubjective sense as well. What a cognizing subject comes to know in logical Objectivity (hence in such a way that this presents no index of a dependency of its truth-content upon the subject or upon anything subjective) can be similarly known by any cognizing subject as long as he fulfills the conditions *any* subject must satisfy to know such Objects. That is, he must experience the things and the *very same things,* and he must, if he is also to know this identity, stand in a relation of empathy to the other cognizing subjects, and for that he must have Corporeality and belong to the same world, etc.

It pertains to *perception's very sense,* as well as to that of *experience* in general, that things come to presence there which are to be determined in themselves and distinguished from all other things. And it pertains to the sense of experiential *judgment* to make a claim to Objective validity. If a thing is determined in itself and distinct from every other, then it has to allow for judgmental, therefore predicative, determination in such a way that its distinctiveness as regards all other things stands out.

The thing given in perception and experience is, in accordance with perception's very sense, something *spatio-temporal* from the first, having form and duration and also having a position in space and time. So we have to distinguish between the *appearing* form and the *form itself* between the appearing spatial magnitude, the appearing location, and the magnitude and location themselves. Everything that we experience of the thing, even the form, has reference to the experiencing subject. All these appear in changing aspects, in the change of which the things are present as sensibly changed also. In addition, the space between things and the form of this space appear under different aspects according to the subjective circumstances. Always and necessarily, however, the one and the same space "appears" as the form of all possible things, a form that cannot be multiplied or altered. Every subject has his "space of orientation," his "here" and his possible "there," this "there" being determined according to the directional system of right-left, above-below, front-back. But the basic form of all identification of the intersubjective givennesses of a sensuous content is of such a kind that they necessarily belong to one and the same *system of location,* whose Objectivity is manifest in that every "here" is identifiable with every relative "there" as regards every new "here" resulting from the subject's "moving on" and so also as regards every "here" from the viewpoint of another subject. This is an ideal necessity and constitutes an Objective system of location, one that does not allow of being grasped by the vision of the eyes but only by the understanding; that is, it is "visible," in a higher kind of intuition, founded on change of location and on empathy. In this way is solved the problem of the "form of intuition" and of spatial intuition. It is not a matter of the senses, although in another respect it is. The primary intuitive space is sensuously given though this is not yet space itself. Objective space is not sensuous, although it is still intuited on a higher level, and it comes to givenness by means of an identification within a change of orientation, but exclusively one the subject itself carries out freely. Oriented space (and along with it, *eo ipso* Objective space) and all appearing spatial forms already admit of idealization; they are to be grasped in geometrical purity and determined "exactly."

The *Objective form* is Objective as ordered within *Objective space.* Everything *else* about a thing that is Objective (detached from all relativisms) is so through a connection with what is fundamentally Objective, viz., space, time, motion. Real properties manifest themselves as real substantial-causal unities in the motion and deformation of the spatial form. These are the *mechanical properties* which express the causal-lawful dependencies of the spatial determinations of bodies. The thing is always *form* in a *situation.* The form is, however, in every situation a *qualified* one. Qualities are what fills, they extend over the surface and through the corporeality of the form. *Qualifications,* however, extend from the things into empty space: *rays of light, radiations of heat,* etc. That means that thingly qualities condition qualities and qualitative changes in other things and indeed do so in such a way that the effect is a constant function of the situation: to every change of situation there corresponds a change of effect. In virtue of such a subordination to spatial relations which may be determined with exactitude, even the sense qualities become amenable to exact determination. Thus we come to an understanding of the physicalistic world-view or world-structure, i.e., to an understanding of the method of physics as a method which pursues the sense of an intersubjectively-Objectively (i.e., non-

relative and thereby at once intersubjective) determinable sensible world.

g) More precise characterization of the physicalistic thing

"Physicalistic nature," to which we have now advanced, presents itself in the following way in accord with our expositions: *the thing itself in itself* consists of a continuously or discretely filled space in states of motion, states which are called energy forms. That which fills space lends itself to certain groups of differential equations and corresponds to certain fundamental laws of physics. But there are no sense qualities here. And that means there are no qualities here whatever. For the quality of what fills space *is* sense quality. But, now, filled space without quality, how is that thinkable?

To attribute actuality to appearing things with their sense qualities in themselves is out of the question, as the natural scientists quite rightly say. For the sense qualities change according to the kind and the disposition of the sense organs; they are dependent on the sense organs and, more generally, dependent on the Body and the total condition of the experiencing subject. And it turns out that the true physical facts which correspond to the qualitative distinctions of red and green, warm and cold, are *produced* without qualitative transition as mere quantitative distinctions of one and the same domain, for example, temperature, waves in the ether, etc.

Shall we say that God sees the things as they are in themselves while we see them through our sense organs, which are a kind of distorting eyeglasses? That things are filled space with absolute quality and it is only that we know nothing of it? But should the things which appear to us as they appear to us be the same as the things which appear to God as they appear to God, then a unity of mutual understanding would have to be possible between God and us, just as, between different men, only through mutual understanding is there the possibility of *knowing* that the things seen by the one are *the same* as those seen by the other. But how would the identification be thinkable if not in the sense that the supposed absolute spirit sees the things precisely also through sensuous appearances, which, likewise, have to be exchangeable in an understanding that is reciprocal—or, at least, unilateral—as is the case with the appearances we share among us men? And if not in that case, then God would be blind to colors, etc., and men blind to his qualities. Is there any sense, however, to arguing about which are the true qualities? The new qualities would again be secondary and would be eliminated once more by physics, which has to be the same for all, if the things are the same. Obviously, the absolute spirit would also have to have a Body for there to be mutual understanding, and thus the dependency on sense organs would have to be there as well. The result is that we must understand the *sense of the distinction between secondary and primary qualities* correctly and that we are permitted to understand the non-Objectivity of the former only in the sense that in no way do they escape the relativity of appearances, not even in the way we easily overlook insofar as we spontaneously think of ourselves as normally sensing in a world of beings of normal sensibility. A main feature of the relativity consists in the dependence upon the subject. To be sure, an important distinction is to be found here: subjects who in general share a *common* world of things, to which they actually relate, hence to which they can relate through appearances, as is required by thingly being, can in principle be relatively "blind" as regards color, sound, etc., i.e., as regards individual senses which provide their own particular sorts of sense qualities. The senses can also be completely different, provided they make possible a common understanding and constitute a common nature as an appearing one. But in principle subjects cannot be blind as regards *all* the senses and consequently at once blind to space, to motion, to energy. Otherwise there would be no world of things there for them; in any case it would not be the same as ours, precisely *the* spatial world, *the* world of nature.

Nature is an intersubjective reality and a reality not just for me and my companions of the moment but for us and for everyone who can have dealings with us and can come to a mutual understanding with us about things and about other people. There is always the possibility that new spirits enter into this nexus; but they must do so by means of their Bodies, which are represented through possible appearances in our consciousness and through corresponding ones in theirs.

The thing is a rule of possible appearances. That means that the thing is a reality as a unity of a manifold of appearances connected according to rules. Moreover, this unity is an intersubjective one. It is a unity of states; the thing has its real properties, and to each moment there corresponds an active state (for the properties express faculties; they are causal properties, related to an "if-then"). Whereas, however, for the *former* consideration, supported by *direct experience,* the *state* is identical with the space that is filled with sensuous qualities (schema), a space which can be an intersubjective unity only as related to a totality of normal "like-sensing" subjects, on the other hand the real possibility and actuality of *subjects endowed with different sense faculties* and the knowledge of the *dependence,* present in each individual, of the sense qualities on physiological processes lead to a consideration of this dependence precisely *as a new dimension of relativities* and lead to the construction, in *thought,* of the purely physicalistic thing. Then to the same Objective-physicalistic state of the thing pertain multiple "filled spaces" related to various sense faculties and individual sense aberrations. The physicalistic thing is *intersubjectively* common in that it has validity for all individuals who stand in possible communion with us. The *Objective determination* determines the thing through that which belongs to it and must belong to it if it is going to be able to appear to me or to anyone else in communion with me and if it is going to be able to count as the same for every member of the communicating society—even for me throughout all possible modifications of my sensibility. The determinations of space and time are common, as is common a lawfulness which, in virtue of its concepts related to the "physicalistic thing," is a unitary rule for all the appearances, of the intersubjective community, which constitute the same thing and which must constitute it in rational mutual understanding. It is only from the appearances (and the intersubjective nexus) that we can draw the sense of what a thing is in "Objective actuality," i.e., in the actuality which appears, and which appears to all communicating subjects, and which is identifiable by means of intersubjective identification.

The Objectively real is not in my "space," or in anyone else's, as "phenomenon" ("phenomenal space") but exists in *Objective space,* which is a formal *unity* of identification in the midst of the changing qualities. Whereas it holds for my space-phenomena that they can only be given with sensuous qualities, it holds for Objective space that it cannot be given with sensuous qualities but can appear only within subjective spaces that have sensuous qualities. This is valid for the *solus ipse* as well and for the space already being constituted therein as Objective, though still not as intersubjective. (Thus the intersubjective thing is the "Objective" spatial form with "Objective" qualities, the physicalistic ones.) *Pure space* (the purely Objective spatial form) arises out of my appearing space *not through abstraction* but *through an Objectification* which takes as "appearance" any sensuously appearing spatial form endowed with sensuous qualities and posits it in manifolds of appearances which do not belong to an individual consciousness but to a societal consciousness as a total group of possible appearances that is constructed out of individual groups. Each subject has the totality of space and has particular spatial forms, but in intersubjectivity these are appearances.

In principle, the thing is given and is to be given only through appearances, whose appearing content can vary with the subjects. This content (the appearing thing just as it appears, as red, as warm, etc.) is what it is as appearance to an actual subject or to a possible subject in actual connection with the former. We find ourselves led back to a multiplicity of actual subjects and, in connection with them,

still possible subjects who intuit a thing, accomplish an experience, etc., in which, as correlate, something appearing as such comes to consciousness in a varying mode with moments of appearance such as red, warm, sweet, round, etc. These subjects stand in a relationship of empathy and, in spite of the variation in the givennesses of appearances, can intersubjectively assure themselves of the identity of what appears therein.

Thus in principle the thing is something intersubjectively identical yet is such that it has no sensuous-intuitive content whatsoever that could be given as identical intersubjectively. Instead, it is only an empty identical something as a correlate of the identification possible according to experiential-logical rules and grounded through them, the identification of what appears in the changing "appearances" with their various contents, the identification carried out by the subjects that stand in the intersubjective nexus along with their corresponding acts appropriate to appearance and to experiential-logical thinking. In physics as the mere natural study of the intersubjective-Objective thing existing "in itself," the thing is Objectively determined as an empty something, determined through the intersubjectively constituted forms of space and time and through the "primary qualities" related to space and time. All secondary qualities, indeed precisely *everything* that can be given intuitively, including all *intuitive spatial and temporal forms* which are quite unthinkable without secondary filling, all differences in orientation, etc.—these do not belong there.

H) THE POSSIBILITY OF THE CONSTITUTION OF AN "OBJECTIVE NATURE" AT THE LEVEL OF INTERSUBJECTIVE EXPERIENCE

Let us now examine analogously, for the intersubjective level of experience as we have done for the solipsistic, which conditions have to be fulfilled so that the constitution of an "Objective" nature can arise, and indeed must arise. We began with relationships as they are present *de facto:* we found that individual differences stand out from a fundamental set of common experiences and lead to the distinction between determinations which belong to the thing "itself" versus ones that are merely subjectively conditioned. Now other conditions, as well, are to be constructed a priori. We can imagine a human world in which there would be no illness, in which there would occur no illusions, hallucinations, or the like. We can furthermore assume that all the persons who have commerce with one another apprehend the world completely alike (abstraction made from the always necessary differences in orientation). In that case would the things with their secondary qualities simply count as the ultimate Objectivity? Or would it be recognized that this state of affairs is contingent and not necessary? It is to be noted in this regard that the constitution of the *sensible world* is obviously to be distinguished from the constitution of the *"true" world*, the world for the *scientific* subject, whose activity is a *spontaneous* "free" thinking and, in general, researching. That is to say: if we live passively, in the manner of animals, "in the world" and in commerce with others who are like us, who are as "normal" as we are, then a world of experience is constituted common to us all. Now, we are, however, *free intelligent beings*. Even if we encounter no abnormalities, we can still perform *gratuitous operations* on our Bodies or on others', and then *"anomalies"* do appear. We pursue, in thought, the causal nexuses and form for ourselves the "physicalistic world-image."

In any case, we see that on the one hand there exists already on the solipsistic level the *possibility of advancing to the constitution of the "Objective" (physicalistic) thing*. On the other hand, there does not exist, even on the intersubjective level, the unconditioned *necessity* to reach that far. But there is—abstracting from the circumstance that *de facto* constitution is accomplished intersubjectively—a distinction in principle between these two possible ways of constructing an "Objective

nature." The solipsistic subject could indeed have over against itself an Objective nature, however this subject could *not apprehend itself as a member of nature*, could not apperceive itself as psychophysical subject, as animal, the way this does happen on the intersubjective level of experience.* Obviously, this can become evident only if the constitution of animal nature is examined. As has indeed been shown in general by the exhibition of the relations of dependency between experienced nature and experiencing subject, the study of subjectivity is unconditionally required for a full clarification of the sense and structure of physical nature.

The Self-Constitution of the Body†

§35. Transition to the study of the constitution of "man as nature"

Now, the theme of the following considerations is to be the constitution of the *natural reality, man* (or animal being), i.e., the constitution of man as he presents himself to a naturalistic point of view: as material body upon which are constructed new strata of being, the Bodily-psychic. It is possible that in this constitutive consideration much will have to be included that subsequent investigation will show as belonging to the personal or spiritual Ego. It will be possible to provide the ultimate distinction between "man as nature" and "man as spirit," as well as the establishment of their reciprocal relations, only when both these Objectivities have been subject to constitutive study.

If we now look for a point of departure for our constitutive analysis, then we must take into account what came to light for us as regards the constitution of material nature, namely, that it, with its entire intuitive content, is related to animal subjects. Hence when

---

*Cf. pp. 183ff. below.
†*Ideas II*, pp. 151–169 (Sections 35–42).

we approach the constitution of the natural Object, "man," we may not already presuppose his Body as a fully constituted material thing but instead must at first pursue what is already constituted prior to, or correlative with, material nature, as regards the psychophysical subject. And here, as before, let us first try to see how far we can advance in a solipsistic consideration.

§36. Constitution of the Body as bearer of localized sensations (sensings)

We have seen that in all experience of spatio-thingly Objects, *the Body* "is involved"* as the perceptual organ of the experiencing subject, and now we must investigate the constitution of this Corporeality. We can thereby choose immediately the special case in which the spatially experienced body, perceived by means of the Body, is the Corporeal body itself. For this too is perceived from the outside, although within certain limits, preventing it from being considered, without qualification, as a thing like any other in a thingly nexus. Thus there are parts of this body which can indeed be perceived by touch but cannot be seen.† At first, however, we may disregard these and begin instead with parts that we can both touch and see. I can look at them and feel them, just like other things, and in this respect the appearances have entirely the same nexus as do other appearances of things. But now there is a distinction between the *visual* appearances and the *tactual* regarding, e.g., a hand. Touching my left hand, I have touch-appearances, that is to say, I do not just sense, but I perceive and have appearances of a soft, smooth hand, with such a form. The indicational sensations of movement and the representational sensations of touch, which are Objectified as features of the thing, "left hand," belong in fact to my right hand. But when I touch the left hand I also find in it, too, series of touch-sensations, which are "*localized*" in it, though these are

not constitutive of properties (such as roughness or smoothness of the hand, of this physical thing). If I speak of the *physical* thing, "left hand," then I am abstracting from these sensations (a ball of lead has nothing like them and likewise for every "merely" physical thing, every thing that is not my Body). If I do include them, then it is not that the physical thing is now richer, but instead *it becomes Body, it senses.* "Touch"-sensations belong to every appearing Objective spatial position on the touched hand, when it is touched precisely at those places. The hand that is touching, which for its part again appears as a thing, likewise has its touch-sensations at the place on its corporeal surface where it touches (or is touched by the other). Similarly, if the hand is pinched, pressed, pushed, stung, etc., touched by external bodies or touching them, then it has its sensations of contact, of being stung, of pain, etc. And if this happens by means of some other part of one's Body, then the sensation is *doubled* in the two parts of the Body, since each is then precisely for the other an external thing that is touching and acting upon it, and each is at the same time Body. All the sensations thus produced have their *localization,* i.e., they are distinguished by means of their place on the appearing Corporeality, and they belong phenomenally to it. Hence the Body is originally constituted in a double way: first, it is a physical thing, *matter;* it has its extension, in which are included its real properties, its color, smoothness, hardness, warmth, and whatever other material qualities of that kind there are. Secondly, I find on it, and I *sense* "on" it and "in" it: warmth on the back of the hand, coldness in the feet, sensations of touch in the fingertips. I sense, extended over larger Bodily areas, the pressure and pull of my clothes. Moving my fingers, I have motion sensations, whereby a sensation in an ever changing way extends itself over and traverses the surface of the fingers, but within this sensation-complex there is at the same time a content hav-

*Cf. pp. 163ff.
†As to the constitution of the Body as a thing, cf. pp. 183ff. below.

ing its localization in the interior of the digital space. My hand is lying on the table. I experience the table as something solid, cold, and smooth. Moving my hand over the table, I get an experience of it and its thingly determinations. At the same time, I can at any moment pay attention to my hand and find on it touch-sensations, sensations of smoothness and coldness, etc. In the interior of the hand, running parallel to the experienced movement, I find motion-sensations, etc. Lifting a thing, I experience its weight, but at the same time I have weight-sensations localized in my Body. And thus, my Body's entering into physical relations (by striking, pressing, pushing, etc.) with other material things provides in general not only the experience of physical occurrences, related to the Body and to things, but also the experience of specifically Bodily occurrences of the type we call *sensings*. Such occurrences are missing in "merely" material things.

The localized sensations are not properties of the Body *as* a physical thing, but on the other hand, they *are* properties of the thing, Body, and indeed they are effect-properties. They arise *when* the Body is touched, pressed, stung, etc., and they arise there *where* it is touched and at the time *when* it is touched: only under certain circumstances do they still endure after the touching takes place. Touching refers here to a physical event. Even two lifeless things can touch one another, but the touching of the Body provides sensations on it or in it.

We must now give heed to the following: in order to bring to perception here the tactual thing, paperweight, I touch it, with my fingers, for example. I then experience tactually the smooth surface of the glass and the delicate crystal edges. But if I attend to the hand and finger, then they have touch sensations which still linger when the hand is withdrawn. Likewise, my finger and hand have kinesthetic sensations, and precisely the same sensations which function as indicational or presentational with respect to the thing, paperweight, function as touch-*effects* of the paperweight on the hand and as sensings produced in it. In the case of the hand lying on the table, the same sensation of pressure is apprehended at

one time as perception of the table's surface (of a small part of it, properly speaking) and at another time produces, with a "different direction of attention," in the actualization of an other stratum of apprehension, sensations of digital pressure. In the same way are related the coldness of the surface of a thing and the sensation of cold in the finger. In the case of one hand touching the other, it is again the same, only more complicated, for we have then two sensations, and each is apprehendable or experienceable in a double way.

Necessarily bound to the tactual perception of the table (this perceptual apprehension) is a perception of the Body, along with its concomitant sensation of touch. This nexus is a necessary connection between two possible apprehensions: pertaining correlatively to that, however, is a connection between two thinghoods that are being constituted. It is shown empirically by the possibility of a representation of the world in those blind from birth that everything can come into play in the extra-visual sphere and that here the apperceptions have to be ordered in such a way that these correlations can be constituted.

§37. *Differences between the visual and tactual realms*

We find now a striking difference between the sphere of the visual and that of the tactual. In the tactual realm we have the *external Object,* tactually constituted, and a second Object, the *Body,* likewise tactually constituted, e.g., the touching finger, and, in addition, there are fingers touching fingers. So here we have that double apprehension: the same touch-sensation is apprehended as a feature of the "external" Object and is apprehended as a sensation of the Body as Object. And in the case in which a part of the Body becomes equally an external Object of an other part, we have the double sensation (each part has its own sensations) and the double apprehension as feature of the one or of the other Bodily part as a physical object. But in the case of an *Object constituted purely visually* we have *nothing* comparable. To be sure, sometimes it is said that the eye is, as it were, in touch with the Object by casting its glance over it. But we immediately sense the difference. An eye does not appear to one's own vision, and it is not the case that the colors which would appear visually on the eye as localized sensations (and indeed visually localized corresponding to the various parts of its visual appearance) would be the same as those attributed to the object in the apprehension of the seen external thing and Objectified in it as features. And similarly, we do not have a kind of extended occularity such that, by moving, one eye could rub past the other and produce the phenomenon of double sensation. Neither can we see the seen thing as gliding over the seeing eye, continually in contact with it, as we can, in the case of a real organ of touch, e.g., the palm of the hand, glide over the object or have the object slip past the hand. I do not see myself, my Body, the way I touch myself. What I call the seen Body is not something seeing which is seen, the way my Body as touched Body is something touching which is touched.* A visual appearance of an object that sees, i.e., one in which the sensation of light could be intuited just as it is in it—that is denied us. Thus what we are denied is an analogon to the touch sensation, which is actually grasped along with the touching hand. The role of the visual sensations in the correlative constitution of the Body and external things is thus different from that of the sensations of touch. All that we can say here is that if no eye is open there are no visual appearances, etc. If, ultimately, the eye as organ and, along with it, the visual sensations are in fact attributed to the Body, then that happens indirectly by means of the properly localized sensations.

Actually, the eye, *too,* is a field of localization but *only for touch sensations,* and, like every organ "freely moved" by the subject, it is a field of localized muscle sensations. It is an Object of touch for the hand; it belongs originally to the merely touched, and not seen, Objects. "Originally" is not used here in a temporal-causal sense; it has to do with a primal group of Objects constituted directly in intuition. The eye can be touched, and it itself provides touch and kinetic sensations; that is why it is necessarily apperceived as belonging to the Body. All this is said from the standpoint of straightforward empirical intuition. The relation of the seen color of the thing to the seeing eye, the eye "with which" we see, the "being directed" of the open eye onto the seen thing, the reference back to this direction of the eye which is part of having visual appearances, and, furthermore, growing out of this, the relation of the color sensations to the eye—all that will not be confused with the givenness of these sensations in the manner of localized "sensings."

The same applies to *hearing.* The ear is "involved," but the sensed tone is not localized in the ear. (I would not even say that the case of the "buzzing" in the ears and similar tones subjectively sensed in the ear are exceptions. They are in the ear just as tones of a violin are outside in space, but, for all that, they do not yet have the proper character of sensings and the localization proper to them.) It would be an important task to thoroughly examine in this regard the groups of sensations of the various senses. However important that would be for a completely elaborated theory of the phenomenological constitution of material thinghood, on the one hand, and of the Body, on the other hand, for us now the broad distinctions will suffice. To make ourselves sure of them, we must be perfectly clear on the fact that *localization of sensings* is in fact something *in principle different from the extension of all material determinations of a thing.* The sensings do indeed spread out in space, cover, in their way, spatial surfaces, run through them, etc. But this *spreading out* and spreading into are precisely something that differs essentially from *extension* in the sense of all the deter-

---

*Obviously, it cannot be said that I see my eye in the mirror, for my eye, that which sees *qua* seeing, I do not perceive. I see something, of which I judge indirectly, by way of "empathy," that it is identical with my eye as a thing (the one constituted by touch, for example) in the same way that I see the eye of an other.

minations that characterize the *res extensa*. The sensing which spreads over the surface of the hand and extends into it is not a real quality of a thing (speaking always within the frame of intuitions and their givenness) such as, for example, the roughness of the hand, its color, etc. These real properties of a thing are constituted through a sensuous schema and manifolds of adumbrations. To speak in a similar way of sensings would be quite absurd. If I turn my hand, bring it closer or take it away, then, for one, the unchanged color of the hand is given to me as constantly different. Yet the color itself presents itself, and the color constituted first (that of the sensuous schema) manifests a real optical property of the hand. Roughness, too, presents itself and does so tactually in manifolds of touch sensations which constantly flow into one another and to each of which a spreading-out belongs. The touch-sensings, however, the sensations which, constantly varying, lie on the surface of the touching finger, are, such as they are lying there spread out over the surface, nothing given through adumbration and schematization. They have nothing at all to do with the sensuous schema. The touch-sensing is not a *state* of the material thing, hand, but is precisely the *hand itself,* which for us is more than a material thing, and the way in which it is mine entails that I, the "subject of the Body," can say that what belongs to the material thing is its, not mine. All sensings pertain to my soul; everything extended to the material thing. *On this surface of the hand I sense the sensations of touch*, etc. And it is precisely thereby that this surface manifests itself immediately as my Body. One can add here as well: if I convince myself that a perceived thing does not exist, that I am subject to an illusion, then, along with the thing, everything extended in its extension is stricken out too. But the sensings do not disappear. Only what is *real* vanishes from being.

Connected to the privilege of the localization of the touch sensations are differences in the complexion of the visual-tactual apprehensions. Each thing that we see is touchable and, as such, points to an immediate relation to the Body, though it does not do so in virtue of its visibility. *A subject whose only sense was the sense of vision could not at all have an appearing Body;* in the play of kinesthetic motivations (which he could not apprehend Bodily) this subject would have appearances of things, he would see real things. It cannot be said that this subject who only sees sees his Body, for its specific distinctive feature as Body would be lacking him, and even the free movement of this "Body," which goes hand in hand with the freedom of the kinesthetic processes, would not make it a Body. In that case, it would only be as if the Ego, in unity with this freedom in the kinesthetic, could immediately and freely move the material *thing, Body.*

The Body as such can be constituted originally only in tactuality and in everything that is localized with the sensations of touch: for example, warmth, coldness, pain, etc. Furthermore, the kinetic sensations play an important role. I see how my hand moves, and without it touching anything while moving, I sense kinetic sensations, though as one with sensations of tension and sensations of touch, and I localize them in the moving hand. And the same holds for all the members of the Body. If, while moving, I do touch something, then the touch sensation immediately acquires localization in the touching surface of the hand. At bottom, it is owing only to their constant interlacing with these primarily localized sensations that the kinetic sensations receive localization. But because there obtains here no parallelism which is exactly stratified as there is between temperature sensations and touch sensations, so the kinesthetic sensations do not spread out in a stratified way over the appearing extension, and they receive only a rather indeterminate localization. Yet this is indeed not without significance; it makes the unity between the Body and the freely moveable thing more intimate.

Obviously, the Body is also to be seen just like any other thing, but it becomes a *Body* only by incorporating tactile sensations, pain sensations, etc.—in short, by the localization of the sensations as sensations. In that case the visual Body also participates in the localization, because it coincides with the tactual Body, just as other things (or phantoms) coincide, ones which are constituted both visually and tactually, and thus there arises the idea of a sensing thing which "has" and which can have, under certain circumstances, certain sensations (sensations of touch, pressure, warmth, coldness, pain, etc.) and, in particular, have them as localized in itself primarily and properly. This is then a precondition for the existence of all sensations (and appearances) whatsoever, the visual and acoustic included, though these do not have a primary localization in the Body.

§38. The Body as organ of the will and as seat of free movement

The distinctive feature of the Body as a field of localization is the presupposition for its further distinctive features setting it off from all material things. In particular, it is the precondition for the fact that it, already taken as Body (namely, as the thing that has a stratum of localized sensations) is an *organ of the will,* the *one and only Object* which, for the will of my pure Ego, is *moveable immediately and spontaneously* and is a means for producing a mediate spontaneous movement in other things, in, e.g., things struck by my immediately spontaneously moved hand, grasped by it, lifted, etc. *Sheer material things are only moveable mechanically and only partake of spontaneous movement in a mediate way.* Only Bodies are immediately spontaneously ("freely") moveable, and they are so, specifically, by means of the free Ego and its will which belong to them. It is in virtue of these free acts that, as we saw earlier, there can be constituted for this Ego, in manifold series of perceptions, an Object-world, a world of spatial-corporeal things (the Body as thing included). The subject, constituted as counter-member of material nature, is (as far as we have seen up to now) an Ego, to which a Body belongs as field of localization of its sensations. The Ego has the "faculty" (the "I can") to freely move this Body—i.e., the organ in which it is articu-

lated—and to perceive an external world by means of it.

§39. Significance of the Body for the constitution of higher Objectivities

Now, besides this, the Body is involved in all other "conscious functions," and that has its various sources. Not only the sensations which exercise a constitutive function as regards the constitution of sense-things, appearing spatial Objects, not only these sensations have a localization given in immediate intuition along with the relation to a Body grounded therein, but that is also true of *sensations belonging to totally different groups,* e.g., the "sensuous" feelings, the sensations of pleasure and pain, the sense of well-being that permeates and fills the whole Body, the general malaise of "corporeal indisposition," etc. Thus here belong groups of *sensations which, for the acts of valuing,* i.e., for intentional lived experiences in the sphere of feeling, or *for the constitution of values* as their intentional correlates, *play a role, as matter, analogous to that played by the primary sensations for what is intentionally lived in the sphere of experience,* or for the constitution of Objects as spatial things. Moreover, all kinds of sensations, difficult to analyze and discuss, belong here as well, ones that form the material substrate for the life of desire and will, sensations of energetic tension and relaxation, sensations of inner restraint, paralysis, liberation, etc. All these groups of sensations, as *sensings,* have an immediate Bodily localization. Thus, for every human being, they *belong, in a way that is immediately intuitable, to the Body as to his particular Body,* i.e., as a subjective objectivity distinguished from the Body as a mere material thing by means of this whole stratum of localized sensations. *The intentional functions, however, are bound to this stratum;* the matter receives a spiritual forming, just as, discussed above, the primary sensations undergo *apprehension,* are taken up in perceptions, upon which, then, perceptual judgments are built, etc. Hence in this way *a human being's total consciousness is in a certain sense, by means of its hyletic substrate, bound to the Body,* though, to be sure, the intentional lived experiences themselves are *no longer* directly and properly *localized;* they no longer form a stratum on the Body. Perception, as the touching apprehension of form, does not have its seat in the touching finger in which the touch sensation is localized; thinking is not actually localized intuitively in the head, the way the impressions of tension are, etc. That we very often speak as if it were so is no proof that we actually apprehend it that way in intuition. The co-intertwined contents of sensation have a localization which is actually intuitively given, but the intentionalities do not, and only metaphorically are they said to be related to the Body or to be in the Body.

§40. More precision concerning the localization of the sensings and concerning the non-thingly properties of the Body

Now, if all that belongs to the matter is Bodily localized or is, by means of localization, related to the Body and is constitutive, therewith, for the Body in the Objectivity proper to it, then we need to ask how this constitution is to be understood and *what it is that institutes unity here.* The physical Body is, of course, a constituted unity, and only to it does the stratum of the sensings belong. How is the content of the sensation connected to what is constituted, and how does the Body, which is equally a material thing, have in itself and on itself the contents of sensation? It is certainly not in the way in which the sensation-content, tone quality, and the sensation-content, intensity, have an essential unity, nor is it the way in which the sensation-content, color, is unified with the moment of spread (we do not mean here spatial extension, talk of which makes no sense with regard to sensation-contents). Here we have on the one side not sensation-contents but constituted real unities instead, and is it really the case that we have mere sensation-contents on the other side? Let us reflect. If an object moves mechanically over the surface of my skin, touching it, then I

obviously have a succession of sensings ordered in a determinate way. If it always moves in the same way, with the same pressure, touching the same parts of the Body at the same pace, then the result is obviously always the same. All this is "obvious," it is there in the apprehension; precisely under such circumstances this Corporeal body behaves in such a way that it is not to be stimulated in just any way but is stimulatable in a definite way under definite circumstances, and such that all effects of stimulation have their system, and to the system of thingly bodies appearing in it there correspond distinctions as to place, whereby, however, to each such place pertains a definite, dependent on the type of the stimulation-effect, further dimension of possible distinctions. To the place in the extension corresponds a place-moment in the sensation, and to the degrees of stimulation and kinds of stimulation correspond definite moments which render the sensation concrete and modifiable according to more or less known ways. Thus there lies in the sensations an order which "coincides" with the appearing extension; but that is already implicit in the apprehension from the outset, in such a way that the stimulation-effects do not appear as something alien and as just an effect, but rather as something *pertaining* to the appearing Corporeal body and to the extensive order, and as something ordered in a *coincident* order. In each Bodily sensation, the mere sensation is not grasped, but it is apprehended as belonging to a system of possible functional consequences which corresponds exactly to the extensive order, consequences that the material real must undergo in consistent parallels with possible material effects. We must also note that the fields of sensation in question here are always completely filled, and each new stimulation does not provoke a sensation as if for the first time, but rather, it provokes in the sensation-field a corresponding change in the sensation. Hence the field undergoes an apprehension as something changeable in manifold ways and as dependent on extension in the type of its changeableness. The field receives localization, and in the field each new change receives localization as a consequence of the particular stimulating circumstances. The new stratum the thing has received by means of the localization of the field acquires, with respect to the constancy of the field, the character of a kind of real property. The Body, we can say, always has states of sensation, and which particular ones it has depends on the concomitant system of real circumstances under which it senses. Under the real circumstances of the "sting" in this or that part of the Body, there emerges in the sensation field (as a field of states) the state of sensation, "sting-sensation." Under the real circumstances we call entrance into a hot room, a change occurs in the total localized field with respect to its total stratum of warmth sensation in the sense of rising temperature, etc. The sensitiveness of the Body thus is constituted throughout as a "conditional" or psychophysical property. And that enters into the apprehension of the Body, as it is perceived "externally." To the apprehension of Corporeality as such belongs not only the apprehension of a thing but also the *co*-apprehension of the sensation fields, and indeed these are given as belonging, in the mode of localization, to the appearing Corporeal body. "Belonging": phenomenologically, this term expresses relations of the phenomenal "if-then": if my hand is touched or struck, then I sense it. We do not here have the hand as physical body and, connected with it, an extra-physical consequence. From the very outset it is apperceptively characterized as a hand *with* its field of sensation, with its constantly co-apprehended state of sensation which changes in consequence of the external actions on it, i.e., as a *physical-aesthesiological unity*. In the abstract, I can separate the physical and aesthesiological strata but can do so precisely only in the abstract. In the concrete perception, the Body is there as a new sort of unity of apprehension. It is constituted as an Objectivity in its own right, which fits under the formal-universal concept of reality, as a thing that preserves its identical properties over against changing external circumstances. The relations of dependency under which it stands toward external nature are thereby, however,

other than the ones material things have amongst themselves. (It has already been mentioned, and it will be discussed with more precision in what follows, that the Body, in addition, as a material thing like all others, is fit within the nexus of reality in a more strict sense, namely, the one of causal regulation.)

It pertains in general to the intuition of something real to leave open, in this intuition's apprehension, further real dependencies which do not yet belong to the content of the executed apprehension in a determinate way (although they may be determinate in their specific nature). The real can therefore be related, in new apprehensions and in extensions of old ones, to new circumstances as something dependent on them, whereby real properties of the same real object are constituted. The sense of the expanded apprehension then prescribes the type which the course of experience has to bear out and determine more precisely. With this more precise determination the apprehension itself then necessarily takes on fuller form.

In this way, even the Body is apprehended not only as dependent with respect to the primary stratum of sensation, its properly localized one, but also with respect to the fields of sensation and groups of sensation that pertain to it mediately and are not properly localized, thus, e.g., with respect to the field of vision. How the visual field of sensation is filled, which motivations can occur therein, and consequently what in the visual field can be experienced by the subject, and in which modes of appearance it must be exhibited, this all depends on certain qualities of the Body, especially on those of the eye, and, furthermore, on the eye's Bodily connections, especially its connections with the central nervous system, and even more particularly it depends on this system itself and, on the other hand, on the concomitant external stimulations. Along with that, hence, are constituted new real properties of the Body, which, thereby, is obviously involved as already constituted from elsewhere. So the capacity to be stimulated in general becomes a universal title for a class of real properties which have quite another source than

the properly extensive (and therewith material) properties of the thing and which in fact
pertain to a quite different dimension. For
through this stratum, through this new group
of real properties which display themselves
as real insofar as they are constituted through
a relation to real circumstances within the
real, the material Body is intertwined with the
soul. What can be apprehended as localized
stratum of the Body as well as what can be apprehended as dependent on the Body (in the
full sense of Body, including this stratum already) and on the "sense organs," all this forms,
under the heading of the matter of consciousness, an underlying basis of consciousness and
undergoes its realizing apprehension in unity
with this consciousness as soul and psychic
Ego. To say that this Ego, or the soul, "has" a
Body does not merely mean that there exists a
physical-material thing which would, through
its material processes, present real preconditions for "conscious events" or even, conversely, that in its processes there occur dependencies on conscious events within a "stream
of consciousness." Causality belongs, if the
word is to retain its pregnant sense, to reality,
and conscious events participate in reality only
as psychic states or as states of a psychic Ego.
Soul and psychic Ego "have" a Body; there
exists a material thing, of a certain nature,
which is not merely a material thing but is a
Body, i.e., a material thing which, as localization field for sensations and for stirrings of
feelings, as complex of sense organs, and as
phenomenal partner and counter-part of all
perceptions of things (along with whatever
else could be said about it, based on the above),
makes up a fundamental component of the
real givenness of the soul and the Ego.

§41. Constitution of the Body as material thing in contrast to other material things*

We have seen how, correlative to the material world, a subject of Bodily-psychic facul-

ties (sense faculties, faculties of free movement, of apperception, etc.) is constituted,
whereby the Body comes to light, at one and
the same time, as Body and as material thing.
In this regard, however, we made the restriction that the Body emerges as a thing of a
particular type, so that one cannot, without
qualification, assign it to nature as a part just
like any other part. This is what we must discuss somewhat more precisely.

A) The Body as center of orientation

If we consider the characteristic way in
which the Body presents itself and do the
same for things, then we find the following situation: each Ego has its own domain of perceptual things and necessarily perceives the
things in a certain orientation. The things appear and do so from this or that side, and in
this mode of appearing is included irrevoca-
bly a relation to a here and its basic directions.
All spatial being necessarily appears in such
a way that it appears either nearer or farther, above or below, right or left. This holds
with regard to all points of the appearing
corporeality, which then have their differences
in relation to one another as regards this nearness, this above and below, etc., among which
there are hereby peculiar qualities of appearance, stratified like dimensions. The Body then
has, for its particular Ego, the unique distinction
of bearing in itself the *zero point* of all these
orientations. One of its spatial points, even if
not an actually seen one, is always characterized in the mode of the ultimate central here:
that is, a here which has no other here outside of itself, in relation to which it would
be a "there." It is thus that all things of the
surrounding world possess an orientation to
the Body, just as, accordingly, all expressions of orientation imply this relation. The
"far" is far from me, from my Body; the "to
the right" refers back to the right side of my
Body, e.g., to my right hand. In virtue of its
faculty of free mobility, the subject can now

*Cf. pp. 176f.

induce the flow of the system of its appearances and, along with that, the orientations.
These changes do not have the significance
of changes of the things of the environment
themselves, and specifically, they do not signify a movement of the things. The Body of
the subject "alters its position" in space; the
things appearing in the environment are constantly oriented thereby; all appearances of
things preserve their fixed system according
to form. The form of intuition, the lawful character of the adumbrations, and, therewith, the
form of the order of orientation around a
center, all this is necessarily preserved. But
whereas the subject is always, at every now,
in the center, in the here, whence it sees the
things and penetrates into the world by vision,
on the other hand the Objective place, the
spatial position, of the Ego, or of its Body, is
a changing one.

Nevertheless, at the present stage of our
investigation we are not at all so advanced
that we could assign to the Ego such an "Objective place." Provisionally, we must say: I
have all things over and against me; they are
all "there"—with the exception of one and
only one, namely the Body, which is always
"here."

B) PECULIARITY OF THE MANIFOLDS OF APPEARANCE OF THE BODY

Other peculiar properties of the Body are
conjoined with its distinctive character as
we have described it. Whereas, with regard to
all other things, I have the freedom to change
at will my position in relation to them and
thereby at the same time vary at will the manifolds of appearance in which they come to
givenness for me, on the other hand I do not
have the possibility of distancing myself
from my Body, or my Body from me, and accordingly the manifolds of appearance of the
Body are restricted in a definite way: certain
of my corporeal parts can be seen by me only
in a peculiar perspectival foreshortening, and
others (e.g., the head) are altogether invisible to me. The same Body which serves me
as means for all my perception obstructs me

in the perception of it itself and is a remarkably imperfectly constituted thing.

C) THE BODY AS INTEGRAL PART OF THE CAUSAL NEXUS

If, despite all this, we apprehend the Body
as a real thing, it is because we find it integrated into the causal nexus of material nature. We
spoke of the peculiarity the Body has (as Body)
of being moved "spontaneously" or "freely"
by the will of the Ego. Besides these free kinesthetic processes, others emerge which, instead of being "done by," are characterized as
being "done to," i.e., as passive processes in
which spontaneity plays no part. In that case,
we have at the same time an experiencing of
the mechanical process of the movement of
the Body and a givenness of this process with
the "psychic" character of enduring something—not as if it were something painful or
repugnant but simply in the sense that "my
hand is moved, my foot is struck, pushed," etc.
Similarly, I experience the mechanical movement of the Body as the movement of a material thing like any other thing even in the
case of spontaneity, and I find it characterized
at the same time as a spontaneous movement
in the sense, "I move my hand," etc.

Thus movements of my Body are apprehended as mechanical processes like those of
external things, and the Body itself is apprehended as a thing which affects others and
upon which the others have effects. All the
cases mentioned earlier of conditional relations between things and the Body also admit
of changes in apprehension, thanks to which
the processes in question appear as merely
physical ones. If a heavy body is resting on
my hand (or perhaps the one hand on the other) then I have, abstracting from the resultant sensation of pressure or pain, the physical
phenomenon of one body pressing on another,
perhaps deforming it by its pressure. If I cut
my finger with a knife, then a physical body is
split by the driving into it of a wedge, the fluid
contained in it trickles out, etc. Likewise, the
physical thing, "my Body," is heated or cooled
through contact with hot or cold bodies; it can

become electrically charged through contact with an electric current; it assumes different colors under changing illumination; and one can elicit noises from it by striking it. The last two cases, however, are different from the earlier ones where there was a psychophysical process that could be split apart abstractively into a physical process and its "psychical" consequence (or vice versa). But the physical process, "red illumination of my hand," is not followed by the sensation of red in the same way that the sensation of warmth follows the heating of my hand, and the physical process to which the sensation of the color is linked —red light rays striking my eyes—is not given to me at all. The "turning point," which lies in the Body, the point of the transformation from causal to conditional process, is hidden from me.

§42. *Character of the Body as constituted solipsistically*

If we now try, in a short summary, to characterize the way a Body is constituted for the solipsistic subject, then we find that:

1) viewed from "within"—in the "inner attitude"—it appears as a freely moving organ (or system of such organs) by means of which the subject experiences the external world. Furthermore, the Body appears as a bearer of sensations, and, thanks to their intertwining with the rest of psychic life in its totality, it appears as forming, with the soul, a concrete unity.

2) Approached from the outside—in the "outer attitude"—it presents itself as a reality *sui generis*. That is: on the one hand, as a material thing of special modes of appearance, a thing "inserted" between the rest of the material world and the "subjective" sphere (the subject together with what was just mentioned in 1), as a center around which the rest of the spatial world is arranged, and as being in causal relationship with the real external world. On the other hand, the Body appears here at the same time as a "turning point" where the causal relations are transformed into conditional relations between the external world and the Bodily-psychic subject. And in virtue of that, the Body appears as pertaining integrally to this subject and its properties, both the specifically Corporeal and the psychic ones bound up with them. That which is constituted in the outer attitude is there co-present together with what is constituted in the inner attitude.

In solipsistic experience, however, we do not attain the givenness of our self as a spatial thing like all others (a givenness which certainly is manifest in our factual experience) nor that of the natural Object, "man" (animal being), which we came to know as correlate of the "naturalistic attitude," a material thing upon which the higher strata of what is specifically animal are built and into which they are, in a certain way, inserted, "introjected." In order to attain that, a different path has to be followed; one must go beyond his own subjectivity and turn to the animalia encountered in the external world.

11. A Phenomenology of the Consciousness of Internal Time

Analysis of the Consciousness of Time*

§7. Interpretation of the grasping of temporal objects as momentary grasping and as enduring act

How are we to understand the apprehension of transcendent temporal objects that are extended over a duration, continuously filling it in the same way (as unchanging things do) or filling it as constantly changing (as in the case, for example, of physical processes, motion, alteration, and the like)? Objects of this kind become constituted in a multiplicity of immanent data and apprehensions, which themselves run off as a succession. Is it possible to unite these successively elapsing representing data in one now-moment? In that case, the entirely new question arises: How, in addition to "temporal objects," immanent and transcendent, does time itself—the duration and succession of objects—become constituted? These different lines of description (indicated only in passing here and requiring still further differentiation) must indeed be kept in mind during the analysis, although all of these questions belong closely together and no one of them can be answered apart from the others. It is certainly evident that the perception of a temporal object itself has temporality, that the perception of duration itself presupposes the duration of perception, that the perception of any temporal form itself has its temporal form. If we disregard all transcendencies, there remains to perception in all of its phenomenological constituents the phenomenological temporality that belongs to its irreducible essence. Since objective temporality always becomes constituted phenomenologically and stands before us in appearance as an objectivity or as a moment of an objectivity only through this constitution, a phenomenological analysis of time cannot clarify the constitution of time without considering the constitution of temporal objects. By *temporal objects in the specific sense* we understand objects that are not only unities in time but that also contain temporal extension in themselves. When a tone sounds, my objectivating apprehension can make the tone itself, which endures and fades away, into an object and yet not make the duration of the tone or the tone in its duration into an object. The latter—the tone in its duration—is a temporal object. The same is true of a melody, of any change whatsoever, but also of any persistence without change, considered as such. Let us take the example of a melody or of a cohesive part of a melody. The matter seems very simple at first: we hear the melody, that is, we perceive it, for hearing is indeed perceiving. However, the first tone sounds, then comes the second tone, then the third, and so on. Must we not say: When the second tone sounds, I hear *it*, but I no longer hear the first tone, etc.? In truth, then, I do not hear the melody but only the single present tone. That the elapsed part of the melody is something objective for me, I owe—or so one will be inclined to say—to memory; and that I do not presuppose, with the appearance of the currently intended tone, that this is *all*, I owe to anticipatory expectation. But we cannot be content with this explanation, for everything that we have said carries over to the individual tone. Each tone has a temporal extension itself. When it begins to sound, I hear it as now; but while it continues to sound it has an ever new now, and the now that immediately precedes it changes into a past. Therefore at any given time I hear only the actually present phase of the tone, and the ob-

*PCIT, pp. 23 (line 15)–46, 52–75 (Sections 7–18 and 23–33), with reconstructed Appendix I (pp. 119 [lines 30–35], 105 [line 6]–107 [line 16], 119 [line 39]–120 [line 33]) to Section 11.

jectivity of the whole enduring tone is constituted in an act-continuum that is in part memory, in smallest punctual part perception, and in further part expectation. This seems to lead back to Brentano's theory. Here, then, a deeper analysis must begin.

§8. *Immanent temporal objects and their modes of appearance*

We now exclude all transcendent apprehension and positing and take the tone purely as a hyletic datum. It begins and ends; and after it has ended, its whole duration-unity, the unity of the whole process in which it begins and ends, "recedes" into the ever more distant past. In this sinking back, I still "hold onto it," have it in a "retention." And as long as the retention lasts, the tone has its own temporality; it is the same, its duration is the same. I can direct my attention to the way in which it is given. I am conscious of the tone and of the duration it fills in a continuity of "modes," in a "continual flow." And one point, one phase of this flow is called "consciousness of the commencing tone"; and in this phase I am conscious of the first time-point of the tone's duration in the mode of the now. The tone is given; that is, I am conscious of it as now. But I am conscious of it as now "as long as" any one of its phases is intended as now. However, if any temporal phase (corresponding to a time-point of the tone-duration) is an actually present now (with the exception of the initial phase), then I am conscious of a continuity of phases as "immediately past" and of the whole extent of the temporal duration from the beginning-point up to the now-point as elapsed. I am not yet conscious of the remaining extent of the duration, however. When the final point is reached, I am conscious of this point itself as the now-point and of the whole duration as elapsed (or I am conscious of it as elapsed at the beginning-point of the new extent of time, which is no longer a tonal extent). "Throughout" this whole flow of consciousness, one and the same tone is intended as enduring, as now enduring. "Beforehand" (in the event that it was not expected), it is not intended. "Afterwards," it is "still" intended

"for a time" in "retention" as having been; it can be held fast and stand or remain fixed in our regard. The whole extent of the tone's duration or "the" tone in its extension then stands before me as something dead, so to speak— something no longer being vitally generated, a formation no longer animated by the generative point of the now but continuously modified and sinking back into "emptiness." The modification of the whole extent, then, is analogous to or essentially identical with the modification that the elapsed part of the duration undergoes in the transition of consciousness to ever new productions during the time that the tone is actually present.

What we have described here is the manner in which the object in immanent time "appears" in a continual flow, the manner in which it is "given." To describe this manner does not mean to describe the appearing temporal duration itself, for it is the same tone with the duration belonging to it that, indeed, was not described but presupposed in the description. The same duration is present duration actually building itself up and then is past, "elapsed" duration, duration that is still intended or that is produced in recollection "as if" it were new. It is the same tone that now sounds of which it is said in the "later" flow of consciousness that it has been, that its duration has elapsed. The points of the temporal duration recede for my consciousness in a manner analogous to that in which the points of an object stationary in space recede for my consciousness when I remove "myself" from the object. The object keeps its place, just as the tone keeps its time. Each time-point is fixed, but it flies into the distance for consciousness. The distance from the generative now becomes greater and greater. The tone itself is the same, but the tone "in the manner in which" it appears is continually different.

§9. *The consciousness of the appearances of immanent objects*

On closer examination, we can distinguish still other lines of description here. 1. We can make evident statements about the immanent object in itself: that it now endures; that a certain part of the duration has elapsed; that the point of the tone's duration grasped in the now (with its tone-content, of course) continuously sinks back into the past and that an ever new point of the duration enters into the now or is now; that the elapsed duration moves away from the actually present now-point, which is constantly filled in some way, and recedes into the ever more "distant" past, and the like. 2. But we can also talk about the way in which we are "conscious" of all such differences pertaining to the "appearing" of the immanent tone and of its duration-content. We speak of perception in connection with the tone-duration that reaches into the actually present now and say that the tone, the enduring tone, is perceived, and that at any given instant, of the extended duration of the tone, only the point of the duration characterized as now is perceived in the fully proper sense. We say of the elapsed extent that it is intended in retentions; specifically, the parts of the duration or phases of the duration lying closest to the actually present now-point, and which cannot be sharply delimited, are intended with diminishing clarity. The more remote phases —those lying further back in the past—are entirely obscure and emptily intended. And the situation is the same after the whole duration has elapsed: What lies nearest to the actually present now, depending on its distance from it, perhaps has a little clarity; the whole [then] disappears into obscurity, into an empty retentional consciousness, and finally disappears altogether (if one is permitted to assert that) as soon as retention ceases.*

We find in the sphere of clarity a greater distinctness and separation (the more so the closer the sphere lies to the actually present now). But the further we move from the now, the greater the fusion and compression that manifests itself. A reflective penetration of the unity of a many-membered process lets us observe that an articulated part of the process "contracts" as it sinks back into the past—a

sort of temporal perspective (within the original temporal appearance) as an analogue of the spatial perspective. In receding into the past, the temporal object contracts and in the process also becomes obscure.

Now it is a matter of investigating more closely what we are able to find and describe here as the phenomenon of time-constituting consciousness, of the consciousness in which temporal objects with their temporal determinations become constituted. We distinguish the enduring, immanent object and the object in its way of appearing, the object intended as actually present or as past. Every temporal being "appears" in some running-off mode that changes continuously, and in this change the "object in its mode of running off" is always and ever a different object. And yet we continue to say that the object and each point of its time and this time itself are one and the same. We will not be able to term this appearance—the "object in its mode of running off" —"consciousness" (any more than we will give the name "consciousness" to the spatial phenomenon, the body in its way of appearing from this side or that, from near or far). The "consciousness," the "experience," is related to its object by means of an appearance in which precisely the "object in its way of appearing" ["Objekt im Wie"] stands before us. Obviously we must recognize our references to intentionality as ambiguous, depending on whether we have in view the relation of the appearance to what appears or the relation of consciousness, on the one hand, to "what appears in its way of appearing" and, on the other hand, to what appears *simpliciter.*

§10. *The continua of the running-off phenomena. The diagram of time*

We would prefer to avoid, then, the use of the word "appearances" for the phenomena that constitute immanent temporal objects; for these phenomena are themselves imma-

---

*It obviously suggests itself to put these modes of appearance and consciousness of temporal objects in parallel to the modes in which a spatial thing appears and is intended in its changing orientation; moreover, it suggests itself to investigate the "temporal orientations" in which spatial things (which are indeed also temporal objects) appear. Nevertheless, we remain for the present within the immanent sphere.

nent objects and are "appearances" in an entirely different sense. We speak here of the "running-off phenomena," or better still, of the "modes of temporal orientation"; and with respect to the immanent objects themselves, we speak of their "running-off characters" (e.g., now, past). We know that the running-off phenomenon is a continuity of constant changes. This continuity forms an inseparable unity, inseparable into extended sections that could exist by themselves and inseparable into phases that could exist by themselves, into points of the continuity. The parts that we single out by abstraction can exist only in the whole running-off; and this is equally true of the phases, the points that belong to the running-off con-

steady progression of the running-off modes we then find the remarkable circumstance that each later running-off phase is itself a continuity, a continuity that constantly expands, a continuity of pasts. To the continuity of running-off modes of the object's duration, we contrast the continuity of running-off modes belonging to each point of the duration. This second continuity is obviously included in the first, the continuity of running-off modes of the object's duration. The running-off continuity of an enduring object is therefore a continuum whose phases are the continua of the running-off modes belonging to the different time-points of the duration of the object. If we proceed along the concrete continuity, we

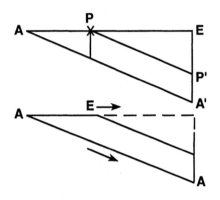

AE – The series of now-points.

AA' – Sinking into the past.

EA' – Continuum of phases (now-point with horizon of the past).

E → – The series of nows perhaps filled with other objects.

tinuity. We can also say of this continuity, with evidence, that in a certain sense it is immutable; that is, with regard to its form. It is inconceivable that the continuity of phases would contain the same phase-mode twice or even contain it as stretched over an entire component section. Just as each point of time (and each extent of time) differs "individually," so to speak, from every other one and just as no one of them can occur twice, so no running-off mode can occur twice. We will still have to make further distinctions and provide clearer descriptions here, however. First of all, we emphasize that the running-off modes of an immanent temporal object have a beginning, a source-point, so to speak. This is the running-off mode with which the immanent object begins to exist. It is characterized as now. In the

move forward in a process of constant modifications; and in this process, the running-off-mode—that is, the running-off continuity of the time-points in question—changes continuously. Since a new now is always entering on the scene, the now changes into a past; and as it does so, the whole running-off continuity of pasts belonging to the preceding point moves "downwards" uniformly into the depths of the past. In our diagram, the continuous series of ordinates illustrates the running-off modes of the enduring object. They grow from A (one point) into a determinate extent, which has the last now as its final point. Then the series of running-off modes that no longer include a now (that is, a now belonging to this duration) begins; the duration is no longer actually present but past, and continuously sinking deeper into the past. The diagram therefore gives a complete picture of the double continuity of running-off modes.

§11. Primal impression and retentional modification

The "source-point" with which the "production" of the enduring object begins is a primal impression. This consciousness is in a state of constant change: the tone-now present "in person" continuously changes *(scil.* consciously, "in" consciousness) into something that has been; an always new tone-now continuously relieves the one that has passed over into modification. But when the consciousness of the tone-now, the primal impression, passes over into retention, this retention itself is a now in turn, something actually existing. While it is actually present itself (but not an actually present tone), it is retention *of* the tone that has been. A ray of meaning can be directed towards the now: towards the retention; but it can also be directed towards what is retentionally intended: towards the past tone. Every actually present now of consciousness, however, is subject to the law of modification. It changes into retention of retention and does so continuously. Accordingly, a fixed continuum of retention arises in such a way that each later point is retention for every earlier point. And each retention is already a continuum. The tone begins and "it" steadily continues. The tone-now changes into a tone-having-been; the *impressional* consciousness, constantly flowing, passes over into ever new *retentional* consciousness. Going along the flow or with it, we have a continuous series of retentions pertaining to the beginning-point. Beyond that, however, each earlier point of this series is adumbrated *in its turn* as a now in the sense of retention. Thus a continuity of retentional modifications attaches itself to each of these retentions, and this continuity itself is again an actually present point that is retentionally adumbrated. This does not lead to a simple infinite regress, since each retention is in itself continuous modification that carries within, so to speak, the heritage of the past in the form of a series of adumbrations. But it is not the case here that in the horizontal direction of the flow each earlier retention is simply replaced by a new one, even if continuously. Rather, each later retention is not only continual modification that has arisen from primal impression; each is also continual modification of all earlier continuous modifications of that same initial point.

Up to now we have taken into consideration principally the perception or original constitution of temporal objects and have attempted to understand analytically the time-consciousness given in them. But consciousness of temporality is not achieved solely in this form. When a temporal object has elapsed, when the actual duration is finished, the consciousness of the now-past object by no means expires with the object, although it now no longer functions as perceptual consciousness, or said better perhaps, as impressional consciousness. (As before, we have immanent objects in view here, which properly speaking are not constituted in a "perception.") Primary memory, or as we said, retention, continuously attaches itself to the "impression." At bottom, we have already analyzed this consciousness in the case considered earlier. For the continuity of phases that attached itself to the actual "now" was nothing other than such a retention or continuity of retentions. In the case of the perception of a temporal object (whether we take an immanent or transcendent object makes no difference in the present consideration), the perception terminates at any moment in a now-apprehension, in a perception in the sense of a positing-as-now. During the time that a motion is being perceived, a grasping-as-now takes place moment by moment; and in this grasping, the actually present phase of the motion itself becomes constituted. But this now-apprehension is, as it were, the head attached to the comet's tail of retentions relating to the earlier now-points of the motion. However, if perception no longer occurs, if we no longer see the motion, or—if it is a melody that is in question—the melody has run its course and silence has ensued, then the perception's final phase is not followed by a new phase of the perception but simply by a phase of fresh memory, which in its turn is followed by another phase of fresh memory, and so on. Thus a pushing back into the past continually occurs. The same continuous complex incessantly undergoes a modification until it disappears; for a weakening, which finally ends in imperceptibility, goes hand in hand with the modification. The original temporal field is manifestly limited, precisely as in perception's case. Indeed, on the whole, one might dare to assert that the temporal field always has the same extension. It moves, as it were, over the perceived and freshly remembered motion and its objective time in the same way as the visual field moves over objective space.*, †

§12. Retention as a unique kind of intentionality

It still remains for us to discuss in a more precise way what sort of modification it is that we have designated as retentional. One speaks of the dying-away, the fading, and so on, of the contents of sensation when perception proper passes over into retention. Now it is already clear, following our explanations up to this point, that the retentional "contents" are not at all contents in the original sense. When a tone dies away, it itself is sensed at first with particular fullness (intensity); and then there follows a rapid weakening in intensity. The tone is still there, still sensed, but in mere reverberation. This genuine tone-sensation must be distinguished from the tonal moment in retention. The retentional tone is not a present tone but precisely a tone "primarily remembered" in the now: it is not really on hand in the retentional consciousness. But neither can the tonal moment that belongs to this consciousness be a different tone that is really on hand; it cannot even be a very weak tone equivalent in quality (such as an echo).

A present tone can indeed "remind" one of a past tone, exemplify it, pictorialize it; but that already presupposes another representation of the past. The intuition of the past cannot itself be a pictorialization. It is an original consciousness. We cannot deny, of course, that there are echoes. But when we recognize and distinguish them, we can easily confirm that they obviously do not belong to retention as retention but to perception. The reverberation of a violin tone is precisely a feeble present violin tone and is absolutely different from the retention of the loud tone that has just passed. The echoing itself and after-images of any sort left behind by the stronger data of sensation, far from having to be ascribed necessarily to the essence of retention, have nothing at all to do with it.

But it surely does belong to the essence of the intuition of time that in each point of its duration (which we can make into an object reflectively) it is consciousness *of what has just been* and not merely consciousness of the now-point of the object that appears as enduring. And what has just been is intended in this consciousness in its corresponding continuity, and in each phase it is intended in a determinate "mode of appearance" with the distinctions of "content" and "apprehension." We focus our attention on the whistle that is now sounding: in each point an extension stands before me, and it stands before me in an extension of "appearance." In each phase of this extension, the appearance has its moment of quality and its moment of apprehension. On the other hand, the moment of quality is not a real quality, not a tone that would really exist at present—that is, that could be taken as a now-existing, though immanent, tone-content. The real content of the consciousness of the now possibly contains sensed tones; these sensed tones must then necessarily be characterized in objectivating apprehension as perceived tones, as present tones, but in no way

---

*The limitation of the temporal field is not taken into consideration in the diagram. No ending of retention is foreseen there, and *idealiter* a consciousness is probably even possible in which everything remains preserved retentionally.

†With respect to the foregoing, cf. Appendix I: Primal Impression and Its Continuum of Modifications, pp. 210ff.

as past. Retentional consciousness really contains consciousness of the past of the tone, primary memory of the tone, and must not be divided into sensed tone and apprehension as memory. Just as a phantasy-tone is not a tone but the phantasy of the tone, or just as tone-phantasy and tone-sensation are essentially different things and not by any chance the same thing only differently interpreted or apprehended, so too the tone primarily remembered in intuition is something *fundamentally and essentially* different from the perceived tone; and correlatively, primary memory (retention) of the tone is something different from sensation of the tone.

§13. The necessity that an impression precede every retention. Evidence pertaining to retention

Now does there exist a law according to which primary memory is possible only in continuous annexation to a preceding sensation or perception? A law according to which each retentional phase is conceivable only as a phase; that is, a law according to which the retentional phase cannot be expanded into an extent that would be identical in all of its phases? One will say decisively: That is absolutely evident. The empirical psychologist, who is accustomed to treating everything psychic as mere matter of fact, will deny it, of course. He will say: Why should a beginning consciousness that commences with a fresh memory, without having been preceded by a perception, not be conceivable? Perception may in fact be necessary to the production of fresh memory. It may in fact be the case that a human consciousness can have memories, even primary memories, only after it has had perceptions; but the opposite is also conceivable. Over against this, we teach the a priori necessity that a corresponding perception, or a corresponding primal impression, precede the retention. Above all, we will have to insist that a phase is conceivable only as a phase, without the possibility of extension. And the now-phase is conceivable only as the limit of a continuity of retentions, just as every reten-

tional phase is itself conceivable only as a point belonging to such a continuum; and this is true of every now of time-consciousness. But then even a completely finished series of retentions would not be conceivable without a corresponding perception preceding it. This implies that the series of retentions that belongs to a now is itself a limit and necessarily undergoes modification; what is remembered "sinks further and further into the past." But not only that—it is necessarily something sunken, something that necessarily permits an evident recollection that traces it back to a now that is given once again.

But then one will say: Can I not have a memory of A, even a primary memory, when in fact A has not even taken place? Certainly. Indeed, I can go even further than that. I can also have a perception of A although A is not occurring in reality at all. And consequently when we have a retention of A (provided that A is a transcendent object), we by no means assert the having of the retention as evidence that A must have preceded it; but we do indeed assert it as evidence that A must have been perceived. Now whether A was heeded primarily or not, it was there "in person" for my consciousness, even if it was unnoticed or noticed only incidentally. But if it is a question of an immanent object, the following obtains: when a succession, a change, or an alteration of immanent data "appears," it too is absolutely certain. And within a transcendent perception, the immanent succession that belongs to its structure essentially is also absolutely certain. It is *fundamentally wrongheaded* to argue: How, in the now, can I know of a not-now, since I cannot compare the not-now —which, of course, no longer exists—with the now (namely, with the memory image that I have on hand in the now)? As if it belonged to the essence of memory that I take an image on hand in the now for another thing similar to it and that I could and must compare them as I do in the case of pictorial representation. Memory—and this is equally true of retention—is not image-consciousness; it is something totally different. What is remembered, of course, does not now *exist*—otherwise it would not be something that has been but something present; and in memory (retention) it is not given as now, otherwise memory, or retention, would precisely not be memory but perception (or, respectively, primal impression). A comparing of what is no longer perceived but merely intended retentionally with something beyond it makes no sense whatsoever. Just as I see being-now in perception and enduring being in the extended perception as it becomes constituted, so I see the past in memory, insofar as the memory is primary memory. The past is given in primary memory, and givenness of the past is memory.

Now if we again take up the question whether a retentional consciousness is conceivable that would not be the continuation of an impressional consciousness, we must say: Such a consciousness is impossible, for every retention intrinsically refers back to an impression. "Past" and "now" exclude one another. Identically the same thing can indeed be now and past, but only because it has endured between the past and the now.

§14. Reproduction of temporal objects (secondary memory)

We characterized primary memory or retention as a comet's tail that attaches itself to the perception of the moment. Secondary memory, recollection, must be distinguished absolutely from primary memory or retention. After the primary memory is over with, a new memory of this motion, of that melody, can emerge. We must now clarify in more detail the difference, already indicated, between the two. If retention attaches itself to the actually present perception, whether during its perceptual flow or in continuous union with it after it has completely elapsed, it is natural to say at first (as Brentano did) that the actually present perception becomes constituted as presentation on the basis of sensations and that primary memory becomes constituted as representation *[Repräsentation]*, as re-presentation *[Vergegenwärtigung]*, on the basis of phantasies. Now just as re-presentations can attach themselves immediately to perceptions,

they can also occur independently without being joined to perceptions, and these are secondary memories. But serious objections arise against this view (as we have already pointed out in the criticism of Brentano's theory). Let us consider a case of secondary memory: We recall, say, a melody that we recently heard at a concert. It is obvious in this case that the whole memory-phenomenon has exactly the same constitution, *mutatis mutandis,* as the perception of the melody. Like the perception, it has a privileged point: to the now-point of the perception corresponds a now-point of the memory. We run through the melody in phantasy; we hear, "as it were," first the initial tone, then the second tone, and so on. At any particular time there is always a tone (or tone-phase) in the now-point. The preceding tones, however, are not erased from consciousness. Primary memory of the tones that, as it were, I have just heard and expectation (protention) of the tones that are yet to come fuse with the apprehension of the tone that is now appearing and that, as it were, I am now hearing. The now-point once again has for consciousness a temporal fringe, which is produced in a continuity of memorial apprehensions; and the total memory of the melody consists in a continuum of such continua of temporal fringes and, correlatively, in a continuum of apprehension-continua of the kind described. But when the re-presented melody has finally run its course, a retention attaches itself to this quasi-hearing; what is quasi-heard continues to fade away for a while—a continuity of apprehension is still there, but no longer as heard. Consequently everything is *like* perception and primary memory and yet is not itself perception and primary memory. Of course, we do not actually hear and we have not actually heard when we let a melody run its course tone by tone in memory or phantasy. In the earlier case we said: We do actually hear, the temporal object itself is perceived, the melody itself is the object of perception. And the times, temporal determinations, and temporal relations are equally given and perceived themselves. And again: After the melody has died away, we no longer have it perceived as present, but we do still have it in consciousness. It is not a present melody but one just past. Its being just past is not merely something meant but a given fact, given itself and therefore "perceived." In opposition to this, the temporal present in recollection is a remembered, re-presented present; and the past too is a remembered, re-presented past but not an actually present past, not a perceived past, not a past primarily given and intuited.

On the other hand, the recollection itself is presently and originally constituted recollection and afterwards just past recollection. It itself is built up in a continuum of primal data and retentions and in union with them constitutes (or rather: re-constitutes) an immanent or transcendent enduring objectivity (depending on whether the recollection is directed towards something immanent or towards something transcendent). Retention, on the other hand, produces no enduring objectivities (either originally or reproductively) but only holds in consciousness what has been produced and stamps on it the character of the "just past."

§15. Reproduction's modes of accomplishment

Now recollection can occur in different forms of accomplishment. Either we execute it in a simple grasping, as when a memory "rises to the surface" and we look at what is remembered in a flash. In this case what is remembered is vague; perhaps the memory brings forward, intuitively, a privileged momentary phase, but it does not repeat its object. Or we execute a memory that actually does reproduce and repeat, a memory in which the temporal object is completely built up afresh in a continuum of re-presentations and in which we perceive it again, as it were—but only "as it were." The whole process is a re-presentational modification of the perceptual process with all of the latter's phases and stages right down to and including the retentions: but everything has the index of reproductive modification.

We also find the simple looking-at or apprehending [occurring] immediately on the ba-

sis of retention, as when a melody has elapsed that lies within the unity of a retention and we turn our attention back to (reflect on) a part of it without producing it afresh. This is an act that is possible for everything that has developed in successive steps, even in steps of spontaneity—for example, in the successive steps of the spontaneity of thinking. Certainly objectivities produced by thinking are also constituted successively. It therefore seems that we can say: Objectivities that are built up originally in temporal processes, becoming constituted member by member or phase by phase (as correlates of unitary acts that are continuously and complexly connected), can be grasped in a retrospective viewing as if they were objects complete in one time-point. But then this givenness definitely points back to another and "original" givenness.

The looking-toward or looking-back at what is given retentionally—and the retention itself—is then fulfilled in re-presentation proper: what is given as just having been shows itself to be identical with what is recollected.

Further differences between primary and secondary memory will emerge if we put them in relation to perception.

§16. Perception as presentation in distinction from retention and recollection

The use of the word *"perception"* requires, of course, some further elucidation at this point. In the case of the "perception of the melody," we distinguish the tone *given now,* calling it the "perceived" tone, and the tones that are *over with,* calling them "not perceived." On the other hand, we call the *whole melody* a perceived melody, even though only the now-point is perceived. We proceed in this way because the extension of the melody is not only given point by point in the extension of the act of perceiving, but the unity of the retentional consciousness still "holds on to" the elapsed tones themselves in consciousness and progressively brings about the unity of the consciousness that is related to the unitary temporal object, to the melody. An objectivity such as a melody cannot be "perceived" or originally given itself otherwise than in this form. The constituted act,* built from consciousness of the now and retentional consciousness, is *adequate perception of the temporal object.* This object must include temporal distinctions, and temporal distinctions are constituted precisely in such acts—in primal consciousness, retention, and protention. If the intentional act of meaning is aimed at the melody, at the whole object, then we have nothing but perception. But if it is aimed at the single tone all by itself or at a measure by itself, then we have perception precisely as long as what is meant is perceived and sheer retention as soon as it is past. With respect to objectivity, the measure then no longer appears as "present" but as "past." But the whole melody appears as present as long as it still sounds, as long as tones belonging to it and meant in *one* nexus of apprehension still sound. It is past only after the final tone is gone.

Considering our earlier explanations, we must say that this relativity carries over to the *individual tones.* Each tone becomes constituted in a continuity of tone-data; and at any given time, only one punctual phase is present as now, while the others are attached as a retentional tail. But we can say: A temporal object is perceived (or intended impressionally) as long as it is still being generated in continuously emerging new primal impressions.

We have, then, characterized the *past* itself as *perceived.* In point of fact, do we not perceive the passing, are we not directly conscious in the cases described of the just-having-been, of the "just past" in its self-givenness, in the mode of being given itself? Obviously the sense of "perception" obtaining here does not coincide with the earlier one. Further distinctions are needed. If, in the grasping of a temporal object, we distinguish between perceptual and memorial (retentional) consciousness, then to the opposition between perception and primary memory there corresponds on the side of the object the opposition between "now present" and "past." Temporal objects—and this pertains to their essence—spread their matter over an

extent of time, and such objects can become constituted only in acts that constitute the very differences belonging to time. But time-constituting acts are—essentially—acts that constitute the present and the past; they have the character of those "perceptions of temporal objects" that we have fully described with respect to their remarkable apprehensional constitution. Temporal objects must become constituted in this way. That implies: an act claiming to give a temporal object itself must contain in itself "apprehensions of the now," "apprehensions of the past," and so on; specifically, as originally constituting apprehensions.

Now if we relate the use of the word "perception" to the differences in givenness with which temporal objects present themselves, the antithesis of perception is the primary memory and the primary expectation (retention and protention) that occur here; in which case, perception and nonperception continuously blend into one another. In the consciousness that belongs to the directly intuitive grasp of a temporal object—of a melody, for example—the measure or tone or part of a tone now being heard is perceived, and what is momentarily intuited as past is not perceived. The apprehensions continuously blend into one another here; they terminate in an apprehension that constitutes the now, but which is only an ideal limit. There is a continuum that ascends towards an ideal limit, just as the continuum of the species red converges towards an ideal pure red. But in our case we do not have individual apprehensions corresponding to individual nuances of red that could be given by themselves; instead we always have—and, according to the essence of the matter, can only have—continuities of apprehensions, or rather a single continuum that is continuously modified. If in some way we divide this continuum into two adjoining parts, then the part that includes the now or is capable of constituting it is distinguished from the other part and constitutes the "rough" now; as soon as we divide this rough now further, it in turn im-

*On acts as constituted unities in the original consciousness of time, cf. §37, pp. 213f.

mediately breaks down into a finer now and a past, and so on.

Perception here is therefore an act-characteristic that joins together a continuity of act-characteristics and is distinguished by the possession of that ideal limit. A similar continuity without this ideal limit is bare memory. In the ideal sense, then, perception (impression) would be the phase of consciousness that constitutes the pure now, and memory would be every other phase of the continuity. But the now is precisely only an ideal limit, something abstract, which can be nothing by itself. Moreover, it remains to be said that even this ideal now is not something *toto coelo* different from the not-now but is continuously mediated with it. And to this corresponds the continuous transition of perception into primary memory.

§17. Perception as the act that gives something itself in opposition to reproduction

In addition to the contrast between perception, or the giving of the present itself, [and primary memory], which has its correlate in the given past, there is another opposition: between perception and recollection or secondary memory. In recollection a now "appears" to us, but it "appears" in an entirely different sense than the sense in which the now appears in perception. This now is not "perceived"—that is, given itself—but represented. It represents a now that is not given. And so too the running-off of a melody in *recollection* represents a "just past" but does not *give* it. Even in mere phantasy every individual is extended in time in some way, having its now, its before, and its after; but the now, before, and after are merely imagined, as is the whole object. Here, therefore, *an entirely different concept of perception* is in question. Perception in this case is the act that places something before our eyes as the thing itself, the act that *originally constitutes* the object. Its opposite is *re-presentation [Vergegenwärtigung, Re-Präsentation]*, understood as the act that does not place an object itself before our eyes but just *represents* it; that places it before our eyes in

image, as it were, although not exactly in the manner of a genuine image-consciousness. Here we do not say anything at all about a continuous mediation of perception with its opposite. Up to this point, the consciousness of the past—the primary consciousness of the past, that is—was not <called> perception because perception was taken as the act that originally constitutes the now. But the consciousness of the past does not constitute a now; it rather constitutes a "just past," something that has preceded the now intuitively. But if we call perception the *act in which all "origin"* lies, the act that *constitutes originally,* then *primary memory* is *perception.* For only in primary memory do we *see* what is past, only in it does the past become constituted—and constituted presentatively, not re-presentatively. The just past, the before in opposition to the now, can be directly seen only in primary memory; it is its essence to bring this new and original past to primary, direct intuition, just as it is the essence of the perception of the now to bring the now directly to intuition. On the other hand, recollection, like phantasy, merely offers us re-presentation; recollection is *as it were* the same consciousness as the act aimed at the now and the act aimed at the past, the acts that create time—*as it were the same,* but nonetheless modified. The phantasied now represents a now but does not give a now itself; the phantasied before and after only represent a before and after, and so on.

§18. The significance of recollection for the constitution of the consciousness of duration and succession

The constitutive significance of primary and secondary memory presents itself somewhat differently, if, instead of the givenness of *enduring objectivities,* we consider the givenness of *duration and succession themselves.*

Let us assume that A emerges as primal impression and endures for a while and that, together with the retention of A at a certain stage of development, B enters on the scene and becomes constituted as enduring B. Throughout this whole process, the consciousness is consciousness of the same A "receding into the past"; of the same A in the flow of these manners of givenness; and of the same A with respect to its form of being, "duration," which belongs to the content of its being, and with respect to all the points of this duration. The same is true of B and of the interval between the two durations or their time-points. But in addition something new appears here: *B follows A;* a succession of two enduring data is given with a definite temporal form, an extent of time that encompasses the succession. The *consciousness of succession* is consciousness that gives its object originally: it is "perception" of this succession. We now consider the reproductive modification of this perception —specifically, the recollection. I *"repeat" the consciousness of this succession;* I re-present it to myself memorially. I *"can"* do this and do it "as often as I choose." A priori the re-presentation of an experience lies within the domain of my *"freedom."* (The "I can" is a practical "I can" and not a "mere idea.") Now what does the re-presentation of the experiential succession look like, and what pertains to its essence? Initially one will say: I re-present to myself first A and then B; if originally I had A – B, I now have (if the index signifies memory) A' – B'. But this is inadequate, for it would mean that I now have, in the consciousness of a succession of these memories, a memory A' and "afterwards" a memory B'. But then I would have a "perception" of the succession of these memories and not a memorial consciousness of the succession. I must therefore set the situation forth by means of (A – B)'. This consciousness does in fact include an A', B', but also an –'. The succession, of course, is not a third part, as if the way of writing down the signs one after the other signified the succession. Still, I can write down the law:

$$(A - B)' = A' -' B'$$

in the sense that there is a consciousness of the memory of A and of B on hand, but also a modified consciousness of "B follows A."

Now if we ask about the consciousness that originally gives a succession of enduring objectivities—and, indeed, the succession of the durations themselves—we find that it necessarily requires retention *and* recollection. Retention constitutes the living horizon of the now; in it I have a consciousness of the "just past." But what becomes originally constituted here—say, in holding on to the just heard tone—is only the being-pushed-back of the now-phase or, as the case may be, of the completely constituted duration, which in this completeness no longer becomes constituted and is no longer perceived. I can, however, undertake a reproduction in "coincidence" with this "result" that is being pushed back. Then the past of the duration is given to me, given precisely as the "re-givenness" of the duration *simpliciter.* And we must note: It is only past durations that I can originally intuit in acts that repeat their objects—only past durations that I can actually intuit, identify, and have objectively as the identical object of many acts. I can relive the present, but it cannot be given again. If I return to one and the same succession, as I can at any time, and identify it as the same temporal object, I produce a succession of recollecting experiences in the unity of an overlapping consciousness of succession; therefore:

$$(A - B) - (A - B)' - (A - B)'' \ldots$$

The question is: What does this process of identifying look like? Above all, the succession is a succession of experiences: the first is the original constitution of the succession of A – B; the second is the memory of this succession; then the same again, and so on. The total succession is originally given as presence. I can again have a memory of this succession, and I can again have a memory of such a memory, and so on *in infinitum.* By an eidetic law, every memory is reiterable not only in the sense that an unrestricted number of levels is possible but also in the sense that this is a sphere of the "I can." Each level is essentially an activity of freedom (which does not exclude obstacles).

What does the first recollection of that succession look like?

$$[(A - B) - (A - B)']'.$$

I can then deduce, in conformity with the earlier law, that $(A - B)'$ and $[(A - B)']'$ are involved in this formula, therefore that a memory of the second level is involved in it—specifically, in succession; and naturally the memory of the succession $(-')$ would be included as well. If I repeat it again, I have still higher modifications of memory and, together with them, the consciousness that I have executed several times and in succession a re-presentation that repeats its object. This is a quite ordinary occurrence. I rap twice on the table. I re-present the succession to myself; then I observe that first I had the succession given perceptually and then remembered it; then I observe that I had just carried out precisely this observing—specifically, as the third member of a series that I can repeat to myself, and so on. All of this is quite commonplace, particularly in the phenomenological method of working.

In the sequence of objects that are perfectly alike (identical in content) and that are given only in succession and not as coexisting, we have a peculiar coinciding in the unity of one consciousness: a successive coinciding. Naturally we are speaking loosely, for the objects are indeed set apart from one another, are intended as forming a succession, and are separated by an extent of time.

And yet: if we have in succession unlike objects with like prominent moments, then "lines of likeness," as it were, run from one to the other, and in the case of similarity, lines of similarity. We have here an interrelatedness that is not constituted in an act of contemplation that relates what it contemplates; we have an interrelatedness that lies *before* all "comparison" and all "thinking" as the presupposition of the intuitions of likeness and difference. Only the similar is truly "comparable"; and "difference" presupposes "coincidence"—that is, that real union of like things

interconnected in the transition [from one to another] (or in their coexistence).

§23. Coinciding of the reproduced now with a past. Distinction between phantasy and recollection

After we have differentiated the reproductive from the original consciousness of the past, a further problem arises. When I reproduce a melody I have heard, the phenomenal now of the recollection re-presents a past: In phantasy, in recollection, a tone now sounds. This tone reproduces, let us say, the first tone of the melody, which is a past melody. The consciousness of the past given along with the second tone re-presents the "just past" that earlier was given originally, hence a past "just past." Now how does the reproduced now happen to re-present a past? Surely a reproduced now immediately represents precisely a now. How does the reference to something past that can be given originally only in the form of the "just past" come about?

To answer this question, it is necessary that we occupy ourselves with a distinction we have only alluded to up to this point—namely, the distinction between mere phantasy of a temporally extended object and recollection. In mere phantasy no positing of the reproduced now and no coinciding of this now with a past now is given. Recollection, on the other hand, posits what is reproduced and in this positing gives it a position in relation to the actually present now and to the sphere of the original temporal field to which the recollection itself belongs. Only in original time-consciousness can the relation between a reproduced now and a past be brought about. The re-presentational flow is a flow of experiential phases that is structured in precisely the way in which any time-constituting flow is structured, and which is therefore a time-constituting flow itself. All the adumbrations and modifications that constitute the temporal form are found here; and just as the immanent tone becomes constituted in the flow of tone-phases, so the unity of the re-presentation of the tone becomes constituted in the flow of the phases of the re-presentation of the tone. It holds quite universally that we are led back in phenomenological reflection from everything that in the widest sense appears, is represented, thought, and so on, to a flow of constituting phases that undergo an immanent objectivation: specifically, the objectivation [that turns them] into perceptual appearances (external perceptions), memories, expectations, wishes, etc., as unities belonging to internal consciousness. Thus re-presentations of every sort, as flows of experience possessing the universal time-constituting formation, also constitute an immanent object: "an enduring process of re-presentation running off in such and such a way."

But on the other hand, re-presentations have the peculiar property that in themselves and in all of their experiential phases they are re-presentations *of*. . . in another sense, that they have a second and different sort of intentionality, one proper to them alone and not to all experiences. Now this new intentionality has the peculiarity that, in form, it is a "replica" *[Gegenbild]* of the intentionality that constitutes time; and as it reproduces in each of its elements a moment of a presentational flow and in its elements taken as a whole a whole presentational flow, so it produces a reproductive consciousness of a re-presented immanent object. It therefore constitutes something twofold: first, through its form as a flow of experience it constitutes the re-presentation as an immanent unity; then, since the moments of experience belonging to this flow are reproductive modifications of moments belonging to a parallel flow (which in the ordinary case consists of nonreproductive moments), and since these reproductive modifications involve an intentionality, the flow is joined together to make up a constitutive whole in which I am conscious of an intentional unity: the unity of what is remembered.

§24. Protentions in recollection

Now in order to understand the insertion of this constituted unity of experience "memory"

into the unitary stream of experience, we must take the following into account: every memory contains expectation-intentions whose fulfillment leads to the present. Every process that constitutes its object originally is animated by protentions that emptily constitute what is coming as coming, that catch it and bring it toward fulfillment. However, the recollective process does not merely renew these protentions memorially. They are not only there in the process of catching what is coming; they have also *caught* it. They have been fulfilled, and we are conscious of this in the recollection. The fulfillment in the recollective consciousness is re-fulfillment (precisely in the modification that belongs to memorial positing). And if the original protention belonging to the perception of the event was indefinite and left open the possibility of things being otherwise or not being at all, in the recollection we have an expectation settled in advance that does not leave all of that open, unless in the form of an "unfinished" recollection, which has a different structure from the indefinite original protention. And yet this too is included in the recollection. Thus there are already difficulties of intentional analysis here for the event considered separately, and then in a new way for the expectations that concern the succession of events up to the present: Recollection is not expectation, but it does have a horizon directed towards the future, specifically, towards the future of what is recollected; and this horizon is fixed. As the recollective process advances, this horizon is disclosed in ever new ways and becomes richer and more vital. And in this process the horizon is filled with ever new recollected events. Those that formerly had only been indicated in advance are now *quasi*-present—*quasi* in the mode of the actualizing present.

§25. The double intentionality of recollection

If, in connection with a temporal object, we distinguish the content with its duration —which can have a different place in the context of "the" time—from its temporal position, then, in the reproduction of an enduring being, we have in addition to the reproduction of the filled duration the intentions that concern its position; and we have them necessarily. A duration cannot even be represented, or better, cannot even be posited, without its being posited in a temporal context, without the presence of intentions aimed at the temporal context. Moreover, it is necessary that these intentions have the form either of intentions aimed at the past or of intentions aimed at the future. To the duality of intentions—to those directed towards the filled duration and to those directed towards the filled duration's place in time —there corresponds a dual fulfillment. The total complex of intentions that makes up the appearance of the past enduring object has its possible fulfillment in the system of appearances that belong to that same enduring object. The intentions aimed at the temporal context are fulfilled by the production of filled connections up to the actual present. Hence we must distinguish within every re-presentation between the reproduction of the consciousness in which the past enduring object was given, that is to say, was perceived or in some way originally constituted, and that which attaches to this reproduction as constitutive of the consciousness "past" or "present" (simultaneous with the actually present now) or "future."

Now is the latter also reproduction? This question can easily mislead us. Naturally the whole is reproduced, not only the then-present of consciousness with its flow but *"implicite"* the whole stream of consciousness up to the living present. That means—and this is a fundamental part of a priori phenomenological genesis—that memory flows continuously, since the life of consciousness flows continuously and does not merely piece itself together link by link into a chain. Rather, everything new reacts on the old; the forward-directed intention belonging to the old is fulfilled and determined in this way, and that gives a definite coloring to the reproduction. Thus a retroactive effect, necessary and a priori, shows itself here. The new points again to the new, which,

in making its appearance, becomes determined and modifies the reproductive possibilities for the old, and so on. Moreover, the retroactive power extends back along the chain, for the reproduced past bears the character *past* and an indeterminate intention aimed at a certain location in time in relation to the now. Thus it is not as if we had a mere chain of "associated" intentions, one bringing to mind another, this one recalling the next (in the flow); rather we have *one* intention that in itself is an intention aimed at the series of possible fulfillments.

But this is a nonintuitive, an "empty" intention. Its object is the objective series of events in time, and this series is the obscure surroundings of what is actually recollected. Does this not universally characterize "surroundings": a unitary intention related to a multitude of interconnected objectivities and coming to fulfillment in the gradual, separate, and multifarious givenness of those objectivities? This is also the case with the spatial background. And thus each thing in perception has its reverse side as background (for it is not a question of the background of attention but of apprehension). The component "nonpresentive perception," which belongs to every transcendent perception as an essential part, is a "complex" intention that can be fulfilled in connections of a determinate sort, in connections of data. Foreground is nothing without background. The appearing side is nothing without the nonappearing side. So too in the unity of time-consciousness: the reproduced duration is the foreground; the intentions directed towards the insertion [of the duration into time] make conscious a background, a temporal background. And this is continued in a certain fashion in the constitution of the temporality of the enduring object itself with its now, before, and after. We have the analogies: for the spatial thing, its insertion into the surrounding space and spatial world; on the other hand, the spatial thing itself with its foreground and background. For the temporal thing: its insertion into the temporal form and the temporal world; on the other hand, the temporal thing itself and its shifting orientation in relation to the living now.

§26. Differences between memory and expectation

We must also investigate whether memory and expectation stand on the same footing. Intuitive memory offers me the living reproduction of the elapsing duration of an event, and only the intentions that point back at what preceded the event and point ahead up to the living now remain nonintuitive.

In the intuitive representation of a future event, I now have intuitively the reproductive "image" of an event that runs off reproductively. Fastened to this image are indeterminate intentions aimed at the future and at the past, that is, intentions that from the beginning of the event concern its temporal surroundings, which terminate in the living now. To that extent, the intuition belonging to expectation is memorial intuition turned upside down, for in memory's case the intentions aimed at the now do not "precede" the event but follow after it. As empty intentions directed towards the surroundings, they lie "in the opposite direction." Now what about the way in which the event itself is given? Does it make an essential difference that in memory the content of the event is determined? But memory can also be intuitive and yet not very determinate, since many of its intuitive components do not have the character of actual memory at all. In the case of "perfect" memory, of course, everything down to the smallest detail would be clear and would be characterized as memory. But *idealiter* this is also possible in the case of expectation. In general, expectation leaves much open, and this remaining-open is again a characteristic of the components in question. But as a matter of principle, a prophetic consciousness (a consciousness that passes itself off as prophetic) is conceivable; that is, a consciousness for which every characteristic belonging to the expectation of what is coming to be lies within view: as when, for example, we have a precisely defined plan and, intuitively representing what is planned, accept it, so to speak, lock, stock, and barrel as future reality. Yet in the intuitive anticipation of the future there will also be much that is insignificant, which as stopgap fills

out the concrete image but which in many respects can exist otherwise than the image offers it: from the beginning it is characterized as being open.

But there are fundamental differences in the manner of fulfillment. Intentions aimed at the past are necessarily fulfilled by bringing to light the contexts that belong to intuitive reproductions. The reproduction of a past event with respect to its validity (in internal consciousness) admits of completion and of the confirmation of its memorial indeterminacies only by being converted into a reproduction in which each and every component is characterized as reproductive. Here it is a matter of such questions as: Have I actually seen this? Have I actually perceived it? Have I actually had this appearance with precisely this content? At the same time, all of this must be inserted into a nexus of like intuitions extending up to the now. A different question, of course, is the following: Was what appears, real? Expectation, on the other hand, finds its fulfillment in a perception. It belongs to the essence of what is expected that it is something that is going to be perceived. Moreover, it is evident that when something expected occurs, that is, has become something present, then the state of expectation itself is over with; if what was future has become something present, then what was present has become something relatively past. This is also the case with the intentions aimed at the surroundings. They too are fulfilled through the actuality of an impressional experiencing.

These differences notwithstanding, the intuition belonging to expectation is something just as original and unique as the intuition of the past.

§27. Memory as consciousness of having-been-perceived

The following is of the greatest significance for the characterization of the positing reproductions we have been analyzing: not only the reproductive positing of temporal being belongs to their essence, but also a certain relation to internal consciousness. That it is consciousness of having-been-perceived belongs fundamentally to the essence of memory. If I remember an external event intuitively, I have a reproductive intuition of it. And it is a positing reproduction. But this reproduction of something external is necessarily given in consciousness by means of a reproduction of something internal. Since the external event is given in a determinate mode of appearance, an appearing of something external must be reproduced. The appearing of the external, as an experience, is a unity belonging to the consciousness of the internal; and to the consciousness of the internal corresponds the reproduction of the internal. Now there exist two possibilities for the reproduction of an event: the reproduction of what is internal can be a positing reproduction, and therefore the appearance of the event can be posited in the unity of immanent time; or the reproduction of what is external can also be a positing reproduction that posits the temporal event in question in objective time but does not posit the appearance itself as an event belonging to internal time, and thus also does not posit the time-constituting stream in the unity of the total life-stream.

Therefore memory is not immediately memory of earlier perception. But since the memory of an earlier event includes the reproduction of the appearances in which it came to be given, there also exists at any time the possibility of a memory of the earlier perception of the event (or the possibility of a reflection *in* the memory that makes the earlier perception something given). The whole complex of the earlier consciousness is reproduced, and what is reproduced has the character of reproduction and the character of the past.

Let us make these relationships clear by an example. I remember the illuminated theater—that cannot mean: I remember having perceived the theater. Otherwise the latter would mean: I remember having perceived that I perceived the theater, and so on. I remember the illuminated theater means: "in my interior" I see the illuminated theater as having been. In the now I see the not-now. Perception consti-

tutes the present. In order to have a now stand before me as now, I must perceive. In order to represent a now intuitively, I must bring about a perception "in image," modified re-presentatively. But I must not do it in such a way that I represent the perception; rather I represent the *perceived,* that which appears as present in the perception. Memory therefore does actually imply a reproduction of the earlier perception, but the memory is not in the proper sense a representation of it: the perception is not meant and posited in the memory; what is meant and posited is the perception's object and the object's now, which, in addition, is posited in relation to the actually present now. I remember yesterday's illuminated theater; that is, I bring about a "reproduction" of the perception of the theater. The theater then hovers before me in the representation as something present. I mean this present theater, but in meaning it I apprehend this present as situated in the past in relation to the actual present of the perceptions occurring right now. Naturally it is now evident that the perception of the theater did exist, that I did perceive the theater. What is remembered appears as having been present, doing so immediately and intuitively; and it appears in this way thanks to the fact that a present that has a distance from the present of the actual now appears intuitively. The latter present becomes constituted in actual perception; the former intuitively appearing present, the intuitive representation of the not-now becomes constituted in a replica of perception, in a "re-presentation of the earlier perception" in which the theater comes to be given "as if it were now." This re-presentation of the perception of the theater must not be understood to imply that, living in the representation, I mean the act of perceiving; on the contrary, I mean the being-present of the perceived object.

§28. Memory and image-consciousness. Memory as positing reproduction

We still need to consider what sort of representation is involved here. What is not in question is a re-presentation by means of a re-sembling object, as in the case of conscious depiction (paintings, busts, and the like). In contrast to such image-consciousness, reproductions have the character of the re-presentation of something itself. The reproductions are distinguished in turn according to whether they are nonpositing ("mere" phantasies) or positing. And then the temporal characteristics are added to this. Memory is the re-presentation of something itself in the sense of the past. The present memory is a phenomenon wholly analogous to perception. It has the appearance of the object in common with the corresponding perception, except that the appearance has a modified character, in consequence of which the object does not stand before me as present but as having been present.

What is essential to the sort of reproductions called memory and expectation lies in the insertion of the reproduced appearance into the context of the being of internal time, the flowing sequence of my experiences. The positing normally extends also to what is given objectively in the external appearance. But this positing can be annulled, can be contradicted, and yet memory—or, respectively, expectation—will still remain; that is, we will not cease to speak of memory and expectation, even if we designate the earlier perception or the perception to come as merely "supposed." If, from the beginning, it is a question of the reproduction of immanent objects rather than transcendent objects, then the hierarchical structure we have described as pertaining to reproductive intuitions disappears, and the positing of what is reproduced coincides with its insertion into the sequence of experiences, into immanent time.

§29. Memory of the present

Yet another type of immediate reproductive intuition of temporal objects must be taken into consideration in the sphere of the intuition of external time and external objectivity (all of our explanations, of course, have been limited to the immediate intuition of temporal

objects and have left the mediate, or nonintuitive, expectations and memories out of account).

Whether on the basis of earlier perceptions or according to a description or in some other way, I can also represent to myself something present as now existing without now having it before me "in person." In the first case, I do indeed have a memory, but I give to what is remembered duration up to the actually present now; and for this duration I have no internally remembered "appearances." The "memory image" does serve me, but I do not posit what is remembered as remembered; I do not posit the object of the internal memory in the duration belonging to it. We posit what endures as it presents itself in this appearance, and we posit the appearing now and the ever new now, and so on; but we do not posit it *as* "past."

We know that the "past" in memory's case also does not imply that in the present act of remembering we make a picture for ourselves of what existed earlier or that we produce other constructions of this sort. On the contrary, we simply posit what appears, what is intuited, which in conformity with its temporality, of course, is intuitable only in temporal modes. And to what thereby appears we give, in the mode of memory by means of the intention aimed at the surroundings of the appearance, a position in relation to the actually present now. Thus, in the case of the re-presentation of something that presently exists but is absent, we must also ask about the intentions directed towards the surroundings of the intuition. And in this case, naturally, these intentions are of an entirely different sort: they have no relation whatsoever to the actually present now through a continuous series of internal appearances that would be posited in their entirety. Of course, this reproductive appearance is not without a context. It is supposed to be something enduring that appears there, something that has been and now is and will be. Thus by some route or other I "can" go and see the thing, still find it; and I can then go back again and in repeated "possible" appearance-series produce the intuition. And had I set out a short time ago and gone there (and this is a prescribed possibility to which possible appearance-series correspond), I would now have this intuition as a perceptual intuition, and so on. Thus the appearance that hovers before me reproductively is indeed not characterized as having existed internally and impressionally, and what appears is not characterized as having been perceived in its temporal duration. But a relation to the *hic et nunc* exists here too, and the appearance also bears a certain positing-character: it belongs in a determinate nexus of appearances (and of appearances that would be "positing," position-taking appearances throughout). And in relation to the latter it has a motivating character: the intentions aimed at the surroundings always furnish a halo of intentions for the "possible" appearances themselves. This is also the case with the intuition of an enduring being that I am now perceiving and that I posit as having existed previously without my having perceived it previously and without my now remembering it, and that I posit as something that will exist in the future.

§30. The preservation of the objective intention in the retentional modification

It often happens that while the retention of something just past is still living, a reproductive image of the thing emerges: but naturally an image of the thing as it was given in the now-point. We recapitulate, so to speak, what was just experienced. This internal renewal in re-presentation puts the reproductive now into relation with the now that is still living in fresh memory, and here the consciousness of identity takes place that brings out the identity of the one and the other. (This phenomenon also shows that, in addition to the intuitive part, there belongs to the sphere of primary memory an empty part that extends very much further. While we still have something past in fresh—although empty—memory, an "image" of that something can simultaneously emerge.) It is a universal and fundamentally essential fact that every now, in sinking back into the past, main-

tains its strict identity. Expressed phenomenologically: The consciousness of the now, which becomes constituted on the basis of material "A," is continuously transmuted into a consciousness of the past while simultaneously an ever new consciousness of the now is built up. During this transmutation, the consciousness undergoing modification preserves its objective intention (and this belongs to the essence of time-consciousness).

Every original temporal field contains the continuous modification with respect to the act-characteristics constituting the field. This modification must not be understood as if, in the series of apprehensions belonging to a phase of the object—that is, the series beginning with the emergence of the apprehensions as now-positing and descending into the last accessible phenomenal past—there took place a continuous modification in the objective intention. On the contrary: the objective intention remains absolutely the same and identical. For all that, however, a phenomenal shading-off does exist, and not only with respect to the apprehension-contents that have their fading-away—a certain descent from the highest pinnacle of sensation in the now to the point of imperceptibility. The now-moment is characterized above all as the new. The now that is just sinking into the past is no longer the new but that which the new has pushed aside. In this being-pushed-aside there lies an alteration. But while what has been pushed aside has lost its characteristic of being now, it remains absolutely unchanged in its objective intention, which is an intention—specifically, an intuitive intention—aimed at individual objectivity. In this respect, therefore, no alteration at all presents itself. But here we must surely consider what "preservation of the objective intention" signifies. The total apprehension of the object contains two components: one of them constitutes the object with regard to its extra-temporal determinations; the other produces the temporal position, the being-now, the having-been, and so on. The object as the temporal material, as that which possesses a temporal position and temporal extension, as that which endures or changes, as that which now is and then has been, springs purely from the objectivation of the apprehension-contents; and therefore, in the case of sensuous objects, from the objectivation of sensuous contents. In saying this, we do not lose sight of the fact that these contents are nevertheless temporal objects, that they are produced in a succession as a continuum of primal impressions and retentions, and that these temporal adumbrations of the data of sensation have their significance for the temporal determinations of the objects constituted by their means. But in their property as representants of the qualities of a physical thing as far as the pure "what" of the qualities is concerned, their temporal character plays no role. The data of apprehension that are apprehended nontemporally constitute the object in its specific composition, and where this is preserved we can already speak of an identity. But when we spoke a short time ago about preserving the relation to something objective, that signified that the object remains preserved not only in its specific composition but also as an individual object, and therefore as a temporally determinate object that sinks back in time together with its temporal determination. This sinking-back is an original phenomenological modification of consciousness through which an ever-growing distance forms in relation to the actually present now, which is always being freshly constituted. This growing distance comes about by virtue of the continuous series of changes leading away from the actual now.

§31. Primal impression and the objective individual time-point

At this point we are seemingly led to an antinomy: the object, in sinking back, constantly changes its place in time; and yet in sinking back it is supposed to preserve its place in time. In truth, the object of the primary memory, which is being pushed back continuously, does not change its place in time at all, but only its distance from the actually present now. And this is the case because the actually present now is taken to be an ever new objective time-point,

while the past temporal moment remains what it is. Now this raises the question: How, in the face of the phenomenon of the constant change of time-consciousness, does the consciousness of objective time and, above all, of identical temporal positions come about? This question is very closely connected with the question about the constitution of the objectivity of individual temporal objects and events: all objectivation is accomplished in time-consciousness; without clarification of the identity of the temporal position, there can be no clarification of the identity of an object in time either.

Set forth in more detail, the problem is the following. The now-phases belonging to the perception continuously undergo a modification; they are not preserved simply as they are: they flow away. What we designate as sinking-back in time is constituted in this process. The tone now sounds, and it immediately sinks into the past—it, the same tone, sinks into the past. This concerns the tone in each of its phases and therefore the whole tone as well. Now the sinking into the past appears to be intelligible to some extent by means of our reflections up to this point. But how does it happen that in the face of the tone's sinking into the past, we nevertheless say that a fixed position in time belongs to it, that time-points and temporal durations can be identified in repeated acts, as our analysis of reproductive consciousness has shown? The tone and every time-point in the unity of the enduring tone certainly does have its absolutely fixed position in "objective" (even if immanent) time. Time is fixed, and yet time flows. In the flow of time, in the continuous sinking down into the past, a nonflowing, absolutely fixed, identical, objective time becomes constituted. This is the problem.

To start with, let us consider somewhat more closely the situation of the same tone sinking into the past. Why do we speak of the same tone that sinks into the past? The tone is built up in the temporal flow by means of its phases. We know that each phase (say, the phase belonging to an actually present now), subject to the law of continuous modification, must nevertheless appear, so to speak, as objectively the same, as the same tone-point, since an apprehension-continuum presents itself here that is governed by the identity of sense and exists in continuous coincidence. The coincidence concerns the extratemporal material, which is preserved in the flow precisely as the identity of objective sense. This is true for each now-phase. But every new now is precisely new and is characterized as new phenomenologically. Even if the tone continues so utterly unchanged that not the least alteration is apparent to us, hence even if each new now possesses precisely the same apprehension-content with respect to moments of quality, intensity, etc., and carries precisely the same apprehension—even if all of this is the case, an original difference nevertheless presents itself; a difference that belongs to a new dimension. And this difference is a continuous one. Considered phenomenologically, only the now-point is characterized as an actually present now, that is, as new; the preceding now-point appears as having undergone its modification, the point prior to that its further modification, and so on. This continuum of modifications in the apprehension-contents and the apprehensions built on them produces the consciousness of the extension of the tone together with the continual sinking into the past of what is already extended.

But how, in the face of the phenomenon of the continuous change of time-consciousness, does the consciousness of objective time and, above all, the consciousness of identical position in time and extension in time come about? The answer runs as follows: It comes about by virtue of the fact that over against the flow of the process of being pushed back in time, over against the flow of the modifications of consciousness, the object that appears pushed back remains apperceptively preserved precisely in absolute identity—specifically, the object together with the positing as "this" that it underwent in the now-point. The continuous modification of the apprehension in the continuous flow does not concern the apprehension's "as what," its sense. The modification intends no new object and no new object-phase. It yields

no new time-points, but constantly the same object with the same time-points. Each actually present now creates a new time-point because it creates a new object, or rather a new object-point, which is held fast in the flow of modification as one and the same individual object-point. And the continuity in which a new now becomes constituted again and again shows us that it is not a question of "newness" as such but of a continuous moment of individuation in which the temporal position has its origin. The essence of the modifying flow is such that this temporal position stands before me as identical and as necessarily identical. The now as actually present now is the givenness of the present of the temporal position. When the phenomenon recedes into the past, the now receives the characteristic of being a past now; but it remains the same now, except that it stands before me as past in relation to the currently actual and temporally new now.

The objectivation of the temporal object therefore rests on the following moments: the content of sensation that belongs to the different actually present now-points of the object can remain absolutely unchanged in quality, yet still not possess true identity in this identity of content, however far it may extend. The same sensation now and in a different now possesses a difference—specifically, a phenomenological difference—that corresponds to the absolute temporal position; this difference is the primal source of the individuality of the "this," and thereby of the absolute temporal position. Each phase of the modification has "essentially" the same qualitative content and the same temporal moment, although modified; and it has them in itself in such a way that, by their means, the subsequent apprehension of identity is made possible. This applies to the side of sensation or, correlatively, to the side of the apprehensional basis. The different moments support different sides of apprehension, of objectivation proper. One side of objectivation finds its basis purely in the qualitative content of the material of sensation: this yields the temporal material—the tone, for example. This material is maintained as identical in the flow of the modification of the past. A second side of objectivation derives from the apprehension of the representants of the temporal positions. This apprehension too is continuously maintained in the flow of modification.

To summarize: The tone-point in its absolute individuality is held fast in its matter and in its temporal position, and it is the latter that first constitutes individuality. Add to this, finally, the apprehension that belongs essentially to the modification and that, while holding on to the extended objectivity with its immanent absolute time, lets the continuous process of being pushed back into the past appear. In our example of the tone, therefore, each now-point of the ever new sounding and fading-away has its material of sensation and its objectivating apprehension. The tone stands before me as the sound of a violin string that has been struck. If we again disregard the objectivating apprehension and look purely at the material of sensation, then, as far as its matter is concerned, it is constantly tone c, its tonal quality and timbre unchanged, its intensity perhaps fluctuating, and so forth. This content, understood purely as content of sensation underlying the objectivating apperception, is extended—that is to say, each now has its content of sensation, and each different now has an individually different content, even if the content is exactly the same materially. Absolutely the same c now and later is perfectly alike as far as sensation is concerned, but the c now is individually different from the c later.

What "individual" means here is the original temporal form of sensation, or, as I can also put it, the temporal form of original sensation, here of the sensation belonging to the current now-point and only to this. But the now-point itself must, in strictness, be defined through original sensation, so that the proposition asserted has to be taken only as an indication of what is supposed to be meant. The impression, as opposed to the phantasm, is distinguished by the character of originalness. Now within the impression we have to call special attention to the primal impression, over against which there stands the continuum of modifications in pri-

mary memorial consciousness. The primal impression is something absolutely unmodified, the primal source of all further consciousness and being. Primal impression has as its content that which the word "now" signifies, insofar as it is taken in the strictest sense. Each new now is the content of a new primal impression. Ever new primal impressions continuously flash forth with ever new matter, now the same, now changing. What distinguishes primal impression from primal impression is the individualizing moment of the impression of the original temporal position, which is something fundamentally different from the quality and other material moments of the content of sensation. The moment of the original temporal position is naturally nothing by itself; the individuation is nothing in addition to what has individuation. The whole now-point, the whole original impression, under-goes the modification of the past; and only by means of this modification have we exhausted the complete concept of the now, since it is a relative concept and refers to a "past," just as "past" refers to the "now." This modification also touches the sensation above all, without nullifying its universal impressional character. It modifies the total content of the primal impression both with respect to its matter and with respect to its temporal position, but it modifies precisely in the sense in which a phantasy-modification does; that is to say, modifying through and through and yet not altering the intentional essence (the total content).

Thus the matter is the same matter, the temporal position the same temporal position, only the mode of givenness has changed: it is givenness of the past. The objectivating apprehension, then, bases itself on this material of sensation. Even if we look purely at the contents of sensation (disregarding the transcendent apperceptions which may perhaps be based on them), we carry out an apperception: the "temporal flow," the duration, then lies within our view as a kind of objectivity. Objectivity presupposes consciousness of unity, consciousness of identity. Here we apprehend the content of every primal sensation as itself. The primal impression gives a tone-point-individual, and this individual is identically the same in the flow of the modification of the past: the apperception relative to this point abides in continuous coincidence in the modification of the past, and the identity of the individual is *eo ipso* identity of temporal position. The continuous welling-up of ever new primal impressions, apprehended as individual points, again and again yields new and different temporal positions. The continuity yields a continuity of temporal positions. In the flow of the modification of the past, therefore, a continuous portion of time filled with sound stands before me, but in such a way that only one of its points is given through primal impression and that from there on the temporal positions continuously appear in different degrees of modification, receding into the past.

Every perceived time is perceived as a past that terminates in the present. And the present is a limit. Every apprehension, however transcendent it may be, is bound by this law. If we perceive a flight of birds or a troop of cavalry at the gallop and the like, we find in the substratum of sensation the described differences: ever new primal sensations carrying with them the characteristic that determines their temporal position and gives rise to their individuation; and, on the other side, we find the same modes in the apprehension. It is precisely in this way that something objective itself—the flight of birds—appears as primally given in the now-point but as fully given in a continuum of the past that terminates in the now and continually terminates in an ever new now, while what has continuously preceded recedes ever further into the continuum of the past. The appearing event constantly possesses the identical absolute temporal value. As its elapsed portion is pushed further and further back into the past, the event is pushed into the past together with its absolute temporal positions, and accordingly with its entire temporal extent: that is, the same event with the same absolute temporal extension continually appears (as long as it appears at all) as identically the same, except that the form of its givenness is different. On the other hand, in the living source-point of being, in the now, ever new primal being si-

multaneously wells up, in relation to which the distance of the event's time-points from the actually present now continuously expands; and consequently the appearance of sinking backwards, of moving away, grows up.

§32. *The role of reproduction in the constitution of the one objective time*

With the preservation of the individuality of the time-points as they sink back into the past, however, we still do not have the consciousness of a unitary, homogeneous, objective time. In the bringing about of this consciousness, reproductive memory (intuitive memory as well as memory in the form of empty intentions) plays an important role. By virtue of a reproductive memory, every point that has been pushed back in time can be made—and made repeatedly—the zero-point of a temporal intuition. The earlier temporal field, in which what is presently pushed back was a now, is reproduced; and the reproduced now is identified with the time-point still living in fresh memory: the individual intention is the same. The reproduced temporal field extends further than the actually present field. If we take a point of the past in this field, the reproduction, in partially coinciding with the temporal field in which this point was the now, yields a further regress into the past, and so on. This process must evidently be conceived as capable of being continued without limit, although in practice the actual memory will soon fail. It is evident that each time-point has its before and after, and that the points and extended sections that are before cannot be compressed in the fashion of an approach to a mathematical limit, such as the limit of intensity. If there were a limit, a now would correspond to it which nothing had preceded, and that is evidently impossible. A now is always and essentially a border-point of an extent of time. And it is evident that this whole extent must sink backwards and that, as it does so, its whole magnitude and complete individuality are preserved. Of course, phantasy and reproduction do not make possible an extension of the intuition of time in the sense that the extent of temporal shadings really given in the simultaneous consciousness would be increased. One will perhaps ask in this respect how, in these temporal fields succeeding one another, the one objective time with its one fixed order comes about. The continuous coinciding of the temporal fields, which in truth is not a mere ordering of temporal fields in temporal succession, offers the answer. The coinciding parts are individually identified during their intuitive and continuous regression into the past. Let us assume that we proceed back into the past from any actually experienced time-point—that is, from any time-point originally given in the temporal field of perception or from some time-point that reproduces a remote past—and that we move, as it were, along a fixed chain of connected objectivities that are identified over and over again. Now how is the linear order established here according to which any extent of time whatsoever, even one that is reproduced without continuity with the actually present temporal field, must be part of a single chain continuing up to the actually present now? Even every arbitrarily phantasied time is subject to the requirement that it must exist as an extent within the one and only objective time if one is going to be able to think of it as actual time (that is, as the time of some temporal object).

§33. Some a priori temporal laws

Obviously, this a priori requirement is grounded in the validity of the fundamental temporal evidences that can be immediately grasped and that become evident on the basis of the intuitions of the data of the temporal positions.

If, to begin with, we compare two primal sensations—or rather, correlatively, two primal data—both actually appearing in one consciousness as primal data, as now, then they are distinguished from one another by their matter. They are, however, simultaneous: they have identically the same absolute position in time; they are both now; and in the same now they necessarily have the same value as far as their temporal position is concerned. They have the same form of individuation; they both become constituted in impressions belonging to the same impressional level. They are modified in this identity, and they continually preserve the identity in the modification of the past. A primal datum and a modified datum of different or equivalent content necessarily have different positions in time. And two modified data have either the same or different temporal positions: the same, if they spring from the same now-point; different, if they spring from different now-points. The actually present now is *one* now and constitutes *one* temporal position, however many objectivities are separately constituted in it: they all have the same temporal present and preserve their simultaneity in flowing off. That the temporal positions have intervals, that these are magnitudes, and the like, can be seen with evidence here; so too can further truths, such as the law of transitivity or the law that if a is earlier than b, then b is later than a. It belongs to time's a priori essence that it is a continuity of temporal positions, sometimes filled with identical and sometimes with changing objectivities, and that the homogeneity of absolute time becomes constituted indefeasibly in the flow of the modifications of the past and in the continuous welling-up of a now, of the generative time-point, of the source-point of all temporal positions whatsoever.

Furthermore, it belongs to the a priori essence of the situation that sensation, apprehension, the taking of a position—all of these—take part in the *same* temporal flow and that the objectivated absolute time is necessarily identically the same as the time that belongs to sensation and apprehension. The preobjectivated time belonging to sensation necessarily founds the unique possibility of an objectivation of temporal positions, which corresponds to the modification of sensation and to the degree of this modification. To the objectivated time-point in which, for example, bells begin to ring, there corresponds the time-point of the matching sensation. In the beginning-phase, the sensation has the same time; that is, if it is subsequently made into an object, then it necessarily keeps the temporal position that coincides with the corresponding temporal position of the ringing of the bells. So too the time of the perception and the time of the perceived are identically the same. The perceptual act sinks backwards in time just as what is perceived in its appearance does, and in reflection identically the same temporal position must be given to each phase of the perception as is given to what is perceived.

APPENDIX I: Primal Impression and Its Continuum of Modifications*

"A"—a tone, for example—becomes constituted in a time-point belonging to a specific phase from among the phases forming its duration by means of a primal impression α, on which follows such and such a modification together with the primal generation of new impressions (new now-moments). Let β be a simultaneous immanent unity, a color, say, and let it be fixed in view as a point "simultaneous" with the tone-point mentioned above. The primal impression β corresponds to b, the color, in the process of constitution. Now what do α and β have in common? What brings it about that they constitute simultaneity and that two modifications α' and β' constitute a having-been-simultaneous?

Every primal impression is characterized as primal impression, and every modification is characterized as modification. Furthermore, every modification is continuous modification. The latter, indeed, is what distinguishes this sort of modification from phantasy-modification and pictorial modification. Each of these temporal modifications is a non-self-sufficient limit in a continuum. And this continuum has the character of a "rectilinear" multiplicity limited on one side. It has a beginning in primal impression and proceeds as modification in one direction. Pairs of points on this continuum having a certain distance from one another constitute temporal phases of the object that, on the objective side, have an equivalent distance from one another.

When we speak of "modification," we first of all have in view the change according to which the primal impression continuously

"dies away." However, each modification can obviously be regarded in the same sense as modification of any preceding modification whatsoever. If we select any one phase of the continuum, we can say that it dies away; and we can say the same thing about every further phase. This, indeed, is inherent in the essence of this and of any such (one-sidedly directed) continuum. The situation is precisely the same as it is in the case of the continuum of intensities spreading out from 0. The process of being augmented is the modification that every intensity undergoes here. Each intensity is in itself what it is, and each new intensity is precisely a new intensity. But in relation to any already given intensity, every intensity later in the series can be regarded as the result of an operation. If b is the intensification of a, then c is the intensification of an intensification in relation to a. In virtue of the continuity, each point is not simply intensification in relation to a preceding point but intensification of intensification of intensification, and so on *in infinitum* and infinitesimally. An infinity of interpenetrating modifications. Only in this case there is no beginning-point that can be taken as an intensity itself. The beginning here is the zero-point. It is inherent in the essence of every linear continuum that, starting from any point whatsoever, we can think of every other point as continuously produced from it; and every continuous production is a production by means of continuous iteration. We can indeed divide each interval *in infinitum* and, in the case of each division, think of the later point of the division as produced mediately through the earlier points; and thus any point whatsoever is finally produced through a division of infinitely many intensifications (each of which is the same infinitely small intensification). Now this is also true in the case of temporal modification—or rather, while the use of the word "production" is a metaphor in the case of other continua, here it is used authentically. The time-constituting continuum is a flow of continuous production of modifications of

*To §11, titled "Primal Impression and Retentional Modification." [This is a reconstruction of the published Appendix I, based on new evidence from Husserl's manuscripts uncovered by Rudolf Bernet. —Ed.]

modifications. The modifications in the sense of iterations proceed from the actually present now, the actual primal impression i; but they go forwards continuously and are not only modifications in relation to i but also, in succession, modifications of one another in the order in which they flow away. This is what characterizes continuous production. Modification continuously generates ever new modification. The primal impression is the absolute beginning of this production, the primal source, that from which everything else is continuously produced. But it itself is not produced; it does not arise as something produced but through *genesis spontanea;* it is primal generation. It does not spring from anything (it has no seed); it is primal creation. If it is said: A new now continuously forms on the now that becomes modified into a not-now, or a source quite suddenly engenders it or originates it, these are metaphors. It can only be said: Consciousness is nothing without impression. When something endures, then a passes over into xa', xa' into yx'a'', and so on. But the production for which consciousness is responsible only reaches from a to a', from xa' to x'a''; the a, x, y, on the other hand, is nothing produced by consciousness. It is what is primally produced— the "new," that which has come into being alien to consciousness, that which has been received, as opposed to what has been produced through consciousness's own spontaneity. The peculiarity of this spontaneity of consciousness, however, is that it creates nothing "new" but only brings what has been primally generated to growth, to development. Of course, what from an empirical point of view we call becoming or production refers to objectivity, and that lies somewhere else altogether. Here it is a question of the spontaneity of consciousness; or put more carefully: of a primal spontaneity of consciousness.

Now depending on whether it is a question of the primal source for the respective now of the constituted content or of the spontaneous productions of consciousness in which the identity of this now is maintained on into the past, the moment of origin is either primal impression or primal memory, primal phantasy, and

so on. If we follow the series of strata, each moment of origin belonging to a stratum is the primal source of spontaneous productions that run throughout the further strata in their continuous modifications and that represent this moment of origin in these strata (that is, the moment of origin that belongs uniquely and alone to the stratum we first had in view). Furthermore, each moment of origin is a phase of a continuous series of moments of origin that blend into one another throughout a succession of strata. Or each moment of origin helps to constitute a concrete duration, and it belongs to the constitution of a concrete duration that an actually present now corresponds to each of its points. The now, for its part, requires its own moment of origin for its constitution. These moments are continuously united in the succession; they "pass over into one another continuously." The transition is mediated "qualitatively" and also temporally: the *quasi*-temporal character is a continuous character.

Multiple primal impressions, primal phantasms, etc.—in short, multiple original moments (we can also say: primal moments of internal consciousness)—can belong to one stratum of internal consciousness. All of the original moments belonging to one stratum have the same character of consciousness, which is essentially constitutive of the respective "now": the now is the same for all of the constituted contents. This common character constitutes simultaneity, the "same-nowness" *["Gleich-Jetzigkeit"].*

By virtue of the original spontaneity of internal consciousness, each primal moment is the source-point for a continuity of productions, and this continuity is of one and the same form. The manner of production, of primal temporal modification, is the same for all primal moments; one and the same law governs throughout all the modifications. This law reads: The continuous producing that belongs to internal consciousness has the form of a one-dimensional "rectilinear" multiplicity; all primal moments within one stratum undergo the same modification (they produce the same moments of the past). Therefore the modifications of two primal moments belonging to the same stratum, modifications that have the same distance from their corresponding primal moments, belong to one and the same stratum; or, the modifications belonging to one stratum again and again produce out of themselves only modifications that belong to one and the same stratum. The production always proceeds at the same speed.

Within each stratum, the different points of the continuous series are at a different distance from the primal moment. This distance on the part of any point is identical with the distance the same point has from its primal moment in the earlier stratum. The constituting primal field of time-consciousness is a continuous extension consisting of a primal moment and a determinate series of reiterated modifications—reiterated modifications with regard to form, not content. As far as form is concerned, the determinations pertaining to these modifications are always and ever the same in all primal fields (in their succession). Each primal moment is precisely a primal moment (now-consciousness); each past, consciousness of the past; and the degree of being past is something determined: a firmly determined formal character corresponds to it in the primally constituting consciousness.

In the succession of strata, moments with "contents" that are perfectly alike, that is, moments whose internal make-up is perfectly alike, can come onto the scene over and over again as primal moments. These primal moments belonging to different strata and possessing internal contents that are entirely alike are individually distinct.

Levels of Constitution of Time and Temporal Objects*

§34. *Differentiation of the levels of constitution*

Now that we have studied time-consciousness—starting from its most obvious phenomena—in some of its principal dimensions and

in its various strata, it would be good to establish and run through systematically for once the different levels of constitution in their essential structure.

We found:

1. the things of empirical experience in objective time (in connection with which we would have to distinguish still different levels of empirical being, which up to this point have not been taken into consideration: the experienced physical thing belonging to the individual subject, the intersubjectively identical thing, the thing of physics);

2. the constituting multiplicities of appearance belonging to different levels, the immanent unities in pre-empirical time;

3. the absolute time-constituting flow of consciousness.

§35. *Difference between constituted unities and the constituting flow*

Now to begin with, this absolute consciousness that lies before *all* constitution should be discussed somewhat more closely. Its peculiarity stands out distinctly in contrast to the constituted unities belonging to the most different levels:

1. Each individual object (each unity, whether immanent or transcendent, constituted in the stream) endures, and necessarily endures—that is, it continuously exists in time and is something identical in this continuous existence, which at the same time can be regarded as a process. Conversely: what exists in time continuously exists in time and is the unity belonging to the process that carries with it inseparably the unity of what endures in the process as it unfolds. The unity of the tone that endures throughout the process lies in the tonal process; and conversely, the unity of the tone is unity in the filled duration, that is, in the process. Therefore, if anything at all is defined as existing in a time-point, it is conceivable only as the phase of a process, a phase in which the duration of an individual being also has its point.

2. Individual or concrete being is necessar-

*PCIT, pp. 77–88 (Sections 34–39), with Appendices VIII and IX (pp. 120–124) to Section 39.

ily changing or unchanging; the process is a process of change or of rest, the enduring object itself a changing object or one at rest. Moreover, every change has its rate or acceleration of change (to use an image) with respect to the same duration. As a matter of principle, any phase of a change can be expanded into a rest, and any phase of a rest can be carried over into a change. Now if we consider the *constituting* phenomena in comparison with the phenomena just discussed, we find a *flow,* and each phase of this flow is a *continuity of adumbrations.* But as a matter of principle, no phase of this flow can be expanded into a continuous succession; and therefore the flow cannot be conceived as so transformed that this phase would be extended in identity with itself. Quite to the contrary, we necessarily find a flow of continuous "change"; and this change has the absurd character that it flows precisely as it flows and can flow neither "faster" nor "slower." If that is the case, then any object that changes is missing here; and since "something" runs its course in every process, no process is in question. There is nothing here that changes, and for that reason it also makes no sense to speak of something that endures. It is therefore nonsensical to want to find something here that remains unchanged for even an instant during the course of its duration.

§36. The time-constituting flow as absolute subjectivity

Time-constituting phenomena, therefore, are evidently objectivities fundamentally different from those constituted in time. They are neither individual objects nor individual processes, and the predicates of such objects or processes cannot be meaningfully ascribed to them. Hence it also can make no sense to say of them (and to say with the same signification) that they exist in the now and did exist previously, that they succeed one another in time or are simultaneous with one another, and so on. But no doubt we can and must say: A certain continuity of appearance—that is, a continuity that is a phase of the time-constituting flow— *belongs* to a now, namely, to the now that it *constitutes;* and to a before, namely, as that

which is constitutive (we cannot say "was") of the before. But is not the flow a succession, does it not have a now, an actually present phase, and a continuity of pasts of which I am now conscious in retentions? We can say nothing other than the following: This flow is something we speak of *in conformity with what is constituted,* but it is not "something in objective time." It is *absolute subjectivity* and has the absolute properties of something to be designated *metaphorically* as "flow"; of something that originates in a point of actuality, in a primal source-point, "the now," and so on. In the actuality-experience we have the primal source-point and a continuity of moments of reverberation. For all of this, we lack names.

§37. Appearances of transcendent objects as constituted unities

We must note, in addition, that when we speak of the "perceptual act" and say that it is the point of genuine perceiving to which a continuous series of "retentions" is attached, we have not described thereby any unities in immanent time, but just moments of the flow. That is, the *appearance*—say, the appearance of a house—is a temporal being, a being that endures, changes, and so on, just as much as the immanent tone, which is not an appearance. But the house-appearance is not the perceptual consciousness and retentional consciousness. The latter can be understood only as time-constituting consciousness, as moments of the flow. In the same way, the memorial appearance (or the remembered immanent object, perhaps the remembered immanent primary content) must be distinguished from the memorial consciousness with its memorial retentions. Everywhere we have to distinguish: *consciousness* (flow), *appearance* (immanent object *[Objekt]*), transcendent *object [Gegenstand]* (when the immanent object is not a primary content). Not all consciousness refers to something in "objective" (that is, transcendent) time, to objective individuality, as the consciousness that belongs to external perception does, for example. In every consciousness we find an "immanent content." In the case of contents that are called "appearances," this immanent content is either the appearance of something individual (of something in external time) or the appearance of something not in time. In judging, for example, I have the appearance "judgment," namely, as a unity in immanent time; and *in this unity* the judgment in the logical sense "appears."* The judging always has the character of the flow. Consequently, what we called "act" or "intentional experience" in the *Logical Investigations* is in every instance a flow in which a unity becomes constituted in immanent time (the judgment, the wish, etc.), a unity that has its immanent duration and that may progress more or less rapidly. These unities, which become constituted in the absolute stream, exist in immanent time, which is *one;* and in this time the unities can be simultaneous or have durations of equal length (or perhaps have the same duration, that is, in the case of two immanent objects that endure simultaneously). Moreover, the unities have a certain determinability with respect to before and after.

§38. The unity of the flow of consciousness and the constitution of simultaneity and succession

We have already occupied ourselves with the constitution of such immanent objects, with their growth from ever new primal sensations and modifications.† Now in reflection we find a single flow that breaks down into many flows, but this multitude nevertheless has a kind of unity that permits and requires us to speak of *one* flow. We find many flows because many series of primal sensations begin and end. But we find a connecting form because the law of the transformation of the now into the no-longer—and, in the other direction, of the not-yet into the now—applies to each of them, but not merely to each of them taken separately; there rather exists something like a common form of the now, a universal and perfect likeness in the mode of flowing. Several, many pri-

mal sensations occur "at once." And when any one of them elapses, the multitude elapses "conjointly" and in absolutely the same mode with absolutely the same gradations and in absolutely the same tempo: except that, in general, one ceases while another still has its not-yet before it—that is to say, its new primal sensations that further prolong the duration of what is intended in it. Or described more adequately: The many primal sensations flow away and from the beginning have at their disposal the same running-off modes, except that the series of primal sensations constitutive of the enduring immanent objects are variously prolonged, corresponding to the varying durations of the immanent objects. They do not all make use of the formal possibilities in the same way. Immanent time is constituted as *one* for all immanent objects and processes. Correlatively, the time-consciousness of what is immanent is an all-inclusive unity. The "being-together" *[Zusammen]*, the "being-all-at-once" *[Zugleich]* of actually present primal sensations is all-embracing; all-embracing too is the "before," the "having-gone-before" of all the immediately preceding primal sensations, the steady transmutation of each ensemble of primal sensations into such a before. This before is a continuity, and each of its points is a homogeneous, identical running-off form for the entire ensemble. The *whole* "being-together" of primal sensations is subject to the law according to which it changes into a steady continuum of modes of consciousness, of modes of having elapsed, and according to which in the same continuity an ever new being-together of primal sensations arises originally, in order in its turn to pass continuously over into the condition of having elapsed. What is a being-together as an ensemble of primal sensations remains a being-together in the mode of having elapsed. Primal sensations have their continuous "succession" in the sense of a continuous running-off, and primal sensations have their being-together, their "being-

---

* "Appearance" is used here in the expanded sense.
† Cf. §11, pp. 190ff.

all-at-once." Actual primal sensations exist all at once; in the succession, however, one sensation or group of sensations existing together is actual primal sensation, while the others have elapsed. But what does that mean? One can say nothing further here than "look": a primal sensation or a group of primal sensations that has an immanent now as object of consciousness (a tone-now, in the same now a color, and so on) continuously changes into modes of the consciousness of the before, in which the immanent object is intended as past; and "all at once," together with these, an ever new primal sensation emerges, an ever new now is established, and thereby an ever new tone-now, form-now, etc., is intended. In a group of primal sensations, primal sensation is distinguished from primal sensation by means of content; only the now is the same. The consciousness, in its form as primal sensation-consciousness, is identical.

But "together" with the primal sensation-consciousness there exist continuous series of modes pertaining to the flowing-away of "earlier" primal sensations, of earlier now-consciousness. *This* being-together is a being-together of modes of consciousness continuously *modified* with respect to form, while the being-together of primal sensations is a being-together of modes purely *identical in form*. We can extract a point in the continuity of running-off modes, and we then find in this point too a being-together of running-off modes perfectly alike in form; or rather, we find an identical running-off mode. One must make an essential distinction between these two ensembles. One is the site for the constitution of simultaneity, the other the site for the constitution of temporal succession—although it is also the case that simultaneity is nothing without temporal succession and temporal succession is nothing without simultaneity, and consequently simultaneity and temporal succession must become constituted correlatively and inseparably. We can differentiate terminologically between the retentional being-all-at-once of fluxions *[fluxionalem Vor-Zugleich]* and the impressional being-all-at-once of fluxions *[impressionalem Zugleich von Fluxionen]*. We cannot call the

one or the other being-all-at-once a being simultaneous. We can no longer speak of a time that belongs to the ultimate constituting consciousness. The simultaneity of a color and of a tone, for example—their being in an "actually present now"—originally becomes constituted with the primal sensations that introduce the retentional process. But the primal sensations are not themselves simultaneous, and we can no more call the phases of the retentional being-all-at-once of fluxions simultaneous phases of consciousness than we can call the succession of consciousness a temporal succession.

We know what this retentional being-all-at-once is from our earlier analyses: the continuum of phases that attach themselves to a primal sensation, each of which is retentional consciousness of the earlier now ("original memory" of it). Here we must note: When the primal sensation recedes and is continuously modified, we not only have in general an experience that is a modification of the earlier experience, but we are also able to turn our glance in it in such a way that we "see," so to speak, the earlier nonmodified experience in the modified experience. When a tonal succession runs off (not too rapidly), we are not only able to "look at" the first tone, after it has elapsed, as a tone that is "still present" although no longer sensed, but we can also take heed of the fact that the mode of consciousness that this tone just now possesses is a "memory" of the primal sensation's mode of consciousness in which it was given as now. But then we must differentiate sharply between the consciousness of the past (the retentional consciousness as well as the consciousness that represents something "again") in which an immanent temporal object is intended as immediately past, and the retention or (depending on whether the original flow of the modification of sensation or its re-presentation is in question) the recollective "reproduction" of the earlier primal sensation. And this we must do for every other fluxion.

If any phase of the duration of an immanent object is a now-phase and therefore intended in primal sensation, then, in the retentional being-all-at-once, retentions that are continuously joined to one another are united with this primal sensation. These retentions are characterized in themselves as modifications of the primal sensations that belong to all of the rest of the points of the constituted duration; that is, to those that have elapsed in time. Each of these retentions has a determinate mode to which distance in time from the now-point corresponds. Each is the consciousness of the past of the corresponding earlier now-point and gives it in the mode of the immediate past that corresponds to its position in the elapsed duration.

§39. The double intentionality of retention and the constitution of the flow of consciousness*

The duality in the intentionality of retention gives us a clue to the solution of the difficulty concerning how it is possible to be aware of a unity belonging to the ultimate constituting flow of consciousness. Without doubt a difficulty does present itself here: If a self-contained flow (one that belongs to an enduring process or object) has elapsed, I can nevertheless look back on it; it forms, so it seems, a unity in memory. Hence the flow of consciousness obviously becomes constituted in consciousness as a unity too. The unity of a tone-duration, for example, becomes constituted in the flow, but the flow itself becomes constituted in turn as the unity of the consciousness of the tone-duration. And must we then not also go on to say that this unity becomes constituted in an altogether analogous way and is every bit as much a constituted temporal series, and that one must therefore surely speak of a temporal now, before, and after?

In the light of our latest explanations, we can give the following answer: There is one, unique flow of consciousness in which both the unity of the tone in immanent time and the unity of the flow of consciousness itself become constituted at once. As shocking (when not initially even absurd) as it may seem to say that the flow of consciousness constitutes its own unity, it is nonetheless the case that it does. And this can be made intelligible on the basis of the flow's essential constitution. Our regard can be directed, in the one case, *through* the phases that "coincide" in the continuous progression of the flow and that function as intentionalities of the tone. But our regard can also be aimed *at* the flow, at a section of the flow, at the passage of the flowing consciousness from the beginning of the tone to its end. Every adumbration of consciousness of the species "retention" possesses a double intentionality: one serves for the constitution of the immanent object, of the tone; it is this intentionality that we call "primary memory" of the (just sensed) tone, or more precisely, just retention of the tone. The other intentionality is constitutive of the unity of this primary memory in the flow; namely, retention, because it is a still-being-conscious, a consciousness that holds back—because it is, precisely, retention—is also retention of the elapsed tone-retention: in its process of being continuously adumbrated in the flow, it is continuous retention of the continuously preceding phases. If we fix our regard on some one phase of the flow of consciousness (a phase in which there appears a tone-now and an extent of the tone-duration in the mode of the just-having-elapsed), then this phase comprehends a continuity of retentions united in the retentional being-all-at-once. This continuity is retention of the total momentary continuity of the continuously preceding phases of the flow. (In its initial member it is new primal sensation; in the member that then follows next in the continuity—in the first phase of adumbration—it is immediate retention of the preceding primal sensation; in the next momentary phase, it is retention of the retention of the primal sensation preceding the one above, and so on.) Now if we allow the flow to flow on, we then have the flow-continuum running off, which causes the continuity we have just described to be modified

---

*Cf. Appendix VIII: The Double Intentionality of the Stream of Consciousness, pp. 218ff.

retentionally; and in this process, each new continuity of phases existing together in one moment is retention in relation to the total continuity belonging to the being-all-at-once in the preceding phase. Thus there extends throughout the flow a horizontal intentionality* that, in the course of the flow, continuously coincides with itself. In the absolute passing-on, in the flowing process, the first primal impression becomes changed into a retention of itself, this retention becomes changed into a retention of this retention, and so on. But together with the first retention there is a new "now," a new primal sensation, and the latter is combined continuously with the former in one moment in such a way that the second phase of the flow is primal sensation of the new now and retention of the earlier now; the third phase is again new primal sensation together with retention of the second primal sensation and retention of the retention of the first; and so on. We must also take into account here that the retention of a retention has intentionality not only in relation to what is immediately retained but also in relation to what, in the retaining, is retained of the second degree, and ultimately in relation to the primal datum, which is objectivated throughout the process. The situation is analogous to the representation of an appearance of a physical thing, which possesses intentionality not only in relation to the thing-appearance but also in relation to the appearing thing; or better still, it is analogous to the memory [of a memory] of A, which makes us conscious not only of the memory but also of the A as what is remembered in the memory.

We believe, therefore, that the unity of the flow itself becomes constituted in the flow of consciousness as a one-dimensional *quasi-temporal* order by virtue of the continuity of

retentional modifications and by virtue of the circumstance that these modifications are, continuously, retentions of the retentions that have continuously preceded them. If I direct my interest towards the tone, if I immerse myself attentively in the "transverse intentionality"† (in the primal sensation as sensation of the actually present tone-now, in the retentional modifications as primary memories of the series of elapsed tone-points and as continually experiencing the unity in the flow of retentional modifications of the primal sensations and of the retentions that are already on hand), then the enduring tone stands before me, constantly expanding in its duration. If I focus on the "horizontal intentionality" and on what is becoming constituted in it, I turn my reflective regard away from the tone (which has endured for such and such a length of time) towards what is new in the way of primal sensation at one point in the retentional being-all-at-once and towards what is retained "all at once" with this new primal sensation in a continuous series. What is retained is the past consciousness in its series of phases (first of all, its preceding phase). And then, in the continuous flowing-on of consciousness, I grasp the retained series of the elapsed consciousness together with the limit of the actual primal sensation and the continuous being-pushed-back of this series, along with the new addition of retentions and primal sensations.

Here we can ask: Can I find and apprehend in one glance the whole retentional consciousness, included in a retentional being-all-at-once, of the past course of consciousness? Obviously, the process necessary in this case is the following: I must first grasp the retentional being-all-at-once itself, and this is continuously modified; indeed, it is what it is only in the flow. Now the flow, inasmuch as it modifies this

---

Längsintentionalität, which Churchill translates as "longitudinal intentionality." I use "horizontal" because I take the intentionality in this case to be the flow's intending of itself in its flowing; this intentionality, in other words, may be said to run lengthwise along the flow, which the term "horizontal" is intended to suggest. —Translator's note.

†*Querintentionalität.* Here I follow Churchill's translation. I interpret the flow's intentionality in this case to be directed towards the immanent object enduring or running off in immanent time (and towards a transcendent object if the immanent object is an act of the appropriate kind). I take the immanent object to be on a different level from the absolute flow that intends or constitutes it; the intentionality directed towards the immanent temporal object may, therefore, be said to cut across the direction of the flow. —Translator's note.

retentional being-all-at-once, coincides with itself intentionally, constituting a unity in the flow. And what is one and identical receives and maintains a continuous mode of being-pushed-back; something new is always being added "in front" in order to flow away immediately in its turn, together with what is connected with it in that moment. Throughout this process my look can remain fixed on the momentary being-all-at-once that sinks into the past, but the constitution of the retentional unity reaches beyond this, always adding something new. My look can be turned towards that in this process, and I am always conscious of it in the flow as constituted unity.

Consequently, *two* inseparably united *intentionalities,* requiring one another like two sides of one and the same thing, are interwoven with each other in the one, unique flow of consciousness. By virtue of one of the intentionalities, immanent time becomes constituted—an objective time, a genuine time in which there is duration and the alteration of what endures. In the other intentionality, it is the *quasi*-temporal arrangement of the phases of the flow that becomes constituted—of the flow that always and necessarily possesses the flowing "now"-point, the phase of actuality, and the series of phases that have preceded the phase of actuality or that will follow it (those that are not yet actual). This prephenomenal, preimmanent temporality becomes constituted intentionally as the form of the time-constituting consciousness and in it itself. The flow of the consciousness that constitutes immanent time not only *exists* but is so remarkably and yet intelligibly fashioned that a self-appearance of the flow necessarily exists in it, and therefore the flow itself must necessarily be apprehensible in the flowing. The self-appearance of the flow does not require a second flow; on the contrary, it constitutes itself as a phenomenon in itself. The constituting and the constituted coincide, and yet naturally they cannot coincide in every respect. The phases of the flow of consciousness in which phases of the same flow of consciousness become constituted phenomenally cannot be identical with these constituted phases, nor are they. What is brought to appearance in the actual momentary phase of the flow of consciousness—specifically, in its series of retentional moments—are the past phases of the flow of consciousness.

APPENDIX VIII: The Double Intentionality of the Stream of Consciousness*

We have a double intentionality in the stream of consciousness. Either we consider the content of the flow together with its flow-form: then we are looking at the primal-experience series, which is a series of intentional experiences, consciousness of. . . . Or we direct our regard to the intentional unities, to what is intended as something unitary in the streaming on of the flow: then an objectivity stands before us in objective time, the temporal field proper as opposed to the temporal field of the stream of experience.

The stream of experience with its phases and extents is itself a unity identifiable through memory together with the directing of one's regard towards what flows: impressions and retentions; the emerging, changing in conformity with law, and disappearing or becoming obscure. This unity becomes constituted originally through the fact of the flow itself; that is to say, it is the flow's proper essence not only simply to exist but to be a unity of experience and to be given in internal consciousness, in which a ray of attention can extend towards it. (This ray is not itself an object of attention. It enriches but does not alter the stream to be considered; it rather "fixes" it and makes it objective.) The attentive perception of this unity is an intentional experience with variable content; and a memory can be directed towards what has passed away and can modify it repeatedly, compare it with what is like it, etc. That this identification is possible, that an object is constituted here, depends on the structure of the experiences: namely, that each phase of the stream changes into retention "of . . . ," that the latter in turn changes in the same way, and so on. Without that process, a content would be inconceivable as experience; without it, as a matter of principle, experience would not and could not be given as a unity to the subject and consequently would be nothing. The flowing consists in the passing of each phase of the original field (thus of a linear continuum) over into a retentional modification of the same, only just past, phase. And so it continues.

In the case of the second intentionality, I do not follow the flow of fields, the flow of the form "now (original)-retentional modification of different degrees" as a unitary sequence of change. Instead, I direct my attention to what is intended in each field and in each phase that the field as a linear continuum possesses. Each phase is an intentional experience. In the case of the foregoing objectification, the constituting experiences were the acts of internal consciousness whose objects are precisely the "phenomena" of time-constituting consciousness. The latter are therefore intentional experiences themselves; their objects are the time-points and temporal durations with their respective objective fillings. While the absolute temporal flow flows, the intentional phases are displaced, but in such a way that they constitute unities in an interrelated manner; they pass over into one another precisely as phenomena of one thing, which is adumbrated in the flowing phenomena in such a way that we have "objects in their ways of appearing" [*"Gegenstände im Wie"*] and in ever new ways of appearing. The form of the way of appearing is the orientation: the now, the just past, the future. With regard to the objects, then, we can once again speak of the flow in which the now changes into the past, and so on. And this is necessarily prescribed a priori by the structure of the experience-flow as the flow of intentional experiences.

Retention is a peculiar modification of the perceptual consciousness, which is primal impression in the original time-constituting consciousness and immananent (adequate) perception with respect to the temporal objects —at least when they are immanent, such as an enduring tone in the tonal field or even a color or datum in the visual field. If P(t) is the perception of a sensed tone, grasping it as an enduring tone, then P(t) changes into a continuity of retentions $R_{p(t)}$. But P(t) is also given as an experience in internal consciousness. If P(t) changes into $R_{p(t)}$, then precisely the internal consciousness of $R_{p(t)}$ necessarily changes in internal consciousness. For here indeed being and being-internally-intended coincide. But then the internal consciousness of P(t) also changes into the retentional modification of this internal consciousness, and this retentional modification itself is intended internally. Thus it is that the just-having-perceived is intended.

When a tone-perception passes over into its corresponding retentions (the consciousness of the tone that just was), a consciousness of the perceiving that just was is found there (in internal consciousness, as experience), and both coincide; I cannot have one without the other. Put differently, both necessarily belong together: the change of a perception of an object into a retentional modification of this perception and the change of the act of perceiving into a retentional modification of the act of perceiving. Thus we necessarily have two kinds of retentional modifications given with every perception that is not perception of internal consciousness. Internal consciousness is a flow. If experiences that are not "internal perceptions" are to be possible in this flow, two kinds of retentional series must be given. Therefore, in addition to the constitution of the flow as a unity through retentions of the "internal," a series of retentions of the "external" must also be given. The latter series constitutes objective time (a constituted immanence, external to the first but nonetheless immanent). Here we must note that the consciousness of the internal does not have as its correlate immanent data that endure (such as a tonal datum, or enduring joys and sorrows, or enduring processes called judgments) but the phases constituting these unities.

APPENDIX IX: Primal Consciousness and the Possibility of Reflection*

Retention is not a modification in which impressional data are really preserved, only in modi-fied form: on the contrary, it is an intentionality—indeed, an intentionality with a specific character of its own. When a primal datum, a new phase, emerges, the preceding phase does not vanish but is "kept in grip" (that is to say, precisely "retained"); and thanks to this retention, a looking-back at what has elapsed is possible. The retention itself is not a looking-back that makes the elapsed phase into an object: while I have the elapsed phase in my grip, I live through the present phase, take it—thanks to retention—"in addition" to the elapsed phase; and I am directed towards what is coming (in a protention).

But since I keep the elapsed phase in my grip, I can direct my regard to it in a new act that we call reflection (immanent perception) or recollection, depending on whether the elapsed experiencing is still being generated in new primal data and is therefore an impression, or on whether it has already elapsed as a whole and "is receding into the past." These acts stand to retention in the relation of fulfillment. Retention itself is not an "act" (that is, an immanent duration-unity constituted in a series of retentional phases) but a momentary consciousness of the elapsed phase and at the same time a foundation for the retentional consciousness of the next phase. Each phase, by being retentionally conscious of the preceding phase, includes in itself the entire series of elapsed retentions in the form of a chain of mediate intentions: it is precisely in this way that duration-unities, which are reproduced by the vertical series of the time-diagram and which are the objects of retrospective acts, become constituted. In these acts, the series of constituting phases comes to be given along with the constituted unity (e.g., the unchanging tone continuously preserved in retention).

We therefore owe it to retention that consciousness can be made into an object.

We can now pose the question: What about the beginning-phase of an experience that is in the process of becoming constituted? Does it also come to be given only on the basis of retention, and would it be "unconscious" if no retention were to follow it? We must say in response to this question: The beginning-phase can become an object only *after* it has elapsed in the indicated way, by means of retention and reflection (or reproduction). But if it were intended *only* by retention, then what confers on it the label "now" would remain incomprehensible. At most, it could be distinguished negatively from its modifications as that one phase that does not make us retentionally conscious of any preceding phase; but the beginning-phase is by all means characterized in consciousness in quite positive fashion. It is just nonsense to talk about an "unconscious" content that would only subsequently become conscious. Consciousness is necessarily *consciousness* in each of its phases. Just as the retentional phase is conscious of the preceding phase without making it into an object, so too the primal datum is already intended—specifically, in the original form of the "now"—without its being something objective. It is precisely this primal consciousness that passes over into retentional modification—which is then retention of the primal consciousness itself and of the datum originally intended in it, since the two are inseparably united. If the primal consciousness were not on hand, no retention would even be conceivable: retention of an unconscious content is impossible. Moreover, the primal consciousness is not something inferred on the basis of reasoning; it is rather something that can be seen as a constituting phase in reflection on the constituted experiencing, exactly like the retentions. But we must not misunderstand this primal consciousness, this primal apprehension or whatever one wants to call it, to be an apprehending act. Apart from the fact that this would be an evidently false description of the situation, it would entangle us in irresolvable difficulties. If one says that every content comes to consciousness only by means of an act of apprehension directed towards it, then the question immediately arises about the consciousness in which this act of apprehension, which is surely a content itself, becomes conscious, and an infinite regress is unavoidable. But if every "content" is "primally conscious"* in itself and necessarily, the question about a further giving consciousness becomes meaningless.

Furthermore, every act of apprehension is itself a constituted immanent duration-unity. While it is being built up, that which it is supposed to make into an object is long since past and would no longer be accessible to it at all —if we did not already presuppose the whole play of primal consciousness and retentions. But since primal consciousness and retentions are there, the possibility exists, in reflection, of looking at the constituted experience *and* at the constituting phases, and even of grasping the distinction that obtains, for example, between the original flow as it was intended in the primal consciousness and its retentional modification. All the objections that have been raised against the method of reflection are explained on the basis of ignorance of the essential constitution of consciousness.

12. Horizons and the Genesis of Perception†

§1. *Original consciousness and the perspectival adumbration of spatial objects*‡

External perception is a constant pretension to accomplish something that, by its very nature, it is not in a position to accomplish. Thus, it harbors an essential contradiction, as it were. My meaning will soon become clear to you once you intuitively grasp how the objective sense exhibits itself as unity [in and through] the unending manifolds of possible appearances; and seen upon closer inspection, how the continual synthesis, as a unity of coinciding, allows the same sense to appear; and how a consciousness of ever new possibilities of appearance constantly persists over against the factual, limited courses of appearance, transcending them.

Let us begin by noting that the aspect, the perspectival adumbration through which every spatial object invariably appears, only manifests the spatial object from one side. No matter how completely we may perceive a thing, it is never given in perception with the characteristics that qualify it and make it up as a sensuous thing from all sides at once. We cannot avoid speaking of these or those sides of the object that are actually perceived. Every aspect, every continuity of single adumbrations, regardless how far this continuity may extend, only offers us sides. And to our mind this statement is not just a mere fact: it is inconceivable that external perception would exhaust the sensuous-material content of its perceived object; it is inconceivable that a perceptual object could be given in the entirety of its sensuously intuitive features, literally,

---

*"*Urbewusst*" in *Husserliana X*; "*unbewusst*" in the publication of 1928. The original manuscript for this appendix has not been located. —Translator's note.

†Excerpted from Edmund Husserl, *Analyses Concerning Passive and Active Synthesis: Lectures on Transcendental Logic*. Translated by Anthony J. Steinbock (Boston: Kluwer Academic Publishers, forthcoming). The originally published title of this selection from APS, "Self-Giving in Perception," has been modified with permission of the translator. Reprinted with permission of the translator.

‡I would like to thank Stephanie Windolph and Tanja Stähler for their helpful remarks on an earlier draft of this translation. —Translator's note.

from all sides at once in a self-contained perception.

Thus, this fundamental division between what is genuinely perceived and what is not genuinely perceived belongs to the primordial structure of the correlation: external perception and bodily "object." When we view the table, we view it from some particular side, and this side is thereby what is genuinely seen. Yet the table has still other sides. It has a non-visible back side, it has a non-visible interior; and these are actually indexes for a variety of sides, a variety of complexes of possible visibility. That is a very curious situation peculiar to the very essence of the matter at hand. For proper to the very sense of every perception is perception's perceived object as its objective sense *[gegenständlicher Sinn],* that is, this thing, the table that is seen. But this thing is not [merely] the side genuinely seen in this moment; rather (according to the very sense of perception) the thing is precisely the full-thing that has still other sides, sides that are not brought to genuine perception in this perception, but that would be brought to genuine perception in other perceptions.

Generally speaking, perception is original consciousness. We have, however, a curious schism in external perception: Original consciousness is only possible in the form of an actually and genuinely original conscious-having of sides and a co-conscious-having of other sides that are precisely not originally there. I say co-conscious, since the non-visible sides are certainly also there somehow for consciousness, "co-meant" as co-present. But they do not appear as such, genuinely. They are not there like reproductive aspects are, as intuitions that exhibit them; we can nevertheless produce such intuitive presentifications any time we like. Viewing the front side of the table we can, whenever we like, orchestrate an intuitive presentational course, a reproductive course of aspects through which the non-visible side of the thing would be presented to us. But here we are doing nothing more than presentifying a course of perceptions to ourselves in which we would see the object—passing from a perception to new ones—from ever new sides in original aspects. Still, that only happens in exceptional circumstances. It is clear that a non-intuitive pointing beyond or indicating is what characterizes the side actually seen as a mere side, and what provides for the fact that the side is not taken for the thing, but rather, that something transcending the side is intended in consciousness as perceived, by which precisely *that* is actually seen. Noetically speaking, perception is a mixture of an actual exhibiting that presents in an intuitive manner what is originally exhibited, and of an empty indicating that refers to possible new perceptions. In a noematic regard, what is perceived is given in adumbrations in such a way that the particular givenness refers to something else that is not-given, as what is not given belonging to the same object. We will have to understand the meaning of this.

Let us first note that every perception, or noematically speaking, every single aspect of the object in itself points to a continuity, to multifarious continua of possible new perceptions, and precisely to those in which the same object would show itself from ever new sides. In every moment of perceiving, the perceived is what it is in its mode of appearance [as] a system of referential implications *[Verweisen]* with an appearance-core on which appearances have their hold. And it calls out to us, as it were, in these referential implications: "There is still more to see here, turn me so you can see all my sides, let your gaze peruse me, draw closer to me, open me up, divide me up; keep on looking me over again and again, turning me to see all sides. You will get to know me like this, all that I am, all my surface qualities, all my inner sensuous qualities," etc.

You understand the meaning of this suggestive manner of speaking. In the particular present perception I have just these aspects and their modifications, and no others, just these aspects that are always limited ones. In each moment the objective sense is the same with respect to the object as such, the object that is meant; and it coincides with the continual course of momentary appearances, as for instance this table here. But what is identical is a constant x, a constant substrate of actually appearing table-moments, but also of indications *[Hinweisen]* of moments not yet appearing.

These indications are at the same time tendencies, indicative tendencies that push us toward the appearances not given. They are, however, not single indications, but entire indicative systems, indications functioning as systems of rays that point toward corresponding manifold systems of appearance. They are pointers into an emptiness since the non-actualized appearances are neither consciously intended as actual nor presentified. In other words, everything that genuinely appears is an appearing thing only by virtue of being intertwined and permeated with an intentional empty horizon, that is, by virtue of being surrounded by a halo of emptiness with respect to appearance. It is an emptiness that is not a nothingness, but an emptiness to be filled-out; it is a determinable indeterminacy. For the intentional horizon cannot be filled out in just any manner; it is a horizon of consciousness that itself has the fundamental trait of consciousness as the consciousness of something.

In spite of its emptiness, the sense of this halo of consciousness is a prefiguring that prescribes a rule for the transition to new actualizing appearances. Seeing the front side of the table, I am also conscious of the back side along with everything else that is non-visible, through an empty pointing ahead, even though it be rather indeterminate. But no matter how indeterminate it may be, it is still a pointing ahead to a bodily shape, to a bodily coloring, etc. And only appearances that adumbrate things of that kind and that determine more closely what is indeterminate in the framework of this prefiguring can be integrated concordantly; only they can stay the course of an identical x of determination as the same, being determined here newly and more closely. This holds time and again for every perceptual phase of the streaming process of perceiving, for every new appearance, only that the intentional horizon has altered and shifted. Proper to every appearing thing of each perceptual phase is a new empty horizon, a new system of determinable indeterminacy, a new system of progressing tendencies with corresponding possibilities of entering into determinately ordered systems of possible appearances, of possible ways that the aspects can run their course, to-

gether with horizons that are inseparably affiliated with these aspects. In the concordant coinciding of sense, they would bring the same object as being ever newly determined to actual, fulfilling givenness. To our mind, the aspects are nothing for themselves; they are appearances-of only through the intentional horizons that are inseparable from them.

We thereby distinguish further between an inner horizon and an outer horizon of the respective aspect-appearance. It should be recognized that the division applying to what is genuinely perceived and what is only co-present entails a distinction between determinations with respect to the content of the object (a) that are actually there, appearing in the flesh, and (b) those that are still ambiguously prefigured in full emptiness. Let us also note that what actually appears is, in itself, also laden with a similar distinction. Indeed, the call resounds as well with respect to the side that is already actually seen: "Draw closer, closer still; now fix your eyes on me, changing your place, changing the position of your eyes, etc. You will get to see even more of me that is new, ever new partial colorings, etc. You will get to see structures of the wood that were not visible just a moment ago, and that formerly were only viewed indeterminately and generally," etc. Thus, even what is already seen is laden with an anticipatory intention. It, what is already seen, is a constant framework that prefigures something new; it is an x to be determined more closely. There is a constant process of anticipation, of preunderstanding. In addition to this inner horizon there are then also outer horizons, prefigurings for what is still devoid of any intuitively given framework that would require only more differentiated ways of sketching it in.

§2. The relationship of fullness and emptiness in the perceptual process and the acquisition of knowledge

In order to gain a deeper understanding we must pay attention to how fullness and emptiness stand in relation to one another at each moment, how emptiness adopts fullness in the flow of perception, and how fullness becomes emptiness again. We must understand the structure of interconnections for every appearance as well as the structure that unites all series of appearances. In the continual progression of perception, as in the case of every perception, we have protentions that are continuously fulfilled by what occurs anew, occurring in the form of the primordial-impressional Now. And here as well. In every progression of external perceiving, the protention has the shape of continuous anticipations that become fulfilled. That is to say, out of the indicative systems of the horizons, certain indicative lines are continually being actualized as expectations; the latter are continuously fulfilled in aspects that are being determined more closely.

In the previous lecture we approached the unity of every external perception from different directions. External perception is a temporal run-off of lived-experience where appearances concordantly pass into one another forming the unity of coincidence corresponding to the unity of sense. We came to understand this flux as a systematic network of progressive fulfillment of intentions that obviously, when viewed from the other side, goes hand in hand with an emptying of intentions that are already full. Every momentary phase of perception is in itself a network of partially full and partially empty intentions. For, in every phase we have genuine appearances, that is, a fulfilled intention, albeit only gradually fulfilled, since there remains an inner horizon of unfulfilledness and an indeterminacy that is still determinable. Moreover, proper to every phase is a fully empty outer horizon that tends toward fulfillment and, in the transition toward a definite direction of progress, strives toward it in the manner of empty anticipation.

Viewed more precisely, we now have to describe the process of perception as a process of acquiring knowledge; and we have to distinguish further (in the following manner) between fulfillment and the process of determining more closely. While the empty horizon—both inner and outer—fashions its next fulfillment in the march of perception, this fulfillment does not merely consist in tracing over in intuition the prefigured sense of which one is emptily conscious. Indeterminacy, as we said, belongs essentially to the empty premonition which is, as it were, the presentiment of what is to come. We spoke as well of determinate indeterminacy. Indeterminacy is a primordial form of generality whose nature it is to be fulfilled in the coincidence of sense only by "specification." As long as this specification itself has the character of indeterminacy (the specific indeterminacy as opposed to the general indeterminacy just mentioned), it can attain further specification, etc., in new steps. But now we should consider that this process of fulfillment, which is a specifying fulfillment, is also a process of knowing something more closely; it is not only a momentary knowledge acquisition, but at the same time a process of acquisition within knowledge that is abiding and that becomes habitual. This will become clearer shortly.

Let us note in advance that the primordial place of this accomplishment is the continuously co-functioning retention. First, let us recall that the continually progressing fulfillment is at the same time a continually progressing emptying. For, as soon as a new side becomes visible, a side that has just been visible gradually disappears from sight, becoming finally completely non-visible. But what has become non-visible is not cognitively lost for us. Thematic perception does not merely drive at continually possessing some new aspect of the object that would be intuitively grasped from moment to moment, as if what was formerly given would slip away from the grasp of [perceptual] interest. Rather, as perception progresses it drives at fashioning a unity of originary acquisitions of knowledge through which the object, according to its specific content, would reach an original acquisition, and through it would become an abiding epistemic possession.* And in fact we understand the original acquisition of knowledge by observing the following situation: The process of determining more closely, which comes about

---

*Every content of an unaltered thing can be reached time and again through perception; I can go around the surface; ideally the thing can be divided, and can be viewed time and again from all surface sides, etc.

with fulfillment, imparts afresh a specific moment of sense. While it vanishes from the field of genuine perception in the progression to new perceptions, it remains held retentionally. (That already takes place prethematically, already in background perceiving. In thematic perception, retention has the thematic character of keeping-a-hold-of.) Accordingly, the empty horizon (into which what is new enters by virtue of retention) has a character other than the empty horizon peculiar to the stretch of perception, that is, before the latter originarily appeared. Having already once seen the back side of an unfamiliar object and, turning back to perceive the front side, the empty premonition of the back side now has a determinate prefiguring that it did not have previously. The unfamiliar object is thereby transformed in the perceptual process into a familiar object; in the end, I have exactly what I had started with, namely, a perspectival appearance. And if the object has moved entirely out of our field of perception, then we have an altogether fully empty retention of it. Nevertheless, we still have the entire epistemic acquisition of it, and we still have a hold on it in thematic perceiving. Our empty-consciousness now has an articulated, systematic sense that is sketched in, that did not exist previously and especially at the beginning of the perception. What was previously a mere framework of sense, a wide ranging generality, is now specified meaningfully in an articulated manner; to be sure, it awaits further experience in order to take on still richer epistemic contents as contents of determination. If I turn back again to the perceptions of the earlier determination, they will issue in the consciousness of recognition, in the consciousness: "I already know all that." Now a mere bringing to intuition takes place, and with it fulfilling confirmation of the empty intentions, but no longer the process of determining more closely.

§3. The possibility of our acquired knowledge being freely at our disposal

By acquiring knowledge originally, perception also acquires permanent, lasting possession of what it has acquired; it is a possession that is at our disposal any time. How is something freely at our disposal? Although this thing that is already familiar to me has become empty, it is freely at my disposal insofar as the empty retention remaining behind can be freely filled up at any time; it can be made present at any time by a re-perception in the sense of a re-cognition. By walking around it, drawing nearer to it, touching it with my hands, etc., I can once more see all the sides that are already familiar to me; I can experience them again, they are ready for perception. And this holds true likewise for the next time. The fact that a re-perception, a renewed perception of the same thing, is possible for transcendence characterizes the fundamental trait of transcendent perception, alone through which an abiding world is there for us, a reality that can be pregiven for us and can be freely at our disposal.

To this we must add yet another essential observation. If we have become familiar with a thing and a second thing appears in our field of vision, and if, with respect to the side genuinely seen, it accords with the earlier and familiar thing, then according to an essential law of consciousness (by virtue of an inner coinciding with the earlier thing awakened through the "association of similarity"), the new thing receives the entire epistemic prefiguring from the earlier one. It is apperceived, as we say, with the same non-visible qualities as the previous one. And even this prefiguring, this acquisition of an inner tradition, is also freely at our disposal in the form of actualizing perception.

But how does this having something freely at our disposal look now upon closer inspection? What makes possible the free foray into our world that is thoroughly interwoven with anticipations; what makes all existing knowledge and new knowledge possible? Let us privilege here the normal and basic instance of the constitution of external existence, namely, the constitution of unaltered spatial things. Whether alterations of things can occur without being perceived and yet can be known in all their unperceived elements in a variety of perceptions and experiences that follow—this is a theme for a clarification existing on a higher level, a theme that already presupposes clarifying the possibility of knowing existence in rest.

Thus, in order to understand at least this basic feature of the constitutive problematic, we ask what having acquisitions of knowledge freely at our disposal looks like—acquisitions I already have, however incompletely; what does it look like specifically in the case of unaltered thingliness? What makes it possible?

From what we have said above, we see that every perception *implicite* invokes an entire perceptual system; every appearance that arises in it implies an entire system of appearance, specifically in the form of intentional inner and outer horizons. We cannot even imagine a mode of appearance in which the appearing object would be given completely. No final presentation in the flesh is ever reached in the mode of appearance as if it would present the complete, exhausted Self of the object. Every appearance implies a *plus ultra* in the empty horizon. And since perception does indeed pretend to give the object [completely] in the flesh in every appearance, it in fact and by its very nature constantly pretends to accomplish more than it can accomplish. In a peculiar way, every perceptual givenness is a constant mixture of familiarity and unfamiliarity, a givenness that points to new possible perceptions that would issue in familiarity. And that will continue to hold in a new sense, differently from what has come to light up to now.

Let us now take a look at the formation of unity through coinciding as it pertains to sense by examining the transition of appearances, for instance, when approaching or walking around an object or in eye movement. The fundamental relationship in this dynamic transition is that of intention and fulfillment. The empty pointing ahead acquires its corresponding fullness. It corresponds roughly to the rich possibilities prefigured; but since its nature is determinable indeterminacy, it also brings, together with the fulfillment, a closer determination. Thus here we have a new "primordial-institution," or as we can say here again, a primordial-impression, since a moment of primordial originality emerges. That of which we are already conscious in a primordial-impressional

manner points to new modes of appearance through its halo which, when occurring, emerge as partly confirming, partly determining more closely. By virtue of inner intentions—unfulfilled and those now in the process of being fulfilled—what has already appeared itself becomes enriched. Moreover, in this progression, the empty outer horizon that was intertwined with the appearances achieves its next fulfillment, at least a partial one. The part of the horizon that remains unfulfilled passes over into the horizon of the new appearance, and it goes on like this continually. That aspect of the object which has already appeared is partially lost again as it progresses out of the givenness of the appearance; the visible becomes non-visible again. But it is not lost. I remain conscious of it retentionally and in such a way that the empty horizon of the appearance present at this time receives a new prefiguring that points in a determinate manner to what has already been given earlier as co-present. Having seen the back side and having turned back to the front side, the perceptual object has kept a determination of sense for me; likewise in emptiness, it points to what was previously seen. They all belong now abidingly to the object. The process of perception is a constant process of acquiring knowledge that holds on to what was acquired epistemically in sense; it thereby fashions an ever newly altered and ever more enriched sense. During the ongoing perceptual process, this sense is added to the grasped object itself in its presumed [complete] presentation in the flesh.

Now, it depends upon the direction of the perceptual processes as to which lines from the system of unfulfilled intentions are brought to fulfillment, that is, which continuous series of possible appearances out of the entire system of possible appearances of the object will be realized. Advancing along this line, the empty intentions are transformed respectively into expectations. Once the path is pursued, the series of appearances runs its course in the sense of continuously arousing and steadily fulfilling expectations that stem from the current kinaestheses, while the remaining empty horizons are left in dead potentiality.

Lastly, we still have to mention that the harmony in the coinciding of adumbration-appearances that pass over into one another by way of intention and fulfillment not only concerns the appearances taken as wholes, but also all their moments and parts that can be differentiated. Thus, there is something corresponding to every filled spatial point of the object in the entire series of appearances; they continuously pass into one another such that this point in the appearance exhibits itself as a moment of the appearing spatial form.

If we ask, finally, what gives unity within every temporal point of the momentary appearance—unity considered as the entire aspect in which the particular side is exhibited—we will also come across reciprocal intentions that are fulfilled simultaneously and reciprocally. The transition of appearances following one after the other are all in dynamic displacement, enrichment, and impoverishment.

The object appearing constantly new, constantly different is constituted as the same in these exceedingly complicated and wondrous systems of intention and fulfillment that make up the appearances. But the object is never finished, never fixed completely.

We must point here to a side of the noematic constitution that is essential for the objectivation of the perceptual object—to the side of kinaesthetic motivation. We mentioned in passing time and again that the courses of appearance go hand in hand with the orchestrating movements of the lived-body *[Leib]*. But that must not remain something that we only mention haphazardly in passing. The lived-body is constantly there, functioning as an organ of perception; and here, it is in itself moreover an entire system of compatibly harmonizing organs of perception. The lived-body is in itself characterized as the perceiving-lived-body. We recognize it then purely as a lived-body, subjectively movable and in perceiving activity, as subjectively self-moving. In this regard it does not come into consideration as a perceived spatial thing, but rather with respect to the system of so-called "movement-sensations" that run their course during perception, in eye movements, head movements, etc. And they do not simply run parallel to the flow of appearances there; rather the kinaesthetic series under consideration and the perceptual appearances are related to one another through consciousness. By viewing an object I am conscious of the position of my eyes and at the same time—in the form of a novel systematic empty horizon—I am conscious of the entire system of possible eye positions that rest at my disposal. And now, what is seen in the given eye position is so enmeshed with the entire system that I can say with certainty that if I were to move my eyes in this direction or in that, specific visual appearances would accordingly run their course in a determinate order. If I were to let the eye movements run this way or that in another direction, different series of appearances would accordingly run their course as expected. This holds likewise for head movements in the system of these possibilities of movement, and again for the movement of walking, etc., that I might bring into play.

Every series of kinaestheses proceeds in its own way, in a manner totally different from the series of sensuous data. It runs its course in such a way as to be freely at my disposal, free to inhibit, free to orchestrate once again, as an originally subjective realization. Thus, the system of lived-body movements is in fact characterized with respect to consciousness in a special way as a subjectively free system. I run through this system in the consciousness of the free "I can." It may happen that I unintentionally dwell upon something, that for instance my eyes turn this way or that. But I can exercise my will at any time and pursue such a path of movement or whatever path of movement I like. As soon as I have an appearance of the thing in such a situation, a system of internally coherent manifold appearances of the same thing is thereby prefigured in the original consciousness of the sequence of appearances.

A propos the appearances I am not free: when I undertake a series of movements in the free system, "I move myself," the appearances that are arriving are already prefigured. The appearances form dependent systems. Only as dependent upon kinaestheses can they continually pass into one another and constitute a unity of one sense. Only by running their course in these ways do they unfold their intentional indicators. Only through this interplay of independent and dependent variables is that which appears constituted as a transcendent perceptual object, precisely as an object that is more than what we directly perceive, as an object that can completely vanish from my perception and yet still persist. We can also say it is constituted as such only by the fact that its appearances are kinaesthetically motivated, and consequently that it is in my freedom —in accordance with the knowledge that I have acquired—to let the appearances run their course randomly as original appearances in their system of concordance. Through the appropriate eye movements and other lived-bodily movements I can, in the case of a familiar object, turn back at any time to the old appearances that give me back the object from the same sides. Or, by freely returning to the appropriate place, I can once again perceive and identify the object no longer perceived.

Thus, in every perceptual process we see a constitutive duet being played: (1) The system of my free possibilities of movement is intentionally constituted as a practical, kinaesthetic horizon. This system is actualized each time I run through single paths of movements with the character of familiarity, that is, of fulfillment. We are not only thereby conscious of every eye position that we have at the moment, every position of the physical-body as the momentary sensation of movement, but we are also conscious of them as a place in a system of places; thus we are conscious of them with an empty horizon which is a horizon of freedom. (2) Every visual sensation or visual appearance that arises in the visual field, every tactile appearance that arises in the field of touch is ordered with respect to consciousness, to the current situation of the consciousness of the parts of the lived-body, creating a horizon of further possibilities that are ordered together, creating a horizon of possible series of appearances belonging to the freely possible series of movement.

In relation to the constitution of transcendent temporality we should note here that ev-

ery path of actualization that we would de facto enter down in realizing this freedom would yield continuous series of appearances of the object. All of these series would exhibit the object for one and the same span of time; they would all exhibit the same object in the same duration, only from different sides. In accordance with the sense of what is constituted, all determinations that would be known through this process would be co-existent.

§4. The relation of esse and percipi in immanent and transcendent perception

All this holds only for transcendent objects. An immanent object, like a lived-experience-of-black, offers itself as a lasting object, and in a certain way through "appearances" as well. But it only does so like any temporal object in general. The temporally extending duration requires the constant modification of the modes of givenness in accordance with the modes of appearance of the temporal orientation. Now, the spatial object is also a temporal object, so the same holds for it too. But it still has a second, special way to appear. By directing our attention to the temporal fullness and especially to the primordial-impressional phases, we come up against the radical difference between the appearance of transcendent and immanent objects. The immanent object has only one possible way to be given in the original in every Now, and therefore every mode of the past also has only one single series of temporal modifications, namely that of presentification, with the changing past objects being constituted in it. But the spatial object has infinitely many ways [to be given in the original] since it can appear in the Now, that is, in an original way from its different sides. Though it appears de facto from this side, it could have been able to appear from other sides, and accordingly every one of its past phases have infinitely many ways in which it could exhibit its past fulfilled points of time. We can also say: the concept of appearance has a new and unique sense for the transcendent object.

If we consider exclusively the Now phase, then in the case of the immanent object, appearance and that which appears cannot be separated in the Now phase. What arises anew in the original is the particular, new black-phase itself, and without being exhibited. And appearing means here nothing other than a to-be devoid of any exhibiting that points beyond, and a to-be-conscious-of in the original.

But on the other hand, with respect to the transcendent object, it is clear that the thing of which we are conscious in the flesh as a thing in the new Now is consciously intended only in and through an appearance; that is, exhibiting and that which is exhibited, adumbration and that which is adumbrated part. If we exchange the noematic attitude that we have privileged up to now with the noetic attitude in which we turn our reflective regard toward the lived-experience and its "intimately inherent"* components, we can also say that a transcendent object such as a thing can only be constituted when an immanent content is constituted as substratum. Now, this immanent content for its part is substituted, as it were, for the peculiar function of the "adumbration," of an exhibiting appearance, of a being exhibited in and through it. When we do not regard the appearing thing-object, but the optical lived-experience itself, the thing-appearance that arises anew in each Now—as we say, the optical appearance—is a complex of surface color moments that are extended in this way or that, which surface color moments are immanent data, and thus we are conscious of them in themselves just as originally as, say, red or black. The manifold changing red-data in which, e.g., any surface side of a red cube and its unaltered red is exhibited, are immanent data.

Yet, on the other hand, the matter does not rest with this mere immanent existence. In the immanent data, something is exhibited in the unique manner of adumbration, which the immanent data themselves are not; in the visual field, a sameness, an identical spatially extended body-color is exhibited in the alteration of the immanently sensed colors. All the noematic moments that we, in the natural attitude, see contained in the object and as related to it, are constituted by means of the immanent data† of sensation, and by virtue of the consciousness that, as it were, animates them. In this regard we speak of apprehension as of transcendent apperception: It characterizes consciousness's accomplishment which is to bestow on the mere immanent contents of sensuous data, on the so-called data of sensation or hyletic data, the function of exhibiting something objectively "transcendent." It is dangerous here to speak of represented and representing, of interpreting data of sensation, or to speak of a function that outwardly signifies through this "interpreting" [*"durch dieses 'Deuten' hinausdeutenden Funktion"*]. Adumbrating, exhibiting in data of sensation, is totally different from an interpretation through signs [*signitives Deuten*].

"Immanent" object-like formations [*Gegenständlichkeiten*], accordingly, are for their part not consciously intended through apperception. In their case, "being consciously intended in the original" and "being," "*percipi*" and "*esse*" converge. And indeed for every Now. However, they are to a large extent bearers of apperceptive functions, at which time something non-immanent is exhibited in and through them. Now the *esse* (for transcendent objects) is in principle distinguished from the *percipi*. In every Now of external perception we do have an original consciousness, but genuine perceiving in this Now, that is, that feature in genuine perceiving that is primordial-impressional (and not simply retentional consciousness of the past phases of the perceptual object) is a conscious-having of what is being adumbrated *originaliter*.† This is not a pure and simple hav-

---

* "*reell.*" Whereas "*real*" for Husserl designates the type of existence or "reality" peculiar to transcendent things, "*reell*" for Husserl depicts what is actual [*wirklich*] without it sharing the ontological status of a real transcendent entity [*res*]. Accordingly, *reell* concerns the intimate immanence of consciousness. What is "*irreal*" from the perspective of the "*real*" can also be "*irreell*" from the perspective of the "*reell*"; this would bear on what Husserl understood generally as "noema" or "sense." —Translator's note.

†Perception is original consciousness of an individual object, of a temporal object, and for every Now we have in perception its primordial-impression in which the object in the Now, in its momentary point of originality, is originally grasped. But it must be shown that original adumbration necessarily goes hand in hand with appresentation.

ing of the object in which conscious-having and being coincide, but a mediate consciousness, provided that only one apperception is had immediately, a store of sense-data referring to kinaesthetic data, and an apperceptive apprehension through which an exhibiting appearance is constituted; in and through it, we are conscious of the transcendent object as adumbrating or exhibiting *originaliter.* Time and again we have the following situation in the process of ongoing perceiving in every Now: in principle, the external object is never purely and simply had in its original Selfness. It appears in principle only through apperceptive exhibition and in ever new exhibitions; as they progress, they bring something that is new to original presentation from its empty horizons.

Yet, it is more important for our ends to recognize that it is inconceivable that something like a spatial object, which gets its original sense genuinely by means of external perception as adumbrating perception, would be given through immanent perception, be it human or superhuman intellect. But from this it follows as inconceivable that a spatial object and everything like it (for instance, an object of the world in the natural sense), could be exhibited in a discrete, self-contained manner from one point of time to the next, along with their entire ensemble of features (as fully determined) that make up their temporal content in this Now. In this respect we also speak of adequate givenness as opposed to inadequate givenness. To express this theologically and in a drastic manner, we do God poor service by conceding him able to make an odd number even and to transform every absurdity into truth. Inadequate modes of givenness belong essentially to spatial structure of things; any other way of givenness is simply absurd. We can never think the given object without empty horizons in any phase of perception and, what amounts to the same thing, without apperceptive adumbration. With adumbration there is simultaneously a pointing beyond what is exhibiting itself in a genuine sense. Genuine exhibition is itself, again, not a pure and simple having on the model of immanence with its *esse = percipi;* instead, it is a partially fulfilled intention that

contains unfulfilled indications that point beyond. The originality of exhibiting the transcendent thing in the flesh necessarily implies that the object as sense has the originality of apperceptive fulfillment and that this harbors inseparably a mixture of actually fulfilling and not yet filled moments of sense. This is the case whether they be moments of sense only prefigured according to the general structure, and apart from that open indeterminate and possible moments, or whether they be moments already distinguished by being specially prefigured. This is why the talk of inadequation as a haphazard lack that a higher intellect could overcome is an unsuitable way of speaking, indeed totally preposterous.

We can formulate a principle here that will become much clearer in our future analyses. Whenever we speak of objects, no matter what category of objects they may be, the sense of this manner of speaking about objects originally stems from perceptions as lived-experiences originally constituting sense and therefore an object-like formation. But the constitution of an object as sense is an accomplishment of consciousness that is in principle unique for every basic type of object. Perception does not consist in staring blankly at something lodged in consciousness, inserted there by some strange wonder as if something were first there and then consciousness would somehow embrace it. Rather, for every imaginable ego-subject, every object-like existence with a specific content of sense is an accomplishment of consciousness. It is an accomplishment that must be new for every novel object. Every basic type of object in principle requires a different intentional structure. An object that *is,* but is not and in principle could not be an object of a consciousness, is pure non-sense.

Every possible object of a possible consciousness is however also an object for a possible originarily giving consciousness; and that we call, at least for individual objects, "perception." To demand of a material object a perception that has the general structure of an immanent perception, and conversely, to demand of an immanent object a perception that has the structure of external perception, is absurd.

Both sense-giving and sense require one another essentially—and this concerns the essential typicality of their correlative structures.

In this way it is the nature of originally transcendent sense-giving, which external perception carries out, that the accomplishment of this original sense-giving is never finished as one span of perception progresses to another and so forth in whatever manner the process of perception may advance. This accomplishment does not simply consist in bringing to intuition something new in a fixed pregiven sense, as if the sense would already be prefigured in a finished manner from the very beginning; rather in the process of perceiving, the sense itself is continually cultivated and is genuinely so in steady transformation, constantly leaving open the possibility of new transformations.

Let us note here that in the sense of concordantly and synthetically progressing perception, we can always distinguish between an unceasingly changing sense and an identical sense running through the changing sense. Every phase of perception has its sense insofar as it has the object given in the How of the determination of the original exhibition and in the How of the horizon. This sense is flowing; it is a new sense in every phase. But the unity of the substrate x, which holds sway in a steady coinciding, and which is determined ever more richly—this unity of the object itself, that is, everything that the process of perception and all further possible perceptual processes determine in it and would determine in it—this unity runs through this flowing sense, through all the modes, "object in the How of determination." In this way an idea that lies in infinity belongs to every external perception, the idea of the fully determined object, of the object that would be determined through and through, known through and through, where every one of its determinations would be purified of all indeterminacy, and where the full determination itself would be devoid of any *plus ultra* with respect to what is still to be determined, what is still remaining open.

I spoke of an idea lying in infinity, that is, of an unattainable idea. For, the essential structure of perception itself excludes a perception (as a self-contained process of courses of appearance, continually passing into one another) that would furnish absolute knowledge of the object in which the tension would collapse between the object in the How of determination (which is changing and relative, remaining incomplete), and the object itself. For evidently, the possibility of a *plus ultra* is in principle never excluded. It is thus the idea of the absolute Self of the object and of its absolute and complete determination, or as we can also put it, of its absolute individual essence. In relation to this infinite idea which is to be seen, but which as such is not realizable, every perceptual object in the epistemic process is a flowing approximation. We always have the external object in the flesh (we see, grasp, seize it), and yet it is always at an infinite distance mentally. What we do grasp of it pretends to be its essence; and it is it too, but it remains so only in an incomplete approximation, an approximation that grasps something of it, but in doing so it also constantly grasps into an emptiness that cries out for fulfillment. What is constantly familiar is constantly unfamiliar, and from the very beginning all knowledge seems to be hopeless. To be sure, I said "seems." And we do not wish to commit ourselves here straight away to a hasty skepticism.

(Of course, the situation is entirely different with immanent objects. Perception constitutes them and appropriates them in their absoluteness. They are not constituted by constant sense modification in the sense of an approximation; only insofar as they become in a future are they laden with protentions and protentional indeterminacies. But what has been constituted as present in the Now is an absolute Self that does not have any unfamiliar sides.)

We have rejected a hasty skepticism. In this regard we should have initially, at all events, made the following distinction. Given that an object is perceived and that we progressively come to know it in the perceptual process, we had to distinguish (a) the particular empty horizon that is prefigured by the process running its course and that is attached to the momentary perceptual phase with its prefiguring, and

(b) a horizon of empty possibilities without this prefiguring. Prefiguring means that an empty intuition is there that provides its general framework of sense. It belongs to the essence of such a prefiguring intention that when pursuing a suitable, appropriate direction of perception this would have to occur: [either] the process of determining more closely, which is a fulfilling process, or as we shall address later as a counterpart, disappointment, annulment of sense, and crossing-out. There are also, however, partial horizons without such a firm prefiguring. In other words, aside from definite prefigured possibilities, there are counter-possibilities for which there is no support and which remain constantly open.

Speaking purely in terms of the sense-giving process of perception itself, we can say, for example, that when something like an illuminated appearance, a shooting star and the like flashes in my visual field, e.g., while gazing at a star-studded sky, it is a fully empty possibility that is not prefigured in the sense, but is left open by it. So, if we confine ourselves to the positive sense-giving process of perception together with its positive prefigurings, the question we pose is both understandable and obvious: whether no enduring and ultimately abiding Self of the object is even attainable in going from the non-intuitable empty prefiguring to the fulfilling process of determining it more closely; put differently, whether not only newer and newer object-like features can enter into the horizon of perception, but whether, in the process of determining more closely, even these features already grasped imply a further determinability, *in infinitum,* hence themselves continually and constantly maintaining the character of the unfamiliar x which can never gain final determinacy. Is then perception an "exchange" that can in principle never be "cashed in" or "realized" by new, similar exchanges, whose realization leads again to exchange and likewise *in infinitum?* The fulfillment of an intention is carried out by being exhibited in the flesh, to be sure, with empty inner horizons.

But is there nothing at all in what has already become exhibited in the flesh that would bring with it a definitiveness so that in fact we are left stuck in an ostensibly empty business of exchange?

We feel that it cannot be so, and in fact—looking more deeply into the structure of the series of perception—we come up against the peculiarity that is summoned to solve the difficulty initially for praxis and its intuitive sensuous world. Also in the case of incomplete fulfillment, that is, in the case of fulfillment laden with indications, it is the nature of genuine appearances as fulfillments of prefigured intentions to point ahead to ideal limits as goals of fulfillment that would be reached by continuous series of fulfillment. But that does not happen right away for the entire object, but rather for the features that have already come to actual intuition in each case. In view of what is genuinely exhibited in the appearance, every appearance belongs systematically to some type of series of appearances to be realized in kinaesthetic freedom in which at least some moment of the shapes would achieve its optimal givenness, and therefore its true Self.

The phantom* as a sensuously qualified bodily surface functions as a basic frame for the object of perception. The bodily surface can exhibit itself in continually diverse appearances, and likewise every partial aspect that comes into relief. For each of them we have distant appearances and near appearances. And again, inside each of these spheres we have more favorable and less favorable appearances, and in ordered series we arrive at optima. In this sense, the distant appearance of a thing and manifold of distant appearances already point back to near appearances in which the form given at first glance [*oberflächliche Gestalt*] and its fullness appear at best in the total overview. This [optimal] form itself given at first glance, which we have for instance when looking at a house from a well chosen standpoint, gives a framework for sketching in further optimal determinations that <would be

---

*The "phantom" for Husserl is the "schema" of the concrete material object, that is, examined without regard to a possible nexus of causality. —Translator's note

brought about by> drawing closer, where only single parts would be given, but then, optimally. The thing itself in its saturated fullness is an idea located in a sense belonging to consciousness and in the manner of its intentional structures; and it is, as it were a <system> of all optima that would be won by sketching in the optimal frameworks. Thematic interest that lives itself out in perceptions is guided by practical interests in our scientific life. And that thematic interest comes to a rest when certain optimal appearances—in which the thing shows so much of its ultimate Self as this practical interest demands—are won for the respective interest. Or rather, the thematic interest as practical interest prefigures a relative Self: what suffices as practical counts as the Self. Thus the house itself and in its true being, and specifically with respect to its pure bodily thingly nature, is quickly given optimally, i.e., experienced as complete for that person who regards it as a buyer or a seller. For the physicist and the chemist, such ways of experience would seem completely superficial and miles away from its true being.

I can only say in a word that all such highly ramified intentional analyses, which are difficult in themselves, belong for their part to a universal genesis of consciousness, and here especially in the genesis of the consciousness of a transcendent reality. If the theme of constitutive analyses is to make understandable how perception brings about its sense-giving and how the object is constituted through all empty intending as always only exhibiting optimal appearance-sense in a relative manner, and to make this understandable from perception's unique intentional constitution according to intimately inherent components of lived-experience itself, according to the intentional noema and sense, then it is the theme of genetic analyses to make understandable how, in the development proper to the structure of every stream of consciousness, which is at the same time the development of the ego—how those complicated intentional systems develop, through which finally an external world can appear to consciousness and to the ego.

VIII.

Transcendental Analytics

13. Formal and Transcendental Logic

The Discipline of Formal Logic*

§5. Provisional delimitation of logic as a priori theory of science

We shall attempt a first delimitation of the province that should be assigned to logic, by keeping to the most universal part of the original historical sense of that science, the part which has been, on the whole, its guiding sense up to within our own time. Significations and signification-bestowing acts can be divided into visibly heterogeneous classes, such that concrete "senseful" locutions are grouped accordingly: statements (in the specific sense of assertive statements), as expressions of judgments and their modalities; expressions of affective acts such as wishes; of volitional acts such as commands. Obviously connected with the differences among these sorts of acts is the differentiation of sorts of reason: judicative reason (including specifically theoretical reason), valuing reason, and practical reason.

If we follow the signification of the word logos which is the richest in content and has been, so to speak, raised to a higher power, namely reason, and if we also give pre-eminence to *scientific reason,* we have thereby delimited at the same time a distinctive sphere of acts and significations, precisely as a sphere to which science, as a rational activity, relates particularly. Scientific thinking, the continual activity of the scientist, is *judicative*

thinking: not just any judicative thinking, but one that is formed, ordered, connected, in certain manners—according to final ideas of reason. The *formations* generated in the course of such thinking—in science, formations expressed in language and permanently documented—have a coherence that is "logical" in the sense specific to theoretical reason: the coherence of theories and, at a higher level, the coherence of "systems." They are built up in determinate forms, out of fundamental propositions or principles, theorems, arguments, proofs, and so forth; lingually they are built up in multi-membered locutions, which, in any one science, all belong together as making up the unity of a locution that is internally connected by the rational sense of all the significations. By virtue of the fact that this significational unity is Objectively documented and can be regenerated by anyone, the generated formations become common property for mankind. Each science, in its theoretical work, has aimed exclusively at "logical" formations, formations produced by the theoretical logos. In this sense, each is itself a "logic." But logic as usually conceived is the science of all that is logical: first, in the sense applicable to all such formations produced by judicative reason—but then, on the other hand, in the sense applicable to judicative reason itself and consequently to any judicative subjectivity whatever as generating such formations.

*FTL, pp. 26–47 (Sections 5–11).

Language is taken into consideration here secondarily, because in science there is combined with the primary purposes of theoretical reason, which lie on the significational side and consist in the attainment of truths, an epistemo-technical purpose, namely that of furthering the work of judging by a suitable scientific language. A maximally durable documentation of the results, in the Objective cultural world, is also relevant to this purpose.

In our further considerations pertaining to the systematic clarification of the idea of logic, we shall address ourselves exclusively to the significational side of scientific locutions —that is to say: purely to judicative reason itself and the formations it produces. That the cognitive subject's primary and true aim lies on this side becomes apparent in the fact that, although the statement-formations are the first to make their appearance in his field of consciousness among its prominences (in the so-called *Blickfeld der Aufmerksamkeit* [field of possible attentive regard]), still his thematizing regard is never directed to the locutions as sensuous phenomena, but always "clear through them" to what is meant. They are not thematic ends but theme-indicators, pointing beyond themselves to the true themes of logic.

Following the historical logical tradition, we have framed the concept of logic as the science of logos in a pregnant sense: as the science of logos in the form of science, or as the science of the essential parts that make up genuine science, as genuine. We could, however, have left the concept of a science of logos in its broader universality from the start; in other words, we could have framed this concept as the concept of a science that, with absolute universality, explores all judicative thinking and its products—including, therefore, rationally judicative thinking and its rational products (among them, those of the sub-scientific level). But, because *scientifically* judicative reason, in the manner characteristic of a highest level, presupposes all the lower levels of productions effected by thinking and, when taken concretely as a theme, includes them all, the reference to science, and therefore the conception of *logic as theory of science,* involves no re-striction; it simply has the advantage of directing attention to the highest final idea of judicative reason.

As a theory of science concerned with principles, logic intends to bring out *"pure" universalities, "a priori" universalities.* As already said in the Introduction, it does not intend to investigate empirically the so-called sciences that are given beforehand—the cultural formations, going by that name, which have in fact come into existence—and abstract their empirical types; on the contrary, free from every restriction to the factual (which supplies it only with points of departure for a criticism of examples), it intends to make completely clear the final ideas that hover dimly before us whenever we are actuated by a purely theoretical interest. Constantly investigating the pure possibilities of a cognitive life, as such, and those of the cognitional formations, as such, attained therein, logic intends to bring to light the essential forms of genuine cognition and genuine science in all their fundamental types, as well as the essential presuppositions by which genuine cognition and genuine science are restricted and the essential forms of the true methods, the ones that lead to genuine cognition and genuine science.

We have spoken of *genuine* cognition, *genuine* science, *genuine* method. Without exception the ideas with which logic is concerned are ideas of "genuineness." The genuine is what reason aims at ultimately—even in its decadent mode, the mode of unreason. The genuine is what is "missed" in obscurity or confusion; whereas, with clarity of goal and way and in the essential forms pertaining to such clarity, it is attained.

§6. *The formal character of logic. The formal a priori and the contingent a priori*

The universality of logic, as concerned with principles, is not simply an a priori or eidetic universality; rather it is, more particularly, a *formal* universality. Not only the narrow and vaguely bounded discipline usually called formal logic (a discipline restricted by a particular concept of the formal, with which we shall have to occupy ourselves greatly), but all logic whatever, in its universal and (as universal) its only philosophic sense, is "formal" throughout all its disciplines. We could say equally well: *Reason itself,* including theoretical reason in particular, *is a form-concept.*

To characterize the most universal and most important concept of form which is involved in these propositions, we may state the following. In a certain sense every eidetic cognition is a product of "pure" reason—*pure from all empeiria* (a characteristic likewise indicated, from another side, by the word a priori); but not every eidetic cognition is pure in a *second sense,* the one pertaining to *form as a principle.* An a priori proposition about all *sounds* as such, about sounds meant with "pure" universality, is pure only in the first sense; it is, as we may say for certain reasons, a *"contingent" a priori.* It has in the eidos *sound* a materially determinate core, which goes beyond the realm of the universality of "principles" in the most radical sense, and restricts it to the "contingent" province of ideally possible sounds. *"Pure" reason is not only above everything empirically factual, but also above every sphere of hyletic, materially determinate, essences.* It is the title for the self-contained system of pure principles that precede every hyletic, materially determinate, a priori and all the sciences concerned with such an a priori, but that, on the other hand, govern these sciences themselves as rational products—govern them, that is, with respect to form.

To acquaint us more closely with the concept of the contingent a priori, the following exposition will suffice within the bounds of our present, merely anticipatory, observations: A subjectivity as such (whether solitary or in communication) is thinkable only as having an essential form, whose highly multifarious constituents we obtain with progressive evidence when we uncover to intuition our own concrete subjectivity and then, with the aid of a free changing of its actuality into "other" possibilities of any concrete subjectivity as such, direct our regard to the invariable that can be seen throughout—that is to say: the essentially

necessary. If we stipulate, from the beginning of this variation, that the subjectivity shall always have the capacity to be and remain a "rational" and, in particular, a judicatively cognizing subjectivity, we encounter restrictive essential structures that fall under the heading of pure reason and, in particular, pure judicative reason. Such a subjectivity also involves as a presupposition a continual and essentially necessary relatedness to some hyletic components or other: as apperceptional foundations for the possible experiences that judging necessarily presupposes. Therefore, if we define the concept of form, as a principle, by the essentially necessary components of any rational subjectivity whatever, the concept *hyle* (exemplified by every "Datum of sensation") is a form-concept and not what we shall define as the opposite of this, a contingent concept. On the other hand, there is no essential requirement that a judicatively cognizing subjectivity (or a rational subjectivity of any kind) be capable of sensing colors or sounds, that it be capable of sensuous feelings having just such and such a differentia, or the like—though the concepts of such matters too can be framed as a priori (as freed from everything empirically factual). Accordingly they too have their a priori, which, however, is contingent and not an a priori of pure reason; or, as we may also say, introducing an old word that tended blindly in the same direction, it is not an "innate" a priori.

If we restrict ourselves to judicative reason, then, as pure reason, as the complete system of this *formal a priori in the most fundamental sense,* it designates at the same time the highest and widest conceivable theme of logic, of "theory of science." Consequently we may say that logic is the *self-explication of pure reason* itself or, ideally, the science in which pure theoretical reason accomplishes a complete investigation of its own sense and perfectly Objectivates itself in a system of principles. In this system pure reason or, correlatively, logic is related reflexively to itself; the self-explication of pure reason is itself a purely rational activity and comes under the very principles that thereby attain explication.

§7. The normative and practical functions of logic

The pre-eminent normative function of logic is obvious. Any a priori science is called on to exercise normative functions, with respect namely to those sciences of matters-of-fact that are subordinate to it. But logic alone is a universal norm in the highest sense and with the greatest conceivable universality. The norms applied by logic are the principles of pure reason itself and the tests of rationality as such. Its formal cognitions are the standards for measuring the extent to which ostensible science conforms to the idea of genuine science, the extent to which the single cognitions of ostensible science are genuine cognitions and its methods genuine methods—methods that, so far as their essential form is concerned, square with the formally universal norms of pure reason.

In taking on normative functions, logic also assumes functions pertaining to the practical shaping of science; and accordingly it can also be included in a logico-practical technology and perhaps combined with an empirical anthropological component. In exercising such functions, logic is related reflexively to itself, not only as a science but also normatively: as a science because, as has already been said, logic is the a priori science of all science as such and is at the same time itself a science; normatively because, in its progressive practical work, it must utilize its already-gained results as norms, going back, perhaps, to apply them to what it has already fashioned in naive evidence.

Logic *becomes* normative, it becomes practical; with a suitable change of attitude, one can convert it into a normative-technological discipline. But intrinsically it is itself not a normative discipline but precisely a science in the pregnant sense, a work of purely theoretical reason—like all the other sciences. As we were saying, a priori sciences, by virtue of being a priori, always *function* normatively and technologically; but, for that reason, they *are* sciences and not technologies. The attitude of the technologist (not the technician but the person devising a technology) is essentially different

from that of the scientist. It is a practical and not a theoretical attitude—even when the technologist incidentally runs into scientific problems and solves them in the interest of technology. His theorizing is then but a means to some (extra-theoretical) practice. It makes no essential difference that here the problem concerns, not an individual instance of practice, but a universal *sort* of practice, which is to be examined, subjected to rules, and furthered—universally, by practical reason. The situation is the same if we consider by itself the mere applying of the norm, prior to any question of a corresponding refashioning of practice. The aim is to help oneself or others "practically" in a certain manner, and not to satisfy purely theoretical interests.

To be sure, the distinction is after all a relative one: because even purely theoretical activity is indeed activity—that is to say, a practice (when the concept of practice is accorded its natural breadth); and, as a practice, it is part of the universal nexus comprising all practical activities and is subject to formal rules of universal practical reason (the principles of ethics), rules with which a *science pour la science* can hardly be compatible. But then there remains the essential difference that all sciences come under the *idea* of an interest of theoretical reason that operates *ad infinitum*. This idea, moreover, is conceived relatively to the idea of a community of scientific investigators, which goes on working *ad infinitum*, a community united in respect of activities and habitualities of theoretical reason. Here we shall mention only the working of investigators for and with one another and their criticizing of one another's results, those obtained by one investigator being taken over as works that pave the way for others, and so forth. But a life lived by single individuals and by the many according to this idea is a life compatible, for example, with the conviction that all the theoretical results thus acquired in common, and the infinite science itself, have a hypertheoretical human function; just as, in the case of the single individual, his abiding scientific vocation, with the always-intermittent exercising of it, is compatible with his other, extra-theoretical, purposes as a father, a citizen, and so forth, and must find its place within the highest practical idea, that of an all-embracing ethical life, the individual's own and the life of the open community of human beings.

§8. The two-sidedness of logic; the subjective and the Objective direction of its thematizing activity

Logic, as the science of all the logical as such and—in its highest form, which embraces all other forms of the logical—as the science of all science as such, inquires *in two opposite directions.* Everywhere it is a matter of rational productions, in a double sense: on one side, as *productive activities and habitualities;* on the other side, as *results* produced by activities and habitualities and afterwards persisting.

On the side where the results lie, we have as the theme of logic the manifold forms of judgment-formations and cognitional formations, which accrue to cognitive subjects during the performance of their thinking activities and do so, moreover, in the particular manner characteristic of a "theme." The formations accruing on the particular occasion are indeed what the thinking subject is aiming at and intends to make his abiding acquisition; while at the same time they are meant to serve him as means for gaining similar new acquisitions. At any particular time, something has come into being, not just somehow or other, but rather as the thing aimed at in his thinking action: In a particular manner the thinking subject *"directs himself" to it;* he has it before him *"Objectively."* In their higher forms, to be sure, these formations transcend the current sphere of presence to consciousness. But they remain nevertheless component parts of a more extensive, thematically encompassed "field," a peculiar realm of products generated by practice, products to which one can always "return" and by means of which one can always generate new formations: new concepts, judgments, arguments, proofs, and theories. In the *unity of a science* all such formations, and the whole field of products that have arisen within the unity pertaining to a theoretical interest, are

unitarily combined to make up an all-embracing *theory,* the systematically continuous development of which, *ad infinitum,* is the common aim of the scientists, as they work with and for one another in open community. By means of this theory the particular scientific "province" is to be made a province of systematic *cognition,* in an all-inclusive unity of cognitional formations, called theoretical truths, which are built one upon another to produce the unity-form of a truth-system.

These Objective affairs all have more than the fleeting factual existence of what comes and goes as a formation actually present in the thematic field. They have also the being-sense of abiding validity; nay, even that of Objective validity in the special sense, reaching beyond the subjectivity now actually cognizing and its acts. They remain identical affairs when repeated, are recognized again in the manner suitable to abiding existents; in documented form they have Objective factual existence, just like the other objectivities of the cultural world: Thus they can be found in an Objective duration by everyone, can be regeneratively understood in the same sense by everyone, are intersubjectively identifiable, are factually existent even when no one is thinking them.

The opposite direction of logic's thematizing activity is *subjective.* It concerns the deeply hidden subjective forms in which theoretical "reason" brings about its productions. The first question here concerns *reason in its present activity*—in other words: that intentionality, as it flows on during its living execution, in which the aforesaid Objective formations have their "origin." Stated more particularly, the effect produced by this intentionality is that, in the executing subject's thematic field, the formations generated on the particular occasion, the judgment-objectivities and cognitional objectivities, make their appearance "Objectively," with the character of generated products. While the corresponding intentionality is being executed, while it is flowing in this manner as an Objectivatingly productive living, it is "unconscious"—that is to say: it *makes* thematic, but it itself is, for that very reason and as a matter of essential necessity, non-thematic. It remains hidden, as long as it has not been uncovered by a reflection and has not thus itself become a theme, the theoretical theme of that logical research which is directed to the subjective. The subject who is straightforwardly judging or thinking in any manner (for example: generating conceptual formations, no matter how complicated) has "consciously" before him, thematically, only the formations undergoing production at that time. Everything that by itself is, in this sense, Objectively logical has, as its "subjective" correlate, the intentionalities constituting it; and, as a matter of essential necessity, there corresponds to each form of the formations a system of productive intentionality, a system that may be called a subjective form. But there is also involved the *further subjective production* by virtue of which the affair *now* actually constituted is, for the cognitive subjects (thanks to sources pertaining to their habituality), more than this momentarily thematic affair of the actual present. This production makes it possible for the constituted to be consciously intended to as something *Objective,* something abidingly valid for the corresponding subjectivity, and makes the constituted take on, in and for the cognitive community, the sense of an ideal Objectivity existing *"in itself."*

The two-sidedness of everything logical, in consequence of which the problem-groups become separated and again combined, places in the way of an explication of their true sense, and in the way of their correct organization, quite extraordinary difficulties. These, one can say, account for the fact that logic, after thousands of years, has not yet entered the steady course of a truly rational development—that it has not become, as its peculiar vocation unconditionally demanded, a science that has pressed onward to a clear consciousness of its goals and, progressing surely from stage to stage, made them actual. Nearly everything that concerns the fundamental sense of logic, of its problems and method, is infected with incomprehensibilities from this turbid source, this perpetually uncomprehended and never rightly examined Objectivity deriving from subjective production. Everything is therefore

disputed; but in the dispute nothing is clarified. Even the ideal Objectivity of logical formations and the a priori character of the logical doctrines relating to them specifically, and then again the sense of this a priori, are stricken with this same obscurity: since the ideal does indeed appear as located within the subjective sphere; it does indeed arise from this sphere as a produced formation.

Accordingly, what we have said so far about logic expresses a precursory survey and an insight yet to be confirmed by more concrete explications and, so far as appears useful, by coming to terms with historical motivations and with interpretations of logic that have arisen from them.

§9. The straightforward thematizing activity of the "Objective" or "positive" sciences. The idea of two-sided sciences

As is already plain, even from our first elucidations, the two-sidedness of everything logical *does not signify a parity of the two sides,* the Objective and the subjective. To think with simple devotedness to the matters in question is to create a coherent thematic field, which contains exclusively the pertinent products of thinking. They are what the thinkers aim at; they are results of thinking and at the same time bases for new thinking actions. The thinking itself—understood concretely as the intentionality, qualified one knows not how, in whose "synthesis" the products of thinking become constituted as "unities of sense"—still requires uncovering, which would take place in a new thinking.

The thinking of scientists is—actionally and habitually, privately and intersubjectively—coherent thinking. It has coherence by virtue of the unity of a theoretical interest and the correlative unity of the scientific province that is to be systematically explored and cognized. Whatever accrues in the process of scientific thinking, as judgment-results or cognitional results pertaining to that province, makes up an openly endless *thematic field by itself,* the expanding unity of the *science as theory,* a multiplicity of themes belonging together and thematically combined.

This thematic field is *overstepped* by reflections turned toward the subjective. In general, therefore, the scientist, because of the exclusiveness of his theoretical interest in his particular province, will not introduce the investigation of any subjective theme into his research. Thus the geometer, for example, will not think of exploring, besides geometrical shapes, geometrical thinking. It may be that shifts to the subjective focus are occasionally helpful or even necessary to what he truly has in view, namely the theory of his province; as in other far-seeing actions, so in theoretical actions the need may arise to deliberate reflectively and ask, "What method shall I try now? What premises can serve me?" But the subjective that then comes into view does not itself belong to what the science is aiming at, its proper theme, which, as a universal theory, embraces all its separate themes. The same is true of other cases where subjects and their acts are brought into scientific discourse; the subjective—the thinking or the subjects themselves who think—is not thereby introduced into the theme, into the particular scientific province and its theory. Thus it is in all *"Objective" or "positive" sciences,* which are, as a rule, the only ones we think of when speaking simply of sciences. This is because the idea of *sciences that have systematically two-sided themes,* themes that combine the theory of the scientific province systematically with a theory of the cognition of that theory, has emerged only in modern times and, moreover, so obscurely that it must still contend for its peculiar sense and its legitimacy.

The positive sciences operate exclusively on the plane of the theory that can be fashioned straightforwardly, when the theorizer directs himself to the province of cognition as his theme—fashioned, that is, by the continuous categorial forming of experiential objectivities belonging to the province, as they come within the scope of determining processes of thinking, and by the systematic connecting of the formations thus acquired, to make cognitional formations at higher and higher levels:

the openly endless, and yet systematically unitary, edifice of the scientific theory of the province.

This plane of theory delimits the themes of science, and does so to such a degree that the positive sciences make a conscious effort to frame the concept of theoretical Objectivity even more rigorously: in such a manner that positive sciences will exclude, as merely subjective, many a thing that the pre-scientifically experiencing and thinking subject finds as an Objective theme. In this manner the scientific investigator of Nature excludes "sensuous qualities." The single experiencing subject finds natural Objects as sensuously qualified, but nevertheless as Objects, as existing in and by themselves, not affected in their existence by the reflectively apprehensible acts of experiencing and of experiential thinking, neither determined nor determinable by the contents of those acts. Yet, with the effecting of an intersubjective communion of experiencing and thinking, the contents of sensuously experienced Objectivity and the descriptive concepts fitted to its contents show a dependence on the experiencing subjects; though the identity of the Objects in question nevertheless remains intersubjectively cognizable and determinable. A purely Objective science aims at a theoretical cognizing of Objects, not in respect of such subjectively relative determinations as can be drawn from direct sensuous experience, but rather in respect of strictly and purely Objective determinations: determinations that obtain for everyone and at all times, or in respect of which, according to a method that everyone can use, there arise theoretical truths having the character of "truths in themselves"—in contrast to mere subjectively relative truths.

§10. Historically existing psychology and scientific thematizing activity directed to the subjective

Though the positive sciences shut themselves off in this manner from all that belongs to the merely subjective of the experiencing and thinking of the matters in question, and do so in order to satisfy the requirements imposed by the idea of pure Object as their exclusive theme, nevertheless a particular positive science of subjects makes its appearance among them, the science of men and brutes—namely *psychology*—that makes the psychic, the specifically subjective, in these its chief theme. If this psychology were in fact the science of everything subjective, it would stand in a remarkable relationship of perfect correlation with all the sciences. All of them are subjectively produced formations; all of them get their Objective themes from hidden producings. Even the object-provinces of the sciences are there pre-theoretically, for persons investigating them, as provinces that come from subjective sources comprised in the harmonious experience that gives "those provinces" beforehand; as experienced or experienceable, they arouse the theoretical interest and take on categorial forms—among these, the forms of scientific truth, given in scientific evidence. Accordingly the universal science of the subjective would embrace every conceivable existent, precisely as something experienceable and theoretically true. It would be the science of universal subjectivity, the science in which everything that is truth—deriving from an actual or possible living, with the possibilities of experience and theory predelineated within that living itself—would receive the sense: true being. In relation to each science, as a developed and still developing production, it would be the perfectly correlative science of precisely that production. Since this psychology itself would be a science, it would be reflexively related to itself; as the science of everything subjective, it would include the science of those subjective sources by virtue of which it accomplished its own productions. And this would be repeated in it at an infinitude of levels.

Obviously none of the historically developed psychologies of ancient or modern times has ever satisfied this requirement of universality or even thought it through seriously as a problem. Without any question an anthropology and a zoology, including a psychology and a psychophysics of men and brutes, have a valid sense. But the extent to which they are capable of the indicated universal correlational tasks

concerning all the sciences and all that ever exists for us—this may be characterized as the great enigma of the modern age, with its peculiar and always freshly reattempted transcendental philosophies, critiques of knowledge, theories of knowledge, theories of the understanding, theories of reason, or whatever the chosen names may be. We ourselves shall have to consider this question more precisely, on the basis of our structural researches concerning the idea of logic. In the present context, all that matters is sharp illumination of the contrast between the "straightforward" thematizing activity of the positive sciences, which is determined by a particular object-province given beforehand by (intersubjective) experience—a province to which that activity is devoted with an exclusive interest—and, on the other hand, the thereby-excluded but still openly possible reflective thematizing, which would concern experiencing-cognizing-producing subjectivity.

§11. *The thematizing tendencies of traditional logic*

A) LOGIC DIRECTED ORIGINALLY TO THE OBJECTIVE THEORETICAL FORMATIONS PRODUCED BY THINKING

From consideration of the sciences we now pass on to *logic,* which indeed, as theory of science, has adjusted itself to the sciences as examples; and we ask how the above-described essential relationships between the Objective and the subjective work out in the historical development of logic.

Obviously, from the beginning and, indeed, up to within our times, logic had none but Objective, none but "positive," sciences—though at very different stages of development—before its eyes to guide it. Accordingly it could find, as its *first universal theme,* nothing but the *realm of thematic formations* produced by scientific thinking in relation to some Objective provinces or other that were somehow given beforehand—that is to say: judgments (with the "concepts" occurring in them), arguments, proofs, complete theories, with their modalities and the normative differences between truth and falsity. To explore all these actual and ostensible knowledge-formations with respect to their formal types and the conditions for possible truth involved by their formal types, was the first task presented.

To be sure, the logicians' naturally predominant epistemo-practical interest, their aiming at a rational production by cognitional strivings and actions, directed their regard precisely to these. But that in no way involved a revelatory penetration of constitutive intentionality, which takes place out of sight in the cognitionally striving and acting subjects; on the contrary, it involved only "a viewing of" what—in this case, as in that of any other volitive aiming and acting—goes on in the field of consciousness, as it were visibly and outstandingly, in union with the goal-setting and with the realizing genesis of the results: namely what goes on under the heading, "I am striving for such and such; I generate it; it is coming into being by the volition of my Ego." In this connection the produced formations, with their multiform constituents and articulations and the intermediate formations at various stages, are, as in any other case, what can be properly described, rather than the uniform and unvarying "I am aiming at it and realizing it member by member."

We shall discuss this important point in more detail. Here we point out, first of all, the following essential difference. Theoretical formations offer themselves, not as Ego-acts do (as transient and merely reiterable), but as *Objects* do; and that signifies: as, so to speak, seizable objectivities, steadfast under observation, always re-identifiable, and accessible to repeated observation, analysis, and description—not much otherwise than objectivities of external experience. Except that theoretical formations are not, like the latter, given beforehand and accepted passively, but rather are, as categorial objectivities, given in the first place only in consequence of theoretical action. But then they too are strictly there: first of all, as in process of construction; and then, with a reiteration of the activity, as identifiable. Thus from each judging on one's own part, at every level of complication, theoretical formations can be

taken, as its result; likewise from each actual or phantasied judging *[Urteil]* on another's part, which one performs in "following" him (and, in this case, depending on whether the judging is actual or phantasied, the formations are taken from it either as the judgments actually "made" or as possible judgments). As the objects of experience are given, in any other experiencing, so here, in "categorial experience," the categorial formations (the expression being taken very broadly in this context) are given evidently, in the manner that characterizes original intuition. Later, however, we shall learn that here, with different focusings of regard, different objectivities can become—and, for the logician, must become—identifiable, experienceable in corresponding evidences.

Thus the logician had steadfast objects as examples, to serve as substrates for "ideations"; consequently there arose the possibility of those "pure formalizations" that yield concepts of analytic-logical "forms." These forms, in turn, were similarly but even more thoroughly firm and steadfast objects, which could be described with respect to their elementary formal components and considered, moreover, operationally. Ways of modifying and of connecting forms—constructively, in reiterable operations—were given as open possibilities, ways in which one could always generate new forms from forms already given: as one does in the combinative constructing of complex judgment-forms out of simpler judgment-forms or in the free constructing of syllogistic forms out of judgment-forms. Accordingly the logician projected in advance, with formal universality, the conceivably possible forms of judgments, and of cognitions, that can be produced concretely in any conceivable province of cognition.

Understandably, therefore, even beginning logic, in its sense-investigations concerning knowledge and science *[Wissen und Wissenschaft]*, was attracted predominantly by the Objective theoretical formations; though at first, and for a long time afterward, there was no thought of limiting the theme quite consciously and expressly to pure judgment-formations and cognitional formations, which nevertheless made up the field in which the work of logic was actually being done. Once work had started in this manner, the internal consistency of the matters in question kept things going automatically. The situation, after all, is not essentially different from that obtaining in fields of research that come from any sort of experience. Once theoretical interest has become fixed on data of experience in some sphere or other, it carries on consistently. The data taken by logic, as we again emphasize, were *also,* after their own manner, data of experience, identifiable and viewable objects— whether or not it is customary to speak in this connection of experience and, indeed, even if the essential analogy between the manner in which *they* are given originally and the manner in which objects are given originally in what is generally called experience has never been grasped. And this "experience" of logical data (with its modifications as memory, "possible" experience, and the like) functions like any other as a basis for the forming of descriptive concepts and the effecting of descriptive cognitions, including, in particular, eidetic cognitions.

b) Logic's interest in truth and the resultant reflection on subjective insight

Now logic was focused, not on just any judgments, on supposed knowledge, but ultimately on *genuine* knowledge and its typical formations. In the first place, that unavoidably produced a sort of *turning toward the subjective.* The logician said something like this to himself: Genuine knowledge, truth, is seized upon in the activities of *"reason,"* in *insight*—which, once it has been exercised, can be repeated by the same subject, and likewise by any other rational subject, and remains as an intellectual possession. Propositions that are immediate objects of insight lead, in evident elementary arguments, to propositions that become evident therewith as consequent truths. A deductive theory, a genuine one, is a complex of elementary steps, built entirely with steps of *insight* and thus making up a unity of truth. Also in the case of "concrete" arguments, starting

from non-evident premises and having their hypothetical cognition-value. In their case, after all, the includedness of the conclusions, as consequences, in the premises is seen; and at the same time it is seen that the consequences would become truths, *if* the premises were to show themselves in insight as truths. Thus, in genuine science, nothing in the way of propositions or proposition-complexes occurs on the Objective side, unless it has acquired its "cognition-value"—its validity-characteristic of trueness, of hypothetical consequence, or the like—from *insights.*

In such reflections—which, as initial, obviously determine logic originally—one cannot avoid speaking continually about the *subjective,* above all about *reason* and *insight* (a word, by the way, that usually connotes an enduring accessibility to insight—an accessibility originally acquired, to be sure, by virtue of an actually operative act of insight). But, although this subjective manner of speaking presupposes a turning of regard toward the psychic, still *everything* that becomes ascertained as a *result* in science lies purely on the Objective side; and accordingly what the logician intends to bring out thematically with such reflections and treat as theory of theory, is likewise only what is Objectively logical.

It must be particularly heeded here that *the "true," or "consequent," or "non-contradictory," acquired in insight, makes its appearance as a characteristic and predicate attached to the judgment-formations themselves;* that is to say, it makes its appearance on the Objective side, and is accordingly a theme in the formal theories that are to be treated by a pure logic of significations. Everything that is "logical" in the pregnant sense—the "rational"—has these characteristics attached to it as Objective characteristics; and logic must name them expressly and seek out the conditions under which they belong to something legitimately. "Truth" is the Objective locution; "insight," "reason," is the subjective and perfectly correlative one. Similarly in the case of each particular mode among the validity-predicates. Every unitarily self-contained and unqualified scientific statement has, or claims to have, this predicate truth, as a predicate derived from insight. In the sciences, since it goes without saying and its repetition would be burdensome and useless, it is not stated, except perhaps with reference to some previous doubt or controversy. In logic, however, it is, in its relation to the bare forms of judgments, precisely the chief thematic consideration.

Frequent reflection on subjective doing is, by the way, something the sciences have in common with the other provinces of technical action. The sense of thought-formations themselves, as formations that have sprung from actions of thinking, involves reference to the corresponding acts, in their order and connection. Accordingly one can describe the formations also from the side belonging to the agent and his doing. For example: instead of saying "$a - b + b = a$," one can say, "Subtract b from a and then add b again," and so forth; or, instead of saying, "Q follows from the premises M and N," one can say, "Q can be concluded from the judgments M and N." But one has gained nothing essential by this: There is, to be sure, a reference to the more or less complex rhythm of the Ego's acts (the steps of *ego cogito); but,* properly speaking, no description of these acts themselves has been made. To count is to generate numbers, to subtract is to generate differences, to multiply is to generate products, and so forth; and, in the same way, to conclude is to generate judgment-consequences from judgments. One has one's eye on the generated products, on what one strives for and generates, and here lies what is solid and seizable; whereas the empty I-count, I-conclude, signifies no more than the conative aiming and the allowing of the products to come into being *[und die Erzeugnisse in ihrem Werden ablaufen lassen].* Naturally that is not to say that there can be no analyses or descriptions of the subjective; it is only to say that, over and above the generated products and their subjective initiation (?) *[Ablaufen]* in the mode of step-by-step actualization, an intentional subjectivity is to be explored, in which the products coming into being and those already generated are constituted as synthetic unities—a subjectivity that is not yet opened up at all by such a mere turning to the "I think."

c) Result: the hybridism of historically existing logic as a theoretical and normative-practical discipline

After all this we understand why logic, throughout its whole development up to within recent times (as long as transcendental-philosophic motives had not become radically effective upon it), necessarily had as its principal thematic sphere the field of theory, the manifold judgment-formations and cognitional formations, and why the thematizing of subjective actions of thinking, though superficially it stood out in bold relief, was completely secondary.

Yet we must not overlook the following: While we were describing the thematizing tendencies of traditional logic and how they were motivated by taking the positive sciences as a guide, we, in our reflections, had to dissect the intentional interconnections with an awareness and a sharpness that were still foreign to logic itself or to logicians who dealt with them. The thing to which we have paid particular attention, namely the Objectivity of theoretical formations as data of a specific "experience" ("categorial experience," as we called it), was far from gaining acceptance in the tradition; and even today it still has to fight for its legitimacy. One must not shun the indispensable broadening of the Object-concept to cover not only real but also irreal ("ideal") Objects; to it there corresponds the broadening of the concept of experience, which, with this amplification, retains precisely the essential property: seizing upon something itself (having of something itself, giving of something itself).*

The logicians' naturally predominant focusing on norms and on techniques of cognition, as we said above, brought thinking, as a mental doing, into the foreground for them; and thus it gave prominence to the real psychic pro-

---

*See Part II, Chapter 1, §§57–59; also *Logische Untersuchungen, II. Bd., II. Teil,* pp. 142ff., the passage introducing the concept of categorial intuition.

cess in which the irreal object, the ideal formation produced by thinking, makes its appearance at a particular time. Rules for this doing, or for the psychic subject as a subject who is active in thinking, were to be ascertained. The intrusive interest in providing norms tended understandably *to mask the ideal Objectivity of the produced formations themselves* and also to prevent the rise of a theoretical thematizing activity relating to them consciously and *purely*. And this was the case, even though the logician's work, as we saw above, dealt continually with these ideal formations, identifying them, subsuming them under form-concepts, and so forth. In spite of this, they remained thematically unseparated from the subjective. In this connection—we shall have to speak of this again—there are also objective difficulties; because the matters dealt with are not external products, but products generated inside the psychic sphere itself.

Now, however, our only concern is to gain an understanding of the essential character of historically existing logic, by means of an explication of the intentionality determining the sense of logic most originally. Briefly summarized, the first requisite was to understand the historically existing logic in respect of its hybridism, as both a theoretical and a normative-practical discipline, and in respect of the consequent hybridism of its theme as, on the one hand, the ideal significations (the categorial formations) and, on the other hand, the actions of thinking and the regulation of these by norms. But it was further requisite to understand that the theoretically seizable and solid constituent of this hybrid, the part to be found in the historically existing syllogistic theories, was essentially nothing other than a *theory of a theory,* though not grasped purely—a theory, therefore, of the produced *judgment-formations and cognitional formations* making up the field of ideal Objects. Whatever went beyond that, in locutions and thoughts relating to the subjective, brought (as we pointed out) no essentially new content but only obvious subjective variants. To this were added, though

not until a very late date (with the instituting of psychologistic or anti-psychologistic transcendental philosophy), actually new and substantial investigations of the subjective, over which, to be sure, no lucky star held sway and which, in any case, must still struggle for their true sense. These we left out of consideration; and, for the time being, we shall continue to do so. Meanwhile, guided by the insight that we have acquired for ourselves concerning the purely Objective theme of logic, and taking the original logical apophantics as our point of departure, we shall first explore the *essentially determined structures of an Objective apophantic logic*—one that is "analytic," "formal"—and shall then deal with the problems involved in ascertaining its essentially determined boundaries. Here we shall start with the modern mathematical disciplines that should likewise be characterized as "analytic" and "formal" and direct our attention to the obscure questions that concern the relationship of this "analytic" mathematics to traditional formal logic, and consequently the relationship between the idea of formal ontology and the idea of formal apophantics.

Formal Logic as Apophantic Analysis*

§12. Discovery of the idea of the pure judgment-form

From our general explanations it is already understandable that, as historically the first part of a systematically executed logic, Aristotelian analytics arose, a first commencement of a logic of theoretical formations. Within the limits imposed by focusing on this theme, it was a *"formal" logic in a particular sense;* though, even as that, it did not attain the full purity and breadth prescribed by its essence. In a survey of the (always materially determinate) judgments of life and science, the most universal groupings of judgments according to types, the perfect likenesses of form among

*FTL, pp. 48–71 (Sections 12–22).

judgments pertaining even to heterogeneous provinces, immediately came to the fore. Aristotle was the first to bring out the idea of form which was to determine the fundamental sense of a "formal logic," as we understand such a discipline today and as Leibniz already understood it in effecting his synthesis of formal logic (as apophantic) and formal analysis to make the unity of a *mathesis universalis.* Aristotle was the first, we may say, to execute in the *apophantic* sphere—the sphere of assertive statements ("judgments" in the sense expressed by the word in traditional logic)— that "formalization" or algebraization which makes its appearance in modern algebra with Vieta and distinguishes subsequent formal "analysis" from all material mathematical disciplines (geometry, mechanics, and the rest). In the materially determinate statements taken as examples, Aristotle substituted algebraic letters for the words (terms) indicating the material: that which is spoken about in the statements, that which determines judgments as judgments relating to divers material provinces or single matters. As concerning the sense, this implied that he substituted the moment "anything whatever" for each materially filled "core" in the judgments, while the remaining judgment-moments were held fast as moments of form, moments that persist without change when one changes the relatedness of the given judgment to matters—or interchanges judgments pertaining to different material spheres —at pleasure. With this taking of the materially filled cores as indeterminate optional affairs—lingually, as indeterminate terms, *S, p,* and the like—the exemplificative determinate judgment becomes converted into the universal and pure form-idea: the pure concept of any judgment whatever that has, as the case may

be, the determinate judgment-form *"S is p,"* the form "If *S* is *p,* then *Q* is *r,"* or the like.

To be sure, in Aristotle the variability of the terms is not completely free, and consequently the idea of form is not quite pure: since, as a matter of course, Aristotle relates his analytics to the real world and, in so doing, has not yet excluded from his analytics the categories of reality. For modern thinkers it was the emergence of algebra that made possible for the first time the advance to a purely formal logic; yet it seems that the Middle Ages, in the treatise *De modis significandi,* ascribed to Duns Scotus, had already attained the conception of the purely formal,* admittedly without making that insight prevail.

§13. The theory of the pure forms of judgments as the first discipline of formal logic

A) THE IDEA OF THEORY OF FORMS

The possibility of subsuming all judgments under pure concepts of configuration or form immediately suggested the thought of a descriptive classification of judgments, exclusively from this formal point of view: regardless, that is, of all other distinctions and lines of inquiry, like those concerning truth or noncontradiction. Thus one distinguished, in respect of form, simple and composite judgments; among simple forms, one distinguished those of the singular, the particular, and the universal judgment; and one went on to the complex configurations of the conjunctive, the disjunctive, the hypothetical, and the causal judgment—judgments among which the judgment-complexes called arguments or syllogisms also belonged. Furthermore one took into consider-

---

*See Martin Heidegger, *Die Kategorien- und Bedeutungslehre des Duns Scotus [Duns Scotus's Theory of Categories and Signification* (Tübingen, 1916)], particularly p. 34. Also Martin Grabmann, *"Die Entwicklung der mittelalterlichen Sprachlogik* [The development of medieval linguistic logic] *(Tractatus de modis significandi),"* *Philosophisches Jahrbuch der Görresgesellschaft,* 1922, pp. 121ff. and 199ff., and the same article, revised and expanded, in Grabmann, *Mittelalterliches Geistesleben: Abhandlungen zur Geschichte der Scholastik und Mystik* (Munich, 1926). On the *Grammatica speculativa,* previously attributed to Duns Scotus, as in fact a work by Thomas of Erfurt, see op. cit., particularly pp. 118–125.

ation the modalizations that judgments (as certainties) undergo and the judgment-forms arising from such modalizations.

Systematically consistent and clean execution of such a description would have permitted the sharp isolation of a peculiar discipline, first defined in the *Logische Untersuchungen* and characterized there as *theory of the pure forms of significations* (or *grammar of pure logic*). This theory of the pure forms of judgments is the intrinsically first discipline of formal logic, implanted as a germ in the old analytics but not yet developed. According to our explanations, it concerns the *mere possibility of judgments, as judgments,* without inquiry whether they are true or false, or even whether, merely as judgments, they are compatible or contradictory.*

B) UNIVERSALITY OF THE JUDGMENT-FORM; THE FUNDAMENTAL FORMS AND THEIR VARIANTS

To have grasped the idea of this theory of pure forms, one would have had to make clear to oneself that, when one aims at a classification of all possible judgments with regard to their forms, "fundamental forms" emerge, or a closed system of fundamental forms emerges, out of which, in accordance with a set of appertinent eidetic laws, ever new, ever more highly differentiated forms, and finally the system of all conceivable judgment-forms without exception, can be generated by construction, with the infinity of their differentiated and always-further-differentiable configurations. It is remarkable that neither this nor the fundamental logical task implicit in it was ever seen.

Stated more precisely, one would have had to make clear to oneself, first of all, that each judgment-form, no matter how it may have been acquired, is a generic universality, not only with regard to possible determinate judgments but also with regard to pure forms sub-

ordinate to it. Thus, for example, the form "*Sp* is *q*" is subordinate to the form "*S* is *p*"; and the form "(*Sp*)*q* is *r*" is subordinate in turn to "*Sp* is *q*." But each judgment-form also bears within itself a universality with a wholly different sense, since each takes in a multiplicity of possible forms as its "modifications"; for example, the form "*S* is *p*" takes in the modifications "if *S* is *p*," "then *S* is *p*," and so forth, which can occur as component parts of whole judgment-forms. The like is true of each and every form. One would have to take heed expressly that the forms standing thus as different under a universal form can be derived from it by *construction*. Furthermore, that not every form can be regarded as such a constructional differentiation of another form, but that, on the contrary, in every case we get back to *primitive forms*. Thus the form of the determining judgment, "*S* is *p*" (where *p* designates a determination, and *S* its substrate), is a primitive form, from which one can derive particularizations and modifications. It is a primitive form: more precisely, it is primitive within the highest genus of apophantic logic, "apophansis," if this genus is extended exclusively to predicative judgment-certainties, while judgment-modalities (which, in themselves, are not subsumed under this genus) become included in its scope by undergoing a transmutation into judgment-certainties with an altered content: namely certainties about possibilities, probabilities, and the like.

Naturally the genus apophansis, with its universality left without differentiation into particular forms, can likewise be designated as a form; and, with this universality, it can be included in form-constructions. Thus, letting the literal signs designate closed assertive statements, we might form "*A* and *A'*" (this being understood as the formation that a conjunctive judgment has; *in forma*, then, as the type pertaining to the corresponding generation of forms), likewise "if *A*, then *A'*," and so forth.

---

*For the thorough legitimation of the idea of this "grammar of pure logic," see *Logische Untersuchungen*, II. Bd., I. Teil, Abschnitt IV.

We might then determine the undetermined forms, A and A', first of all by primitive forms of particularizations, and go on from these to new forms, continuing thus without limit, according to any of the principles of form-construction. Such universal formation-forms as the conjunctive and the hypothetical must likewise be called fundamental forms, since they indicate *fundamental kinds of "operations"* that we can undertake with any two judgments or judgment-forms.

c) Operation as the guiding concept in the investigation of forms

If we have become attentive to the *point of view of "operation"* (with *laws of operation* in which, mathematically speaking, "existential propositions" are implicit), we shall naturally choose the concept of operation as a guide in our investigation of forms; we shall have to conduct this research in such a way that it leads to an *exhibition of the fundamental operations and their laws,* and to the *ideal construction of the infinity of possible forms* according to these laws. Consequently the fundamental forms will not stand side by side, but will be graded one above another. Thus, for example, the form "*S* is *p*" is more original than the form "*Sp* is *q*," which is an operational transformation of it, namely by the operation of converting a predicate into an attribute. But the form "*Sp* is *q*" makes its appearance in the definition of this operation, and forthwith bears within itself a new principle for the construction of forms.

Finally one will be able to take the point of view of operation so broadly that one regards even the fundamental form "*S* is *p*" as an operation: the operation of determining a determinable substrate, *S*. Similarly, one will then regard every modalization as a form-productive operation that transmutes the sense in a certain manner, so that, relative to the series of modalities, the form of the apophansis (in the original sense: assertoric certainty) is characterized for essential reasons as the primitive form, and the other forms are characterized as its variants. To be sure, one then sees

forthwith that operation, in the sense of a free changing of any judgment into another one, yields a narrower concept, since modalization is plainly not a matter of arbitrary transmutation.

This, moreover, should be emphasized expressly: *Every operative fashioning of one form out of others has its law;* and this law, in the case of operations proper, is of such a nature that the generated form can itself be submitted to a repetition of the same operation. *Every law of operation thus bears within itself a law of reiteration.* Conformity to this law of *reiterable operation* extends throughout the whole province of judgments, and makes it possible to construct reiteratively (by means of fundamental forms and fundamental operations, which can be laid down) the infinity of possible forms of judgments.

§14. Consequence-logic (logic of non-contradiction) as the second level of formal logic

From the theory of the pure forms of judgments there is differentiated, as a higher level of the formal logic of judgments, the science of the *possible forms of true judgments.* It has been developed at least in part as a historical fact, though not in a systematic context such as this, and not with purity. Indeed, the obvious procedure was to inspect the mere forms of judgments with a view to determining the extent to which, separately or as fashioned into complex forms, they involve eidetically universal conditions for possible truth or falsity, conditions that apply to all conceivable judgments with corresponding forms. Particularly in the case of argument-forms (complex proposition-forms in which valid and fallacious arguments proceed) it was evident that not all proposition-forms can be combined to make forms of genuine arguments, *actually "consequent"* arguments. It can be seen that certain argument-forms have, at the same time, the value of formal *eidetic laws,* namely as general truths about *judgment-consequence:* about the *("analytic") includedness* of judgments having such and such a form in premise-judgments having an appropriate form; likewise that other argument-forms have the value of eidetic laws of *analytic anti-consequence, analytic "contradictions"*—that properly they are forms, not of implicative arguments *[von Schlüssen]* but, so to speak, of "exclusions" *[von Ausschlüssen].*

With deeper consideration of the sense of this analytic includedness and excludedness, logical research could have attained the cognition that the *traditional formal logic is not a pure "logic of non-contradiction"* and that, with the bringing out of such a logic in its purity, a most significant *division* would have to be made *within the complex of problems and the theory of logic.*

To seek out systematically the eidetic laws that govern *just the analytic includedness and excludedness,* just the internal and external *analytic non-contradictoriness* of judgments, singly or in combination, is a *separate problem.* In such inquiry one is *not yet concerned with the truth* of judgments, but is concerned *merely* with whether the judgment-members included in a whole judgment, no matter how simple or how complex it may be, are *"compatible" with one another or contradict one another* and thereby make the whole judgment itself a contradictory judgment, one that cannot be made "properly." Reference to logical laws that, on the basis of form, govern the *mere non-contradictoriness* of judgments must be understood in a corresponding sense. It is an important insight that questions concerning consequence and inconsistency can be asked about judgments *in forma,* without involving the least inquiry into truth or falsity and therefore without ever bringing the concepts of truth and falsity, or their derivatives, into the *theme.* In view of this possibility, we distinguish a level of formal logic that we call *consequence-logic* or *logic of non-contradiction.*

The problem of non-contradiction naturally extends to the compossibility of quite arbitrarily assembled judgment-collections, so far as, in thinking of these, one normally thinks also of the connection of the judgments to form the unity of one collective judgment—which, accordingly, is meant by one judging subject in one judging process of meaning. Equally it concerns the non-contradictory unifiability of judgments in other judgment-compounds: for example, judgments that have unity as judgment-members in any ostensible theory —such unity being indeed that of a single judgment, though a very complicatedly founded judgment, which belongs to a higher order. The like is true when we descend from complex judgments to judgments that are simple in the usual sense. Any self-contained apophansis whose members are not themselves judgments that likewise have an apophantic self-containedness is accepted as simple in this sense. But even such an apophansis still has members that must be called "judicial" unities, though they are not self-sufficient unities. Therefore the difference between non-contradictory unifiability and contradiction extends also to the "simple" apophansis; and so do the laws of formal analytics.

This determines a pregnant and self-contained concept of a *"pure apophantic analytics,"* an analytics in which belong not only the whole of syllogistics, so far as its essential content is concerned, but also (as we shall show) many other disciplines, namely those of formal-mathematical "analysis." Nevertheless, as may be emphasized forthwith, the original concept of analytics as an *analytics in the broader sense* will also be indispensable; and, as our investigations progress, we shall be able to determine its peculiar sense more strictly—precisely on the basis of the narrower concept.

The fundamental concepts of pure analytics in the pregnant sense include, *as fundamental concepts of validity* (norm-concepts), *only analytic consequence and analytic contradiction;* as already said, *truth and falsity,* along with their modalities, are *not present* among them. This must be rightly understood: They are not present as fundamental concepts pertaining to the *thematic* sphere. Therefore, in this pure analytics, they play only the role that is theirs in all the sciences, so far as all sciences strive for truths and consequently talk about truth and falsity; but that is not to say that truth and falsity belong among the "fundamental concepts" of every science, the concepts pertaining to the proper essence of its particular scientific *province*.

§15. Truth-logic and consequence-logic

Inquiry for formal laws of possible *truth* and its modalities would be a higher logical inquiry, *after* the isolation of pure analytics. If a logic restricts itself to the bare forms of the significations of statements—that is, the judgment-forms—what means does it have of becoming a genuine logic of truth? One can see forthwith that *non-contradiction* is an essential condition for possible *truth,* but also that mere analytics becomes converted into a *formal truth-logic* only by virtue of a *connection* between these intrinsically separable concepts, a connection that determines an eidetic law and, in a logic, *must be formulated separately.* More about that later. For the present, let us restrict ourselves to the domain of pure apophantic analytics.

§16. The differences in evidence that substantiate the separating of levels within apophantics. Clear evidence and distinct evidence

A) Modes of performing the judgment. Distinctness and confusion

Mere predelineation of the separations with which the last sections were concerned, separations that must be made in formal logic, is not enough. There is need of more penetrating substantiations, which explicate the correspondingly differentiated evidences; only with such substantiations, moreover, can an actual insight into the necessity and the scope of these separations be opened up.

A judgment can be given as evidently the same judgment in very different manners of subjective givenness. It can make its appearance as something completely vague that comes to mind or perhaps as the completely vague signification of a statement read, understood, and believingly accepted. In such cases not the slightest bit of an *explicit performance belonging to judicative spontaneity* need take

place: not the slightest bit of an explicit subject-positing, of a positing-thereupon as predicate, of a passing on relatingly to another Object, which is posited separately, or of any like process. If the "vaguely," "confusedly," *judging process of meaning* something that comes to mind is followed by such a process of *explicit judging,* then we say, on the basis of the synthesis of fulfilling identification that comes about: The confused meaning or opinion *"becomes distinct";* now, for the first time, something is *"properly judged";* and the judgment, which previously was meant only expectantly, now is *properly* and itself *given.*

Similarly in the case of *reading* or *hearing.* In this case we have, it is true, a *sensuous unity* and mutual congruity of the seen or heard *verbal signs* in their *sensuous configuration;* but, in ordinary reading, *we by no means have, combined with that, an accompanying articulation of actual thinking, of thinking produced from the Ego, member by member, in synthetic activity.* Rather, this course of thinking proper is *only indicated* (by the passively flowing synthesis of the sensuous verbal sounds) as a course of thinking *to be* performed.

Let us examine the situation somewhat more closely.

The verbal sounds have their indications, which, in themselves, refer interdependently to one another and are built one on another. The sounds conjoin to make the unity of a word-formation, which in turn consists of relatively self-contained formations. Each of these is bearer of a unity of indication; and the whole is a self-contained unity, which has noetically the phenomenological characteristic of associative self-containedness and on the parallel side (noematically) the phenomenological characteristic that consists in the self-containedness of an indicated "significational" unity, built correspondingly out of indicated formations.

Now, on the significational side, the indicated formations, *the judgments themselves,* can make their appearance in the *"evidence" of a progressive fulfillment of the indicating intentions*—that is, in the manner that distinguishes judgments proper, *judgments that are not only indicated but at the same time gener-ated in originary activity; or,* as happens in passive reading, they can be *indicated in an empty manner.*

Here we have a particular case of a quite universal regularity. Within every species of *empty consciousness* the following difference in the empty intendedness can occur: The con-sciousness can flow in an internally unseparat-ed manner, in such a manner that it does *not* have particular empty meanings as its mem-bers; or else as an articulated, articulatedly ex-ercised, empty consciousness. For example, I may be non-intuitively conscious of, and even paying attention to, the street in front of my house "confusedly, all at the same time"; on the other hand, perhaps subsequently, I may be conscious of it in explicitly "going through" it, as, in an articulative manner, I become con-scious of the windings of the street, the trees and houses along it—but still non-intuitively or perhaps with some points where members emerge momentarily as intuited. Thus a non-articulated empty consciousness can become converted into a "corresponding" articulated empty consciousness, the confusedly meant sense-content (while entering into identify-ing coincidence of the sort peculiar to "expli-cation") becoming "spread out" as the *expli-cate,* the meaning proper of the previously con-fused unitary content.

The same is true in the particular case of indicated judicial significations, whether they are the significations of (one's own or anoth-er's) actually given judgings or those of judg-ings intended to in phantasy as possible. In this connection the following is to be noted: In understanding another's judgings, I "fol-low"; and this, the mode understanding-in-following-another (and perhaps judging *with* him), is to be carefully distinguished from the judging that is originally one's own and from the different modes of this: from the judging that is now being done actively, and likewise from one's own past, but confusedly "reawak-ened," judging, which is only "still in force," and so on.

Accordingly we have to make a distinction that, in a certain manner, cuts across these: We

have to distinguish, on the one hand, a *non-explicit judgment,* indicated by a sentence that makes its appearance explicitly, and, on the other hand, a corresponding *explicit judg-ment* or, as the case may be, a subsequent explication with identification of the meant.

But we have to distinguish two cases of making distinct: besides the one to which we have paid exclusive attention up to now—namely the case in which the distinct explicate is *non-contradictory* and simply identifiable <with the confusedly meant>—we must note the case in which the explicate is *contradic-tory.* In witnessing non-contradictory coinci-dence, I see that the explicated is the same as the unexplicated, or that what was meant by the judger in the earlier confused meaning is merely made distinct. In the contrasting case, that of contradiction, the unity of the con-fused total meaning, as a *unitary belief,* is presupposed. Now, as explication progresses, this or that newly appearing *particular be-lief* can undergo cancellation, annulment, by the particular beliefs that have already been exercised explicitly and remain firmly in force. When that occurs, the underlying total belief, the one that is being explicated, forthwith and necessarily assumes the characteristic of nullity. What has happened now to the coinci-dence of identity between the total explicand and the total explicate? Obviously we must say: With the cancellation, the belief that has suffered this cancellational modification is still there in a certain manner, as a belief hav-ing this sense—no longer, indeed, as a belief now actually exercised by the Ego or root-ed in him as his continuingly accepted con-viction, but still in his consciousness as his *earlier* belief, with the whole sense in its sense-articulations and the corresponding dox-ic positings.

If it is a matter of another's judging, then, in case I do not believe too, I have the "mere idea" of the other's belief that has such and such a content: I have a presentation *[Vergegen-wärtigung]* analogous to a memory of some past belief of my own "in which I no longer join" but which I nevertheless accept now, in memory, as my previously exercised believing. My judgment—which I made *just now* but must reject upon explication, which therefore, from this moment on, is no longer my judgment now but only my just-past judgment—now has, according to the explication, such and such an explicit sense; and the situation is the same in the case of my *earlier* past judgment and similar in the case of the other's appresented judgment. In this connection it is to be noted that, throughout the cancellational change, there continues to be a coincidence of identity, which concerns the mere judgment-"material." The cancellation alters nothing in the judgment that is presentiated retentionally, or recollectively, or in the manner characteristic of empathy; and, if I explicate what is implicit in it, then the judgment presentiated in one of those manners coincides with the explicate, even though, while explicating, I make my cancellation. Naturally that is not to say that the other subject or I knew beforehand what explication would yield as a distinct proposition; otherwise no one could overlook contradictions, whether immediate or mediate.

After these clarifications we understand the essential difference between the *vague or "confused" manners of judging [Urteilsweisen]* and the *"distinct"* ones and can see at once that there is *no* question of whether judgings *[Urteile]* have *evidence* (intuitiveness) *with regard to their predicatively formed affair-complexes [hinsichthich ihrer Sachverhalte]* or not. On the one side, *within vagueness itself,* the difference that is so important in relation to verbal thinking emerged for us: Even the sensuousness of the verbal sounds and of their articulations can be vague; then again there can be sharp articulation in this respect and, with it, an *articulation of the indications.* But even then the very important *distinctness of the judicative meanings themselves is lacking:* They are indeed believings and to that extent judgings; yet they are not "proper" judgings.

In the case of verbal judging, an explicit performance of the judging, concurrent with the

indications, is called with good reason *"judging* actually and *properly":* because it alone has the essential characteristic of the originariness in which the judgment is given originaliter, given as the judgment itself—in that (this being the same thing here) the judgment is built up "syntactically" in the judger's actual action proper. The following is only a different expression: Explicit judging, *"distinct" judging, is the evidence appropriate to the "distinct judgment,"* as the *ideal objectivity* that becomes constituted originarily in such a synthetic action, and identified in the repetition of such an action.

This evidence is an original emerging of the judgment as it itself, but not yet an evidentially experiencing <act of> *seizing upon and regarding it thematically.* Subsequently what has become constituted in this evidence, in this polythetic action, is graspable "monothetically," in one grasping ray; the polythetic formation becomes an object.*

Naturally confusion and distinctness of judging can be intermingled; as they are if, when we are reading, we actually and properly perform a few judgment-steps and -sequences, and then let ourselves be carried along for a while by the mere indications belonging to the word-formations—which in turn, as we said, can have their own distinctness or indistinctness, of quite a different sort.†

b) Distinctness and Clarity

But there is also a mingling of another sort and therefore, with appropriate purification, another important contrast for us to take into consideration: namely the mingling of *"distinctness"* and *"clarity,"* and the purely apprehended difference between them.

Two evidences become separated here. First, the evidence wherein the *judgment itself, qua judgment,* becomes itself given—the judgment that, as itself given, is called also a distinct judgment, taken from the actual and proper

*Cf. *Ideen,* pp. 247f. [English translation, pp. 335ff.]
†On this whole exposition cf. Appendix II.

judgment-performing. Second, *the evidence wherein *that* becomes itself given *which the judger wants to attain "by way of" his judgment*—the judger, that is, as wanting to *cognize,* which is the way logic always conceives him.

To judge explicitly is not *per se* to judge with *"clarity":* Judging with "clarity" has at once *clarity of the affairs,* in the performance of the judgment-steps, and *clarity of the predicatively formed affair-complex* in the whole judging *[im ganzen Urteil].* An unclear and a clear judging can judge one and the same judgment; thus evidence of the self-identity of the judgment can extend throughout essentially different modes of givenness. But only a *judging with full clarity* can be *actual present cognition;* and, as such, it is a *new evidence,* pertaining to a givenness originaliter of the affairs themselves, of the predicatively formed affair-complex itself, at which one aims in the judging that strives toward cognition—even where the judging is still quite unclear, intuitionally quite unfulfilled.

c) Clarity in the Having of Something Itself and Clarity of Anticipation

But here the differences are again ramified, since "clarity" may designate either judging in the mode of the judging that gives its meant affair-complex *itself*—that is, what one usually has in mind as *evident judging*—or else judging in the mode of a judging that makes intuited in that it *prefigures* the meant affair-complex. In the latter case, what is *itself* given is not the predicatively formed affair-complex but precisely a prefiguration, an *intuitional* anticipation, yet to be confirmed by the having of the affair-complex itself. Perfect clarity signifies, in the one case, clarity of "seeing," of "seizing upon," in the actual and proper sense: so that the predicatively formed affair-complex and the affairs entering into it—they themselves—are seized upon; in the other case, perfectly prefigurative clarity of the goal not yet actualized but only striven toward in judging. Here the cognitional striving tends *from "confusion" toward distinctness;* and, if the latter yields a still imperfectly intuitional judgment or, worse yet, a judgment completely devoid of intuition, despite being constituted explicitly, then the striving tends *through* this judgment, *perhaps at first toward only a prefiguration* of the cognitional goal. The phenomenon of transition to synthetic coincidence is then called, in the usual sense of the word, *clarification* of the judgment qua meaning or opinion (making one's meaning clear to oneself). The cognitional striving, however, has not thereby reached its goal; it tends farther, toward that *other clarity,* toward *evidence as the having of the meant itself,* the final goal.

These two modes of clarity have their degrees of perfection, with the appertinent ideas of perfect obscurity and perfect clarity.* Moreover, with the transition to clarity—accordingly, among "clarifications"—those cases become isolated in which only single parts of what has become posited acquire clarity, or can acquire it: because, though they indeed combine to make up either a clear picture or

*To speak of a "limit" rather than an idea of clarity would not always be appropriate, though limit is the word that first comes to mind. Not always should one think of something like a *limes.* Perfect evidence of external experience, for example, is a regulative idea in the Kantian sense. External experience is, a priori, never a perfect giving of anything itself; but, as long as external experience goes on with consistent harmony, it bears within itself, as an intentional implication, the idea of an infinite self-contained system of possible experiences that we, starting from *de facto* experience, could have gone through, or could go through now or in the future—experiences such that, as harmonious continuations of *de facto* experience, they would have shown (or would show) what the physical thing is, "in and of itself," besides what it has already shown itself to be. As the correlate of this phenomenologically clarifiable infinite anticipation (which, as an infinite anticipation, has an evidence of its own) the physical thing existing in itself is, for its part, an idea, one that rightly guides the thinking done in natural science and enables such thinking to progress by degrees of approximation, each having its relative evidence. For our purposes we can content ourselves with a crude initial description of "clarity." (On the concept of the physical thing as an idea in the Kantian sense, cf. *Ideen,* pp. 390ff. [English translation pp. 411ff.].)

an evidently given affair-complex "itself," they do so in such a fashion that this, which has become intuited, does not fulfill the judging intention but, on the contrary, annuls it—in the manner appropriate to an impossibility, or else (in the other case) to an "untruth," that becomes evident.

§17. The essential genus, "distinct judgment," as the theme of "pure analytics"

Pure apophantic analytics, in our pregnant sense, has as the superordinate concept determining its province the concept of the *judgment:* the judgment *proper,* which derives its being-sense originaliter from the explicit properness of the judgment-performing and from that alone. The cognitional striving—which often tends *through* a merely explicit judging and which the logician (with his interest in scientific judging—correlatively, scientific judgments as judgments aimed in the direction of truth as cognition) has pre-eminently in mind—remains quite beside the question in the sphere of pure analytics; it is abstracted from. The identical judgment—whether clarified or even at all clarifiable, whether or not it can be converted into cognition, provided only that it is, or can be, derived actually *from distinct evidence*—that is the theme.

Like all logic as an a priori science, pure analytics has to do, not with actual judgments—that is to say, judgments actually made sometime and somewhere—but with a priori possibilities, to which all corresponding actualities are subordinated in an easily understood sense. If the logician, in order to obtain eidetic universality in pure analytics, must begin with examples, which he uses as a basis for seeing essences, he can take actual judgments of his own; on the other hand, he can take other persons' judgments, which he perhaps rejects entirely but which, in following and understanding them in a proper quasi-performing, he nevertheless grasps evidently as possible judgments. But he can likewise project himself in-

to a phantasy-world and become immersed in a judging (his own or another's) within it—provided only that he produces the variant of distinct evidence that has the significance of evidence of possible judgments as possible. Thus the *purely* analytic logician has the *essential genus, distinct judgment,* with its sphere of possible judgments, as his *province.*

§18. The fundamental question of pure analytics

The question now is: While remaining *entirely within* this province, what can we state about possible distinct judgments *in forma,* after the antecedent logical discipline, the theory of pure forms (which, in any case, contains the forms of distinct judgments), has constructed the multiplicity of possible forms and placed it at our disposal?

Restricted as we are to what appertains to the own-essentiality of judgments—that is, the constituent properties belonging to them *as* judgments—we can expect, in addition to the own-essentiality explicated by the theory of forms, only relationships founded a priori on the own-essentiality of judgments. And we do in fact encounter here relationships with which we are acquainted and which belong a priori purely to distinct judgments as distinct: *consequence* (includedness); *inconsistency* (analytic contradiction, excludedness); and the *tertium,* judgment-compatibility, which is neither one nor the other—*empty non-contradiction,* as the unifiability of judgments that "have nothing to do with one another."

On closer inspection we discover that what has just been said applies even to the *judgment-members* of apophantic wholes—namely as members posited, or positable, with distinctness. They too, as we indicated in advance,* are *"judgments" in the broader sense* (but not self-sufficient ones), since, when cognition is the goal, they are destined to become judgment-members of apophantic wholes (judgments in the pregnant sense), and only thus do they acquire cognitional significance. These

*See §14.

judgments *in an unusually amplified sense*—which shall henceforth determine our concept of the judgment—also stand in the above-indicated fundamental analytic relationships: As standing in consequence-relationships, they can demand or exclude one another; and, in case they are mutually exclusive, they are incompatible in the unity of a whole judgment.

Since, as closer consideration shows, all pure analytic relationships are relationships in which different judgments—we are referring exclusively to judgments falling under the concept of the distinct judgment, the judgment proper—either go together to form the unity of one judgment or else are impossible in such a unity, the *fundamental question of pure analytics* can be formulated as follows:

When, and in what relations, are any judgments—as judgments, and so far as mere form is concerned—possible within the unity of one judgment?

Naturally they are thus possible, only as either standing in a consequence-relation or unrelated in respect of a possible consequence.

"Non-contradiction" therefore signifies the possibility that the judger can judge distinct judgments *within the unity* of a judgment performable with distinctness. In this connection it should be noted that even mere judging *together* involves a judgment-unity, a unity of co-positedness.

In formal and pure analytics the inquiry concerns judgment-*forms:* Which forms can be known, and known a priori, to be *universal* forms pertaining to the performing of a distinct judging; and which can be known not to be such forms? In that question the following is included: Which forms of judgment-combinations at any level are a priori forms of unitary judgments that are distinctly evident as properly performable?

§19. Pure analytics as fundamental to the formal logic of truth. Non-contradiction as a condition for possible truth

In these researches, then, we must never go outside the proper essence of judgments or judgment-forms, never go beyond distinct evidence. But we go beyond this a priori sphere,

as soon as we ask *questions concerning truth* or as soon as, with regard to the objects taken at first only as distinct judgments, we ask questions concerning their adequation to the affairs themselves: in short, as soon as we bring the concept of truth into our theme. The predicate truth does indeed relate to judgments and only to judgments, whether we take the above-characterized narrower judgment-concept (the concept of apophansis) or the broader one as our basis. But, as long as we restrict ourselves to merely distinct evidence and what is identifiable in it under the name judgment, although every contradiction (every *analytic countersense*) is indeed excluded, an opening remains for every *material countersense* and for every other untruth. After all, we are abstracting from every effect produced by clarification, by resorting to material possibility or to truth; we are abstracting, in other words from all questions of verification.

What then does it signify, to seek formally universal eidetic insight concerning possible judicial truth? It obviously signifies phantasying possible judgments as possibly undergoing verification, as possibly standing in a relationship of adequation to the corresponding judgments that give the supposed affairs themselves. *Now* the judgments are thought of from the very beginning, not as mere judgments, but as judgments pervaded by a dominant *cognitional striving,* as meanings that have to become *fulfilled,* that are not objects by themselves, like the data arising from mere distinctness, but passages to the "truths" themselves that are to be attained.

If, in this manner, one exchanges the theoretical focusing on mere judgments for the *focusing on cognition,* on the predicatively formed affair-complexes that are judgingly cognized or, correlatively, on the verifying adequation, then one grasps forthwith, as an eidetic insight, that whatever is incompatible in the unity of a distinct judgment is incompatible also in the truth, or that a contradiction in the mere judgments of course excludes the possibility of adequation. *Truth* and falsity are predicates that can *belong only to a judgment that is distinct* or can be made distinct, *one that can be performed actually and prop-*

erly. Logic has never made clear to itself that *this* concept of the judgment is at the basis of the old thesis that truth and falsity (in the original sense) are predicates of judgments. *Thus, in a mediated fashion, a pure analytics, by virtue of its essence, is at the same time a fundamental part of a formal logic of truth.* The division of the universe of judg-ment-forms into those that are law-forms belonging to consequence, those that are law-forms belonging to inconsistency, and those that, as standing outside both classes, are non-contradictory in the "trivial" sense (as the mathematician would express it), acquires immediate significance for the possibility of adequation or truth. Any *consequence-relationship of judgments,* if it can be effected with intuitiveness, becomes a *consequence-relationship of truths* or of material possibilities. Any contradiction, on the other hand, excludes from the start all questions of adequation; it is *a limine* a falsity.

§20. The principles of logic and their analogues in pure analytics

The separation of a pure consequence-logic from truth-logic results in a two-sidedness that also extends to the so-called principles of traditional logic—that is, the principles explicating the concepts truth and falsity.

The *double principle of contradiction and excluded middle,* as a principle of truth-logic, says the following:

"If a judgment is true, then its contradictory opposite is false"; and "of two contradictory judgments, one is necessarily true"; combining the two propositions: "any judgment is exclusively one or the other, true or false."

The *analogue* of these propositions in consequence-logic is a principle that appertains to the essence of judgments proper (judgments that are themselves given in distinct evidence). It reads:

If two judgments are contradictory, it is not the case that both are possible as judgments proper, that both can become given in distinct evidence; it is not the case that both have ideal "mathematical existence." Nevertheless one of them has it; one of them can become given in distinct evidence.*

The *principles that originally connect truth and consequence* must also be reckoned among the highest truth-principles of apophantic logic. Traditional logic offers them in the impure form of the *modus ponens* and the *modus tollens.* Here too we have the same analogy. Already, in the sphere of mere analytic consequence-relationships, there are a *modus ponens* and a *modus tollens,* which, naturally, say nothing about truth or falsity thematically, but rather appertain, as a particular consequence-law, purely to the essence of judgments proper and to the relationships of analytic consequence peculiar to these. Solely in this form are the *modus ponens* and the *modus tollens* a genuine <purely analytic> logical *principle.* This principle reads:

"N" follows analytically from two judgments of the forms, "If *M,* then *N"* and *"M."* In the same manner, "Not *M"* follows from two judgments of the forms, "If *M,* then *N"* and "Not *N."*

The corresponding *truth-principle* then reads:

If an immediate relationship of total analytic antecedent and total analytic consequent obtains between any two judgments, *M* and *N,* then the truth of the antecedent entails the truth of the consequent, and the falsity of the consequent entails the falsity of the antecedent.

We have introduced the phrases "total antecedent" and "total consequent" to indicate

---

*It may be that the intent of this paragraph would be indicated less misleadingly as follows.

A judgment in which two mutually contradictory judgments are conjoined is not possible as a judgment proper; it cannot become given as a possible judgment in distinct evidence; it does not have ideal "mathematical existence." But at least one of any two mutually contradictory judgments has such "existence"; at least one of them can become given as a possible judgment in distinct evidence.

For a justification of the main changes involved in this rendering, see §14, *supra,* the first sentence in the fourth paragraph. —Translator's note.

the *immediacy* of the relationship. We understand by these phrases nothing but the actual members of a relationship of immediate consequence, no matter how they may be divisible afterwards. It is only as parts of total antecedents and total consequents that the component premises and the component consequents determine consequence-relationships, which therefore are already *mediate.* If, in one of the consequent-wholes (which is the total consequent, only as being the complete whole), a single consequent is false, it immediately determines the falsity of the total consequent, and only thus the falsity of the total premise.

When applied to the above-stated *modus ponens* and *modus tollens*—understood as a principle of immediate pure consequence-relationships—the principle laid down by us yields immediately the correct modes belonging to truth-logic:

If the antecedent in a hypothetical judgment is true, its consequent is true; if the consequent is false, so is the antecedent. Or, put formally:

If, at the same time, "If *M,* then *N*" and *"M"* are true (if they "hold good" at the same time), then *"N"* is true. If, at the same time, "If *M,* then *N*" and "Not *N*" are true, then "Not *M*" is true (or, equivalently, *"M"* is false).

As for *mediacies* of analytic consequence: In the first place, it is a pure law of analytic consequence-relationships (pertaining therefore to "mere," but distinct, judgments and prior all questions concerning their possible truth), that *an immediate analytic consequent of an immediate analytic consequent is itself an analytic consequent of the antecedent;* whence it follows, as itself a consequence, that a consequent with any degree of mediacy is also a consequent of the antecedent. If we combine this law with our truth-principle concerning immediate analytic consequence-relationships then it follows—and, indeed, with mere analytic consequence—that this principle, when broadened, retains its validity for analytic consequences having any degree of mediacy.

§21. The evidence in the coinciding of "the same" confused and distinct judgment. The broadest concept of the judgment

If we cast a backward glance at *"confused" judgments,* which we have contrasted with judgments in the pregnant sense belonging to analytics (judgments as distinct), we see that, in the identification of "confused" judgments, each with the corresponding distinct judgment, yet a *third evidence* is concealed, by virtue of which a *third concept of the judgment* receives being-sense. With the transition, with the making distinct to oneself of what one truly meant in the vague judging process of meaning (what was truly said by oneself or by another, what was truly thought in having something vaguely come to mind)—with this transition the distinct judgment becomes given as an *evident mere explication of the true sense or meaning.* There comes to pass a coincidence of identity belonging to an originally peculiar type, which indicates a *fundamental type of "evidence."* This evidence, like any other (any "experience" in the widest conceivable sense), has its degrees of perfection and its idea—here indeed an ideal limit* of perfection, at which the synthetic coincidence would in fact be absolutely perfect.

These two manners of judging *[Urteilsweisen]*—with their respective correlates, the *confused judgment* and the *distinct judgment* themselves—obviously have *a relationship similar to that between distinct but empty* (or else imperfectly intuitive) judging and *distinct* judging *with insight,* the judging in which the possible being, or the true being, of the affairs aimed at in cognitional judging is itself given in insight. Confused judging bears within itself—not always, but (as we have already said) in the nexus of a theoretical interest—an *aiming,* which is directed to the distinct judgment and which, if it attains this, becomes *fulfilled* therein. Now, in the case of a clarifying fulfillment-synthesis, a focusing of regard

*Cf. §16 c, p. 253, note, *supra.* —Translator's note.

and an identification are possible, by virtue of which an *empty* judgment and a *full* judgment become identified, *merely as judgments,* and gain an objectivity of their own as the *same* judgment; and the like is true of the parallel fulfillment-synthesis that effects the coincidence of a *confused* and a *distinct* judgment. Or, to put it differently: Just as the cognition, the having of the predicatively formed affair-complex itself, is *also* intrinsically a distinct judgment (as truly a distinct judgment as the corresponding empty judgment is), so the judgment with vagueness and the judgment with distinctness are "the same judgment." That is not to say that every confused judgment admits of being converted into "the same" distinct judgment—any more than every distinct judgment admits of being converted into a material insight, whether as a possibility or as a truth.

The *broadest concept of the judgment* is therefore the one that is unaffected by the differences among confusion, distinctness, and clarity, or that consciously abstracts from these differences. When this concept is taken as a basis, there corresponds to each insightfully cognitive judgment, and to each distinct judgment (in view of the essential possibility—and, genetically, the constant necessity—of its becoming confused), a like judgment, or rather the same one, in the confused mode; and therefore the concept of the confused judgment embraces, in a certain manner, all judgments in the broadest sense, including those that can be made distinct and those that can be made clear.

§22. The concept defining the province belonging to the theory of apophantic forms, as the grammar of pure logic, is the judgment in the broadest sense

The importance of this discrimination of the third evidence and its correlative, the new and broadest concept of the judgment, lies in our having now acquired the basis for understanding the province belonging to the theory of the pure forms of judgments. Obviously the concept defining that province is the judgment in the broadest sense; and all the laws of form that go to make up the theory are tied

to the proper essence of *these* judgments. As confused, every judgment is possible that, as distinct, is impossible; and again, as distinct, every judgment is possible that, as an evident cognition, is impossible. In the theory of forms, the free construction of forms knows as yet no restraining contradictions. The whole support of form-construction is *speech,* with its well-differentiated indications, its references to sense, which attach to the sensuously differentiated signs and their sensuous configurations. And it is therefore not without reason that the theory of the forms of significations was characterized in my *Logische Untersuchungen* as the "grammar of pure logic." In a certain manner, furthermore, it is also not without reason that people often say that formal logic has let itself be guided by grammar. In the case of theory of forms, however, this is not a reproach but a necessity—provided that, for guided by grammar (a word intended to bring to mind *de facto* historical languages and their grammatical description), guidance by the grammatical itself be substituted. Distinctly understanding a statement and framing it as a possible judgment—this can and often does signify a distinct grasping of the *word*-sequences (accompanied by an internal explicit following, in a quasi-speaking) and also of their *reference-articulations,* with which there accrues the unity of a judgment, confused and yet articulated in a definite form. Thus we can understand quite definitely and articulatedly: "No quadrangle has four angles," or "All *A's* are *B's,* including some that are not *B's,*" or the like. Such examples too pass muster in the "grammar of pure logic"; and thus all forms of contradictory judgments belong in the system of forms. Without the definite articulation of vague judgments by means of the sensuous articulation of verbal signs, no theory of forms, no logic whatever, would be possible—and, of course, no science either.

By these analyses the sense of the threefold stratification of formal logic, briefly characterized in §§13–15, has been clarified from the most original sources, and the essential necessity of this stratification has been established. Up to now, this stratification has remained foreign to logic; only the isolation of a theory of pure forms had already been effected in the *Logische Untersuchungen;* in the present context, however, the separation has been established on incomparably deeper grounds. Needless to say, our separation of the formal logic of non-contradiction from the formal logic of truth is something fundamentally and essentially new, however familiar its wording may be to everyone. For the words in question meant something entirely different, namely the distinction between, on the one hand, all the problems of formal logic, which, as formal, leave out all the non-formal "material of cognition," and, on the other hand, the somehow broader problems (broader in a sense that was not exactly clear) to be propounded by a logic— problems that take into account precisely this non-formal material: for example, questions concerning the possibility of a cognition of real actuality or the possibility of fashioning truths about the real world.

The Transcendental Grounds of Logic*

§56. The reproach of psychologism cast at every consideration of logical formations that is directed to the subjective

Let us begin by considering the demand that logical researches be *two-sided,* a demand that we stated in our preparatory considerations,† but without a sufficient clarification of the thematizing activity directed to the subjective. This demand was stated as quite universal and therefore as valid in the case of the logic that is first in itself, namely analytic logic. *The sense and the legitimacy of this thematizing of the subjective by logic*—a thematizing that, to say it forthwith, will not claim the significance of a separate logical discipline, to be set apart from analytics as directed to the Objective and ideal—are now in question.

But here at the entrance stands the bogy of

psychologism. Against the demand for logical researches directed to the subjective, an appeal is made to the first volume of my *Logische Untersuchungen* (which bears the significant title, *"Prolegomena zur reinen Logik"* [Prolegomena to *Pure* Logic]); and the objection is raised that the *"Prolegomena"* were intended to effect the radical elimination of everything psychological from the theme of logic, first from that of traditional logic and then from that of logic as amplified to become the full *mathesis universalis.* The empiricism that had become dominant (anti-Platonism in its historical origin) was blind to the peculiar Objectivity of all ideal formations; everywhere it re-interpreted them psychologistically as the concomitant psychic activities and habitualities: This was true, in particular, respecting those objectivities (irreal, according to their own sense) which—as statements, as judgments, as truths, as arguments, proofs, and theories, and as categorial objectivities that occur as formed within all these—make up the thematic province of logic. The judgments of which logic speaks in its laws are not the mental judgment-processes (the judgings); the truths are not the mental evidence-processes; the proofs are not the subjective-psychic provings; and so forth.

The theory of cardinal numbers (which, as we know, is itself a part of logic) has to do, not with mental processes of collecting and counting, but with numbers; the theory of ordered sets and ordinal numbers has to do, not with mental processes of ordering, but with ordered sets themselves and their forms; and, in like manner, syllogistics does not have to do with the psychic processes of judging and inferring. The same is true of the other Objective sciences. No one would designate as the province of natural science the psychic processes of experiencing Nature and thinking about it, rather than Nature itself. Here the psychologistic temptations, to which recent logic had yielded almost universally, did not exist. And, according to all this, every thematizing of the

*FTL, pp. 151–174 (Sections 56–67).
†See §8.

subjective (instead of which most people will immediately say "psychological thematizing") seems to be excluded for logic, as it is for every other Objective science (except human and animal psychology). The subjective belongs in the province, not of logic, but of psychology.

But then what about our demand that correlative investigations of the subjective be included in logic? Is it not on a par with the corresponding demand in the case of any other science?

Soon after publication of the *Logische Untersuchungen* the reproach was cast that the phenomenological investigations demanded there under the name "clarification" of the fundamental concepts of pure logic, investigations which the second volume attempted to block out in broad outline, signified a relapse into psychologism.

It is noteworthy that readers regarded the *"Prolegomena zur reinen Logik"* as an unqualified overcoming of psychologism and failed to take notice that nowhere in that volume was psychologism pure and simple (as a *universal* epistemological aberration) the theme. Rather the discussion concerned *a psychologism with a quite particular sense,* namely the psychologizing of the irreal significational formations that are the theme of logic. The obscurity still generally prevalent today concerning the problem of a universal epistemological psychologism, an obscurity that affects the fundamental sense of the whole of transcendental philosophy (including so-called "theory of knowledge") is something that, at the time, I myself had not entirely overcome; though precisely the "phenomenological" investigations in the second volume, so far as they paved the way to a transcendental phenomenology, opened up at the same time the necessary avenues to the setting and the radical overcoming of the problem of transcendental psychologism.

Thus it is very necessary to go into detail again concerning the *particular problem of psychologism* treated in the *"Prolegomena."* But we intend, not to confine ourselves to our earlier presentations, which need improvement in particular points, but rather to give the problem a purer form and also set it in more general contexts, which will provide a transition to the clarification of the necessary sense of a "two-sidedly" inquiring logic, one that is, in the genuine sense, philosophic. Our chief purpose is to show that a logic directed straightforwardly to its proper thematic sphere, and active exclusively in cognizing that, remains stuck fast in a naivete which shuts it off from the philosophic merit of radical self-understanding and fundamental self-justification, or, what amounts to the same thing, the merit of being most perfectly scientific, the attainment of which is the raison d'être of philosophy, above all as theory of science.

§57. Logical psychologism and logical idealism

A) The motives for this psychologism

We have already* spoken of the difficulty of separating from psychological subjectivity the psychically produced formations making up the thematic domain of logic—the difficulty, that is, of regarding judgments (and likewise sets, cardinal numbers, and so forth) as anything other than psychic occurrences in the human beings who are doing the judging. What accrues originaliter in the judicative doing, as subjects and predicates, premise-propositions, conclusion-propositions, and so forth, does indeed make its appearance, member by member, in the field of the judger's consciousness. It is nothing alien to the psychic, nothing like a physical process, a physical formation accruing in physical action. On the contrary, the judgment-members and the whole judgment-formation make their appearance in the psychic activity itself, which goes on as a process of consciousness; they make their appearance in it without separation from it and not outside but inside. Indeed, the misled followers of English Empiricism do not even succeed in making a distinction

*See §10.

here between the judging mental process and the formation that takes shape "in it," member by member. What is true of originally generative actions of thinking is true also of the secondary modes of thinking—for example: having something come to mind confusedly and other processes of meaning "indistinctly" (and equally true of originally generative actions belonging to the parallel types of rational consciousness, rational emotional and volitional consciousness, and true also of *their* corresponding secondary modes). It is in the confused thinking consciousness itself, and not as something external, that these confused thoughts make their appearance. How then, in logic, have we stepped outside the field of "psychic phenomena," "phenomena of internal experience"? It would follow that all the Data for logic are real occurrences belonging to the sphere of psychology; and, as such, according to the usual view, they would be unambiguously determined within the universal causal nexus of the real world and explainable by causal laws.

But this latter point may be left out of consideration. Our main concern here is the *equating of the formations produced by judging* (and then, naturally, of all similar formations produced by rational acts of any other sort) *with phenomena appearing in internal experience.* This equating is based on their making their appearance "internally," in the act-consciousness itself. Thus concepts, judgments, arguments, proofs, theories, would be psychic occurrences; and logic would be, as John Stuart Mill said it is, a "part, or branch, of psychology."* This highly plausible conception is *logical psychologism.*

B) THE IDEALITY OF LOGICAL FORMATIONS
AS THEIR MAKING THEIR APPEARANCE
IRREALLY IN THE LOGICO-PSYCHIC SPHERE

In opposition to this we say: There is an original evidence that, in repeated acts, which are quite alike or else similar, the produced judgments, arguments, and so forth, are not merely quite alike or similar but *numerically, identically, the same* judgments, arguments, and the like. Their "making an appearance" in the domain of consciousness is multiple. The particular formative processes of thinking are temporally outside one another (viewed as real psychic processes in real human beings, they are outside one another in Objective time); they are individually different and separated. Not so, however, the thoughts that are thought in the thinking. To be sure, the thoughts do not make their appearance in consciousness as something "external." They are not real objects, not spatial objects, but irreal formations produced by the mind; and their peculiar essence excludes spatial extension, original locality, and mobility. Like other products of the mind, they admit, however, of a physical embodiment: in their case, an embodiment by the sensuous verbal signs; and thus they gain a secondary spatial existence (that of the spoken or written sentence). Every sort of irreality, of which the ideality of significations and the different† ideality of universal essences or species are particular cases, has manners of possible participation in reality. Yet this in no way alters the essential separation between the real and the irreal.

But more deeply penetrating clarifications are indispensable here. By studying and paralleling the evidence of the real and the irreal we shall gain an understanding of the universal homogeneity of objectivities—*as* objectivities.

§58. The evidence of ideal objects analogous to that of individual objects

The evidence of irreal objects, objects that are ideal in the broadest sense, is, in its effect, quite analogous to the evidence of ordinary so-called internal and external experience, which alone—on no other grounds than prejudice—is commonly thought capable of effecting an original Objectivation. The identity and, therefore, the *objectivity* of something ideal can be

---

*An Examination of Sir William Hamilton's Philosophy, chap. XX. —Translator's note.
†The exposition substantiating this distinction, not yet made in the "Prolegomena," will be offered in my Logische Studien *[Logical Studies]*, which will soon appear. [See Edmund Husserl, EJ, §64c.]

directly "seen" (and, if we wished to give the word a suitably amplified sense, directly experienced) with the same originality as the identity of an object of experience in the usual sense—for example: an experienced object belonging to Nature or an experienced immanent object (any psychic Datum). In repeated experiences—before any repetition, in the continuous modification of the momentary perception in retention and protention, then in possible recollections, repeatable at will—there comes about, with their synthesis, the consciousness of The Same, moreover as an "experience" of this self-sameness. The possibility of such original identification belongs, as essential correlate, to the sense of *every* object of *experience* in the usual and pregnant sense, a sense determined to the effect that experience is an *evident seizing* upon and *having* of either an immanent or a real *individual* Datum *itself.*

In just the same fashion, we say, there belongs to the sense of an *irreal* object the possibility of its identification on the basis of its own manners of being itself seized upon and had. Actually the effect of this "identification" is like that of an "experience," except that an irreal object is *not individuated in consequence of a temporality belonging to it originally.**

The *possibility of deception* is inherent in the evidence of experience and does not annul either its fundamental character or its effect; though becoming evidentially aware of <actual> deception "annuls" the deceptive experience or evidence itself. The evidence of a new experience is what makes the previously uncontested experience undergo that modification of believing called "annulment" or "cancellation"; and it alone can do so. Evidence of experience is therefore always presupposed by the process. The conscious "dispelling" of a deception, with the originality of "now I *see* that it is an illusion," is itself a species of evidence, namely evidence of the nullity of something experienced or, correlatively, evidence of the "annulment" of the (previously unmodi-

fied) experiential evidence. This too holds for *every* evidence, for every "experience" in the amplified sense. Even an ostensibly apodictic evidence can become disclosed as deception and, in that event, presupposes a similar evidence by which it is "shattered."

§59. A universal characterization of evidence as the giving of something itself

The continual obstacle that may have been sensed during this exposition is owing solely to the usual, fundamentally wrong, interpretation of evidence, an interpretation made possible by the utter lack of a serious phenomenological analysis of the effective performance common to all forms of evidence. Thus it happens that evidence is usually conceived as an *absolute apodicticity,* an absolute security against deceptions—an apodicticity quite incomprehensibly ascribed to a single mental process torn from the concrete, essentially unitary, context of subjective mental living. The usual theorist sees in evidence an absolute criterion of truth; though, by such a criterion, not only external but also, in strictness, all internal evidence would necessarily be done away with. If, being unable to explicate evidence as a functioning intentionality, the theorist, by a kind of sensualistic substitution, falls back on so-called feelings of evidence, then their attainment of truth itself (an attainment he still ascribes to evidence) becomes a miracle, nay, at bottom a countersense.

Let no one upbraid us with the renowned evidence of "internal perception," as an instance counter to these statements. For internal perception's giving of its "immanent percept" itself—about this we shall have more to say—is, by itself alone, the giving of something-itself which is only a preliminary to an object; it is not the giving of something-itself which is an object in the proper sense. Perception *alone* is never a full Objectivating performance, if we understand such a performance to be indeed

---

*Irreal objectivities can very well assume an extra-essential relatedness to time, likewise an extra-essential relatedness to space and an extra-essential reification.

the seizing upon an *object* itself. We accept internal perception as a seizing upon an object itself, only because we are tacitly taking into account possible recollection, repeatable at will. When actualized, recollection gives for the first time original certainty of the being of a subjective *object* in the full sense, a so-called psychic Datum, as something acquired originaliter and identifiable at will, something to which one can "always go back again" and which one can recognize in a reactivation as the selfsame. Naturally, the concomitant intentional relation to such a *"synthesis of recognition"* plays a similar role in the case of each external objectivity—which is by no means to say that it makes up the full performance effected by external experience.

Evidence, as has already become apparent to us by the above explanations, designates *that performance on the part of intentionality which consists in the giving of something-itself [die intentionale Leistung der Selbstgebung].* More precisely, it is the universal pre-eminent form of "intentionality," of "consciousness of something," in which there is consciousness of the intended-to objective affair in the mode itself-seized-upon, itself-seen—correlatively, in the mode: being with it itself in the manner peculiar to consciousness. We can also say that it is the primal consciousness: I am seizing upon *"it itself"* originaliter, as contrasted with seizing upon it in an image or as some other, intuitional or empty, fore-meaning.

Still we must immediately point out here that evidence has *different* modes of originality. *The primitive mode of the giving of something-itself* is *perception.* The being-with is for me, as percipient, consciously my now-being-with: I myself with the perceived itself. An intentionally modified and more complicated mode of the giving of something itself is the memory that does not emerge emptily but, on the contrary, actualizes "it itself" *again: clear recollection.* By its own phenomenological composition, clear recollection is intrinsically a "reproductive" consciousness, a consciousness of the object itself as my past object, as (correlatively) the object which was perceived by me (the same Ego, but reproduced in the mode, "past"), and with which I (the active Ego as present for himself) am now "again"—with it itself.

Let us note here, because we might otherwise be misled,* that the modification of itself-giving as perception and recollection plays very different roles for *real* and *ideal* objectivities respectively. This is connected with the circumstance that *the latter have no temporal loci to bind them individuatingly.* Merely because of an essentially possible alteration of attitude or focus, any clear explicit recollection of an ideal species changes into a perception of it—something naturally excluded in the case of temporally individuated objects.

We are not opposing our universal characterization of evidence to the usual one as though ours were a new "theory," an attractive interpretation, which is yet to be tested, who knows how—perhaps in the end even by experiments on thinking. Rather we are presenting it as an evidence attained at a higher level, by the phenomenological explication of any experience and of any actually exercised "insight" (something that others, without reason, have separated quite essentially from what are usually called experiences). This higher evidence, in turn, can be itself explicated and understood in respect of its effect only by means of an evidence belonging to a third level; and so *in infinitum. Only in seeing can I bring out what is truly present in a seeing;* I must make a seeing explication of the proper essence of seeing.

Precisely because it gives its objective affair as the affair itself, any consciousness that gives something-itself can establish rightness, correctness, for another consciousness (for a mental meaning process that is merely unclear or even one that is confused, or for one that is indeed intuitive but merely prefigurative, or that in some other manner fails to give the object itself)—and it does so, as we had occasion

---

*As I was misled at the time of the *Logische Untersuchungen.*

to describe, in the form of *synthetic adequation* to the "affairs themselves"; or else it establishes incorrectness, in the form of inadequation, as the evidentness of nullity. Thus the givings of things themselves are the acts producing evident legitimacy or rightness; they are creative *primal institutings of rightness,* of truth as correctness—precisely because, for the objectivities themselves as existing for us, they are the originally constitutive acts, originally institutive of sense and being. In like fashion, original inadequations, as givings of nullity itself, are primal institutings of falsity, of wrongness as incorrectness *(positio* changed: of the trueness of the nullity or incorrectness). They constitute, not objectivity simpliciter—that is: existing objectivity—but rather, on the basis of supposed or meant objectivity, cancellation of that "meaning"— that is: its nonbeing.

§60. The fundamental laws of intentionality and the universal function of evidence

We have already touched on the fact that the giving of something-itself is, like every other single intentional process, a *function* in the all-embracing nexus of consciousness. The effect produced by a single intentional process, in particular its effect as a giving of something-itself, its effect as evidence, is therefore not shut off singly. The single evidence, by its own intentionality, can implicitly "demand" further givings of the object itself; it can "refer one" to them for a supplementation of its Objectivating effect. Let us turn our attention to that which pervades all conscious life, in order to appropriate a significant cognition that concerns evidence universally.

The concept of any intentionality whatever—any life-process of consciousness-of something or other—and *the concept of evidence, the intentionality that is the giving of something-itself, are essentially correlative.* Let us confine ourselves to "positing" consciousness, positional consciousness. In the case of "neutral" consciousness everything that we shall now state becomes modified in an easily

understood manner; the places of evidence, adequation, and the rest, are taken by their as-if modifications. The following obtains as a *fundamental law of intentionality:*

Absolutely any consciousness of anything whatever belongs a priori to an openly endless multiplicity of possible modes of consciousness, which can always be connected synthetically in the unity-form of conjoint acceptance *(con-posito)* to make one consciousness, as a consciousness of *"the Same."* To this multiplicity belong essentially the modes of a manifold *evidential consciousness,* which fits in correspondingly as an evidential having, either of the Same itself or of an Other itself that evidently annuls it.

Thus *evidence is a universal mode of intentionality, related to the whole life of consciousness.* Thanks to evidence, the life of consciousness has an *all-pervasive teleological structure,* a pointedness toward "reason" and even a pervasive tendency toward it—that is: toward the discovery of correctness (and, at the same time, toward the lasting acquisition of correctness) and toward the cancelling of incorrectnesses (thereby ending their acceptance as acquired possessions).

It is not only with respect to this all-pervasive teleological function that evidence is a theme for far-reaching and difficult investigations. These concern also the universal nature of evidence as a single component of conscious life—and here belongs the property mentioned above: that in every evidential consciousness of an object an intentional reference to a synthesis of recognition is included. They concern furthermore the modes of originality of evidence and their functions, as well as the different regions and categories of objectivities themselves. For though, in characterizing evidence as the giving (or, relative to the subject, the having) of an object itself, we were indicating a universality relating to all objectivities in the same manner, that does not mean that the structure of evidence is everywhere quite alike.

Category of objectivity and category of evidence are perfect correlates. To every fundamental species of objectivities—as intentional unities maintainable throughout an intentional synthesis and, ultimately, as unities belonging to a possible "experience"—*a fundamental species of "experience," of evidence, corresponds,* and likewise a fundamental species of intentionally indicated evidential style in the possible enhancement of the perfection of the having of an objectivity itself.

Thus a great *task* arises, the task of exploring all these modes of the evidence in which the objectivity intended to *shows itself,* now less and now more perfectly, of making understandable the extremely complicated performances, fitting together to make a synthetic harmony and always pointing ahead* to new ones. To declaim from the heights about evidence and "the self-confidence of reason" is of no avail here. And to stick to tradition—which, for motives long forgotten and, in any case, never clarified, reduces evidence to an insight that is apodictic, absolutely indubitable, and, so to speak, absolutely finished in itself—is to bar oneself from an understanding of any scientific production. Natural science, for example, *must* rely on *external experience,* only because external experience is precisely that *mode of the having of something itself which pertains to natural Objects,* and therefore without it there would be absolutely nothing conceivable to which believing about Nature (spatial things) might adjust itself. And again, only because imperfect experience is still experience, still a consciousness that is a having of something itself *[Bewusstsein der Selbsthabe],* can experience adjust itself to experience and correct itself by experience. For this same reason, moreover, it is wrong for a criticism of sensuous experience, which naturally brings out its essential imperfection (that is: its being at the mercy of further experience!), to end with rejecting it—whereupon the critic in his extremity appeals to hypotheses and indirect arguments, with which he attempts to seize the phantom of some (absurdly) transcendent "In-Itself." All transcendental-realistic theories, with their arguments leading from the "imma-

nent" sphere of purely "internal" experience to an extra-psychic transcendency, are attributable to a blindness to the proper character of "external" experience as a performance that gives us something itself and would otherwise be unable to provide a basis for natural-scientific theories.

I do not find that sufficient attention has been paid to the clarification of evidence and of all the pertinent relationships between mere *"intention"* and *"fulfillment,"* which was first effected in the *Logische Untersuchungen, II. Teil,* and deepened in my *Ideen.* It is certainly in great need of improvement; still I believe that I am right in seeing in this first clarification a decisive advance of phenomenology beyond the philosophic past. I am of the certain conviction that only by virtue of the resultant insight into the essence, and the genuine problems, of evidence has a seriously scientific transcendental philosophy ("critique of reason") become possible, as well as, at bottom, a seriously scientific psychology, conceived centrally as the science of the proper essence of the psychic, an essence that (as Brentano discovered) consists in *intentionality.* The new doctrine admittedly has one inconvenience: The appeal to evidence ceases to be, so to speak, a trick of epistemological argumentation; instead it raises tremendous reaches of evidently seizable and soluble problems—ultimately those of phenomenological constitution, which we shall develop in Chapters 6 and 7.

§61. Evidence in general in the function pertaining to all objects, real and irreal, as synthetic unities

Returning now to irreal objectivities, particularly those belonging to the sphere of analytic logic, we recall that in Part I we became acquainted with the evidences that in their case, and according to their various strata, are legitimizing evidences, evidences that give something-itself. In the case of the irreal objectivities of each stratum such evidences, then, are the corresponding "experiences"; and they have the *essential property of all experiences* or evidences of whatever sort—that is to say: with the repetition of the subjective life-processes, with the sequence and synthesis of different experiences of the Same, they make evidently visible *something that is indeed numerically identical (and not merely things that are quite alike),* namely *the* object, which is thus an object experienced many times or, as we may also say, one that *"makes its appearance" many times* (as a matter of ideal possibility, infinitely many times) in the domain of consciousness. If one substituted for the ideal objectivities those temporal occurrences in the life of consciousness in which they "make their appearance," then, to be consistent, one would have to do likewise in the case of Data of experience <in the usual narrower sense>. For example, psychic Data, the Data of "internal experience," are experienced as in immanent time and thus as intentionally identical Data given in the flow of subjective temporal modes. We should therefore have to put the immanent constitutive complexes of "original time-consciousness"* in their place.

But the constitutive that pertains to the identical of external experience is more easily accessible. Physical objects too make their appearance "in the field of consciousness"; and, in respect of what is most general, no differently than ideal objects—that is to say: as intentional unities (though in the mode: "itself given") making their appearance in the flow of multiple manners of appearance built one upon another. In this making-of-their-appearance within the mental experience-processes, they are, in a legitimate sense, "immanent" in these, but not in the usual sense, that of real immanence.

If one intends to understand what consciousness does and, in particular, what evidence does, it is not enough, here or anywhere else, to speak of the "directedness" of consciousness, particu-

larly of experiencing consciousness, to objects and, at most, to distinguish superficially among internal and external experience, ideation, and the like. The *multiplicities of consciousness* coming under these headings must be brought to sight in phenomenological reflection and dissected structurally. One must then trace them with regard to their *synthetic transitions;* and, down to the most elementary structures, one must seek out the intentional role or function. One must make it understood how, in the immanence of the multiplicities of mental processes (or <in the immanence> of the changing modes of appearance occurring in these multiplicities), their *being-directed-to* and that *to which* they are directed are *made;* and one must also make it understood wherein, now, *inside the sphere of vision belonging to the synthetic experience itself,* the transcendent object consists—as the *identical pole immanent in the single mental processes and yet transcending them by virtue of having an identity that surpasses them.* It is a giving of something-itself and yet a giving of something-itself that is "transcendent": an at first *"indeterminately"* itself-given identical pole, which subsequently displays itself, in "its" (likewise ideally identical) "determinations," throughout the giving of it-itself, a giving that can be continued in the synthetic form: "explication." But, in the manner of something instituted originally, *this transcendence lies in the proper essence of the experience itself.* What it signifies can be learned only by interrogating experience; just as what a legal property-right signifies and what demonstrates it at any time (incidentally, a matter that itself belongs within our province) can be found out only by going back and examining the "primal instituting" of that right.

The following great, and so often neglected, truism must therefore be made the center of all investigations of essential sense *[aller prinzipiellen Besinnungen].* Such an affair as an object (even a physical object) draws the *ontic sense* peculiar to it (by which it then sig-

---

*Regarding analysis of the constitution of temporal Data, see my PCIT.

nifies what it signifies in all possible modes of consciousness) *originally from the mental processes of experience alone*—from such processes as are intrinsically characterized as awarenesses-of in the mode "it-itself," as appearances-of a Something itself, and (in the case of physical objects) as our being confronted by something itself, the being of which is certain. The *primitive form* here is *showing-itself-as-present,* which belongs to perception, or *showing-itself-"again,"* which belongs to recollection in the mode of the past.

Experience is the primal instituting of the being-for-us of objects as having their objective sense. Obviously that holds good equally in the case of *irreal* objects, whether their character is the ideality of the specific, or the ideality of a judgment, or that of a symphony, or that of an irreal object of some other kind. Everywhere, and therefore even in the case of external experience, it is true that an evidential giving of something itself must be characterized as a process of constitution, a process whereby the object of experience arises *[ein Prozess . . . eines Sichbildens des Erfahrungsgegenstandes]* — though, to be sure, this constitution is at first restricted, since the object claims an existence extending beyond the multiplicities of actual present experience. (This moment of the object's being-sense also requires constitutional clarification; and, by virtue of the intentionality implicit in experience itself and always uncoverable, it permits such clarification.) Essentially in the continuous and discrete syntheses of manifold experiences, the experiential object, as such, is built up "visibly": in the varying show of ever new sides, ever new moments belonging to its own essence. And from this constitutive *[aufbauenden]* life, which predelineates its own possible harmonious flow, the sides and moments and the object itself (as showing itself only thus, variously) draw their respective senses, each as the Identical that belongs to possible and— after their actualization—repeatable shapings of something itself *[Selbstbildungen].* Here too the identity is evident: The object is evidently not itself the actual and openly possible expe-

riential processes constituting it; nor is it the evident possibility, connected with this process, the possibility, namely, of repetitive synthesis (as a possibility pertaining to "I can").

§62. The ideality of all species of objectivities over against the constituting consciousness. The positivistic misinterpretation of Nature is a type of psychologism

Consequently a certain *ideality* lies in the sense of every experienceable object, including every physical object, over against the manifold "psychic" processes *separated* from each other by individuation in immanent time —the processes of an experiencing life, then too of potential experiencing life, and finally of potential and actual becoming-conscious of all sorts, including the non-experiencing sorts. It is the *universal ideality of all intentional unities* over against the *multiplicities* constituting them.

In it consists the *"transcendence" belonging to all species of objectivities over against the consciousness of them* (and, in an appropriately altered but corresponding manner, the transcendence belonging to this or that Ego of a consciousness, understood as the subject-pole of the consciousness).

If, in spite of this, we still *separate immanent from transcendent objects,* that can involve a division only *within* this broadest concept of transcendence. In no respect does it alter the fact that likewise the transcendence belonging to the real, and, at the highest level, the intersubjectively real (the Objective in a preeminent sense), is constituted in respect of its being and sense exclusively in the immanent sphere, the sphere of the multiplicities of consciousness, and that the *transcendence belonging to the real, as such, is a particular form of "ideality"* or, better, of a *psychic irreality:* the irreality of something that *itself,* with all that belongs to it in its own essence, actually or possibly *makes its appearance* in the purely phenomenological sphere of consciousness, *and yet* in such a manner that it is evidently *no real part or moment of consciousness,* no real psychic Datum.

Accordingly we find a *precise analogue of the psychologistic interpretation of logical,* and of all other, *irrealities* (we might say: the amplified region of Platonic ideas) in that well-known type of *positivism* which we could also designate as Humeianism. It is represented, for example, by the Machian philosophy and the "philosophy of as-if"—though in a manner that, so far as originariness and depth of problematics are concerned, falls far short of Hume. For this positivism, physical things become reduced to empirically regular complexes of psychic Data ("sensations"); their identity and therefore their whole being-sense become sheer fictions. It is not merely a false doctrine, completely blind to the essential phenomenological facts; it is also countersensical, because of its failure to see that even fictions have their mode of being, their manner of evidence, their manner of being unities of multiplicities, and therefore carry with them the same problem that was to be theorized away by means of them.

§63. Originally productive activity as the giving of logical formations themselves; the sense of the phrase, their production

We have often spoken of a *producing of logical formations* in consciousness. In connection with this locution, warning must be given against a misunderstanding, which, *mutatis mutandis,* concerns all speaking of a constitution of objectivities in consciousness.

In other cases where we speak of a producing, we are referring to a *real* sphere. We mean thereby an active bringing forth of real physical things or real processes: Something real, already there within the sphere of the surrounding world, is suitably treated, is rearranged or transformed. In our case, however, we have before us *irreal* objects, given in real psychic processes—irreal objects that we treat and, by acting, form thus and so, with a practical thematizing directed to *them* and not at all to the *psychic realities.* Accordingly, it is not as though the statement might be weakened, that

here, and *in all seriousness,* a *formative doing,* an acting, a practical directedness to aims or ends, took place; as though something new were not actually produced here, by purposeful action, out of something given beforehand as a basis for practice. As a matter of fact, *judging too* (and naturally, in a particular manner, cognitive judging with its originality) *is acting;* the only difference is that, by its essential nature, judging is not a treating of something real, no matter how self-evidently any acting whatever is itself something psychically real (Objectively real, where, with the psychological attitude, we take judging as a human activity). But, from the beginning and in all its formings at different levels, this acting has exclusively the irreal in its thematic sphere; in judging, something irreal becomes intentionally constituted. In the active formation of new judgments out of judgments already given beforehand, we are, in all seriousness, productively active. As in every other acting the ends of our action, the new judgments to be produced, are consciously intended to by us beforehand in modes of an anticipation which is empty, still undetermined in respect of content, or in any case still unfulfilled; we are conscious of them thus as the things toward which we are striving and the bringing of which to an actualizing givenness of them-themselves makes up the action, as accomplished step by step.

Thus the objectivities "treated" here are no realities: The peculiar sense that ideal objectivities possess, in being (as we have said) exactly as originally certain to us in an evidence of their own as are the real objectivities coming from experience, is unalterable. Equally unalterable, on the other hand, is the fact that they too are producible ends, final ends and means, and that they are what they are, only "as coming from" an original production. But that is not at all to say that they are what they are, only *in* and *during* the original production. That they are "in" the original production signifies that they are intended to in it, as a certain intentionality having the form of *spontaneous activity,* and more particularly in the mode belonging to the *original objectivity it-*

self. This manner of givenness—givenness as something coming from such original activity— is nothing other than *the sort of "perception" proper to them.* Or, what is the same thing, this originally acquiring activity is the *"evidence" appropriate to these idealities.* Evidence, quite universally, is indeed nothing other than the mode of consciousness—built up, perhaps, as an extraordinarily complex hierarchical structure—that offers its intentional objectivity in the mode belonging to the original "it itself." This evident-making activity of consciousness—in the present case a spontaneous activity hard to explore—is the "original constitution," stated more pregnantly, the primally institutive constitution, of ideal objectivities of the sort with which logic is concerned.

§64. The precedence of real to irreal objects in respect of their being

In concluding this investigation, let us add that much vehement opposition—which to be sure disregards our phenomenological findings—arises from a misunderstanding of the sense in which we put ideal objectivities and also categorial variants of realities (such variants as predicatively formed affair-complexes) on a par with realities themselves. For us it is merely a matter of the legitimacy of the *broadest sense, "any object whatever"* or "anything whatever," and, *correlatively, of the most universal sense of evidence,* evidence as the giving of something itself. Otherwise than with respect to the legitimate subsumption of ideas under the concept of object, and consequently under the concept of substrate of possible predications, there is no parity at all between real and ideal objectivities, as can be understood precisely on the basis of our tenets. *In respect of its being, reality has precedence to every irreality whatsoever,* since all irrealities relate back essentially to an actual or possible reality. "The attempt" to survey these relations on every side and attain systematic cognition of all that actually or possibly exists, the realities

and the irrealities "—that attempt" leads to the highest philosophic problems, those of a universal ontology.

§65. A more general concept of psychologism

The extraordinary broadening and, at the same time, radicalizing of the refutation of logical psychologism, which we have effected in the foregoing investigation, have brought us an extreme *generalization of the idea of psychologism,* in a *quite definite*—but not the only—*sense.* Psychologism in this sense is to be distinguished by the circumstance that some species or other of possibly evident objectivities (or even all species, as is the case in Hume's philosophy) are *psychologized,* because, as is obvious, they are constituted in the manner peculiar to consciousness—that is to say: their being-sense is built up, in and for subjectivity, by experience or other modes of consciousness that combine with experience. That they are "psychologized" signifies that their objective sense, their *sense as a species of objects* having a peculiar essence, is *denied* in favor of the subjective mental occurrences, the Data in immanent or psychological temporality.

But it is not important here, whether these Data be regarded as real* Data for *psychology* (a science of men and brutes as Objective realities) or as Data belonging to something distinguished, no matter how, as *"transcendental" subjectivity* (a subjectivity antecedent to all Objective realities, including human subjects); nor, in the latter case, does it matter whether the Data be regarded as a bundle or collection of absolutely posited sensations or as intentional mental processes in the teleological unity of a concrete Ego and a community of Egos. Still the expression psychologism is more appropriate to any interpretation which converts objectivities into something psychological in the proper sense; and the *pregnant* sense of psychologism should be defined accordingly.

---

*Reading *reale* instead of *irreale.* —Translator's note.

§66. *Psychologistic and phenomeno-logical idealism. Analytic and transcendental criticism of cognition*

This psychologism, conceived so universally and (purposely) in hybrid fashion, is the fundamental characteristic of every bad *"idealism" (lucus a non lucendo!)* like Berkeley's or Hume's. Yet it extends far beyond the conception one usually connects with the word "idealism," as this conception usually fails to take into consideration precisely the genuine idealities of the amplified Platonic sphere (though the Humeian conception is indeed to be excepted here). But the *phenomenological idealism* developed by me should not be mistaken for this idealism, as it is, time after time, by superficial readers of my works (even phenomenological readers); it gets its *fundamentally different and novel sense* precisely by radical criticism of the aforesaid psychologism, on the basis of a phenomenological clarification of evidence.

The following is pertinent here and can help to characterize phenomenological idealism.

Every "seeing" and, correlatively, everything identified in "evidence" has its own legitimacy; likewise every self-contained realm of possible "experience," as the *province* of a science, as its *theme* in the *first* and most proper sense. At the same time, there belongs to each science a *secondarily thematic sphere,* the sphere of its *criticism:* This is a criticism of "cognition" in a first sense "of the term criticism of cognition"—that is to say: relating to the ideal cognitional results (those belonging to the "theory") and, on the subjective side, relating to what is ideal in a correlative sense, namely the acting (concluding, proving) that corresponds to these idealities. Through this criticism, which we may designate as *analytic criticism of cognition,* each science gets its relation to analytics as a universal science of theory conceived with formal universality and, correlatively, its relation to the correspondingly delimited analytic practical discipline.

Finally, however, every science has a *third thematic sphere,* likewise a sphere of criticism, but of a criticism *turned in a different direc-*

tion. This criticism concerns the *constituting subjectivity* corresponding to each province and to each scientific performance busied with a province. Over against criticism of the prior data, the actions, and the results, that make their appearance openly in the field of consciousness, we have here a criticism of cognition that has quite a different nature: criticism of the constitutive sources from which the positional sense and the legitimacy of cognition originate; accordingly criticism of the *effective performances that remain hidden* during the inquiring and theorizing directed straightforwardly to the province. This is the criticism of *"reason"* (taken either psychologically or transcendentally); or, contrasting it with analytic criticism of cognition, we may say it is *transcendental criticism of cognition.* What we have said holds good for logic as well as for every other science; and already, in our general preparatory considerations, we asserted it under the heading, the *two-sidedness* of logical thematizing, though not with the distinctness and precision that have been possible here.

§67. *The reproach of psychologism as indicating failure to understand the necessary logical function of transcendental criticism of cognition*

Now the *reproach of psychologism* was, as we remember, directed against precisely that two-sidedness—with regard to the *Logische Untersuchungen* because, in the *"Prolegomena,"* they combatted psychologism and yet, in Part II, went over to investigations of phenomenological subjectivity, to investigations concerning the intentional structures of stating and signifying, of objectivation and the content (sense) of an objectivation, of perception and the sense of a perception, of judging and the supposed predicatively formed affair-complex, of categorial acts and the constitution of categorial objects as contrasted with sensuous ones, of symbolic-empty consciousness as contrasted with intuitive, of the intentional relationships between bare intention and fulfillment, of evidential consciousness, of adequation, of the constitution of true being and predicational truth, and so forth. Such "descriptive-psychological" researches in the psychology of cognition were said to be psychologistic transgressions of a pure logic. This was the objection; though it was not intended to involve the rejecting of epistemo-critical researches concerning all sciences (logic presumably included). On the contrary, such researches were highly regarded by everyone. But the opinion was that they should follow quite a different line; they must not take our concretely actual and possible cognitive living, they must not take its intentional analysis, as their problem. That was said to be psychology and to signify epistemological psychologism.

Such criticism and the whole ruling conception involve *separating science and the criticism of reason;* they involve granting science a separate existence in its own right and taking criticism of reason as a science of a new sort, relating to all science and enjoying a higher dignity, but not disturbing the rightful independence of the sciences. This is above all the case with analytic logic; it holds in advance as an absolute norm, which all rational cognition presupposes. The worth of my criticism of logical psychologism, and all similar criticisms before and after mine, is seen to lie precisely in their bringing out a pure (analytic) logic, which is to be separated from all psychology as a *self-sufficient* science, like geometry or natural science in this respect. The criticism of reason may have questions to ask about pure logic; but they must not disturb its independent course and must on no account delve into the concreteness of logical conscious life, for that would be psychology.

As against this, let us first bear in mind that the war against logical psychologism was in fact meant to serve no other end than the supremely important one of making the specific *province* of analytic logic visible in its purity and ideal peculiarity, freeing it from the psychologizing confusions and misinterpretations in which it had remained enmeshed from the beginning. — Its "province": that is to say, its thematic field in the first and chief sense, such a field as any science has. But that does not preclude the possibility that secondarily—for the sake of cognition of the province—something that is not part of it, but is essentially connected with it, will also be made a theme. Indeed, this is already the case, as mentioned earlier, with respect to the field of "analytic" criticism indispensable to every science: the field comprising, on the one hand, its theory and all its judgments relating to the province and, on the other hand, the corresponding ideal actions.

And now cannot something similar be the case, and must it not be the case, with respect to the total field comprising the intentional acts, the manners of appearance, the modes of consciousness of every sort, in which the scientific province and its objects and complexes of objects are given beforehand for the subject who judges, and comprising, in like fashion, those in which his whole theoretical living and striving relating to the province goes on intentionally, those in which the theory and the scientifically true being of the province are intentionally constituted? Should not this too be in fact a field for a criticism necessary to all sciences, a transcendental criticism—necessary, if they are to have any capability whatever of being genuine sciences? If this could be made evident and the great field of tasks awaiting this last and deepest criticism could be displayed, logic would naturally be served thereby; for, as the universal, and not the merely analytic, theory of science (not mere *mathesis universalis),* logic would relate not only to all genuine sciences, with respect to their universal essential possibilities, but also to any and all criticism pertaining to them and their genuineness, and here likewise with respect to its essential universalities. *Universal theory of science is ipso facto universal theory of genuine science as such, a criticism belonging to its own essence,* whether as criticism of judgments as produced formations, ideal components of its ideal theories, or as criticism of the intentional life that constitutes province and theory.

It is not our present task to inquire about any traditional or now-accepted criticisms of reason, or about their paralyzing fears of a concrete consideration of cognitive subjectivity (a consideration interdicted under the name psychologism), their fears of every introduction of psychology into observations proper to a theory of science. We are asking only about what pertains to the essential possibility of genuine science. If the investigation of constitutive consciousness, the inquiry into the whole teleology of the intentionalities belonging to cognitive life, could be proved essentially necessary for making genuineness of the sciences possible, it would have to be accepted by us. And if, in this regard, a "psy-chologism" should still have to be obviated (a psychologism with a different sense from that of the phychologism which we have treated up to now, though allied to it), then we should have to learn this by considering the requirements themselves for logic. Without any commitment on our part, the thematizing of the subjective—more distinctly: of the intentional-constitutive—a thematizing whose essential function is still to be clarified, shall henceforth be designated as *phenomenological*.

14. Individuals and Sets

Explication of Individuals*

§24. The activity of explicative contemplation and the explicative synthesis

A) The explicative synthesis as the locus of origin of the categories "substrate" and "determination" and the problem of their analysis

Let us now proceed to the next level of objectifying activity, that of *explicative contemplation*. Provisionally, it has already been characterized as an orientation of perceptual interest in the sense of an entering into the internal horizon of the object, a horizon which is immediately coawakened by the givenness of the object. This signifies the following: assuming the case of an unobstructed exercise of perceptual interest, the ego cannot long remain with a merely simple contemplation and apprehension; rather, the tendency inherent in the contemplation of an object immediately pushes it beyond this. In streaming forth in a linear continuity, the act of contemplation would become a simple fixed view if it did not disengage itself and pass over into a chain of individual apprehensions, of individual acts, in a discrete succession of separate steps which, bound internally to one another, form a *polythetic unity* of the individual theses. The individual apprehensions fall into sequence with one another, directed toward singularities *in* the object. The object, *every* object, has its peculiarities, its internal determinations. In the terms of phenomenology, this means that every object conceivable in general as an object of possible experience has its subjective modes of givenness: it can rise up out of the obscure background of consciousness and from there affect the ego and determine it to an attentive apprehension. It has thereby its differences of appearance according to "near" and "far," it has its own way of moving from distance to proximity, which allows ever more individual moments to come to prominence and to determine particular affections and orientations. For example, what first strikes the eye is its total surface color or its shape; then a certain part of the object becomes prominent—in the case of a house, for example, the roof; finally, the particular properties of this part—its color, shape,

*EJ, pp. 112–119, 205–209 (Sections 24a-c and 50a).

and so on. And, in conformity with the nature and mode of givenness of the object, the expectations, which are immediately coawakened and refer to what it exhibits of itself by way of its properties, are more or less determined. The object is present from the very first with a character of familiarity; it is already apprehended as an object of a type more or less vaguely determined and already, in some way, known. In this way the direction of the expectations of what closer inspection will reveal in the way of properties is prescribed.

Disregarding the fact that each stage of the originally intuitive explication already takes place within this horizon of familiarity and is not the sheer bringing-to-givenness of an object completely new, but is only the more precise determination and correction of anticipations, we seek at first to bring out the *general essence* through which the process of explication is distinguished from a pure and simple act of contemplation. Only after this is done should we take into account the different *modes of accomplishment* of explication which are possible in view of the full concretion of the consciousness of horizon wherein explication is always situated—for these modes of accomplishment are all of the same fundamental structure.

Let us take an object, call it *S,* and its internal determinations α, β, . . . ; the process set going by the interest in *S* does not simply give the series: apprehension of *S,* apprehension of α, of β, etc., as if the apprehensions had nothing to do with one another, as if there had been a change of themes. This process is, therefore, not like the case where, after the weakening of the interest of cognition in an object, this interest having been supplanted by interest in a second and then in a third, we turn toward those which have forced attention on themselves by an affection of appropriate power. On the contrary, in the whole process of individual acts which lead from the apprehension of *S* to the apprehension of α, β, . . . *we come to know S.* This process is a *developing contemplation,* a unity of articulated contemplation. Through the entire process the *S* retains the character of *theme;* and while, step by step, we gain pos-

session of the moments, the parts, one after the other—and each one of them is precisely a moment or part, i.e., what is generally called a property or determination—each is nothing in itself but something of the object *S,* coming from it and in it. In the apprehension of the properties we come to know *it,* and we come to know the properties only as belonging to it. In the development, the indeterminate theme *S* turns into the *substrate* of the properties which emerge, and they themselves are constituted in it as its *determinations.*

But how does it happen that the ego, in the apprehension of α, β, etc., is conscious of knowing *S in them?* In what way is α present to consciousness in another way than *S* or as some other *S'* toward which we turn after *S?* In other words, what makes *S* the general theme in a privileged sense, so that α, β, . . . , even if they are apprehended successively and thus in a certain way also become thematic, still lack, in comparison to *S,* equal status? Indeed, why is it that they are simply themes *in which* is realized in a coherent way the dominant interest in *S,* and why is the transition to them not an entering into another object, and therewith a turning away from and weakening of the interest in *S,* but a continuing fulfillment and augmentation of this interest? It is necessary, therefore, to describe the intentional functions which determine that the "object" of explication is presented to us in the sense-form "substrate" and that the moments explicated are presented in a wholly different form, namely, as *"properties,"* as *"determinations,"* of the object, in such a way that we can speak of an *explication,* of a development of *S* in *its* determinations, and say that it is *the S* which is determined *as* α, *as* β, and so on.

The process of explication in its originality is that in which an object given at first hand is brought to explicit intuition. The analysis of its structure must bring to light how a *twofold constitution of sense [Sinngebung]* is realized in it: "object as substrate" and "determination α . . ."; it must show how this constitution of sense is realized in the form of a process which goes forward in separate steps, through which, however, extends continuously a *unity of coincidence*—a unity of coincidence of a special kind, belonging exclusively to these sense-forms. We can also say that it is necessary to show that this process is one of "self-evidence," for in it something is originally intuited as *"object-substrate"* as such, and, as such, having something on the order of "determinations." With this, we are at the *place of origin of the first of the so-called "logical categories."* It is true, we can only begin to speak of logical categories in the proper sense in the sphere of predicative judgment, as elements of determination which belong necessarily to the form of possible predicative judgments. But all categories and categorial forms which appear there are erected on the prepredicative syntheses and have their origin in them.

b) Explicative coincidence as a particular mode of the synthesis of overlapping [*Überschiebung*]

What strikes us first of all in the process of explication, in the transition from the apprehension of S to that of α, is a certain mental overlapping of the two apprehensions. But this is by no means sufficient to characterize explication. For such an overlapping of all apprehensions is common to explication and all cases in which the ego advances from apprehension to apprehension in a synthetic activity unified by the bond of a single interest. This overlapping is realized just as much when a thing is apprehended at first in undivided unity and then in view of its peculiar form, sound, or odor, i.e., whatever elements stand out, as when what is apprehended synthetically is at first a thing and then, as separated from it and not belonging to its determination, a form, a sound, an odor. *In every synthesis of this kind,* even if wholly dissimilar objects are contemplated as a unity, *an overlapping takes place.* The ego plays a continually active role through the series of steps run through; in the second, it is still directed toward the object of the first; it is directed, therefore, in spite of the privileged position of the new object of primary apprehension, on both of them together: with the new and, through the new, on the old. The

two are together actively taken up by the ego; the indivisible ego is in both. The succession of the rays of attention and of apprehension has become *a single double ray.*

But there is an essential difference, depending on whether, in this synthetic activity, it is *according to the objective sense* that a synthesis of *coincidence* is produced, thus in an entirely special identity-synthesis, or whether such a thing does not take place. If we pass from a color over to a sound, then this is not the case. But if we pass, always synthetically, from one color to another, there is already a synthesis of coincidence; the moments which overlap one another coincide according to likeness or similarity. If we now take the case of the synthesis "thing and property of the thing" and, in general, the synthesis "object and objective property," then a completely unique synthesis of the coincidence of identity confronts us here. The synthesis relative to the intentional objects (the sense-content of acts of individual apprehension) appearing here one by one is a synthesis of a certain coincidence of identity which goes forward continuously and through the sharply separated stages of the act.

This *explicative coincidence,* as we will call it, should not be confused with the *total coincidence of identity* with regard to objective sense, such as occurs when we pass synthetically from one representation (mode of givenness) to others of the same object and thereby identify that object with itself. Such a coincidence belongs, for example, to every perception of a thing which goes forward continuously, as the continuous synthesis of the multifariously changing appearances in the consciousness of the same thing (of a thing which remains continuously one); but it also belongs to every synthesis of identity of sensuous intuitions; for example, of a perception and a remembrance of the same object. But in the case of explicative coincidence, it is a question of an identification which is wholly other, completely unique, in which continuity and discreteness are bound together in a remarkable way. Substrate and determination are constituted originally in the process of explication as correlative members of a kind of coincidence. When α is present to our consciousness as a determination, we are not simply conscious of it as being absolutely the same as S, nor are we conscious of it as something completely other. In every explicative determination of S, *S is present* in one of its particularities; and in the different determinations which appear in the form of explicates, it remains the same, but in conformity with the different particularities which are its properties.

c) The retaining-in-grasp of explication in contrast to the retaining-in-grasp of simple apprehension

The special nature of explicative coincidence becomes clearly evident in the contrast to simple apprehension. If we carry out simple apprehension, still without explicative contemplation—for example, if for a certain time we are turned toward an object enduring in time in order to apprehend it but without determining anything about it—then this apprehension is an activity of the ego, a spontaneity which springs originally from the ego-pole. We thus distinguish the active *laying-hold-of,* which begins discretely, and the continuous *holding-fast-to* into which it is transformed. This laying-hold-of is an original springing-forth of the grasping activity of the ego which is carried on continuously.

Let us now turn to partial apprehension. We observe, for example, a copper bowl which is before us: our glance "runs over" it, remains fixed for a moment on the roundness, and returns to it again, attracted by a spot which stands out, a variation from the uniform roundness. Then our glance jumps to a large shiny spot and goes on a bit farther, following the shimmering glitter; then it is struck by the bosses; the cluster is thrown into relief as a unity; we run over these bosses one by one, etc. In all this we are continuously oriented toward the entire object; we have apprehended it and hold fast to it as a thematic substrate. While we apprehend the singularities in particular, we actively carry out afresh particular orientations and apprehensions which cause what is apprehended to stand out in a privileged way. These partial apprehensions naturally are active "operations," just like the first simple apprehension.

If we now carry out a partial apprehension, what happens during this time to the total apprehension, the apprehension of the bowl? It still always remains what we "look at." We are continually turned toward it in an apprehension, but the partial apprehensions coincide with the total apprehension in such a way that in each partial apprehension we apprehend the whole to the degree that, in the coincidence, the whole overlaps the particularity which is apprehended and is present to consciousness in this overlapping. But here again there is the difference, which we have already noted regarding simple apprehension, between original grasping and still-retaining-in-grasp. In the initial apprehension of the whole, without consideration of its particularities, a flux of activity, springing originally from the ego, is directed toward the undifferentiated unified object. If the explicative contemplation is put into play, a new flux of original activity is directed toward the properties in question. But now, on the other hand, the activity springing up initially is not maintained and directed toward the whole as it was before. As soon as the explicative contemplation begins, its intentional mode manifestly changes; to be sure, we are and remain directed toward the entire object which we apprehend—which is precisely the object of contemplation—but the active apprehension of the whole does not remain in the original form which first gave it life but is a *maintaining of the activity in an intentional modification,* precisely as a still-retaining-in-grasp.

The same thing is true in the passage from one explicate to the next. The moment no longer apprehended momentarily in virtue of being partial, but apprehended as just having been, continues to be retained in grasp in the transition to a new stage of activity. This *retaining* grasp, a grasp in the mode of the "still," is *a state of activity which endures;* it is not a laying-hold-of or an apprehension which is carried on continuously as an act. Just as in simple contemplation, such a grasping in the mode of retaining can be more or less firm and then become loose, or it can be loose and again become firmer; but it can also stop completely: the object is let go, it slips from our grasp. In the explication being considered here, it hardly needs particular mention that the retaining-in-grasp is impressional.

Exactly as in continuous simple apprehension, therefore, there is *at each stage of explication a retaining-in-grasp of the substrate.* But here the retaining-in-grasp is totally different from that which is likewise under consideration in simple apprehension. That is, the apprehension of the object which is included in the constant retaining-in-grasp of the substrate takes upon itself, step by step, all of the particularities which have been thrown into relief: the having-in-grasp of the object being explicated is not a having-in-grasp which is unchanged with regard to content, i.e., a still-having-in-grasp of the *same,* "such as" it was for consciousness before this stage; on the contrary, thanks to constantly new partial coincidences, it is an always different having-in-grasp. In every step, what is gotten hold of as singular is incorporated by the coincidence into the sense content of the substrate. The individual graspings are transformed, not into merely retentive individual graspings such as occur when something is still retained in simple contemplation or when one passes on to a new object, but into *modifications of a total grasp,* in other words, into enrichments of its content.

In the clarifications presented up to now, it is already implied that the way in which S is still retained is essentially different from the ways in which α, β, . . . , are retained. On the one side we have the activity, constantly springing up originally, of the inaugurative grasping and actually holding-in-grasp—which is a grasping and a having-in-grasp carried on in a continuous way—up to the point in which the explication begins, and, after that, the modified activity of the secondary still-retaining-in-grasp. Both forms coalesce into a permanent unity; in them, the active ego is and remains

constantly turned toward S. On the side of the explicates, on the other hand, the phenomena are different. The inaugurative activity, carried on in an original springing-forth, is one in which an explicate comes to original apprehension and persists until its time is elapsed; this activity again changes when a new explicate is apprehended. However, the first is certainly not abandoned; it remains valid during the entire continuing process. To this extent, we also say here that it still remains in grasp. But here, this continuing-to-be-retained has its exclusive source in the intentionality, already described, of active coincidence, by means of which the explicate, and everything which constitutes an element of determination of S, is included as *a sense-determinative precipitate of S* which subsists unchanged. After the explication of the α, the S becomes $S\alpha$; after the emergence of the β, $(S\alpha)\beta$, and so on. Thus α, β, etc., are no longer apprehended—either primarily or secondarily; the ego is no longer directed toward them; it is directed toward S, which contains them as precipitates. Accordingly, we see that the intentionality of an explication is constantly in movement, in a continuous internal transformation, and that, at the same time, it consists of a series of discrete steps, whose intentionality, however, is traversed by a continuity. This continuity is a permanent synthesis of coincidence which concerns the content of apprehensions as well as the activities themselves: the active apprehending and being-directed toward the "whole," or, to speak more precisely, the being-directed toward the substrate S, is implicitly "co"-directed toward the α, . . . ; and, in the "emergence" of the α, it is the S which is apprehended and displayed "in its relation to" α.

§50. The fundamental structure of predication

A) The two-membered nature of the predicative process

We will therefore take our point of departure from the simple perception and explication of an as yet undetermined substrate *S* and, for reasons to be discussed later, will limit ourselves at first to its explication according to a dependent internal determination, a moment which we will designate as *p*. The simplest case is one in which the explication (as the contemplation of an object) does not go on to ever new moments at all. In our example, the contemplation stops at once and leads only to *p*, and immediately thereafter it proceeds to a fresh determination. What is the new achievement which occurs when, on the basis of explication, we come to the predicative determination "*S* is *p*"?

We have seen that, in the explication of a substrate *S*, a coincidence takes place between *S* and its determining moment *p*. As a substrate still remaining in grasp, the substrate has obtained in this synthesis of transition from *S* to *p* an accretion of sense. But when, retaining *S* in grasp, we pass to its moment *p*, therefore when we witness this coincidence, this "contraction" of *S* in *p*, we have not yet, for all that, posited *S* *as subject* in a predicative judgment, and we have not yet determined it as having the moment *p* in the manner "*S* is *p*." This, rather, is the *achievement of a new kind of activity*. Already in the act of apprehension and receptive explication there were active steps: in an active turning-toward, the substrate *S* was first apprehended in its undifferentiated unity, made a theme, and then its determination *p* was actively apprehended in the explicative synthesis. The work of the activity of the ego went thus far. Beyond this, the explicative coincidence arose *passively* between the substrate *S*, still retained in grasp, and its determination *p*, and the thematic object-substrate found its enrichment of sense in this passive modification (cf. above, §24).

When the transition from *S* to *p* has taken place in this way, there then develops on the basis of active contemplation an *interest of higher level* in the object-substrate, an interest, proceeding from this contemplation, *in retaining* the accretion of sense arising from it, the *S* in its enrichment of sense. *S* which, at the end of the process of contemplation, is other than in the beginning, the *S* which has receded and remains only retained in grasp, which no longer stands at the "focal point" of interest, returns again to this focal point inasmuch as it now shows itself as extended in sense. We go back to the *S*, thus identifying it with itself, which only means, however, that, in the return, it "again" stands there as *S*: in this new thematic apprehension we have its enrichment of sense as mere protention, in connection with the retention of the transition which has just taken place. The interest now betakes itself in the direction of *S* in its enrichment of sense, which supposes that we *again* pass to *p*. For originally, *p* emerges as the enrichment of sense [of *S*] only in the synthetic transition [from *S* to *p*] in the explicative coincidence. But the transition is now guided by the cognitive will to retain *S* in its determination. An *active* intention aims at apprehending what previously was a merely *passive* coincidence, therefore, in the active transition to *p*, at producing in an original activity what accrues to *S*. As an active ego, directed toward *S* in its accretion of sense, and in my interest focused on this accretion itself, I bring about the transition and the partial coincidence as free activity and thus bring about the fulfillment of the determining intention, the intention toward *S* in the sense accruing from the transition and coincidence. I have *S* as the substrate of a determination and actively determine it. The object-substrate takes the form of the predicative subject; it is the subject-theme as *terminus a quo,* and the activity goes over to the predicate as the opposed *terminus ad quem.* It is only then that there is realized in a productive activity—which is not only a synthetic activity in general but, at the same time, the *activity of synthesis itself*—the consciousness that *S* receives a determination *by p* in the mode "*S* is *p*."

We have said that what is peculiar to the predicative synthesis consists in the active accomplishment of the synthetic transition from *S* to *p*, in the active accomplishment of the unity of identity between *S* and *p*. We are therefore directed in a certain way toward the unity of identity. But this must not be understood as if we (noetically) were directed *toward the identifying process,* toward the multiplicity of lived experience in which the synthetic unity between S and p is established. We are in this attitude *now,* when we phenomenologically elucidate the predicative synthesis; but when we accomplish this synthesis itself, we are *directed objectively* toward S in its partial identity with p. On the other hand, this does not mean that we then explicate the result of the receptive explication, namely, this successively constituted unity of identity which is preconstituted in the explication. This would mean running through the succession anew, therefore renewing the explication "in memory." Such a repetition of the explication generally takes place in receptive experience (cf. §25) [only] when we endeavor to impress an object on ourselves in its intuitive determinations ("attributes"). For this, a simply apprehending regard is first directed toward the unity of coincidence already constituted; this unity becomes a theme in a simple thesis with a single ray of attention, and then the explication is accomplished anew. But this still does not lead to a predication.

On the contrary, in order for the substrate of the explication to become a subject and for the explicates to become predicates, it is necessary that the regard turn back to the unity which is passively preconstituted within the receptive activity of the process of explication and is in a sense concealed. *Being turned toward this unity in order to apprehend it* implies *repeating the process in a changed attitude,* making an active synthesis from a passive one. This synthesis is not something which can be originally apprehended in a simple turning-toward in the manner in which, at the lower level, everything was apprehended in acts of simple turning-toward; rather, they can be perceived only by repeating the act of running-through. This takes place, as was mentioned, in a change of attitude: we do not again carry out a merely contemplative explication but an activity of predicative identification, and this is an *apprehending consciousness,* whose *activity* is characterized not by a single ray but by *several rays (a polythetic activity).* The action

of determinative identification goes from the spontaneous apprehension of S as subject to p: the apprehending regard lives in the apprehension of its being determined as p. In the activity of explication, the object is already implicitly "determined" as p, i.e., it is clarified and made explicit as such, but the "being-determined-as" is not apprehended. It is first apprehended in the repeated active accomplishment of the synthesis, an accomplishment which presupposes the preceding explication. As present to consciousness, the S must be already explicated, but it is now posited predicatively simply as S, which is identical, no matter how it may be explicated. On the other hand, it pertains to its form that it is the explicand; it is posited in the form of subject, and p expresses the determination. In the "is," the form of the synthesis between explicand and explicate is expressed in its active accomplishment, i.e., as the apprehension of being-determined-as, and in the predication this form is a component of the total "state of affairs" which attains expression.

To sum up: *essentially, the predicative synthesis always has two levels:*

1. In the transition from S to the moments $p, q, \ldots$, emerging in coincidence: the $p, q,$ are apprehended for themselves. The interest which followed the objective sense of the preconstitution, or, correlatively, the quidditive content of the object coming to prominence therein, drains off into the determinations, but S and each of the moments already apprehended remains in grasp.

2. But then there is something new; namely, the ego in its interest turns back to S and, for example, first taking p particularly in grasp again and directing a new ray of attention toward it, becomes aware of the enrichment of sense and is saturated with it, while it again reproduces it by an original activity in a new passage to p; and thus for each of the determinations. *Determination always has two members.*

Thus is described the process of predication which tradition always already had in view under the terms "synthesis" and "diaeresis" without actually being able to come to grips with it.

Constituting Sets*

§24. The activity of explicative contemplation and the explicative synthesis

D) EXPLICATION AND APPREHENSION OF PLURALITY

Now that we have made sure of this specific mode of the process of explication, it is easy to contrast it with a mode of synthesis related to it but from which it must be rigorously differentiated, namely, the synthesis which occurs in the *apprehension of plurality.* To be sure, a plurality—for example, a cluster of stars, a cluster of colored dots—can also, on the basis of a unified prominence and affection, become a unitary theme, and its objective particulars can be explicated as determinative parts. Then we have before us only a special case of explication. It is also an ideal limiting case if plurality is apprehended as a unitary whole and all apperception of plurality is lacking.

But the normal case is one in which the unity of configuration is apperceived from the first as existing in a pluralistic way, as a plurality of objects, and this apperception is "realized." This means that the coming-into-prominence of plural existents does not lead to a unitary objective turning-toward but that, on the contrary, it is the *individual* members of the plurality which excite the interest in advance and which are immediately thematized as individuals—but not as mere isolated individuals but as individuals linked together thematically. This linking occurs to the extent that the interest follows the likeness or similarity already given by an association in the background with other moments of a configuration, and each individual interest works not only to the benefit of each new particular, by a kind of coincidence of interest which flows over it, but also to the benefit of everything which has already been apprehended previously and to which it remains attached. In that the interest is now fulfilled through the particular and continues on to new particulars, a uniform active process grows up in which each of the aspects already apprehended still remains in grasp in such a way that in fact not only a *succession of activities* but also *a unity of activity grows up which persists throughout the succession.* In this way the pervading activity moves constantly on the permanent background which this plurality constitutes by appearing continuously in a uniform configuration; thus, we have to do here in a certain way with partial apprehensions within what is present to consciousness as a whole.

But however far the analogy with the case of the explication of a particular object extends, and however true it may be that what we have shown, up to the last point, with respect to the process of running through a plurality also holds in its essentials for explication in our sphere, still an essential difference comes into view. The thematic object which is explicated belongs to the explication and in it assumes the character of substrates for its explicates. But in the present case, however much it may appear as a uniform configuration in original intuition, the plurality is *not a goal of effective activity;* it is not a goal of knowledge gained through experience. It is not seized in advance and retained in active grasp in particular apprehensions; in the progress of these apprehensions, that specific partial identification which we have called explicative coincidence does not take place—a coincidence in which activities of both sides have a share. It is also clear that the individual activities of running through a plurality, precisely for this reason, are not united according to the same principle as those of explication. In general: *the unity of the activities in the running-through of a plurality has its source, not in activity itself, but in connection arising from passivity.* If, when a plurality is run through, it is also actively taken together, then matters evidently stand otherwise. But then the uniting activity is obviously completely other than that which gives unity

---

*EJ, pp. 119–121, 244–248 (Sections 24d and 61).

to an explication. It is an activity of a higher level, one to be described later on, a spontaneity in which the plurality is constituted as a specific object, as a "set." But in explication as such we do not perform separate acts taking the explicates together; it requires a special interest of a new kind in order to bring about, in addition, an explication in the form of an explicating which collectively links the explicates together. However, such a collective assemblage *[Zusammennehmen]* of the explicates is not necessary for explication considered in its normal course. From the very first, the explication has its unity in that the object is continuously the theme and as such remains constantly in grasp in a modified activity such as we have described.

§61. The set as a further example of an objectivity of understanding. Its constitution in productive spontaneity

States of affairs are not the only objectivities of the understanding which are constituted in predicatively productive spontaneity. They have a privileged position which is grounded in the basic function of the predicative judgment in the narrow sense of the copulative unity of linkage. We have contrasted the copulative linkage to the collective, which, to be sure, does not lead to the logical formation of sense, to deposits of sense in object-substrates in the same way as copulative spontaneity, but which is still to be counted as predicative spontaneity in the broader sense. It leads, like all predicative spontaneity, to the preconstitution of a new objectivity, that of the object "set."

In the domain of receptivity there is already an act of plural contemplation in the act of collectively taking things together; it is not the mere apprehension of one object after the other but a retaining-in-grasp of the one in the apprehension of the next, and so forth (cf. §24d). But this unity of taking-together, of collection, does not yet have *one* object: the pair, the collection, more generally, the set of the two objects. In a limited consciousness, we are turned toward one object in particular, then toward

another in particular, and nothing beyond this. We can then, while we hold on to the apprehension, again carry out a new act of taking-together [of, let us say,] the inkwell and a noise that we have just heard, or we retain the first two objects in apprehension and look at a third object, as one separate from the others. The connection of the first two is not loosened thereby. It is another thing to take the third object into the combination or to take a new object into consideration in addition to the two objects already in special combination. And then we have a unity of apprehension in the form of *([A, B], C):* likewise *([A, B], [C, D]),* etc. It is necessary to say again here that each apprehension of complex form has as objects *A B C . . .* and not, for example *(A, B)* as *one* object, and so on.

On the other hand, we can direct the regard of attention *[Zuwendung]* and the apprehension toward the *pair,* toward the one and the other of the pair, whereby *these* are objects. If we do this, then the repeated individual concentration, the concentrated partial apprehension, now of the *A* and then of the *B,* functions as a kind of explication, as an act of running-through the total object *A + B.* Looking into the matter more closely, the act of representation *(A, B)* has priority over the act of collection *(A + B),* in which the *sum* is the object. That, is, in order that the sum may be given, in order that it may be apprehended in self-givenness and contemplated. as such, we must apprehend the *A* and *B* together; in the unity of this apprehension of the two objects, the new object is preconstituted as its result, so to speak, as something which we now apprehend as one and which we can explicate in the individual apprehension of *A, B. . . .*

Thus, in order for the collective connection, originally sprung from the act of plural explication of *A* and *B* to become a substrate—i.e., a true object, something identifiable—a *turning of regard* is first required. But this implies that, as long as we carry out a merely collective assemblage, we have, more than ever, only a *preconstituted object,* a *"plurality,"* and only in retrospective apprehension, following the active constitution, do we have *as an object plurality as unity: as set.* It is the same here as with all objects produced in predicative spontaneity: a syntactical objectivity is preconstituted in a spontaneity, but only after it is completed *can it become a theme, it being an object only in retrospective apprehension [Rückgreifen].* The collective synthesis, the "*A* and *B* and *C*," is, indeed, the noetic unity of a consciousness but not yet the unity of an object in the proper sense, that is, in the sense of a thematic object-substrate. Here *A,* then *B,* then *C* is thematic, but the collective is not yet thematic. The colligating consciousness contains several objects encompassed in unity but not a unique object having several members. Nevertheless, through every synthetically unified consciousness, a new object is essentially preconstituted, precisely one having many members; there is then required only an act of thematic apprehension, possible at any time, to make what is thus preconstituted into an object and thereby a substrate of judgment. In the present case, the colligating is a *polythetic operation* through which a collective is essentially *pre*constituted. It becomes a thematic object after completion of the act of colligation through a *retrospective apprehension [rückgreifendes Erfassen]* by which the set is given to the ego as an object, as something identifiable. Subsequently, it is an object like any other; not only can it be totally identified as the identical element of many modes of givenness, but it can be explicated in an ever renewed identification; and this act of explication in its turn is always an act of colligation. But, like any substrate-objectivity, it can again also enter as subject in new connections of judgment, etc.

Naturally, sets can also be colligated in their turn with other disjunctive sets and can therefore be constituted as *sets of a higher order* and then be thematically objectified. The objects, disjunctively united in a set, can thus be sets in their turn. But finally, every set, preconstituted in intuition, leads to ultimate constituents, to particularities which are no longer sets. For it belongs to the idea of such a set that in its first givenness as substrate there is already present a pregiven multiplicity of particular affections which we actualize by its apprehension. To be sure, it is not precluded that, by "approaching," intuition can put new affections into play which previously were not yet available, so that the intended unities are again resolved into pluralities. But, in spite of this, *every set must be conceived a priori as capable of being reduced to ultimate constituents,* therefore to constituents *which are themselves no longer sets.*

But we can still add that, within the unity of a set, it is possible to delimit different partial sets by affectively particularizing connections, that in this way *mutually overlapping sets are possible,* and that, in general, sets in relation to other sets can exhibit all possible relations of containment.

Consequently, a set is an original objectivity, preconstituted by an activity of colligation which links disjunct objects to one another; the active apprehension of this objectivity consists in a simple reapprehension or laying-hold of that which has just been preconstituted. As a pure formation of spontaneity, the set represents a pre-eminent form in which thematic objects of every conceivable kind enter as members and with which they can themselves function again as members of determining judgments of every kind. One of the syntheses of predicative objectivation is the "and," and one of the syntheses of relation—which, to be sure, belongs to a wholly different orientation—is the "disjunct." These are the basic components of the particular syntactical form which is the collection or set.

There are, therefore, no originally passively preconstituted sets. Passivity can only create the preconditions; but it is not necessary that, in advance, the many objects as preconstituted in disjunction be already available and exercise their combined affective power. The objects can also enter into the thematic field of vision one after the other; and while we are already occupied with judging in various ways what has gone before, they fulfill by their succession the described conditions of the collection. The unity of affection is constituted successively, it provides the channels for changes of interest; and if the emerging objects are disjunctive, the collection can make its appearance. But it can also spring into activity from the first, as when an S is explicated step by step in its disjunctive properties and these properties at the very beginning attain collective connection. In any case, a turning of regard which makes the collective into an object is always possible here.

15. Universals

The Constitution of Empirical Universals*

§81. The original constitution of the universal

A) THE ASSOCIATIVE SYNTHESIS OF LIKE WITH LIKE AS THE BASIS OF THE PROMINENCE OF THE UNIVERSAL

The fact that all objects of experience are from the first experienced as known according to their type has its basis in the sedimentation of all apperceptions and in their habitual continued action on the basis of associative awakening. Association originally produces the passive synthesis of like with like, and this not only within a field of presence but also through the entire stream of lived experience, its immanent time, and everything which is constituted in it. Thus the synthesis of like with like is constituted by associative awakening, and the two terms can then be brought together in the unity of a presentifying intuition. If we would seek out the universal in its most original production, we must not first have recourse to syntheses of likeness which lead to empirical types, because in this case what is brought together through association is not necessarily self-given. To be sure, associative relations of likeness also subsist between the self-given in an actual perception and the more or less clearly remembered; these relations found the characteristics of typical knowledge, through which the empirical types are preconstituted. Of all this, therefore, we must first take no account and limit ourselves to what is self-given in the unity of a presence in a perception, in order to track down how generalities are originally constituted in self-givenness on the basis of the self-given.

We return to the result of our analysis of the associative constitution of unity. Every object affects us from a plurality of cogiven objects present in a field, and it may happen that the plurality as such, as a multiplicity of distinct objects, can also affect us as a unity. It is not a mere assemblage of distinct givens, but already in the passivity of its preconstitution it essentially includes a bond of internal affinity insofar as the individual objects belonging to it have common properties, on the basis of which they can then be taken together as entering into the unity of one thematic interest. In the activity of colligation which runs through the individual members there takes place a coincidence of similarity as regards what is common to them, and a distinction as regards what is different. In conformity with the "magnitude" of similarity, the common elements have a power of mutual evocation of corresponding importance; in a pair of objects closely bound together in this way there may come to prominence colors which are alike or very similar;

*EJ, pp. 321–338 (Sections 81–85).

in another pair the shapes may become prominent; and so on. As we carry out a colligation, each of the members coincides with its partner in that it is an identical substrate, namely, the substrate of the moments of similarity or likeness. In the moment of coincidence, the similar blends with the similar in proportion to their similarity, while the consciousness of a duality of what is united in this blending still persists. These similarities have their degrees, which are called contrasts of similarity, or "differences" in a determinate sense. In the case of complete likeness, the blending is, for consciousness, a perfect blending, that is, a blending without contrast and without difference. These are all processes taking place entirely within passivity. Blending and the coincidence of likeness arise quite independently of whether we actually spontaneously run through and colligate individual members coming into coincidence or whether there is only a passive preconstitution of multiplicity.

As has already been shown, the form of the states of affairs of the judgment of relation can be constituted on the basis of such syntheses of likeness. As we pass from one ink spot to another, a coincidence is accomplished in the form of a synthesis of likeness, and the state of affairs "*A* is like *B*" is engendered by the fact that they are both kept apart and synthetically combined.

But the act of judgment can go in still another direction: whereas on the basis of the associative awakening of like by like, an object no longer affects us merely for itself but in community with those akin to it, likewise, every judgment which is valid for an object taken for itself can enter into connection with judgments which are valid for kindred objects. Otherwise expressed: in the unity of a plurality founded on kinship, a singular judgment can enter into community with another singular judgment, whereby new kinds of judgments going beyond singularities arise. This becomes intelligible in view of the unique character of the synthesis of like with like. Its peculiarity lies in the fact that, though it indeed very much resembles a synthesis of identity, it still is not one. It resembles such a synthesis so much that

as we pass from like to like we often simply say: "This is surely the same thing." But the like are two distinct objects, and not one and the same. And yet *in every such duality,* and in any manifold of like things, there is actually a *unity and a sameness in the strictest sense.* It makes its appearance in the synthesis of the coincidence of likeness; in other words, it is preconstituted originally as an object through this synthesis. It is on this that a new mode of judging is then grounded.

B) The universal as constituted in productive spontaneity. Individual judgment and general [*generelles*] judgment

To begin with, we assume that the thematically determinative interest concentrates and particularizes itself on *S* and does this without loss of the general interest in what is connected with *S*. The affection which provides the impulse for the excitation of an ongoing interest, bringing about an encompassing synthesis and a continuous activity of unification, is constantly efficacious. In the restriction to *S,* the moment *p,* which comes to prominence as its property, is first apprehended in the form *S is p.* Suppose that the interest now shifts over to *S'*—which coaffects us on the basis of a completely like moment *p,* an individual moment *belonging to S'.* This *S'* must become predicatively determined by its moment *p* in the same way that just previously was true of *S.* The passive synthesis of coincidence between *S* and *S',* which was the ground of the common affection, can now be actively apprehended; we say that *S* and *S'* are the same—are *p:* although *S* still has *its* moment *p,* and *S',* in turn, has *its* moment *p.* Like the substrates, their properties are separated; but in the thematic transition we make, they are coincident, and there is an activity of identification. But this does not mean that the qualitative moments on both sides, or even that the *S* and the *S',* are present to consciousness as identical, although we say that *S* and *S'* are the same. With this, obviously, there is no question of a total identification; but, on the other hand, there is also no question of a *partial identification* of the kind which we have called explicative coincidence and to which we owe the qualitative moment as determination.

In any case, it is clear that when we pass from like moment to like moment a unity emerges in the coincidence, a unity in the duality of elements which are both separated and linked together, and that this unity emerges over and over again as totally and identically the same when we pass to a new member *S''*, then again to *S'''*, in which we have a moment *p* which is always like. The unity first emerges on the basis of the passive coincidence of likeness of the individual moments; and if one comes back to it, it can then be apprehended for itself. We must, therefore, distinguish the *first series of judgments,* in which there is predicated of each substrate *its own individual moment—S'* is *p'*, *S''* is *p''*, etc.—and, in contrast to this, *the judgments in which the* same *p, as everywhere* like, is predicated as the *universal,* as the identically one in all, that which emerges in *p', p'',* and so on. This means that the unity is preconstituted in the passive coincidence of likeness of the moments *p', p'',* and so on, *as the unity of the species p:* on the strength of this, an act of judgment oriented in a new direction is possible, in which, if we return to *S'* and re-effect the identification, we no longer determine *S'* by *p'* as its individual moment but by *p* as *identically the same in S, S',* and so on. There result the judgments *S'* is *p, S''* is *p,* and so on, in which *p* no longer designates an individual predicative core but a general one, namely, the universal as that which is common to two or more *S's* successively apprehended. Instead of being determined by the fleeting and variable moment, this is determined, therefore, by an *element ideally and absolutely identical,* which, in the mode of repetition or assimilation, goes through all the individual objects and their multiform moments as an ideal unity. As we will see later on, this is a unity which is not at all a function of the actuality of the moments; it does not come into being and disappear with them, and,

though it is individualized in them, it is not in them as a part.

First of all, we take note of the fact that here different forms of judgment must be distinguished from one another and that a new form is constituted, different from those which we have considered up to now. The judgment *S* is *p** in which *p* designates the *individual moment* in the individual object *S* is completely different from the judgment *S* is *p* in which *p* designates the *universal, the eidos,* and, in the same way, the judgment *p'* is *p* (the individual moment *p'* is of the kind *p*). In the one case, there is an identification between the substrate and its individual moment, in the other, a universal is predicated of the substrate. It is determined as being of the kind *p;* or *p',* on the basis of coincidence with other like moments *p'',* is determined as being of the kind *p*. In the one case we thus have a judgment which contains individual cores in itself and predicates something individual of them; we call it an *individual judgment.* In the other case, new cores appear, namely, generalities, at least on one side: the judgment is a *universal judgment.* This is a new *form of judging* because the difference of the cores has as a consequence a *modification of the form of the synthesis of identity* in contrast to the simple explicative synthesis, such as we conceived it as originally underlying our basic form of the categorical judgment: *S* is *p;* this is a synthesis which naturally can occur only on the basis of such a simple explicative synthesis or a plurality of such syntheses.

Speaking genetically and as a matter of principle, such a general core, a *hen epi pollōn,* naturally can be present to consciousness as the unity of an a priori generality, and can be ready for a possible thematic apprehension, only after the active accomplishment of the separate apprehension of like objects in a synthetic transition. But no act of relational judgment of comparison need necessarily have preceded, for example a judgment of the form *pS* (the moment *p* of *S*) is like *pS';* rather, this requires another attitude. The direction of in-

---

*Reading *p* instead of *p'*. —Translator's note.

terest toward the universal, toward unity as opposed to multiplicity, does not aim at the determination of the like in relation to another as its like. Hence it is not the synthesis of coincidence of the like, presenting itself passively, which is actualized in the form of an "is"-predication. What awakens interest is rather *what is passively preconstituted in the coincidence of the like as individually apprehended;* this is the *one* which comes into prominence on the basis of the coincidence, the identical which is one and always the same, no matter in what direction we may continue; it is this which is *actively apprehended.*

Furthermore, what is achieved is obviously no longer something on the order of an *explication* of like objects. The *one* which comes to light here is not in the objects as their part, as a partial-identical; otherwise, it would indeed be only a like which is present everywhere, and the like elements would be in a relation of intersection.

Hence, the *one* does not repeat itself in the like; it is given only once, but in many. It confronts us as an *objectivity of a new kind,* as an objectivity of understanding, *arising from original sources of activity,* although obviously on the foundation of sensibility; for the activity of apprehending and running through particulars and bringing them into coincidence is necessary if the universal is to be preconstituted at all and then become a thematic object. Its original apprehension has a field of interest of a different sort, which the interest must run through as in the case of an individual object of simple receptivity. The glancing ray of attention must go *through* the individual objects already constituted; and, as it pursues the bond of likeness and brings about the coincidence, the one which is thus constituted is thematized as something which is *inherent* in the individual objects and yet is not part of them; for the objects compared can also be completely separated.

c) PARTICIPATION IN THE IDENTITY OF THE UNIVERSAL, AND MERE LIKENESS

This kind of self-giving inherent in particulars points to *a wholly unique relation of iden-* *tity,* different from all other such relations. If the universal α which is brought into prominence in the same way in *A* and *B* is apprehended objectively, it gives itself as *in A, in B,* and in the corresponding transitions. States of affairs of a new kind can arise: *A* is an instance of the universal, it participates in the universal, it is *conceived* through α. If we make α the subject, this means: α, the predicate, belongs to the particular, to *A,* to *B;* the concept dwells in the particular *(koinōnia).* To express the first state of affairs in ordinary language, we say, for example: "This is red, that is also red." We should notice here that the adjectival form belongs essentially to the state of affairs and is not an accident of grammar. It will be necessary later on to discuss the way in which the forms of judging "in general" emerge on the basis of these relations.

The relation of *participation* is not to be confused with that of *mere likeness.* We must not think that the identity of the universal is only an exaggerated way of speaking. Through overlapping, the like here and there stands out from the different. But just as the concrete individual objects are separated in multiplicity or plurality, wherein the coincidence by overlapping which makes its appearance in the active accomplishment of colligation changes nothing, so also the moments of likeness which become objects of attention are separated and, in the same way, the moments which differ; each object has *its* indwelling moment, for example, that of redness, and each of the many objects which are red has its proper individual moment, but in likeness.

As against this, it should be emphasized that *likeness is only* a correlate of the identity of a universal, which in truth can be considered as one and the same and as a "counterpart" of the individual. This identical moment is first "particularized" *[vereinzelt]* into two, and then, as we will soon see, into as many as desired. All of these particularizations have a relation to one another through their relation to the identical and are then said to be like. Metaphorically speaking, the concrete objects which have such particularizations in themselves are then said to be like "with regard to red" and can themselves be considered in an improper sense as particularizations of the universal.

§82. *Empirical generalities and their extension. The ideality of concepts*

We first thought of the universal as given to us by the cohesion of two substrates. And, in fact, a universal is already constituted in this case; it is, to be sure, a universal of the *lowest level*—precisely, what is common to *two* objects. However, the comparison can go further, at first from *A* to *B*, then from *B* to *C*, to *D*, etc.; and, with each new step, the universal acquires a greater *extension*. As we have already indicated, not only the singular judgments *A* is red, *B* is red, *C* is red, and so on can emerge on the basis of this coincidence of likeness, but also *new forms of the state of affairs as plural: A and B are red, A and B and C are red,* where "red" designates the species. By inverting the terms, the judgments read: Red (now as the main substrate, as the subject in a new syntactical form) belongs to *A, B, C.* . . . In the first form there is then a multiple subject, a plural; a synthetic ray goes out from each member, directed toward the general predicate, which is posited only once. Conversely: the one general term as subject discharges a multiple ray of predication. Each individual ray terminates in a member of the collection: *A* and *B*, etc.

In these cases, the comparison which leads to a universal concerns individually determined objects, which appear in a finite closed experience in their individual determinateness. Although opposite to them as irreal, yet still bound to them, the universal then appears as something standing out *in* them, as a concept dwelling in them. However, as soon as the experience broadens and leads to new like objects, while the first are still in hand or associatively awakened in a recollection, a resumption of the synthesis immediately occurs; new elements of likeness are immediately recognized as particularizations of the same universal. This can proceed to infinity. As soon as an *open horizon* of like objects is present to consciousness as a horizon of presumptively actual and really possible objects, and as soon as it becomes intuitive as an open infinity, it gives itself as *an infinitude of particularizations of the* SAME *universal.* The generalities individually apprehended and combined then get an infinite extension and lose their tie to precisely those individuals from which they were first abstracted.

In addition, it should be noted that a synthetic linking-on to an original constitution of the generality is by no means required in order to apprehend a particular object as the particular instance of a universal. If the concept, e.g., the concept *flower,* previously appeared in an original comparison, then a new flower making its appearance is recognized on the basis of associative awakening of the type "flower," established in the past, without an intuitive recollection of the earlier cases of comparison being necessary. But actual givenness of the universal then requires that we pass beyond what is particular in the likenesses, eventually toward an open horizon of possible continuation. Whether the earlier cases are individually represented in addition does not matter. Thus it is evident that *the universal is not bound to any particular actuality.*

We can now also go beyond experience, and the comparison of objects actually given in experience, and pass over to free imagination. We imagine similar particulars—similar to actualities which have been actually experienced to begin with—and thereupon as many as we choose, that is, always new, individually different from one another, as similar particulars, and such that, if the experience had continued, they could actually have been given to us. Thus, to every concept belongs *an infinite extension of purely possible particulars,* of purely possible conceptual objects. If I imagine things, I apprehend in them as pure possibilities the concept of a thing. I can find this same concept in actual things; stated more precisely, in intended things which I posit as actualities on the basis of actual experience. In the transition from imagination to actual experience, these give themselves as particulars realizing the same universal which, in imagination, is not truly realized but only quasi-realized in the possibilities discerned.

Consequently, *the possibility of the formation of general objectivities,* of "concepts," extends *as far as there are associative syntheses of likeness.* On this rests the *universality of the operation of the formation of concepts;* everything which, in some way or other, is objectively constituted in actuality or possibility, as an object of actual experience or of imagination, can occur as a term in relations of comparison and be conceived through the activity of eidetic identification and subsumption under a universal.

The concept in its ideality must be understood as something objective which has a *purely ideal being,* a being which does not presuppose the actual existence of corresponding particulars; it is what it is even if the corresponding particulars are only pure possibilities, though, on the other hand, in the realm of experienced actuality, it can also be the realized concept of actual particulars. And *if there are* actual particulars, other like ones can just as well be taken in their place. *Correlative to the pure being of the universal is the being of the pure possibilities* which participate in it and which must be constructed as its bases and as an ideally infinite extension of the bases of the pure abstraction giving access to the universal.

Naturally, concepts as *pure* concepts can, from the first, originate *outside of all relation to current actuality,* namely, by the comparison of pure possibilities of the imagination. It is clear thereby that every actual likeness, acquired in this way, of possibilities given as existing (as existing, not in the sense of a reality of experience, but precisely *as* a possibility) intentionally includes in itself a possible likeness of possible actualities and a possible universal in which they can possibly participate. On the other hand, even if they were formed originally on the basis of experience as actual generalities, concepts can always be apprehended as pure concepts.

Despite all the Platonic turns of phrase by which we have described its relation to the particular, the ideality of the universal must not be understood as if it were a question here of a being-in-itself devoid of reference to any subject. On the contrary, like *all* objectivities of understanding, it refers essentially *to the processes of productive spontaneity* which belong to it correlatively and in which it comes to original givenness. The *being of the universal* in its different levels is essentially a *being-constituted* in these processes.

In accordance with our starting from experience and from the comparison and formation of concepts taking place on the basis of experience, we have, up to this point, not yet been able to deal with pure generalities. What we have described is the acquisition of *empirical* generalities. All the concepts of natural life bring with them, without harm to their ideality, the copositing of an empirical sphere in which they have the place of their possible realization in particulars. If we speak of animals, plants, cities, houses, and so on, we intend therewith in advance *things of the world,* and in fact the world of our actual, real experience (not of a merely possible world); accordingly, we think of these concepts as *actual* generalities, that is, as bound to this world. The extension of such concepts is indeed infinite, but it is an *actual* extension, the extension of things actually and really possible in the given world. These real possibilities, which belong to the extension of empirical concepts, must not be confused with the *pure* possibilities to which pure generalities refer. On this, more later on.

§83. *Empirico-typical generality and its passive preconstitution*

A) THE ATTAINMENT OF EMPIRICAL CONCEPTS FROM TYPES IN NATURAL EXPERIENTIAL APPERCEPTION

In the first place, there are still important distinctions to be made in the domain of empirical generalities; above all, it is necessary to examine more closely the path which leads from passively preconstituted typifications to empirical concepts, specifically to empirical concepts understood not only in the sense of everyday concepts but, on a higher level, to concepts of the empirical sciences.

We return to what has been said previously. The factual world of experience is experienced as a typified world. Things are experienced as trees, bushes, animals, snakes, birds; specifically, as pine, linden, lilac, dog, viper, swallow, sparrow, and so on. The table is characterized as being familiar and yet new. What is given in experience as a new individual is first known in terms of what has been genuinely perceived; it calls to mind the like (the similar). But what is apprehended according to type also has a horizon of possible experience with corresponding prescriptions of familiarity and has, therefore, types of attributes not yet experienced but expected. When we see a dog, we immediately anticipate its additional modes of behavior: its typical way of eating, playing, running, jumping, and so on. We do not actually see its teeth; but although we have never yet seen this dog, we know in advance how its teeth will look—not in their individual determination but according to type, inasmuch as we have already had previous and frequent experience of "similar" animals, of "dogs," that they have such things as "teeth" and of this typical kind. To begin with, what is experienced about a perceived object in the progress of experience is straightway assigned "apperceptively" to every perceived object with similar components of genuine perception. We anticipate this, and actual experience may or may not confirm it. In the confirmation, the content of a type is extended, but the type can also be subdivided into particular types; on the other hand, every concrete real thing still has its *individual attributes,* though at the same time they have their *typical form.*

Everything apprehended according to type can lead us to the *general concept of the type* in which we apprehend it. On the other hand, we are not *necessarily* directed toward the universal in this way; notwithstanding the possible utilization of the name "dog" in its general signification, we need not thematize a dog according to its type *as* a particular of the universal "dog"; rather, we can also be directed toward it as an individual: then, the passively preconstituted reference to its type, in which it is apprehended from the first, remains unthematic. But on the basis of this reference we can always constitute a general concept "dog," represent other dogs known by experience to ourselves; in an arbitrary creation of the imagination we can also represent other dogs to ourselves in an open multiplicity and hence discern the universal "dog." If we are once attuned to apprehension of the universal, then in conformity with the synthesis discussed in §81, each part, each particular moment in an object, furnishes us something to apprehend conceptually as general; every analysis will then go hand in hand with a general predication. Thus the uniform general type, the universal first apprehended on the basis of the associatively awakened relation of the likeness of one object with other objects, will be a universal, a concept which includes many *particular concepts.* But if the objects are real objects, then a sensuous type coming to prominence does not exhaust every like element which we can find in continuing experience and, consequently, in the exposition of the true being of these objects as that in which they are like. The more the objects reveal themselves as they are, the more each of them enters into intuition, then all the more numerous are the possibilities which present themselves of finding likenesses. But it then also becomes evident that further determinations are as a rule in regular connection with the determinations already apprehended or, what is the same thing, that in the course of experience they must be expected as copresent.

To the type "dog," e.g., belongs a stock of typical attributes with an open horizon of anticipation of further such attributes. This implies that, according to the "universal," one dog is like every other, specifically, in such a way that the universal, which, through the previous experiences of dogs, even if these were only superficial and wholly incomplete, has been prescribed as characterizing all dogs and which is already known according to its type, brings with itself an indeterminate horizon of typical attributes still unknown. If we were to go on in experience, at first to this or that particular dog, we would in the end constantly discover ever new attributes, belonging not merely to *these* dogs but to dogs *in general* and determined by the typical attributes which we have ascribed to them up to that point. Thus, superseding the *actual* concept, specifically acquired in actual experience, a *presumptive idea* arises, *the idea of a universal,* to which belongs, in addition to the attributes already acquired, a horizon, indeterminate and open, of unknown attributes (conceptual determinations). Specifically, this is a horizon in the sense of a constant presumption, of a constant empirical certainty, according to which what is identified as a dog through the known attributes will also have, through empirical induction relative to dogs given and examined more closely, new attributes which are found in conformity with a rule, and so on and on. Thus empirical concepts are changed by the continual admission of new attributes but according to an empirical idea of an open, ever-to-be-corrected concept which, at the same time, contains in itself the rule of empirical belief and is founded on the progress of actual experience.

B) ESSENTIAL AND NONESSENTIAL TYPES.
SCIENTIFIC EXPERIENCE AS LEADING TO THE
EXPOSITION OF THE ESSENTIAL TYPES

To be sure, there are certain typical generalities of experience already passively preconstituted and then apprehended thematically, e.g., grass, shrubs, and the like, in connection with which no such infinitely open typical horizon is linked to the attributes which are determinative in the beginning. This means that, in conformity with the nature of experience, the eventual presupposition that there will always be typical attributes to discover is not confirmed. Immediate experience often separates and distinguishes things solely on the basis of certain obvious differences which can mask an actually existing internal correlation; for example, the membership of the animals called "whales" in the class of mammals is masked by the outward analogy which whales have with fishes with regard to their mode of

life, something already indicated in the verbal designation.* In such cases we speak of *nonessential types.* In the comprehensive experience of concrete nature, individuals are ordered increasingly under *essential types,* in different levels of generality. Scientific investigation of empirical natural history is based on this. Necessarily underlying it is *the prescientific and multifariously nonessential typification carried out by natural experiential apperception.* Scientific concepts of species seek to determine essential types by a systematic and methodical experience. Scientific concepts can include only *a finite number of determinate attributes,* but they also carry, with a scientifically extraordinary probability, an infinitely open horizon of typical attributes, codetermined by this conceptual content, although these attributes are at first unknown; this horizon can be explored and circumscribed in subsequent investigations. In addition, the typical also concerns causality: the causality of the "life" of animals or plants of the relevant types (species) under the conditions of life, the mode of their "development," their reproduction, etc., with regard to which it is not necessary to go into more detail at this point.

§84. Levels of generality

A) CONCRETE GENERALITY AS THE GENERALITY DERIVED FROM THE REPETITION OF COMPLETELY LIKE INDIVIDUALS. INDEPENDENT AND ABSTRACT, SUBSTANTIVAL AND ADJECTIVAL GENERALITIES

The typical generalities under which the content of experience is ordered are of different levels. For example, when we juxtapose the types "fir" and "conifer," which we come by in the course of experience, the latter has a greater "extension" and is, therefore, a higher generality. The levels of generality are conditioned by the degrees of likeness of the members of the extension.

If we start from the experience of individu-

*One of the elements in the German word for "whale," *Walfisch,* is the word for "fish." —Translator's note.

al objects, then the lowest universal, which, from a genetic point of view, we come upon from the very first, is that one which arises from the mere "repetition" of individuals capable of being experienced as independent and completely like. We call it a *concretum*. Every individual object can be thought more than once; a second object completely like it is always conceivable in comparison with it. Every individual is an individual particular of its *concretum;* it is a concrete individual. *This universal, born of the repetition of like independent objects* (that is, from individuals), is *the lowest generality,* the most *independent;* this implies that it is one which is not founded in other generalities, therefore, which does not presuppose them. Thus, e.g., the universal "brightness" is founded in the universal "color," which includes brightness; in turn, color is only conceivable as formed color; and this—in other words, the colored shape (the spatial shape), more precisely, the formed spatial thing itself—is the complete *concretum,* i.e., the universal, which, as a universal, is completely independent.

We see by this that the lowest concrete generalities found other generalities, those of their abstract moments, which, in turn, naturally yield a universal of repetition, but one that is dependent: a member of the class of the lowest dependent generalities, the *abstract species.* As generalities which have an extension of originally dependent particulars, predestined to an originally adjectival apprehension, they are themselves originally *adjectival generalities.* To them we contrast the originally independent generalities as *substantival generalities.*

B) HIGHER-LEVEL GENERALITIES AS GENERALITIES ON THE BASIS OF MERE SIMILARITY

If the likeness of the individual members of the extension of a generality is no longer *complete* likeness, then generalities of higher levels emerge. We have understood complete likeness as the limit of similarity. With the transition from the similar to the similar a coincidence appears which is still not a complete coincidence. The similar members which have overlapped one another are *divergent.* Different similarities can have different divergences, and the divergences are themselves again comparable, have, themselves, their own similarities. Similarity, therefore, has a gradation, and its limit, complete similarity, signifies an absence of divergence in coincidence, i.e., the coincidence of elements which merely repeat themselves. It is the foundation for the lowest level of similarity. In what concerns the mere similarity in which the higher levels of generality are grounded, we have found as its principal differences those of *total similarity* (similarity in relation to all the individual moments of the similar objects) and *partial similarity* (similarity in relation to individual moments, each with its limit of likeness, while the others are not similar).* Generalities of different levels emerge, depending on these differences. Levels of generality are thus conditioned not only by *the magnitude of the divergences in similarity* of all the similar moments which are found in the individual members of the extension of the generality in question—in the case of total similarity these are *all* the moments—but also by the *number of similar moments,* i.e., by the degree of approximation to total similarity. Stated more precisely, *complete likeness* is the *limit of total similarity,* while, in the case of merely partial similarity (even if, in relation to the *individual moments,* this attains the limit of complete likeness), this limit can never be attained in relation to the *whole.* It always remains the merely similar. Nevertheless, the universal of similarity also contains, by virtue of its relation to its limit, a universal of likeness, but only of a partial, mediate likeness, likeness "in relation to this or that moment." Thus, even in the coincidence of likeness, a *common* moment comes to light, or, rather, a moment which originally shines

---

*On the concepts "total similarity" and "partial similarity," as well as "distance of similarity," cf. §§44, 45.

through as a common moment. It comes to perfect givenness in the process of the transition from the universal of the repetition of completely like members to the next-higher species, to the universal of mere similarity—of total similarity, to begin with, and then to the universal of partial similarity (likeness), which does not include the absolutely like or totally similar but the like (similar) in relation to this or that moment.

The universal of mere similarity is one of a higher level since the members of its extension, even if it is formed only by the coincidence of *two* similar objects, can already be conceived as a universal arising from the possible repetition of like members. It is thus a *specific universal,* which already has under itself two or more concrete generalities; later on we come to higher species, genera, and so on. These are *dependent generalities,* and this because they spring from the comparison of generalities (at the lowest level those of repetition). Thus, universals can be compared like other objects, e.g., red and blue; and in this synthetic activity a generality of a higher level is constituted. In this activity, the generality comes to self-givenness as a generality which has generalities under itself as particulars. Thus, on the basis of like *concreta* there arises a *"concrete" species* and, from concrete species, a "concrete" genus. Naturally, this is not to say that the "concrete" species, and so on, would itself be a *concretum.* We call it a "concrete species" only to call attention to its origin from the concrete, since there are also species which have under them dependent generalities, universals arising from the repetition of abstract moments, e.g., species of shapes and so on. In contrast to generalities of higher levels, we call these *abstract:* abstract genera and species.

It hardly needs to be emphasized that empirical types, as the kind of generality which first thrusts itself on our attention and rests on the passive preconstitution of typical familiarities, are for the most part universals which belong to a higher level, to that of the generality of species or genus; for the lowest universal, arising from the mere repetition of the completely like, is obviously a limiting case.

§85. Material generalities and formal generalities

Another important difference is that between *material* and *formal* generalities. In order to understand it, we must remember our breakdown of objectivities into those devoid of logicosyntactical form and those which are syntactically formed, namely, the objectivities of the understanding. Depending on the kinds of objects compared for the purpose of apprehending the universal, two kinds of fundamentally different generalities result.

1. The synthesis of coincidence of the like can obviously link objects as objects of simple experience, thus objects which still have undergone no syntactical formation. They acquire a syntactical form only from this synthesis of coincidence and the abstraction inherent in it. Thus concepts arise which are *purely material* as well as concrete—concepts which, to be sure, do not have a name. For concepts expressed verbally, like tree, house, etc., already include, in addition, a variety of predicates acquired in the activity of judgment. However, it is important to fix the simple limiting case at the outset. It is a matter here of concrete concepts preceding all explication and syntactical linking of predicates.

2. But if we then compare syntactical structures, *new likenesses* appear in them, namely:

a) Those which belong to contents elicited from passive experience by explication, which thus depend on a material community. They yield *material general concepts.*

b) Likenesses which belong to the syntactical forms springing from spontaneous production, i.e., those which refer to *merely formal communities.* For example, in the statement "Red is different from blue," in addition to the material concepts red and blue, pure forms are also expressed in our talk about difference and in the whole form of the proposition: subject-form, predicate-form, object-form. Concepts such as likeness, difference, unity, plurality, group, whole, part, object, property—in short, *all so-called purely logical concepts* and all concepts which can and must be expressed in the diversity of state-of-affairs forms and, verbally, in statement forms are, if we merely allow what is material in the propositions to be undetermined, *purely formal concepts,* formal generalities.

Eidetic Variation and the Acquisition of Pure Universals*

§86. *The contingency of empirical generalities and a priori necessity*

Empirical generalities, we said, have an extension of actual and really possible particulars. Acquired at first on the basis of the repetition of like and then merely similar objects given in actual experience, these generalities refer not only to this limited and, so to speak, denumerable extension of actual particulars, from which they have been originally acquired, but as a general rule they have a *horizon* which presumptively exhibits a broader experience of particulars which can be acquired in free arbitrariness by opening up this presumptive horizon of being. When it is a question of the realities of the infinite pregiven world, we can imagine *an arbitrary number of particulars capable of being given later on,* which likewise includes this empirical generality as a *real possibility.* The extension is then an infinitely open one, and still the unity of the empirically acquired species and the higher genus is a "contingent" one. This means that a contingently given particular object was the point of departure of the formation of the concept, and this formation led beyond the likewise contingent likenesses and similarities—contingent because the member acting as the point of departure for the comparison was contingent, given in actual experience. The concept opposed to this contingency is that of *a priori necessity.* It will be necessary to show how, in contrast to these

empirical concepts, pure concepts are formed, concepts whose constitution does not thus depend on the contingency of the element actually given as the point of departure and its empirical horizons. These concepts do not envelop an extension which, as it were, is open merely *after the event,* but beforehand, *a priori.* This envelopment beforehand signifies that they must be capable of *prescribing rules to all empirical particulars.* With empirical concepts, infinity of extension implies only that I can imagine an arbitrary number of like particulars without its actually being evident whether, in the progress of actual experience, this presumptively posited "again and again" might perhaps undergo a cancellation, whether this being able to continue might one day actually reach a limit. With pure concepts, on the other hand, this infinity of actually being-able-to-continue is *given with self-evidence,* precisely because, *before* all experience, these concepts prescribe rules for its later course and, consequently, rule out a sudden change, a cancellation. This idea of a priori generality and necessity will become even clearer in the course of our presentation.

§87. *The method of essential seeing*

A) Free variation as the foundation of essential seeing

From the preceding it has already become clear that, for the acquisition of pure concepts or concepts of essences, an empirical comparison cannot suffice but that, by special arrangements, the universal which first comes to prominence in the empirically given must from the outset be freed from its character of contingency. Let us attempt to get a first concept of this operation. It is based on the modification of an experienced or imagined objectivity, turning it into an arbitrary example which, at the same time, receives the character of a guiding "model," a point of departure for the production of an infinitely open multiplicity of vari-

---

*EJ, pp. 339–354 (Sections 86–90).

ants. It is based, therefore, on a *variation*. In other words, for its modification in pure imagination, we let ourselves be guided by the fact taken as a model. For this it is necessary that ever new similar images be obtained as copies, as images of the imagination, which are all concretely similar to the original image. Thus, by an act of volition we produce free variants, each of which, just like the total process of variation itself, occurs in the subjective mode of the "arbitrary." It then becomes evident that a unity runs through this multiplicity of successive figures, that in such free variations of an original image, e.g., of a thing, an *invariant* is necessarily retained as the *necessary general form,* without which an object such as this thing, as an example of its kind, would not be thinkable at all. While what differentiates the variants remains indifferent to us, this form stands out in the practice of voluntary variation, and as an absolutely identical content, an invariable *what,* according to which all the variants coincide: *a general essence.* We can direct our regard toward it as toward the necessarily invariable, which prescribes limits to all variation practiced in the mode of the "arbitrary," all variation which is to be variation of the same original image, no matter how this may be carried out. The essence proves to be that without which an object of a particular kind cannot be thought, i.e., without which the object cannot be intuitively imagined as such. This general essence is the *eidos,* the *idea* in the Platonic sense, but apprehended in its purity and free from all metaphysical interpretations, therefore taken exactly as it is given to us immediately and intuitively in the vision of the idea which arises in this way. Initially, this givenness was conceived as a givenness of experience. Obviously, a mere imagining, or rather, what is intuitively and objectively present in it, can serve our purpose just as well.

For example, if we take a sound as our point of departure, whether we actually hear it or whether we have it present as a sound "in the imagination," then we obtain the *eidos* sound as that which, in the course of "arbitrary" variants, is necessarily common to all these variants. Now if we take as our point of departure

another sound-phenomenon in order to vary it arbitrarily, in the new "example" we do not apprehend *another eidos* sound; rather, in juxtaposing the old and the new, we see that it is *the same,* that the variants and the variations on both sides join together in a single variation, and that the variants here and there are, in like fashion, *arbitrary particularizations of the one eidos.* And it is even evident that in progressing from one variation to a new one we can give this progress and this formation of new multiplicities of variation the character of an arbitrary progress and that, furthermore, in such progress in the form of arbitrariness the same *eidos* must appear "again and again": the same general essence "sound in general."

b) The arbitrary structure of the process of the formation of variants

That the *eidos* depends on a freely and arbitrarily producible multiplicity of variants attaining coincidence, on an open infinity, does not imply that an *actual* continuation to infinity is required, an actual production of all the variants—as if only then could we be sure that the *eidos* apprehended at the end actually conformed to all the possibilities. On the contrary, what matters is that the variation as a process of the formation of variants should itself have a *structure of arbitrariness,* that the process should be accomplished in the consciousness of an arbitrary development of variants. This does not mean—even if we break off—that we intend an actual multiplicity of particular, intuitive variations which lead into one another, an actual series of objects, offering themselves in some way or other and utilized arbitrarily, or fictively produced in advance; it means, rather, that, just as each object has the character of *exemplary arbitrariness,* so the multiplicity of variations likewise always has an arbitrary character: it is a matter of indifference what might still be joined to it, a matter of indifference what, in addition, I might be given to apprehend in the consciousness that "I could continue in this way." This remarkable and truly important consciousness of "and so on, at my pleasure" belongs essentially to every multiplicity of variations. Only in this way is given what we call an "infinitely open" multiplicity; obviously, it is the same whether we proceed according to a long process, producing or drawing arbitrarily on anything suitable, thus extending the series of actual intuitions, or whether we break off prematurely.

c) THE RETAINING-IN-GRASP OF THE ENTIRE MULTIPLICITY OF VARIATIONS AS THE FOUNDATION OF ESSENTIAL SEEING

In this multiplicity (or, rather, on the groundwork of the open process of the self-constitution of variation, with the variants actually appearing in intuition) is grounded as a higher level *the true seeing of the universal as eidos.* Preceding this seeing, there is the transition from the initial example, which gives direction and which we have called a model, to ever new images, whether these are due to the aimless favor of association and the whims of passive imagination (in which case we only seize upon them arbitrarily as examples) or whether we have obtained them by our own pure activity of imaginative invention from our original model. In this transition from image to image, from the similar to the similar, all the arbitrary particulars attain overlapping coincidence in the order of their appearance and enter, in a purely passive way, into a synthetic unity in which they all appear as modifications of one another and then as arbitrary sequences of particulars in which the same universal is isolated as an *eidos.* Only in this continuous coincidence does something which is the same come to congruence, something which henceforth can be seen purely for itself. This means that it is *passively preconstituted* as such and that the seeing of the *eidos* rests in the *active intuitive apprehension* of what is thus preconstituted— exactly as in *every* constitution of objectivities of the understanding, and especially of general objectivities.

Naturally, the presupposition for this is that the multiplicity *as such* is present to consciousness as a *plurality* and never slips completely from our grasp. Otherwise, we do not attain the *eidos* as the ideally identical, which only *is* as

hen epi pollōn. If, for example, we occupy ourselves with the inventive imagining of a thing or a figure, changing it into arbitrarily new figures, we have something always new, and always only one thing: the last-imagined. Only if we retain in grasp the things imagined earlier, as a multiplicity in an open process, and only if we look toward the congruent and the purely identical, do we attain the *eidos.* Certainly, we need not ourselves actively and expressly bring about the overlapping coincidence, since, with the successive running-through and the retaining-in-grasp of what is run through, it takes place of itself in a purely passive way.

d) THE RELATION OF ESSENTIAL SEEING TO THE EXPERIENCE OF INDIVIDUALS. THE ERROR OF THE THEORY OF ABSTRACTION

The peculiar character of essential seeing on the basis of variation will become still clearer if we contrast it with the intuitive experience of individual objects. Over against the specific *freedom* of variation, there is in all experience of the individual a wholly determined *commitment.* This means that when we receptively experience an individual on the basis of a passive pregivenness, when we turn toward it in order to apprehend it, when we take it in as existing, we thereby take our stand, so to speak, on the ground of this apperception. By it, horizons are prescribed for further possible experiences which will take place on this ground, pregiven from the first step. Everything which we further experience must be brought into a context of unanimity if it is to count as an object for us; failing this, it is canceled, nullified, is not taken in receptively as actual; unanimity must prevail on the ground of a unity of experience, a ground already prescribed for each individual object of experience; every conflict is excluded or, rather, leads to a cancellation. Every *experience in the pregnant sense,* which includes activity, at least of the lowest level, thus signifies *"taking a stand on the ground of experience."*

The same thing holds for *imagination* insofar as we imagine within a context such that the individual imaginings are to be linked together in the unity of one act of imagination. Here, in the mode of the quasi, is repeated all that has already been said about actual experience. We have a quasi-world as a unified world of imagination. It is the "ground" on which we can take our stand in the course of a unified act of imagination—only with this difference: that it is left to our free choice to decide how far we will allow this unity to extend; we can enlarge such a world at our pleasure, whereas fixed boundaries are set to the unity of an actual world by what was given previously.

In contrast to this constraint in the experience of the individual object, the specific *freedom of essential seeing* becomes intelligible to us: in the free production of the multiplicity of variations, in the progress from variant to variant, we are not bound by the conditions of unanimity in the same way as in the progress of experience from one individual object to another on the ground of the unity of experience. If, for example, we envisage to ourselves an individual house now painted yellow, we can just as well think that it could be painted blue or think that it could have a slate instead of a tile roof or, instead of this shape, another one. The house is an object which, in the realm of the possible, could have other determinations in place of, and incompatible with, whatever determinations happen to belong to it within the unity of a representation. This house, the same, is thinkable as *a* and as *non-a* but, naturally, if as *a*, then not *at the same time* as *non-a*. It cannot be both simultaneously; it cannot be actual while having *each* of them at the same time; but at any moment it can be *non-a* instead of *a*. It is, therefore, thought as an identical something in which opposite determinations can be exchanged. "Intuitively," in the attainment of this self-evidence, the existence of the object is certainly bound to the possession of one *or* the other of the opposing predicates and to the requirement of the exclusion of their joint possession; however, an *identical substrate* of concordant attributes is evidently present, except that its *simple* thesis is not possible, but only the *modified* thesis: if this identical something determined as *a* ex-

ists, then *a'* belongs to it in the canceled form *non-a*, and conversely. To be sure, the identical substrate is not an individual pure and simple. The sudden change is that of an individual into a second individual incompatible with it in coexistence. An individual pure and simple is an existing individual (or one capable of existing). However, *what is seen as unity in the conflict is not an individual* but a concrete hybrid unity of individuals mutually nullifying and coexistentially exclusive: a unique consciousness with a unique content, whose correlate signifies concrete unity founded in conflict, in incompatibility. This remarkable hybrid unity is at the bottom of essential seeing.

The old theory of abstraction, which implies that the universal can be constituted only by abstraction on the basis of individual, particular intuitions, is thus in part unclear, in part incorrect. For example, if I construct the general concept tree—understood, of course, as a pure concept—on the basis of individual, particular trees, the tree which is present in my mind is not posited in any way as an individually determined tree: on the contrary, I represent it in such a way that it is the same in perception and in the free movement of imagination, that it is not posited as existing or even called into question, and that it is not in any way held to be an individual. The *particular*, which is at the bottom of essential seeing, *is not in the proper sense an intuited individual as such.* The remarkable unity which is at the bottom here is, on the contrary, an "individual" in the exchange of "nonessential" constitutive moments (those appearing, as complementary moments, outside the essential moments, which are to be apprehended as identical).

E) CONGRUENCE AND DIFFERENCE IN THE OVERLAPPING COINCIDENCE OF MULTIPLICITIES OF VARIATION

What has already been said implies the following: with the *congruence* present in the coincidence of the multiplicities of variation there is connected, on the other hand, a *difference* in various aspects. If, for example, we pass from a given red color to a series of any other red colors whatsoever—whether we actually see them or whether they are colors floating "in the imagination"—we obtain the *eidos* "red," which, as the necessarily common, is what is congruent in the alteration of the "arbitrary" variants, while the different extensions in the coincidence, instead of being congruent, on the contrary come to prominence in conflict.

The *idea of the difference,* therefore, is only to be understood *in its involvement with the idea of the identically common element which is the eidos.* Difference is that which, in the overlapping of the multiplicities, is not to be brought into the unity of the congruence making its appearance thereby, that which, in consequence, does not make an *eidos* visible. To say that a unity of congruence is not attained means that in the coincidence the different elements are in conflict with one another. Consider, for example, an identical color; at one time it is the color of this extension and shape, at another time of that. In the overlapping, the one conflicts with the other, and they mutually supplant each other.

But, on the other hand, it is clear that *things cannot enter into conflict which have nothing in common.* In our example, not only is an identical color already presupposed; it is even more important that, even if the one colored object were square, they still could not enter into conflict if both were not extended figures. Thus, every difference in the overlapping with others and in conflict with them points toward a new universal to be brought out (in our example, shape) as the universal of the superimposed differences which have momentarily come into the unity of conflict. This point will be of great importance for the theory of the hierarchical structure of ideas up to the highest regions.

By way of summary, we survey the three principal steps which pertain to the process of ideation:

1. The productive activity which consists in running through the multiplicity of variations.

2. The unitary linking in continuous coincidence.

3. The active identification which brings out the congruent over against the differences.

f) VARIATION AND ALTERATION

One point still requires clarification. We speak of *variation* and of variants, not of *alteration* and phases of alteration. In fact, the two concepts are essentially different, despite a certain affinity.

An alteration is always alteration of a real thing, understood in a completely general sense as a temporal existent, something which endures, which continues through a duration. Every real thing is subject to change and *is* only in alteration or nonalteration. Nonalteration is only a limiting case of alteration. Alteration signifies a continual being-other or, rather, a becoming-other and yet being the same, individually the same, in this continual becoming-other: the alteration of a color, its fading, and so on, is an example of this. A real thing changes as this individual real thing; its state changes, but it retains its individual identity in this change of state. Nonalteration, on the other hand, implies: being the same in duration but, in addition, remaining continually the same in every phase of duration. With alteration, the state of being in duration and through the phases of duration is a state of being-other, or becoming-other, in each new phase, i.e., certainly remaining individually the same but, at the same time, not remaining continually the same.

When we direct our attention to the *phases* of the duration of the real thing and to that which occupies these phases, we have a multiplicity of figurations of the same thing: the same thing now, the same then, and so on, and, correspondingly, from phase to phase, the same as like or unlike. But when we change the orientation of our regard, directing our attention to the one enduring thing which presents itself in the phases, which "gradates" itself through time as the same, we experience the unity, the identity, which alters or does not alter, which continues and endures through the flux of multiplicities of figurations. This unity is not the universal of the individual temporal phases, any more than these are its variants. This unity is precisely what constitutes the unity of the individual which endures and which, as enduring, changes or remains the same. *In all alteration, the individual remains identically the same.* On the other hand, variation depends precisely on this: that we drop the identity of the individual and change it imaginatively into another possible individual.

On the other hand, it pertains to the alteration of an individual that we can also deal with its phases as variants (although by changing our point of view). Then we see that *no alteration is possible in which all the phases of the alteration do not belong together generically.* A color can change only into a color and not, e.g., into a sound. From this it is clear that every possible alteration is accomplished within a highest genus, which it can never contravene.

§88. The meaning of the phrase: "seeing" generalities

We speak of an essential "seeing" and, in general, of the seeing of generalities. This way of talking still requires justification. We use the expression "to see" here in the completely broad sense which implies nothing other than the *act of experiencing things oneself,* the fact of having seen things themselves, and, on the basis of this self-seeing, of having similarity before one's eyes, of accomplishing, on the strength of it, that mental overlapping in which the common, e.g., the red, the figure, etc., "itself" emerges—that is, attains intuitive apprehension. This, naturally, does *not* mean a *sensuous seeing.* One cannot see the universal red as one sees an individual, particular red; but the extension of the expression "seeing," which not without reason is customary in ordinary language, is unavoidable. With this, we wish to indicate that we appropriate, *directly and as itself,* a common and general moment of as many examples as desired, seen one by one, in a manner wholly analogous to the way in which we appropriate an individual particular in sensuous perception; although, to be sure, the

seeing is more complex here. It is a seeing resulting from the actively comparative overlapping of congruence. This is true of every kind of intuitive apprehension of commonalities *[Gemeinsamkeiten]* and generalities, though where a pure *eidos* is to be seen as an a priori, this seeing has its special methodological form—precisely that which has been described, namely, that indifference with regard to actuality which is generated in variation, whereby what presents itself as actual acquires the character of an arbitrary example, an indifferent point of departure of a series of variations.

§89. The necessity of an explicit exclusion of all positing of being for the purpose of attaining pure generality

It might now be thought that our description of essential seeing makes the task appear too difficult and that it is unnecessary to operate with the multiplicities of variation, which are stressed as allegedly fundamental, and likewise with the functions of imagination which participate therein in so peculiar a way. Would it not be enough to say that any arbitrary red here and red there, any arbitrary, pregiven plurality of red things, pertaining to experience or to any other representation, furnishes the possibility of an essential seeing of the *eidos* red? What would be necessary to describe is only the activity of running through what is given in overlapping coincidence and bringing the universal into view. However, it should be noted here that the word "arbitrary" in the context of our remarks must not be taken as a mere manner of speaking, or as constituting a nonessential attitude on our part, but that *it belongs to the fundamental character of the act of seeing ideas.*

But if in such a way of talking there is the notion that a determinate plurality of similar objects is enough to enable us to obtain a universal by a comparative coincidence, it is necessary to emphasize the following once more: certainly we obtain for this red here and that red there an identical and general element present in both, but precisely only as what is common to this and that red. We do not obtain pure red in general as *eidos*. To be sure, taking account of a third red or several, whenever they present themselves to us, we can recognize that the universal of the two is identically the same as the universal of the many. But in this way we always obtain only commonalities and generalities relative to empirical extensions; the possibility of progress *in infinitum* is still not given intuitively by this. However, as soon as we say that every arbitrary like moment, newly to be taken account of, *must* yield the same result, and if we repeat once more: the *eidos* red is *one* over against the infinity of possible particulars which belong to this and any other red capable of being in coincidence with it, then we are already in need of an infinite variation in our sense as a foundation. This variation provides us with what belongs to the *eidos* as its inseparable correlate, the so-called *extension of the eidos,* of the "purely conceptual essence," as the infinity of possible particulars which fall under it as its "particular exemplifications" and, Platonically speaking, are found with it in a relation of participation; every conceivable particular in general is referred to the essence, participates in it and in its essential moments. How the *totality* of the particulars which fall under the pure universal belong correlatively to it as its extension we will discuss forthwith.

First of all, it is necessary to point out that *even totally free variation is not enough* to actually give us the universal as pure. Even the universal acquired by variation must not yet be called *pure* in the true sense of the word, i.e., free from all positing of actuality. Although the relation to the contingent example, actually existing as a point of departure, is already excluded by the variation, a relation to actuality can still cling to the universal, and in the following way: For a pure *eidos,* the factual actuality of the particular cases by means of which we progress in the variation is completely irrelevant. And this must be taken literally. The actualities must be treated as possibilities among other possibilities, in fact as arbitrary possibilities of the imagination. This treatment is achieved only when every con-

nection to pregiven actuality is most carefully excluded. If we practice variation freely but cling secretly to the fact that, e.g., these must be arbitrary sounds *in the* world, heard or able to be heard by men on earth, then we certainly have an essential generality as an *eidos* but one *related to our world of fact* and bound to this universal fact. It is a secret bond in that, for understandable reasons, it is imperceptible to us.

In the natural development of universal *[universalen]* experience, the unity of which is continually being realized, the experienced world is granted to us as the universal permanent ground of being and as the universal field of all our activities. As the firmest and most universal of all our habitualities, the world is valid and remains in its actual validity for us, no matter what interests we may pursue; like all interests, those involving eidetic cognition are also related to it. With all exercise of imagination, like the one which we have already considered, set in motion by the supposition of possible particulars, chosen arbitrarily and falling under a concept attained empirically, and so also with every imaginative variation involving the intention of seeing ideas, the world is coposited; every fact and every *eidos* remains related to the factual world, belonging to this world. Because of its universality, we, of course, do not notice in the natural attitude this hidden positing of the world and this bond to being.

Only if we become conscious of this bond, *putting it consciously out of play,* and so also free this broadest surrounding horizon of variants from all connection to experience and all experiential validity, do we achieve perfect purity. Then we find ourselves, so to speak, in a pure world of imagination, a *world of absolutely pure possibility.* Every possibility of this kind can then be a central member for possible pure variations in the mode of the arbitrary. From each of these possibilities results an absolutely pure *eidos,* but from any other only if the series of variations of the one and the other are linked together in a *single* series in the manner described. Thus for colors and for sounds a different *eidos* emerges; they are different in kind, and this with respect to what is purely intuited in them.

A pure *eidos,* an essential generality, is, e.g., the species red or the genus color, but only if it is apprehended as a pure generality, thus free from all presupposition of any factual existent whatsoever, any factual red or any real colored actuality. Such is also the sense of the statements of geometry, e.g., when we designate the circle as a kind of conic section, that is, when we apprehend it in an eidetic intuition; we are then not speaking of an actual surface as an instance belonging to a real actuality of nature. Accordingly, *a purely eidetic judging "in general,"* such as the geometrical, or that concerned with ideally possible colors, sounds, and the like is, in its generality, *bound to no presupposed actuality.* In geometry, we speak of conceivable figures, in eidetic color-theory of conceivable colors, which constitute the extension of purely seen generalities.

The whole of mathematics also operates with concepts originally created in this way; it produces its immediate eidetic laws (axioms) as truths which are "necessary and universal in the strict sense," "admitting of no possible exception" (Kant). It sees them as general *[generelle]* essence-complexes *[Wesensverhalte],* producible in an absolute identity for every conceivable exemplification of its pure concepts—for those rigorously circumscribed multiplicities of variations or a priori extension—and, *as such,* self-evidently cognizable. From them, in a deductive intuition (a priori "self-evidence" of a necessary inference), mathematics then produces its theories and derived "theorems," again as ideal identities, perceptible in the arbitrary repetition of the activity which produced them.

§90. Pure generality and a priori necessity

We now turn to the problem, already touched upon above, of the *extension of pure generalities* and to the problems, closely linked to this, concerning the relation of pure possibility and empirico-factual actuality.

In conformity with its origin in the method

of free variation and the consequent exclusion of all positing of actual being, pure generality naturally can have *no extension consisting of facts,* of empirical actualities which bind it [to experience], but only an *extension of pure possibilities.* On the other hand, eidetic generality must always be posited in relation to admitted actualities. Every color occurring in actuality is certainly, at the same time, a possible color in the pure sense: each can be considered as an example and can be changed into a variant. Thus, in the realm of arbitrary freedom we can lift all actuality to a plane of pure possibility. But it then appears that even arbitrary freedom has its own peculiar constraint. What can be varied, one into another, in the arbitrariness of imagination (even if it is without connection and does not accord with the understanding of a reality conceivable in the imagination) bears in itself a necessary structure, an *eidos,* and therewith *necessary laws* which determine what must necessarily belong to an object in order that it can be an object of this kind. This necessity then also holds for everything factual: we can see that everything which belongs inseparably to the pure *eidos* color, e.g., the moment of brightness, must likewise belong to every actual color.

The universal truths, in which we merely display what belongs to pure essential generalities, precede all questions bearing on facts and the truths which concern them. Hence, these essential truths are called *a priori;* this means, *by reason of their validity, preceding all factuality,* all determinations arising from experience. Every actuality given in experience, and judged by the thinking founded on experience, is subject, insofar as the correctness of such judgments is concerned, to the unconditional norm that it must first comply with all the a priori "conditions of possible experience" and the possible thinking of such experience: that is, with the conditions of its pure possibility, its representability and positability as the objectivity of a uniformly identical sense.

Such a priori conditions are expressed for nature (for the actuality of physical experience) by the mathematics of nature with all its propositions. It expresses them "a priori," i.e., without dealing with "nature" as a fact. The reference to facts is the business of the *application,* which is always possible a priori and is self-evidently intelligible in this possibility. And now we can say in general: *judging actualities according to the laws of their pure possibility,* or judging them according to "laws of essences," a priori laws, *is a universal and absolutely necessary task which must be carried out for all actuality.* What is easy to make clear in the example of mathematical thinking and mathematical natural science is valid in a completely general way *for every objective sphere.* To each belongs the possibility of an a priori thinking, consequently an a priori science having the same functional application as this science—insofar as we give the a priori everywhere the same strict sense, the only one which is significant. There is not the slightest reason to consider the methodological structure of a priori thinking, as we have exhibited it in its general essential features in mathematical thinking, as an exclusive property of the mathematical sphere.* Indeed, in view of the general essential relationship of actuality and possibility, of experience and pure imagination, even to admit such a limitation would be completely absurd. From *every* concrete actuality, and every individual trait actually experienced in it or capable of being experienced, a path stands open to the realm of ideal or pure possibility and consequently to that of a priori thinking. And in conformity with this completely general method, the method of formation of pure individual possibilities, as well as of the infinite "extensions" of the possibilities which merge into one another in the transformations of variation, is everywhere the same, and thus naturally also the originally intuitive formation of pure essential generalities pertaining to them: "ideas" (essences, pure concepts) and laws of essences.

16. The Genesis of Judgment†

§82. Reduction of judgments to ultimate judgments. The primitive categorial variants of Something; the primitive substrate, individual

We must start by *going back from the judgment to the judgment-substrates,* from truths to their *objects-about-which.*

In the first place, we require here an important supplementation of the pure logic of noncontradiction, a supplementation that, to be sure, goes beyond formal mathematics proper, but still does not belong to truth-logic. It is a matter, so to speak, of a *transitional link* between them.

As we remember, the formalization which analytics carries out, and which determines its peculiar character, consists in thinking of the syntactical stuffs, or "cores," of judgments as mere anythings whatever, so that only the syntactical form, the specifically judicial (including the core-forms, such as the forms substantivity and adjectivity), becomes determinant for the conceptual essences that, as "judgment-forms," enter into the logical laws of analytics. Here we must note the *relativity* in which these laws leave *the indeterminately universal cores.* For example, the forms of the categorical judgment, and more particularly of the adjectively determining categorical judgment, says nothing

---

*In this connection, however, it should be emphasized that the method of mathematical thinking of essences is, as a *method of idealization,* in important points to be distinguished from the intuition of essences in other subjects, whose fluid types cannot be apprehended with exactitude; this analogy thus holds only in the most general respects. On this difference, see also Edmund Husserl, CES, esp. pp. 17ff., 48ff.

†FTL, pp. 202–212 (Sections 82–86).

about whether the subject or predicate of the judgment already contains a syntactical form in the core itself. The subject *S,* taken as a form, is formally particularized equally well by "*S,* which is *a,*" "*S,* which is *a, b,*" "*S,* which has a relation to *Q,*" or the like. Meanwhile it remains undetermined whether, in each of these forms, the *S* itself already has syntactical structures of the same sort within it. In the same manner, on the predicate side, the *p* may already bear within itself a categorial determination (perhaps "*p,* which is *q*"—for example: blood-red); and thus there may be forms within forms, to any degree of complexity. But it can be seen a priori that *any actual or possible judgment leads back to ultimate cores* when we follow up its syntaxes; accordingly that it is a syntactical structure built ultimately, though perhaps far from immediately, out of *elementary cores, which no longer contain any syntaxes.* Also, in following up the sense of the *substantivized adjective,* we are led back to the *original adjective* and to the more original judgment of which it is a member and in which it occurs as an irreducible primitive form. In the same manner, a universality of a higher level (for example: the logical form-genus, judgment-form) leads us back to universalities of a lower level (in our example, the particular judgment-forms). And always it is clear that, by reduction, we reach a corresponding *ultimate,* that is: *ultimate substrates*—from the standpoint of formal logic, *absolute subjects* (subjects that are not nominalized predicates, relations, or the like), *ultimate predicates* (predicates that are not predicates of predicates, or the like), *ultimate universalities, ultimate relations.*

But this must be understood correctly. In the logic of judgments, judgments (as we have explained) are senses, judicial meanings (or opinions) as objects. Consequently the reduction signifies that, *purely by following up the meanings,* we reach *ultimate something-meanings;* first of all, then, as regards the meant or supposed judgment-objects, *supposed absolute objects-about-which.* — Furthermore that, in the ultimate judgments, the ones on which the other judgments at different levels are built, we get back to the *primitive categorial variants of the sense, absolute something:* absolute properties, relations, and so forth, as *senses.*

For *mathesis universalis,* as formal mathematics, these ultimates have no particular interest. Quite the contrary for *truth-logic:* because ultimate substrate-objects are *individuals,* about which very much can be said in formal truth, and *back to which all truth ultimately relates.* If one keeps to the formal of pure analytics, if the evidence—the evidence serving this discipline—accordingly relates only to pure judgment-senses as distinct, one cannot establish this last proposition; it is by no means an "analytic" proposition. To have insight into it, one must *make ultimate cores intuited,* one must draw fullness of adequation, not from evidence of the judgment-senses, but instead from evidence of the "matters" or "affairs" corresponding to them. In analytic logic one can go so far, and only so far, as to say that, in the sense, there must be certain sense-elements as the ultimate core-stuffs in all syntactical forms, and that one is brought back to judgment-complexes of ultimate judgments having "individual" substrates. *Analytically one can assert nothing about the possibility or the essential structure of individuals.* Even that, for example, a *time-form* necessarily belongs to them—duration, qualitative filledness of duration, and so forth—is something one can know only from a material evidence; and it can enter the judgment-sense only by virtue of an antecedent syntactical performance.

§83. Parallel reduction of truths. Relation of all truths to an antecedent world of individuals

To the reduction of judgments to ultimate judgments with an ultimate sense, there corresponds a *reduction of truths:* of the truths belonging to a higher level to those belonging on the *lowest level,* that is: to truths that relate directly to their matters and material spheres, or (because the substrates play the leading role here) that relate directly *to individual objects* in their object-spheres—individual objects, objects that therefore contain within themselves no judgment-syntaxes and that, in their experienceable factual being, are *prior to all judging.* That judgments (not judgment-senses) relate to objects signifies that, in the judgment itself, these objects are meant as substrates, as the objects about which something is stated; and reductive deliberation teaches, as an a priori, that *every conceivable judgment ultimately* (and either definitely or indefinitely) *has relation to individual objects* (in an extremely broad sense, real objects), and therefore has *relation to a real universe,* a "world" or a *world-province,* "for which it holds good." (The second thesis takes us further and is yet to be grounded.)

To ground the first thesis more strictly let us point out that universal judgments say nothing with definiteness about individuals, but that extensionally, according to their sense, they bear an immediate or a mediate relation ultimately to individual singles. This is clear, first of all, in the case of universalities with a material content. However much, as upper-level universalities, they may relate extensionally to other universalities, they evidently must lead back by a finite number of steps to singles with a material content that are themselves not universalities but individuals. But, if it is a case of formal-analytic universalities—numbers, for example, or multiplicities—then "everything and anything" belongs to their extension or that of their units. That involves their possible determination by any arbitrarily selectable objects whatever; and these could themselves be analytico-formal formations, with respect to whose units the same is true; and so *in infinitum.* But, according to their sense, it also involves their possible application to arbitrarily selectable objects with material content; which would take us back to the preceding case. Thus it is indeed true that absolutely every universality has an ultimate extensional relation of applicability to individuals that are either delimited by universalities with material content or else themselves left open to choice in this respect. Now, in accordance with its sense, formal logic—and therefore all forming of formal-analytic universalities, as a function of the theory of science—is intended to serve the ends of sciences that have

material content. With all its freedom in the reiterative forming of forms, and with all its reflexive relatedness to its own scientific character, formal logic still intends—and even *in* these reiterations and this reflexiveness—not to remain a playing with empty thoughts, but to become an aid to cognition that has material content. Thus the ultimate applicability of formal analytics to individuals is, at the same time, a *teleological* relatedness to all possible spheres of *individuals.* And therefore these spheres are, for logic, what is first in itself.

§84. The hierarchy of evidences; the intrinsically first evidences those of experience. The pregnant concept of experience

Now, if truth is in question and, correlatively, an evidence by which it becomes one's own originarily, then what has just been stated is of obvious significance. The *hierarchy of evidences* goes with that of judgments and their senses; and *the truths and evidences that are first in themselves* must be the *individual* ones. A priori, the judgments made subjectively in the form belonging to the evidence which is *actually most original,* the evidence that seizes upon its substrates and predicatively formed affair-complexes originally and *quite directly,* must be *individual judgments.*

Individuals are given by experience, *experience in the first and most pregnant sense,* which is defined as a direct relation *to something individual.* In this connection however, if we take as *experiential judgments* the group of judgments that have the most original evidence, then in a certain manner we must take experience in a broad sense: not only as the simple giving of an individual existence itself —that is: with certainty of its being—but also as extending to the *modalizations* of this certainty, which can, after all, change into likelihood, probability, and so forth. But, over against *all* these forms of "actual" (that is: positional) experience, there comes into question "neutralized" experience, *"as-if experience,"* we can also say *"experience in phantasy,"* which, with a suitable and freely possible alteration of one's attitude, becomes positional experience of a possible individual. Naturally, as-if experience has parallel as-if modalities of its primitive mode, as-if certainty of being.

§85. The genuine tasks of so-called judgment-theory. The sense-genesis of judgments as a clue in our search for the hierarchy of evidences

The considerations just pursued give us access to an understanding of the *proper task of judgment-theory,* a discipline that, although much discussed, has remained rather fruitless, because it has lacked all understanding of the specific character of the investigations directed to the subjective that are necessary in the case of judgments, in the logical sense, and in the case of the fundamental concepts relating to these.

1. If the general confusion was reduced to the extent that (overcoming the psychologistic confounding of them) one distinguished *judging* and *the judgment itself* (the ideal formation, the stated proposition), it then was even less possible to set a senseful *problem concerning the subjective* as long as the peculiar essence of all intentionality, as a constitutive performance, was not understood and therefore judicative intentionality in particular was not understood as the constitutive performance in the case of ideal judgment-formations—and, still more particularly, the intentionality of evidential judging was not understood as the constitutive performance in the case of ideal truth-formations. Therefore, after the aforesaid distinction between judging and judgment has been made, the *first judgment-problem* that must be set in logic, starting from there, is that of going back to the variously effective intentionality and carrying out the reflective phenomenological clarifications in which *logic's different concepts of the judgment* become separated, according to their origins, as *fundamental concepts* for its disciplines and become, at the same time, understandable in their interrelatedness.

2. If this first series of investigations has been carried out—the ones we attempted in the earlier parts of this book—then *reductive deliberations* such as were occupying us a little while ago* become necessary. They uncover the *hidden intentional implications* included in judging and in the judgment itself as the product of judging. *Judgments as senses accordingly have a sense-genesis.*

What that signifies can be understood from the phenomenological *pointing back* that, for example, a nominalized predicate (as expressible by such nouns as "red" and "the red") bears, in that it points back to a nominalizing activity, on the noetic side, and to the original predicate (as expressible by such adjectives as "red"), on the noematic side. Such phenomenological pointings-back are shown by every other nominalized sense-formation (like "the similarity" and "this, that *S* is *p*")—pointings back to the corresponding more original formation and, correlatively, to the pertinent nominalizing activities; likewise, each attributive determination in the subject points back to the originality of that determination as a predicate; and so forth.

This yields, *even for the theory of forms* and, subsequently, for procedure in *an analytics of consequence-relationships, a principle of genetic order,* which at the same time determines the specifically logical aim conferred on analytics with the concepts and laws of *truth.* With respect to the subjective, that signifies that the predelineated *order of judgment-forms involves a* predelineated *order in the process of making materially evident* and in the different levels of *true materialities themselves.*

Uncovering the sense-genesis of judgments signifies, more precisely, an unravelling of the sense-moments that are implicit in, and belong essentially to, the sense that has plainly come to light. Judgments, as the finished products of a "constitution" or "genesis," can and must be asked about this genesis. The essential peculiarity of such products is precisely that they are senses that bear within them, as a sense-implicate of their genesis, a sort of historical-

*See §§82 and 83.

ness; that in them, level by level, sense points back to original sense and to the corresponding noetic* intentionality; that therefore each sense-formation can be asked about its *essentially necessary sense-history.*

This wonderful peculiarity is concomitant with the universality of consciousness of every sort as effective intentionality. All intentional unities come from an intentional genesis, are "constituted" unities; and everywhere one can ask the "finished" unities about their constitution, about their total genesis, and particularly about the eidetically apprehensible essential form of this genesis. This fundamental fact, embracing in its universality the whole of intentional living, is what *determines the proper sense of intentional analysis, its sense as an uncovering of the intentional implications,* with which there come to the fore, as contrasted with the overt, the finished, sense of the unities, their *hidden* sense-moments and "causal" sense-relations. At any rate, we understand this so far as the judgment is concerned; and it now becomes understandable in particular that *not only the overt, or finished, but likewise the implied sense must always have its say,* and that it too exercises an essential function, particularly in the process of making evident—here, in our logical sphere, the process of making logical principles evident. But, as will be seen forthwith, that applies not only to the syntactical implications but also to the deeper-lying genesis pertaining to the ultimate "cores" and pointing back to their origination from experiences. Without being clear about all that, we cannot actually have the principles of logic at our command, we do not know what hidden presuppositions may lie within them.

§86. The evidence of pre-predicative experience as the intrinsically primary theme of transcendental judgment-theory. The experiential judgment as the original judgment

The lowest level reached by tracing back the clue of sense-genesis brings us, as we already know, to *judgments about individuals;* and consequently, in the case of evident judgments, in the sense of seeings of the predicatively formed affair-complexes themselves, it brings us to those evidences of something individual that belong to the simplest type. These are the pure and simple *experiential judgments,* judgments about data of possible perception and memory, which give norms for the correctness of categorical judicial meanings at the lowest level concerning individuals.

Let us utilize a proposition from the general theory of consciousness—more particularly, from the phenomenology of universal genesis in consciousness. It states that, for objectivities of every sort, *consciousness in the mode, giving them-themselves, precedes* all other modes of consciousness relating to them, all these other modes being genetically secondary. Consciousness that gives us something itself is indeed always passing over, by way of retention and protention, into consciousness that does *not* give us something itself: empty consciousness. Even recollection, though it can be intuitive, is the awakening of an empty consciousness and points back to earlier original consciousness. Accordingly, from these genetical points of view, *the intrinsically first judgment-theory is the theory of evident judgments, and the intrinsically first thing in the theory of evident judgments* (and therefore in judgment-theory as a whole) *is the genetical tracing of predicative evidences back to the non-predicative evidence* called *experience.* With suitable further intentional formings, the experience enters into the judging done at the lowest genetic level, and the product of experience enters into the judgment-formation itself.

Here one has indeed reached the intrinsically *first beginning of a systematic judgment-theory,* as a theory that traces the essentially determined systematic genesis pertaining to the judgment employed originally on the matters themselves (the "evidential" judgment) and then follows the predelineated ways leading upward from what is intrinsically first in this genesis.

.

---

*Reading *noetische* instead of *noematische.* —Translator's note.

This beginning, moreover, is the place systematically, *starting from the judgment, to discover* that certainty and modalities of certainty, suppositive intention and fulfillment, identical existent and identical sense, evident having of something itself, trueness of being (being "actual") and truth as correctness of sense—that *none of these is a peculiarity exclusively within the predicational sphere, that, on the contrary, they all belong already to the intentionality of experience.* Starting from there, one can trace them into the givings of things themselves, the evidences, on a higher level—for example: those of the *proximate variants of the individual* (property, relation, and so forth) and particularly the evidence of the *universal* (derivable from the experience of individuals), with its extensional sense as embracing individuals.

Thus one comes *from the experiential judgment*—more particularly, from the most immediate experiential judgment having the categorical form—*to experience* and to *the motive for that broadening of the concept of judgment* already indicated by Hume's concept of *belief*. Historically, to be sure, the apprehension of this broadest concept remains crude, even countersensical. Its inadequacy is shown by the mere fact that the identification of judgment and "belief" presently necessitates introduction of a "presentation *[Vorstellung]*" allegedly founding this belief. This is not the place to submit the doctrine to extensive criticism. Lockean sensualism, which reaches completion in Hume and John Stuart Mill and becomes almost all-prevailing in modern philosophy, finds in this *belief a mere Datum of "internal sense,"* not much different from a Datum of "external sense," such as a sound-Datum or a smell-Datum. To those prepossessed by the *parallelizing of "internal" and "external" experience*—correlatively, the sphere of individual psychic being (the sphere grasped in its real being by immanent experience, so they supposed) and the sphere of physical being— it appeared to be without question that, at bottom, *problems concerning judgment* and psychic problems generally must have *essentially the same sense as problems concerning physical Nature* and should be treated by the same method: as *problems concerning reality,* problems for a psychology as the science of "psychic phenomena," of Data of "internal experience," including belief-Data. Because of this blindness to all intentionality and—even after intentionality had been insisted upon by Brentano—because of a blindness to its Objectivating function, *all the actual problems concerning judgment* were indeed *lost from view.* If their genuine sense is brought out, the intentionality of predicative judgments leads back ultimately to the intentionality of experience.

According to what was indicated above, the theory of the evidence of the pure and simple categorical experiential judgment should be called the "intrinsically primary" judgment-theory because, in respect of intentional genesis, the non-evident judgment, even the countersensical judgment, points back to an origin from experiential judgments. It should be emphasized that this referring back, just like the predicational sense-genesis discussed a little while ago, is not inferred from an *inductive empeiria* on the part of the psychological observer, perchance the experimentalist in the "psychology of thinking"; on the contrary, as can be shown in phenomenology, it is an *essential component of the intentionality,* a component uncoverable among the intentional contents thereof in the corresponding productions of fulfillment. Accordingly it is the case that, *for us,* to be sure, as carrying on a philosophico-logical sense-investigation, *the non-evident and the evident judgment are presented on an equal plane* and the course of *naively positive logic* is therefore the *natural* one; whereas, considered in itself, the evident judgment—most fundamentally, *the experiential judgment—is nevertheless the original judgment.* From its syntaxes, the ones that are first in themselves, genesis of the higher syntaxes goes upward, the ones with which formal analytics is exclusively occupied in its theories, concerning itself with the conditions for possible judicative evidence that are implicit in the a priori forms of distinct judgings and of their intentional correlates.

Now, even though formal analytics, in respect of its province and its theory, has to do only with the *forms* of possible judgments and truths, and even though no such thing as evidence or experience is to be found <as thematic> in its province or its theory, still, in its "epistemo-critical" investigations of the subjective, which concern the radical method of intentional performances, it must investigate the categorial mediacies of evidence and verification, and accordingly must clarify the *performance of the original judgments.* Through these all truth and all judicative evidence, so we see, are related back to the primitive basis, experience; and, because experience itself functions *in* and *not beside* the original judgments, *logic needs a theory of experience*—in order to be able to give scientific information about the legitimating bases, and the legitimate limits, of its a priori, and consequently about its own legitimate sense. If experience itself is accounted as judgment in the broadest sense, then this theory of experience is to be characterized as itself the first and most fundamental judgment-theory. Naturally this explication of experience, as the activity that precedes the specifically categorial activities and takes on shape in them, must be restricted to a *"formal" universality* consistent with the purpose of formal logic—a universality that is "formal" in the sense that, on the subjective side, is the *correlate* of the sense in which analytics is formal. The relevant and by no means easy unravelling of the multiform experiential performance carried out in the experiential judgment, and the unravelling of this original judgment itself, will be done elsewhere.* Here let us mention in particular only the fact that even this founding experience has its style of syntactical performances, which, however, are still free from all the conceptual and grammatical formings that characterize the categorial as exemplified in the predicative judgment and the statement.†

---

*In the studies in logic that were announced above. [See *Erfahrung und Urteil,* I. Abschnitt and II. Abschnitt.]

†In my *Logische Untersuchungen, II. Bd., II. Teil, 6. Untersuchung,* the concept of the categorial was first introduced with exclusive attention to that which is syntactical in the judgment. No separation was yet made between, on the one hand, the syntactical as such, which makes its appearance already in the pre-predicational sphere and, moreover, has its analogues in the spheres of emotion and volition and, on the other hand, the syntactical that belongs to the specific sphere comprising judgments.

IX.

Static and Genetic Phenomenology

17. Time and the Self-Constitution of the Ego*

*§30. The transcendental ego insepa-
rable from the processes making up his
life*

Objects exist for me, and are for me what
they are, only as objects of actual and possible
consciousness. If this is not to be an empty
statement and a theme for empty speculations,
it must be shown what makes up concretely
this existence and being-thus for me, or what
sort of actual and possible consciousness is
concerned, what the structure of this consciousness is, what "possibility" signifies here, and
so forth. This can be done solely by constitutional investigation—first, in the broader sense
introduced initially, and then in the narrower
sense just now described. Moreover there is
but one possible method, the one demanded
by the essence of intentionality and of its horizons. Even from the preparatory analyses leading us upward to the sense of the problem, it
becomes clear that the transcendental ego (in
the psychological parallel, the psyche) is what
it is solely in relation to intentional objectivities. Among these, however, are necessarily
included for the ego existing objects and, for
him as related to a world, not only objects
within his (adequately verifiable) sphere of
immanent time but also world Objects, which
are shown to be existent only in his inadequate,
merely presumptive, external experience—in
the harmoniousness of its course. It is thus an
essential property of the ego, constantly to have
systems of intentionality—among them, harmonious ones—partly as going on within him
<actually>, partly as fixed potentialities, which,
thanks to predelineating horizons, are available for uncovering. Each object that the ego
ever means, thinks of, values, deals with, likewise each that he ever phantasies or can phantasy, indicates its correlative system and exists
only as itself the correlate of its system.

*§31. The Ego as identical pole of the
subjective processes*

Now, however, we must call attention to a
great gap in our exposition. The ego is himself
existent for himself in continuous evidence;
thus, in himself, he is *continuously constituting himself as existing.* Heretofore we have
touched on only one side of this self-constitution, we have looked at only the *flowing cogito.*
The ego grasps himself not only as a flowing life but also as *I,* who live this and that
subjective process, who live through this and
that cogito, *as the same I.* Since we were busied up to now with the intentional relation of
consciousness to object, cogito to cogitatum,
only that synthesis stood out for us which "po-
larizes" the multiplicities of actual and possible consciousness toward identical objects,
accordingly in relation to *objects as poles,* synthetic unities. Now we encounter a second po-

*CM, pp. 65–81 (Sections 30–39).

larization, a *second kind of synthesis,* which embraces all the particular multiplicities of *cogitationes* collectively and in its own manner, namely as belonging to the identical Ego, who, *as the active and affected subject of consciousness,* lives in all processes of consciousness and is related, *through* them, to all object-poles.

§32. The Ego as substrate of habitualities

But it is to be noted that *this centering Ego is not an empty pole of identity,* any more than any *object* is such. Rather, according to a law of "transcendental generation," with every *act* emanating from him and having a *new* objective sense, he acquires *a new abiding property.* For example: If, in an act of judgment, I decide for the first time in favor of a being and a being-thus, the fleeting act passes; but from now on *I am abidingly the Ego who is thus and so decided,* "I am of this conviction." That, however, does not signify merely that I remember the act or can remember it later. This I can do, even if meanwhile I have "given up" my conviction. After cancellation it is no longer my conviction; but it has remained abidingly my conviction up to then. As long as it is accepted by me, I can "return" to it repeatedly, and repeatedly find it as mine, habitually my own opinion or, correlatively, find myself as the Ego who *is* convinced, who, as the persisting Ego, is determined by this abiding *habitus* or state. Likewise in the case of decisions of every other kind, value-decisions, volitional decisions. I decide; the act-process vanishes but the decision persists; whether I become passive and sink into heavy sleep or live in other acts, the decision continues to be accepted and, correlatively, I am so decided from then on, as long as I do not give the decision up. If it aims at a terminating deed, it is not "revoked" by the deed that fulfills it; in the mode characteristic of fulfilled decision it continues to be accepted: "I continue to stand by my deed." *I myself,* who am persisting in my abiding volition, *become changed* if I "cancel" my decisions or repudiate my deeds. The persisting, the tem-

poral enduring, of such determining properties of the Ego, or the peculiar change that the Ego undergoes in respect of them, manifestly is not a continuous filling of immanent time with subjective processes—just as the abiding Ego himself, as the pole of abiding Ego-properties, is not a process or a continuity of processes, even though, with such habitual determining properties, he is indeed related back to the stream of subjective processes. Since, by his *own active generating,* the Ego constitutes himself as *identical substrate of Ego-properties,* he constitutes himself also as a "fixed and abiding" *personal Ego*—in a maximally broad sense, which permits us to speak of sub-human "persons." Though convictions are, in general, only relatively abiding and have their modes of alteration (through modalization of the active positings—for example, "cancellation" or negation, undoing of their acceptance), the Ego shows, in such alterations, an abiding style with a unity of identity throughout all of them: a "personal character."

§33. The full concretion of the Ego as monad and the problem of his self-constitution

From the Ego as identical pole, and as substrate of habitualities, we distinguish *the ego taken in full concreteness*—in that we take, in addition, that without which the Ego cannot after all be concrete. (The ego, taken in full concreteness, we propose to call by the Leibnizian name: monad.) The Ego can be concrete only in the flowing multiformity of his intentional life, along with the objects meant—and in some cases constituted as existent for him —in that life. Manifestly, in the case of an object so constituted, its abiding existence and being-thus are a correlate of the habituality constituted in the Ego-pole himself by virtue of his position-taking.

That is to be understood in the following manner. As ego, I have a surrounding world, which is continually "existing for me"; and, in it, objects as "existing for me"—already with the abiding distinction between those with which I am acquainted and those only anticipated as objects with which I may become acquainted. The former, the ones that are, in the first sense, existent for me, are such by original acquisition—that is: by my original taking cognizance of what I had never beheld previously, and my explication of it in particular intuitions of its features. Thereby, in my synthetic activity, the object becomes constituted originally, perceptively, in the explicit sense-form: "something identical having its manifold properties," or "object as identical with itself and undergoing determination in respect of its manifold properties." This, my activity of positing and explicating being, sets up a habituality of my Ego, by virtue of which the object, as having its manifold determinations, is mine abidingly. Such abiding acquisitions make up my surrounding world, so far as I am acquainted with it at the time, with its horizons of objects with which I am unacquainted—that is: objects yet to be acquired but already anticipated with this formal object-structure.

I exist for myself and am continually given to myself,* by experiential evidence, as *"I myself."* This is true of the transcendental ego and, correspondingly, of the psychologically pure ego; it is true, moreover, with respect to any sense of the word ego. Since the monadically concrete ego includes also the whole of actual and potential conscious life, it is clear that the problem of *explicating this monadic ego phenomenologically* (the problem of his constitution for himself) must include *all constitutional problems without exception.* Consequently the phenomenology of this *self-constitution* coincides with *phenomenology as a whole.*

§34. A fundamental development of phenomenological method. Transcendental analysis as eidetic

With the doctrine of the Ego as pole of his acts and substrate of habitualities, we have already touched on the *problems of phenomenological genesis* and done so at a significant point. Thus we have touched the level of *genetic phenomenology.* Before we clarify the more precise sense of genetic phenomenology, a *renewed meditation concerning phenomenological method is needed.* At last we must bring to bear a fundamental methodological insight, which, once it is grasped, pervades the whole phenomenological method (and likewise, in the natural realm, the method of a genuine and pure internal psychology). We have delayed mentioning it, only to facilitate entrance into phenomenology. The excessively great multiplicity of novel discoveries and problems was meant to act at first in the simpler attire of a merely empirical description (though conducted purely within the sphere of transcendental experience). The *method of eidetic description,* however, signifies a transfer of all empirical descriptions into a new and fundamental dimension, which at the beginning would have increased the difficulties of understanding; on the other hand, it is easy to grasp after a considerable number of empirical descriptions.

By the method of transcendental reduction each of us, as Cartesian meditator, was led back to his transcendental ego—naturally with its concrete-monadic contents as this de facto ego, the one and only absolute ego. When I keep on meditating, I, as this ego, find descriptively formulable, intentionally explicatable types; and I was able to progress step by step in the intentional uncovering of my "monad" along the fundamental lines that offer themselves. For good reasons, in the course of our descriptions such expressions as "essential necessity" and "essentially determined" forced themselves upon us—phrases in which a definite concept of the a priori, first clarified and delimited by phenomenology, receives expression.

What is involved here will become clear directly in particular examples. Let us pick out no matter what type of intentional processes (of perception, retention, recollection, declaration, liking something, striving for it, and

---

*Reading: *Ich bin fur mich selbst und \<bin\> mir . . . gegeben.* —Translator's note.

so forth) and think of it as explicated and described in respect of its sort of intentional performance—accordingly: in respect of noesis and noema. This can signify (and so we have understood it up to now) that types of de facto occurrences in the de facto transcendental ego are in question and that the transcendental descriptions are therefore meant to have an "empirical" significance. But involuntarily we confined our description to such a universality that its results remain unaffected, regardless of what the situation may be with respect to the empirical factualness of the transcendental ego.

Let us make this clear to ourselves, and then fruitful for our method. Starting from this table-perception as an example, we vary the perceptual object, table, with a completely free optionalness, yet in such a manner that we keep perception fixed as perception of something, no matter what. Perhaps we begin by fictively changing the shape or the color of the object quite arbitrarily, keeping identical only its perceptual appearing. In other words: Abstaining from acceptance of its being, we change the fact of this perception into a pure possibility, one among other quite "optional" pure possibilities—but possibilities that are possible perceptions. We, so to speak, shift the actual perception into the realm of non-actualities, the realm of the as-if, which supplies us with "pure" possibilities, pure of everything that restricts to this fact or to any fact whatever. As regards the latter point, we keep the aforesaid possibilities, not as restricted even to the co-posited de facto ego, but just as a completely free "imaginableness" of phantasy. Accordingly from the very start we might have taken as our initial example a phantasying ourselves into a perceiving, with no relation to the rest of our de facto life. Perception, the universal type thus acquired, floats in the air, so to speak—in the atmosphere of pure phantasiableness. Thus removed from all factualness, it has become the pure "eidos" perception, whose "ideal" extension is made up of all ideally possible perceptions, as purely phantsiable processes. Analyses of perception are then "essential" or

"eidetic" analyses. All that we have set forth concerning syntheses belonging to the type, perception, concerning horizons of potentiality, and so forth, holds good, as can easily be seen, "essentially" for everything formable in this free variation, accordingly for all imaginable perceptions without exception—in other words: with absolute "essential universality," and with "essential necessity" for every particular case selected, hence for every de facto perception, since every fact can be thought of merely as exemplifying a pure possibility.

The variation being meant as an evident one, accordingly as presenting in pure intuition the possibilities themselves as possibilities, its correlate is an intuitive and apodictic consciousness of something universal. The eidos itself is a beheld or beholdable universal, one that is pure, "unconditioned"—that is to say: according to its own intuitional sense, a universal not conditioned by any fact. It is prior to all "concepts," in the sense of verbal significations; indeed, as pure concepts, these must be made to fit the eidos.

Though each singly selected type is thus elevated from its milieu within the empirically factual transcendental ego into the pure eidetic sphere, the intentional outer horizons pointing to its uncoverable connexus within the ego do not vanish; only this nexus-horizon itself becomes eidetic. In other words: With each eidetically pure type we find ourselves, not indeed inside the de facto ego, but inside an eidos ego; and constitution of one actually pure possibility among others carries with it implicitly, as its outer horizon, a purely possible ego, a pure possibility-variant of my de facto ego. We could have started out by imagining this ego to be freely varied, and could set the problem of exploring eidetically the explicit constitution of any transcendental ego whatever. The new phenomenology did so from the beginning; and accordingly all the descriptions and all the problem-delimitations treated by us up to now have in fact been translations from the original eidetic form back into that of an empirical description of types. Therefore, if we think of a phenomenology developed as an intuitively a priori science *purely according to the eidetic method,* all its eidetic researches are nothing else but *uncoverings of the all-embracing eidos, transcendental ego as such,* which comprises all pure possibility-variants of my de facto ego and this ego itself qua possibility. Eidetic phenomenology, accordingly, explores the universal a priori without which neither I nor any transcendental Ego whatever is "imaginable"; or, since every eidetic universality has the value of an unbreakable law, eidetic phenomenology explores the all-embracing laws that prescribe for every factual statement about something transcendental the possible sense (as opposed to the absurdity or inconsistency) of that statement.

To me as the meditating ego, guided by the idea of a philosophy as the all-embracing science, grounded with absolute strictness, a science whose possibility I took as a tentative basis, it becomes evident after these last considerations that, *first of all,* I must develop a purely *eidetic phenomenology* and that in the latter alone the first actualization of a philosophical science—the actualization of a "first philosophy"—takes place or can take place. After transcendental reduction, my true interest is directed to my pure ego, to the uncovering of this de facto ego. But the uncovering can become genuinely scientific only if I go back to the apodictic principles that pertain to this ego as exemplifying the eidos ego: the essential universalities and necessities by means of which the fact is to be related to its rational grounds (those of its pure possibility) and thus made scientific (logical). It should be noted that, in the transition from my ego to an ego as such, neither the actuality nor the possibility of other egos is presupposed. I phantasy only myself as if I were otherwise; I do not phantasy others. "In itself," then, the science of pure possibilities precedes the science of actualities and alone makes it possible, as a science. With this we attain the methodological insight that, *along with phenomenological reduction, eidetic intuition is the fundamental form of all particular transcendental methods* (that both of them determine, through and

through, the legitimate sense of a transcendental phenomenology).

§35. Excursus into eidetic internal psychology

We go outside the closed sphere of our meditations, which restricts us to transcendental phenomenology, if we cannot repress the remark that, with only slight modifications (which, to be sure, abolish its transcendental sense), the whole content of the fundamental methodological observation that has just been made remains ours when, on the basis of the natural world view, we strive for a psychology as a positive science and, in that connection, strive primarily for the psychology that is first in itself and necessary to any psychology: purely intentional psychology. To the concrete transcendental ego there corresponds then the human Ego, concretely as the psyche taken purely in itself and <as it is> for itself, with the psychic polarization: I as pole of my habitualities, the properties comprised in my character. Instead of eidetic transcendental phenomenology we then have an eidetic pure psychology, relating to the eidos psyche, whose eidetic horizon, to be sure, remains unexamined. If, however, it did become examined, the way to overcome this positivity would become open—that is, the way leading over into absolute phenomenology, the phenomenology of the transcendental ego, who indeed no longer has a horizon that could lead beyond the sphere of his transcendental being and thus relativize him.

§36. The transcendental ego as the universe of possible forms of subjective process. The compossibility of subjective processes in coexistence or succession as subject to eidetic laws

After the significant new formulation of the idea of a transcendental phenomenology according to the eidetic method, when we return to the task of discovering the problems of phenomenology, we naturally confine ourselves thenceforth within the limits of a purely eidetic phenomenology, in which the de facto transcendental ego and particular data given in transcendental experience of the ego have the significance merely of examples of pure possibilities. Likewise we understand the already discovered problems as eidetic, in that we think of the possibility of making them eidetically pure (a possibility shown in our example) as actualized. Satisfying the ideal problem of an actually systematic discovery of the essential components belonging to a concrete ego as such, or initiating an actually *systematic sequence of problems and investigations,* involves extraordinary difficulties. Only in the last decade has this system begun to make itself clear, above all because we have gained new ways of access to the *specifically universal* problems of the transcendental ego's constitution. The universal a priori pertaining to a transcendental ego as such is an eidetic form, which contains an infinity of forms, an infinity of a priori types of actualities and potentialities of life, along with the objects constitutable in a life as objects actually existing. But in a *unitarily possible* ego not all singly possible types are *compossible,* and not all compossible ones are compossible in just any order, at no matter what loci in that ego's own temporality. If I form some scientific theory or other, my complex rational activity, with its rationally constituted existent, belongs to an essential type that is possible, not in every possible ego, but only in one that is "rational" in a particular sense, the same that, with the mundanization of the ego, presents itself in the essential form: man ("rational" animal). When I reduce my de facto theorizing to its eidetic type, I have varied myself too (regardless of whether I am aware of it)—not however in a wholly optional manner, but within the frame of the corresponding essential type, "rational" being. Manifestly I cannot imagine the theorizing I do or can do now as shifted arbitrarily within the unity of my life; and this too carries over into the eidetic. Eidetic apprehension of my (transcendentally reduced) childhood life and its possibilities of constitution produces a type, such that in its further devel-

opment, but not in its own nexus, the type "scientific theorizing" can occur. Restriction of this kind has its grounds in an a priori universal structure, in a conformity to universal eidetic laws of coexistence and succession in egological time. For indeed whatever occurs in my ego, and eidetically in an ego as such —in the way of intentional processes, constituted unities, Ego habitualities—has its temporality and, in this respect, participates in the system of forms that belongs to the all-inclusive temporality with which every imaginable ego, every possibility-variant of my ego, constitutes himself for himself.

§37. Time as the universal form of all egological genesis

The eidetic laws of compossibility (rules that govern simultaneous or successive existence and possible existence together, in the fact) are laws of causality in a maximally broad sense —laws for an If and Then. Yet it is better to avoid here the expression causality, which is laden with prejudices (deriving from naturalism), and to speak of *motivation* in the transcendental sphere (and in the sphere of "pure" psychology). The *universe of subjective processes,* which are the "really inherent" consciousness-constituents of the transcendental ego, is a universe of compossibilities only in the universal *unity-form of the flux,* in which all particulars have their respective places as processes that flow within it. Accordingly even this most universal form, which belongs to all particular forms of concrete subjective processes (with the products that are flowingly constituted in the flux of such processes) is the form of a motivation, connecting all and governing within each single process in particular. We can call it furthermore a *formal regularity pertaining to a universal genesis,* which is such that past, present, and future, become unitarily constituted over and over again, in a certain noetic-noematic formal structure of flowing modes of givenness.

But, within this form, life goes on as a motivated course of particular constitutive performances with a multiplicity of particular motivations and motivational systems, which, according to *universal laws of genesis,* produce a unity of *universal genesis of the ego.* The ego constitutes himself for himself in, so to speak, the unity of a "history." We said that the constitution of the ego contains all the constitutions of all the objectivities existing for him, whether these be immanent or transcendent, ideal or real. It should now be added that the *constitutive systems* (systems actualizable by the Ego), by virtue of which such and such objects and categories of objects exist for him, are themselves possible only within the frame of a genesis in conformity with laws. At the same time they are bound, in their constituting, by the universal genetic form that makes the concrete ego (the monad) possible as a unity, as having particular constituents of his being that are compossible. That a Nature, a cultural world, a world of men with their social forms, and so forth, exist for me signifies that possibilities of corresponding experiences exist for me, as experiences I can at any time bring into play and continue in a certain *synthetic style,* whether or not I am at present actually experiencing objects belonging to the realm in question. It signifies furthermore that other modes of consciousness corresponding to them—vague intendings and the like—exist as possibilities for me, and also that these other modes of consciousness have possibilities of becoming fulfilled or disappointed by experiences of predelineated types. This involves a firmly developed habituality, acquired by a certain genesis in conformity with eidetic laws.

We are reminded here of the long-familiar problems concerning the *psychological origin* of the "idea of space," the "idea of time," the "idea of a physical thing," and so forth. In phenomenology such problems present themselves as transcendental and, naturally, as *problems of intentionality,* which have their particular places among the problems of a universal genesis.

Access to the ultimate universalities involved in problems of eidetic phenomenology is, however, very difficult. This is particularly true with respect to an *ultimate genesis.* The beginning phenomenologist is bound in-

voluntarily by the circumstance that he takes himself as his initial example. Transcendentally he finds himself as the ego, then as generically an ego, who already has (in conscious fashion) a world—a world of our universally familiar ontological type, with Nature, with culture (sciences, fine art, mechanical art, and so forth), with personalities of a higher order (state, church), and the rest. The phenomenology developed at first is merely "static"; its descriptions are analogous to those of natural history, which concern particular types and, at best, arrange them in their systematic order. Questions of universal genesis and the genetic structure of the ego in his universality, so far as that structure is more than temporal formation, are still far away; and, indeed, they belong to a higher level. But even when they are raised, it is with a restriction. At first, even eidetic observation will consider an ego as such with the restriction that a constituted world already exists for him. This, moreover, is a necessary level; only by laying open the law-forms of the genesis pertaining to this level can one see the possibilities of a *maximally universal* eidetic phenomenology. In the latter the ego varies himself so freely that he does not keep even the ideal restrictive presupposition that a world having the ontological structure accepted by us as obvious is essentially constituted for him.

§38. Active and passive genesis

If we inquire first about principles of constitutive genesis that have universal significance for us, as possible subjects related to a world, we find them to be divided according to two fundamental forms, into principles of *active* and principles of *passive* genesis. In active genesis the Ego functions as productively constitutive, by means of subjective processes that are specifically acts of the Ego. Here belong all the works of *practical reason,* in a maximally broad sense. In this sense even logical reason is practical. The characteristic feature (in the case of the realm of logos) is that Ego-acts, pooled in a sociality—whose transcendental sense, to be sure, we have not yet brought to light—become combined in a manifold, specifically active synthesis and, on the basis of objects already given (in modes of consciousness that give beforehand), *constitute new objects originally.* These then present themselves for consciousness *as products.* Thus, in collecting, the collection <is constituted>; in counting, the number; in dividing, the part; in predicating, the predicate and the predicational complex of affairs; in inferring, the inference; and so forth. Original universality-consciousness is likewise an activity, one in which the universal becomes constituted objectively. On the Ego side there becomes constituted a consequent habituality of continuing acceptance, which thereupon is part of the constitution of the object as simply existing for the Ego: an object that can always be seized again, be it in reiterated producings, with synthetic consciousness of the same objectivity as given again in *"categorial intuition,"* or be it in a synthetically appertinent vague consciousness. The transcendental constitution of such objects (cultural objects, for example), in relation to *intersubjective* activities, presupposes the antecedent constitution of a transcendental intersubjectivity—about which we shall not speak until later.

As already mentioned, the higher forms of such activities of "reason" in a specific sense and, correlatively, the higher forms of *products* of reason, all of which have the character of *irreality* (that of "ideal" objects), cannot be regarded forthwith as belonging to every concrete ego as such. This is already shown by memory of our childhood. However, as regards the *lowest levels,* such as experiential grasping, explicating the experienced in respect of its parts, taking together, relating, and the like, the situation may well turn out to be different. In any case, anything built by activity necessarily presupposes, as the lowest level, a passivity that gives something beforehand; and, when we trace anything built actively, we run into constitution by passive generation. The "ready-made" object that confronts us in life as an existent mere physical thing (when we disregard all the "spiritual" or "cultural"

characteristics that make it knowable as, for example, a hammer, a table, an aesthetic creation) is given, with the originality of the "it itself," in the synthesis of a passive experience. As such a thing, it is given beforehand to "spiritual" activities, which begin with active grasping.

While these are making their synthetic products, the passive synthesis that supplies all their "material" still goes on. The physical thing given beforehand in passive intuition continues to appear in a unitary intuition; and, no matter how much the thing may be modified therein by the activity of explication, of grasping parts and features, it continues to be given beforehand during and in this activity: The manifold modes of appearance, the unitary visual or tactual "perceptual images" continue their flow; and, in their manifestly passive synthesis, the one physical thing, with its one shape and other unitary features, appears. Yet precisely this synthesis, as a synthesis having this form, has its "history," evinced in the synthesis itself. It is owing to an essentially necessary genesis that I, the ego, can experience a physical thing and do so even at first glance. This is true, moreover, not only as regards phenomenological genesis but also as regards genesis in the usual sense, psychological genesis. With good reason it is said that in infancy we had to learn to see physical things, and that such modes of consciousness of them had to precede all others genetically. In "early infancy," then, the field of perception that gives beforehand does not as yet contain anything that, in a mere look, might be explicated as a physical thing. Yet, without putting ourselves back into the realm of passivity, to say nothing of using the external psycho-physical point of view of psychology, we can, the meditating ego can, penetrate into the intentional constituents of experiential phenomena themselves—thing-experiencing phenomena and all others—and thus find intentional references leading back to a "history" and accordingly making these phenomena knowable as formations subsequent to other, essentially antecedent formations (even if the latter cannot be related to precisely the same constituted object). There, however, we soon encounter eidetic laws governing a passive forming of perpetually new syntheses (a forming that, in part, lies prior to all activity and, in part, takes in all activity itself); we encounter a passive genesis of the manifold apperceptions, as products that persist in a habituality relating specifically to them. When these habitual apperceptions become actually operative, the already given objects formed for the central Ego appear, affect him, and motivate activities. Thanks to the aforesaid passive synthesis (into which the performances of active synthesis also enter), the Ego always has an environment of "objects." Even the circumstance that everything affecting me, as a "developed" ego, is apperceived as an "object," a substrate of predicates with which I may become acquainted, belongs here, since this is an already familiar goal-form for possible explications as acquaintive explications—explications that would constitute an object as an abiding possession, as something accessible again and again; and this goal-form is understandable in advance as having arisen from a genesis. It itself points back to a "primal instituting" of this form. Everything known to us points to an original becoming acquainted; what we call unknown has, nevertheless, a known structural form: the form "object" and, more particularly, the form "spatial thing," "cultural Object," "tool," and so forth.

§39. Association as a principle of passive genesis

The *universal principle of passive genesis,* for the constitution of all objectivities given completely prior to the products of activity, bears the title *association.* Association, it should be clearly noted, is a matter of *intentionality,* descriptively demonstrable as that, in respect of its primal forms, and standing, in respect of its intentional performances, under *eidetic laws.* Owing to these, each and every passive constitution is to be made understandable—both the constitution of subjective processes, as objects in immanent time, and the constitution of all real natural objects belonging to the Objective spatiotemporal world. Association is a *fundamental concept belonging to transcendental phenomenology* (and, in the psychological parallel, a fundamental concept belonging to a purely intentional psychology). The old concepts of association and of laws of association, though they too have usually been related to the coherencies of pure psychic life by Hume and later thinkers, are only naturalistic distortions of the corresponding genuine, intentional concepts. From phenomenology, which was very late in finding avenues to the exploration of association, this concept receives a completely new aspect, an essentially new delimination, with new fundamental forms. Here belongs, for example, sensuous configuration in coexistence and in succession. It is phenomenologically evident, but strange to the tradition-bound, that association is not a title merely for a conformity to empirical laws on the part of complexes of data comprised in a "psyche"—according to the old figure, something like an intrapsychic gravitation—but a title (moreover an extremely comprehensive one) for a conformity to eidetic laws on the part of the constitution of the pure ego. It designates a *realm of the "innate" a priori,* without which an ego as such is unthinkable. Only through the phenomenology of genesis does the ego become understandable: as a nexus, connected in the unity of an all-embracing genesis, an infinite nexus of synthetically congruous performances—at levels, all of which fit the universal persisting form, *temporality,* because the latter itself is built up in a continual, passive and completely universal genesis, which, as a matter of essential necessity, embraces everything new. In the developed ego, this many-leveled structure is conserved as a persistent form-system of apperception and consequently of constituted objectivities—among them, the ones belonging to an Objective universe having a fixed ontological structure; and this conserving is itself only a form of genesis. In all of that, the particular fact is irrational; but it is possible only in the a priori form-system pertaining to it as an egological fact. Nor should it be overlooked here that *"fact,"* with its *"irrationality,"* is itself a *structural concept within the system of the concrete a priori.* Now that the problems of phenomenology have been reduced to the unitary comprehensive title, "the (static and genetic) constitution of objectivities of possible consciousness," phenomenology seems to be rightly characterized also as *transcendental theory of knowledge.*

18. Static and Genetic Phenomenological Method*

We must make the following distinction under the rubric of the laws of genesis:

(1) Laws of genesis in the sense of the demonstration of laws for the sequences of particular events in the stream of lived-experience. They are either laws of immediate, necessary succession for concrete events or for abstract phases, moments of such events like the necessary connection of retentions to lived-experiences that have lapsed, or the necessary connection of retentional phases to the respective impressional phase. Or they are also laws of a mediated sequence, for instance, the laws of association, laws for the emergence of reproductions for a present lived-experience within the present and the like for the emergence of intentions of expectation—in the widest sense of empty intentions, fulfilled or unfulfilled processes of pointing-toward or pointing-back.

(2) Lawful regularities that regulate the formation of apperceptions. Apperceptions are intentional lived-experiences that are conscious of something as perceived which is not self-given in these lived-experiences (not completely); and they are called apperceptions to the extent that they have this trait, even if in this case they also consciously intend what in truth is self-given in them. Apperceptions transcend their immanent content, and belonging essentially to this transcending is the fact that within the same stream of consciousness whose segments are being continually connected, a fulfilling lived-experience is possible that, in the synthesis of fulfillment, supplies its self-given† as the same, and in that other lived-experience supplies what is not-self-given and the same [self-given]. Insofar as this is the case, there is a law here regulating the future, but a law merely for future possibilities, concerning a possible continuation of the stream of consciousness, one that is ideally possible.

Defined in this general way, apperception is a concept that encompasses every self-giving, thus every intuitive consciousness.‡ Originary apperception is perception, and every modi-

*Excerpted from Edmund Husserl, *Analyses Concerning Passive and Active Synthesis: Lectures on Transcendental Logic.* Translated by Anthony J. Steinbock (Boston: Kluwer Academic Publishers, forthcoming). Reprinted with permission of the translator.

From 1921. —Editor's note.

†What is meant here is not immanently inherent, adequate givenness, but being perceived in the genuine sense.

‡Consider how the concept of apperception is to be circumscribed. Apperception: a consciousness that is conscious of something individual that is not self-given in it (self-given does not mean being contained in perception in an intimately inherent manner); and it is called apperception to the extent that it has this trait, even if it has something in addition that is self-given in it. Namely, a consciousness can be apperceptively conscious of something, and that same something can also still be self-given in the same consciousness that extends even further than this apperceiving. For example, if in this way we call a consciousness of a sign an apperception, then that which is signified *[das Bezeichnete]* can also be self-given along with the consciousness of a sign in the unity of a consciousness. Or in the unity of a perception of a hexagon there appears a hexagonal plane and at the same time another; but one of them appears with

fication of apperception in imagination contains an apperception precisely in the shape of this modification. If we consider here that every present consciousness (every span of presence belonging to the stream of lived-experience) not only is, but is "perceived," that is, is present now to consciousness in an impressional manner, then we also mean that an "apperception" lies in every present consciousness. In fact, we cannot even conceive of a consciousness that would not go beyond the strict present in its essential flux from presence to new presences; consciousness is inconceivable without retentional and protentional horizons, without a co-consciousness (although a necessarily non-intuitive one) of the past of consciousness and an anticipation of an approaching consciousness (no matter how indeterminate it may be). Thus if something "arises out of something" at all in the stream of consciousness, then apperceptions necessarily arise from apperceptions. We do not need to consider here whether there are primordial apperceptions that could be placed at the "beginning" of the stream of consciousness. In any case, there are apperceptive horizons, kinds of such horizons, kinds of apperceptive intentions (I also say appresenting intentions) that must arise at each place in the stream according to the universal lawful regularities of conscious life—like the examples given above show. But this also holds likewise for those that can arise—even if they must not arise—at every place in the stream, namely, insofar as they are bound to conditions that are possible at each place.

To the latter belong the intentions that customarily come into question under the rubric of association. At each place in the stream it is possible for constellations that are similar (I use an empty term [constellations] whose scientific content is still to be specified) to be produced again with earlier ones, to recall the earlier similar ones, to point back to them, to bring them perhaps to intuitive presence, and then as fulfillments to show them synthetically unified with the present ones, etc. Yet even these apperceptions, and likewise these apperceptive combinations—which exhibit the unities of a combined phenomenon, whose combinations presuppose apperceptions and encompass them—these apperceptions can only take place when other, especially suited apperceptions have preceded them.

(Could we not also define apperception in the following way: a consciousness that is not only conscious of something within itself in general, but at the same time intends this something as a motivation for a consciousness of something else; thus, a consciousness that is not merely conscious of something, and then still something else that it does not include, but rather, a consciousness that points to this other one as one that belongs to it, as what is motivated through it. In any case, we will have to expand and give sharper contours to our previous definition.)

In addition, types of complicated apperceptions can occur, which, once they are there, are repeated in a further stream of consciousness according to primordial laws under universally

---

reference to the other one, and the other one is itself appearing. This holds in general with respect to the components of self-givenness peculiar to external appearing phenomena.

Every motivation is apperception. The emergence of a lived-experience *A* motivates the lived-experience of a *B* in the unity of a consciousness; the consciousness of *A* is equipped with an intention that points beyond, "indicating" a coexistence. But here we must add that every unfulfilled intention, every unfulfilled horizon contains motivations, systems of motivations. It is a potentiality of motivation. When fulfillment takes place, a current motivation is there. One can also say that apperception is itself a motivation, that it motivates whatever may occur as fulfilling, that it motivates beyond itself into an emptiness. But that will depend upon more precise definitions of apperception and motivation. Moreover, one will certainly not be able to say that a sign *[Zeichen]* motivates if it is not an indication *[Anzeichen]*, a word-sign, for example. But we must also ask whether one will want to speak of apperception in that case. Admittedly, we have formulated our concept in an extraordinarily broad manner. Deeper investigations are needed here. If one speaks of apperception, perception will not necessarily express a positing consciousness, for the co-perceived is then not necessarily co-posited, to say nothing of perceived in the [broader] sense of "perception" *[perzipiert im Sinne von "wahrgenommen"]*.

Fundamental for the theory of consciousness is the universal exploration of the relations of consciousness intending beyond itself (beyond its Self)—what we call here apperception—to association.

producible conditions; indeed, they run through this stream of consciousness steadily, like all natural apperceptions, all objective apperceptions of reality, apperceptions which in accordance with their essence themselves have a history, a genesis according to primordial laws. Thus, it is a necessary task to establish the universal and primitive laws under which stands the formation of an apperception arising from a primordial apperception, and to derive systematically the possible formations, that is, to clarify every given structure according to its origin.

This "history" of consciousness (the history of all possible apperceptions) does not concern bringing to light a factical genesis for factical apperceptions or factical types in a factical stream of consciousness, or even in all factical human beings; thus it is not at all similar to the development of plant or animal species. Rather, every shape of apperception is an essential shape and has its genesis in accordance with essential laws; accordingly, included in such an idea of apperception is that it must undergo a "genetic analysis." And what is given is not the necessary becoming of the particular, single apperception (when it is understood as a fact); rather, the mode of genesis is only given with the genesis of essence; in this mode of genesis any kind of apperception of this type must have arisen originally (in one stroke or piecemeal) in an individual stream of consciousness. And after it had arisen (as primordially instituting, so to speak), individual apperceptions of the same type were able to arise in an entirely different manner, namely as genetic after-effects of the earlier ones already formed—in accordance with intelligible laws of a primitive form. The theory of consciousness is directly a theory of apperceptions; the stream of consciousness is a stream of a constant genesis; it is not a mere series *[Nacheinander]*, but a development *[Auseinander]*, a process of becoming according to

laws of necessary succession in which concrete apperceptions of different typicalities (among them all the apperceptions that give rise to the universal apperception of a world) grow out of primordial apperceptions or out of apperceptive intentions of a primitive kind.

Every apperception exhibits the structure of noesis and noema. Every apperception carries out in its own way a sense-giving and a positing of objects in doxic modalities. We have to undertake a unique form of analysis in order to elucidate the intentionality of an apperception, in order to describe, according to their noetic and noematic structures, the possible types of fulfillment and the systems of possible omni-faceted, complete fulfillment, or the systems of a fulfillment that is continually in the process of becoming complete. With these descriptions, namely the constitutive ones, we are in no way inquiring into an explanatory genesis. In our descriptions of all the modal modifications in retentions, rememberings, expectations, etc., we likewise do not inquire into genesis when we pass from the original impressions (perceptions) as a generally typical generic character that concerns all apperceptions, over to a constitutive character, and therefore tracing a principle of systematic ordering of apperceptions, a principle of ordering that intersects the division of apperceptions according to the highest genera of objects (actual and possible existing regions of objects). A universal doctrine of consciousness is thus a universal doctrine of apperceptions, correlative to a universal doctrine of the highest categories of possible objects and their categorial modifications—a universal constitutive phenomenology. The latter is preceded by a universal phenomenology of the most general structures and modalities that encompass all categories of apperceptions. To this one must add a universal theory of genesis.*

In a certain way, we can therefore distinguish "explanatory" phenomenology as a phenom-

---

*Phenomenology:
1) Universal phenomenology of the general structures of consciousness
2) Constitutive Phenomenology
3) Phenomenology of Genesis

enology of regulated genesis, and "descriptive" phenomenology as a phenomenology of possible, essential shapes (no matter how they have come to pass) in pure consciousness and their teleological ordering in the realm of possible reason under the headings, "object" and "sense." In my lectures, I did not say "descriptive," but rather "static" phenomenology. The latter offers an understanding of intentional accomplishment, especially of the accomplishment of reason and its *negata*. It reveals to us the graduated levels of intentional objects that emerge in founded apperceptions of a higher level as objective senses and in functions of sense-giving, and it reveals to us how they function in them, etc. But in these investigations we are concerned in the first place with apperceptive forms, with modes of consciousness that are conceived so generally (that is, left so indeterminate) that they must belong to the make-up of every monad (e.g., perception, memory, etc.). Other ones have a different universality and necessity. If we take as our point of departure the "natural concept of the world" and the human ego as subject of knowledge, then what we have gained through an eidetic analysis is the idea of a monad that is precisely in relation to a "world" of this corresponding concept, and in this way we have a pure range of monads in whose stream of consciousness "necessarily" emerge the corresponding types of apperceptions (spatial-causal thing, animal being, human being), although perhaps they do not necessarily belong to the idea of a monad as such—what in any case is not immediately certain a priori from the start.

Further, in monads that correspond to human beings within the natural attitude, we find factically peculiar occurrences of reason in particular shapes. We <want to investigate> the intentional typicality that is made available to us through the phenomenological-eidetic analysis of the ideas "human being" and "world," we want to investigate it systematically according to all possible nexuses of reason (that is, we want to investigate its nexuses and ultimately the entire world of these monads most basically in the possible nexuses of "concor-

dant," ratifying experience of the respective object-like formations), and we want to gain its essential shape. Likewise, we investigate in the free realm of possibility the essential structures of the formal lawful regularity of a reason in general as formal-logical reason, etc. Aside from the fact that we form the corresponding thoughts and realize truths in ourselves—we recognize through them how possible rational subjects would think; through this we construe in an indeterminate generality subjects of pure reason and their shapes of rational activities in which they live toward and attain true being and truths, as well as true values and goods. But even with all this, we do not gain knowledge concerning how a monad, as it were, looks in its completeness, and which possibilities are prefigured for such complete monadic individualities, and through which lawful regularity of individuation.

Let us note that we remain here within the sphere of reason, within the realm of the active ego, and that we cannot describe a shape of active apperception, that is, any coherent unity of active configuration (which as a unity of consciousness is intentional and accordingly is apperceptive configuration) without also constantly speaking of genesis. Every inferring is an active apperceiving, and as an active process of configuring, it is a judging, because another judging has preceded it—one judgment is passed on other judgments that have been passed. The conclusion follows from the premises, it is generated from them; the lived-experience genetically issues from the grounding lived-experiences, even if other genetic interconnections play a founding role there. Thus, every activity is motivated, and we have pure genesis in the sphere of acts as a pure act-genesis in such a form that I, who execute acts, am determined by the fact that I have executed other acts. Further, we have acts that are motivated through affections and that stand in a genetic relation to spheres that fall outside of the sphere of activity. We have, finally, genesis in the sphere of pure passivity, even though formations which have their origin in an earlier activity may play their part in them; but now they themselves emerge passively.

Accordingly, in the doctrine of genesis, in "explanatory" phenomenology, we have:

(1) Genesis of passivity, that is, a general lawful regularity of genetic becoming in passivity that is always there and, without a doubt, has origins that lie further back, just as apperception itself does. Special types that belong to the general idea of passive genesis.

(2) The participation of the ego and relationships between activity and passivity.

(3) Interrelations, formations of pure activity; genesis as an active accomplishment of ideal objects and as an accomplishment of real generation. Secondary sensibility: general laws of the consciousness of what is habitual. Everything habitual belongs to passivity. Even the activity that has become habitual.

(4) Once we have gained all the kinds of genesis and their laws, we will then ask to what extent one can assert something about the individuality of a monad, about the unity of its "development," about the regulative system that essentially unites all the particular geneses in the form of one monad, and about which types of individual monads are a priori possible and construable.

(5) And connected to all of the preceding we ask: in what sense the genesis of a monad can be implicated in the genesis of another, and in what sense a unity of genesis can, according to laws [of genesis], combine a multiplicity of monads. On the one hand, passive genesis, which in the case of the constitution of an anthropological world (or rather, an animal world) refers to the constituted physiological processes and to their conditions in the unity of the physical world with the lived-body of another; on the other hand, active genesis in the form of the motivation of my thinking, valuing, willing through that of others. Thus, considering the individuality of the monad leads to the question of the individuality of a multiplicity of coexisting monads, monads genetically combined with one another. With respect to "our" world it leads to the question of mak-

ing understandable monadologically the natural psychophysical world and the communal world.*

(6) Again, all this relates to the question concerning the genetic explanation of a monad within which a unitary nature and a world in general is constituted genetically, and how a unitary nature and a world in general remain constituted from this point onward throughout its entire life, or through an exceptional span of life, and further how a world with animals and humans is constituted in a constant process of identifying itself.

Having preceded this is the static elucidation of world-apperception and of the sense-giving that is carried out in it. But, it seems, it is only possible to undertake an absolute consideration of the world, a "metaphysics," and to understand the possibility of a world first through a genetic consideration of individuation.

(7) My passivity stands in connection with the passivity of all others: one and the same thing-world is constituted for us, one and the same time as objective time such that through this, my Now and the Now of every other—and thus his life-present (with all immanences) and my life-present—are objectively "simultaneous." Accordingly, my objectively experienced and ratified locations and the locations of every other share the same locality; they are the same locations, and these are indices for ordering my and others' phenomenal systems, not as separated orders, but coordinated orders in "the same time." That is, my life and the life of another do not merely exist, each for themselves; rather, one is "directed" toward the other. Not only have sensations occurred in me in this or that order such that, in accordance with the laws of genesis, a nature had to be constituted for me, and not only has this nature endured, but a typically stable lived-body is mediated in this process. Realized is also the possibility that there are things similar to my lived-body in the nature that is given to me.

*The expression "our" world designates a first person plural world constituted through various historical and intersubjective processes of appropriation and disappropriation; as such it becomes for Husserl in the 1930s a term for the "generative" phenomenon of "homeworld." —Translator's note.

Furthermore, not only has empathy ensued, but this empathy has been ratified by the fact that the interior life of the other ego has expressed itself in a regular manner, and from then on newly determined and ratified my appresentations again and again.

Primordial laws of genesis are the laws of original time-consciousness, the primordial laws of reproduction and then of association and associative expectation. In relation to this there is genesis on the basis of active motivation.

If we compare static and genetic nexuses, then we will have to ask whether one can achieve a systematic phenomenology of static nexuses (like that of noesis and noema), that is, whether the genetic dimension can be fully suspended here. On the whole, the question is how the investigations are to be ordered. It is clear that one will initially proceed from particular fundamental types, some of which—as I already said above—will occur necessarily, others which will be presented as possibilities. The question concerns the leading clues of the system. As leading clues, we have types of objects, that is, leading clues from the standpoint of ontology. And with this constitutive teleologies. Here ideal possibilities of concordant modes of givenness are elaborated, ideal possibilities of monadic streams in which the unity of an accomplishment is constituted, and other possibilities outside of these are to be considered as opposing forms.

Another leading clue is the unity of a monad as a unity of a genesis, and then the investigation of the typicality of possible monads, namely, of possible types of the unity of an individual monad, of an individual ego, and of that which it had to find [in its environing-world], and how it had to encounter itself, or how it bears within itself a rule of individual character traits that are then recognizable (perhaps through others).

Beginning with the natural attitude, one can also take the "natural concept of the world" as a leading clue. One raises the natural world to the eidetic level, analyzes it according to its strata, extracts types of constituting objects and describes constituting consciousness, and finally the constitution of this type, world—all without paying any attention to genesis.

Perhaps I can be more clear by writing:

Necessary successions in the open sphere of lived-experience: that which is arriving is then not only arriving, but following necessarily according to the evident law of necessary succession. Naturally, one can call that a law of genesis.

All "horizons" or all "apperceptions" naturally arise in this way. But in a "static" regard, we have "finished" apperceptions. Here apperceptions emerge and are awakened as finished, and have a "history" reaching way back. A constitutive phenomenology can regard the nexuses of apperceptions in which the same object is constituted eidetically, in which it shows itself in its constituted ipseity in the way it is expected and can be expected. Another "constitutive" phenomenology, the phenomenology of genesis, follows the history, the necessary history of this objectivation and thereby the history of the object itself as the object of a possible knowledge. The primordial history of objects leads back to hyletic objects and to the immanent ones in general, that is, to the genesis of them in original time-consciousness. Contained within the universal genesis of a monad are the histories of the constitution of objects that are there for this monad, and within the universal eidetic phenomenology of genesis this very process is [explicated as] accomplished for all conceivable objects in relation to all conceivable monads. And conversely, one gains graduated levels of monads corresponding to the levels of objects.

I must now go through the *Ideas* once more to become clearer about what still distinguishes the doctrine of the structures of consciousness from the constitutive considerations if I also regard everything immanent "constitutively."

X.

Transcendental Phenomenology and the Way through the Science of Phenomenological Psychology

19. Phenomenological Psychology and Transcendental Phenomenology*

"Phenomenology"†

Introduction

The term 'phenomenology' designates two things: a new kind of descriptive method which made a breakthrough in philosophy at the turn of the century, and an a priori science derived from it; a science which is intended to supply the basic instrument *(Organon)* for a rigorously scientific philosophy and, in its consequent application, to make possible a methodical reform of all the sciences. Together with this philosophical phenomenology, but not yet separated from it, however, there also came into being a new psychological discipline parallel to it in method and content: the a priori pure or "phenomenological" psychology, which raises the reformational claim to being the basic methodological foundation on which alone a scientifically rigorous empirical psychology

can be established. An outline of this psychological phenomenology, standing nearer to our natural thinking, is well suited to serve as a preliminary step that will lead up to an understanding of philosophical phenomenology.

I. Pure Psychology: Its Field of Experience, Its Method, and Its Function

1. Pure natural science and pure psychology

Modern psychology is the science dealing with the "psychical" in the concrete context of spatiotemporal realities, being in some way so to speak what occurs in nature as egoical, with all that inseparably belongs to it as psychic processes like experiencing, thinking, feeling, willing, as capacity, and as *habitus*. Experience presents the psychical as merely a stra-

*SW, pp. 22–35. This article appeared in the *Encyclopaedia Britannica* (1927).

†The translator gratefully acknowledges the help he received from Professor Herbert Spiegelberg (Washington University, St. Louis, Missouri) and Professor Gisela Hess (MacMurray College, Jacksonville, Illinois) in the preparation of the original translation. The translator has revised his earlier effort in accordance with corrections received from various sources. Principally, the translator wishes to thank Herbert Spiegelberg for his continued help as well as Karl Schuhmann, who forwarded a marked-up copy of the translation, which he had used as the text for a seminar in parallel with the German original. Under the impetus of the criticisms of Professor Schuhmann, the translator has reviewed the entire text and devised many new renderings (not always those suggested by Professor Schuhmann) which he hopes have improved the present translation.

tum of human and animal being. Accordingly, psychology is seen as a branch of the more concrete science of anthropology, or rather zoology. Animal realities are first of all, at a basic level, physical realities. As such, they belong in the closed nexus of relationships in physical nature, in Nature meant in the primary and most pregnant sense as the universal theme of a pure natural science; that is to say, an objective science of nature which in deliberate one-sidedness excludes all extra-physical predications of reality. The scientific investigation of the bodies of animals fits within this area. By contrast, however, if the psychic aspect of the animal world is to become the topic of investigation, the first thing we have to ask is how far, in parallel with the pure science of nature, a pure psychology is possible. Obviously, purely psychological research can be done to a certain extent. To it we owe the basic concepts of the psychical according to the properties essential and specific to it. These concepts must be incorporated into the others, into the psychophysical foundational concepts of psychology.

It is by no means clear from the very outset, however, how far the idea of a pure psychology—as a psychological discipline sharply separate in itself and as a real parallel to the pure physical science of nature—has a meaning that is legitimate and necessary of realization.

2. The purely psychical in self-experience and community experience. The universal description of intentional experiences

To establish and unfold this guiding idea, the first thing that is necessary is a clarification of what is peculiar to experience, and especially to the pure experience of the psychical—and specifically the purely psychical that experience reveals, which is to become the theme of a pure psychology. It is natural and appropriate that precedence will be accorded to the most immediate types of experience, which in each case reveal to us our own psychic being.

Focusing our experiencing gaze on our own psychic life necessarily takes place as reflection, as a turning about of a glance which had previously been directed elsewhere. Every experience can be subject to such reflection, as can indeed every manner in which we occupy ourselves with any real or ideal objects—for instance, thinking, or in the modes of feeling and will, valuing, and striving. So when we are fully engaged in conscious activity, we focus exclusively on the specific thing, thoughts, values, goals, or means involved, but not on the psychical experience as such, in which these things are known *as* such. Only reflection reveals this to us. Through reflection, instead of grasping simply the matter straight-out—the values, goals, and instrumentalities—we grasp the corresponding subjective experiences in which we become "conscious" of them, in which (in the broadest sense) they "appear." For this reason, they are called "phenomena," and their most general essential character is to exist as the "consciousness-of" or "appearance-of" the specific things, thoughts (judged states of affairs, grounds, conclusions), plans, decisions, hopes, and so forth. This relatedness [of the appearing to the object of appearance] resides in the meaning of all expressions in the vernacular languages which relate to psychic experience—for instance, perception *of* something, recalling *of* something, thinking *of* something, hoping *for* something, fearing something, striving *for* something, deciding on something, and so on. If this realm of what we call "phenomena" proves to be the possible field for a pure psychological discipline related exclusively to phenomena, we can understand the designation of it as *phenomenological psychology.* The terminological expression, deriving from Scholasticism, for designating the basic character of being as consciousness, as consciousness of something, is *intentionality.* In unreflective holding of some object or other in consciousness, we are turned or directed towards it: our *"intentio"* goes out towards it. The phenomenological reversal of our gaze shows that this "being directed" *[Gerichtetsein]* is really an immanent essential feature of the respective experiences involved; they are "intentional" experiences.

An extremely large and variegated number of kinds of special cases fall within the general scope of this concept. Consciousness of something is not an empty holding of something; every phenomenon has its own total form of intention *[intentionale Gesamtform]*, but at the same time it has a structure, which in intentional analysis leads always again to components which are themselves also intentional. So for example in starting from a perception of something (for example, a die), phenomenological reflection leads to a multiple and yet synthetically unified intentionality. There are continually varying differences in the modes of appearing of objects, which are caused by the changing of "orientation"—of right and left, nearness and farness, with the consequent differences in perspective involved. There are further differences in appearance between the "actually seen front" and the "unseeable" *["unanschaulichen"]* and relatively "undetermined" reverse side, which is nevertheless "meant along with it." Observing the flux of modes of appearing and the manner of their "synthesis," one finds that every phase and portion [of the flux] is already in itself "consciousness-of"—but in such a manner that there is formed within the constant emerging of new phases the synthetically unified awareness that this is one and the same object. The intentional structure of any process of perception has its fixed essential type *[seine feste Wesenstypik]*, which must necessarily be realized in all its extraordinary complexity just in order for a physical body simply to be perceived as such. If this same thing is intuited in other modes—for example, in the modes of recollection, fantasy or pictorial representation—to some extent the whole intentional content of the perception comes back, but all aspects peculiarly transformed to correspond to that mode. This applies similarly for every other category of psychic process: the judging, valuing, striving consciousness is not an empty having knowledge of the specific judgments, values, goals, and means. Rather, these constitute themselves, with fixed essential forms cor-

responding to each process, in a flowing intentionality. For psychology, the universal task presents itself: to investigate systematically the elementary intentionalities, and from out of these [unfold] the typical forms of intentional processes, their possible variants, their syntheses to new forms, their structural composition, and from this advance towards a descriptive knowledge of the totality of mental process, towards a comprehensive type of a life of the psyche *[Gesamttypus eines Lebens der Seele]*. Clearly, the consistent carrying out of this task will produce knowledge which will have validity far beyond the psychologist's own particular psychic existence.

Psychic life is accessible to us not only through self-experience but also through experience of others. This novel source of experience offers us not only what matches our self-experience but also what is new, inasmuch as, in terms of consciousness and indeed as experience, it establishes the differences between own and other, as well as the properties peculiar to the life of a community. At just this point there arises the task of also making phenomenologically understandable the mental life of the community, with all the intentionalities that pertain to it.

3. The self-contained field of the purely psychological. — Phenomenological reduction and true inner experience

The idea of a phenomenological psychology encompasses the whole range of tasks arising out of the experience of self and the experience of the other founded on it. But it is not yet clear whether phenomenological experience, followed through in exclusiveness and consistency, really provides us with a kind of closed-off field of being, out of which a science can grow which is exclusively focused on it and completely free of everything psychophysical. Here [in fact] difficulties do exist, which have hidden from psychologists the possibility of such a purely phenomenological psychology even after Brentano's discovery of intentionality. They are relevant already to the construction of a really pure self-experience, and therewith of a really pure psychic datum. A particular method of access is required for the pure phenomenological field: the method of "phenomenological reduction." This *method of "phenomenological reduction"* is thus the foundational method of pure psychology and the presupposition of all its specifically theoretical methods. Ultimately the great difficulty rests on the way that already the self-experience of the psychologist is everywhere intertwined with external experience, with that of extra-psychical real things. The experienced "exterior" does not belong to one's intentional interiority, although certainly the experience itself belongs to it as experience— *of* the exterior. Exactly this same thing is true of every kind of awareness directed at something out there in the world. A consistent epoché of the phenomenologist is required, if he wishes to break through to his own consciousness as pure phenomenon or as the totality of his purely mental processes. That is to say, in the accomplishment of phenomenological reflection he must inhibit every co-accomplishment of objective positing produced in unreflective consciousness, and therewith [inhibit] every judgmental drawing-in of the world as it "exists" for him straightforwardly. The specific experience of this house, this body, of a world as such, is and remains, however, according to its own essential content and thus inseparably, experience "*of* this house," this body, this world; this is so for every mode of consciousness which is directed towards an object. It is, after all, quite impossible to describe an intentional experience—even if illusionary, an invalid judgment, or the like— without at the same time describing the object of that consciousness *as* such. The universal epoché of the world as it becomes known in consciousness (the "putting it in brackets") shuts out from the phenomenological field the world as it exists for the subject in simple absoluteness; its place, however, is taken by the world as given in *consciousness* (perceived, remembered, judged, thought, valued, etc.)— the world *as such,* the "world in brackets," or in other words, the world, or rather individual things in the world as absolute, are replaced

by the respective meaning of each in *consciousness [Bewusstseinssinn]* in its various modes (perceptual meaning, recollected meaning, and so on).

With this, we have clarified and supplemented our initial determination of the phenomenological experience and its sphere of being. In going back from the unities posited in the natural attitude to the manifold of modes of consciousness in which they appear, the unities, as inseparable from these multiplicities— but as "bracketed"—are also to be reckoned among what is purely psychical, and always specifically in the appearance-character in which they present themselves. The method of phenomenological reduction (to the pure "phenomenon," the purely psychical) accordingly consists (1) in the methodical and rigorously consistent epoché of every objective positing in the psychic sphere, both of the individual phenomenon and of the whole psychic field in general; and (2) in the methodically practiced seizing and describing of the multiple "appearances" as appearances of their objective units and these units as units of component meanings accruing to them each time in their appearances. With this is shown a twofold direction—the *noetic* and *noematic* of phenomenological description. Phenomenological experience in the methodical form of the phenomenological reduction is the only genuine "inner experience" in the sense meant by any well-grounded science of psychology. In its own nature lies manifest the possibility of being carried out continuously in infinitum with methodical preservation of purity. The reductive method is transferred from self-experience to the experience of others insofar as there can be applied to the envisaged *[vergegenwärtigten]* mental life of the Other the corresponding bracketing and description according to the subjective "How" of its appearance and what is appearing ("noesis" and "noema"). As a further consequence, the community that is experienced in community experience is reduced not only to the mentally particularized intentional fields but also to the unity of the community life that connects them all together, the community mental life in its phenomenological purity (intersubjective reduction). Thus results the perfect expansion of the genuine psychological concept of "inner experience."

To every mind there belongs not only the unity of its multiple *intentional life-process [intentionalen Lebens]* with all its inseparable unities of sense directed towards the "object." There is also, inseparable from this life-process, the experiencing *I-subject* as the identical *I-pole* giving a center for all specific intentionalities, and as the carrier of all habitualities growing out of this life-process. Likewise, then, the reduced intersubjectivity, in pure form and concretely grasped, is a community of pure "persons" acting in the intersubjective realm of the pure life of consciousness.

4. Eidetic reduction and phenomenological psychology as an eidetic science

To what extent does the unity of the field of phenomenological experience assure the possibility of a psychology exclusively based on it, thus a pure phenomenological psychology? It does not automatically assure an empirically pure science of *facts* from which everything psychophysical is abstracted. But this situation is quite different with an a priori science. In it, every self-enclosed field of possible experience permits *eo ipso* the all-embracing transition from the factual to the essential form, the *eidos*. So here, too. If the phenomenological actual fact as such becomes irrelevant; if, rather, it serves only as an example and as the foundation for a free but intuitive variation of the factual mind and communities of minds *into* the a priori possible (thinkable) ones; and if now the theoretical eye directs itself to the necessarily enduring invariant in the variation; then there will arise with this systematic way of proceeding a realm of its own, of the "a priori." There emerges therewith the eidetically necessary typical form, the *eidos;* this *eidos* must manifest itself throughout all the potential forms of mental being in particular cases, must be present in all the synthetic combinations and self-enclosed wholes, if it is to be at all "thinkable," that is, intuitively conceivable.

Phenomenological psychology in this manner undoubtedly must be established as an "eidetic phenomenology"; it is then exclusively directed toward the invariant essential forms. For instance, the phenomenology of perception of bodies will not be (simply) a report on the factually occurring perceptions or those to be expected; rather it will be the presentation of invariant structural systems without which perception of a body and a synthetically concordant multiplicity of perceptions of one and the same body as such would be unthinkable. If the phenomenological reduction contrived a means of access to the phenomenon of real and also potential inner experience, the method founded in it of "eidetic reduction" provides the means of access to the invariant essential structures of the total sphere of pure mental process.

5. The fundamental function of pure phenomenological psychology for an exact empirical psychology

A phenomenological pure psychology is absolutely necessary as the foundation for the building up of an "exact" empirical psychology, which since its modern beginnings has been sought according to the model of the exact pure sciences of physical nature. The fundamental meaning of "exactness" in this natural science lies in its being founded on an a priori form-system—each part unfolded in a special theory (pure geometry, a theory of pure time, theory of motion, etc.)—for a Nature conceivable in these terms. It is through the utilization of this a priori form-system for factual nature that the vague, inductive empirical approach attains to a share of eidetic necessity *[Wesensnotwendigkeit]* and empirical natural science itself gains a new sense—that of working out for all vague concepts and rules their indispensable basis of rational concepts and laws. As essentially differentiated as the methods of natural science and psychology may remain, there does exist a necessary common ground: that psychology, like every science, can only draw its "rigor" ("exactness") from the rationality of the essence. The uncovering of the a priori set of types without which "I," "we," "consciousness," "the objectivity of consciousness," and therewith mental being as such would be inconceivable—with all the essentially necessary and essentially possible forms of synthesis which are inseparable from the idea of a whole comprised of individual and communal mental life—produces a prodigious field of exactness that can immediately (without the intervening link of *Limes-Idealisierung*) be carried over into research on the psyche. Admittedly, the phenomenological a priori does not comprise the complete a priori of psychology, inasmuch as the psychophysical relationship as such has its own a priori. It is clear, however, that this a priori will presuppose that of a pure phenomenological psychology, just as on the other side it will presuppose the pure a priori of a physical (and specifically the organic) Nature as such.

The systematic construction of a phenomenological pure psychology demands:

(1) The description of the peculiarities universally belonging to the essence of intentional mental process, which includes the most general law of synthesis: every connection of consciousness with consciousness gives rise to a consciousness.

(2) The exploration of single forms of intentional mental process which in essential necessity generally must or can present themselves in the mind; in unity with this, also the exploration of the syntheses they are members of for a typology of their essences: both those that are discrete and those continuous with others, both the finitely closed and those continuing into open infinity.

(3) The showing and eidetic description *[Wesensdeskription]* of the total structure *[Gesamtgestalt]* of mental life as such; in other words, a description of the essential character *[Wesensart]* of a universal "stream of consciousness."

(4) The term "I" designates a new direction for investigation (still in abstraction from the social sense of this word) in reference to the essence-forms of "habituality"; in other words, the "I" as subject of lasting beliefs or thought-tendencies—"persuasions"—(convictions about being, value-convictions, volitional decisions, and so on), as the personal subject of habits, of trained knowing, of certain character qualities.

Throughout all this, the "static" description of essences ultimately leads to problems of genesis, and to an all-pervasive genesis that governs the whole life and development of the personal "I" according to eidetic laws *[eidetischen Gesetzen]*. So on top of the first "static phenomenology" will be constructed in higher levels a dynamic or genetic phenomenology. As the first and founding genesis it will deal with that of passivity—genesis in which the "I" does not actively participate. Here lies the new task, an all-embracing eidetic phenomenology of association, a latter-day rehabilitation of David Hume's great discovery, involving an account of the a priori genesis out of which a real spatial world constitutes itself for the mind in habitual acceptance. There follows from this the eidetic theory dealing with the development of personal habituality, in which the purely mental "I" within the invariant structural forms of consciousness exists as personal "I" and is conscious of itself in habitual continuing being and as always being transformed. For further investigation, there offers itself an especially interconnected stratum at a higher level: the static and then the genetic phenomenology of reason.

II. Phenomenological Psychology and Transcendental Phenomenology

6. *Descartes's transcendental turn and Locke's psychologism*

The idea of a purely phenomenological psychology does not have just the function described above, of reforming empirical psychology. For deeply rooted reasons, it can also serve as a preliminary step for laying open the essence of a transcendental phenomenology. Historically, this idea too did not grow out of the peculiar needs of psychology proper. Its history leads us back to John Locke's notable basic work, and the significant development in Berkeley and Hume of the impetus it contained. Already Locke's restriction to the purely subjective was determined by extra-psychological interests: psychology here stood in the service of the transcendental problem awakened through Descartes. In Descartes's *Meditations,* the thought that had become the guiding one for "first philosophy" was that all of "reality," and finally the whole world of what exists and is so *for us,* exists only as the presentational content of our presentations, as meant in the best case and as evidently reliable in our own cognitive life. This is the motivation for all transcendental problems, genuine or false. Descartes's method of doubt was the first method of exhibiting "transcendental subjectivity," and his *ego cogito* led to its first conceptual formulation. In Locke, Descartes's transcendentally pure *mens* is changed into the "human mind," whose systematic exploration through inner experience Locke tackled out of a transcendental-philosophical interest. And so he is the founder of *psychologism*—as a transcendental philosophy founded *through* a psychology of inner experience. The fate of scientific philosophy hangs on the radical overcoming of every trace of psychologism, an overcoming which not only exposes the fundamental absurdity of psychologism but also does justice to its transcendentally significant kernel of truth. The sources of its continuous historical power are drawn from out of a double sense [an ambiguity] of all the concepts of the subjective, which arises as soon as the transcendental question is broached. The uncovering of this ambiguity involves [us in the need for] at once the sharp separation, and at the time the parallel treatment, of pure phenomenological psychology (as the scientifically rigorous form of a psychology purely of inner experience) and transcendental phenomenology as true transcendental philosophy. At the same time this will justify our advance discussion of psychology as the means of access to true philosophy. We will begin with a clarification of the true transcendental problem, which in the initially obscure unsteadiness of its sense makes one so very prone (and this applies already to Descartes) to shunt it off to a side track.

7. The transcendental problem

To the essential sense of the transcendental problem belongs its all-inclusiveness, in which it places in question the world and all the sciences investigating it. It arises within a general reversal of that "natural attitude" in which everyday life as a whole as well as the positive sciences operate. In it [the natural attitude] the world is for us the self-evidently existing universe of realities which are continuously before us in unquestioned givenness. So this is the general field of our practical and theoretical activities. As soon as the theoretical interest abandons this natural attitude and in a general turning around of our regard directs itself to the life of consciousness—*in which* the "world" is for us precisely that, the world which is present *to us*—we find ourselves in a new cognitive attitude [or situation]. Every sense which the world has for us (this we now become aware of), both its general indeterminate sense and its sense determining itself according to the particular realities, is, within the internality of our own perceiving, imagining, thinking, valuing life-process, a conscious sense, and a sense which is formed in subjective genesis. Every acceptance of something as validly existing is effected within us ourselves; and every evidence in experience and theory that establishes it, is operative in us ourselves, habitually and continuously motivating us. This [principle] concerns the world in every determination, even those that are self-evident: that what belongs *in and for itself* to the world, is how it is, whether or not I, or whoever, become by chance aware of it or not. Once the world in this full universality has been related to the subjectivity of consciousness, in whose living consciousness it makes its appearance precisely as "the" world in its varying sense, then its whole mode of being acquires a dimension of unintelligibility, or rather of questionableness. This "making an appearance" *[Auftreten],* this being-for-us of the world as only subjectively having come to acceptance and only subjectively brought and to be brought to well-grounded evident presentation, requires clarification. Because of its empty generality, one's first awakening to the relatedness of the world to consciousness gives no understanding of *how* the varied life of consciousness, barely discerned and sinking back into obscurity, accomplishes such functions: how it, so to say, manages in its immanence that something which manifests itself can present itself *as* something existing in itself, and not only as something meant but as something authenticated in concordant experience. Obviously the problem extends to every kind of "ideal" world and its "being-in-itself" (for example, the world of pure numbers, or of "truths in themselves"). Unintelligibility is felt as a particularly telling affront to *our* very mode of being [as human beings]. For obviously we are the ones (individually and in community) in whose conscious life-process the real world which is present for us as such gains sense and acceptance. As human creatures, however, we ourselves are supposed to belong to the world. When we start with the sense of the world *[weltlichen Sinn]* given with our mundane existing, we are thus again referred back to ourselves and our conscious life-process as that wherein for us this sense is first formed. Is there conceivable here or anywhere another way of elucidating [it] than to interrogate consciousness itself and the "world" that becomes known in it? For it is precisely as meant by us, and from nowhere else than in us, that it has gained and can gain its sense and validity.

Next we take yet another important step, which will raise the "transcendental" problem (having to do with the being-sense of "transcendent" relative to consciousness) up to the final level. It consists in recognizing that the relativity of consciousness referred to just now applies not just to the brute fact of *our* world but in eidetic necessity to every conceivable world whatever. For if we vary our factual world in free fantasy, carrying it over into random conceivable worlds, we are implicitly varying *ourselves* whose environment the world is: we each change ourselves into a possible subjectivity, whose environment would always have to be the world that was thought of, as a world of its [the subjectivity's] possible ex-

periences, possible theoretical evidences, possible practical life. But obviously this variation leaves untouched the pure ideal worlds of the kind which have their existence in eidetic universality, which are in their essence invariable; it becomes apparent, however, from the possible variability of the subject knowing such identical essences *[Identitäten]*, that their cognizability, and thus their intentional relatedness does not simply have to do with our de facto subjectivity. With the eidetic formulation of the problem, the kind of research into consciousness that is demanded is the eidetic.

8. The solution by psychologism as a transcendental circle

Our distillation of the idea of a phenomenologically pure psychology has demonstrated the possibility of uncovering by consistent phenomenological reduction what belongs to the conscious subject's own essence in eidetic, universal terms, according to all its possible forms. This includes those forms of reason [itself] which establish and authenticate validity, and with this it includes all forms of potentially appearing worlds, both those validated in themselves through concordant experiences and those determined by theoretical truth. Accordingly, the systematic carrying through of this phenomenological psychology seems to comprehend in itself from the outset in foundational (precisely, eidetic) universality the whole of correlation research on being and consciousness; thus it would seem to be the [proper] locus for all transcendental elucidation. On the other hand, we must not overlook the fact that psychology in all its empirical and eidetic disciplines remains a "positive science," a science operating within the natural attitude, in which the simply present world is the thematic ground. What it wishes to explore are the psyches and communities of psyches that are [actually] to be found in the world. Phenomenological reduction serves as psychological only to the end that it gets at the psychical aspect of animal realities in its pure own essential specificity and its pure own specific essential interconnections. Even in eidetic research [then], the psyche retains the sense of being which belongs in the realm of what is present in the world; it is merely related to possible real worlds. Even as eidetic phenomenologist, the psychologist is transcendentally naive: he takes the possible "minds" ("I"-subjects) completely according to the relative sense of the word as those of men and animals considered purely and simply as present in a possible spatial world. If, however, we allow the transcendental interest to be decisive, instead of the natural-worldly, then psychology as a whole receives the stamp of what is transcendentally problematic; and thus it can by no means supply the premises for transcendental philosophy. The subjectivity of consciousness, which, as psychic being, is its theme, cannot be that to which we go back in our questioning into the transcendental.

In order to arrive at an evident clarity at this decisive point, the thematic sense of the transcendental question is to be kept sharply in view, and we must try to judge how, in keeping with it, the regions of the problematical and unproblematical are set apart. The theme of transcendental philosophy is a concrete and systematic elucidation of those multiple intentional relationships, which in conformity with their essences belong to any possible world whatever as the surrounding world of a corresponding possible subjectivity, for which it [the world] would be the one present as practically and theoretically accessible. In regard to all the objects and structures present in the world for these subjectivities, this accessibility involves the regulations of its possible conscious life, which in their typology will have to be uncovered. [Among] such categories are "lifeless things," as well as men and animals with the internalities of their psychic life. From this starting point the full and complete being-sense of a possible world, in general and in regard to all its constitutive categories, shall be elucidated. Like every meaningful question, this transcendental question presupposes a ground of unquestioned being, in which all means of solution must be contained. This ground is here the [anonymous] subjectivity of that kind of conscious life in which a possible

world, of whatever kind, is constituted as present. However, a self-evident basic requirement of any rational method is that this ground presupposed as beyond question is not confused with what the transcendental question, in its universality, puts into question. Hence the realm of this questionability includes the whole realm of the transcendentally naive and therefore every possible world simply claimed in the natural attitude. Accordingly, all possible sciences, including all their various areas of objects, are transcendentally to be subjected to an epoché. So also psychology, and the entirety of what is considered the psychical in its sense. It would therefore be circular, a transcendental circle, to base the answer to the transcendental question on psychology, be it empirical or eidetic-phenomenological. We face at this point the paradoxical ambiguity: the subjectivity and consciousness to which the transcendental question recurs can thus really not be the subjectivity and consciousness with which psychology deals.

9. The transcendental-phenomenological reduction and the semblance of transcendental duplication

Are we then supposed to be dual beings—psychological, as human objectivities in the world, the subjects of psychic life, and at the same time transcendental, as the subjects of a transcendental, world-constituting life-process? This duality can be clarified through being demonstrated with self-evidence. The psychic subjectivity, the concretely grasped "I" and "we" of ordinary conversation, is experienced in its pure psychic ownness through the method of phenomenological-psychological reduction. Modified into eidetic form it provides the ground for pure phenomenological psychology. Transcendental subjectivity, which is inquired into in the transcendental problem, and which subjectivity is presupposed in it as an existing basis, is none other than again "I myself" and "we ourselves"; not, however, as found in the natural attitude of everyday or of positive science; i.e., apperceived as components of the objectively present world before us, but rather as subjects of conscious life, *in which* this world and all that is present—for "us"—"makes" itself through certain apperceptions. As men, mentally as well as bodily present in the world, we are for "ourselves"; we are appearances standing within an extremely variegated intentional life-process, "our" life, *in which* this being on hand constitutes itself "for us" apperceptively, with its entire sense-content. The (apperceived) I and we on hand presuppose an (apperceiving) I and we, *for* which they are on hand, which, however, is not itself present again in the same sense. To this transcendental subjectivity we have direct access through a transcendental experience. Just as the psychic experience requires a reductive method for purity, so does the transcendental.

We would like to proceed here by introducing the *transcendental reduction* as built on the psychological reduction—as an additional part of the purification which can be performed on it any time, a purification that is once more by means of a certain epoché. This is merely a consequence of the all-embracing epoché which belongs to the sense of the transcendental question. If the transcendental relativity of every possible world demands an all-embracing bracketing, it also postulates the bracketing of pure psyches and the pure phenomenological psychology related to them. Through this bracketing they are transformed into transcendental phenomena. Thus, while the psychologist, operating within what for him is the naturally accepted world, reduces to pure psychic subjectivity the subjectivity occurring there (but still within the world), the transcendental phenomenologist, through his absolutely all-embracing epoché, reduces this psychologically pure element to transcendental pure subjectivity, [i.e.,] to that which performs and posits within itself the apperception of the world and therein the objectivating apperception of a "psyche [belonging to] animal realities." For example, my actual current mental processes of pure perception, fantasy, and so forth, are, in the attitude of positivity, psychological givens [or data] of psychological inner experience. They are transmuted into

my transcendental mental processes if through a radical epoché I posit as mere phenomena the world, including my own human existence, and now follow up the intentional life-process wherein the entire apperception "of" the world, and in particular the apperception of my mind, my psychologically real perception-processes, and so forth, are, formed. The content of these processes, what is included in their own essences, remains in this fully preserved, although it is now visible as the core of an apperception practiced again and again psychologically but not previously considered. For the transcendental philosopher, who through a previous all-inclusive resolve of his will has instituted in himself the firm habituality of the transcendental "bracketing," even this "mundanization" [*Verweltlichung,* treating everything as part of the world] of consciousness which is omnipresent in the natural attitude is inhibited once and for all. Accordingly, the consistent reflection on consciousness yields him time after time transcendentally pure data, and more particularly it is intuitive in the mode of a new kind of experience, *transcendental "inner" experience.* Arisen out of the methodical transcendental epoché, this new kind of "inner" experience opens up the limitless transcendental field of being. This field of being is the parallel to the limitless psychological field, and the method of access [to its data] is the parallel to the purely psychological one, i.e., to the psychological-phenomenological reduction. And again, the transcendental I [or ego] and the transcendental community of egos, conceived in the full concretion of transcendental life are the transcendental parallel to the I and we in the customary and psychological sense, concretely conceived as mind and community of minds, with the psychological life of consciousness that pertains to them. My transcendental ego is thus evidently "different" from the natural ego, but by no means as a second, as one *separated* from it in the natural sense of the word, just as on the contrary it is by no means bound up with it or intertwined with it, in the usual sense of these words. It is just the field of transcendental self-experience (conceived in full concreteness) which in every case can, *through mere alteration of attitude,* be changed into psychological self-experience. In this transition, an identity of the I is necessarily brought about; in transcendental reflection on this transition the psychological Objectivation becomes visible as self-objectivation of the transcendental I, and so it is as if in every moment of the natural attitude the I finds itself with an apperception imposed upon it. If the parallelism of the transcendental and psychological experience-spheres has become comprehensible out of a mere alteration of attitude, as a kind of identity of the complex interpenetration of senses of being, then there also becomes intelligible the consequence that results from it, namely the same parallelism and the interpenetration of transcendental and psychological phenomenology implied in that interpenetration, whose whole theme is pure intersubjectivity, in its dual sense. Only that in this case it has to be taken into account that the purely psychic intersubjectivity, as soon as it is subjected to the transcendental epoché, also leads to its parallel, that is, to transcendental intersubjectivity. Manifestly this parallelism spells nothing less than theoretical equivalence. Transcendental intersubjectivity is the concretely autonomous absolute existing basis *[Seinsboden]* out of which everything transcendent (and, with it, everything that belongs to the real world) obtains its existential sense as that of something which only in a relative and therewith incomplete sense is an existing thing, namely as being an intentional unity which in truth exists from out of transcendental bestowal of sense, of harmonious confirmation, and from an habituality of lasting conviction that belongs to it by essential necessity.

10. *Pure psychology as propaedeutic to transcendental phenomenology*

Through the elucidation of the essentially dual meaning of the subjectivity of consciousness, and also a clarification of the eidetic science to be directed to it, we begin to understand on very deep grounds the historical insurmountability of psychologism. Its power

lies in an *essential transcendental semblance* which [because] undisclosed had to remain effective. Also from the clarification we have gained we begin to understand on the one hand the independence of the idea of a transcendental phenomenology, and the systematic developing of it, from the idea of a phenomenological pure psychology; and yet on the other hand the propaedeutic usefulness of the preliminary project of a pure psychology for an ascent to transcendental phenomenology, a usefulness which has guided our present discussion here. As regards this point [i.e., the independence of the idea of transcendental phenomenology from a phenomenological pure psychology], clearly the phenomenological and eidetic reduction allows of being *immediately* connected to the disclosing of transcendental relativity, and in this way transcendental phenomenology springs directly out of the transcendental intuition. In point of fact, this direct path was the historical path it took. Pure phenomenological psychology as eidetic science in positivity was simply not available. As regards the second point, i.e., the propaedeutic preference of the indirect approach to transcendental phenomenology through pure psychology, [it must be remembered that] the transcendental attitude involves a change of focus from one's entire form of life-style, one which goes so completely beyond all previous experiencing of life that it must, in virtue of its absolute strangeness, needs be difficult to understand. This is also true of a transcendental science. Phenomenological psychology, although also relatively new, and in its method of intentional analysis completely novel, still has the accessibility which is possessed by all positive sciences. Once this psychology has become clear, at least according to its sharply defined idea, then only the clarification of the true sense of the transcendental-philosophical field of problems and of the transcendental reduction is required in order for it to come into possession of transcendental phenomenology as a mere reversal of its doctrinal content into transcendental terms. The basic difficulties for penetrating into the terrain of the new phenomenology fall into these two stages, namely that of understanding the true method of "inner experience," which already belongs to making possible an "exact" psychology as rational science of facts, and that of understanding the distinctive character of the transcendental methods and questioning. True, simply regarded in itself, an interest in the transcendental is the highest and ultimate scientific interest, and so it is entirely the right thing (it has been so historically and should continue) for transcendental theories to be cultivated in the autonomous, absolute system of transcendental philosophy; and to place before us, through showing the characteristic features of the natural in contrast to the transcendental attitude, the possibility within transcendental philosophy itself of reinterpreting all transcendental phenomenological doctrine [or theory] into doctrine [or theory] in the realm of natural positivity.

III. Transcendental Phenomenology and Philosophy as Universal Science with Absolute Foundations

11. Transcendental phenomenology as ontology

Remarkable consequences arise when one weighs the significance of transcendental phenomenology. In its systematic development, it brings to realization the Leibnizian idea of a universal ontology as the systematic unity of all conceivable a priori sciences, but on a new foundation which overcomes "dogmatism" through the use of the transcendental phenomenological method. Phenomenology as the science of all conceivable transcendental phenomena and especially the synthetic total structures in which alone they are concretely possible—those of the transcendental single subjects bound to communities of subjects is *eo ipso* the a priori science of all conceivable beings. But [it is the science] then not merely of the Totality of objectively existing beings, and certainly not in an attitude of natural positivity; rather, in the full concretion of being in general which derives its sense of being and its validity from the correlative intentional constitution. This also comprises the being of tran-

scendental subjectivity itself, whose nature it is demonstrably to be constituted transcendentally in and for itself. Accordingly, a phenomenology properly carried through is the truly universal ontology, as over against the only illusory all-embracing ontology in positivity— and precisely for this reason it overcomes the dogmatic one-sidedness and hence unintelligibility of the latter, while at the same time it comprises within itself the truly legitimate content [of an ontology in positivity] as grounded originally in intentional constitution.

12. Phenomenology and the crisis in the foundations of the exact sciences

If we consider the how of this inclusion, we find that what is meant is that every a priori is ultimately prescribed in its validity of being precisely *as* a transcendental achievement; i.e., it is together with the essential structures of its constitution, with the kinds and levels of its givenness and confirmation of itself, and with the appertaining habitualities. This implies that in and through the establishment of the a priori the subjective *method* of this establishing is itself made transparent, and that for the a priori disciplines which are founded within phenomenology (for example, as mathematical sciences) there can be no "paradoxes" and no "crises of the foundations." The consequence that arises [from all this] with reference to the a priori sciences that have come into being historically and in transcendental naivete is that only a radical, phenomenological grounding can transform them into true, methodical, fully self-justifying sciences. But precisely by this they will cease to be positive (dogmatic) sciences and become dependent branches of the one phenomenology as all-encompassing eidetic ontology.

13. The phenomenological grounding of the factual sciences in relation to empirical phenomenology

The unending task of presenting the complete universe of the a priori in its transcendental relatedness-back-to-itself [or self-reference], and thus in its self-sufficiency and perfect methodological clarity, is itself a function of the method for realization of an all-embracing and hence fully grounded science of empirical fact. Within [the realm of] positive reality *[Positivität]*, genuine (relatively genuine) empirical science demands the methodical establishing-of-a-foundation *[Fundamentierung]* through a corresponding a priori science. If we take the universe of all possible empirical sciences whatever and demand a *radical* grounding that will be free from all "foundation crises," then we are led to the all-embracing a priori of the radical and that is [and must be] *phenomenological* grounding. The genuine form of an all-embracing science of fact is thus the phenomenological [form], and as this it is the universal science of the factual transcendental intersubjectivity, [resting] on the methodical foundation of eidetic phenomenology as knowledge applying to any possible transcendental subjectivity whatever. Hence *the idea of an empirical phenomenology* which follows after the eidetic is understood and justified. It is identical with the complete systematic universe of the positive sciences, provided that we think of them from the beginning as absolutely grounded methodologically through eidetic phenomenology.

14. Complete phenomenology as all-embracing philosophy

Precisely through this is restored the most primordial concept of philosophy—as all-embracing science based on radical self-justification, which is alone [truly] science in the ancient Platonic and again in the Cartesian sense. Phenomenology rigorously and systematically carried out, phenomenology in the broadened sense [which we have explained] above, is identical with this philosophy which encompasses all genuine knowledge. It is divided into eidetic phenomenology (or all-embracing ontology) as *first philosophy*, and as *second philosophy*, [it is] the science of the universe of *facta*, or of the transcendental intersubjectivity that synthetically comprises all *facta*. First philosophy is the universe of methods for the second, and is related back into itself for its methodological grounding.

15. The "ultimate and highest" problems as phenomenological

In phenomenology all rational problems have their place, and thus also those that traditionally are in some special sense or other philosophically significant. For out of the absolute sources of transcendental experience, or eidetic intuiting, they first [are able to] obtain their genuine formulation and feasible means for their solution. In its universal relatedness-back-to-itself, phenomenology recognizes its particular function within a possible life of mankind *[Menschheitsleben]* at the transcendental level. It recognizes the absolute norms which are to be picked out intuitively from it [life of mankind], and also its primordial teleo-logical-tendential structure in a directedness towards disclosure of these norms and their conscious practical operation. It recognizes itself as a function of the all-embracing reflective meditation of (transcendental) humanity, [a self-examination] in the service of an all-inclusive praxis of reason; that is, in the service of striving towards the universal ideal of absolute perfection which lies in infinity, [a striving] which becomes free through [the process of] disclosure. Or, in different words it is a striving in the direction of the idea (lying in infinity) of a humanness which in action and throughout would live and move [be, exist] in truth and genuineness. It recognizes its self-reflective function [of self-examination] for the relative realization of the correlative practical idea of a genuine human life *[Menschheitsleben]* in the second sense (whose structural forms of being and whose practical norms it is to investigate), namely as one [that is] consciously and purposively directed towards this absolute idea. In short, the metaphysically teleological, the ethical, and the problems of philosophy of history, no less than, obviously, the problems of judging reason, lie within its boundary, no differently from all significant problems whatever, and all [of them] in their inmost synthetic unity and order as [being] of transcendental spirituality *[Geistigkeit]*.

16. The phenomenological resolution of all philosophical antitheses

In the systematic work of phenomenology, which progresses from intuitively given [concrete] data to heights of abstraction, the old traditional ambiguous antitheses of the philosophical standpoint are resolved—by themselves and without the arts of an argumentative dialectic, and without weak efforts and compromises: oppositions such as between rationalism (Platonism) and empiricism, relativism and absolutism, subjectivism and objectivism, ontologism and transcendentalism, psychologism and antipsychologism, positivism and metaphysics, or the teleological versus the causal interpretation of the world. Throughout all of these, [one finds] justified motives, but throughout also half-truths or impermissible absolutizing of only relatively and abstractively legitimate one-sidednesses.

Subjectivism can only be overcome by the most all-embracing and consistent subjectivism (the transcendental). In this [latter] form it is at the same time objectivism [of a deeper sort], in that it represents the claims of whatever objectivity is to be demonstrated through concordant experience, but admittedly [this is an objectivism which] also brings out its full and genuine sense, against which [sense] the supposedly realistic objectivism sins by its failure to understand transcendental constitution. *Relativism* can only be overcome through the most all-embracing relativism, that of transcendental phenomenology, which makes intelligible the relativity of all "objective" being [or existence] as transcendentally constituted; but at one with this [it makes intelligible] the most radical relativity, the relatedness of the transcendental subjectivity to itself. But just this [relatedness, subjectivity] proves its identity to be the only possible sense of [the term] "ab-

solute" being—over against all "objective" being that is relative to it—namely, as the "for-itself"—being of transcendental subjectivity. Likewise: *Empiricism* can only be overcome by the most universal and consistent empiricism, which puts in place of the restricted [term] "experience" of the empiricists the necessarily broadened concept of experience [inclusive] of intuition which offers original data, an intuition which in all its forms (intuition of *eidos,* apodictic self-evidence, phenomenological intuition of essence, etc.) shows the manner and form of its legitimation through phenomenological clarification. Phenomenology as eidetic is, on the other hand, rationalistic: it overcomes restrictive and dogmatic rationalism, however, through the most universal rationalism of inquiry into essences, which is related uniformly to transcendental subjectivity, to the I, consciousness, and conscious objectivity. And it is the same in reference to the other antitheses bound up with them. The tracing back of all being to the transcendental subjectivity and its constitutive intentional functions leaves open, to mention one more thing, no other way of contemplating the world than the *teleological.* And yet phenomenology also acknowledges a kernel of truth in naturalism (or rather sensationism). That is, by revealing associations as intentional phenomena, indeed as a whole basic typology of forms of passive intentional synthesis with transcendental and purely passive genesis based on essential laws, phenomenology shows Humean fictionalism to contain anticipatory discoveries; particularly in his doctrine of the origin of such fictions as thing, persisting existence, causality—anticipatory discoveries all shrouded in absurd theories.

Phenomenological philosophy regards itself in its whole method as a pure outcome of methodical intentions which already animated Greek philosophy from its beginnings; above all, however, [it continues] the still vital intentions which reach, in the two lines of rationalism and empiricism, from Descartes through Kant and German idealism into our confused present day. A pure outcome of methodical intentions means real method which allows the problems to be taken in hand and completed. In the way of true science this path is endless. Accordingly, phenomenology demands that the phenomenologist foreswear the ideal of a philosophic system and yet as a humble worker in community with others, live for a perennial philosophy *[philosophia perennis]*.

XI.

Transcendental Phenomenology and the Way through the Life-World

20. The Mathematization of Nature*

§8. The origin of the new idea of the universality of science in the reshaping of mathematics

The first thing we must do is understand the fundamental transformation of the idea, the task of universal philosophy which took place at the beginning of the modern age when the ancient idea was taken over. From Descartes on, the new idea governs the total development of philosophical movements and becomes the inner motive behind all their tensions.

The reshaping begins with prominent special sciences inherited from the ancients: Euclidean geometry and the rest of Greek mathematics, and then Greek natural science. In our eyes these are fragments, beginnings of our developed sciences. But one must not overlook here the immense change of meaning whereby *universal* tasks were set, primarily for mathematics (as geometry and as formal-abstract theory of numbers and magnitudes)— tasks of a style which was *new in principle,* unknown to the ancients. Of course the ancients, guided by the Platonic doctrine of ideas, had already idealized empirical numbers, units of measurement, empirical figures in space, points, lines, surfaces, bodies; and they had transformed the propositions and proofs of geometry into ideal-geometrical propositions and proofs. What is more, with Euclidean ge-

ometry had grown up the highly impressive idea of a systematically coherent deductive theory, aimed at a most broadly and highly conceived ideal goal, resting on "axiomatic" fundamental concepts and principles, proceeding according to apodictic arguments—a totality formed of pure rationality, a totality whose unconditioned truth is available to insight and which consists exclusively of unconditioned truths recognized through immediate and mediate insight. But Euclidean geometry, and ancient mathematics in general, knows only finite tasks, a finitely closed a priori. Aristotelian syllogistics belongs here also, as an a priori which takes precedence over all others. Antiquity goes this far, but never far enough to grasp the possibility of the infinite task which, for us, is linked as a matter of course with the concept of geometrical space and with the concept of geometry as the science belonging to it. To ideal space belongs, for us, a universal, systematically coherent a priori, an infinite, and yet—in spite of its infinity—self-enclosed, coherent systematic theory which, proceeding from axiomatic concepts and propositions, permits the deductively univocal construction of any conceivable shape which can be drawn in space. What "exists" ideally in geometric space is univocally decided, in all its determinations, in advance. Our apodictic thinking, proceeding stepwise to infinity through concepts, propositions, infer-

*CES, pp. 21–59, 68–73 (Sections 8–9 and 14–15).

ences, proofs, only "discovers" what is already there, what in itself already exists in truth.

What is new, unprecedented, is the conceiving of this idea of a rational infinite totality of being with a rational science systematically mastering it. An infinite world, here a world of idealities, is conceived, not as one whose objects become accessible to our knowledge singly, imperfectly, and as it were accidentally, but as one which is attained by a rational, systematically coherent method. In the infinite progression of this method, every object is ultimately attained according to its full being-in-itself *[nach seinem vollen An-sich-sein]*.

But this is true not only in respect to ideal space. Even less could the ancients conceive of a similar but more general idea (arising from formalizing abstraction), that of a formal mathematics. Not until the dawn of the modern period does the actual discovery and conquest of the infinite mathematical horizons begin. The beginnings of algebra, of the mathematics of continua, of analytic geometry arise. From here, thanks to the boldness and originality peculiar to the new humanity, the great ideal is soon anticipated of a science which, in this new sense, is rational and all-inclusive, or rather the idea that the infinite totality of what is in general is intrinsically a rational all-encompassing unity that can be mastered, without anything left over, by a corresponding universal science. Long before this idea comes to maturity, it determines further developments as an unclear or half-clear presentiment. In any case it does not stop with the new mathematics. Its rationalism soon overtakes natural science and creates for it the completely new idea of *mathematical natural science*—Galile-

an science, as it was rightly called for a long time. As soon as the latter begins to move toward successful realization, the idea of philosophy in general (as the science of the universe, of all that is) is transformed.

§9. *Galileo's mathematization of nature*

For Platonism, the real* had a more or less perfect methexis in the ideal. This afforded ancient geometry possibilities of a primitive application to reality. [But] through Galileo's *mathematization of nature, nature itself* is idealized under the guidance of the new mathematics; nature itself becomes—to express it in a modern way—a mathematical manifold *[Mannigfaltigkeit]*.

What is the meaning of this mathematization of nature? How do we reconstruct the train of thought which motivated it?

Prescientifically, in everyday sense-experience, the world is given in a subjectively relative way. Each of us has his own appearances; and for each of us they count as *[gelten als]* that which actually is. In dealing with one another, we have long since become aware of this discrepancy between our various ontic validities.† But we do not think that, because of this, there are many worlds. Necessarily, we believe in *the* world, whose things only appear to us differently but are the same. [Now] have we nothing more than the empty, necessary idea of things which exist objectively in themselves? Is there not in the appearances themselves a content we must ascribe to true nature? Surely this includes everything which pure geometry, and in general the mathematics of the pure form of space-time, teaches us, with the self-evidence of absolute, universal

das Reale. I have used "real" almost exclusively for the German *real* and its derivatives. For Husserl this term refers to the spatiotemporal world as conceived by physics (or to the psychic when it is mistakenly conceived on the model of the physical). The more general *Wirklichkeit* has usually been translated by the etymologically correct term "actuality." —Translator's note.

†*Seinsgeltungen. Geltung* is a very important word for Husserl, especially in this text. It derives from *gelten,* which is best translated "to count (as such and such) (for me)," as in the previous sentence, or "to be accepted (as, etc.)," or "to have the validity (of such and such) (for me)." *Gültigkeit* is the more common substantive but is less current in Husserl. Thus *"validity"* ("our validities," etc.) seems an appropriate shortcut for such more exact but too cumbersome expressions as "that which counts (as)," "those things which we accept (as)," etc., in this case, "those things that we accept as existing." I have used "ontic" when Husserl compounds *Sein* with this and other words, e.g., *Seinssinn, Seinsgewissheit.* —Translator's note.

validity, about the pure shapes it can construct *idealiter*—and here I am describing, without taking a position, what was "obvious"* to Galileo and motivated his thinking.

We should devote a careful exposition to what was involved in this "obviousness" for Galileo and to whatever else was taken for granted by him in order to motivate the idea of a mathematical knowledge of nature in his new sense. We note that he, the philosopher of nature and "trail-blazer" of physics, was not yet a physicist in the full present-day sense; that his thinking did not, like that of our mathematicians and mathematical physicists, move in the sphere of symbolism, far removed from intuition; and that we must not attribute to him what, through him and the further historical development, has become "obvious" to us.

A) "PURE GEOMETRY"

Let us first consider "pure geometry," the pure mathematics of spatiotemporal shapes in general, pregivent to Galileo as an old tradition, involved in a process of lively forward development—in other words, in generally the same way we still find it: [on the one hand] as a science of "pure idealities" which is, on the other hand, constantly being practically applied to the world of sense-experience. So familiar to us is the shift between a priori theory and empirical inquiry in everyday life that we usually tend not to separate the space and the spatial shapes geometry talks about from the space and spatial shapes of experiential actuality, as if they were one and the same. If geometry is to be understood as the foundation for the meaning *[Sinnesfundament]* of exact physics, however, we must be very precise here as elsewhere. In order to clarify the formation of Galileo's thought we must accordingly reconstruct not only what consciously motivated him. It will also be instructive

to bring to light what was implicitly included in his guiding model of mathematics, even though, because of the direction of his interest, it was kept from his view: as a hidden, presupposed meaning it naturally had to enter into his physics along with everything else.

In the intuitively given surrounding world, by abstractively directing our view to the mere spatiotemporal shapes, we experience "bodies"—not geometrical-ideal bodies but precisely those bodies that we actually experience, with the content which is the actual content of experience. No matter how arbitrarily we may transform these bodies in fantasy, the free and in a certain sense "ideal" possibilities we thus obtain are anything but geometrical-ideal possibilities: they are not the geometrically "pure" shapes which can be drawn in ideal space—"pure" bodies, "pure" straight lines, "pure" planes, "pure" figures, and the movements and deformations which occur in the "pure" figures. Thus geometrical space does not mean anything like imaginable space or, generally speaking, the space of any arbitrarily imaginable (conceivable) world. Fantasy can transform sensible shapes only into other sensible shapes. Such shapes, in actuality or fantasy, are thinkable only in gradations: the more or less straight, flat, circular, etc.

Indeed, the things of the intuitively given surrounding world fluctuate, in general and in all their properties, in the sphere of the merely typical: their identity with themselves, their self-sameness and their temporally enduring sameness, are merely approximate, as is their likeness with other things. This affects all changes, and *their* possible samenesses and changes. Something like this is true also of the abstractly conceived shapes of empirically intuited bodies and their relations. This gradualness can be characterized as that of greater or less perfection. Practically speaking there is, here as elsewhere, a simple perfection in

---

Selbstverständlichkeit is another very important word in this text. It refers to what is unquestioned but not necessarily unquestionable. "Obvious" works when the word is placed in quotation marks, as it is here. In other cases I have used various forms of the expression "taken for granted." —Translator's note.

†*vorgegeben*. Implying "already there," as material to be worked with. This term is much used later on as applied to the life-world. —Translator's note.

the sense that it fully satisfies special practical interests. But when interests change, what was fully and exactly satisfactory for one is no longer so for another; and of course there is a limit to what can be done by means of the normal technical capacity of perfecting, e.g., the capacity to make the straight straighter and the flat flatter. But technology progresses along with mankind, and so does the interest in what is technically more refined; and the ideal of perfection is pushed further and further. Hence we always have an open horizon of *conceivable* improvement to be further pursued.

Without going more deeply into the essential interconnections involved here (which has never been done systematically and is by no means easy), we can understand that, out of the praxis of perfecting, of freely pressing toward the horizons of *conceivable* perfecting "again and again," *limit-shapes** emerge toward which the particular series of perfectings tend, as toward invariant and never attainable poles. If we are interested in these ideal shapes and are consistently engaged in determining them and in constructing new ones out of those already determined, we are "geometers." The same is true of the broader sphere which includes the dimension of time: we are mathematicians of the "pure" shapes whose universal form is the coidealized form of space-time. In place of real praxis—that of action or that of considering empirical possibilities having to do with actual and really [i.e., physically] possible empirical bodies—we now have an *ideal* praxis of "pure thinking" which remains exclusively within the realm of pure limit-shapes. Through a method of idealization and construction which historically has long since been worked out and can be practiced intersubjectively in a community, these limit-shapes have become acquired tools that can be used habitually and can always be applied to something new—an infinite and yet self-enclosed world of ideal objects as a field for study. Like all cultural acquisitions which arise out of human accomplishment, they remain objectively knowable and available without requiring that the formulation of their meaning be repeatedly and explicitly renewed. On the basis of sensible embodiment, e.g., in speech and writing, they are simply apperceptively† grasped and dealt with in our operations. Sensible "models" function in a similar way, including especially the drawings on paper which are constantly used during work, printed drawings in textbooks for those who learn by reading, and the like. It is similar to the way in which certain cultural objects (tongs, drills, etc.) are understood, simply "seen," with their specifically cultural properties, without any renewed process of making intuitive what gave such properties their true meaning. Serving in the methodical praxis of mathematicians, in this form of long-understood acquisitions, are significations which are, so to speak, sedimented in their embodiments. And thus they make mental manipulation possible in the geometrical world of ideal objects. (Geometry represents for us here the whole mathematics of space-time.)

But in this mathematical praxis we attain what is denied us in empirical praxis: "exactness"; for there is the possibility of determining the ideal shapes in absolute identity, of recognizing them as substrates of absolutely identical and methodically, univocally determinable qualities. This occurs not only in particular cases, according to an everywhere similar method which, operating on sensibly intuitable shapes chosen at random, could carry out idealizations everywhere and originally create, in objective and univocal determinateness, the pure idealities which correspond to them. For this, [rather,] certain structures stand out, such as straight lines, triangles, circles. But it is possible—and this was the discovery which created geometry—using these elementary shapes, singled out in advance as universally available, and according to universal operations which can be carried out with them,

---

Limesgestalten. Husserl has in mind the mathematic concept of limit. —Translator's note.

†*apperzeptiv.* Husserl uses this term in the Leibnizian sense to denote a self-conscious act (but not necessarily an act of reflection) under a certain point of view or "attitude" *(Einstellung),* here the mathematical. —Translator's note.

to *construct* not only more and more shapes which, because of the method which produces them, are intersubjectively and univocally determined. For in the end the possibility emerges of producing constructively and univocally, through an a priori, all-encompassing systematic method, *all* possibly *conceivable* ideal shapes.

The geometrical methodology of operatively determining some and finally all ideal shapes, beginning with basic shapes as elementary means of determination, points back to the methodology of determination by surveying and measuring in general, practiced first primitively and then as an art in the prescientific, intuitively given surrounding world. The undertaking of such measurement has its obvious origin in the essential form of that surrounding world. The shapes in it that are sensibly experienceable and sensibly-intuitively conceivable, and the types [of shapes] that are conceivable at any level of generality, fade into each other as a continuum. In this continuity they fill out (sensibly intuited) space-time, which is their form. Each shape in this open infinitude, even if it is given intuitively in reality as a *fact,* is still without "objectivity"; it is not thus intersubjectively determinable, and communicable in its determinations, for everyone—for every other one who does not at the same time factually see it. This purpose [of procuring objectivity] is obviously served by the *art of measuring.* This art involves a great deal, of which the actual measuring is only the concluding part: on the one hand, for the bodily shapes of rivers, mountains, buildings, etc., which as a rule lack strictly determining concepts and names, it must create such concepts —first for their "forms" (in terms of pictured similarity), and then for their magnitudes and relations of magnitude, and also for the determinations of position, through the measurement of distances and angles related to known places and directions which are presupposed as being fixed. The art of measuring discovers *practically* the possibility of picking out as [standard] measures certain empirical basic shapes, concretely fixed on empirical rigid bodies which are in fact generally available; and

by means of the relations which obtain (or can be discovered) between these and other body-shapes it determines the latter intersubjectively and in practice univocally—at first within narrow spheres (as in the art of surveying land), then in new spheres where shape is involved. So it is understandable how, as a consequence of the awakened striving for "philosophical" knowledge, knowledge which determines the "true," the objective being of the world, the empirical art of measuring and its empirically, practically objectivizing function, through a change from the practical to the theoretical interest, was idealized and thus turned into the purely geometrical way of thinking. The art of measuring thus becomes the trailblazer for the ultimately universal geometry and its "world" of pure limit-shapes.

b) The basic notion of Galilean physics: nature as a mathematical universe

The relatively advanced geometry known to Galileo, already broadly applied not only to the earth but also in astronomy, was for him, accordingly, already pregiven by tradition as a guide to his own thinking, which [then] related empirical matters to the mathematical ideas of limit. Also available to him as a tradition, of course—itself partially determined in the meantime by geometry—was the art of measuring, with its intention of ever increasing exactness of measurement and the resulting objective determination of the shapes themselves. If the empirical and very limited requirements of technical praxis had originally motivated those of pure geometry, so now, conversely, geometry had long since become, as "applied" geometry, a means for technology, a guide in conceiving and carrying out the task of systematically constructing a methodology of measurement for objectively determining shapes in constantly increasing "approximation" to the geometrical ideals, the limit-shapes.

For Galileo, then, this was given—and of course he, quite understandably, did not feel the need to go into the manner in which the accomplishment of idealization originally arose (i.e., how it grew on the underlying basis of the pregeometrical, sensible world and its practical arts) or to occupy himself with questions about the origins of apodictic, mathematical self-evidence. There is no need for that in the attitude of the geometer: one has, after all, studied geometry, one "understands" geometrical concepts and propositions, is familiar with methods of operation as ways of dealing with precisely defined structures and of making proper use of figures on paper ("models"). It did not enter the mind of a Galileo that it would ever become relevant, indeed of fundamental importance, to geometry, as a branch of a universal knowledge of what is (philosophy), to make geometrical self-evidence—the "how" of its origin—into a problem. For us, proceeding beyond Galileo in our historical reflections, it will be of considerable interest to see how a shift of focus became urgent and how the "origin" of knowledge had to become a major problem.

Here we observe the way in which geometry, taken over with the sort of naivete of a priori self-evidence that keeps every normal geometrical project in motion, determines Galileo's thinking and guides it to the idea of physics, which now arises for the first time in his life-work. Starting with the practically understandable manner in which geometry, in an old traditional sphere, aids in bringing the sensible surrounding world to univocal determination, Galileo said to himself: Wherever such a methodology is developed, there we have also overcome the relativity of subjective interpretations which is, after all, essential to the empirically intuited world. For in this manner we attain an identical, nonrelative truth of which everyone who can understand and use this method can convince himself. Here, then, we recognize something that truly is—though only in the form of a constantly increasing approximation, beginning with what is empirically given, to the geometrical ideal shape which functions as a guiding pole.

However, all this *pure* mathematics has to do with bodies and the bodily world only through an abstraction, i.e., it has to do only with *abstract shapes* within space-time, and with these, furthermore, as purely "ideal" limit-shapes. *Concretely,* however, the actual and possible empirical shapes are given, at first in empirical sense-intuition, merely as "forms" of a "matter," of a sensible plenum;* thus they are given together with what shows itself, with its own gradations, in the so-called "specific" sense-qualities:† color, sound, smell, and the like.

To the concreteness of sensibly intuitable bodies, of their being in actual and possible experience, belongs also the fact that they are restricted by the [type of] changeability that is essential to them. Their changes of spatiotemporal position, or of form- or plenum-characteristics, are not accidental and arbitrary but depend on one another in sensibly *typical* ways. Such types of relatedness between bodily occurrences are themselves moments of everyday experiencing intuition. They are ex-

---

einer sinnlichen Fülle. I have used the word *plenum* to translate this strange use of *Fülle:* the sensible content which "fills in" the shapes of the world, the "secondary qualities" that are left over after pure shape has been abstracted. Cf. the related but not identical use of *Fülle* in LI, Investigation VI, §21. —Translator's note.

†It is a bad legacy of the psychological tradition since Locke's time that the sense-qualities of actually experienced bodies in the everyday, intuited surrounding world-colors, touch-qualities, smells, warmth, heaviness, etc., which are perceived as belonging to the bodies themselves, as their properties—are always surreptitiously replaced by the [so-called] "sense data" *[sinnliche Daten, Empfindungsdaten.* Both terms must be translated by the same expression. — Translator's note]; these are also indiscriminately called sense-qualities and, at least in general, are not at all differentiated from [properties as such]. Where a difference is felt, instead of thoroughly describing the peculiarities of this difference, which is quite necessary, one holds to the completely mistaken opinion (and we shall speak of this later) that "sense-data" constitute what is immediately given. What corresponds to them in the [perceived] bodies themselves is then ordinarily replaced by their mathematical-physical [properties]—when it is precisely the origin of the meaning [of these properties] that we are engaged in investigating. Here and everywhere we shall speak—giving faithful expression to actual experience—of *qualities* or *properties* of the bodies which are actually perceived through these properties. And when we characterize them as the *plena* of shapes, we also take these shapes to be "qualities" of the bodies themselves, indeed sense-qualities; except that, as αἰσθητὰ κοινά they are not related to sense-organs belonging to them alone, as are the αἰσθητὰ ἴδια.

perienced as that which gives the character of *belonging together* to bodies which *exist together* simultaneously and successively, i.e., as that which *binds* their being *[Sein]* to their being-such *[Sosein]*. Often, though not always, we are clearly confronted in experience with the connected elements which make up these real-causal interdependencies. Where that is not the case, and where something happens which is strikingly new, we nevertheless immediately ask why and look around us into the spatiotemporal circumstances. The things of the intuited surrounding world (always taken as they are intuitively there for us in everyday life and count as actual) have, so to speak, their "habits"—they behave similarly under typically similar circumstances. If we take the intuitable world as a whole, in the flowing present in which it is straightforwardly there for us, it has even as a whole its "habit," i.e., that of continuing habitually as it has up to now. Thus our empirically intuited surrounding world has an *empirical over-all style*. However we may change the world in imagination or represent to ourselves the future course of the world, unknown to us, in terms of its possibilities, "as it might be," we necessarily represent it according to the style in which we have, and up to now have had, the world. We can become explicitly conscious of this style by reflecting and by freely varying these possibilities. In this manner we can make into a subject of investigation the invariant general style which this intuitive world, in the flow of total experience, persistently maintains. Precisely in this way we see that, universally, things and their occurrences do not arbitrarily appear and run their course but are *bound* a priori by this style, by the invariant form of the intuitable world. In other words, through a *universal causal regulation, all that is together in the world* has a universal immediate or mediate way of *belonging together;* through this the world is not merely a totality *[Allheit]* but an all-encompassing unity *[Alleinheit]*, a *whole* (even though it is infinite). This is self-evident a priori, no matter how little is actually experienced of the particular causal dependencies, no matter how little of this is known from past

experience or is prefigured about future experience.

This universal causal style of the intuitively given surrounding world makes possible hypotheses, inductions, predictions about the unknowns of its present, its past, and its future. In the life of prescientific knowing we remain, however, in the sphere of the [merely] approximate, the typical. How would a "philosophy," a scientific knowledge of the world, be possible if we were to stop at the vague consciousness of totality whereby, amidst the vicissitudes of temporary interests and themes of knowledge, we are also conscious of the world as horizon? Of course we can, as has been shown, also thematically reflect on this world-whole and grasp its causal style. But we gain thereby only the empty, general insight that any experienceable occurrence at any place and at any time is causally determined. But what about the specifically determined world-causality, the specifically determined network of causal interdependencies that makes concrete all real events at all times? Knowing the world in a seriously scientific way, "philosophically," can have meaning and be possible only if a method can be devised of *constructing*, systematically and in a sense in advance, the world, the infinitude of causalities, starting from the meager supply of what can be established only relatively in direct experience, and of compellingly *verifying* this construction in spite of the infinitude [of experience]. How is this thinkable?

But here mathematics offers its services as a teacher. In respect to spatiotemporal shapes it had already blazed the trail, in two ways in fact. *First:* by idealizing the world of bodies in respect to what has spatiotemporal shape in this world, it created ideal objects. Out of the undetermined universal form of the lifeworld, space and time, and the manifold of empirical intuitable shapes that can be imagined into it, it made for the first time an objective world in the true sense—i.e., an infinite totality of ideal objects which are determinable univocally, methodically, and quite universally for everyone. Thus mathematics showed for the first time that an infinity of objects that are subjectively relative and are thought only in a vague, general representation is, through an a priori all-encompassing method, objectively determinable and can actually be thought as determined in itself or, more exactly, as an infinity which is determined, decided in advance, in itself, in respect to all its objects and all their properties and relations. It can be thought in this way, I said—i.e., precisely because it is constructible *ex datis* in its objectively true being-in-itself, through its method which is not just postulated but is actually created, apodictically generated.*

Second: coming into contact with the art of measuring and then guiding it, mathematics —thereby descending again from the world of idealities to the empirically intuited world —showed that one can universally obtain objectively true knowledge of a completely new sort about the things of the intuitively actual world, in respect to that aspect of them (which all things necessarily share) which alone interests the mathematics of shapes, i.e., a [type of] knowledge related in an approximating fashion to its own idealities. All the things of the empirically intuitable world have, in accord with the world-style, a bodily character, are *res extensae,* are experienced in changeable collocations which, taken as a whole, have their total collocation; in these, particular bodies have their relative positions, etc. By means of pure mathematics and the practical art of measuring, one can produce, for everything in the world of bodies which is extended in this way, a completely new kind of inductive prediction; namely, one can "calculate" with compelling necessity, on the basis of given and measured events involving shapes, events which are unknown and were never accessible to direct measurement. Thus ideal geometry, estranged from the world, becomes "applied" geometry and thus becomes in a certain respect a general method of knowing the real.

But does not this manner of objectifying, to be practiced on one abstract aspect of the world, give rise to the following thought and the conjectural question:

Must not something similar be possible for the concrete world as such? If one is already firmly convinced, moreover, like Galileo— thanks to the Renaissance's return to ancient philosophy—of the possibility of philosophy as *epistēmē* achieving an objective science of the world, and if it had just been revealed that pure mathematics, applied to nature, consummately fulfills the postulate of *epistēmē* in its sphere of shapes: did not this also have to suggest to Galileo the idea of a nature which is constructively determinable in the same manner in all its *other aspects?*

But is this not possible only if the method of measuring through approximations and constructive determinations extends to *all* real properties and real-causal relations of the intuitable world, to everything which is ever experienceable in particular experiences? But how can we do justice to this general anticipation, [and] how can it become a practicable method for a concrete knowledge of nature?

The difficulty here lies in the fact that the material plena—the "specific" sense-qualities —which concretely fill out the spatiotemporal shape-aspects of the world of bodies *cannot,* in their own gradations, be *directly* treated as are the shapes themselves. Nevertheless, these qualities, and everything that makes up the concreteness of the sensibly intuited world, must count as manifestations of an "objective" world. Or rather, they must continue to count as such; because (such is the way of thinking which motivates the idea of the new physics) the certainty, binding us all, of one and the same world, the actuality which exists in itself, runs uninterrupted through all changes of subjective interpretation; all aspects of experiencing intuition manifest something of this world. It becomes attainable for our objective knowledge when those aspects which, like sensible qualities, are abstracted away in the pure mathematics of spatiotemporal form and its possible particular shapes, and are not themselves

---

*Reading *erzeugte* for *erzeugende.* —Translator's note.

directly mathematizable, nevertheless become mathematizable *indirectly*.

c) The problem of the mathematiza-bility of the "plena"

The question now is what an *indirect mathematization* would mean.

Let us first consider the more profound reason why a direct mathematization (or an analogue of approximative construction), in respect to the specifically sensible qualities of bodies, is impossible in principle.

These qualities, too, appear in gradations, and in a certain way measurement applies to them as to all gradations—we "assess" the "magnitude" of coldness and warmth, of roughness and smoothness, of brightness and darkness, etc. But there is no exact measurement here, no growth of exactness or of the methods of measurement. Today, when we speak of measuring, of units of measure, methods of measure, or simply of magnitudes, we mean as a rule those that are already related to idealities and are "exact"; so it is difficult for us to carry out the abstract isolation of the plena which is so necessary here: i.e., to consider —experimentally, so to speak—the world of bodies exclusively according to the "aspect" of those properties belonging under the title "specific sense-qualities," through a universal abstraction opposed to the one which gives rise to the universal world of shapes.

What constitutes "exactness"? Obviously, nothing other than what we exposed above: empirical measuring with increasing precision, but under the guidance of a world of idealities, or rather a world of certain particular ideal structures that can be correlated with given scales of measurement—such a world having been objectified in advance through idealization and construction. And now we can make the contrast clear in a word. We have not two but only *one* universal form of the world: not two but only *one geometry*, i.e., one of shapes, without having a second for plena. The bodies of the empirical-intuitable world are such, in accord with the world-structure belonging to this world—a priori, that each body has—abstractly speaking—an extension of its own and that all these extensions are yet shapes of the one total infinite extension of the world. As world, as the universal configuration of all bodies, it thus has a total form encompassing all forms, and *this* form is idealizable in the way analyzed and can be mastered through construction.

To be sure, it is also part of the world-structure that all bodies have their specific sense-qualities. But the qualitative configurations based purely on these are not analogues of spatiotemporal shapes, are not incorporated into a world-form peculiar to them. The limit-shapes of these qualities are not idealizable in an analogous sense; the measurement ("assessing") of them cannot be related to corresponding idealities in a constructible world already objectivized into idealities. Accordingly, the concept of "approximation" has no meaning here analogous to that within the mathematizable sphere of shapes—the meaning of an objectifying achievement.

Now with regard to the "indirect" mathematization of that aspect of the world which in itself has no mathematizable world-form: such mathematization is thinkable only in the sense that the specifically sensible qualities ("plena") that can be experienced in the intuited bodies are closely related in a quite peculiar and *regulated* way with the shapes that belong essentially to them. If we ask what is predetermined a priori by the universal world-form with its universal causality—i.e., if we consult the invariant, general style of being to which the intuited world, in its unending change, adheres: on the one hand the form of space-time is predetermined, and everything that belongs to it a priori (before idealization), as encompassing all bodies in respect to shape. It is further predetermined that, in each case of real bodies, factual shapes require factual plena and vice versa; that, accordingly, *this* sort of general causality obtains, binding together aspects of a *concretum* which are only abstractly, not really, separable. What is more, considering everything as a totality, there obtains a universal *concrete* causality. This causality contains the necessary anticipation that the intuitively given world can be intuited as a world only as an endlessly open horizon and hence that the infinite manifold of particular causalities can be anticipated only in the manner of a horizon and is not itself given. We are thus in any case, and a priori, certain, not only that the total shape-aspect of the world of bodies generally requires a plenum-aspect pervading all the shapes, but also that *every change,* whether it involves aspects of shape or of plenum, occurs according to certain causalities, immediate or mediate, which make it necessary. This is the extent, as we said, of the undetermined general anticipation a priori.

This is not to say, however, that the total behavior of plenum-qualities, in respect to what changes and what does not change, follows causal rules in such a way that this whole abstract aspect of the world is dependent in a consistent way on what occurs causally in the shape-aspect of the world. In other words, we do not have an a priori insight that every change of the specific qualities of intuited bodies which is experienced or is conceivable in actual or possible experience refers causally to occurrences in the abstract shape-stratum of the world, i.e., that every such change has, so to speak, a counterpart in the realm of shapes in such a way that any total change in the whole plenum has its causal counterpart in the sphere of shapes.

Put in this way, this conception might appear almost fantastic. Still, let us take into account the long-familiar idealization of the form of space-time with all its shapes, carried out (in large areas, though by no means completely) for thousands of years, together with the changes and configurations of change relating to this form. The idealization of the art of measurement was, as we know, included in this, not merely as the art of measuring things but as the art of empirical causal constructions (in which deductive inferences helped, of course, as they do in every art). The theoretical attitude and the thematization of pure idealities and constructions led to pure geometry (under which we include here all pure mathematics of shapes); and later —in the reversal which has by now become understandable—applied geometry (as we re-

member) arose, as the practical art of measuring, guided by idealities and the constructions ideally carried out with them: i.e., an objectification of the concrete causal world of bodies within corresponding limited spheres. As soon as we bring all this to mind, the conception proposed above, which at first appeared almost eccentric, loses its strangeness for us and takes on—thanks to our earlier scientific schooling—the character of something taken for granted. What we experienced, in prescientific life, as colors, tones, warmth, and weight belonging to the things themselves and experienced causally as a body's radiation of warmth which makes adjacent bodies warm, and the like, indicates in terms of physics, of course, tone-vibrations, warmth-vibrations, i.e., pure events in the world of shapes. This universal indication is taken for granted today as unquestionable. But if we go back to Galileo, as the creator of the conception which first made physics possible: what came to be taken for granted only through his deed could not be taken for granted by him. He took for granted only pure mathematics and the old familiar way of applying it.

If we adhere strictly to Galileo's motivation, considering the way in which it in fact laid the foundation for the new idea of physics, we must make clear to ourselves the *strangeness* of his basic conception in the situation of his time; and we must ask, accordingly, how he could hit upon this conception, namely, that everything which manifests itself as real through the specific sense-qualities must have its *mathematical index* in events belonging to the sphere of shapes—which is, of course, already thought of as idealized—and that there must arise from this the possibility of an *indirect* mathematization, in the fullest sense, i.e., it must be possible (though indirectly and through a particular inductive method) to construct *ex datis,* and thus to determine objectively, *all* events in the sphere of the plena. The whole of infinite nature, taken as a concrete universe of causality—for this was inherent in that strange conception—became [the object of] a *peculiarly applied mathematics.*

But first let us answer the question of what, in the pregiven world which was already mathematized in the old limited way, could have incited Galileo's basic conception.

D) THE MOTIVATION OF GALILEO'S CONCEPTION OF NATURE

Now there were some occasions, rather scanty, to be sure, of manifold but disconnected experiences, within the totality of prescientific experience, which suggested something like the indirect quantifiability of certain sense-qualities and thus a certain possibility of characterizing them by means of magnitudes and units of measurement. Even the ancient Pythagoreans had been stimulated by observing the functional dependency of the pitch of a tone on the length of a string set vibrating. Many other causal relations of a similar sort were, of course, generally known. Basically, all concrete intuitively given events in the familiar surrounding world contain easily discernible dependencies of plenum-occurrences on those of the sphere of shapes. But there was generally no motive for taking an analytical attitude toward the nexus of causal dependencies. In their vague indeterminateness they could not incite interest. It was different in cases where they took on the character of a determinateness which made them susceptible to determining induction; and this leads us back to the measurement of plena. Not everything which concomitantly and visibly changed on the side of shapes was measurable through the old, developed measuring methods. Also, it was a long way from such experiences to the universal idea and hypothesis that all specifically qualitative events function as indices for precisely corresponding constellations and occurrences of shape. But it was not so far for the men of the Renaissance, who were inclined to bold generalizations everywhere and in whom such exuberant hypotheses immediately found a receptive audience. Mathematics as a realm of genuine objective knowledge (and technology under its direction)—that was, for Galileo and even before him, the focal point of "modern" man's guiding interest in a philosophical knowledge of the world and a rational praxis. There must be measuring methods for everything encompassed by geometry, the mathematics of shapes with its a priori ideality. And the whole concrete world must turn out to be a mathematizable and objective world if we pursue those individual experiences and actually measure everything about them which, according to the presuppositions, comes under applied geometry—that is, if we work out the appropriate method of measuring. If we do that, the sphere of the specifically qualitative occurrences must *also* be mathematized *indirectly*.

In interpreting what was taken for granted by Galileo, i.e., the universal applicability of pure mathematics, the following must be noted: In every application to intuitively given nature, pure mathematics must give up its abstraction from the intuited plenum, whereas it leaves intact what is idealized in the shapes (spatial shapes, duration, motion, deformation). But in one respect this involves the performance of coidealization of the sensible plena belonging to the shapes. The extensive and intensive infinity which was substructed through the idealization of the sensible appearances, going beyond all possibilities of actual intuition—separability and divisibility *in infinitum,* and thus everything belonging to the mathematical continuum—implies a substruction of infinities for the *plenum*-qualities which themselves are *eo ipso* cosubstructed. The whole concrete world of bodies is thus charged with infinities not only of shape but also of plena. But it must also be noted once again that the "indirect mathematizability" which is essential for the genuine Galilean conception of physics is not yet given thereby.

As far as we have come, only a general idea has been attained or, more precisely, a general hypothesis: that a universal inductivity* obtains in the intuitively given world, one which announces itself in everyday experiences but whose infinity is hidden.

To be sure, this inductivity was not understood by Galileo as a hypothesis. For him a physics was immediately almost as certain as

---

*eine universale Induktivität, i.e., that all types of occurrence in the world are such as to be susceptible to induction. —Translator's note.

the previous pure and applied mathematics. The hypothesis also immediately traced out for him [its own] path of realization (a realization whose success necessarily has the sense, in our eyes, of a *verification of the hypothesis* —this by no means obvious hypothesis related to the [previously] inaccessible factual structure of the concrete world).* What mattered for him first, then, was the attainment of farther reaching and ever more perfectible *methods* in order actually to develop, beyond those which had thus far in fact been developed, all the methods of measuring that were prefigured as ideal possibilities in the ideality of pure mathematics—to measure, for example, speeds and accelerations. But the pure mathematics of shapes itself required a richer development as constructive quantification —which later on led to analytic geometry. The task now was to grasp systematically, by means of these aids, the universal causality— or, as we may say, the peculiar universal inductivity—of the world of experience which was presupposed in the hypothesis. It is to be noted, [then,] that along with the new, concrete, and thus two-sided idealization of the world, which was involved in Galileo's hypothesis, the obviousness of a universal, exact causality was also given—a universal causality which is not, of course, first arrived at by induction through the demonstration of individual causalities but which precedes and guides all induction of particular causalities—this being true even of the concretely general, intuitable causality which makes up the concretely intuitable form of the world as opposed to particular, individual causalities experienceable in the surrounding world of life *[Lebensumwelt]*.

This universal idealized causality encompasses all factual shapes and plena in their idealized infinity. Obviously, if the measurements made in the sphere of shapes are to bring about truly objective determinations, occurrences on the side of the plena must also be dealt with methodically. All the fully concrete things and occurrences—or rather the ways in which factual plena and shapes stand in causal relation— must be included in the method. The application of mathematics to plena of shape given in reality makes, because of the concreteness involved, causal presuppositions which must be brought to determinateness. How one should actually proceed here, how one should regulate methodically the work to be accomplished completely within the intuitively given world; how the factually accessible bodily data, in a world charged through hypothetical idealization with as yet unknown infinities, are to be brought to causal determination in *both* aspects;† how the hidden infinities in these data are to be progressively disclosed according to methods of measuring; how, through growing approximations in the sphere of shapes, more and more perfect indices of the qualitative plena of the idealized bodies become apparent; how the bodies themselves, as concrete, become determinable through approximations in respect to all their ideally possible occurrences: all this was a matter of *discovery* in physics. In other words, it was a matter for the passionate *praxis of inquiry* and not a matter for prior systematic reflection upon what is possible in principle, upon the essential presuppositions of a mathematical objectification which is supposed to be able to determine the concretely real within the network of universal concrete causality.

Discovery is really a mixture of instinct and method. One must, of course, ask whether such a mixture is in the strict sense philosophy or science—whether it can be knowledge of the world in the ultimate sense, the only sense that could serve us as a [genuine] understanding of the world and ourselves. As a discoverer, Galileo went directly to the task of realizing his idea, of developing methods for measuring the nearest data of common experience; and actual experience demonstrated (through a method which was of course not radically clarified) what his hypothetical anticipation in

---

*"Our eyes," referring to us who are engaged in this historical reflection. Once we have removed our own prejudices, we see this as a strange hypothesis rather than simply taking it for granted. —Translator's note.

†I.e., the aspect of shape and the aspect of plenum. —Translator's note.

each case demanded; he actually found causal interrelations which could be mathematically expressed in "formulae."

The actual process of measuring, applied to the intuited data of experience, results, to be sure, only in empirical, inexact magnitudes and their quantities. But the art of measuring is, in itself, at the same time the art of pushing the exactness of measuring further and further in the direction of growing perfection. It is an art not [only] in the sense of a finished method for completing something; it is at the same time a method for improving [this very] method, again and again, through the invention of ever newer technical means, e.g., instruments. Through the relatedness of the world, as field of application, to pure mathematics, this "again and again" acquires the mathematical sense of the *in infinitum,* and thus every measurement acquires the sense of an approximation to an unattainable but ideally identical pole, namely, one of the definite mathematical idealities or, rather, one of the numerical constructions belonging to them.

From the beginning, the whole method has a *general* sense, even though one always has to do with what is individual and factual. From the very beginning, for example, one is not concerned with the free fall of *this* body; the individual fact is rather an *example,* embedded from the start in the concrete totality of types belonging to intuitively given nature, in its empirically familiar invariance; and this is naturally carried over into the Galilean attitude of idealizing and mathematizing. The indirect mathematization of the world, which proceeds as a methodical objectification of the intuitively given world, gives rise to general numerical formulae which, once they are formed, can serve by way of application to accomplish the factual objectification of the particular cases to be subsumed under them. The formulae obviously express general causal interrelations, "laws of nature," laws of real dependencies in the form of the "functional" dependencies of numbers. Thus their true meaning does not lie in the pure interrelations between numbers (as if they were formulae in the purely arithmetical sense); it lies in what the Galilean idea of

a universal physics, with its (as we have seen) highly complicated meaning-content, gave as a task to scientific humanity and in what the process of its fulfillment through successful physics results in—a process of developing particular methods, and mathematical formulae and "theories" shaped by them.

e) The verificational character of natural science's fundamental hypothesis

According to our remark [above, pp. 347–348]—which of course goes beyond the problem of merely clarifying Galileo's motivation and the resulting idea and task of physics—the Galilean idea is a *hypothesis,* and a very remarkable one at that; and the actual natural science throughout the centuries of its verification is a correspondingly remarkable sort of verification. It is remarkable because the hypothesis, in spite of the verification, continues to be and is always a hypothesis; its verification (the only kind conceivable for it) is an endless course of verifications. It is the peculiar essence of natural science, it is a priori its way of being, to be unendingly hypothetical and unendingly verified. Here verification is not, as it is in all practical life, merely susceptible to possible error, occasionally requiring corrections. There is in every phase of the development of natural science a perfectly correct method and theory from which "error" is thought to be eliminated. Newton, the ideal of exact natural scientists, says *"hypotheses non fingo,"* and implied in this is the idea that he does not miscalculate and make errors of method. In the total idea of an exact science, just as in all the individual concepts, propositions, and methods which express an "exactness" (i.e., an ideality)—and in the total idea of physics as well as the idea of pure mathematics—is embedded the *in infinitum,* the permanent form of that peculiar inductivity which first brought geometry into the historical world. In the unending progression of correct theories, individual theories characterized as "the natural science of a particular time," we have a progression of hypotheses which are in every respect hypotheses *and* verifications. In the progression there is growing perfection, and for all of natural science taken as a totality this means that it comes more and more to itself, to its "ultimate" true being, that it gives us a better and better "representation" *["Vorstellung"]* of what "true nature" is. But true nature does not lie in the infinite in the same way that a pure straight line does; even as an infinitely distant "pole" it is an infinity of theories and is thinkable only as verification; thus it is related to an infinite historical process of approximation. This may well be a topic for philosophical thinking, but it points to questions which cannot yet be grasped here and do not belong to the sphere of questions we must now deal with. For our concern is to achieve complete clarity on the idea and task of a physics which in its Galilean form originally determined modern philosophy, [to understand it] as it appeared in Galileo's own motivation, and to understand what flowed into this motivation from what was traditionally taken for granted and thus remained an unclarified presupposition of meaning, as well as what was later added as seemingly obvious, but which changed its actual meaning.

In this connection it is not necessary to go more concretely into the first beginnings of the enactment of Galileo's physics and of the development of its method.

f) The problem of the sense of natural-scientific "formulae"

But one thing more is important for our clarification. The *decisive accomplishment* which, in accord with the total sense of natural-scientific method, makes determined, systematically ordered predictions immediately possible, going beyond the sphere of immediately experiencing intuitions and the possible experiential knowledge of the prescientific life-world, is the establishment of the actual correlation among the mathematical idealities which are hypothetically substructed in advance in undetermined generality but still have to be demonstrated in their determined form. If one still has a vivid awareness of this correlation in its original meaning, then a mere thematic focus of attention on this meaning is sufficient in order to grasp the ascending orders of *intuitions* (now conceived as approximations) indicated by the functionally coordinated quantities (or, more briefly, by the formulae); or rather one can, following these indications, bring the ascending orders of intuitions vividly to mind. The same is true of the coordination itself, which is expressed in functional forms; and thus one can outline the empirical regularities of the practical life-world which are to be expected. In other words, if one has the formulae, one already possesses, in advance, the practically desired prediction of what is to be expected with empirical certainty in the intuitively given world of concretely actual life, in which mathematics is merely a special [form of] praxis. Mathematization, then, with its realized formulae, is the achievement which is decisive for life.

Through these considerations we see that, from the very first conceiving and carrying-out of the method, the passionate interest of the natural scientist was concentrated on this decisive, fundamental aspect of the above-mentioned total accomplishment, i.e., on the *formulae*, and on the technical* method ("natural-scientific method," "method of the true knowledge of nature") of acquiring them and grounding them logically and compellingly for all. And it is also understandable that some were misled into taking these formulae and their formula-meaning for the true being of nature itself.

This "formula-meaning" requires a more detailed clarification, now, in respect to the superficialization of meaning† which unavoidably accompanies the technical development and practice of method. Measurements give rise to numbers on a scale, and, in general proposi-

---

kunstmässig, i.e., having the character of a technique. — Translator's note.
†*Sinnesveräusserlichung,* literally, "externalization of meaning," but with the sense of rendering it superficial, separating it from its origin. —Translator's note.

tions about functional dependencies of measured quantities, they result not in determined numbers but in numbers in general, stated in general propositions which express laws of functional dependencies. Here we must take into account the enormous effect—in some respects a blessing, in others portentous—of the algebraic terms and ways of thinking that have been widespread in the modern period since Vieta (thus since even before Galileo's time). Initially this means an immense extension of the possibilities of the arithmetic thinking that was handed down in old, primitive forms. It becomes free, systematic, a priori thinking, completely liberated from all intuited actuality, about numbers, numerical relations, numerical laws. This thinking is soon applied in all its extensions—in geometry, in the whole pure mathematics of spatiotemporal shapes—and the latter are thoroughly formalized algebraically for methodical purposes. Thus an "arithmetization of geometry" develops, an arithmetization of the whole realm of pure shapes (ideal straight lines, circles, triangles, motions, relations of position, etc.). They are conceived in their ideal exactness as measurable; the units of measurement, themselves ideal, simply have the meaning of spatiotemporal magnitudes.

This arithmetization of geometry leads almost automatically, in a certain way, to the emptying of its meaning. The actually spatiotemporal idealities, as they are presented firsthand [*originär*] in geometrical thinking under the common rubric of "pure intuitions," are transformed, so to speak, into pure numerical configurations, into algebraic structures. In algebraic calculation, one lets the geometric signification recede into the background as a matter of course, indeed drops it altogether; one calculates, remembering only at the end that the numbers signify magnitudes. Of course one does not calculate "mechanically," as in ordinary numerical calculation; one thinks, one invents, one may make great discoveries—but they have acquired, unnoticed, a displaced, "symbolic" meaning. Later this becomes a fully conscious methodical displacement, a methodical transition from geometry, for example, to pure *analysis,* treated as a science in its own right; and the results achieved in this science can be applied to geometry. We must go into this briefly in more detail.

This process of method-transformation, carried out instinctively, unreflectively in the praxis of theorizing, begins in the Galilean age and leads, in an incessant forward movement, to the highest stage of, and at the same time a surmounting of, "arithmetization"; it leads to a completely universal "formalization." This happens precisely through an improvement and a broadening of the algebraic theory of numbers and magnitudes into a universal and thus purely formal "analysis," "theory of manifolds," "logistic"—words to be understood sometimes in a narrower, sometimes a broader, sense, since until now, unfortunately, there has been no unambiguous characterization of what in fact, and in a way practically understandable in mathematical work, a coherent mathematical field is. Leibniz, though far ahead of his time, first caught sight of the universal, self-enclosed idea of a highest form of algebraic thinking, a *mathesis universalis,* as he called it, and recognized it as a task for the future. Only in our time has it even come close to a systematic development. In its full and complete sense it is nothing other than a formal logic carried out universally (or rather to be carried out *in infinitum* in its own essential totality), a science of the forms of meaning of the "something-in-general" which can be constructed in pure thought and in empty, formal generality. On this basis it is a science of the "manifolds" which, according to formal elementary laws of the noncontradiction of these constructions, can be built up systematically as in themselves free of contradiction. At the highest level it is a science of the universe of the "manifolds" as such which can be conceived in this way. "Manifolds" are thus in themselves compossible totalities of objects in general, which are thought of as distinct only in empty, formal generality and are conceived of as defined by determinate modalities of the something-in-general. Among these totalities the so-called "definite" manifolds are distinctive. Their definition through a "complete axiomatic system" gives a special sort of totality in all deductive determinations to the formal substrate-objects contained in them. With this sort of totality, one can say, the formal-logical idea of a "world-in-general" is constructed. The "theory of manifolds" in the special sense is the universal science of the *definite* manifolds.*

G) The emptying of the meaning of mathematical natural science through "technization"†

This most extreme extension of the already formal but limited algebraic arithmetic has immediate applications, in its a priori fashion, within all "concretely material" *[konkret sachhaltige]* pure mathematics, the mathematics of "pure intuitions," and can thus be applied to mathematized nature; but it also has applications to itself, to previous algebraic arithmetic, and, again by extension, to all its own formal manifolds; in this way it is related back to itself. Like arithmetic itself, in technically developing its methodology it is drawn into a process of transformation, through which it becomes a sort of *technique;* that is, it becomes a mere art of achieving, through a calculating technique according to technical rules, results the genuine sense of whose truth can be attained only by concretely intuitive thinking actually directed at the subject matter itself. But now [only] those modes of thought, those types of clarity which are indispensable for a technique as such, are in action. One operates with letters and with signs for connections and relations (+, ×, =, etc.), according to *rules of the game* for arranging them together in a way essentially not different, in fact, from a game of cards or chess. Here the *original* thinking that genuinely gives meaning to this technical process and truth to the correct results (even the "formal truth" peculiar to the formal *mathesis universalis)* is excluded; in this manner it is also excluded in the formal theory of

manifolds itself, as in the previous algebraic theory of number and magnitude and in all the other applications of what has been obtained by a technique, without recourse to the genuine scientific meaning; this includes also the application to geometry, the pure mathematics of spatiotemporal shapes.

Actually the process whereby material mathematics is put into formal-logical form, where expanded formal logic is made self-sufficient as pure analysis or theory of manifolds, is perfectly *legitimate,* indeed necessary; the same is true of the technization which from time to time completely loses itself in merely technical thinking. But all this can and must be a method which is understood and practiced in a fully conscious way. It can be this, however, only if care is taken to avoid dangerous shifts of meaning by keeping always immediately in mind the original bestowal of meaning *[Sinngebung]* upon the method, through which it has the sense of achieving knowledge about the *world.* Even more, it must be freed of the character of an *unquestioned tradition* which, from the first invention of the new idea and method, allowed elements of obscurity to flow into its meaning.

Naturally, as we have shown, the *formulae* —those obtained and those to be obtained— count most for the predominant interest of the discovering scientist of nature. The further physics has gone in the actual mathematization of the intuited, pregiven nature of our surrounding world, the more mathematical-scientific propositions it has at its disposal, the further the instrument destined for it, the *mathesis universalis,* has been developed: the greater is the range of its possible deductive conclusions concerning new facts of quantified nature and thus the range of indicated corresponding verifications to be made. The latter devolve upon the experimental physicist, as does the whole work of ascending from the intuitively given surrounding world, and the experiments and measurements performed in it,

---

*For a more exact exposition of the concept of the definite manifold, see *Ideas I,* §72. On the idea of the *mathesis universalis,* see LI, I, §§60, 69, 70, and, above all, FTL, §23.
†*Technisierung,* i.e., the process of becoming a technique. —Translator's note.

to the ideal poles. Mathematical physicists, on the other hand, settled in the arithmetized sphere of space-time, or at the same time in the formalized *mathesis universalis,* treat the mathematical-physical formulae brought to them as special pure structures of the formal *mathesis,* naturally keeping invariant the constants which appear in them as elements of functional laws of factual nature. Taking into account all the "natural laws already proved or in operation as working hypotheses," and on the basis of the whole available formal system of laws belonging to this *mathesis,* they draw the logical consequences whose results are to be taken over by the experimenters. But they also accomplish the formation of the available logical possibilities for new hypotheses, which of course must be compatible with the totality of those accepted as valid at the time. In this way, they see to the preparation of those forms of hypotheses which now are the only ones admissible, as hypothetical possibilities for the interpretation of causal regularities to be empirically discovered through observation and experiment in terms of the ideal poles pertaining to them, i.e., in terms of exact laws. But experimental physicists, too, are constantly oriented in their work toward ideal poles, toward numerical magnitudes and general formulae. Thus in *all* natural-scientific inquiry these are at the center of interest. All the discoveries of the old as well as the new physics are discoveries in the formula-world which is coordinated, so to speak, with nature.

The formula-meaning of this world lies in idealities, while the whole toilsome work of achieving them takes on the character of a mere pathway to the goal. And here one must take into consideration the influence of the above-characterized technization of formal-mathematical thinking: the transformation of its experiencing, discovering way of thinking, which forms, perhaps with great genius, constructive theories, into a way of thinking with transformed concepts, "symbolic" concepts. In this process purely geometrical thinking is also depleted, as is its application to factual nature in natural-scientific thinking. In addition, a technization takes over all other methods

belonging to natural science. It is not only that these methods are later "mechanized." To the essence of all method belongs the tendency to superficialize itself in accord with technization. Thus natural science undergoes a many-sided transformation and covering-over of its meaning. The whole cooperative interplay between experimental and mathematical physics, the enormous intellectual work constantly accomplished here, takes place within a transformed horizon of meaning. One is, of course, to some degree conscious of the difference between τέχνη and science. But the reflection back upon the actual meaning which was to be obtained for nature through the technical method stops too soon. It no longer reaches far enough even to lead back to the position of the idea of mathematizing nature sketched out in Galileo's creative meditation, to what was wanted from this mathematization by Galileo and his successors and what gave meaning to their endeavors to carry it out.

h) The life-world as the forgotten meaning-fundament of natural science

But now we must note something of the highest importance that occurred even as early as Galileo: the surreptitious substitution of the mathematically substructed world of idealities for the only real world, the one that is actually given through perception, that is ever experienced and experienceable—our everyday life-world. This substitution was promptly passed on to his successors, the physicists of all the succeeding centuries.

Galileo was himself an heir in respect to pure geometry. The inherited geometry, the inherited manner of "intuitive" conceptualizing, proving, constructing, was no longer original geometry: in this sort of "intuitiveness" it was already empty of meaning. Even ancient geometry was, in its way, τέχνη, removed from the sources of truly immediate intuition and originally intuitive thinking, sources from which the so-called geometrical intuition, i.e., that which operates with idealities, has at first derived its meaning. The geometry of idealities was preceded by the practical art of surveying, which knew nothing of idealities. Yet such a pregeometrical achievement was a meaning-fundament for geometry, a fundament for the great invention of idealization; the latter encompassed the invention of the ideal world of geometry, or rather the methodology of the objectifying determination of idealities through the constructions which create "mathematical existence." It was a fateful omission that Galileo did not inquire back into the original meaning-giving achievement which, as idealization practiced on the original ground of all theoretical and practical life—the immediately intuited world (and here especially the empirically intuited world of bodies)—resulted in the geometrical ideal constructions. He did not reflect closely on all this: on how the free, imaginative variation of this world and its shapes results only in possible empirically intuitable shapes and not in exact shapes; on what sort of motivation and what new achievement was required for genuinely geometric idealization. For in the case of inherited geometrical method, these functions were no longer being *vitally* practiced; much less were they reflectively brought to theoretical consciousness as methods which realize the meaning of exactness from the inside. Thus it could appear that geometry, with its own immediately evident a priori "intuition" and the thinking which operates with it, produces a self-sufficient, absolute truth which, as such—"obviously" —could be applied without further ado. That this obviousness was an illusion—as we have pointed out above in general terms, thinking for ourselves in the course of our exposition of Galileo's thoughts—that even the meaning of the application of geometry has complicated sources: this remained hidden for Galileo and the ensuing period. Immediately with Galileo, then, begins the surreptitious substitution of idealized nature for prescientifically intuited nature.

Thus all the occasional (even "philosophical") reflections which go from technical [sci-entific] work back to its true meaning always stop at idealized nature; they do not carry out the reflection radically, going back to the ultimate purpose which the new science, together with the geometry which is inseparable from it, growing out of prescientific life and its surrounding world, was from the beginning supposed to serve: a purpose which necessarily lay *in* this prescientific life and was related to its life-world. Man (including the natural scientist), living in this world, could put all his practical and theoretical questions only to *it*—could refer in his theories only to it, in its open, endless horizons of things unknown. All knowledge of laws could be knowledge only of predictions, grasped as lawful, about occurrences of actual or possible experiential phenomena, predictions which are indicated when experience is broadened through observations and experiments penetrating systematically into unknown horizons, and which are verified in the manner of inductions. To be sure, everyday induction grew into induction according to scientific method, but that changes nothing of the essential meaning of the pregiven world as the horizon of all meaningful induction. It is this world that we find to be the world of all known and unknown realities. To it, the world of actually experiencing intuition, belongs the form of space-time together with all the bodily *[körperlich]* shapes incorporated in it; it is in this world that we ourselves live, in accord with our bodily *[leiblich],** personal way of being. But here we find nothing of geometrical idealities, no geometrical space or mathematical time with all their shapes.

This is an important remark, even though it is so trivial. Yet this triviality has been buried precisely by exact science, indeed since the days of ancient geometry, through that substitution of a methodically idealized achievement for what is given immediately as actuality presupposed in all idealization, given by a [type of] verification which is, in its own way, unsurpassable. This actually intuited, actual-

---

Körper means a body in the geometric or physical sense; *Leib* refers to the body of a person or animal. Where possible, I have translated *Leib* as "living body" (*Leib* is related to *Leben); Körper* is translated as "body" or sometimes "physical body." In cases where adjectival or adverbial forms are used, as here, it is sometimes necessary to insert the German words or refer to them in a footnote. —Translator's note.

ly experienced and experienceable world, in which practically our whole life takes place, remains unchanged as what it is, in its own essential structure and its own concrete causal style, whatever we may do with or without techniques. Thus it is also not changed by the fact that we invent a particular technique, the geometrical and Galilean technique which is called physics. What do we actually accomplish through this technique? Nothing but *prediction* extended to infinity. All life rests upon prediction or, as we can say, upon induction. In the most primitive way, even the ontic certainty* of any straightforward experience is inductive. Things "seen" are always more than what we "really and actually" see of them. Seeing, perceiving, is essentially having-something-itself *[Selbsthaben]* and at the same time having-something-in-advance *[Vor-haben]*, meaning-something-in-advance *[Vor-meinen]*. All praxis, with its projects *[Vorhaben]*, involves inductions; it is just that ordinary inductive knowledge (predictions), even if expressly formulated and "verified," is "artless" compared to the artful "methodical" inductions which can be carried to infinity through the method of Galilean physics with its great productivity.

In geometrical and natural-scientific mathematization, in the open infinity of possible experiences, we measure the life-world—the world constantly given to us as actual in our concrete world-life—for a well-fitting *garb of ideas,* that of the so-called objectively scientific truths. That is, through a method which (as we hope) can be really carried out in every particular and constantly verified, we first construct numerical indices for the actual and possible sensible plena of the concretely intuited shapes of the life-world, and in this way we obtain possibilities of predicting concrete occurrences in the intuitively given life-world, occurrences which are not yet or no longer actually given. And this kind of prediction infinitely surpasses the accomplishment of everyday prediction.

Mathematics and mathematical science, as a garb of ideas, or the garb of symbols of the symbolic mathematical theories, encompasses everything which, for scientists and the educated generally, *represents* the life-world, *dresses it up* as "objectively actual and true" nature. It is through the garb of ideas that we take for *true being* what is actually a *method* —a method which is designed for the purpose of progressively improving, *in infinitum,* through "scientific" predictions, those rough predictions which are the only ones originally possible within the sphere of what is actually experienced and experienceable in the life-world. It is because of the disguise of ideas that the true meaning of the method, the formulae, the "theories," remained unintelligible and, in the naive formation of the method, was *never* understood.

Thus no one was ever made conscious of the radical problem of *how* this sort of naivete actually became possible and is still possible as a living historical fact; how a method which is actually directed toward a goal, the systematic solution of an endless scientific task, and which continually achieves undoubted results, could ever grow up and be able to function usefully through the centuries when no one possessed a real understanding of the actual meaning and the internal necessity of such accomplishments. What was lacking, and what is still lacking, is the actual self-evidence through which he who knows and accomplishes can give himself an account, not only of what he does that is new and what he works with, but also of the implications of meaning which are closed off through sedimentation or traditionalization, i.e., of the constant presuppositions of his [own] constructions, concepts, propositions, theories. Are science and its method not like a machine, reliable in accomplishing obviously very useful things, a machine everyone can learn to operate correctly without in the least understanding the inner possibility and necessity of this sort of accomplishment? But was geometry, was science,

---

Seinsgewissheit, i.e., certainty of being. —Translator's note.

capable of being designed in advance, like a machine, without* an understanding which was, in a similar sense, complete—scientific? Does† this not lead to a *regressus in infinitum?*

Finally, does this problem not link up with the problem of the instincts in the usual sense? Is it not the problem of *hidden reason,* which knows itself as reason only when it has become manifest?

Galileo, the discoverer—or, in order to do justice to his precursors, the consummating discoverer—of physics, or physical nature, is at once a discovering and a concealing genius *[entdeckender und verdeckender Genius].* He discovers mathematical nature, the methodical idea, he blazes the trail for the infinite number of physical discoveries and discoverers. By contrast to the universal causality of the intuitively given world (as its invariant form), he discovers what has since been called simply the law of causality, the "a priori form" of the "true" (idealized and mathematized) world, the "law of exact lawfulness" according to which every occurrence in "nature"—idealized nature—must come under exact laws. All this is discovery-concealment, and to the present day we accept it as straightforward truth. In principle nothing is changed by the supposedly philosophically revolutionary critique of the "classical law of causality" made by recent atomic physics. For in spite of all that is new, what is essential in principle, it seems to me, remains: namely, nature, which is in itself mathematical; it is given in formulae, and it can be interpreted only in terms of the formulae.

I am of course quite serious in placing and continuing to place Galileo at the top of the list of the greatest discoverers of modern times. Naturally I also admire quite seriously the great discoverers of classical and postclassical physics and their intellectual accomplishment, which, far from being merely mechanical, was in fact astounding in the highest sense. This accomplishment is not at all disparaged by

the above elucidation of it as τέχνη or by the critique in terms of principle, which shows that the true meaning of these theories—the meaning which is genuine in terms of their origins—remained and had to remain hidden from the physicists, including the great and the greatest. It is not a question of a meaning which has been slipped in through metaphysical mystification or speculation; it is, rather, with the most compelling self-evidence, the true, the only real meaning of these theories, as opposed to the meaning of being a *method,* which has its own comprehensibility in operating with the formulae and their practical application, technique.

How what we have said up to now is still one-sided, and what horizons of problems, leading into new dimensions, have not been dealt with adequately—horizons which can be opened up only through a reflection on this life-world and man as its subject—can be shown only when we are much further advanced in the elucidation of the historical development according to its innermost moving forces.

i) Portentous misunderstandings resulting from lack of clarity about the meaning of mathematization

With Galileo's mathematizing reinterpretation of nature, false consequences established themselves even beyond the realm of nature which were so intimately connected with this reinterpretation that they could dominate all further developments of views about the world up to the present day. I mean Galileo's famous doctrine of the merely subjective character of the specific sense-qualities,‡ which soon afterward was consistently formulated by Hobbes as the doctrine of the subjectivity of all concrete phenomena of sensibly intuitive nature and world in general. The phenomena are only in the subjects; they are there only as causal results of events taking place in true nature,

*Reading *ohne ein* for *aus einem.* —Translator's note.
†Reading *führt* for *führte.* —Translator's note.
‡This doctrine is perhaps best expressed in Galileo's *Il Saggiatore (The Assayer).* See *Discoveries and Opinions of Galileo,* trans. Stillman Drake (Garden City: Doubleday Anchor Original, 1957), pp. 274ff. —Translator's note.

which events exist only with mathematical properties. If the intuited world of our life is merely subjective, then all the truths of pre- and extrascientific life which have to do with its factual being are deprived of value. They have meaning only insofar as they, while themselves false, vaguely indicate an in-itself which lies behind this world of possible experience and is transcendent in respect to it.

In connection with this we arrive at a further consequence of the new formation of meaning, a self-interpretation of the physicists which grows out of this new formation of meaning as "obvious" and which was dominant until recently:

Nature is, in its "true being-in-itself," mathematical. The *pure* mathematics of space-time procures knowledge, with apodictic self-evidence, of a set of laws of this "in-itself" which are unconditionally, universally valid. This knowledge is immediate in the case of the axiomatic elementary laws of the a priori constructions and comes to be through infinite mediations in the case of the other laws. In respect to the space-time form of nature we possess the "innate" faculty (as it is later called) of knowing with definiteness true being-in-itself as mathematically ideal being (before all actual experience). Thus implicitly the space-time form is itself innate in us.

It is otherwise with the more concrete universal lawfulness of nature, although it, too, is mathematical through and through. It is inductively accessible a posteriori through factual experiential data. In a supposedly fully intelligible way, the a priori mathematics of spatiotemporal shapes is sharply distinguished from natural science which, though it applies pure mathematics, is inductive. Or, one can also say: the purely mathematic relationship of ground and consequent is sharply distinguished from that of real ground and real consequent, i.e., that of natural causality.

And yet an uneasy feeling of obscurity gradually asserts itself concerning the relation between the mathematics of nature and the mathematics of spatiotemporal form, which, after all, belongs to the former, between the latter "innate" and the former "non-innate"

mathematics. Compared to the absolute knowledge we ascribe to God the creator, one says to oneself, our knowledge in pure mathematics has only one lack, i.e., that, while it is always absolutely self-evident, it requires a systematic process in order to bring to realization as knowing, i.e., as explicit mathematics, all the shapes that "exist" in the spatiotemporal form. In respect to what exists concretely in nature, by contrast, we have no a priori self-evidence at all. The whole mathematics of nature, beyond the spatiotemporal form, we must arrive at inductively through facts of experience. But is nature in itself not thoroughly mathematical? Must it not also be thought of as a coherent mathematical system? Must it not be capable of being represented in a coherent mathematics of nature, precisely the one that natural science is always merely seeking, as encompassed by a system of laws which is "axiomatic" in respect of form, the axioms of which are always only hypotheses and thus never really attainable? Why is it, actually, that they are not? Why is it that we have no prospect of discovering nature's own axiomatic system as one whose axioms are apodictically self-evident? Is it because the appropriate innate faculty is lacking in us in a factual sense?

In the superficialized, more or less already technized meaning-pattern of physics and its methods, the difference in question was "completely clear": it is the difference between "pure" (a priori) and "applied" mathematics, between "mathematical existence" (in the sense of pure mathematics) and the existence of the mathematically formed real (i.e., that of which mathematical shape is a component in the sense of a real property). And yet even such an outstanding genius as Leibniz struggled for a long time with the problem of grasping the correct meaning of the two kinds of existence—i.e., universally the existence of the spatiotemporal form as purely geometrical and the existence of universal mathematical nature with its factual, real form—and of understanding the correct relation of each to the other.

The significance of these obscurities for the Kantian problem of synthetic judgments a priori and for his division between the synthetic judgments of pure mathematics and those of natural science will concern us in detail later [see §25].

The obscurity was strengthened and transformed still later with the development and constant methodical application of pure formal mathematics. "Space" and the purely *formally* defined "Euclidean manifold" were confused; the *true axiom* (i.e., in the old, customary sense of the term), as an ideal norm with unconditional validity, grasped with self-evidence in pure geometric thought or in arithmetical, purely logical thought, was confused with the *inauthentic [uneigentliches]* "axiom"—a word which in the theory of manifolds signifies not judgments ("propositions") but forms of propositions as components of the definition of a "manifold" to be constructed formally without internal contradiction.

k) Fundamental significance of the problem of the origin of mathematical natural science*

Like all the obscurities exhibited earlier, [the preceding] follow from the transformation of a formation of meaning which was originally vital, or rather of the originally vital consciousness of the task which gives rise to the methods, each with its special sense. The developed method, the progressive fulfillment of the task, is, as method, an art (τέχνη) which is handed down; but its true meaning is not necessarily handed down with it. And it is precisely for this reason that a theoretical task and achievement like that of a natural science (or any science of the world)—which can master the infinity of its subject matter only through infinities of method† and can master the latter infinities only by means of a technical thought and activity which are empty of meaning—can only be and remain meaningful in a true and original sense *if* the scientist has developed in himself the ability to *inquire*

back into the *original meaning* of all his meaning-structures and methods, i.e., into the *historical meaning of their primal establishment*, and especially into the meaning of all the *inherited meanings* taken over unnoticed in this primal establishment, as well as those taken over later on.

But the mathematician, the natural scientist, at best a highly brilliant technician of the method—to which he owes the discoveries which are his only aim—is normally not at all able to carry out such reflections. In his actual sphere of inquiry and discovery he does not know at all that everything these reflections must clarify is even in *need* of clarification, and this for the sake of that interest which is decisive for a philosophy or a science, i.e., the interest in true knowledge of the *world itself, nature itself*. And this is precisely what has been lost through a science which is given as a tradition and which has become a τέχνη, insofar as this interest played a determining role at all in its primal establishment. Every attempt to lead the scientist to such reflections, if it comes from a nonmathematical, nonscientific circle of scholars, is rejected as "metaphysical." The professional who has dedicated his life to these sciences must, after all—it seems so obvious to him—know best what he is attempting and accomplishing in his work. The philosophical needs ("philosophicomathematical," "philosophicoscientific" needs), aroused even in these scholars by historical motives to be elucidated later, are satisfied by themselves in a way that is sufficient for them—but of course in such a way that the whole dimension which must be inquired into is not seen at all and thus not at all dealt with.

l) Characterization of the method of our exposition

In conclusion let us say a word about the *method* we have followed in the very intricate

---

*There is no section "j." In German one does not distinguish between "i" and "j" in an enumeration of this sort. — Translator's note.

†I.e., the infinite pursuit of its method. —Translator's note.

considerations of this section, in the service of our over-all aim. The historical reflections we embarked upon, in order to arrive at the self-understanding which is so necessary in our philosophical situation, demanded clarity concerning the *origin of the modern spirit* and, together with that—because of the significance, which cannot be overestimated, of mathematics and mathematical natural science— clarity concerning the origin of these sciences. That is to say: clarity concerning the original motivation and movement of thought which led to the conceiving of their idea of nature, and from there to the movement of its realization in the actual development of natural science itself. With Galileo the idea in question appears for the first time, so to speak, as full-blown; thus I have linked all our considerations to his name, in a certain sense simplifying and idealizing the matter; a more exact historical analysis would have to take account of how much of his thought he owed to his "predecessors." (I shall continue, incidentally, and for good reasons, in a similar fashion.) In respect to the situation as he found it and to the way in which it had to motivate him and did motivate him according to his known pronouncements, much can be established immediately, so that we understand the beginning of the whole bestowal of meaning *[Sinngebung]* upon natural science. But in this very process we come upon the shifts and concealments of meaning of later and most recent times. For we ourselves, who are carrying out these reflections (and, as I may assume, my readers), stand under the *spell* of these times. Being caught up in them, we at first have no inkling of these shifts of meaning—we who all think we know so well what mathematics and natural science "are" and do. For who today has not learned this in school? But the first elucidation of the original meaning of the new natural science and of its novel methodical style makes felt something of the later shifts in meaning. And clearly they influence, or at least make more difficult, the analysis of the motivation [of science].

Thus we find ourselves in a sort of circle. The understanding of the beginnings is to be gained fully only by starting with science as given in its present-day form, looking back at its development. But in the absence of an understanding of the *beginnings* the development is mute as a *development of meaning.* Thus we have no other choice than to proceed forward and backward in a zigzag pattern; the one must help the other in an interplay. Relative clarification on one side brings some elucidation on the other, which in turn casts light back on the former. In this sort of historical consideration and historical critique, then, which begins with Galileo (and immediately afterward with Descartes) and must follow the temporal order, we nevertheless have constantly to make *historical leaps* which are thus not digressions but necessities. They are necessities if we take upon ourselves, as we have said, the task of self-reflection which grows out of the "breakdown" situation of our time, with its "breakdown of science" itself. Of first importance for this task, however, is the reflection on the original meaning of the new sciences, above all that of the exact science of nature; for the latter was and still is, through all its shifts of meaning and misplaced self-interpretations, of decisive significance (in a manner to be pursued further) for the becoming and being of the modern positive sciences, of modern philosophy, and indeed of the spirit of modern European humanity in general.

The following also belongs to the method: readers, especially those in the natural sciences, may have become irritated by the fact —it may appear to them almost as dilettantism—that no use has been made of the natural-scientific way of speaking. It has been consciously avoided. In the kind of thinking which everywhere tries to bring "original intuition" to the fore—that is, the pre- and extrascientific life-world, which contains within itself all actual life, including the scientific life of thought, and nourishes it as the source of all technical constructions of meaning—in this kind of thinking one of the greatest difficulties is that one must choose the naive way of speaking of [everyday] life, but must also use it in a way which is appropriate for rendering evident what is shown.

It will gradually become clearer, and finally be completely clear, that the proper return to the naivete of life—but in a reflection which rises above this naivete—is the only possible way to overcome the philosophical naivete which lies in the [supposedly] "scientific" character of traditional objectivistic philosophy. This will open the gates to the new dimension we have repeatedly referred to in advance.

We must add here that, properly understood, all our expositions are supposed to aid understanding only from the relative [perspective of our] position and that our expression of doubts, given in the criticisms [of Galileo, etc.] (doubts which we, living in the present, now carrying out our reflections, do not conceal), has the methodical function of preparing ideas and methods which will gradually take shape in us as results of our reflection and will serve to liberate us.* All reflection undertaken for "existential" reasons is naturally *critical.* But we shall not fail to bring to a reflective form of knowledge, later on, the basic meaning of the course of our reflections and our particular kind of critique.

§14. Precursory characterization of objectivism and transcendentalism. The struggle between these two ideas as the sense of modern spiritual history

What characterizes objectivism is that it moves upon the ground of the world which is pregiven, taken for granted through experience, seeks the "objective truth" of this world, seeks what, in this world, is unconditionally valid for every rational being, what it is in itself. It is the task of *epistēmē, ratio,* or philosophy to carry this out universally. Through these one arrives at what ultimately is; beyond this, no further questions would have a rational sense.

Transcendentalism, on the other hand, says: the ontic meaning *[Seinssinn]* of the pregiven life-world† is a *subjective structure [Gebilde],* it is the achievement of experiencing, prescientific life. In this life the meaning and the ontic validity *[Seinsgeltung]* of the world are built up—of that particular world, that is, which is actually valid for the individual experiencer. As for the "objectively true" world, the world of science, it is a structure at a higher level, built on prescientific experiencing and thinking, or rather on its accomplishments of validity *[Geltungsleistungen].* Only a radical inquiry back into subjectivity—and specifically the subjectivity which *ultimately* brings about all world-validity, with its content and in all its prescientific and scientific modes, and into the "what" and the "how" of the rational accomplishments—can make objective truth comprehensible and arrive at the ultimate ontic meaning of the world. Thus it is not the being of the world as unquestioned, taken for granted, which is primary in itself; and one has not merely to ask what belongs to it objectively; rather, what is primary in itself is subjectivity, understood as that which naively pregives‡ the being of the world and then rationalizes or (what is the same thing) objectifies it.

Yet already one is threatened with absurdity here. For it first appears obvious that this subjectivity is man, i.e., psychological subjectivity. Mature transcendentalism protests against psychological idealism and, questioning objective science *as philosophy,* claims to have ini-

*This is a rough guess at a passage which is so obscure that I suspect something is missing. The sense, borne out by subsequent sentences, seems to be: In the historical but also critical reflections of this section, it is not yet clear (at least to the reader) *from what point of view* we are criticizing Galileo, Descartes, *et al.,* or where it will all lead. This point of view or attitude *will* gradually emerge as the phenomenological attitude which takes the form (in this case a historical-critical form) of liberating us from our prejudices. —Translator's note.

†Husserl probably means to include Hume under transcendentalism, as is his usual practice. This sentence would not strictly apply to Kant, according to Husserl (see §28), since Kant's transcendentalism did not penetrate to the role of the pregiven life-world in subjective life. In this sense Hume was for Husserl the more radical transcendental philosopher. —Translator's note.

‡*vorgibt.* A peculiarly Husserlian twist: that which is (pre)given is (pre)given *by subjectivity* through its meaning-bestowing acts. —Translator's note.

tiated a completely new sort of scientific procedure, the transcendental. Past philosophy had not even the slightest conception of a subjectivism in this transcendental style. Effective motives for the appropriate change of attitude were lacking, although such a change might have been conceivable from the direction of ancient skepticism, precisely through its anthropologistic relativism.

The whole history of philosophy since the appearance of "epistemology" and the serious attempts at a transcendental philosophy is a history of tremendous tensions between objectivistic and transcendental philosophy. It is a history of constant attempts to maintain objectivism and to develop it in a new form and, on the other side, of attempts by transcendentalism to overcome the difficulties entailed by the idea of transcendental subjectivity and the method it requires. The clarification of the origin of this internal split in the philosophical development, the analysis of the ultimate motives for this most radical transformation of the idea of philosophy, is of the utmost importance. It affords the first insight into the thoroughgoing *meaningfulness [Sinnhaftigkeit]* which unifies the whole movement of philosophical history in the modern period: a unity of purpose binding generations of philosophers together, and through this a direction for all the efforts of individual subjects and schools. It is a direction, as I shall try to show here, toward a *final form* of transcendental philosophy—as *phenomenology*. This also contains, as a suspended moment *[aufgehobenes Moment]*, the *final form of psychology* which uproots the naturalistic sense of modern psychology.

§15. Reflection on the method of our historical manner of investigation

The type of investigation that we must carry out, and which has already determined the style of our preparatory suggestions, is not that of a historical investigation in the usual sense. Our task is to make comprehensible the *teleology* in the historical becoming of philosophy, especially modern philosophy, and at the same time to achieve clarity about ourselves, who are the bearers of this teleology, who take part in carrying it out through our personal intentions. We are attempting to elicit and understand the *unity* running through all the [philosophical] projects of history that oppose one another and work together in their changing forms. In a constant critique, which always regards the total historical complex as a personal one, we are attempting ultimately to discern the historical task which we can acknowledge as the only one which is personally our own. This we seek to discern not from the outside, from facts, as if the temporal becoming in which we ourselves have evolved were merely an external causal series. Rather, we seek to discern it from the *inside*. Only in this way can we, who not only have a spiritual heritage but have become what we are thoroughly and exclusively in a historical-spiritual manner, have a task which is truly our own. We obtain it not through the critique of some present or handed-down system, of some scientific or prescientific *"Weltanschauung"* (which might as well be Chinese, in the end), but only through a critical understanding of the total unity of history—*our* history. For it has spiritual unity through the unity and driving force of the task which, in the historical process—in the thinking of those who philosophize for one another and with one another across time—seeks to move through the various stages of obscurity toward satisfying clarity until it finally works its way through to perfect insight. Then the task stands before us not merely as factually required but as a task *assigned* to us, the present-day philosophers. For we are what we are as functionaries of modern philosophical humanity; we are heirs and cobearers of the direction of the will which pervades this humanity; we have become this through a primal establishment which is at once a reestablishment *[Nachstiftung]* and a modification of the Greek primal establishment. In the latter lies the *teleological beginning,* the true birth of the European spirit as such.

This manner of clarifying history by inquiring back into the primal establishment of the goals which bind together the chain of future generations, insofar as these goals live on in sedimented forms yet can be reawakened again and again and, in their new vitality, be criticized; this manner of inquiring back into the ways in which surviving goals repeatedly bring with them ever new attempts to reach new goals, whose unsatisfactory character again and again necessitates their clarification, their improvement, their more or less radical reshaping—this, I say, is nothing other than the philosopher's genuine self-reflection on what he is *truly seeking,* on what is in him as a will coming *from* the will and *as* the will of his spiritual forefathers. It is to make vital again, in its concealed historical meaning, the sedimented conceptual system which, as taken for granted, serves as the ground of his private and nonhistorical work. It is to carry forward, through his own self-reflection, the self-reflection of his forebears and thus not only to reawaken the chain of thinkers, the social interrelation of their thinking, the community of their thought, and transform it into a living present for us but, on the basis of the *total unity* thus made present, to carry out a *responsible critique,* a peculiar sort of critique which has its ground in these historical, personal projects, partial fulfillments, and exchanges of criticism rather than in what is privately taken for granted by the present philosopher. If he is to be one who thinks for himself *[Selbstdenker],* an autonomous philosopher with the will to liberate himself from all prejudices, he must have the insight that all the things he takes for granted *are* prejudices, that all prejudices are obscurities arising out of a sedimentation of tradition—not merely judgments whose truth is as yet undecided*— and that this is true even of the great task and idea which is called "philosophy." All judgments which count as philosophical are related back to this task, this idea.

A historical, backward reflection of the sort under discussion is thus actually the deepest kind of self-reflection aimed at a self-understanding in terms of what we are truly seeking as the historical beings we are. Self-reflection serves in arriving at a decision; and here this naturally means immediately carrying on with the task which is most truly ours and which has now been clarified and understood through this historical self-reflection, the task set for us all in the present.

But to every primal establishment *[Urstiftung]* essentially belongs a final establishment *[Endstiftung]* assigned as a task to the historical process. This final establishment is accomplished when the task is brought to consummate clarity and thus to an apodictic method which, in every step of achievement, is a constant avenue to new steps having the character of absolute success, i.e., the character of apodictic steps. At this point philosophy, as an infinite task, would have arrived at its apodictic beginning, its horizon of apodictic forward movement. (It would, of course, be completely wrong to confuse the sense of the apodictic which is indicated here, and which is the most fundamental sense, with the usual sense taken from traditional mathematics.)

But we must be warned of a misunderstanding: Every historical philosopher performs his self-reflections, carries on his dealings with the philosophers of his present and past. He expresses himself about all this, fixes through these confrontations his own position, and thus creates a self-understanding of his own deeds in accord with the way his published theories have grown up within him in the consciousness of what he was striving for.

But no matter how precisely we may be informed, through historical research, about such "self-interpretations" (even about those of a whole series of philosophers), we learn nothing in this way about what, through all these philosophers, "the point of it" ultimately was, in the hidden unity of intentional inwardness which alone constitutes the unity of history. Only in the final establishment is this revealed; only through it can the unified directedness of all philosophies and philosophers open up. From here elucidation can be attained which enables us to understand past thinkers in a way

---

*I.e., prejudices *(Vor-Urteile)* in the literal sense. — Translator's note.

that they could never have understood themselves.

This makes it clear that the peculiar truth of such a "teleological consideration of history" can never be decisively refuted by citing the documented "personal testimony" of earlier philosophers. This truth is established only in the self-evidence of a critical over-all view which brings to light, behind the "historical facts" of documented philosophical theories and their apparent oppositions and parallels, a meaningful, final harmony.

21. Elements of a Science of the Life-World*

§33. The problem of the "life-world" as a partial problem within the general problem of objective science

Briefly reminding ourselves of our earlier discussions, let us recall the fact we have emphasized, namely, that science is a human spiritual accomplishment which presupposes as its point of departure, both historically and for each new student, the intuitive surrounding world of life, pregiven as existing for all in common. Furthermore, it is an accomplishment which, in being practiced and carried forward, continues to presuppose this surrounding world as it is given in its particularity to the scientist. For example, for the physicist it is the world in which he sees his measuring instruments, hears time-beats, estimates visible magnitudes, etc.—the world in which, furthermore, he knows himself to be included with all his activity and all his theoretical ideas.

When science poses and answers questions, these are from the start, and hence from then on, questions resting upon the ground of, and addressed to, the elements of this pregiven world in which science and every other life-praxis is engaged. In this life-praxis, knowledge, as prescientific knowledge, plays a constant role, together with its goals, which are in general satisfactorily achieved in the sense which is intended and in each case usually in order to make practical life possible. But a new civilization (philosophical, scientific civilization), rising up in Greece, saw fit to recast the idea of "knowledge" and "truth" in natural existence and to ascribe to the newly formed idea of "objective truth" a higher dignity, that of a norm for all knowledge. In relation to this, finally, arises the idea of a universal science encompassing all possible knowledge in its infinity, the bold guiding idea of the modern period. If we have made this clear to ourselves, then obviously an explicit elucidation of the objective validity and of the whole task of science requires that we first inquire back into the pregiven world. It is pregiven to us all quite naturally, as persons within the horizon of our fellow men, i.e., in every actual connection with others, as "the" world common to us all. Thus it is, as we have explained in detail, the constant ground of validity, an ever available source of what is taken for granted, to which we, whether as practical men or as scientists, lay claim as a matter of course.

Now if this pregiven world is to become a subject of investigation in its own right, so that we can arrive, of course, at scientifically defensible assertions, this requires special care in preparatory reflections. It is not easy to achieve clarity about what kind of peculiar scientific and hence universal tasks are to be posed under the title "life-world" and about whether something philosophically significant will arise here. Even the first attempt to understand the peculiar ontic sense of the life-world, which

*CES, pp. 121–147 (Sections 33–38).

can be taken now as a narrower, now as a broader one, causes difficulties.

The manner in which we here come to the life-world as a subject for scientific investigation makes this subject appear an ancillary and partial one within the full subject of objective science in general. The latter has become generally, that is, in all its particular forms (the particular positive sciences), incomprehensible as regards the possibility of its objective accomplishment. If science becomes a problem in this way, then we must withdraw from the operation of it and take up a standpoint above it, surveying in generality its theories and results in the systematic context of predicative thoughts and statements, and on the other side we must also survey the life of acts practiced by working scientists, working with one another—their setting of goals, their termination in a given goal, and the terminating self-evidence. And what also comes under consideration here is precisely the scientists' repeated recourse, in different general manners, to the life-world with its ever available intuited data; to this we can immediately add the scientists' statements, in each case simply adapted to this world, statements made purely descriptively in the same prescientific manner of judging which is proper to the "occasional"* statements of practical, everyday life. Thus the problem of the life-world, or rather of the manner in which it functions and must function for scientists, is only a partial subject within the above-designated whole of objective science (namely, in the service of its full grounding).

It is clear, however, that prior to the general question of its function for a self-evident grounding of the objective sciences there is good reason to ask about the life-world's own and constant ontic meaning for the human beings who live in it. These human beings do not always have scientific interests, and even scientists are not always involved in scientific work; also, as history teaches us, there was not always in the world a civilization that lived

habitually with long-established scientific interests. The life-world was always there for mankind before science, then, just as it continues its manner of being in the epoch of science. Thus one can put forward by itself the problem of the manner of being of the life-world; one can place oneself completely upon the ground of this straightforwardly intuited world, putting out of play all objective-scientific opinions and cognitions, in order to consider generally what kind of "scientific" tasks, i.e., tasks to be resolved with universal validity, arise in respect to this world's own manner of being. Might this not yield a vast theme for study? Is it not the case that, in the end, through what first appears as a special subject in the theory of science, that "third dimension" is opening up, immediately destined in advance to engulf the whole subject matter of objective science (as well as all other subject matters on the "plane")? At first this must appear peculiar and unbelievable. Many paradoxes will arise; yet they will be resolved. What imposes itself here and must be considered before everything else is the correct comprehension of the essence of the life-world and the method of a "scientific" treatment appropriate to it, from which "objective" scientific treatment, however, is excluded.

§34. Exposition of the problem of a science of the life-world

A) THE DIFFERENCE BETWEEN OBJECTIVE SCIENCE AND SCIENCE IN GENERAL

Is not the life-world as such what we know best, what is always taken for granted in all human life, always familiar in its typology through experience? Are not all its horizons of the unknown simply horizons of what is just incompletely known, i.e., known in advance in respect of its most general typology? For prescientific life, of course, this type of acquaintance suffices, as does its manner

---

*okkasionelle. A term from the second of the Logische Untersuchungen, §26 (1913 ed., vol. 11, p. 81): an expression is "essentially subjective and occasional" if its actual meaning depends "on the occasion [Gelegenheit], the person speaking, and his situation." —Translator's note.

of converting the unknown into the known, gaining "occasional" knowledge on the basis of experience (verifying itself internally and thereby excluding illusion) and induction. This suffices for everyday praxis. If, now, something more can be and is to be accomplished, if a "scientific" knowledge is supposed to come about, what can be meant other than what objective science has in view and does anyway? Is scientific knowledge as such not "objective" knowledge, aimed at a knowledge substratum which is valid for everyone with unconditioned generality? And yet, paradoxically, we uphold our assertion and require that one not let the handed-down concept of objective science be substituted, because of the century-old tradition in which we have all been raised, for the concept of science in general.

The* title "life-world" makes possible and demands perhaps various different, though essentially interrelated, scientific undertakings; and perhaps it is part of genuine and full scientific discipline that we must treat these all together, though following their essential order of founding, rather than treating, say, just the one, the objective-logical one (this particular accomplishment within the life-world) by itself, leaving the others completely out of scientific consideration. There has never been a scientific inquiry into the way in which the life-world constantly functions as subsoil, into how its manifold prelogical validities act as grounds for the logical ones, for theoretical truths.† And perhaps the scientific discipline which this life-world as such, in its universality, requires is a peculiar one, one which is precisely not objective and logical but which, as the ultimately grounding one, is not inferior but superior in value. But how is this completely different sort of scientific discipline, for which the objective sort has always been substituted up to now, to be realized? The idea of objective truth is predetermined in its whole meaning by the contrast with the idea of the truth in pre- and extrascientific life. This latter

truth has its ultimate and deepest source of verification in experience which is "pure" in the sense designated above, in all its modes of perception, memory, etc. These words, however, must be understood actually as prescientific life understands them; thus one must not inject into them, from current objective science, any psychophysical, psychological interpretation. And above all—to dispose of an important point right away—one must not go straight back to the supposedly immediately given "sense-data," as if *they* were immediately characteristic of the purely intuitive data of the life-world. What is actually first is the "merely subjective-relative" intuition of prescientific world-life. For us, to be sure, this "merely" has, as an old inheritance, the disdainful coloring of the δόξα. In prescientific life itself, of course, it has nothing of this; there it is a realm of good verification and, based on this, of well-verified predicative cognitions and of truths which are just as secure as is necessary for the practical projects of life that determine their sense. The disdain with which everything "merely subjective and relative" is treated by those scientists who pursue the modern ideal of objectivity changes nothing of its own manner of being, just as it does not change the fact that the scientist himself must be satisfied with this realm whenever he has recourse, as he unavoidably must have recourse, to it.

b) The use of subjective-relative experiences *for* the objective sciences, and the science *of* them

The sciences build upon the life-world as taken for granted in that they make use of whatever in it happens to be necessary for their particular ends. But to use the life-world in this way is not to know it scientifically in its own manner of being. For example, Einstein uses the Michelson experiments and the corroboration of them by other researchers, with

---

*This whole paragraph is crossed out in the MS. — Translator's note.
†This sentence was added by Fink. It does not seem to fit in, and it breaks the continuity between the preceding and following sentences. —Translator's note.

apparatus copied from Michelson's, with everything required in the way of scales of measurement, coincidences established, etc. There is no doubt that everything that enters in here —the persons, the apparatus, the room in the institute, etc.—can itself become a subject of investigation in the usual sense of objective inquiry, that of the positive sciences. But Einstein could make no use whatever of a theoretical psychological-psychophysical construction of the objective being of Mr. Michelson; rather, he made use of the human being who was accessible to him, as to everyone else in the prescientific world, as an object of straightforward experience, the human being whose existence, with this vitality, in these activities and creations within the common life-world, is always the presupposition for all of Einstein's objective-scientific lines of inquiry, projects, and accomplishments pertaining to Michelson's experiments. It is, of course, the one world of experience, common to all, that Einstein and every other researcher knows he is in as a human being, even throughout all his activity of research. [But] precisely this world and everything that happens in it, used as needed for scientific and other ends, bears, on the other hand, for every natural scientist in his thematic orientation toward its "objective truth," the stamp "merely subjective and relative." The contrast to this determines, as we said, the sense of the "objective" task. This "subjective-relative" is supposed to be "overcome"; one can and should correlate with it a hypothetical being-in-itself, a substrate for logical-mathematical "truths-in-themselves" that one can approximate through ever newer and better hypothetical approaches, always justifying them through experiential verification. This is the one side. But while the natural scientist is thus interested in the objective and is involved in his activity, the subjective-relative is on the other hand still functioning for him, not as something irrelevant that must be passed through but as that which ultimately grounds the theoretical-logical ontic validity for all objective verification, i.e., as the source of self-evidence, the source of verification. The visible measuring scales, scale-markings, etc., are

used as actually existing things, not as illusions; thus that which actually exists in the life-world, as something valid, is a premise.

c) Is the subjective-relative an object for psychology?

Now the question of the manner of being of this subjective sphere, or the question of the science which is to deal with it in its own universe of being, is normally disposed of by the natural scientist by referring to psychology. But again one must not allow the intrusion of what exists in the sense of objective science when it is a question of what exists in the life-world. For what has always gone under the name of psychology, at any rate since the founding of modern objectivism regarding knowledge of the world, naturally has the meaning of an "objective" science of the subjective, no matter which of the attempted historical psychologies we may choose. Now in our subsequent reflections the problem of making possible an objective psychology will have to become the object of more detailed discussions. But first we must grasp clearly the contrast between objectivity and the subjectivity of the life-world as a contrast which determines the fundamental sense of objective-scientific discipline itself, and we must secure this contrast against the great temptations to misconstrue it.

d) The life-world as universe of what is intuitable in principle; the "objective-true" world as in principle nonintuitable "logical" substruction

Whatever may be the chances for realizing, or the capacity for realizing, the idea of objective science in respect to the mental world (i.e., not only in respect to nature), this idea of objectivity dominates the whole *universitas* of the positive sciences in the modern period, and in the general usage it dominates the meaning of the word "science." This already involves a naturalism insofar as this concept is taken from Galilean natural science, such that the scientifically "true," the objective, world is always thought of in advance as nature, in an expanded sense of the word. The contrast between the subjectivity of the life-world and the "objective," the "true" world, lies in the fact that the latter is a theoretical-logical substruction, the substruction of something that is in principle not perceivable, in principle not experienceable in its own proper being, whereas the subjective, in the life-world, is distinguished in all respects precisely by its being actually experienceable.*

The life-world is a realm of original self-evidences.† That which is self-evidently given is, in perception, experienced as "the thing itself,"‡ in immediate presence, or, in memory, remembered as the thing itself; and every other manner of intuition is a presentification of the thing itself. Every mediate cognition belonging in this sphere—broadly speaking, every manner of induction—has the sense of an induction of something intuitable, something possibly perceivable as the thing itself or rememberable as having-been-perceived, etc. All conceivable verification leads back to these modes of self-evidence because the "thing itself" (in the particular mode) lies in these intuitions themselves as that which is actually, intersubjectively experienceable and verifiable and is not a substruction of thought; whereas such a substruction, insofar as it makes a claim to truth, can have actual truth only by being related back to such self-evidences.

It is of course itself a highly important task, for the scientific opening-up of the life-world, to bring to recognition the primal validity of these self-evidences and indeed their higher dignity in the grounding of knowledge compared to that of the objective-logical self-evi-

dences. One must fully clarify, i.e., bring to ultimate self-evidence, how all the self-evidence of objective-logical accomplishments, through which objective theory (thus mathematical and natural-scientific theory) is grounded in respect of form and content, has its hidden sources of grounding in the ultimately accomplishing life, the life in which the self-evident givenness of the life-world forever has, has attained, and attains anew its prescientific ontic meaning. From objective-logical self-evidence (mathematical "insight," natural-scientific, positive-scientific "insight," as it is being accomplished by the inquiring and grounding mathematician, etc.), the path leads back, here, to the primal self-evidence in which the life-world is ever pregiven.

One may at first find strange and even questionable what has been simply asserted here, but the general features of the contrast among levels of self-evidence are unmistakable. The empiricist talk of natural scientists often, if not for the most part, gives the impression that the natural sciences are based on the experience of objective nature. But it is not in this sense true that these sciences are experiential sciences, that they follow experience in principle, that they all begin with experiences, that all their inductions must finally be verified though experiences; rather, this is true only in that other sense whereby experience [yields] a self-evidence taking place purely in the life-world and as such is the source of self-evidence for what is objectively established in the sciences, the latter never themselves being experiences of the objective. The objective is precisely never experienceable as itself; and scientists themselves, by the way, consider it in

---

*In life the verification of being, terminating in experience, yields a full conviction. Even when it is inductive, the inductive anticipation is of a possible experienceability which is ultimately decisive. Inductions can be verified by other inductions, working together. Because of their anticipations of experienceability, and because every direct perception itself includes inductive moments (anticipation of the sides of the object which are not yet experienced), everything is contained in the broader concept of "experience" or "induction." [Cf. p. 355, above.]

†Husserl's use of *Evidenz* does not permit of its always being translated in the same way. But when used in its most special or technical sense, as it is here, "self-evidence" is better than simply "evidence." As can be seen from the context here, it means "self-givenness"; whereas the English word "evidence" usually has a very different meaning, that of something testifying to the existence of something else (e.g., evidence in a trial). —Translator's note.

‡ *"es selbst."* The use of the word "thing" in this expression is not out of place as long as Husserl is talking about perception. But in another context that which is "itself" given might not be a "thing"; it could be an ideal state of affairs, for example in mathematical or logical intuition. —Translator's note.

this way whenever they interpret it as something metaphysically transcendent, in contrast to their confusing empiricist talk. The experienceability of something objective is no different from that of an infinitely distant geometrical construct and in general no different from that of all infinite "ideas," including, for example, the infinity of the number series. Naturally, "rendering ideas intuitive" in the manner of mathematical or natural-scientific "models" is hardly intuition of the objective itself but rather a matter of life-world intuitions which are suited to make easier the conception of the objective ideals in question. Many [such] conceptual intermediaries are often involved, [especially since] the conception itself does not always occur so immediately, cannot always be made so self-evident in its way, as is the case in conceiving of geometrical straight lines on the basis of the life-world self-evidence of straight table-edges and the like.

As can be seen, a great deal of effort is involved here in order to secure even the presuppositions for a proper inquiry, i.e., in order first to free ourselves from the constant misconstructions which mislead us all because of the scholastic dominance of objective-scientific ways of thinking.

E) THE OBJECTIVE SCIENCES AS SUBJECTIVE CONSTRUCTS—THOSE OF A PARTICULAR PRAXIS, NAMELY, THE THEORETICAL-LOGICAL, WHICH ITSELF BELONGS TO THE FULL CONCRETENESS OF THE LIFE-WORLD

If the contrast [under discussion] has been purified, we must now do justice to the essential interrelatedness [of the elements contrasted]: objective theory in its logical sense (taken universally: science as the totality of predicative theory, of the system of statements meant "logically" as "propositions in themselves," "truths in themselves," and in this sense logically joined) is rooted, grounded in the life-world, in the original self-evidences belonging to it. Thanks to this rootedness objective science has a constant reference of meaning to the world in which we always live, even as scientists and also in the total community of scientists—a reference, that is, to the general life-world. But at the same time, as an accomplishment of scientific* persons, as individuals and as joined in the community of scientific activity, objective science itself belongs to the life-world. Its theories, the logical constructs, are of course not things in the life-world like stones, houses, or trees. They are logical wholes and logical parts made up of ultimate logical elements. To speak with Bolzano, they are "representations-in-themselves" ["Vorstellungen an sich"] "propositions in themselves," inferences and proofs "in themselves," ideal unities of signification whose logical ideality is determined by their *telos,* "truth in itself."

But this or any other ideality does not change in the least the fact that these are human formations, essentially related to human actualities and potentialities, and thus belong to this concrete unity of the life-world, whose concreteness thus extends farther than that of "things." Exactly the same thing is true, correlative to this, of scientific activities—those of experiencing, those of arriving at logical formations "on the basis of" experience—activities through which these formations appear in original form and original modes of variation in the individual scientists and in the community of scientists: the original status of the proposition or demonstration dealt with by all.

But here we enter an uncomfortable situation. If we have made our contrast with all necessary care, then we have two different things: life-world and objective-scientific world, though of course [they are] related to each other. The knowledge of the objective-scientific world is "grounded" in the self-evidence of the life-world. The latter is pregiven to the scientific worker, or the working community, as ground; yet, as they build upon this, what is built is something new, something different. If we cease being immersed in our scientific

---

*The text reads "prescientific persons," which must be a mistake. —Translator's note.

thinking, we become aware that we scientists are, after all, human beings and as such are among the components of the life-world which always exists for us, ever pregiven; and thus all of science is pulled, along with us, into the —merely "subjective-relative"—life-world. And what becomes of the objective world itself? What happens to the hypothesis of being-in-itself, related first to the "things" of the life-world, the "objects," the "real" bodies, real animals, plants, and also human beings within the "space-time" of the life-world—all these concepts being understood, now, not from the point of view of the objective sciences but as they are in prescientific life?

Is it not the case that this hypothesis, which in spite of the ideality of scientific theories has direct validity for the scientific subjects (the scientists as human beings), is but *one* among the many practical hypotheses and projects which make up the life of human beings in this life-world—which is at all times consciously pregiven to them as available? Do not all goals, whether they are "practical" in some other, extrascientific sense or are practical under the title of "theory," belong *eo ipso* to the unity of the life-world, if only we take the latter in its complete and full concreteness?

On the other hand, we have seen also that the propositions, the theories, the whole edifice of doctrine in the objective sciences are structures attained through certain activities of scientists bound together in their collaborative work—or, to speak more exactly, attained through a continued building-up of activities, the later of which always presuppose the results of the earlier. And we see further that all these theoretical results have the character of validities for the life-world, adding themselves as such to its own composition and belonging to it even before that as a horizon of possible accomplishments for developing science. The concrete life-world, then, is the grounding soil *[der gründende Boden]* of the "scientifically true" world and at the same time encompasses it in its own universal concreteness. How is this to be understood? How are we to do justice systematically—that is, with appropriate scientific discipline—to the all-encompassing, so paradoxically demanding, manner of being of the life-world?

We are posing questions whose clarifying answers are by no means obvious. The contrast and the inseparable union [we have been exploring] draw us into a reflection which entangles us in more and more troublesome difficulties. The paradoxical interrelationships of the "objectively true world" and the "life-world" make enigmatic the manner of being of both. Thus [the idea of a] true world in any sense, and within it our own being, becomes an enigma in respect to the sense of this being. In our attempts to attain clarity we shall suddenly become aware, in the face of emerging paradoxes, that all of our philosophizing up to now has been without a ground. How can we now truly become philosophers?

We cannot escape the force of this motivation. It is impossible for us to evade the issue here through a preoccupation with aporia and argumentation nourished by Kant or Hegel, Aristotle or Thomas.

f) THE PROBLEM OF THE LIFE-WORLD NOT AS A PARTIAL PROBLEM BUT RATHER AS A UNIVERSAL PROBLEM FOR PHILOSOPHY

Of course, it is a new sort of scientific discipline that is required for the solution of the enigmas which now disquiet us: it is not mathematical, nor logical at all in the historical sense; it cannot already have before it, as an available norm, a finished mathematics, logic, or logistic, since these are themselves objective sciences in the sense which is presently problematical and, as included in the problem, cannot be presuppositions used as premises. At first, as long as one only makes contrasts, is only concerned with oppositions, it could appear that nothing more than or different from objective science is needed, just as everyday practical life undertakes its rational reflections, both particular and general, without needing a science for them. It just *is* this way, a fact familiar to all, unthinkingly accepted rather than being formulated as a fundamental fact and thought through as a subject for thinking in its own right—namely, that there are two sorts of truth: on the one side, everyday practical situational truths, relative, to be sure, but, as we have already emphasized, exactly what praxis, in its particular projects, seeks and needs; on the other side there are scientific truths, and their grounding leads back precisely to the situational truths, but in such a way that scientific method does not suffer thereby in respect to its own meaning, since it wants to use and must use precisely these truths.

Thus it could appear—if one allows oneself to be carried along by the thoughtless naivete of life even in the transition from the extralogical to the logical, to the objective-scientific praxis of thinking—that a separate investigation under the title "life-world" is an intellectualistic enterprise born of a mania, peculiar to modern life, to theorize everything. But, on the other hand, it has at least become apparent that we cannot let the matter end with this naivete, that paradoxical enigmas announce themselves here: merely subjective relativity is supposedly overcome by objective-logical theory, yet the latter belongs, as the theoretical praxis of human beings, to the merely subjective and relative and at the same time must have its premises, its sources of self-evidence, in the subjective and relative. From here on this much is certain: that all problems of truth and of being, all methods, hypotheses, and results conceivable for these problems—whether for worlds of experience or for metaphysical higher worlds—can attain their ultimate clarity, their evident sense or the evidence of their nonsense, only through this supposed intellectualistic hypertrophy. This will then include, certainly, all ultimate questions of legitimate sense and of nonsense in the busy routine of the "resurrected metaphysics" that has become so vocal and so bewitching of late.

Through this last series of considerations the magnitude, the universal and independent significance, of the problem of the life-world has become intelligible to us in an anticipatory insight. In comparison with this the problem of the "objectively true" world or that of objective-logical science—no matter how pressing it may repeatedly become, and properly so—appears now as a problem of secondary and more specialized interest. Though the peculiar accomplishment of our modern objective science may still not be understood, nothing changes the fact that it is a validity for the life-world, arising out of particular activities, and that it belongs itself to the concreteness of the life-world. Thus in any case, for the sake of clarifying this and all other acquisitions of human activity, the concrete life-world must first be taken into consideration; and it must be considered in terms of the truly concrete universality whereby it embraces, both directly and in the manner of horizons, all the built-up levels of validity acquired by men for the world of their common life and whereby it has the totality of these levels related in the end to a world-nucleus to be distilled by abstraction, namely, the world of straightforward intersubjective experiences. To be sure, we do not yet know how the life-world is to become an independent, totally self-sufficient subject of investigation, how it is supposed to make possible scientific statements—which as such, after all, must have their own "objectivity," even if it is in a manner different from that of our sciences, i.e., a necessary validity to be appropriated purely methodically, which we and everyone can verify precisely through this method. We are absolute beginners, here, and have nothing in the way of a logic designed to provide norms; we can do nothing but reflect, engross ourselves in the still not unfolded sense of our task, and thus secure, with the utmost care, freedom from prejudice, keeping our undertaking free of alien interferences (and we have already made several important contributions to this); and this, as in the case of every new undertaking, must supply us with our method. The clarification of the sense of the task is, indeed, the self-evidence of the goal *qua* goal; and to this self-evidence belongs essentially the self-evidence of the possible "ways" to it. The intricacy and difficulty of the preliminary reflections which are still before us will justify themselves, not only because of the magnitude of the goal, but also because of the essential strangeness and precariousness of the ideas which will necessarily become involved.

Thus what appeared to be merely a problem of the fundamental basis of the objective sciences or a partial problem within the universal problem of objective science has indeed (just as we announced in advance that it would) proven to be the genuine and most universal problem. It can also be put this way: the problem first appears as the question of the relation between objective-scientific thinking and intuition; it concerns, on the one hand, then, logical thinking as the thinking of logical thoughts, e.g., the physicist's thinking of physical theory, or purely mathematical thinking, in which mathematics has its place as a system of doctrine, as a theory. And, on the other hand, we have intuiting and the intuited, in the life-world prior to theory. Here arises the ineradicable illusion of a pure thinking which, unconcerned in its purity about intuition, already has its self-evident truth, even truth about the world—the illusion which makes the sense and the possibility, the "scope," of objective science questionable. Here one concentrates on the separateness of intuiting and thinking and generally interprets the nature of the "theory of knowledge" as theory of science, carried out in respect to two correlative sides* (whereby science is always understood in terms of the only concept of science available, that of objective science). But as soon as the empty and vague notion of intuition—instead of being something negligible and insignificant compared to the supremely significant logical sphere in which one supposedly already has genuine truth—has become the problem of the life-world, as soon as the magnitude and difficulty of this investigation take on enormous proportions as one seriously penetrates it, there occurs the great transformation of the "theory of knowledge" and the theory of science whereby, in the end, science as a problem and as an accomplishment loses its self-sufficiency and becomes a mere partial problem.

What we have said also naturally applies

to logic, as the a priori theory of norms for everything "logical"—in the overarching sense of what is logical, according to which logic is a logic of strict objectivity, of objective-logical truths. No one ever thinks about the predications and truths which precede science, about the "logic" which provides norms within this sphere of relativity, or about the possibility, even in the case of these logical structures conforming purely descriptively to the life-world, of inquiring into the system of principles that give them their norms a priori. As a matter of course, traditional objective logic is substituted as the a priori norm even for this subjective-relative sphere of truth.

§35. Analysis of the transcendental epoché. First step: The epoché of objective science

Because of the peculiar nature of the task which has arisen for us, the method of access to the new science's field of work—which must be attained before the working problems of the science are given—is articulated into a multiplicity of steps, each of which has, in a new way, the character of an epoché, a withholding of natural, naive validities and in general of validities already in effect. The first necessary epoché, i.e., the first methodical step, has already come into view through the preliminary reflections hitherto carried out. But an explicit, universal formulation is needed. Clearly required before everything else is the epoché in respect to all objective sciences. This means not merely an abstraction from them, such as an imaginary transformation, in thought, of present human existence, such that no science appeared in the picture. What is meant is rather an epoché of all participation in the cognitions of the objective sciences, an epoché of any critical position-taking which is interested in their truth or falsity, even any position on their guiding idea of an objective knowledge of the world. In short, we carry out an epoché in regard to all objective theo-

---

*I.e., the subjective and the objective. —Translator's note.

retical interests, all aims and activities belonging to us as objective scientists or even simply as [ordinary] people desirous of [this kind of] knowledge.

Within this epoché, however, neither the sciences nor the scientists have disappeared for us who practice the epoché. They continue to be what they were before, in any case: facts in the unified context of the pregiven life-world; except that, because of the epoché, we do not function as sharing these interests, as coworkers, etc. We establish in ourselves just one particular habitual direction of interest, with a certain vocational attitude, to which there belongs a particular "vocational time."* We find the same thing here as elsewhere: when we actualize one of our habitual interests and are thus involved in our vocational activity (in the accomplishment of our work), we assume a posture of epoché toward our other life-interests, even though these still exist and are still ours. Everything has "its proper time," and in shifting [activities] we say something like: "Now it is time to go to the meeting, to the election," and the like.

In a special sense, of course, we call science, art, military service, etc., our "vocation," but as normal human beings we are constantly (in a broadened sense) involved in many "vocations" (interested attitudes) at the same time: we are at once fathers, citizens, etc. Every such vocation has its time of actualizing activities. Accordingly, this newly established vocational interest, whose universal subject matter is called the "life-world," finds its place among the other life-interests or vocations and it has "its proper time" within the one personal time, the form of the various exercised vocational times.

Of course, to equate the new science in this way with all "bourgeois" [bürgerliche] vocations, or even with the objective sciences, is a sort of trivialization, a disregard for the greatest value-distinction there can be between sciences. Understood in this way, it was so happily criticized by the modern irrationalistic

philosophers. This way of looking at it makes it appear as if, once again, a new, purely theoretical interest, a new "science" with a new vocational technique, is to be established, carried on either as an intellectualistic game with very ideal pretensions or as a higher-level intellectual technique in the service of the positive sciences, useful for them, while they themselves, in turn, have their only real value in their usefulness for life. One is powerless against the misrepresentations of hurried readers and listeners who in the end hear only what they want to hear; but in any case they are part of the indifferent mass audience of the philosopher. The few, for whom one [really] speaks, will know how to restrain such a suspicion, especially after what we have said in earlier lectures. They will at least wait to see where our path leads them.

There are good reasons for my stressing so sharply the vocational character of even the "phenomenologist's" attitude. One of the first things to be described about the epoché in question is that it is a habitual epoché of accomplishment, one with periods of time in which it results in work, while other times are devoted to other interests of work or play; furthermore, and most important, the suspension of its accomplishment in no way changes the interest which continues and remains valid within personal subjectivity—i.e., its habitual directedness toward goals which persist as its validities—and it is for this very reason that it can be actualized again and again, at different times, in this identical sense. This by no means implies, however, that the life-world epoché —to which further significant moments belong, as we shall show—means no more for human existence, practically and "existentially," than the vocational epoché of the cobbler, or that it is basically a matter of indifference whether one is a cobbler or a phenomenologist, or, also, whether one is a phenomenologist or a positive scientist. Perhaps it will even become manifest that the total phenomenological attitude and the epoché be-

---

*Berufszeit, colloq., "working hours." But I have translated it literally as "vocational time" in order to preserve the notion of Beruf, a "calling." —Translator's note.

longing to it are destined in essence to effect, at first, a complete personal transformation, comparable in the beginning to a religious conversion, which then, however, over and above this, bears within itself the significance of the greatest existential transformation which is assigned as a task to mankind as such.

§36. *How can the life-world, after the epoché of the objective sciences, become the subject matter of a science? The distinction in principle between the objective-logical a priori and the a priori of the life-world*

If our interest is exclusively in the "life-world," we must ask: Has the life-world, through the epoché in respect to objective science, already been laid open as a universal scientific subject matter?* Do we already have thereby the subject matter for statements that are generally valid scientifically, statements about facts that are to be established scientifically? How do we have the life-world as a universal field, fixed in advance, of such establishable facts? It is the spatiotemporal world of things as we experience them in our pre- and extrascientific life and as we know them to be experienceable beyond what is [actually] experienced. We have a world-horizon as a horizon of possible thing-experience *[Ding-erfahrung]*. Things: that is, stones, animals, plants, even human beings and human products; but everything here is subjective and relative, even though normally, in our experience and in the social group united with us in the community of life, we arrive at "secure" facts; within a certain range this occurs of its own accord, that is, undisturbed by any noticeable disagreement; sometimes, on the other hand, when it is of practical importance, it occurs in a purposive knowing process, i.e., with the goal of [finding] a truth which is secure for our purposes. But when we are thrown into an alien social sphere, that of the Negroes in the Congo, Chinese peasants, etc., we discover that their truths, the facts that for them are fixed, generally verified or verifiable, are by no means the same as ours. But if we set up the goal of a truth about the objects which is unconditionally valid for all subjects, beginning with that on which normal Europeans, normal Hindus, Chinese, etc., agree in spite of all relativity—beginning, that is, with what makes objects of the life-world, common to all, identifiable for them and for us (even though conceptions of them may differ), such as spatial shape, motion, sense-quality, and the like—then we are on the way to objective science. When we set up this objectivity as a goal (the goal of a "truth in itself") we make a set of hypotheses through which the pure life-world is surpassed. We have precluded *this* [type of] "surpassing" through the first epoché (that which concerns the objective sciences), and now we have the embarrassment of wondering what else can be undertaken scientifically, as something that

---

*First let us recall that what we call science is, within the constantly valid world, as life-world, a particular type of purposeful activities and purposeful accomplishments like all human vocations in the usual sense of the word; to this sphere also belong those practical intentions of a higher level which do not involve types of vocation or goal-oriented interrelations and accomplishments at all, the more or less isolated, incidental, more or less fleeting interests. All these are, from the human point of view, peculiarities of human life and of human habitualities, and they all lie within the universal framework of the life-world into which all accomplishments flow and to which all human beings and all accomplishing activities and capacities always belong. Of course, the new theoretical interest in the universal life-world itself, in its own manner of being, requires a certain epoché in regard to all these interests, i.e., in regard to the pursuit of our ends, in regard to all the criticism, always belonging to the purposeful life, of the means and the goals or ends themselves, e.g., whether we should factually persist in them, whether certain paths should be taken as general directives, etc. Living toward our ends, which are valid for us habitually, we do, of course, live in the horizon of the life-world, no matter which ends are "having their turn"; everything that happens and develops here exists in the life-world and in the manner of the life-world; but being oriented toward what exists within the life-world is not the same as focusing on the [life-world] as the universal horizon, not the same as making thematic the end in view *as* a being within this horizon, the newly thematic life-world. Thus the first thing we must do is refrain from the pursuit of all scientific and other interests. But the epoché alone is not enough: even all setting of ends, all projecting, presupposes something worldly; the *wherewith,* i.e., the life-world, is given prior to all ends. [This last sentence is only a rough guess at the sense of this somewhat garbled stenographic note. —Translator's note.]

can be established once and for all and for everyone.

But this embarrassment disappears as soon as we consider that the life-world does have, in all its relative features, a *general structure*. This general structure, to which everything that exists relatively is bound, is not itself relative. We can attend to it in its generality and, with sufficient care, fix it once and for all in a way equally accessible to all. As life-world the world has, even prior to science, the "same" structures that the objective sciences presuppose in their substruction of a world which exists "in itself" and is determined through "truths in themselves" (this substruction being taken for granted due to the tradition of centuries); these are the same structures that they presuppose as a priori structures and systematically unfold in a priori sciences, sciences of the *logos,* the universal methodical norms by which any knowledge of the world existing "in itself, objectively" must be bound. Prescientifically, the world is already a spatiotemporal world; to be sure, in regard to this spatiotemporality there is no question of ideal mathematical points, of "pure" straight lines or planes, no question at all of mathematically infinitesimal continuity or of the "exactness" belonging to the sense of the geometrical a priori. The bodies familiar to us in the life-world are actual bodies, but not bodies in the sense of physics. The same thing is true of causality and of spatiotemporal infinity. [These] categorical features of the life-world have the same names but are not concerned, so to speak, with the theoretical idealizations and the hypothetical substructions of the geometrician and the physicist. As we already know, physicists, who are men like other men, who know themselves as living in the life-world, the world of their human interests, have, under the title of physics, a particular sort of questions and (in a broader sense) practical projects directed toward the things of the life-world, and their "theories" are the practical results. Just as other projects, practical interests, and their realizations belong to the life-world, presuppose it as ground, and enrich it with their activity, so it is with science, too, as a human project and prax-

is. And this includes, as we have said, everything objectively a priori, with its necessary reference back to a corresponding a priori of the life-world. This reference-back is one of a founding of validity *[Geltungsfundierung].* A certain idealizing accomplishment is what brings about the higher-level meaning-formation and ontic validity of the mathematical and every other objective a priori on the basis of the life-world a priori. Thus the latter ought first to become a subject of scientific investigation in its peculiarity and purity, and then one ought to set the systematic task of understanding how, on this basis and in what manners of new meaning-formation, the objective a priori comes about as a mediated theoretical accomplishment. What is needed, then, would be a systematic division of the universal structures—universal life-world a priori and universal "objective" a priori—and then also a division among the universal inquiries according to the way in which the "objective" a priori is grounded in the "subjective-relative" a priori of the life-world or how, for example, mathematical self-evidence has its source of meaning and source of legitimacy in the self-evidence of the life-world.

This consideration has a particular interest for us even though we have already detached our problem of a science of the life-world from the problem of objective science in that we, caught up through our schooling in the traditional objectivistic metaphysics, at first have no means of access whatever to the idea of a universal a priori belonging purely to the life-world. What we need first is a separation in principle of the latter from the objective a priori which is [always] immediately substituted for it. It is this very separation that is effected by the first epoché of all objective sciences, if we understand it also as the epoché of all objective a priori sciences and make it complete through the considerations we have just carried out. The latter provide us, in addition, with the fundamental insight that the universal a priori of the objective-logical level—that of the mathematical sciences and all others which are a priori in the usual sense—is grounded in a universal a priori which is in itself prior, precisely that of the pure life-world.

Only through recourse to this a priori, to be unfolded in an a priori science of its own, can our a priori sciences, the objective-logical ones, achieve a truly radical, a seriously scientific, grounding, which under the circumstances they absolutely require.

Here we can also say: The supposedly completely self-sufficient logic which modern mathematical logicians *[Logistiker]* think they are able to develop, even calling it a truly scientific philosophy, namely, as the universal, a priori, fundamental science for all objective sciences, is nothing but naivete. Its self-evidence lacks scientific grounding in the universal life-world a priori, which it always presupposes in the form of things taken for granted, which are never scientifically, universally formulated, never put in the general form proper to a science of essence. Only when this radical, fundamental science exists can such a logic itself become a science. Before this it hangs in mid-air, without support, and is, as it has been up to now, so very naive that it is not even aware of the task which attaches to every objective logic, every a priori science in the usual sense, namely, that of discovering how this logic itself is to be grounded, hence no longer "logically" but by being traced back to the universal prelogical a priori through which everything logical, the total edifice of objective theory in all its methodological forms, demonstrates its legitimate sense and from which, then, all logic itself must receive its norms.

Yet this insight surpasses the interest in the life-world which governs us now; for this, as we have said, all that counts is the distinction in principle between the objective-logical and the life-world a priori; and the purpose of this is to be able to set in motion a radical reflection upon the great task of a pure theory of essence of the life-world.

§37. The formal and most general structures of the life-world: thing and world on the one side, thing-consciousness on the other

If we seek out, simply looking around us, what is formal and general, what remains in-variant in the life-world throughout all alterations of the relative, we involuntarily stop at what alone determines for us in life the sense of talking about the world: the world is the universe of things, which are distributed within the world-form of space-time and are "positional" in two senses (according to spatial position and temporal position)—the spatiotemporal *onta*. Here would thus be found the task of a life-world ontology, understood as a concretely general doctrine of essence for these *onta*. For our interest in the present context it suffices to have indicated this. Rather than spend our time here, we prefer to move on to a task which is much greater, as will soon be seen—one which in fact encompasses such a doctrine. In order to prepare the way for this new subject of investigation, which also essentially concerns the life-world but is not ontological, we shall undertake a general reflection—we, that is, as waking, living human beings in the life-world (and thus naturally within the epoché regarding all interference of positive scientific discipline).

This general reflection will at the same time have the function of making evident an essential distinction among the possible ways in which the pregiven world, the ontic universe *[das ontische Universum]*, can become thematic for us. Calling to mind what has repeatedly been said: the life-world, for us who wakingly live in it, is always already there, existing in advance for us, the "ground" of all praxis whether theoretical or extratheoretical. The world is pregiven to us, the waking, always somehow practically interested subjects, not occasionally but always and necessarily as the universal field of all actual and possible praxis, as horizon. To live is always to live-in-certainty-of-the-world. Waking life is being awake to the world, being constantly and directly "conscious" of the world and of oneself as living *in* the world, actually experiencing *[erleben]* and actually effecting the ontic certainty of the world. The world is pregiven thereby, in every case, in such a way that individual things are given. But there exists a fundamental difference between the way we are conscious of the world and the way we are conscious of things or objects (taken in the broadest sense, but still purely in the sense of the life-world), though together the two make up an inseparable unity: Things, objects (always understood purely in the sense of the life-world), are "given" as being valid for us in each case (in some mode or other of ontic certainty) but in principle only in such a way that we are conscious of them as things or objects *within the world-horizon.* Each one is something, "something of" the world of which we are constantly conscious as a horizon. On the other hand, we are conscious of this horizon only as a horizon for existing objects; without particular objects of consciousness it cannot be actual *[aktuell].* Every object has its possible varying modes of being valid, the modalizations of ontic certainty. The world, on the other hand, does not exist as *an* entity, as an object, but exists with such uniqueness that the plural makes no sense when applied to it. Every plural, and every singular drawn from it, presupposes the world-horizon. This difference between the manner of being of an object in the world and that of the world itself obviously prescribes fundamentally different correlative types of consciousness for them.

§38. The two possible fundamental ways of making the life-world thematic: the naive and natural straightforward attitude and the idea of a consistently reflective attitude toward the "how" of the subjective manner of givenness of life-world and life-world objects

These most general features of waking life make up the formal framework within which it now becomes possible to distinguish the different ways this life is carried on, though in all cases the world is pregiven and, within this horizon, objects are given. These ways result in the different manners, we could also say, in which we are awake to the world and to the objects in the world. The first, the naturally normal one which absolutely must precede the others not for accidental but for essential reasons, is that of straightforwardly living toward whatever objects are given, thus toward the world-horizon, in normal, unbroken constancy, in a synthetic coherence running through all acts. This normal, straightforward living, toward whatever objects are given, indicates that all our interests have their goals in objects. The pregiven world is the horizon which includes all our goals, all our ends, whether fleeting or lasting, in a flowing but constant manner, just as an intentional horizon-consciousness implicitly "encompasses" [everything] in advance. We, the subjects, in our normal, unbroken, coherent life, know no goals which extend beyond this; indeed we have no idea that there could be others. All our theoretical and practical themes, we can also say, lie always within the normal coherence of the life-horizon "world." World is the universal field into which all our acts, whether of experiencing, of knowing, or of outward action, are directed. From this field, or from objects in each case already given, come all affections, transforming themselves in each case into actions.

Yet there can be a completely different sort of waking life involved in the conscious having of the world. It would consist in a transformation of the thematic consciousness of the world which breaks through the normality of straightforward living. Let us direct our attention to the fact that in general the world or, rather, objects are not merely pregiven to us all in such a way that we simply have them as the substrates of their properties but that we become conscious of them (and of everything ontically meant) through subjective manners of appearance, or manners of givenness, without noticing it in particular; in fact we are for the most part not even aware of it at all. Let us now shape this into a new universal direction of interest; let us establish a consistent universal interest in the "how" of the manners of givenness and in the *onta* themselves, not straightforwardly but rather as objects in respect to their "how"—that is, with our interest exclusively and constantly directed toward *how,* throughout the alteration of relative validities, subjective appearances, and opinions, the coherent, universal validity *world—the* world—comes into being for us; how, that is, there arises in us the constant consciousness of the universal existence, of the universal horizon, of real, actually existing objects, each of which we are conscious of only through the alterations of our relative conceptions *[Auffassungen]* of it, of its manners of appearing, its modes of validity, even when we are conscious of it in particularity as something simply being there.

In this total change of interest, carried out with a new consistency founded on a particular resolve of the will, we notice that we acquire a number of never thematically investigated types, not only of individual things but also of syntheses, in an inseparable synthetic totality which is constantly produced by intentionally overlapping horizon-validities; and the latter influence each other reciprocally in the form of corroborating verifications of existence, or refuting cancelings-out, or other modalizations. This is the essential character of the synthetic totality in which we can take possession of something previously completely unknown, something never envisioned or grasped as a task for knowledge; this is the universal accomplishing life in which the world comes to be as existing for us constantly in flowing particularity, constantly "pregiven" to us. We can also say: this is the synthetic totality in which we now discover, for the first time, that and how the world, as correlate of a discoverable universe of synthetically connected accomplishments, acquires its ontic meaning and its ontic validity in the totality of its ontic *[ontische]* structures.

But here we do not need to go into more detailed expositions, into everything that can become thematic. What is essential for us here is the distinction between the two types of investigation,* each regarded as a universal investigation.

The natural life, whether it is prescientifically or scientifically, theoretically or practically interested, is life within a universal unthematic horizon. This horizon is, in the natural attitude, precisely the world always pregiven as that which exists. Simply living on in this manner, one does not need the word "pregiven"; there is no need to point out that the world is constantly actuality for us. All natural questions, all theoretical and practical goals taken as themes—as existing, as perhaps existing, as probable, as questionable, as valuable, as project, as action and result of action—have to do with something or other within the world-horizon. This is true even of illusions, nonactualities, since everything characterized through some modality of being is, after all, related to actual being. For, in advance, "world" has the meaning "the universe of the 'actually' existing actualities": not the merely supposed, doubtful, or questionable actualities but the actual ones, which as such have actuality for us only in the constant movement of corrections and revisions of validities *[Umgeltungen von Geltungen]*—all this considered as the anticipation of an ideal unity.

Instead of persisting in this manner of "straightforwardly living into the world," let us attempt a universal change of interest in which the new expression "pregivenness of the world" becomes necessary because it is the title for this differently directed and yet again universal theme of the manners of pregivenness. In other words, nothing shall interest us but precisely that subjective alteration of manners of givenness, of manners of appearing and of the modes of validity in them, which, in its constant process, synthetically connected as it incessantly flows on, brings about the coherent consciousness of the straightforward "being" of the world.

Among the objects of the life-world we also find human beings, with all their human action and concern, works and suffering, living in common in the world-horizon in their particular social interrelations and knowing themselves to be such. All this, too, then, shall be included as we carry out our new universal di-

---

*This could refer either to the "two ways of making the life-world thematic" (cf. section heading) or to the investigation of the "how" of the objects *vs.* the investigation of the subjective syntheses. —Translator's note.

rection of interest. A coherent theoretical interest shall now be directed exclusively toward the universe of the subjective, in which the world, in virtue of the universality of synthetically bound accomplishments in this universe, comes to have its straightforward existence for us. In the natural and normal world-life this subjective manifold constantly goes on, but there it remains constantly and necessarily concealed. How, by what method, is it to be revealed? Can it be shown to be a self-enclosed universe with its own theoretical and consistently maintained inquiry, revealing itself as the all-encompassing unity of ultimately functioning and accomplishing subjectivity which is to account for the existence of the world—the world for us, our natural life-horizon? If this is a legitimate and a necessary task, its execution implies the creation of a new science of a peculiar sort. In opposition to all previously designed objective sciences, which are sciences on the ground of the world, this would be a science of the universal *how* of the pregivenness of the world, i.e., of what makes it a universal ground for any sort of objectivity. And included in this is the creation of a science of the ultimate grounds *[Gründe]* which supply the true force of all objective grounding, the force arising from its ultimate bestowal of meaning.

Our historically motivated path, moving from the interpretation of the interplay of problems between Hume and Kant, has now led us to the postulate of clarifying the pregiven world's character of universally "being the ground" for all objective sciences and—what followed of itself—for all objective praxis; it has led us, then, to the postulate of that novel universal science of subjectivity as pregiving the world. We shall now have to see how we can fulfill this postulate. We notice thereby that the first step which seemed to help at the beginning, that epoché through which we freed ourselves from all objective sciences

as grounds of validity, by no means suffices. In carrying out this epoché, we obviously continue to stand on the ground of the world; it is now reduced to the life-world which is valid for us prescientifically; it is just that we may use no sort of knowledge arising from the sciences as premises, and we may take the sciences into consideration only as historical facts, taking no position of our own on their truth.

But nothing about this affects our interested looking-around in the prescientifically intuited world or our paying attention to its relative features. In a certain way, concern with this sort of thing belongs continually even to [one type of] objective investigation, namely, that of the historians, who must, after all, reconstruct the changing, surrounding life-worlds of the peoples and periods with which they deal. In spite of this, the pregiven world is still valid as a ground [for them] and has not been transposed into the universe of the purely subjective, a universal framework in its own right, which is our concern now.

The same thing holds [even] if we take as our subject of investigation, in the unity of a systematic survey, all [historical] periods and peoples and finally the entire spatiotemporal world, paying constant attention to the relativity of the surrounding life-worlds of particular human beings, peoples, and periods as mere matters of fact. It is clear that the same thing is true of this world survey, in the form of an iterated synthesis of relative, spatiotemporal life-worlds, that is true of a survey of one such life-world individually. It is taken one part at a time and then, at a higher level, one surrounding world, one temporal period, at a time; each particular intuition [yields] an ontic validity, whether in the mode of actuality or possibility. As each intuition occurs, it presupposes others having objective validity—presupposes for us, the observers, the general ground of the validity of the world.

BIBLIOGRAPHY
Works of Edmund Husserl

Books Published in Husserl's Lifetime

Philosophie der Arithmetik: Psychologische und logische Untersuchungen. Vol. 1. Halle a.d. Saale: C.E.M. Pfeffer, 1891.

Logische Untersuchungen. 2 vols. Halle a.d. Saale: Max Niemeyer, 1900 and 1901.

Logische Untersuchungen. 2nd rev. ed. 2 vols. Halle a.d. Saale: Max Niemeyer, 1913 and 1921. [All page references are to this edition.]

Ideen zu einer reinen Phänomenologie und phänomenologischen Philosophie. Vol. 1: *Allgemeine Einführung in die reine Phänomenologie,* in *Jahrbuch für Philosophie und phänomenologische Forschung,* vol. 1. Halle a.d. Saale: Max Niemeyer, 1913. Pp. 1–323. [All page references are to this edition.]

Vorlesungen zur Phänomenologie des inneren Zeitbewusstseins, ed. Martin Heidegger. *Jahrbuch für Philosophie und phänomenologische Forschung,* vol. 9. Halle a.d. Saale: Max Niemeyer, 1928. Pp. viii-ix, 367–498.

Formale und transzendentale Logik: Versuch einer Kritik der logischen Vernunft, in *Jahrbuch für Philosophie und phänomenologische Forschung,* vol. 10. Halle a.d. Saale: Max Niemeyer, 1929. Pp. v-xiii, 1–298.

Méditations Cartésiennes. Trans. E. Levinas and G. Pilfer. Paris: A. Colin, 1931.

Erfahrung und Urteil: Untersuchungen zur Genealogie der Logik, ed. L. Landgrebe. Prague: Academia-Verlag, 1938; Hamburg: Claasen, 1954.

Husserliana Edition

Cartesianische Meditationen und Pariser Vorträge, ed. S. Strasser. *Husserliana,* vol. 1. The Hague: Martinus Nijhoff, 1963.

Die Idee der Phänomenologie: Fünf Vorlesungen. 2nd. ed. Ed. Walter Biemel. *Husserliana,* vol. 2. The Hague: Martinus Nijhoff, 1958.

Ideen zu einer reinen Phänomenologie und phänomenologischen Philosophie. Band 1: *Allgemeine Einführung in die reine Phänomenologie.* Ed. Walter Biemel. *Husserliana,* vol. 3. The Hague: Martinus Nijhoff, 1950.

Ideen zu einer reinen Phänomenologie und phänomenologischen Philosophie. Band 1: *Allgemeine Einführung in die reine Phänomenologie.* Band 2: *Ergänzende Texte (1912–1929).* Ed. Karl Schuhmann. *Husserliana,* vol. 3/a and 3/b. The Hague: Martinus Nijhoff, 1976.

Ideen zu einer reinen Phänomenologie und phänomenologischen Philosophie. Band 2: *Phänomenologische Untersuchungen zur Konstitution.* Ed. Marly Biemel. *Husserliana,* vol. 4. The Hague: Martinus Nijhoff, 1952.

Ideen zu einer reinen Phänomenologie und phänomenologischen Philosophie. Band 3: *Die Phänomenologie und die Fundamente der Wissenschaften.* Ed. Marly Biemel. *Husserliana,* vol. 5. The Hague: Martinus Nijhoff, 1952.

Die Krisis der europäischen Wissenschaften und die transzendentale Phänomenologie: Eine Einleitung in die phänomenologische Philosophie. Ed. Walter Biemel. *Husserliana,* vol. 6. The Hague: Martinus Nijhoff, 1954.

Erste Philosophie (1923/24). Part 1: *Kritische Ideengeschichte.* Ed. Rudolf Boehm. *Husserliana,* vol. 7. The Hague: Martinus Nijhoff, 1956.

Erste Philosophie (1923/24). Part 2: *Theorie der phänomenologische Reduktion.* Ed. Rudolf Boehm. *Husserliana,* vol. 8. The Hague: Martinus Nijhoff, 1959.

Phänomenologische Psychologie: Vorlesungen Sommersemester 1925. Ed. Walter Biemel. *Husserliana,* vol. 9. The Hague: Martinus Nijhoff, 1968.

Zur Phänomenologie des inneren Zeitbewusstseins (1893–1917). Ed. Rudolf Boehm. *Husserliana,* vol. 10. The Hague: Martinus Nijhoff, 1966.

Analysen zur passiven Synthesis: Aus Vorlesungs-

und Forschungsmanuskripten 1918–1926. Ed. Margot Fleischer. *Husserliana,* vol. 11. The Hague: Martinus Nijhoff, 1966.

Philosophie der Arithmetik: Mit ergänzenden Texten (1890–1901). Ed. Lothar Eley. *Husserliana,* vol. 12. The Hague: Martinus Nijhoff, 1970.

Zur Phänomenologie der Intersubjektivität, Erster Teil: 1905–1920. Ed. Iso Kern. *Husserliana,* vol. 13. The Hague: Martinus Nijhoff, 1973.

Zur Phänomenologie der Intersubjektivität, Zweiter Teil: 1921–1928. Ed. Iso Kern. *Husserliana,* vol. 14. The Hague: Martinus Nijhoff, 1973.

Zur Phänomenologie der Intersubjektivität, Dritter Teil: 1929–1935. Ed. Iso Kern. *Husserliana,* vol. 15. The Hague: Martinus Nijhoff, 1973.

Ding und Raum: Vorlesungen 1907. Ed. U. Claesges. *Husserliana,* vol. 16. The Hague: Martinus Nijhoff, 1974.

Formale und transzendentale Logik: Versuch einer Kritik der logischen Vernunft. Ed. P. Janssen. *Husserliana,* vol. 17. The Hague: Martinus Nijhoff, 1974.

Logische Untersuchungen. Vol. 1: Prolegomena zur reinen Logik. Ed. Elmar Holenstein. *Husserliana,* vol. 18. The Hague: Martinus Nijhoff, 1975.

Logische Untersuchungen. Vol. 2: Untersuchungen zur Phänomenologie und Theorie der Erkenntnis, Part 1. Ed. U. Panzer. *Husserliana,* vol. 19. The Hague: Martinus Nijhoff, 1984.

Logische Untersuchungen. Vol. 2: Untersuchungen zur Phänomenologie und Theorie der Erkenntnis, Part 2. Ed. U. Panzer. *Husserliana,* vol. 20. The Hague: Martinus Nijhoff, 1984.

Studien zur Arithmetik und Geometrie: Texte aus dem Nachlaß (1886–1901). Ed. I. Strohmeyer. *Husserliana,* vol. 21. The Hague: Martinus Nijhoff, 1983.

Aufsätze und Rezensionen (1890–1910). Ed. B. Rang. *Husserliana,* vol. 22. The Hague: Martinus Nijhoff, 1979.

Phantasie, Bildbewußtsein, Erinnerung: Zur Phänomenologie der anschaulichen Vergegenwärtigungen: Texte aus dem Nachlaß (1898–1925). Ed. E. Marbach. *Husserliana,* vol. 23. The Hague: Martinus Nijhoff, 1980.

Einleitung in die Logik und Erkenntnistheorie: Vorlesungen 1906/1907. Ed. Ullrich Melle. *Husserliana,* vol. 24. The Hague: Martinus Nijhoff, 1984.

Aufsätze und Vorträge (1911–1921). Ed. Thomas Nenon and Hans Sepp. *Husserliana,* vol. 25. Dordrecht: Martinus Nijhoff, 1987.

Vorlesungen über Bedeutungslehre: Sommersemester 1908. Ed. Ursula Panzer. *Husserliana,* vol. 26. Dordrecht: Martinus Nijhoff, 1987.

Aufsätze und Vorträge (1922–1937). Ed. Thomas Nenon and Hans Rainer Sepp. *Husserliana,* vol. 27. Dordrecht: Kluwer Academic Publishers, 1989.

Vorlesungen über Ethik und Wertlehre, 1908–1914. Ed. Ullrich Melle. *Husserliana,* vol. 28. Dordrecht: Kluwer Academic Publishers, 1988.

Die Krisis der europäischen Wissenschaften und die transzendentale Phänomenologie: Ergänzungsband. Texte aus dem Nachlaß 1934–1937. Ed. Reinhold Smid. *Husserliana,* vol. 29. Dordrecht: Kluwer Academic Publishers, 1993.

Logik und allgemeine Wissenschaftstheorie. Vorlesungen 1917/18, mit ergänzenden Texten aus der ersten Fassung 1910/11. Ed. Ursula Panzer. *Husserliana,* vol. 30. Dordrecht: Kluwer Academic Publishers, 1968.

Other Editions of Husserl's Works

Die phänomenologische Methode: Ausgewählte Texte I. Ed. Klaus Held. Stuttgart: Phillip Reclam, 1985. *Phänomenologie der Lebenswelt: Ausgewählter Texte II.* Ed. Klaus Held. Stuttgart: Phillip Reclam, 1986.

Studienausgabe of the Felix Meiner Verlag, Hamburg

Cartesianische Meditationen: Eine Einleitung in die Phänomenologie [text from *Husserliana,* vol. 1]. Ed. E. Ströker. 1977.

Fünfte Logische Untersuchung: Über intentionale Erlebnisse und ihre "Inhalte" [text from the 1st ed., 1901, of the *Logische Untersuchungen*]. Ed. E. Ströker. 1975.

Grundprobleme der Phänomenologie, 1910/1911. Ed. I. Kern. 1977.

Die Idee der Phänomenologie [text from *Husserliana,* vol. 2]. Ed. P. Janssen. 1986.

Die Konstitution der geistigen Welt [text from *Husserliana,* vol. 4]. Ed. M. Sommers. 1984.

Die Krisis der europäischen Wissenschaften und

die transzendentale Phänomenologie: Eine Einleitug in die phänomenologische Philosophie [text from *Husserliana,* vol. 6]. Ed. E. Ströker. 1982.

Die Phänomenologie und die Fundamente der Wissenschaften [text from *Husserliana,* vol. 5]. Ed. K.-H. Lembeck. 1986.

Texte zur Phänomenologie des inneren Zeitbewusstseins (1893–1917) [text from *Husserliana,* vol. 10]. Ed. Rudolf Bernet. 1985.

Husserl's Correspondence

Briefwechsel. Ed. Karl Schuhmann with Elisabeth Schuhmann. *Husserliana Dokumente,* vol. 3. Dordrecht: Kluwer Academic Publishers, 1994.
Vol. 3/1, *Die Brentanoschule.*
Vol. 3/2, *Die Münchener Phänomenologen.*
Vol. 3/3, *Die Göttinger Schule.*
Vol. 3/4, *Die Freiburger Schule.*
Vol. 3/5, *Die Neukantianer.*
Vol. 3/6, *Philosophische Briefe.*
Vol. 3/7, *Wissenschaftler Korrespondenz.*
Vol. 3/8, *Institutionelle Schreiben.*
Vol. 3/9, *Familienbriefe.*
Vol. 3/10, *Einführung und Register.*
Briefe an Roman Ingarden. The Hague: Martinus Nijhoff, 1968.

Husserliana Documents

Fink, Eugen. *VI. Cartesianische Meditation.* Part 1: *Die Idee einer transzendentalen Methodenlehre.* Part 2: *Ergänzungsband. Husserliana Dokumente,* vol. 2/1 and 2/2. Dordrecht: Kluwer Academic Publishers, 1988. [For the translation of Husserl's textual notations to Fink, see English Translations, below.]

Schuhmann, Karl. *Husserl-Chronik: Denk- und Lebensweg Husserls. Husserliana Dokumente,* vol. 1. The Hague: Martinus Nijhoff, 1977.

Other Works of Husserl

Briefe an Roman Ingarden. The Hague: Martinus Nijhoff, 1968.

"Randbermerkungen Husserls zu Heideggers *Sein und Zeit* und *Kant und das Problem der Metaphysik,*" ed. Roland Breeur. *Husserl Studies* 11 (1994): 3–63.

English Translations

Analyses Concerning Passive and Active Synthesis: Lectures on Transcendental Logic. Trans. Anthony J. Steinbock. Boston: Kluwer Academic Publishers, forthcoming.

"The Apodicticity of Recollection." Trans. Deborah Chaffin. *Husserl Studies* 2 (1985): 10–32. [Translation of *Husserliana,* vol. 11, pp. 365–383.]

Cartesian Meditations: An Introduction to Phenomenology. Trans. Dorion Cairns. The Hague: Martinus Nijhoff, 1960.

The Crisis of European Sciences and Transcendental Phenomenology: An Introduction to Phenomenological Philosophy. Trans. David Carr. Evanston, Ill.: Northwestern University Press, 1970.

Experience and Judgment: Investigations in a Genealogy of Logic. Trans. James S. Churchill and Karl Ameriks. Evanston, Ill.: Northwestern University Press, 1973.

Formal and Transcendental Logic. Trans. Dorion Cairns. The Hague: Martinus Nijhoff, 1969.

Husserl: Shorter Works. Ed. Peter McCormick and Frederick Elliston. Notre Dame, Ind.: University of Notre Dame Press, 1981.

The Idea of Phenomenology. Trans. William Alston and George Nakhnikian. The Hague: Martinus Nijhoff, 1964.

Ideas: General Introduction to Pure Phenomenology. Trans. W. R. Boyce Gibson. London: George Allen & Unwin, 1931.

Ideas Pertaining to a Pure Phenomenology and to a Phenomenological Philosophy. First Book: *General Introduction to a Pure Phenomenology.* Trans. F. Kersten. *Collected Works,* vol. 2. The Hague: Martinus Nijhoff, 1982.

Ideas Pertaining to a Pure Phenomenology and to a Phenomenological Philosophy. Second Book: *Studies in the Phenomenology of Constitution.* Trans. Richard Rojcewicz and André Schuwer. *Collected Works,* vol. 3. Dordrecht: Kluwer Academic Publishers, 1989.

Ideas Pertaining to a Pure Phenomenology and to a Phenomenological Philosophy. Third Book: *Phenomenology and the Foundations of the Sciences.* Trans. Ted Klein and William Pohl. *Collected Works,* vol. 1. The Hague: Martinus Nijhoff, 1980.

"Kant and the Idea of Transcendental Philosophy," *Southwestern Journal of Philosophy* 5 (Fall 1974): 9–56.

Logical Investigations. Trans. J. N. Findlay. 2 vols. London: Routledge & Kegan Paul, 1970.

On the Phenomenology of the Consciousness of Internal Time (1893–1917). Trans. John Brough. *Collected Works,* vol. 4. Dordrecht: Kluwer Academic Publishers, 1991.

The Paris Lectures. Trans. P. Koestenbaum. The Hague: Martinus Nijhoff, 1967.

Phenomenological Psychology: Lectures, Summer Semester, 1925. Trans. John Scanlon. The Hague: Martinus Nijhoff, 1977.

The Phenomenology of Internal Time Consciousness. Trans. James Churchill. Bloomington: Indiana University Press, 1964.

"Philosophy as Rigorous Science," in *Phenomenology and the Crisis of Philosophy.* Trans. Quentin Lauer. New York: Harper and Row, 1965. Pp. 71–147. Reprinted in *Husserl: Shorter Works,* ed. Peter McCormick and Frederick Elliston, 1981.

Textual notations in Eugen Fink, *Sixth Cartesian Meditation: The Idea of a Transcendental Theory of Method.* Trans. Ronald Bruzina. Bloomington: Indiana University Press, 1994.

Thing and Space: Lectures of 1907. Trans. Richard Rojcewicz. *Collected Works,* vol. 7. Dordrecht: Kluwer Academic Publishers, 1998.

INDEX